6·95

Social
Change

SOCIAL CHANGE

Sources, Patterns, and Consequences

2nd edition

Edited by Eva Etzioni-Halevy

and Amitai Etzioni

BASIC BOOKS, INC., PUBLISHERS *New York*

© 1964, 1973 by Basic Books, Inc., Publishers
Library of Congress Catalog Card Number: 73–81392
SBN 465–07855–9
Manufactured in the United States of America
Designed by Sophie Adler

10 9 8 7 6

In memory of Salomon Horowitz

Preface

Assembling this book has proved to be a frustrating experience. Again and again we were tempted to compile a multivolume series, in order to do justice to the rich variety of materials available on social change. Within the space limits we had, it was impossible to include more than a small sample of essays, excerpts from books, and new articles representing the major approaches to the study of social change.

We have tried to select writings that were brief enough in their entirety or that could be excerpted without becoming incomprehensible or distorted* and which, at the same time, would provide keys to the work that could not be included. We generally chose analytical as against descriptive material, hoping that the former would furnish the student and researcher with tools for dealing with the latter. We also tried to include concrete illustrations of analytical propositions and to give at least some examples of empirical study in various aspects of social change; but lengthy descriptions had to be excluded. The teacher may wish to enrich the students' diet by assigning the reading of one or more monographs, now often available in paperback. Or, in more advanced courses, the teacher who wishes to enlarge on one aspect of social change—such as group dynamics, industrialization, or population —may find it desirable to assign additional pertinent readings.

Though this volume draws on a variety of approaches and disciplines, it has been compiled by sociologists, concentrates on the work of sociologists, and is intended for students of sociology. The tyranny of space allowed the inclusion of only a fraction of the relevant work done by anthropologists, political scientists, economists, and psychologists.

The present collection includes rather more discussion than one might expect to find of social change on an international level. We feel that this area of change has been unduly neglected by sociologists and that it will be of much interest in the near future.

* The more important omissions are marked in the text by ellipses.

The brief introductory notes are meant to be neither novel in content nor exhaustive in scope. They are intended to stimulate the reader's interest in the material, to show some of the threads that connect the selections, and to sketch out the main lines of discussion and argument on these issues up to now. The student should also bear in mind that our interpretive comments, like the propositions made in the essays themselves, are open to refutation and should be viewed as food for thought, rather than as *obiter dicta*.

Eva Etzioni-Halevy and Amitai Etzioni

Contents

Preface   vii

Part I   Sources and Patterns of Change:
         Classical Theories

         INTRODUCTION   3

    1 Herbert Spencer
       The Evolution of Societies   9

    2 Auguste Comte
       The Progress of Civilization through Three States   14

    3 Oswald Spengler
       The Life Cycle of Cultures   20

    4 Vilfredo Pareto
       The Circulation of Elites   26

    5 Karl Marx
       Historical Materialism Summarized   30

    6 Karl Marx and Friedrich Engels
       The Class Struggle   32

    7 Max Weber
       The Role of Ideas in History   40

    8 Max Weber
       The Routinization of Charisma   43

    9 Ferdinand Toennies
       From Community to Society   54

Part II Sources and Patterns of Change:
         Modern Theories

         INTRODUCTION   65

10 Talcott Parsons
    A Functional Theory of Change   72

11 Francesca Cancian
    Functional Analysis of Change   87

12 Ralf Dahrendorf
    Toward a Theory of Social Conflict   100

13 Lewis A. Coser
    Social Conflict and the Theory of Social Change   114

14 C. Wright Mills
    The Sources of Societal Power   123

15 Julian H. Steward
    A Neo-Evolutionist Approach   131

16 A. L. Kroeber
    Diffusionism   140

17 Amitai Etzioni
    Toward a Theory of Societal Guidance   145

18 David C. McClelland
    Business Drive and National Achievement   161

Part III Spheres of Change:

The Modern Society

INTRODUCTION   177

19 Kingsley Davis
    The Demographic Transition   183

20 Ernest W. Burgess
    The Family in a Changing Society   191

21 Bernard Barber
    Change and Stratification Systems   199

22 Gaetano Mosca
    The Varying Structure of the Ruling Class   210

23 Will Herberg
    Religious Revival in the United States   223

24 Peter F. Drucker
    The Educational Revolution   232

25 Kenneth Keniston
   A Second Look at the Uncommitted 239

Part IV Modernization

   INTRODUCTION 263

26 Neil J. Smelser
   Toward a Theory of Modernization 268

27 W. W. Rostow
   The Takeoff into Self-Sustained Growth 285

28 Wilbert E. Moore
   Motivational Aspects of Development 301

29 Reinhard Bendix
   Industrialization, Ideologies, and Social Structure 310

30 S. N. Eisenstadt
   Breakdowns of Political Modernization 320

31 Joseph R. Gusfield
   *Tradition and Modernity: Misplaced Polarities
   in the Study of Social Change* 333

32 Alex Inkeles
   *Making Men Modern: On the Causes and Consequences
   of Individual Change in Six Developing Countries* 342

Part V Levels of Change

   INTRODUCTION 365

33 Kurt Lewin
   Group Dynamics and Social Change 371

34 Mason Haire
   *Biological Models and Empirical Histories
   of the Growth of Organizations* 379

35 Robert E. Park
   The Race-Relations Cycle 393

36 Arnold Rose
   *The American Negro Problem in the Context of
   Social Change* 396

37 David Riesman
   From "Inner-Directed" to "Other-Directed" 410

Part VI Processes of Change

INTRODUCTION   423

38 Philip M. Hauser
    *The Chaotic Society: Product of the Social
    Morphological Revolution*   428

39 R. M. MacIver
    The Role of the Precipitant   443

40 Horace M. Kallen
    Innovation   447

41 Ralph Linton
    Discovery, Invention, and Their Cultural Setting   451

42 James Coleman, Herbert Menzel, and Elihu Katz
    *Social Processes in Physicians' Adoption of a
    New Drug*   457

43 Gunnar Myrdal, with Richard Sterner and Arnold Rose
    The Principle of Cumulation   473

44 William F. Ogburn
    The Hypothesis of Cultural Lag   477

45 Morton A. Kaplan
    Essential Rules and Rules of Transformation   481

Part VII Human Initiative in Social Change

INTRODUCTION   489

46 Charles E. Lindblom
    Rational Policy through Mutual Adjustment   493

47 Ralf Dahrendorf
    Market and Plan   500

48 James S. Coleman, et al.
    Enhancing Equality of Educational Opportunity   505

49 Crane Brinton
    The Anatomy of Revolution: Tentative Uniformities   514

50 James C. Davies
    Toward a Theory of Revolution   519

51 Ralph H. Turner
    The Theme of Contemporary Social Movements   535

    Index   543

Social
Change

PART I

SOURCES AND PATTERNS OF CHANGE

Classical
Theories

Introduction

Many of the fathers of sociology were concerned with the general trend of history and its meaning. Mostly they sought to explain the past development of society and sometimes to predict its future in terms of a definite pattern.

For such nineteenth-century thinkers as Herbert Spencer and Auguste Comte, the pattern is one of linear ascent. Spencer saw the development of society as a process of evolution, which, like organic evolution, is a process of growth, increasing complexity, increasing differentiation of structure and function, and increasing interdependence among the differentiated parts. He also believed in the emergence of an industrial order which would increasingly protect the rights of the individual, decrease the emphasis on government, abolish wars, dissolve national borders, and establish a global community.

Comte, too, saw society as a process of evolution and progress and defined his task as one of establishing the uniformities governing this progress. Thus, he formulated his famous law of the three states of the development of human thought—the theological, the metaphysical, and the positive—which were also the bases of the three historical forms of social organization.

As against these optimistic conceptions, Oswald Spengler early in this century put forth an opposing, essentially pessimistic view. For Spengler, human existence is an endless series of ups and downs. Like waves in the ocean, the great cultures appear, rise to great heights, only to subside again while others rise in their turn. Like the individual organism, each culture has a life cycle of birth, childhood, maturity, old age, and death. The cycles have no cumulative meaning. At the end of each cycle, mankind is essentially where it was before. For Spengler, the West has passed its phase of maturity, which he calls "culture," and is already well advanced into the decadent period, which he refers to as "civilization."

Vilfredo Pareto viewed political change—as akin to the rotation of a wheel, which itself remains unchanged. The masses, as he saw it, will continue to be excluded from meaningful participation in their government. Change comes as elites are replaced by still others. (Recently, this view has gained a measure of revival in the "pendulum" theory which sees governments as moving back and forth between dedication to domestic change and to the *status-quo*). As the "superior bloodline" of each elite grows anemic, society's vitality and viability, according to Pareto, is maintained through a changing of the guard, but the guards and their oligarchic nature are immutable. Above all, change occurs not as a response to political mobilization among the masses or particular social classes: it is a purely intra or inter elite affair.

Most other theories presented here derive from either the linear or the cyclical principles; some writers, with differing emphases, incorporate elements of both.

The Marxist theory, too, is basically a theory of progress, although not of linear progress. The advance toward the classless society proceeds through "dialectical" conflicts, in each of which one subordinate class overthrows its ruling class (*e.g.*, the bourgeoisie overthrows the aristocracy), only to establish a new society in which a new subordinate class rises to overthrow it. But these cycles are neither endless nor meaningless. As Marx saw it, the wheel has now reached its last turn; with the proletarian revolution, the story is about to come to an end. The proletariat's victory will give rise to a classless society, one which knows no major conflict and hence no revolutions.

The Marxist theory of history differs from that of the linear progress, not only in that it conceives history as a series of violent conflicts rather than a smooth progress to higher plateaus, but also in its view of the initial state. The typical "enlightenment" theory of progress (*e.g.*, Condorcet's) saw humanity as gradually moving from a dark, ignorant, brutal, primitive state to one of reason, virtue and happiness. For Engels, the initial state was similar to the end state; generalizing the ethnographic researches of Lewis H. Morgan, he viewed early primitive society as a classless commune, to which man is destined to return. The basic similarity of this conception to that common to many religions has often been pointed out. There was a Garden of Eden; there is a state of sin; there will be a return to the Kingdom of God.

One important aspect of Max Weber's theory is in a way quite close to the cyclical approach. According to Weber, when the legitimacy of an old historical structure is exhausted, a charismatic leader emerges outside the structure and gives it its *coup de grâce*. The leader and his followers take over and build a new structure on the ruins of the old one. The subsequent "routinization of charisma" constitutes the foundation of the new structure—which sooner or later will also be faced with the same lack of legitimacy, charismatic upheaval, new routinization, and so on.

Another aspect of Weber's theory approximates the linear-development approach, for he sees the development of culture as a process of constantly increasing rationalization, of growing inner consistency and coherence. This is most evident in the transition from magic to science; the development of religion from polytheism to monotheism is also viewed in this light; and Weber observed the same trend in the development of music.

Thus, Weber's approach to change is two-pronged; he combines a cyclical theory of social development with a linear theory of cultural development. Though Weber never fully relates these two themes, he intimates that the social structure "catches up" with cultural development under the impact of the charismatic periods; at these points, the social structure is opened up to reorganization by ever-more-"rationalized" cultural systems. The role of Calvin and other great reformers in introducing a "Protestant ethic" is a prime illustration.

The work of Toennies is second only to that of Weber in the scope and depth of its influence on contemporary sociology. Toennies, like Spencer, views society as growing more and more complex, in a linear process. Small and simple structures grow to become large and complex ones. He sees the trend from what he calls *Gemeinschaft* to *Gesellschaft* as one in which primitive, traditional, closely knit communities are torn and uprooted, to be replaced by a large, urbanized, industrial society in which human relations are impersonal and instrumental. Like the theorists of linear ascent, he sees a clear, irreversible trend; but, unlike them, he is ambivalent in evaluating this trend. Modern society has provided men with many new freedoms, with new dimensions of knowledge, and with material affluence. But it has also brought about alienation, atomization, and impersonality.

By making the pattern and direction of human history their domain, the early sociologists made certain that their theories would bear directly on the most basic questions of social life. The same holds for their concern with the forces that move history. Can men make their own history or only ride history like a wave? Most thinkers represented here are determinists up to a point; if the sheer contingency of random impulse were all that made the world go round, its course could hardly be as predictable, as "rational," as they felt it is. On the other hand, all these thinkers concede a modicum of leeway for man to interfere with his fate, though they differ greatly in the degree of freedom they grant him.

Spengler sees the course of history as more-or-less given, like the childhood, maturity, and decay of the human body. There is extremely little man can do to alter it. Spencer, too, leaves little room for individual interference. But, whereas Spengler outlines the inevitability of our culture's doom, Spencer believes in the inevitability of human progress. Man's spirit and his history point in the same direction; there is no contradiction between the two. Marx takes somewhat different positions in various writings, but basically he views human fate as predestined. The ruling class, by utilizing the state and the church, means of violence and ideology, might delay the historic process to some extent; the proletariat, if properly organized and acting in concert, might accelerate it. But ultimately the wheels of history are turning, and nobody can stop or reverse them.

Weber left history more open to human guidance. To be sure, man is caught in the institutional web he himself set up; but, at charismatic moments, he breaks in, remodeling the institutional structure to bring it closer to his wish. On the cultural level, the process of increasing rationalization indicates increased submission of the universe to man's mind; but, at the same time, there is no sign that man is free to reverse this process, should he change his mind about it.

The theories represented here view the forces of history as originating from within human society—from its economic structure or its culture. In this sense, they indeed lay the foundations of contemporary sociology, which has completely rejected several other sets of theories that regard society and its changes as determined by forces originating outside the social system. Theories that explain the course of human history predominantly by supernatural forces, environmental factors (*e.g.,* climate), or biological factors (*e.g.,* race) have all been discredited. The supernatural theories have been discarded on the ground that the factors they deal with are not amenable to scientific inquiry; the environmental and biological theories because the factors they deal with change extremely slowly and therefore could hardly explain the changes of human society, which are occasionally quite rapid. The amount of rainfall in Russia and its racial composition hardly changed from 1817 to 1917 and so cannot adequately account for the shift from a tsarist to a communist regime. Unlike the classic theories presented in this volume—many of which have exerted a strong influence on contemporary sociology—the environmental and biological theories have been so completely rejected that they are only of historical interest.

Within the range of the theories which stress that the determinants of social change arise from within society itself, the longest, deepest, and most important controversy lies between those who see the prime moving forces of human history in the "spiritual" spheres and those who see it in the "material" ones; between those who stress the role of ideas and those who stress the role of economic factors; between those who stress the role of culture and those who stress the role of technology.

Thus Comte, though he called on sociology to look, not for causes and effects in history, but rather for uniformities, nevertheless, in his own work, implicitly attributes causal primacy to the cultural sphere by describing the three successive states of human thought as giving rise to three successive states of social organization.

Marx, in contrast, believes that "the method of production in material existence conditions social, political, and mental evolution in general." Since Marxism has frequently been oversimplified, it must be stressed that it does allow for a certain range of independence of the various non-economic spheres; but, as Engels put it: ". . . the *final causes* [italics supplied] of all social changes are to be sought . . . in the modes of production and exchange."

Weber, in *The Protestant Ethic and the Spirit of Capitalism,* brought this primacy into question by demonstrating the crucial importance of the spiritual sphere in determining the economic structure itself. But he was careful to point out that this was only one side of the causal chain, that under other circumstances the economic factors might determine the cultural ones, and that *in toto* the sources of change are neither exclusively economic nor exclusively cultural.

Under the influence of Weber, sociology is outgrowing this controversy by rejecting all deterministic theories. All efforts to explain societal change as originating in one single social factor have so utterly failed, while efforts to show that a variety of factors exert some influence have proved to be so much more satisfactory, that contemporary sociology has almost unanimously adopted the multifactor approach.

Social change, it is now held, may originate in any institutional area, bringing about changes in other areas, which in turn make for further adaptations in the initial sphere of change. Technological, economic, political, religious, ideological, demographic, and stratificational factors are all viewed as potentially independent variables which influence each other as well as the course of society.

The appeal of classical theories, especially to the untutored reader, is large. Their scope is enormous, their claim to applicability limitless, their language nontechnical and arousing. Still, sociology has tended to move away from the effort to form and improve such theories, chiefly because of a drawback they had—a drawback directly related to their virtues: though they supplied valuable insights, when viewed in their entirety, they turned out to be either untestable, and hence scientifically unacceptable, or only partly true at best.

Thus, mankind obviously does not travel smoothly from a lesser to a higher state of enlightenment, as Comte asserted. The melting of national borders and the development of a global community which Spencer envisioned has not been brought about by industrial society so far, and, since he did not specify *when* he expected this to happen, the theory can never be disproved, which makes it untestable.

Similarly, Marx has been proved wrong on almost every single count on which he made a prediction specific enough to be tested: the revolution did not occur in highly industrialized, but rather in industrially "backward," countries; it did not bring about the classless society, nor did it eliminate internal conflicts and contradictions; and the middle class did not diminish in a process of polarization, but instead increased steadily; and so on. On the other hand, the proposition that the "final" causes of social change lie in the economic sphere is untestable. Since no empirical specification for the concept "final" has been provided, any impetus originating in the economic sphere can be viewed as a final cause, whereas any impetus originating in another sphere may be viewed as nonfinal. Moreover, when he predicted the fading away of the state in a classless society, Marx, like Spencer, did not specify the conditions or time at which he expected this to come about. Consequently, this thesis, too, is untestable.

Weber, as we saw, put much stress on the role of charismatic upheavals in bringing about change; his theory makes but little provision for slow, reformatory changes, which come about gradually and without crisis. Changes like these took place, for instance, in modern England and the United States, which were transformed from rural, religious, closed to urban, industrial, highly mobile societies; from what approximated a state of *laissez-faire* to societies controlled to a considerable degree by central governments, societies in which the welfare of the population as well as the growth of the country are guided by the community and its political instruments—all this without revolutionary upheaval.

Toennies, again, did not make sufficient allowance for the survival of elements of *Gemeinschaft* in the *Gesellschaft*—like the nuclear family or friendships—and he did not foresee the development of what could be referred to as elements of *Gemeinschaft* or quasi-*Gemeinschaft* in modern society, expressed for instance in flourishing suburbs, clubs, and professional communities.

Even so, the fact is that sociology has evolved from these theories They have laid the groundwork for modern sociology by calling attention to various areas of inquiry (*e.g.,* Marx—to stratification) and by providing many of the concepts used as a matter of course in present-day sociology. But the totalistic scope of these theories soon had to be abandoned; before it could progress, sociology had largely to give up the quest for overall patterns and for "ultimate" causes of change. Although in general this reaction was well justified, possibly it was overdone by sociologists moving to the other extreme, avoiding not only the study of history in its broadest sense, the inquiry into the study of change of all times, but also the changes of specific societies at particular times. Hopefully, the concepts and tools recently developed will serve as the building stones of a new theory of change that is not only grand, but also testable, and one which when tested will be found true.

CHAPTER 1

HERBERT SPENCER

The Evolution of Societies

A Society Is an Organism

Growth is common to social aggregates and organic aggregates. We do not entirely exclude community with inorganic aggregates. Some of these, as crystals, grow in a visible manner; and all of them, on the hypothesis of evolution, have arisen by integration at some time or another. Nevertheless, compared with things we call inanimate, living bodies and societies so conspicuously exhibit augmentation of mass, that we may fairly regard this as characterizing them both. Many organisms grow throughout their lives; and the rest grow throughout considerable parts of their lives. Social growth usually continues either up to times when the societies divide or up to times when they are overwhelmed.

Here, then, is the first trait by which societies ally themselves with the organic world and substantially distinguish themselves from the inorganic world.

The Evolution of Structures

It is also a character of social bodies, as of living bodies, that, while they increase in size, they increase in structure. Like a low animal, the embryo of a high one has few distinguishable parts; but, while it is acquiring greater mass, its parts multiply and differentiate. It is thus with a society. At first the unlikenesses among its groups of units are inconspicuous in number and degree; but, as population augments, divisions and subdivisions become more numerous and more decided. . . . As we progress from small groups to larger, from simple groups to compound groups, from compound groups to doubly compound ones, the unlikenesses of parts increase. The social aggregate, homogeneous when minute, habitually gains in heterogeneity along

From Herbert Spencer, *Sociology* (New York: Appleton and Co., 1892), Vol. 1, pp. 437-439, 459-463, 473-475, 584-585.

with each increment of growth, and to reach great size must acquire great complexity. Let us glance at the leading stages.

Naturally, in a state like that of the Cayaguas or Wood-Indians of South America, so little social that "one family lives at a distance from another," social organization is impossible; and even where there is some slight association of families, organization does not arise while they are few and wandering. Groups of Esquimaux, of Australians, of Bushmen, of Fuegians, are without even that primary contrast of parts implied by settled chieftainship. Their members are subject to no control but such as is temporarily acquired by the stronger, or more cunning, or more experienced; not even a permanent nucleus is present. Habitually, where larger simple groups exist, we find some kind of head. Though not a uniform rule (for . . . the genesis of a controlling agency depends on the nature of the social activities), this is a general rule. The headless clusters, wholly ungoverned, are incoherent, and separate before they acquire considerable sizes; but along with maintenance of an aggregate approaching to, or exceeding, a hundred, we ordinarily find a simple or compound ruling agency—one or more men claiming and exercising authority that is natural, or supernatural, or both. This is the first social differentiation.

Soon after it, there frequently comes another, tending to form a division between regulative and operative parts. In the lowest tribes, this is rudely represented only by the contrast in status between the sexes: the men, having unchecked control, carry on such external activities as the tribe shows us, chiefly in war; while the women are made drudges who perform the less skilled parts of the process of sustentation. But that tribal growth, and establishment of chieftainship, which gives military superiority, presently causes enlargement of the operative part by adding captives to it. This begins unobtrusively. While in battle the men are killed, and often afterwards eaten, the noncombatants are enslaved. Patagonians, for example, make slaves of women and children taken in war. Later, and especially when cannibalism ceases, comes the enslavement of male captives; whence results, in some cases, an operative part clearly marked off from the regulative part. Among the Chinooks, "slaves do all the laborious work." We read that the Beluchi, avoiding the hard labor of cultivation, impose it on the Jutts, the ancient inhabitants whom they have subjugated. Beecham says it is usual on the Gold Coast to make the slaves clear the ground for cultivation. And among the Felatahs "slaves are numerous: the males are employed in weaving, collecting wood or grass, or on any other kind of work; some of the women are engaged in spinning . . . in preparing the yarn for the loom, others in pounding and grinding corn, etc."

Along with that increase of mass caused by union of primary social aggregates into a secondary one, a further unlikeness of parts arises. The holding together of the compound cluster implies a head of the whole as well as heads of the parts; and a differentiation analogous to that which originally produced a chief now produces a chief of chiefs. Sometimes the combination is made for defense against a common foe, and sometimes it results from conquest by one tribe of the rest. In this last case, the predominant tribe, in maintaining its supremacy, develops more highly its military character, thus becoming unlike the others.

After such clusters of clusters have been so consolidated that their united powers can be wielded by one governing agency, there come alliances with, or subjugations of, other clusters of clusters, ending from time to time in coalescence. When this happens there results still greater complexity in the governing agency, with its king, local rulers, and petty chiefs; and, at the same time, there arise more marked divisions of classes—military, priestly, slave, etc. Clearly, then, complication of structure accompanies increase of mass.

This increase of heterogeneity, which in both classes of aggregates goes along with growth, presents another trait in common. Beyond unlikenesses of parts due to development of the coordinating agencies, there presently follow unlikenesses among the agencies coordinated—the organs of alimentation, etc., in the one case, and the industrial structures in the other.

When animal-aggregates of the lowest order unite to form one of a higher order and when, again, these secondary aggregates are compounded into tertiary aggregates, each component is at first similar to the other components; but in the course of evolution dissimilarities arise and become more and more decided. Among the *Coelenterata* the stages are clearly indicated. From the sides of a common hydra bud out young ones, which, when fully developed, separate from their parent. In the compound hydroids, the young polyps produced in like manner remain permanently attached and, themselves repeating the process, presently form a branched aggregate. When the members of the compound group lead similar and almost independent lives, as in various rooted genera, they remain similar—save those of them which become reproductive organs. But, in the floating and swimming clusters, formed by a kindred process, the differently conditioned members become different while assuming different functions. It is thus with the minor social groups combined into a major social group. Each tribe originally had within itself such feebly marked industrial divisions as sufficed for its low kind of life, and these were like those of each other tribe. But union facilitates exchange of commodities; and if, as mostly happens, the component tribes severally occupy localities favorable to unlike kinds of production, unlike occupations are initiated, and there result unlikenesses of industrial structure. Even between tribes not united, as those of Australia, barter of products furnished by their respective habitats goes on so long as war does not hinder. And evidently, when there is reached such a stage of integration as in Madagascar or as in the chief Negro states of Africa, the internal peace that follows subordination to one government makes commercial intercourse easy. The like parts being permanently held together, mutual dependence becomes possible; and, along with growing mutual dependence, the parts grow unlike. . . .

The Evolution of Functions

Changes of structure cannot occur without changes of function. . . . Indeed, as in societies many changes of structure are more indicated by changes of function than directly seen, it may be said that these last have been already described by implication.

There are, however, certain functional traits not manifestly implied by traits of structure. To these a few pages must be devoted.

If organization consists in such a construction of the whole that its parts can carry on mutually dependent actions, then in proportion as organization is high there must go a dependence of each part on the rest so great that separation is fatal, and conversely. This truth is equally well shown in the individual organism and in the social organism.

The lowest animal-aggregates are so constituted that each portion, similar to every other in appearance, carries on similar actions; and here spontaneous or artificial separation interferes scarcely at all with the life of either separated portion. When the faintly differentiated speck of protoplasm forming a Rhizopod is accidentally divided, each division goes on as before. So, too, is it with those aggregates of the second order in which the components remain substantially alike. The ciliated monads clothing the horny fibers of a living sponge need one another's aid so little, that, when the sponge is cut in two, each half carries on its processes without interruption. Even where some unlikeness has arisen among the units, as in the familiar polyp, the perturbation caused by division is but temporary: the two or more portions resulting need only a little time for the units to rearrange themselves into fit forms before resuming their ordinary simple actions. The like happens for the like reason with the lowest social aggregates. A headless wandering group of primitive men divides without any inconvenience. Each man, at once warrior, hunter, and maker of his own weapons, hut, etc., with a squaw who has in every case the like drudgeries to carry on, needs concert with his fellows only in war and to some extent in the chase; and, except for fighting, concert with half the tribe is as good as concert with the whole. Even where the slight differentiation implied by chieftainship exists, little inconvenience results from voluntary or enforced separation. Either before or after a part of the tribe migrates, some man becomes head, and such low social life as is possible recommences.

With highly organized aggregates of either kind, it is very different. We cannot cut a mammal in two without causing immediate death. Twisting off the head of a fowl is fatal. Not even a reptile, though it may survive the loss of its tail, can live when its body is divided. And, among annulose creatures it similarly happens that, though in some inferior genera bisection does not kill either half, it kills both in an insect, an arachnid, or a crustacean. If in high societies the effect of mutilation is less than in high animals, still it is great. Middlesex, separated from its surroundings, would in a few days have all its social processes stopped by lack of supplies. Cut off the cotton district from Liverpool and other ports, and there would come arrest of its industry followed by mortality of its people. Let a division be made between the coalmining populations and adjacent populations which smelt metals or make broadcloth by machinery, and both, forthwith dying socially by arrest of their actions, would begin to die individually. Though when a civilized society is so divided that part of it is left without a central controlling agency, it may presently evolve one; yet there is meanwhile much risk of dissolution, and before reorganization is efficient a long period of disorder and weakness must be passed through.

So that the *consensus* of functions becomes closer as evolution advances. In low aggregates, both individual and social, the actions of the parts are but little dependent on one another, whereas in developed aggregates of both kinds, that combination of actions which constitutes the life of the whole makes possible the component actions which constitute the lives of the parts.

Summary

. . . The many facts contemplated unite in proving that social evolution forms a part of evolution at large. Like evolving aggregates in general, societies show *integration,* both by simple increase of mass and by coalescence and recoalescence of masses. The change from *homogeneity* to *heterogeneity* is multitudinously exemplified; up from the simple tribe, alike in all its parts, to the civilized nation, full of structural and functional unlikenesses. With progressing integration and heterogeneity goes increasing *coherence.* We see the wandering group dispersing, dividing, held together by no bonds; the tribe with parts made more coherent by subordination to a dominant man; the cluster of tribes united in a political plexus under a chief with subchiefs; and so on up to the civilized nation, consolidated enough to hold together for a thousand years or more. Simultaneously comes increasing *definiteness.* Social organization is at first vague; advance brings settled arrangements which grow slowly more precise; customs pass into laws which, while gaining fixity, also become more specific in their applications to varieties of actions; and all institutions, at first confusedly intermingled, slowly separate, at the same time that each within itself marks off more distinctly its component structures. Thus in all respects is fulfilled the formula of evolution. There is progress toward greater size, coherence, multiformity, and definiteness.

CHAPTER 2

AUGUSTE COMTE

The Progress of
Civilization through
Three States

The Progress of Civilization Follows Laws

The experience of the past proves, in the most decisive manner, that the progressive march of civilization follows a natural and unavoidable course, which flows from the law of human organization and, in its turn, becomes the supreme law of all practical phenomena.

In this place it is manifestly impossible to expound the law in question with precision, or to verify it historically, even in the briefest manner. We only propose to offer some reflections on this fundamental conception.

The first reflection points to the necessity for assuming that such a law does exist in order to explain the political phenomena.

All men who possess a certain knowledge of the leading facts of history, be their historical views what they may, will agree in this, that the cultivated portion of the human race, considered as a whole, has made uninterrupted progress in civilization from the most remote periods of history to our own day. In this proposition, the term "civilization" is understood as including the social organization.

No reasonable doubt can be raised about this fundamental fact as regards the epoch which extends from the eleventh century to the present time, in other words commencing with the introduction of the sciences of observation into Europe by the Arabs and the enfranchisement of the Commons. But the truth is equally incontestable as regards the antecedent period. Savants are now well convinced that the pretensions to advanced scientific knowl-

---

From Auguste Comte, *System of Positive Polity* (London: Longmans, Green and Co., 1877), "General Appendix: Early Essays," Vol. IV, pp. 555-58, 572-73.

edge put forward on behalf of the ancients by *littérateurs* are devoid of all real basis. The Arabians are proved to have surpassed them. Such also has been the case, even more decidedly, as regards industry, at all events in reference to all that calls for real ability and does not result from mere accident. Even if the fine arts were deemed to constitute an exception, their exclusion is susceptible of a natural explanation which would leave the main proposition essentially untouched. Lastly, as regards the social organization, it is perfectly manifest that this, during the same period, made the greatest progress, owing to the establishment of Christianity and the formation of the feudal system, so superior to the organization of Greece and Rome.

It is therefore certain that civilization has, under every aspect, made constant progress.

On the other hand, while discarding the disparaging spirit, alike blind and unjust, introduced by the metaphysical philosophy, we cannot but perceive that, in consequence of the state of infancy which has hitherto characterized political speculations, the practical combinations that have until now guided civilization were not always those best adapted to promote its progress and frequently tended rather to impede than to assist this. There have been epochs the main political activity of which was of a purely stationary character. Such, generally speaking, were those of social systems in their decline; for example, of the Emperor Julian, of Philip II and the Jesuits, and lastly of Bonaparte. Let us also bear in mind that, as already pointed out, the social organization does not regulate the course of civilization, but, on the contrary, results from this.

Frequent cures, effected in spite of a treatment manifestly erroneous, have revealed to physicians the powerful action by which every living body spontaneously tends to rectify accidental derangements of its organization. In like manner the advance of civilization, notwithstanding unfavorable political combinations, clearly proves that civilization is governed by a natural law of progress, independent of all combinations, and dominating them. If this principle were denied, in order to explain such a fact and comprehend how it has come to pass that civilization, in place of being retarded by errors committed, has almost invariably benefited by them, we could only have recourse to direct, continuous supernatural guidance, after the fashion of theological politics.

Lastly, it is well to remark that too frequently events have been regarded as unfavorable to civilization which were only apparently so. The chief cause of this misapprehension has been the insufficient attention paid, even by the best intellects, to an essential law of organized bodies, which applies with equal force to the human race acting collectively as to a single individual. It consists in the necessity for a certain degree of resistance, in order that all forces may be fully developed. But this remark in no way affects the preceding consideration. For, though obstacles are needed to develop forces, they do not produce them.

The conclusion deduced from this fundamental consideration would be much strengthened if we took into account the remarkable identity observable in the development of the civilization of different nations, between which no political intercommunication can with probability be assumed. Such an identity could only have been produced under the influence of a natural progress of civilization, uniformly applicable to all nations as resulting from the fundamental laws of the human organization common to all. Thus, for example, the customs of the early times of Greece, as they are described by Homer, are found to be almost identical with those which subsist among the savage nations of North America. So, likewise, the feudalism of the Malays closely resembles that of Europe in the eleventh century. These points of resemblance, it is clear, can only be explained in the way above mentioned.

A second consideration will render evident the existence of a natural law regulating the progress of civilization.

If, in conformity with the view above submitted, we admit that each phase of the social order is necessarily derived from that of the corresponding civilization, we may in our observations lay out of consideration this complex element; the results arrived at for the residuary facts will equally apply to the organization of society.

Reducing thus the question to its simplest terms, it becomes easy to perceive that civilization follows a determined and invariable course.

A superficial philosophy, which would make this world a scene of miracles, has immensely exaggerated the influence of chance, that is to say of isolated causes, in human affairs. This exaggeration is peculiarly apparent in reference to the sciences and the arts. Among other remarkable examples, everyone knows the great admiration excited even in intelligent minds by the idea that the law of universal gravitation was revealed to Newton by the fall of an apple.

All sensible men in our time admit that chance plays only a very small part in scientific and industrial discoveries, that in none but insignificant discoveries does it rank as chief agent. But to this error has succeeded another which, though in itself much less unreasonable, has nevertheless almost the same disadvantages. The office of chance has been in like manner transferred to genius. This explanation hardly accounts more felicitously for the action of the human mind.

The history of human knowledge clearly proves that all our labors in the sciences and arts are so connected, whether in the same or in succeeding generations, that the discoveries of one age prepare those of the following, as the former had been themselves prepared by those of the preceding. It has been demonstrated that the isolated power of genius is greatly less than that with which it has been credited. The man most justly distinguished by great discoveries almost always owes the largest share of his success to his predecessors in the same career. In a word, the human mind follows, in the development of the sciences and arts, a definite course, one that transcends the greatest intellectual forces, which arise, so to speak, only as instruments destined to produce in due course successive discoveries.

Confining our observations to the sciences whose progress we can follow most easily from remote periods, we see, in truth, that their main historic epoch—that is to say their passage through the theological and metaphysical into the positive stage—are rigorously determined. These three states succeed one another necessarily in an order prescribed by the nature of the human mind. The transition from one to the other takes place according to a course the steps of which resemble one another in all the sciences, nor can the greatest amount of genius dispense with passing through them. Turning from this general review to the subdivisions of the scientific or definitive state, we observe the same law. Thus for example, the great discovery of universal gravitation was prepared by the labors of the astronomers and geometers of the sixteenth and seventeenth centuries, chiefly by those of Kepler and Huygens. They were indispensable to its birth and certain, sooner or later, to produce it.

It appears, therefore, from the preceding remarks that the elementary march of civilization is unquestionably subject to a natural and invariable law which overrules all special human divergencies. But since the state of the social organization of necessity follows that of civilization, the same conclusion applies to civilization, considered as a whole or in its elements.

The two considerations above announced, though insufficient to furnish a complete exposition of the progress of civilization, nevertheless prove its reality. They show the possibility of determining with precision all its attributes by a careful observation of the past and of thus creating positive polity.

Our business is next to fix exactly the practical aim of this science and its general points of contact with the wants of society, especially its connection with the real work of reorganization which is so imperiously required by the actual state of the body politic.

To effect this, it is necessary at the outset to ascertain the limits of all true political action.

The fundamental law which governs the natural progress of civilization rigorously determines the successive states through which the general development of the human race must pass. On the other hand, this law necessarily results from the instinctive tendency of the human race to perfect itself. Consequently, it is as completely independent of our control as are the individual instincts the combination of which produces this permanent tendency.

Since no known fact authorizes us to believe that the human organization is liable to any fundamental alteration, the progress of that civilization which flows from it is in essentials unalterable. To speak more precisely, none of the intermediate steps which it prescribes can be evaded, and no step in a backward direction can really be made.

Nevertheless, the progress of civilization is more or less modifiable and may vary in point of rapidity within certain limits, from various causes, physical and moral, which can be estimated. Among these causes are political combinations. In this sense only is it possible for man to influence the course of his own civilization. . . .

Law of the Three States

I believe that history may be divided into three grand epochs, or states of civilization, each possessing a distinct character, spiritual and temporal. They embrace civilization at once in its elements and its *ensemble;* which . . . evidently constitutes an indispensable condition of success.

Of these the first is the Theological and Military epoch.

In this state of society, all theoretical conceptions, whether general or special, bear a supernatural impress. The imagination completely predominates over the observing faculty, to which all right of inquiry is denied.

In like manner, all the social relations, whether special or general, are avowedly and exclusively military. Society makes conquest its one permanent aim. Industrial pursuits are carried on only so far as is necessary for the support of the human race. Slavery, pure and simple, of the producers, is the principal institution.

Such is the first great social system produced by the material progress of civilization. It existed in an elementary shape from the very commencement of regular and permanent societies. In its entirety it becomes completely established only after a long series of generations.

The second epoch is Metaphysical and Juridical. Its general character is that of possessing no well-defined characteristics. It forms a link and is mongrel and transitional.

. . . Observation is still kept subordinate to imagination, but the former is, within certain limits, allowed to modify the latter. These limits are gradually enlarged, until, in the end, observation conquers the right of examining in every direction. At first it obtains this right in reference to all special theoretical conceptions and gradually, by force of exercise, as to general theoretic ideas, which constitutes the natural termination of the transition. This period is one of criticism and argument.

Under temporal aspects, industry in this second epoch becomes more extended, without as yet acquiring the upper hand. Consequently, society is no longer frankly military and yet has not become frankly industrial, either in its elements or in its *ensemble.* The special social relations are modified. Industrial slavery is no longer direct; the producer, still a slave, begins to obtain some rights in his relations with the military. Industry makes fresh advances which finally issue in the total abolition of individual slavery. After this enfranchisement, the producers still remain subject to a collective arbitrary authority. Nevertheless, the general social relations soon undergo a modification. The two aims of activity, conquest and production, advance *pari passu*. Industry is at first favored and protected as a military resource. Later its importance augments; and finally war is regarded and systematically pursued as a means of favoring industry—which is the last term of the intermediate *régime*.

Lastly, the third epoch is that of Science and Industry. All special theoretic conceptions have become positive, and the general conceptions tend to become so. As regard the former, observation predominates over imagination; while, in reference to the latter, observation has dethroned the imagination, without having as yet taken its place.

Under temporal aspects, industry has become predominant. All the special relations have gradually established themselves on industrial bases. Society, taken collectively, tends to organize itself in the same manner, by making production its only and constant aim.

The last epoch has ended as regards the elements and is commencing as regards the *ensemble*. Its direct point of departure dates from the introduction of the positive sciences into Europe by the Arabs and the enfranchisement of the Commons, that is to say, from about the eleventh century.

In order to prevent all confusion in applying this general view, we should never lose sight of the fact that civilization necessarily progressed in reference to the spiritual and temporal *elements* of the social state before advancing in regard to their *ensemble*. Consequently, the three great and successive phases were inevitably inaugurated as to their elements before they commenced as to the *ensemble*, a circumstance which might occasion some confusion if we did not make a large allowance for this unavoidable difference.

Such, then, are the principal characteristics of the three epochs into which we can divide the entire history of civilization, from the period when the social state began to acquire real solidity until the present time. I venture to submit to savants this primary division of the past, which appears to me to fulfill the essential conditions of a good classification of the *ensemble* of political facts.

CHAPTER 3

OSWALD SPENGLER

The Life Cycle of Cultures

Cultures are organisms, and world history is their collective biography.
Morphologically, the immense history of the Chinese or of the classical culture is the exact equivalent of the petty history of the individual man, or
of the animal, or the tree, or the flower. In the destinies of the several cultures that follow upon one another, grow up with one another, touch, over-
shadow, and suppress one another, is compressed the whole content of human history. And, if we set free their shapes, till now hidden all too deep
under the surface of a trite "history of human progress" and let them
march past us in the spirit, it cannot but be that we shall succeed in distinguishing, amidst all that is special or unessential, the primitive culture-
form, *the* Culture that underlies as ideal all the individual cultures.

I distinguish the *idea* of a culture, which is the sum total of its inner possibilities, from its sensible *phenomenon* or appearance upon the canvas of
history as a fulfilled actuality. It is the relation of the soul to the living body,
to its expression in the light-world perceptible to our eyes. This history of a
culture is the progressive actualizing of its possible, and the fulfillment is
equivalent to the end.

Culture is the *prime phenomenon* of all past and future world history.
The deep and scarcely appreciated idea of Goethe, which he discovered in
his "living nature" and always made the basis of his morphological researches, we shall here apply—in its most precise sense—to all the formations of man's history, whether fully matured, cut off in the prime, half-
opened, or stifled in the seed. It is the method of living into (*erfühlen*) the
object, as opposed to dissecting it. "The highest to which man can attain is
wonder; and, if the prime phenomenon makes him wonder, let him be
content; nothing higher can it give him, and nothing further should he seek
for behind it; here is the limit." The prime phenomenon is that in which the

idea of becoming is presented net. To the spiritual eye of Goethe, the idea of the prime plant was clearly visible in the form of every individual plant that happened to come up or even that could possibly come up. . . . It was a look into the heart of things that Leibniz would have understood, but the century of Darwin is as remote from such a vision as it is possible to be.

At present, however, we look in vain for any treatment of history that is entirely free from the methods of Darwinism—that is, of systematic natural science based on causality. A physiognomic that is precise, clear, and sure of itself and its limits has never yet arisen, and it can only arise through the discoveries of method that we have yet to make. Herein lies the great problem set for the twentieth century to solve—to explore carefully the inner structure of the organic units in and through which world history fulfills itself, to separate the morphologically necessary from the accidental, and, by seizing the *purport* of events, to ascertain the languages in which they speak.

Over the expanse of the water passes the endless uniform wave-train of the generations. Here and there, bright shafts of light broaden out, everywhere dancing flashes confuse and disturb the clear mirror, changing, sparkling, vanishing. These are what we call the clans, tribes, peoples, races which unify a series of generations within this or that limited area of the historical surface. As widely as these differ in creative power, so widely do the images that they create vary in duration and plasticity, and, when the creative power dies out, the physiognomic, linguistic, and spiritual identification marks vanish also, and the phenomenon subsides again into the ruck of the generations. Aryans, Mongols, Germans, Kelts, Parthians, Franks, Carthaginians, Berbers, Bantus are names by which we specify some very heterogeneous images of this order.

But over this surface, too, the great cultures accomplish their majestic wave cycles. They appear suddenly, swell in splendid lines, flatten again, and vanish, and the face of the waters is once more a sleeping waste.

A culture is born in the moment when a great soul awakens out of the protospirituality (*dem urseelenhaften Zustande*) of ever-childish humanity and detaches itself, a form from the formless, a bounded and mortal thing from the boundless and enduring. It blooms on the soil of an exactly definable landscape, to which plant-wise it remains bound. It dies when this soul has actualized the full sum of its possibilities in the shape of peoples, languages, dogmas, arts, states, sciences and reverts into the protosoul. But its living existence, that sequence of great epochs which define and display the stages of fulfillment, is an inner passionate struggle to maintain the Idea against the powers of chaos without and the unconscious muttering deep-down within. It is not only the artist who struggles against the resistance of the material and the stifling of the idea within him. Every culture stands in a deeply symbolical, almost in a mystical, relation to the Extended, the space in which and through which it strives to actualize itself. The aim once attained—the idea, the entire content of inner possibilities, fulfilled and made externally actual—the culture suddenly hardens, it mortifies, its blood congeals, its force breaks down, and it becomes Civilization, the thing which we feel and understand in the words Egypticism, Byzantinism, Mandarinism. As such, they may, like a worn-out giant of the primeval forest, thrust their decaying branches toward the sky for hundreds or thousands of years, as we see in China, in India, in the Islamic world. It was thus that the classical civilization rose gigantic, in the imperial age, with a false semblance of youth and strength and fullness, and robbed the young Arabian culture of the East of light and air.

This—the inward and outward fulfillment, the finality, that awaits every living culture—is the purport of all the historic "declines," among them that decline of the classical which we know so well and fully and another decline, entirely comparable to it in course and duration, which will occupy the first centuries of the coming millennium but is heralded already and sensible in and around us today—the decline of the West. Every culture passes through the age-phases of the individual man. Each has its childhood, youth, manhood, and old age. It is a young and trembling soul, heavy with misgivings, that reveals itself in the morning of Romanesque and Gothic. . . . Childhood speaks to us also—and in the same tones—out of early Homeric Doric, out of early Christian (which is really early Arabian) art and out of the works of the Old Kingdom in Egypt that began with the Fourth Dynasty. . . . The more nearly a culture approaches the noon culmination of its being, the more virile, austere, controlled, intense the form-language it has secured for itself, the more assured its sense of its own power, the clearer its lineaments. In the spring, all this had still been dim and confused, tentative, filled with childish yearning and fears—witness the ornament of Romanesque-Gothic church porches of Saxony[1] and southern France, the early Christian catacombs, the Dipylon[2] vases. But there is now the full consciousness of ripened creative power that we see in the time of the early Middle Kingdom of Egypt, in the Athens of the Pisistratidae, in the age of Justinian, in that of the Counterreformation, and we find every individual trait of expression deliberate, strict, measured, marvelous in its ease and self-confidence. And we find, too, that everywhere, at moments, the coming fulfillment suggested itself; in such moments were created the head of Amenemhet III (the so-called Hyksos Sphinx of Tanis), the domes of Hagia Sophia, the paintings of Titian. Still later, tender to the point of fragility, fragrant with the sweetness of late October days, come the Cnidian Aphrodite and the Hall of the Maidens in the Erechtheum; the arabesques on Saracen

---

[1] By "Saxony," a German historian means not the present-day state of Saxony (which was a small and comparatively late accretion), but the whole region of the Weser and the lower Elbe, with Westphalia and Holstein.—TRANS

[2] Vases from the cemetery adjoining the Dipylon Gate of Athens, the most representative relics that we possess of the Doric or primitive age of the Hellenic culture (about 900 to 600 B.C.).—TRANS

horseshoe-arches; the Zwinger of Dresden, Watteau, Mozart. At last, in the gray dawn of civilization, the fire in the soul dies down. The dwindling powers rise to one more half-successful effort of creation and produce the classicism that is common to all dying cultures. The soul thinks once again and in Romanticism looks back piteously to its childhood; then finally, weary, reluctant, cold, it loses its desire to be and, as in Imperial Rome, wishes itself out of the overlong daylight and back in the darkness of protomysticism, in the womb of the mother, in the grave. . . .

The notion of life duration as applied to a man, a butterfly, an oak, a blade of grass comprises a specific time value, which is quite independent of all the accidents of the individual case. Ten years are a slice of life which is approximately equivalent for all men, and the metamorphosis of insects is associated with a number of days exactly known and predictable in individual cases. For the Romans the notions of *pueritia, adolescentia, iuventus, virilitas, senectus* possessed an almost mathematically precise meaning. . . . The duration of a generation—whatever may be its nature—is a fact of almost mystical significance.

Now, such relations are valid also, and to an extent never hitherto imagined, for all the higher cultures. *Every culture, every adolescence and maturing and decay of a culture, every one of its intrinsically necessary stages and periods, has a definite duration, always the same, always recurring with the emphasis of a symbol.* . . . What is the meaning of that striking fifty-year period, the rhythm of the political, intellectual, and artistic "becoming" of all cultures? [3] Of the 300-year period of the Baroque, of the Ionic, of the great mathematics, of Attic sculpture, of mosaic painting, of counterpoint, of Galilean mechanics? What does the *ideal* life of one millennium for each culture mean in comparison with the individual man's "three-score years and ten"? As the plant's being is brought to expression in form, dress, and carriage by leaves, blossoms, twigs, and fruit, so also is the being of a culture manifested by its religious, intellectual, political, and economic formations. Just as, say, Goethe's individuality discourses of itself in such widely different forms as the *Faust,* the *Farbenlehre,* the *Reineke Fuchs, Tasso, Werther,* the journey to Italy and the Friederike love, the *Westöstliche Diwan* and the *Römische Elegien,* so the individuality of the classical world displays itself in the Persian wars, the Attic drama, the city-state, the Dionysia and not less in the Tyrannis, the Ionic column, the geometry of Euclid, the Roman legion, and the gladiatorial contests and *panem et circenses* of the Imperial age.

In this sense, too, every individual being that has any sort of importance

---

[3] I will only mention here the distances apart of the three Punic Wars, and the series —likewise comprehensible only as rhythmic—Spanish Succession War, Silesian wars, Napoleonic Wars, Bismarck's wars, and the World War.

recapitulates, of intrinsic necessity, all the epochs of the culture to which it belongs. In each one of us, at that decisive moment when he begins to know that he is an ego, the inner life wakens just where and just how that of the culture wakened long ago. Each of us men of the West, in his child's daydreams and child's play, lives again its Gothic—the cathedrals, the castles, the hero sagas, the crusader's *Dieu le veult,* the soul's oath of young Parsifal. Every young Greek had his Homeric age and his Marathon. In Goethe's Werther, the image of a tropic youth, that every Faustian (but no classical) man knows, the springtime of Petrarch and the Minnesänger reappears. When Goethe blocked out the *Urfaust,*[4] he was Parsifal; when he finished *Faust I,* he was Hamlet, and only with *Faust II* did he become the world-man of the nineteenth century who could understand Byron. Even the senility of the classical—the faddy and unfruitful centuries of very late Hellenism, the second childhood of a weary and blasé intelligence—can be studied in more than one of its grand old men. Thus, much of Euripides' *Bacchae* anticipates the life outlook, and much of Plato's *Timaeus,* the religious syncretism of the Imperial age; and Goethe's *Faust II* and Wagner's *Parsifal* disclose to us in advance the shape that *our* spirituality will assume in our next (*in point of creative power our last*) centuries.

Biology employs the term *homology* of organs to signify morphological equivalence, in contradistinction to the term *analogy* which relates to functional equivalence. This important, and in the sequel most fruitful, notion was conceived by Goethe (who was led thereby to the discovery of the *os intermaxillare* in man) and put into strict scientific shape by Owen; this notion, also, we shall incorporate in our historical method.

It is known that for every part of the bone structure of the human head an exactly corresponding part is found in all vertebrated animals right down to the fish and that the pectoral fins of fish and the feet, wings and hands of terrestrial vertebrates are homologous organs, even though they have lost every trace of similarity. The lungs of terrestrial and the swim bladders of aquatic animals are homologous, while lungs and gills on the other hand are analogous—that is, similar in point of use. And the trained and deepened morphological insight that is required to establish such distinctions is an utterly different thing from the present method of historical research, with its shallow comparisons of Christ and Buddha, Archimedes and Galileo, Caesar and Wallenstein, parceled Germany and parceled Greece. More and more clearly as we go on, we shall realize what immense views will offer themselves to the historical eye as soon as the rigorous morphological method has been understood and cultivated. To name but a few examples, *homologous* forms are: classical sculpture and West European orchestration; the Fourth Dynasty pyramids and the Gothic cathedrals; Indian Buddhism and Roman Stoicism (Buddhism and Christianity are *not even*

---

[4] The first draft of *Faust I,* discovered only comparatively recently.—TRANS

analogous); the periods of "the Contending States" in China; the Hyksos in Egypt and the Punic Wars; the age of Pericles and the age of the Ommayads; the epochs of the Rigveda, of Plotinus, and of Dante. The Dionysiac movement is homologous with the Renaissance, analogous to the Reformation. For us, "Wagner is the *résumé* of modernity," as Nietzsche rightly saw; and the equivalent that logically *must* exist in the Classical modernity we find in Pergamene art. . . .

The application of the "homology" principle to historical phenomena brings with it an entirely new connotation for the word "contemporary." I designate as contemporary two historical facts that occur in exactly the same relative positions in their respective cultures and therefore possess exactly equivalent importance. The development of the classical and that of the Western mathematic proceeded in complete congruence, and we might venture to describe Pythagoras as the contemporary of Descartes; Archytas, of Laplace; Archimedes, of Gauss. The Ionic and the Baroque, again, ran their course *contemporaneously*. Polygnotus pairs in time with Rembrandt; Polycletus, with Bach. The Reformation, Puritanism, and, above all, the turn to civilization appear simultaneously in all cultures. In the classical, this last epoch bears the names of Philip and Alexander; in our West, those of the Revolution and Napoleon. Contemporary, too, are the building of Alexandria, of Baghdad, and of Washington; classical coinage and our double-entry bookkeeping; the first Tyrannis and the Fronde; Augustus and Shih-huang-ti; Hannibal and the World War.

. . . All great creations and forms in religion, art, politics, social life, economy, and science appear, fulfill themselves, and die down *contemporaneously* in all the cultures; the inner structure of one corresponds strictly with that of all the others; there is not a single phenomenon of deep physiognomic importance in the record of one for which we could not find a counterpart in the record of every other; and this counterpart is to be found under a characteristic form and in a perfectly definite chronological position. . . .

CHAPTER 4

VILFREDO PARETO

The Circulation of Elites

Let us assume that in every branch of human activity each individual is given an index which stands as a sign of his capacity, very much the way grades are given in the various subjects in examinations in school. The highest type of lawyer, for instance, will be given 10. The man who does not get a client will be given 1—reserving zero for the man who is an out-and-out idiot. To the man who has made his millions—honestly or dishonestly as the case may be—we will give 10. To the man who has earned his thousands we will give 6; to such as just manage to keep out of the poor-house, 1, keeping zero for those who get in. To the woman "in politics," such as the Aspasia of Pericles, the Maintenon of Louis XIV, the Pompadour of Louis XV, who has managed to infatuate a man of power and play a part in the man's career, we shall give some higher number, such as 8 or 9; to the strumpet who merely satisfies the senses of such a man and exerts no influence on public affairs, we shall give zero. To a clever rascal who knows how to fool people and still keep clear of the penitentiary, we shall give 8, 9, or 10, according to the number of geese he has plucked and the amount of money he has been able to get out of them. . . .

So let us make a class of the people who have the highest indices in their branch of activity, and to that class give the name of *élite*.

For the particular investigation with which we are engaged, a study of the social equilibrium, it will help if we further divide that class into two classes: a *governing élite*, comprising individuals who directly or indirectly play some considerable part in government, and a *non-governing élite*, comprising the rest.

So we get two strata in a population: (1) A lower stratum, the *non-élite*, with whose possible influence on government we are not just here con-

From: THE MIND AND SOCIETY: A TREATISE ON GENERAL SOCIOLOGY, by Vilfredo Pareto. Translated by A. Bongiorno and A. Livingston. Published through the sponsorship of the Pareto Fund. Dover Publications, Inc. New York, 1935 copyright by The Pareto Fund, pp. 1422-1432.

cerned; then (2) a higher stratum, *the élite*, which is divided into two: (*a*) a governing *élite*; (*b*) a non-governing *élite*.

In the concrete, there are no examinations whereby each person is assigned to his proper place in these various classes. That deficiency is made up for by other means, by various sorts of labels that serve the purpose after a fashion. Such labels are the rule even where there are examinations. The label "lawyer" is affixed to a man who is supposed to know something about the law and often does, though sometimes again he is an ignoramus. So, the governing *élite* contains individuals who wear labels appropriate to political offices of a certain altitude—ministers, Senators, Deputies, chief justices, generals, colonels, and so on—making the apposite exceptions for those who have found their way into that exalted company without possessing qualities corresponding to the labels they wear.

Such exceptions are much more numerous than the exceptions among lawyers, physicians, engineers, millionaires (who have made their own money), artists of distinction, and so on; for the reason, among others, that in these latter departments of human activity the labels are won directly by each individual, whereas in the *élite* some of the labels—the label of wealth, for instance—are hereditary. In former times there were hereditary labels in the governing *élite* also—in our day hardly more than the label of king remains in that status; but if direct inheritance has disappeared, inheritance is still powerful indirectly; and an individual who has inherited a sizable patrimony can easily be named Senator in certain countries, or can get himself elected to the parliament by buying votes or, on occasion, by wheedling voters with assurances that he is a democrat of democrats, a Socialist, an Anarchist. Wealth, family, or social connexions also help in many other cases to win the label of the *élite* in general, or of the governing *élite* in particular, for persons who otherwise hold no claim upon it.

If all these deviations from type were of little importance, they might be disregarded, as they are virtually disregarded in cases where a diploma is required for the practice of a profession. Everyone knows that there are persons who do not deserve their diplomas, but experience shows that on the whole such exceptions may be overlooked.

One might, further, from certain points of view at least, disregard deviations if they remained more or less constant quantitatively—if there were only a negligible variation in proportions between the total of a class and the people who wear its label without possessing the qualities corresponding.

As a matter of fact, the real cases that we have to consider in our societies differ from those two. The deviations are not so few that they can be disregarded. Then again, their number is variable, and the variations give rise to situations having an important bearing on the social equilibrium. We are therefore required to make a special study of them.

Furthermore, the manner in which the various groups in a population intermix has to be considered. In moving from one group to another an individual generally brings with him certain inclinations, sentiments, attitudes, that he has acquired in the group from which he comes, and that circumstance cannot be ignored.

To this mixing, in the particular case in which only two groups, the *élite* and the *non-élite*, are envisaged, the term "circulation of élites" has been applied—in French, *circulation des élites*.

In conclusion we must pay special attention (1), in the case of one single group, to the proportions between the total of the group and the number of individuals who are nominally members of it but do not possess the qualities requisite for effective membership; and then (2), in the case of various groups, to the ways in which transitions from one group to the other occur, and to the intensity of that movement—that is to say, to the velocity of the circulation. . . .

The upper stratum of society, the *élite*, nominally contains certain groups of people, not always very sharply defined, that are called aristocracies. There are cases in which the majority of individuals belonging to such aristocracies actually possess the qualities requisite for remaining there; and then again there are cases where considerable numbers of the individuals making up the class do not possess those requisites. . . .

Aristocracies do not last. It is an incontestable fact that after a certain length of time they pass away. History is a graveyard of aristocracies. The Athenian "People" was an aristocracy as compared with the remainder of a population of resident aliens and slaves. It vanished without leaving any descent. The various aristocracies of Rome vanished in their time. So did the aristocracies of the Barbarians. Where, in France, are the descendants of the Frankish conquerors? The genealogies of the English nobility have been very exactly kept; and they show that very few families still remain to claim descent from the comrades of William the Conqueror. The rest have vanished. In Germany the aristocracy of the present day is very largely made up of descendants of vassals of the lords of old. The populations of European countries have increased enormously during the past few centuries. It is as certain as certain can be that the aristocracies have not increased in proportion.

They decay not in numbers only. They decay also in quality, in the sense that they lose their vigour, that there is a decline in the proportions of the residues[1] which enabled them to win their power and hold it. The governing class is restored not only in numbers, but—and that is the more important thing—in quality, by families rising from the lower classes and bringing with them the vigour and the proportions of residues necessary for keeping themselves in power. It is also restored by the loss of its more degenerate members.

---

[1] Pareto conceives of residues as manifestations of psychic states, sentiments and instincts.—The Editors.

If one of those movements comes to an end, or worse still, if they both come to an end, the governing class crashes to ruin and often sweeps the whole of a nation along with it. Potent cause of disturbance in the equilibrium is the accumulation of superior elements in the lower classes and, conversely, if inferior elements in the higher classes. If human aristocracies were like thorough-breds among animals, which reproduce themselves over long periods of time with approximately the same traits, the history of the human race would be something altogether different from the history we know.

In virtue of class-circulation, the governing *élite* is always in a state of slow and continuous transformation. It flows on like a river, never being today what it was yesterday. From time to time sudden and violent disturbances occur. There is a flood—the river overflows its banks. Afterwards, the new governing *élite* again resumes its slow transformation. The flood has subsided, the river is again flowing normally in its wonted bed.

Revolutions come about through accumulations in the higher strata of society—either because of a slowing-down in class-circulation, or from other causes—of decadent elements no longer possessing the residues suitable for keeping them in power, and shrinking from the use of force; while meantime in the lower strata of society elements of superior quality are coming to the fore, possessing residues suitable for exercising the functions of government and willing enough to use force.

In general, in revolutions the members of the lower strata are captained by leaders from the higher strata, because the latter possess the intellectual qualities required for outlining a tactic, while lacking the combative residues supplied by the individuals from the lower strata.

Violent movements take place by fits and starts, and effects therefore do not follow immediately on their causes. After a governing class, or a nation, has maintained itself for long periods of time on force and acquired great wealth, it may subsist for some time still without using force, buying off its adversaries and paying not only in gold, but also in terms of the dignity and respect that it had formerly enjoyed and which constitute, as it were, a capital. In the first stages of decline, power is maintained by bargainings and concessions, and people are so deceived into thinking that that policy can be carried on indefinitely. So the decadent Roman Empire bought peace of the Barbarians with money and honours. So Louis XVI, in France, squandering in a very short time an ancestral inheritance of love, respect, and almost religious reverence for the monarchy, managed, by making repeated concessions, to be the King of the Revolution. So the English aristocracy managed to prolong its term of power in the second half of the nineteenth century down to the dawn of its decadence, which was heralded by the "Parliament Bill" in the first years of the twentieth.

CHAPTER 5

KARL MARX

Historical Materialism Summarized

In the social production which men carry on, they enter into definite relations that are indispensable and independent of their will; these relations
of production correspond to a definite stage of development of their material
powers of production. The sum total of these relations of production constitutes the economic structure of society—the real foundation, on which rise
legal and political superstructures and to which correspond definite forms of
social consciousness. The mode of production in material life determines
the general character of the social, political, and spiritual processes of life. It
is not the consciousness (*Bewusstsein*) of men that determines their existence (*sein*), but, on the contrary, their social existence that determines
their consciousness. At a certain stage of their development, the material
forces of production in society come in conflict with the existing relations
of production or—what is but a legal expression for the same thing—with
the property relations within which they had been at work before. From
forms of development of the forces of production, these relations turn into
their fetters. Then comes the period of social revolution. With the change of
the economic foundation, the entire immense superstructure is more or less
rapidly transformed. In considering such transformations, the distinction
should always be made between the material transformation of the economic conditions of production, which can be determined with the precision
of natural science, and the legal, political, religious, aesthetic, or philosophic
—in short, ideological—forms in which men become conscious of this conflict and fight it out. Just as our opinion of an individual is not based on what
he thinks of himself, so can we not judge of such a period of transformation by its own consciousness; on the contrary, this consciousness must

From the author's Introduction to Karl Marx, *A Contribution to the Critique of Political Economy* (Chicago: Charles H. Kerr, 1904), pp. 11-13.

rather be explained from the contradictions of material life, from the existing conflict between the social forces of production and the relations of production. No social order ever disappears before all the productive forces, for which there is room in it, have been developed; and new, higher relations of production never appear before the material conditions of their existence have matured in the womb of the old society. Therefore, mankind always takes up only such problems as it can solve, since, looking at the matter more closely, we will always find that the problem itself arises only when the material conditions necessary for its solution already exist or are at least in the process of formation. In broad outlines we can designate the Asiatic, the ancient, the feudal, and the modern bourgeois methods of production as so many epochs in the progress of the economic formation of society. The bourgeois relations of production are the last antagonistic form of the social process of production—antagonistic not in the sense of individual antagonism, but of one arising from conditions surrounding the life of individuals in society; at the same time, the productive forces developing in the womb of bourgeois society create the material conditions for the solution of that antagonism. This social formation constitutes, therefore, the closing chapter of the prehistoric stage of human society.

CHAPTER 6

KARL MARX AND FRIEDRICH ENGELS

The Class Struggle

Bourgeoisie and Proletariat

The history of all hitherto existing society is the history of class struggles.

Freeman and slave, patrician and plebeian, lord and serf, guildmaster and journeyman, in a word, oppressor and oppressed, stood in constant opposition to one another, carried on an uninterrupted, now hidden, now open fight, a fight that each time ended either in a revolutionary reconstitution of society at large or in the common ruin of the contending classes.

In the earlier epochs of history, we find almost everywhere a complicated arrangement of society into various orders, a manifold gradation of social rank. In ancient Rome we have patricians, knights, plebeians, slaves; in the Middle Ages, feudal lords, vassals, guildmasters, journeymen, apprentices, serfs; in almost all of these classes, again, subordinate gradations.

The modern bourgeois society that has sprouted from the ruins of feudal society has not done away with class antagonisms. It has but established new classes, new conditions of oppression, new forms of struggle in place of the old ones.

Our epoch, the epoch of the bourgeoisie, possesses, however, this distinctive feature: it has simplified the class antagonisms. Society as a whole is more and more splitting up into two great hostile camps, into two great classes directly facing each other—bourgeoisie and proletariat.

The Rise of the Bourgeoisie

From the serfs of the Middle Ages sprang the chartered burghers of the earliest towns. From these burgesses, the first elements of the bourgeoisie were developed.

The discovery of America, the rounding of the Cape, opened up fresh

---

From Karl Marx and Friedrich Engels, *Manifesto of the Communist Party* (New York: International Publishers, 1932), pp. 9-21.

ground for the rising bourgeoisie. The East Indian and Chinese markets, the colonization of America, trade with the colonies, the increase in the means of exchange and in commodities generally gave to commerce, to navigation, to industry, an impulse never before known and, thereby, to the revolutionary element in the tottering feudal society, a rapid development.

The feudal system of industry, in which industrial production was monopolized by closed guilds, now no longer sufficed for the growing wants of the new markets. The manufacturing system took its place. The guildmasters were pushed aside by the manufacturing middle class; division of labor between the different corporate guilds vanished in the face of division of labor in each single workshop.

Meantime, the markets kept ever growing, the demand ever rising. Even manufacture no longer sufficed. Thereupon, steam and machinery revolutionized industrial production. The place of manufacture was taken by the giant, modern industry; the place of the industrial middle class, by industrial millionaires—the leaders of whole industrial armies, the modern bourgeois.

Modern industry has established the world market, for which the discovery of America paved the way. This market has given an immense development to commerce, to navigation, to communication by land. This development has, in its turn, reacted on the extension of industry; and, in proportion as industry, commerce, navigation, railways extended, in the same proportion the bourgeoisie developed, increased its capital, and pushed into the background every class handed down from the Middle Ages.

We see, therefore, how the modern bourgeoisie is itself the product of a long course of development, of a series of revolutions in the modes of production and of exchange.

Each step in the development of the bourgeoisie was accompanied by a corresponding political advance of that class. An oppressed class under the sway of the feudal nobility, it became an armed and self-governing association in the medieval commune; here independent urban republic (as in Italy and Germany), there taxable "third estate" of the monarchy (as in France); afterward, in the period of manufacture proper, serving either the semifeudal or the absolute monarchy as a counterpoise against the nobility and, in fact, cornerstone of the great monarchies in general—the bourgeoisie has at last, since the establishment of modern industry and of the world market, conquered for itself, in the modern representative state, exclusive political sway. The executive of the modern state is but a committee for managing the common affairs of the whole bourgeoisie. . . .

More and more, the bourgeoisie keeps doing away with the scattered state of the population, of the means of production, and of property. It has agglomerated population, centralized means of production, and has concentrated property in a few hands. The necessary consequence of this was political centralization. Independent or but loosely connected provinces with separate interests, laws, governments and systems of taxation became lumped together into one nation, with one government, one code of laws, one national class interest, one frontier, and one customs tariff.

The bourgeoisie, during its rule of scarce one hundred years, has created more massive and more colossal productive forces than have all preceding generations together. Subjection of nature's forces to man, machinery, application of chemistry to industry and agriculture, steam navigation, railways, electric telegraphs, clearing of whole continents for cultivation, canalization of rivers, whole populations conjured out of the ground—what earlier century had even a presentiment that such productive forces slumbered in the lap of social labor?

We see then that the means of production and of exchange, which served as the foundation for the growth of the bourgeoisie, were generated in feudal society. At a certain stage in the development of these means of production and of exchange, the conditions under which feudal society produced and exchanged, the feudal organization of agriculture and manufacturing industry—in a word, the feudal relations of property—became no longer compatible with the already developed productive forces; they became so many fetters. They had to be burst asunder; they were burst asunder.

Into their place stepped free competition, accompanied by a social and political constitution adapted to it and by the economic and political sway of the bourgeois class.

The Rise of the Proletariat

A similar movement is going on before our own eyes. Modern bourgeois society, with its relations of production, of exchange, and of property—a society that has conjured up such gigantic means of production and of exchange—is like the sorcerer who is no longer able to control the powers of the nether world whom he has called up by his spells. For many a decade past, the history of industry and commerce is but the history of the revolt of modern productive forces against modern conditions of production, against the property relations that are the conditions for the existence of the bourgeoisie and of its rule. It is enough to mention the commercial crises that by their periodical return put the existence of the entire bourgeois society on trial, each time more threateningly. In these crises, a great part, not only of the existing products, but also of the previously created productive forces, are periodically destroyed. In these crises, there breaks out an epidemic that, in all earlier epochs, would have seemed an absurdity—the epidemic of overproduction. Society suddenly finds itself put back into a state of momentary barbarism; it appears as if a famine, a universal war of devastation, had cut off the supply of every means of subsistence; industry and commerce seem to be destroyed. And why? Because there is too much civilization, too much means of subsistence, too much industry, too much commerce. The productive forces at the disposal of society no longer tend to further the development of the conditions of bourgeois property; on the contrary, they have become too powerful for these conditions, by which they are fettered, and no sooner do they overcome these fetters than they bring disorder into the whole of bourgeois society, endanger the existence of bourgeois property. The conditions of bourgeois society are too narrow to comprise the wealth created by them. And how does the bourgeoisie get over these crises? On the one hand, by enforced destruction of a mass of productive forces; on the other, by the conquest of new markets and by the more thorough exploitation of the old ones. That is to say, by paving the way for more extensive and more destructive crises and by diminishing the means whereby crises are prevented.

The weapons with which the bourgeoisie felled feudalism to the ground are now turned against the bourgeoisie itself.

But not only has the bourgeoisie forged the weapons that bring death to itself; it has also called into existence the men who are to wield those weapons—the modern working class, the proletarians.

In proportion as the bourgeoisie, *i.e.,* capital, is developed, in the same proportion is the proletariat, the modern working class, developed—a class of laborers who live only so long as they find work and who find work only so long as their labor increases capital. These laborers, who must sell themselves piecemeal, are a commodity, like every other article of commerce, and are consequently exposed to all the vicissitudes of competition, to all the fluctuations of the market.

Owing to the extensive use of machinery and to division of labor, the work of the proletarians has lost all individual character and, consequently, all charm for the workman. He becomes an appendage of the machine, and it is only the most simple, most monotonous, and most easily acquired knack that is required of him. Hence, the cost of production of a workman is restricted almost entirely to the means of subsistence that he requires for his maintenance and for the propagation of his race. But the price of a commodity, and therefore also of labor, is equal to its cost of production. In proportion, therefore, as the repulsiveness of the work increases, the wage decreases. Nay more, in proportion as the use of machinery and division of labor increases, in the same proportion the burden of toil also increases, whether by prolongation of the working hours, by increase of the work exacted in a given time, or by increased speed of the machinery, etc.

Modern industry has converted the little workshop of the patriarchal master into the great factory of the industrial capitalist. Masses of laborers, crowded into the factory, are organized like soldiers. As privates of the industrial army, they are placed under the command of a perfect hierarchy of officers and sergeants. Not only are they slaves of the bourgeois class and of the bourgeois state, they are daily and hourly enslaved by the machine, by the overseer, and, above all, by the individual bourgeois manufacturer himself. The more openly this despotism proclaims gain to be its end and aim, the more petty, the more hateful, and the more embittering it is.

The less the skill and exertion of strength implied in manual labor, in other words, the more modern industry develops, the more is the labor of men superseded by that of women. Differences of age and sex have no longer any distinctive social validity for the working class. All are instruments of labor, more or less expensive to use, according to their age and sex.

No sooner has the laborer received his wages in cash, for the moment escaping exploitation by the manufacturer, than he is set upon by the other portions of the bourgeoisie, the landlord, the shopkeeper, the pawnbroker, etc.

The lower strata of the middle class—the small tradespeople, shopkeepers, and retired tradesmen generally, the handicraftsmen and peasants—all these sink gradually into the proletariat, partly because their diminutive capital does not suffice for the scale on which modern industry is carried on and is swamped in the competition with the large capitalists, partly because their specialized skill is rendered worthless by new methods of production. Thus the proletariat is recruited from all classes of the population.

The proletariat goes through various stages of development. With its birth begins its struggle with the bourgeoisie. At first the contest is carried on by individual laborers; then by the workpeople of a factory; then by the operatives of one trade, in one locality, against the individual bourgeois who directly exploits them. They direct their attacks, not against the bourgeois conditions of production, but against the instruments of production themselves; they destroy imported wares that compete with their labor, they smash machinery to pieces, they set factories ablaze, they seek to restore by force the vanished status of the workman of the Middle Ages.

At this stage the laborers still form an incoherent mass scattered over the whole country and broken up by their mutual competition. If anywhere they unite to form more compact bodies, this is not yet the consequence of their own active union, but of the union of the bourgeoisie, which, in order to attain its own political ends, is compelled to set the whole proletariat in motion and is, moreover, still able to do so for a time. At this stage, therefore, the proletarians do not fight their enemies, but the enemies of their enemies, the remnants of absolute monarchy, the landowners, the nonindustrial bourgeois, the petty bourgeoisie. Thus the whole historical movement is concentrated in the hands of the bourgeoisie; every victory so obtained is a victory for the bourgeoisie.

But, with the development of industry, the proletariat not only increases in number; it becomes concentrated in greater masses, its strength grows, and it feels that strength more. The various interests and conditions of life within the ranks of the proletariat are more and more equalized, in proportion as machinery obliterates all distinctions of labor and nearly everywhere reduces wages to the same low level. The growing competition among the bourgeois and the resulting commercial crises make the wages of the workers ever more fluctuating. The unceasing improvement of machinery, ever more rapidly developing, makes their livelihood more and more precarious; the collisions between individual workmen and individual bourgeois take more and more the character of collisions between two classes. Thereupon the workers begin to form combinations (trade unions) against the bourgeoisie; they club together in order to keep up the rate of wages; they found permanent associations in order to make provision beforehand for these occasional revolts. Here and there the contest breaks out into riots.

Now and then the workers are victorious, but only for a time. The real fruit of their battles lies, not in the immediate result, but in the ever-expanding union of the workers. This union is furthered by the improved means of communication which are created by modern industry and which place the workers of different localities in contact with one another. It was just this contact that was needed to centralize the numerous local struggles, all of the same character, into one national struggle between classes. But every class struggle is a political struggle. And that union, to attain which the burghers of the Middle Ages, with their miserable highways, required centuries, the modern proletarians, thanks to railways, achieve in a few years.

This organization of the proletarians into a class and consequently into a political party is continually being upset again by the competition between the workers themselves. But it ever rises up again, stronger, firmer, mightier. It compels legislative recognition of particular interests of the workers by taking advantage of the divisions among the bourgeoisie itself. Thus the ten-hour bill in England was carried.

Altogether, collisions between the classes of the old society further the course of development of the proletariat in many ways. The bourgeoisie finds itself involved in a constant battle. At first, with the aristocracy; later on, with those portions of the bourgeoisie itself whose interests have become antagonistic to the progress of industry; at all times, with the bourgeoisie of foreign countries. In all these battles, it sees itself compelled to appeal to the proletariat, to ask for its help, and, thus, to drag it into the political arena. The bourgeoisie itself, therefore, supplies the proletariat with its own elements of political and general education; in other words, it furnishes the proletariat with weapons for fighting the bourgeoisie.

Further, as we have already seen, entire sections of the ruling classes are, by the advance of industry, precipitated into the proletariat or are at least threatened in their conditions of existence. These also supply the proletariat with fresh elements of enlightenment and progress.

Finally, in times when the class struggle nears the decisive hour, the process of dissolution going on within the ruling class, in fact within the whole range of old society, assumes such a violent, glaring character, that a small section of the ruling class cuts itself adrift and joins the revolutionary class, the class that holds the future in its hands. Just as, therefore, at an earlier period, a section of the nobility went over to the bourgeoisie, so now a portion of the bourgeoisie goes over to the proletariat and, in particular, a portion of the bourgeois ideologists who have raised themselves to the level of comprehending theoretically the historical movement as a whole.

Of all the classes that stand face to face with the bourgeoisie today, the proletariat alone is a really revolutionary class. The other classes decay and finally disappear in the face of modern industry; the proletariat is its special and essential product.

The lower middle class, the small manufacturer, the shopkeeper, the artisan, the peasant—all these fight against the bourgeoisie, to save from extinction their existence as fractions of the middle class. They are, therefore, not revolutionary, but conservative. Nay more, they are reactionary, for they try to roll back the wheel of history. If by chance they are revolutionary, they are so only in view of their impending transfer into the proletariat; they thus defend, not their present, but their future interests; they desert their own standpoint to adopt that of the proletariat.

The "dangerous class," the social scum (*Lumpenproletariat*), that passively rotting mass thrown off by the lowest layers of old society, may, here and there, be swept into the movement by a proletarian revolution; its conditions of life, however, prepare it far more for the part of a bribed tool of reactionary intrigue.

The social conditions of the old society no longer exist for the proletariat. The proletarian is without property; his relation to his wife and children has no longer anything in common with bourgeois family relations; modern industrial labor, modern subjection to capital, the same in England as in France, in America as in Germany, has stripped him of every trace of national character. Law, morality, religion are to him so many bourgeois prejudices, behind which lurk in ambush just as many bourgeois interests.

All the preceding classes that got the upper hand sought to fortify their already acquired status by subjecting society at large to their conditions of appropriation. The proletarians cannot become masters of the productive forces of society except by abolishing their own previous mode of appropriation and thereby also every other previous mode of appropriation. They have nothing of their own to secure and to fortify; their mission is to destroy all previous securities for, and insurances of, individual property.

All previous historical movements were movements of minorities or in the interest of minorities. The proletarian movement is the self-conscious, independent movement of the immense majority, in the interest of the immense majority. The proletariat, the lowest stratum of our present society, cannot stir, cannot raise itself up, without all the superincumbent strata of official society being sprung into the air.

Though not in substance, yet in form, the struggle of the proletariat with the bourgeoisie is at first a national struggle. The proletariat of each country must, of course, first of all settle matters with its own bourgeoisie.

In depicting the most general phases of the development of the proletariat, we traced the more or less veiled civil war raging within existing society up to the point where that war breaks out into open revolution and where the violent overthrow of the bourgeoisie lays the foundation for the sway of the proletariat.

Hitherto, every form of society has been based, as we have already seen, on the antagonism of oppressing and oppressed classes. But, in order to oppress a class, certain conditions must be assured to it under which it can, at least, continue its slavish existence. The serf, in the period of serfdom, raised himself to membership in the commune, just as the petty bourgeois, under the yoke of feudal absolutism, managed to develop into a bourgeois. The modern laborer, on the contrary, instead of rising with the progress of industry, sinks deeper and deeper below the conditions of existence of his own class. He becomes a pauper, and pauperism develops more rapidly than population and wealth. And here it becomes evident that the bourgeoisie is unfit any longer to be the ruling class in society and to impose its conditions of existence upon society as an overriding law. It is unfit to rule because it is incompetent to assure an existence to its slave within his slavery, because it cannot help letting him sink into such a state that it has to feed him, instead of being fed by him. Society can no longer live under this bourgeoisie; in other words, its existence is no longer compatible with society.

The essential condition for the existence and sway of the bourgeois class is the formation and augmentation of capital; the condition for capital is wage labor. Wage labor rests exclusively on competition between the laborers. The advance of industry, whose involuntary promoter is the bourgeoisie, replaces the isolation of the laborers, due to competition, by their revolutionary combination, due to association. The development of modern industry, therefore, cuts from under its feet the very foundation on which the bourgeoisie produces and appropriates products. What the bourgeoisie therefore produces, above all, are its own gravediggers. Its fall and the victory of the proletariat are equally inevitable.

CHAPTER 7

MAX WEBER

The Role of Ideas in History

In a universal history of culture, the central problem for us is not, in the last analysis, even from a purely economic viewpoint, the development of capitalistic activity as such, differing in different cultures only in form: the adventurer type or capitalism in trade, war, politics, or administration as sources of gain. It is rather the origin of this sober bourgeois capitalism with its rational organization of free labor. Or, in terms of cultural history, the problem is that of the origin of the Western bourgeois class and of its peculiarities, a problem which is certainly closely connected with that of the origin of the capitalistic organization of labor, but is not quite the same thing. For the bourgeois as a class existed prior to the development of the peculiar modern form of capitalism, though, it is true, only in the Western hemisphere.

Now, the peculiar modern Western form of capitalism has been, at first sight, strongly influenced by the development of technical possibilities. Its rationality is today essentially dependent on the calculability of the most important technical factors. But this means fundamentally that it is dependent on the peculiarities of modern science, especially the natural sciences based on mathematics and exact and rational experiment. On the other hand, the development of these sciences and of the technique resting on them now receives important stimulation from these capitalistic interests in its practical economic application. It is true that the origin of Western science cannot be attributed to such interests. Calculation, even with decimals, and algebra have been carried on in India, where the decimal system was invented. But it was only made use of by developing capitalism in the West, while in India it led to no modern arithmetic or bookkeeping. Neither was the origin of mathematics and mechanics determined by capitalistic interests. But the *technical* utilization of scientific knowledge, so important

From the author's Introduction to Max Weber, *The Protestant Ethic and the Spirit of Capitalism,* trans., Talcott Parsons (New York: Charles Scribner's Sons, 1958), pp. 23-27. Used by permission of Charles Scribner's Sons.

for the living conditions of the mass of people, was certainly encouraged by economic considerations, which were extremely favorable to it in the Occident. But this encouragement was derived from the peculiarities of the social structure of the Occident. We must hence ask, from *what* parts of that structure was it derived, since not all of them have been of equal importance?

Among those of undoubted importance are the rational structures of law and of administration. For modern rational capitalism has need, not only of the technical means of production, but of a calculable legal system and of administration in terms of formal rules. Without it, adventurous and speculative trading capitalism and all sorts of politically determined capitalisms are possible, but no rational enterprise under individual initiative, with fixed capital and certainty of calculations. Such a legal system and such administration have been available for economic activity in a comparative state of legal and formalistic perfection only in the Occident. We must hence inquire where that law came from. Among other circumstances, capitalistic interests have in turn undoubtedly also helped, but by no means alone nor even principally, to prepare the way for the predominance in law and administration of a class of jurists specially trained in rational law. But these interests did not themselves create that law. Quite different forces were at work in this development. And why did not the capitalistic interests do the same in China or India? Why did not the scientific, the artistic, the political, or the economic development there enter on that path of rationalization which is peculiar to the Occident?

For in all the cases above it is a question of the specific and peculiar rationalism of Western culture. Now, by this term very different things may be understood, as the following discussion will repeatedly show. There is, for example, rationalization of mystical contemplation, that is, of an attitude which, viewed from other departments of life, is specifically irrational, just as much as there are rationalizations of economic life, of technique, of scientific research, of military training, of law and administration. Furthermore, each one of these fields may be rationalized in terms of very different ultimate values and ends, and what is rational from one point of view may well be irrational from another. Hence, rationalizations of the most varied character have existed in various departments of life and in all areas of culture. To characterize their differences from the viewpoint of cultural history, it is necessary to know what departments are rationalized, and in what direction. It is, hence, our first concern to work out and to explain genetically the special peculiarity of Occidental rationalism and, within this field, that of the modern Occidental form. Every such attempt at explanation must, recognizing the fundamental importance of the economic factor, above all take account of the economic conditions. But at the same time the opposite correlation must not be left out of consideration. For, though the development of economic rationalism is partly dependent on rational technique and law, it is at the same time determined by the ability and disposition of men to adopt certain types of practical rational conduct. When these types have been obstructed by spiritual obstacles, the development of rational economic conduct has also met serious inner resistance. The magical and religious forces and the ethical ideas of duty based on them have in the past always been among the most important formative influences on conduct. In the studies collected here we shall be concerned with these forces.[1]

Two older essays have been placed at the beginning which attempt, at one important point, to approach the side of the problem which is generally most difficult to grasp: the influence of certain religious ideas on the development of an economic spirit, or the *ethos* of an economic system. In this case we are dealing with the connection of the spirit of modern economic life with the rational ethics of ascetic Protestantism. Thus we treat here only one side of the causal chain. Later studies on the economic ethics of the world religions attempt, in the form of a survey of the relations of the most important religions to economic life and to the social stratification of their environment, to follow out both causal relationships, so far as it is necessary in order to find points of comparison with the Occidental development. For only in this way is it possible to attempt a causal evaluation of those elements of the economic ethics of the Western religions which differentiate them from others, with a hope of attaining even a tolerable degree of approximation. . . .

---

[1] That is, in the whole series of *Aufsätze zur Religionssoziologie.*—TRANS

CHAPTER 8

MAX WEBER

The Routinization
of Charisma

The Nature of Charismatic Authority

The term "charisma" will be applied to a certain quality of an individual personality, by virtue of which he is set apart from ordinary men and treated as endowed with supernatural, superhuman, or at least specifically exceptional powers or qualities. These are such as are not accessible to the ordinary person, but are regarded as of divine origin or as exemplary, and on the basis of them the individual concerned is treated as a leader. In primitive circumstances this peculiar kind of deference is paid to prophets, to people with a reputation for therapeutic or legal wisdom, to leaders in the hunt, and heroes in war. It is very often thought of as resting on magical powers. How the quality in question would be ultimately judged from any ethical, aesthetic, or other such point of view is naturally entirely indifferent for purposes of definition. What is alone important is how the individual is actually regarded by those subject to charismatic authority, by his "followers" or "disciples."

For present purposes it will be necessary to treat a variety of different types as being endowed with charisma in this sense. It includes the state of a "berserker" whose spells of maniac passion have, apparently wrongly, sometimes been attributed to the use of drugs. In medieval Byzantium a group of people endowed with this type of charismatic warlike passion were maintained as a kind of weapon. It includes the "shaman," the kind of magician who in the pure type is subject to epileptoid seizures as a means of falling into trances. Another type is that of Joseph Smith, the founder of Mormonism, who, however, cannot be classified in this way with absolute

From Max Weber, *The Theory of Social and Economic Organization* (New York: Oxford University Press, 1947), pp. 358-373. Reprinted by permission of the translator, Talcott Parsons.

certainty since there is a possibility that he was a very sophisticated type of deliberate swindler. Finally it includes the type of intellectual, such as Kurt Eisner,[1] who is carried away with his own demagogic success. Sociological analysis, which must abstain from value judgments, will treat all these on the same level as the men who, according to conventional judgments, are the "greatest" heroes, prophets, and saviors. . . .

Charismatic authority is specifically outside the realm of everyday routine and the profane sphere. In this respect, it is sharply opposed both to rational, and particularly bureaucratic, authority and to traditional authority, whether in its patriarchal, patrimonial, or any other form. Both rational and traditional authority are specifically forms of everyday routine control of action; while the charismatic type is the direct antithesis of this. Bureaucratic authority is specifically rational in the sense of being bound to intellectually analyzable rules, while charismatic authority is specifically irrational in the sense of being foreign to all rules. Traditional authority is bound to the precedents handed down from the past and to this extent is also oriented to rules. Within the sphere of its claims, charismatic authority repudiates the past and is in this sense a specifically revolutionary force. It recognizes no appropriation of positions of power by virtue of the possession of property, either on the part of a chief or of socially privileged groups. The only basis of legitimacy for it is personal charisma, so long as it is proved, that is, as long as it receives recognition and is able to satisfy the followers or disciples. But this lasts only so long as the belief in its charismatic inspiration remains.

The above is scarcely in need of further discussion. What has been said applies to the position of authority of such elected monarchs as Napoleon, with his use of the plebiscite. It applies to the "rule of genius," which has elevated people of humble origin to thrones and high military commands, just as much as it applies to religious prophets or war heroes. . . .

In traditionally stereotyped periods, charisma is the greatest revolutionary force. The equally revolutionary force of "reason" works from without by altering the situations of action and hence its problems, finally in this way changing men's attitudes toward them; or it intellectualizes the individual. Charisma, on the other hand, may involve a subjective or internal reorientation born out of suffering, conflicts or enthusiasm. It may then result in a radical alteration of the central system of attitudes and directions of action, with a completely new orientation of all attitudes toward the different problems and structures of the "world."[2] In prerationalistic periods,

---

[1] The leader of the communistic experiment in Bavaria in 1919.—ED (T.P.)

[2] Weber here uses *Welt* in quotation marks, indicating that it refers to its meaning in what is primarily a religious context. It is the sphere of "worldly" things and interests as distinguished from transcendental religious interests.—ED (T.P.)

tradition and charisma between them have almost exhausted the whole of the orientation of action.

The Necessity of Routinization

In its pure form charismatic authority has a character specifically foreign to everyday routine structures. The social relationships directly involved are strictly personal, based on the validity and practice of charismatic personal qualities. If this is not to remain a purely transitory phenomenon, but to take on the character of a permanent relationship forming a stable community of disciples, or a band of followers, or a party organization, or any sort of political or hierocratic organization, it is necessary for the character of charismatic authority to become radically changed. Indeed, in its pure form charismatic authority may be said to exist only in the process of originating. It cannot remain stable, but becomes either traditionalized or rationalized, or a combination of both.

The following are the principal motives underlying this transformation: (1) the ideal and also the material interests of the followers in the continuation and the continual reactivation of the community; (2) the still stronger ideal and also stronger material interests of the members of the administrative staff, the disciples or other followers of the charismatic leader in continuing their relationship. Not only this, but they have an interest in continuing it in such a way that both from an ideal and a material point of view, their own status is put on a stable everyday basis. This means, above all, making it possible to participate in normal family relationships or at least to enjoy a secure social position, in place of the kind of discipleship which is cut off from ordinary worldly connections, notably in the family and in economic relationships.

The Problem of Succession

These interests generally become conspicuously evident with the disappearance of the personal charismatic leader, and with the problem of succession which inevitably arises. The way in which this problem is met—if it is met at all and the charismatic group continues to exist—is of crucial importance for the character of the subsequent social relationships. The following are the principal possible types of solution:

(1) The search for a new charismatic leader on the basis of criteria of the qualities which will fit him for the position of authority. This is to be found in a relatively pure type in the process of choice of a new Dalai Lama. It consists in the search for a child with characteristics which are interpreted to mean that he is a reincarnation of the Buddha. This is very similar to the choice of the new Bull of Apis.

In this case the legitimacy of the new charismatic leader is bound to certain distinguishing characteristics—thus, to rules with respect to which a tradition arises. The result is a process of traditionalization in favor of which the purely personal character of leadership is eliminated.

(2) By revelation manifested in oracles, lots, divine judgments, or other techniques of selection. In this case, the legitimacy of the new leader is dependent on the legitimacy of the technique of his selection. This involves a form of legalization. It is said that at times the *Schofetim* of Israel had this character. Saul is said to have been chosen by the old war oracle.

(3) By the designation on the part of the original charismatic leader of his own successor and his recognition on the part of the followers. This is a very common form. Originally, the Roman magistracies were filled entirely in this way. The system survived most clearly into later times in the appointment of "dictators" and in the institution of the "interrex." In this case, legitimacy is acquired through the act of designation.

(4) Designation of a successor by the charismatically qualified administrative staff and his recognition by the community. In its typical form, this process should quite definitely not be interpreted as "election," or "nomination," or anything of the sort. It is not a matter of free selection, but of one which is strictly bound to objective duty. It is not to be determined merely by majority vote, but is a question of arriving at the correct designation, the designation of the right person who is truly endowed with charisma. It is quite possible that the minority and not the majority should be right in such a case. Unanimity is often required. It is obligatory to acknowledge a mistake, and persistence in error is a serious offense. Making a wrong choice is a genuine wrong requiring expiation. Originally it was a magical offense.

Nevertheless, in such a case it is easy for legitimacy to take on the character of an acquired right which is justified by standards of the correctness of the process by which the position was acquired, for the most part, by its having been acquired in accordance with certain formalities, such as coronation. This was the original meaning of the coronation of bishops and kings in the Western world by the clergy or the nobility with the "consent" of the community. There are numerous analogous phenomena all over the world. The fact that this is the origin of the modern conception of "election" raises problems which will have to be gone into later.

(5) By the conception that charisma is a quality transmitted by heredity; thus that it is participated in by the kinsmen of its bearer, particularly by his closest relatives. This is the case of hereditary charisma. The order of hereditary succession in such a case need not be the same as that which is in force for appropriated rights, but may differ from it. It is also sometimes necessary to select the proper heir within the kinship group by some of the methods just spoken of; thus in certain Negro states brothers have had to fight for the succession. In China, succession had to take place in such a

way that the relation of the living group to the ancestral spirits was not disturbed. The rule either of seniority or of designation by the followers has been very common in the Orient. Hence, in the house of Osman, it has been obligatory to eliminate all other possible candidates.

Only in medieval Europe and in Japan universally, elsewhere only sporadically, has the principle of primogeniture, as governing the inheritance of authority, become clearly established. This has greatly facilitated the consolidation of political groups in that it has eliminated struggle between a plurality of candidates from the same charismatic family.

In the case of hereditary charisma, recognition is no longer paid to the charismatic qualities of the individual, but to the legitimacy of the position he has acquired by hereditary succession. This may lead in the direction either of traditionalization or of legalization. The concept of "divine right" is fundamentally altered and now comes to mean authority by virtue of a personal right which is not dependent on the recognition of those subject to authority. Personal charisma may be totally absent. Hereditary monarchy is a conspicuous illustration. In Asia there have been very numerous hereditary priesthoods; also, frequently, the hereditary charisma of kinship groups has been treated as a criterion of social rank and of eligibility for fiefs and benefices.

(6) The concept that charisma may be transmitted by ritual means from one bearer to another or may be created in a new person. The concept was originally magical. It involves a dissociation of charisma from a particular individual, making it an objective, transferable entity. In particular, it may become the charisma of office. In this case the belief in legitimacy is no longer directed to the individual, but to the acquired qualities and to the effectiveness of the ritual acts. The most important example is the transmission of priestly charisma by annointing, consecration, or the laying on of hands and of royal authority, by annointing and by coronation. The *caracter indelibilis* thus acquired means that the charismatic qualities and powers of the office are emancipated from the personal qualities of the priest. For precisely this reason, this has, from the Donatist and the Montanist heresies down to the Puritan revolution, been the subject of continual conflicts. The "hireling" of the Quakers is the preacher endowed with the charisma of office.

Routinization and the Administrative Staff

Concomitant with the routinization of charisma with a view to insuring adequate succession, go the interests in its routinization on the part of the administrative staff. It is only in the initial stages and so long as the charismatic leader acts in a way which is completely outside everyday social organization, that it is possible for his followers to live communistically in a community of faith and enthusiasm, on gifts, "booty" or sporadic acquisition.

Only the members of the small group of enthusiastic disciples and followers are prepared to devote their lives purely idealistically to their call. The great majority of disciples and followers will in the long run "make their living" out of their "calling" in a material sense as well. Indeed, this must be the case if the movement is not to disintegrate.

Hence, the routinization of charisma also takes the form of the appropriation of powers of control and of economic advantages by the followers or disciples, and of regulation of the recruitment of these groups. This process of traditionalization or of legalization, according to whether rational legislation is involved or not, may take any one of a number of typical forms:

1. The original basis of recruitment is personal charisma. With routinization, the followers or disciples may set up norms for recruitment, in particular involving training or tests of eligibility. Charisma can only be "awakened" and "tested"; it cannot be "learned" or "taught." All types of magical asceticism, as practiced by magicians and heroes, and all novitiates, belong in this category. These are means of closing the group which constitutes the administrative staff.

Only the proved novice is allowed to exercise authority. A genuine charismatic leader is in a position to oppose this type of prerequisite for membership. His successor is not, at least if he is chosen by the administrative staff. This type is illustrated by the magical and warrior asceticism of the "men's house" with initiation ceremonies and age groups. An individual who has not successfully gone through the initiation, remains a "woman"—that is, is excluded from the charismatic group.

2. It is easy for charismatic norms to be transformed into those defining a traditional social status on a hereditary charismatic basis. If the leader is chosen on a hereditary basis, it is very easy for hereditary charisma to govern the selection of the administrative staff and even, perhaps, those followers without any position of authority. The term "familistic state" will be applied when a political body is organized strictly and completely in terms of this principle of hereditary charisma. In such a case, all appropriation of governing powers, of fiefs, benefices, and all sorts of economic advantages follow the same pattern. The result is that all powers and advantages of all sorts become traditionalized. The heads of families, who are traditional gerontocrats or patriarchs without personal charismatic legitimacy, regulate the exercise of these powers, which cannot be taken away from their family. It is not the type of position he occupies which determines the rank of a man or of his family, but rather the hereditary charismatic rank of his family determines the position he will occupy. Japan, before the development of bureaucracy, was organized in this way. The same was undoubtedly true of China as well, where, before the rationalization which took place in the territorial states, authority was in the hands of the "old families." Other types of examples are furnished by the caste system

in India and by Russia before the *Mjestnitschestvo* was introduced. Indeed, all hereditary social classes with established privileges belong in the same category.

3. The administrative staff may seek and achieve the creation and appropriation of individual positions and the corresponding economic advantages for its members. In that case, according to whether the tendency is to traditionalization or legalization, there will develop (a) benefices, (b) offices, or (c) fiefs. In the first case a praebendal organization will result; in the second, patrimonialism or bureaucracy; in the third, feudalism. These become appropriated in the place of the type of provision from gifts or booty without settled relation to the everyday economic structure.

Case (a), benefices, may consist in rights to the proceeds of begging, to payments in kind, or to the proceeds of money taxes, or finally, to the proceeds of fees. Any one of these may result from the regulation of provision by free gifts or by "booty" in terms of a rational organization of finance. Regularized begging is found in Buddhism; benefices in kind, in the Chinese and Japanese "rice rents"; support by money taxation has been the rule in all the rationalized conquering states. The last case is common everywhere, especially on the part of priests and judges and, in India, even the military authorities.

Case (b), the transformation of the charismatic mission into an office, may have more of a patrimonial or more of a bureaucratic character. The former is much the more common; the latter is found principally in Mediterranean Antiquity and in the modern Western World. Elsewhere it is exceptional.

In case (c), only land may be appropriated as a fief, whereas the position as such retains its originally charismatic character. On the other hand, powers and authority may be fully appropriated as fiefs. It is difficult to distinguish the two cases. It is, however, rare that orientation to the charismatic character of the position disappears entirely; it did not do so in the Middle Ages.

Routinization and Economic Organization

For charisma to be transformed into a permanent routine structure, it is necessary that its anti-economic character should be altered. It must be adapted to some form of fiscal organization to provide for the needs of the group, and hence to the economic conditions necessary for raising taxes and contributions. When a charismatic movement develops in the direction of praebendal provision, the "laity" become differentiated from the "clergy"; that is, the participating members of the charismatic administrative staff which has now become routinized. These are the priests of the developing "church." Correspondingly, in a developing political body, the vassals, the holders of benefices, or officials are differentiated from the "taxpayers." The former, instead of being the "followers" of the leader, become state officials or appointed party officials. This process is very conspicuous in Buddhism and in the Hindu sects. The same is true in all the states resulting from conquest which have become rationalized to form permanent structures, also of parties and other movements which have originally had a purely charismatic character. With the process of routinization, the charismatic group tends to develop into one of the forms of everyday authority, particularly the patrimonial form in its decentralized variant or the bureaucratic. Its original peculiarities are apt to be retained in the charismatic standards of honor attendant on the social status acquired by heredity or the holding of office. This applies to all who participate in the process of appropriation, the chief himself and the members of his staff. It is thus a matter of the type of prestige enjoyed by ruling groups. A hereditary monarch by "divine right" is not a simple patrimonial chief, patriarch, or sheik; a vassal is not a mere household retainer or official. Further details must be deferred to the analysis of social stratification.

As a rule, the process of routinization is not free of conflict. In the early stages personal claims on the charisma of the chief are not easily forgotten, and the conflict between the charisma of office or of hereditary status with personal charisma is a typical process in many historical situations.

1. The power of absolution—that is, the power to absolve from mortal sins—was held originally only by personal charismatic martyrs or ascetics, but became transformed into a power of the office of bishop or priest. This process was much slower in the Orient than in the Occident because in the latter case it was influenced by the Roman conception of office. Revolutions under a charismatic leader, directed against hereditary charismatic powers or the powers of office, are to be found in all types of corporate groups, from states to trade unions. The more highly developed the interdependence of different economic units in a monetary economy, the greater the pressure of the everyday needs of the followers of the charismatic movement becomes. The effect of this is to strengthen the tendency to routinization, which is everywhere operative, and as a rule has rapidly won out. Charisma is a phenomenon typical of prophetic religious movements or of expansive political movements in their early stages. But as soon as the position of authority is well established, and above all as soon as control over large masses of people exists, it gives way to the forces of everyday routine.

2. One of the decisive motives underlying all cases of the routinization of charisma is naturally the striving for security. This means legitimization, on the one hand, of positions of authority and social prestige; on the other hand, of the economic advantages enjoyed by the followers and sympathizers of the leader. Another important motive, however, lies in the objective necessity of adaptation of the patterns of order and of the organization of the administrative staff to the normal, everyday needs and conditions of carrying on administration. In this connection, in particular, there are al-

ways points at which traditions of administrative practice and of judicial decision can take hold, since these are needed both by the normal administrative staff and by those subject to its authority. It is further necessary that there should be some definite order introduced into the organization of the administrative staff itself. Finally, as will be discussed in detail below, it is necessary for the administrative staff and all its administrative practices to be adapted to everyday economic conditions. It is not possible for the costs of permanent, routine administration to be met by "booty," contributions, gifts and hospitality, as is typical of the pure type of military and prophetic charisma.

3. The process of routinization is thus not by any means confined to the problem of succession and does not stop when this has been solved. On the contrary, the most fundamental problem is that of making a transition from a charismatic administrative staff, and the corresponding principles of administration, to one which is adapted to everyday conditions. The problem of succession, however, is crucial, because through it occurs the routinization of the charismatic focus of the structure. In it, the character of the leader himself and of his claim to legitimacy is altered. This process involves peculiar and characteristic conceptions which are understandable only in this context, and do not apply to the problem of transition to traditional or legal patterns of order and types of administrative organization. The most important of the modes of meeting the problem of succession are the charismatic designation of a successor and hereditary charisma.

4. As has already been noted, the most important historical example of designation by the charismatic leader of his own successor is Rome. For the *rex,* this arrangement is attested by tradition; while for the appointment of the "dictator" and of the co-emperor and successor in the principate, it has existed in historical times. The way in which all the higher magistrates were invested with the *imperium* shows clearly that they also were designated as successors by the military commander, subject to recognition by the citizen army. The fact that candidates were examined by the magistrate in office, and that originally they could be excluded on what were obviously arbitrary grounds, shows clearly what was the nature of the development.

5. The most important examples of designation of a successor by the charismatic followers of the leader are to be found in the election of bishops, and particularly of the Pope, by the original system of designation by the clergy and recognition by the lay community. The investigations of U. Stutz have made it probable that, though it was later altered, the election of the German emperor was modeled on that of the bishops. He was designated by a group of qualified princes and recognized by the "people," that is, those bearing arms. Similar arrangements are very common.

6. The classical case of the development of hereditary charisma is that of caste in India. All occupational qualifications, and in particular all the qualifications for positions of authority and power, have there come to be

regarded as strictly bound to the inheritance of charisma. Eligibility for fiefs, involving governing powers, was limited to members of the royal kinship group, the fiefs being granted by the eldest of the group. All types of religious office, including the extraordinarily important and influential position of *guru,* the *directeur de l'âme,* were treated as bound to hereditary charismatic qualities. The same is true of all sorts of relations to traditional customers and of all positions in the village organization, such as priest, barber, laundryman, watchman, etc. The foundation of a sect always meant the development of a hereditary hierarchy, as was true also of Taoism in China. Also in the Japanese "feudal" state, before the introduction of a patrimonial officialdom on the Chinese model, which then led to praebends and a new feudalization, social organization was based purely on hereditary charisma.

This kind of hereditary charismatic right to positions of authority has been developed in similar ways all over the world. Qualification by virtue of individual achievement has been replaced by qualification by birth. This is everywhere the basis of the development of hereditary aristocracies, in the Roman nobility, in the concept of the *stirps regia,* which Tacitus describes among the Germans, in the rules of eligibility to tournaments and monasteries in the late Middle Ages, and even in the genealogical research carried on on behalf of the parvenu aristocracy of the United States. Indeed, this is to be found everywhere where a differentiation of hereditary social classes has become established.

The following is the principal relation to economic conditions: The process of routinization of charisma is in very important respects identical with adaptation to the conditions of economic life, since this is one of the principal continually operating forces in everyday life. Economic conditions in this connection play a leading role and do not constitute merely a dependent variable. To a very large extent, the transition to hereditary charisma or the charisma of office serves in this connection as a means of legitimizing existing or recently acquired powers of control over economic goods. Along with the ideology of loyalty, which is certainly by no means unimportant, allegiance to hereditary monarchy in particular is very strongly influenced by the consideration that all inherited property and all that which is legitimately acquired would be endangered if subjective recognition of the sanctity of succession to the throne were eliminated. It is hence by no means fortuitous that hereditary monarchy is more acceptable to the propertied classes than, for instance, to the proletariat.

Beyond this, it is not possible to say anything in general terms, which would at the same time be substantial and valuable, on the relations of the various possible modes of adaptation to the economic order. This must be reserved to a special investigation. The development of a praebendal structure, of feudalism and the appropriation of all sorts of advantages on a hereditary charismatic basis, may in all cases have the same stereotyping effect on the economic order if they develop from charismatic starting points as if they developed from patrimonial or bureaucratic origins. The immediate effect of charisma in economic as in other connections is usually strongly revolutionary; indeed, often destructive, because it means new modes of orientation. But in case the process of routinization leads in the direction of traditionalism, its ultimate effect may be exactly the reverse.

CHAPTER 9

FERDINAND TOENNIES

From Community to Society

Order—Law—Mores

There is a contrast between a social order which—being based upon consensus of wills—rests on harmony and is developed and ennobled by folkways, mores, and religion and an order which—being based upon a union of rational wills—rests on convention and agreement, is safeguarded by political legislation, and finds its ideological justification in public opinion.

There is, further, in the first instance, a common and binding system of positive law, of enforceable norms regulating the interrelation of wills. It has its roots in family life and is based on land ownership. Its forms are in the main determined by the code of the folkways and mores. Religion consecrates and glorifies these forms of the divine will, *i.e.,* as interpreted by the will of wise and ruling men. This system of norms is in direct contrast to a similar positive law which upholds the separate identity of the individual rational wills in all their interrelations and entanglements. The latter derives from the conventional order of trade and similar relations, but attains validity and binding force only through the sovereign will and power of the state. Thus, it becomes one of the most important instruments of policy; it sustains, impedes, or furthers social trends; it is defended or contested publicly by doctrines and opinions and thus is changed, becoming more strict or more lenient.

There is, further, the dual concept of morality as a purely ideal or mental system of norms for community life. In the first case, it is mainly an expression and organ of religious beliefs and forces, by necessity intertwined with the conditions and realities of family spirit and the folkways and mores. In the second case, it is entirely a product and instrument of public opinion, which encompasses all relations arising out of contractual sociableness, contacts, and political intentions.

From Ferdinand Toennies, *Community and Society—Gemeinschaft und Gesellschaft,* trans. and ed., Charles P. Loomis (East Lansing, Mich.: The Michigan State University Press, 1957), pp. 223-233. Reprinted by permission of the editor and the publisher.

Dissolution

The substance of the body social and the social will consists of concord, folkways, mores, and religion, the manifold forms of which develop under favorable conditions during its lifetime. Thus, each individual receives his share from this common center, which is manifest in his own sphere, *i.e.,* in his sentiment, in his mind and heart, and in his conscience as well as in his environment, his possessions, and his activities. This is also true of each group. It is in this center that the individual's strength is rooted, and his rights derive, in the last instance, from the one original law which, in its divine and natural character, encompasses and sustains him, just as it made him and will carry him away. But under certain conditions and in some relationships, man appears as a free agent (person) in his self-determined activities, and has to be conceived of as an independent person. The substance of the common spirit has become so weak or the link connecting him with the others worn so thin that it has to be excluded from consideration. In contrast to the family and cooperative relationship, this is true of all relations among separate individuals where there is no common understanding and no time-honored custom or belief creates a common bond. This means war and the unrestricted freedom of all to destroy and subjugate one another, or, being aware of possible greater advantage, to conclude agreements and foster new ties. To the extent that such a relationship exists between closed groups or communities or between their individuals or between members and nonmembers of a community, it does not come within the scope of this study. In this connection we see a community organization and social conditions in which the individuals remain in isolation and veiled hostility toward each other so that only fear of clever retaliation restrains them from attacking one another, and, therefore, even peaceful and neighborly relations are in reality based upon a warlike situation. This is, according to our concepts, the condition of *Gesellschaft*-like civilization, in which peace and commerce are maintained through conventions and the underlying mutual fear. The state protects this civilization through legislation and politics. To a certain extent science and public opinion, attempting to conceive it as necessary and eternal, glorify it as progress toward perfection.

But it is in the organization and order of the *Gemeinschaft* that folk life and folk culture persist. The state, which represents and embodies *Gesellschaft,* is opposed to these in veiled hatred and contempt, the more so the further the state has moved away from and become estranged from these forms of community life. Thus, also in the social and historical life of mankind there is partly close interrelation, partly juxtaposition and opposition of natural and rational will.

The People and the State

In the same way as the individual natural will evolves into pure thinking and rational will, which tends to dissolve and subjugate its predecessors, the original collective forms of *Gemeinschaft* have developed into *Gesellschaft* and the rational will of the *Gesellschaft*. In the course of history, folk culture has given rise to the civilization of the state.

The main features of this process can be described in the following way. The anonymous mass of the people is the original and dominating power which creates the houses, the villages, and the towns of the country. From it, too, spring the powerful and self-determined individuals of many different kinds: princes, feudal lords, knights, as well as priests, artists, scholars. As long as their economic condition is determined by the people as a whole, all their social control is conditioned by the will and power of the people. Their union on a national scale, which alone could make them dominant as a group, is dependent on economic conditions. And their real and essential control is economic control, which before them and with them and partly against them the merchants attain by harnessing the labor force of the nation. Such economic control is achieved in many forms, the highest of which is planned capitalist production or largescale industry. It is through the merchants that the technical conditions for the national union of independent individuals and for capitalistic production are created. This merchant class is by nature, and mostly also by origin, international as well as national and urban, *i.e.*, it belongs to *Gesellschaft*, not *Gemeinschaft*. Later all social groups and dignitaries and, at least in tendency, the whole people acquire the characteristics of the *Gesellschaft*.

Men change their temperaments with the place and conditions of their daily life, which becomes hasty and changeable through restless striving. Simultaneously, along with this revolution in the social order, there takes place a gradual change of the law, in meaning as well as in form. The contract as such becomes the basis of the entire system, and rational will of *Gesellschaft*, formed by its interests, combines with authoritative will of the state to create, maintain, and change the legal system. According to this conception, the law can and may completely change the *Gesellschaft* in line with its own discrimination and purpose; changes which, however, will be in the interest of the *Gesellschaft*, making for usefulness and efficiency. The state frees itself more and more from the traditions and customs of the past and the belief in their importance. Thus, the forms of law change from a product of the folkways and mores and the law of custom into a purely legalistic law, a product of policy. The state and its departments and the individuals are the only remaining agents, instead of numerous and manifold fellowships, communities, and commonwealths which have grown up organically. The characters of the people, which were influenced and determined by these previously existing institutions, undergo new changes in adaptation to new and arbitrary legal constructions. These earlier institutions lose the firm hold which folkways, mores, and the conviction of their infallibility gave to them.

Finally, as a consequence of these changes and in turn reacting upon them, a complete reversal of intellectual life takes place. While originally rooted entirely in the imagination, it now becomes dependent upon thinking. Previously, all was centered around the belief in invisible beings, spirits and gods; now it is focalized on the insight into visible nature. Religion, which is rooted in folk life or at least closely related to it, must cede supremacy to science, which derives from and corresponds to consciousness. Such consciousness is a product of learning and culture and, therefore, remote from the people. Religion has an immediate contact and is moral in its nature because it is most deeply related to the physical-spiritual link which connects the generations of men. Science receives its moral meaning only from an observation of the laws of social life, which leads it to derive rules for an arbitrary and reasonable order of social organization. The intellectual attitude of the individual becomes gradually less and less influenced by religion and more and more influenced by science. Utilizing the research findings accumulated by the preceding industrious generation, we shall investigate the tremendous contrasts which the opposite poles of this dichotomy and these fluctuations entail. For this presentation, however, the following few remarks may suffice to outline the underlying principles.

Types of Real Community Life

The exterior forms of community life as represented by natural will and *Gemeinschaft* were distinguished as house, village, and town. These are the lasting types of real and historical life. In a developed *Gesellschaft,* as in the earlier and middle stages, people live together in these different ways. The town is the highest, *viz.,* the most complex, form of social life. Its local character, in common with that of the village, contrasts with the family character of the house. Both village and town retain many characteristics of the family; the village retains more, the town less. Only when the town develops into the city are these characteristics almost entirely lost. Individuals or families are separate identities, and their common locale is only an accidental or deliberately chosen place in which to live. But as the town lives on within the city, elements of life in the *Gemeinschaft,* as the only real form of life, persist within the *Gesellschaft,* although lingering and decaying. On the other hand, the more general the condition of *Gesellschaft* becomes in the nation or a group of nations, the more this entire "country" or the entire "world" begins to resemble one large city. However, in the city and therefore where general conditions characteristic of the *Gesellschaft* prevail, only the upper strata, the rich and the cultured, are really active and alive. They set up the standards to which the lower strata have to conform. These lower classes conform partly to supersede the others, partly in imitation of them in order to attain for themselves social power and independence. The city consists, for both groups (just as in the case of the "nation" and the "world"), of free persons who stand in contact with each other, exchange with each other and cooperate without any *Gemeinschaft* or will thereto developing among them except as such might develop sporadically or as a leftover from former conditions. On the contrary, these numerous external contacts, contracts, and contractual relations only cover up as many inner hostilities and antagonistic interests. This is especially true of the antagonism between the rich or the socalled cultured class and the poor or the servant class, which try to obstruct and destroy each other. It is this contrast which, according to Plato, gives the "city" its dual character and makes it divide in itself. This itself, according to our concept, constitutes the city, but the same contrast is also manifest in every largescale relationship between capital and labor. The common town life remains within the *Gemeinschaft* of family and rural life; it is devoted to some agricultural pursuits but concerns itself especially with art and handicraft which evolve from these natural needs and habits. City life, however, is sharply distinguished from that; these basic activities are used only as means and tools for the special purposes of the city.

The city is typical of *Gesellschaft* in general. It is essentially a commercial town and, insofar as commerce dominates its productive labor, a factory town. Its wealth is capital wealth, which, in the form of trade, usury, or industrial capital, is used and multiplies. Capital is the means for the appropriation of products of labor or for the exploitation of workers. The city is also the center of science and culture, which always go hand in hand with commerce and industry. Here the arts must make a living; they are exploited in a capitalistic way. Thoughts spread and change with astonishing rapidity. Speeches and books through mass distribution become stimuli of farreaching importance.

•

Counterpart of Gemeinschaft

Family life is the general basis of life in the *Gemeinschaft*. It subsists in village and town life. The village community and the town themselves can be considered as large families, the various clans and houses representing the elementary organisms of its body; guilds, corporations, and offices, the tissues and organs of the town. Here original kinship and inherited status remain an essential, or at least the most important, condition of participating fully in common property and other rights. Strangers are accepted and protected as serving-members or guests, either temporarily or permanently. Thus, they can belong to the *Gemeinschaft* as objects, but not easily as agents and representatives of the *Gemeinschaft*. . . . All these relationships can, under special circumstances, be transformed into merely interested and dissolvable interchange between independent contracting parties. In the city such change, at least with regard to all relations of servitude, is only natural and becomes more and more widespread with its development. The difference between natives and strangers becomes irrelevant. Everyone is what he is, through his personal freedom, through his wealth and his contracts. He is a servant only insofar as he has granted certain services to someone else, master insofar as he receives such services. Wealth is, indeed, the only effective and original differentiating characteristic; whereas in *Gemeinschaften* property it is considered as participation in the common ownership, and as a specific legal concept is entirely the consequence and result of freedom or ingenuity, either original or acquired. Therefore, wealth, to the extent that this is possible, corresponds to the degree of freedom possessed.

In the city . . . family life is decaying. The more and the longer their influence prevails, the more the residuals of family life acquire a purely accidental character. For there are only few who will confine their energies within such a narrow circle; all are attracted outside by business, interests, and pleasures, and thus separated from one another. The great and mighty, feeling free and independent, have always felt a strong inclination to break through the barriers of the folkways and mores. They know that they can do as they please. They have the power to bring about changes in their favor, and this is positive proof of individual arbitrary power. The mechanism of money, under usual conditions and if working under high pressure, is means to overcome all resistance, to obtain everything wanted and desired, to eliminate all dangers and to cure all evil. This does not hold always. Even if all controls of the *Gemeinschaft* are eliminated, there are nevertheless controls in the *Gesellschaft* to which the free and independent individuals are subject. For *Gesellschaft* (in the narrower sense), convention takes to a large degree the place of the folkways, mores, and religion. It forbids much as detrimental to the common interest which the folkways, mores, and religion had condemned as evil in and of itself.

The will of the state plays the same role through law courts and police, although within narrower limits. The laws of the state apply equally to everyone; only children and lunatics are not held responsible to them. Convention maintains at least the appearance of morality; it is still related to the folkways, mores, and religious and aesthetic feeling, although this feeling tends to become arbitrary and formal. The state is hardly directly concerned with morality. It has only to suppress and punish hostile actions which are detrimental to the common weal or seemingly dangerous for itself and society. For as the state has to administer the common weal, it must be able to define this as it pleases. In the end it will probably realize that no increase in knowledge and culture alone will make people kinder, less egotistic and more content, and that dead folkways, mores and religions cannot be revived by coercion and teaching. The state will then arrive at the conclusion that in order to create moral forces and moral beings it must prepare the ground and fulfill the necessary conditions, or at least it must eliminate counteracting forces. The state, as the reason of *Gesellschaft,* should decide to destroy *Gesellschaft* or at least reform or renew it. The success of such attempts is highly improbable.

The Real State

Public opinion, which brings the morality of *Gesellschaft* into rules and formulas and can rise above the state, has nevertheless decided tendencies to urge the state to use its irresistible power to force everyone to do what is useful and to leave undone what is damaging. Extension of the penal code and the police power seems the right means to curb the evil impulses of the masses. Public opinion passes easily from the demand for freedom (for the upper classes) to that of despotism (against the lower classes). The makeshift, convention, has but little influence over the masses. In their striving for pleasure and entertainment they are limited only by the scarcity of the means which the capitalists furnish them as price for their labor, which condition is as general as it is natural in a world where the interests of the capitalists and merchants anticipate all possible needs and in mutual competition incite to the most varied expenditures of money. Only through fear of discovery and punishment, that is, through fear of the state, is a special and large group, which encompasses far more people than the professional criminals, restrained in its desire to obtain the key to all necessary and unnecessary pleasures. The state is their enemy. The state, to them, is an alien and unfriendly power; although seemingly authorized by them and embodying their own will, it is nevertheless opposed to all their needs and desires, protecting property which they do not possess, forcing them into military service for a country which offers them hearth and altar only in the form of a heated room on the upper floor or gives them, for native soil, city streets where they may stare at the glitter and luxury in lighted windows forever beyond their reach! Their own life is nothing but a constant alternative between work and leisure, which are both distorted into factory routine and the low pleasure of the saloons. City life and *Gesellschaft* drive the common people to decay and death; in vain they struggle to attain power through their own multitude, and it seems to them that they can use their power only for a revolution if they want to free themselves from their fate. The masses become conscious of this social position through the education in schools and through newspapers. They proceed from class consciousness to class struggle. This class struggle may destroy society and the state which it is its purpose to reform. The entire culture has been transformed into a civilization of state and *Gesellschaft,* and this transformation means the doom of culture itself if none of its scattered seeds remain alive and again bring forth the essence and idea of *Gemeinschaft,* thus secretly fostering a new culture amidst the decaying one.

The Periods

To conclude our theory, two periods stand thus contrasted with each other in the history of the great systems of culture: a period of *Gesellschaft* follows a period of *Gemeinschaft.* The *Gemeinschaft* is characterized by the social will as concord, folkways, mores, and religion; the *Gesellschaft* by the social will as convention, legislation, and public opinion. The concepts correspond to types of external social organization, which may be classed as follows:

A. Gemeinschaft

1. Family life: concord. Man participates in this with all his sentiments. Its real controlling agent is the people (*Volk*).
2. Rural village life: folkways and mores. Into this, man enters with all his mind and heart. Its real controlling agent is the commonwealth.
3. Town life: religion. In this, the human being takes part with his entire conscience. Its real controlling agent is the church.

B. Gesellschaft

1. City life: convention. This is determined by man's intentions. Its real controlling agent is *Gesellschaft* per se.
2. National life: legislation. This is determined by man's calculations. Its real controlling agent is the state.
3. Cosmopolitan life: public opinion. This is evolved by man's consciousness. Its real controlling agent is the republic of scholars.

With each of these categories a predominant occupation and a dominating tendency in intellectual life are related in the following manner:

(A) 1. Home (or household) economy, based upon liking or preference, *viz.,* the joy and delight of creating and conserving. Understanding develops the norms for such an economy.

2. Agriculture, based upon habits, *i.e.,* regularly repeated tasks. Cooperation is guided by custom.

3. Art, based upon memories, *i.e.,* of instruction, of rules followed, and of ideas conceived in one's own mind. Belief in the work and the task unites the artistic wills.

(B) 1. Trade based upon deliberation; namely, attention, comparison, calculation are the basis of all business. Commerce is deliberate action per se. Contracts are the custom and creed of business.

2. Industry based upon decisions; namely, of intelligent productive use of capital and sale of labor. Regulations rule the factory.
3. Science, based upon concepts, as is self-evident. Its truths and opinions then pass into literature and the press and thus become part of public opinion.

Epochs of the Periods

In the earlier period, family life and home (or household) economy strike the keynote; in the later period, commerce and city life. If, however, we investigate the period of *Gemeinschaft* more closely, several epochs can be distinguished. Its whole development tends toward an approach to *Gesellschaft* in which, on the other hand, the force of *Gemeinschaft* persists, although with diminishing strength, even in the period of *Gesellschaft,* and remains the reality of social life.

The first period is formed by the influence of the new basis of social organization which results from the cultivation of the soil: neighborhood relation is added to the old and persisting kinship relations, village to the clan. The other epoch comes into existence when villages develop into towns. The village and town have in common the principle of social organization in space, instead of the principle of time which predominates through the generations of the family, the tribe, and the people. Because it descends from common ancestors, the family has invisible metaphysical roots, as if they were hidden in the earth. The living individuals in the family are connected with each other by the sequence of past and future generations. But in village and town it is the physical, real soil, the permanent location, the visible land, which create the strongest ties and relations. During the period of *Gemeinschaft* this younger principle of space remains bound to the older principle of time. In the period of *Gesellschaft* they become disconnected, and from this disconnection results the city. It is the exaggeration of the principle of space in its urban form. In this exaggeration, the urban form becomes sharply contrasted with the rural form of the same principle, for the village remains essentially and almost necessarily bound to both principles. In this sense, the whole continual development may be considered as a process of increasing urbanization. "It may be said that the whole economic history of *Gesellschaft, i.e.,* of the modern nations, is in essence summarized in the change in the relationship between town and country" (Karl Marx, *Das Kapital,* I, p. 364). That is, from a certain point on, the towns by their influence and importance achieve, in the nation, predominance over the rural organization. In consequence, country and village must use more of their own productive forces for the support and furtherance of the urban areas than they can spare for purposes of reproduction. Therefore, the rural organization is doomed to dissolution. . . .

PART II

SOURCES AND PATTERNS OF CHANGE

Modern
Theories

Introduction

The grand theories gave inadequate guidance for sociological research, but no modern theory of social change has replaced them. There is no adequate theory of social change, just as there is no fully developed general theory of society. Actually, both Talcott Parsons and Wilbert E. Moore have suggested that a theory of society and one of social change are inseparable. Parsons closes his discussion of change in *The Social System* with the statement:

> Perhaps, even, it is not too much to hope that this chapter as a whole will convince the reader that there is a certain falsity in the dilemma between "static" and "dynamic" emphases. If theory is *good theory*, whichever type of problem it tackles most directly, there is no reason whatever to believe that it will not be *equally* applicable to the problems of change and to those of process within a stabilized system.[1]

Moore states: "An 'integrated' theory of social change will be as singular or plural as sociological theory as a whole, and will include about the same subdivisions and topics." [2]

There is little doubt that, once a complete theory of society is developed, it will serve to study both "static" structures and "dynamic" processes, but the search for such a theory must progress on several fronts. Furthermore, even in a fully integrated theory, whereas statements on high levels of abstraction will probably be applicable to both structure and process, concrete statements may deal with one rather than with the other. At any rate, at present one can certainly point to such statements that are exclusively concerned with "static" relationships as: "the more ranks an organization has, the lower the morale of the lower participants." This statement discusses no

---

[1] Talcott Parsons, *The Social System* (Glencoe, Ill.: The Free Press, 1951), p. 535.
[2] Wilbert E. Moore, "A Reconsideration of Theories of Social Change," *American Sociological Review*, XXV (1960), 818.

processes, but compares the morale of lower ranks among organizations that have differing numbers of ranks. On the other hand, we have such statements as: "In order for the process of differentiation of the child's personality to continue, one (or more) of the socialization agents must sanction behavior that is conforming to the next state of equilibrium, whereas another agent (or agents) has to be supportive in a nondirective way." The statement specifies two conditions under which the personality system of a child can be kept changing, but says nothing about the power differential between the two socialization agents, which is a comparatively "static" condition as concerns this process.

The growth of sociological analysis tends to follow two lines: (1) analysis of existing structures based on case studies of social units at one point in time or comparisons of several units at the same time (or at different times, but disregarding this on the assumption that the difference in time is irrelevant); (2) follow-up studies that examine the same variable or a set of variables at different times. While some studies combine both approaches, so far these are the exception, not the rule.

Parsons' most recent work, that of Neil Smelser presented later in this volume, as well as those of several other sociologists, all suggest some elements of a general theory of change. The most important point, represented in the opening paragraphs of Parsons' article, is the progress made since the early 1950's in regarding change not just as a sort of disequilibrium, or as something that maintains equilibrium, but also as a process that can decisively change the state of equilibrium itself. Earlier writings in modern sociological theory dealt mainly with two kinds of change:

(1) A process that removed a social unit from its institutionalized pattern and thus elicited forces of social control that strove to counter it, to return the unit to its initial state. The image was one of a ball that is rolled from the bottom of a bowl against one of its walls. The force of gravity strives to return the ball to its initial position. A simple social parallel would be an increase in unemployment that elicits an increase in federal spending on public works, which reduces the unemployment to its initial state.

(2) The second kind of change or process dealt with in earlier writings, is a necessary condition for equilibrium—for instance, the changing positions of the feet of a bicycle rider, or the turning of the wheels, which are required in order for the bicycle to keep upright and on the move. A simple social illustration would be the need to keep mobility at a given level to maintain an achievement-oriented society.

Both conceptions of change assume that the basic variables (or "framework") remain unchanged. The walls of the bowl, the force of gravity, the bicycle structure, public works, the social value of mobility, are taken as constants. To the degree that their change is studied, they are viewed in a still larger framework, which in turn is assumed to be constant.

The more recent development of sociological theory permits the study of changes within a system itself, *i.e.,* changes in the "basic" variables. The study of change is no longer limited to changing subsystems of stable systems; it now allows for the study of change of an entire unit, of society itself.

The model Parsons offers below for the study of changes of a system is based on the idea of differentiation. Any given social unit has a "simple," "undifferentiated" structure in which the various functions fulfilled by the unit are "fused" together, *i.e.,* are all carried out by the same set of actors, in the same set of relationships. In the process of differentiation the various functions acquire structural units of their own. For instance, production and socialization, once carried out within the family, become vested in distinct social structures, such as the factory (or the occupational realm in general), and the school (and to a degree youth movements, clubs and the like). The process of differentiation requires at the same time that the new units, each specializing in a particular function, be related to each other; differentiation requires reintegration. This is achieved through a normative system which prescribes the relationships between, let us say, the family and the factory; through "bridging" institutions, *e.g.,* the vocational school; or through mechanisms for adjustment of conflicts, such as courts.

In sum, the study of differentiation, and that of the new modes of integration it requires, is a study of the re-formation of social structure. At the beginning of the process we see a system in a state of equilibrium being disturbed, not just in part but in its entirety; at the end of the process we see that a new equilibrium has been established. The model allows us to analyze, and within limits to forecast, the direction of certain structural changes. There can hardly be a question that the model of differentiation does provide the elements of a theory of social change.

Obviously, this model does not presume to cover all possible forms of change. The development of several social units may follow different patterns. The "differentiation model" applies to the pattern in which a developing unit builds up new subunits but serves no new functions. On the other hand, the "epigenesis model" presented below deals with the pattern in which a newly created unit first fulfills only one function autonomously, then expands to serve more and more functional needs. The expansion of international systems from rather limited, intergovernmental treaties to encompassing supranational communities is one striking example. A formal organization developing an informal structure is another.

The possibility of formulating a theory of social change, as an integral part of the structural–functional approach in sociology, is not accepted by all sociologists. Both Francesca Cancian and Ralf Dahrendorf address themselves to this question. Dahrendorf concludes that the answer will have to be found outside the structural-functional tradition. Cancian sees the answer within it.

Cancian explicitly meets the criticism that Parsonian theory is a "static" one, and suggests that the structural-functional theory is indeed able to study change and actually does so. Moreover, the study of change need not be introduced in an ad hoc, unsystematic fashion; it can be made an integral part of the structural-functional approach. Thus, for example, disintegration of a particular system can be predicted: functionalism specifies the prerequisites of a system; remove these, and the system falls apart. In other words, if we make a statement about the prerequisites of a system and give this statement a negative sign—meaning that the prerequisites are not now being fulfilled—we formulate a statement about the conditions of disintegration, which is one form of change.

In addition, according to Cancian, the structural-functional theory can make statements about changes which are prerequisites for the maintenance of stability of the system and about corrective changes, in which deviations from the system's state of equilibrium are followed by attempts to restore it.

Dahrendorf views the structural-functional effort to form a general theory of society as a failure. He regards it as covering one part, one set of elements, and not another. Structural-functional theory, he feels, explores the factors that hold social units together, the forces of integration, but is not adequate to handle the forces of disruption and change. Dahrendorf does not formulate a general theory that would encompass both "statics" and "dynamics," but instead advocates the formation of another partial theory that would cover the elements which he sees as neglected by the structural-functional approach, a theory of conflict and change. Together the two partial theories would cover the full range of sociological phenomena. Dahrendorf proceeds to provide an illustration of what such a partial theory of conflict and change would be like.

As Coser sees it, conflict prevents the ossification of the social system by exerting pressure for innovation and creativity. Conflict can prevent accommodations and habitual relations from progressively impoverishing creativity, e.g., technological improvement stimulated from the conflict activity of trade unions through the raising of wage levels. These processes refer to change within systems. There is also change *of* systems—Marxian type of change. Coser, though, stresses more the integrative effect of conflict, not its undoing-redoing, fundamentally transforming consequences.

While these modes of change do not exhaust the possibilities of the structural-functional approach, they surely suffice to show that the search for one sociological theory that covers both permanence and change need not be given up yet. But it is worth pointing out that it is precisely due to the pressure of criticism by Dahrendorf, Lewis Coser, and others that more and more attention is being paid by functionalists to the study of change.

The work of C. Wright Mills continues the grand-theory line, even though Mills did not make all history and all societies his domain. Actually, compared to earlier "classical" works, Mills's analysis is limited in scope—technical and empirical. But compared to most contemporary sociology, he is urgently concerned with social issues, rather than rigorously scientific. His use of terms is far from precise (his "elite," for instance, stands sometimes for holders of institutional positions, sometimes for a social class)[3] and his combination of sociological analysis and social criticism is in the best Marxist tradition.

Mills's perspective differs from that common among contemporary sociologists also in his incomplete adherence to the multifactor approach. It would be a gross error to view Mills as a pure Marxist, since his work is deeply influenced by Max Weber. He assigns a considerable role to political (*i.e.,* normative and coercive) factors, viewing the government and the military, the church and the courts, not as mere instruments of the propertied classes, but as forces in their own right. Still, Mills puts a strong emphasis on class factors, and his view of a coalition of elites maintaining exclusive access to power certainly comes closer to a neo-Marxist approach than most other contemporary sociological writings on social change.

Anthropologists have maintained or revived approaches which most sociologists have rejected but which are nevertheless of interest, and which, in the future, may yet be reincorporated into sociological theories of change. The old evolutionary theories, mostly implying linear progress, have been rejected on the grounds that human history obviously fails to display a general, encompassing trend toward higher and higher enlightenment; that various sectors of any society are apt to proceed at a different pace and possibly in different directions (science may progress cumulatively while the enforcement of moral standards may show no or only little improvement); and that different societies follow different patterns of development and possibly are oriented to different states of "maturity." Not only did the Russian industrialization follow a different path from that of England, but, in addition, industrialized Russia is quite different from industrialized England.

Julian H. Steward explores a new approach to the study of evolution that avoids these pitfalls. First, following the general trend of the social sciences, his concepts are less value-laden and he does not assume that moral progress is immanent in social development. Second, again in line with the general trend, he does not seek a single path of change, but presents a theory of multilinear evolution. What then is left of the earlier evolutionary framework? Although the multilinear evolutionist assumes that there is more than one path of development, he makes it his working assumption that the number of possible patterns is limited. There are several patterns the course of civilization might follow, but not an endless number, and empirical study may show under what conditions a society will go one way rather than another. Moreover, while societies travel on different paths at a

---

[3] This point was made by Daniel Bell, *The End of Ideology* (Glencoe, Ill.: The Free Press, 1960), pp. 46-47.

different pace, to different destinations, there seem to be some basic similarities between these journeys. Thus, in spite of interruptions, cyclical rhythms of ascent and decline, and so on; societies seem to proceed from the small and simple to the large and complex.

A. L. Kroeber analyzes another anthropological approach markedly different from both the evolutionary and the structural–functional views. Basically, "diffusionism" tends to explain change in one society by finding its origin in another. When pushed to an extreme, it claims that every new pattern of behavior or item of culture has spread from one original source. Most sociologists find it difficult to accept this approach. True, many ideas spread from one society to another, especially in modern times—with the increase and improvement in communication—but at the same time there is undoubtedly much parallel innovation in which two or more cultures discover or work out a similar solution to the same problem. Even more important is the fact that from the multitude of items communicated to any society, only a few are adapted; which ones are utilized and which are not depends not only on the communication (e.g., its vigor, amount, and repetitiveness), but on the needs, interests, and absorptive capacities of the receiving system. Furthermore, identical items communicated will be differently adapted by various societies. Thus, as Kroeber indicates, diffusion is an important variable in the analysis of change, but diffusionism has been pushed too far in an attempt to build a framework for the study of change around this one variable.

What is needed is a combined study of systems of intersocial communication and patterns of intrasocial absorption, related to the study of the conditions under which innovations, whether externally or internally initiated, are integrated into society.

Amitai Etzioni attempts to provide a theoretical framework which combines the voluntaristic elements, emphasized in utopian and revolutionary approaches, with the structural and collectivistic elements stressed by functionalist theories. The core question Etzioni seeks to answer is: what are the conditions under which society can guide the processes which govern their lives and re-shape their society, rather than as in the traditional definition of alienation remaining subject to forces they neither understand nor control. The answer, spelled out in The Active Society, focuses on knowledge, strategy, power, consensus, and mobilization as the variables crucial to transformation.

The psychological approach gained much new attention in recent years, due to David McClelland and Everett E. Hagen's contribution to the study of change, in particular development.[4] According to this approach, the main force that propels societies rests not in environmental factors, ideas, or social

---

[4] David C. McClelland, The Achieving Society (Princeton, N.J.: D. Van Nostrand, 1961); Everett E. Hagen, On the Theory of Social Change (Homewood, Ill.: The Dorsey Press, 1961).

conflict but in individuals with high achievement motivation. If we wish to predict a society's future rate of economic development we should look first at its overall level of "entrepreneurial *spirit*" as reflected, for instance, in the themes of its children's literature, rather than to "external factors" such as the type of economic system-capitalist, socialist or communist. The economic success of a country is deeply affected by the individual achievement motivation of its managers, in business as well as government. This achievement drive is largely attained in the formative years and is effected by the social structure of the family and the culture.

CHAPTER 10

TALCOTT PARSONS

A Functional Theory
of Change

Structure and Process

The subject in general is far too vast for discussion in a brief paper, unless one confined himself to the highest level of generality. I should like, therefore, to concentrate my attention on one major type of change in social systems, that which is most closely analogous to the process of growth in the organism. This usually involves an element of quantitative increase in the "magnitude" of the system, in the social case, *e.g.,* through increase in population, but it also involves what in an important sense is qualitative or "structural" change. The type of the latter on which I should like to concentrate is the process of structural differentiation and the concomitant development of patterns and mechanisms which integrate the differentiated parts.

•

One of the most fundamental canons of scientific method is that it is impossible to study everything at once. Since the basis of generalization in science is always the demonstration of relatedness in process of variation (in one sense change), there must always somewhere be a distinction between the features of the phenomena under observation which do and which do not change under the relevant limitations of time and scope and in the respects which are defined as important for the purposes in hand. The specificities of significant change could not even be identified if there were no *relative* background of nonchange to relate them to.

To me the concept of structure is simply a shorthand statement of this basic point. The structure of a system is that set of properties of its component parts

From Talcott Parsons, "Some Considerations on the Theory of Social Change," *Rural Sociology,* XXVI (1961), No. 3, pp. 219-239. Reprinted by permission of the author and the publisher.

and their relations or combinations which, for a particular set of analytical purposes, can both logically and empirically be treated as constant within definable limits. If, however, there is built up strong empirical evidence that treating such elements as constant for particular types of systems is helpful in understanding the patterning of variation of other elements, then this structure is not simply an arbitrary methodological assumption, but propositions about it and its limits of empirical stability become empirical generalizations which are just as important as are "dynamic" generalizations.

•

Any ordinary system, therefore, is capable of description as on the one hand a structure, a set of units or components with, for the purposes in hand, stable properties, which of course may be relational, and on the other hand of events, of processes, in the course of which "something happens" to change some properties and some relations among them.

The concept of stability has obviously been used here as a defining characteristic of structure. The sense of the former term which must be distinguished from structure is that in which it is used to characterize a system as a whole, or some subsystem of such a system. In this present sense it is equivalent to the more specific concept of stable equilibrium—which in another reference may be either "static" or "moving." A system then is stable or (relatively) in equilibrium when the relation between its structure and the processes which go on within it and between it and its environment are such as to maintain those properties and relations, which for the purposes in hand have been called its structure, relatively unchanged. Very generally, always in "dynamic" systems, this maintenance is dependent on continuously varying processes, which "neutralize" either endogenous or exogenous sources of variability which, if they went far enough, would change the structure. A classic example of equilibrium in this sense is the maintenance of nearly constant body temperature by mammals and birds—in the face of continuing variation in environmental temperature and through mechanisms which operate either to produce heat, including slowing up its loss, or to slow down the rate of heat production or accelerate its dissipation.

Contrasted then with stability or equilibrating processes are those processes which operate to bring about structural change. That such processes exist and that they are of fundamental scientific importance is nowhere in question. Thus even in physics, whereas the mass of the atom of a particular element has been the prototype of the stable structural reference point, the discoveries of modern nuclear physics have now evolved a theory of change by which, through nuclear fission and/or fusion, the structures of "atomic identity" are transformed into others. The reason for insistence on the importance of keeping the concepts of structure and process and of stability and change analytically distinct is not a predilection in favor of one or the other item in each pair, but in favor of orderly procedure in scientific analysis.

As I see it now, the distinction between the two pairs of concepts is one of level of system reference. The structure of a system and of its environment must be distinguished from process *within* the system and in *interchange* between the system and its environment. But processes which maintain the stability of a system, internally through both structure and process, and in interchange with its environment, *i.e.,* states of its equilibrium, must be distinguished from processes by which this balance between structure and more "elementary" process is altered in such a way as to lead to a new and different "state" of the system, a state which must be described in terms of an alteration of its previous structure. To be sure the distinction is relative, but it is an essential and an ordered relativity. What I have been saying is that *at least two* systematically related perspectives on the problem of constancy of variation are essential to any sophisticated level of theoretical analysis.

These considerations constitute the major framework in which I should like to approach the analysis of change in social systems. I should like to attempt to discuss one type of change in the sense in which it has just been contrasted with stability and therefore will presuppose that there is a system or set of systems to which the concept of equilibrium is relevant, but which are conceived as undergoing processes of change which as such are processes of upsetting the initial equilibrium state and later "settling down" into a new equilibrium state. . . .

Let us start with the question of the structure of social systems and introduce both a formal and a substantive consideration. The formal one is that the structure of any empirical system may be treated as consisting in (1) *units,* such as the particle or the cell, and (2) *patterned relations* among units, such as relative distances, "organization" into tissues and organs. For social systems the minimum unit is the *role* of the participating individual actor (or status-role, if you will), and the minimum relation is that of patterned reciprocal interactions in terms of which each participant functions as an actor in relation to (orienting to) the others and, conversely, each is object for all the others. Higher-order units of social systems are collectivities, *i.e.,* organized action systems of the role performance of pluralities of human individuals. Perhaps it is well to speak of units on either level as units of *orientation* when they are treated as actors, as units of *modality* when they are treated as objects.[1]

In social structure the element of "patterned relation" is clearly in part

---

[1] This is the terminology used in "Pattern Variables Revisited," *American Sociological Review,* XXV (1960), 467-483.

"normative." This is to say that from the point of view of the unit it includes a set of "expectations" as to his or its behavior on the axis of what is or is not proper, appropriate, or right. From the point of view of other units with which the unit of reference is in interaction, this is a set of standards according to which positive or negative sanctions can be legitimated. Corresponding to the distinction between role and collectivity for the case of units is that between norm and value for that of relational pattern. A value is a normative pattern which defines desirable behavior for a system in relation to its environment, without differentiation in terms of the functions of units or of their particular situations. A norm, on the other hand, is a pattern defining desirable behavior for a unit or class of units in respects specific to it, and differentiated from the obligations of other classes.

The proposition that the relational patterns of social systems are normative, which is to say that they consist in institutionalized normative culture, can, in fact, be extended to the structure of units as well. One way of making this clear is to point out that what at one level of reference is a unit at another is a system. What we are calling the structural properties of the unit, therefore, are at the next level the relational patterns which order the relations between what in turn are the subunits making *it* up. Therefore, it is justified to assert, in the wider perspective, that the structure of social systems in general *consists* in institutionalized patterns of normative culture. It is of course further essential that these must be understood as applying at the two distinct levels of organization, which we call that of units and relational pattern among units.

To return now to the paradigm of the stable system discussed above, process in a system must be conceived as a process of interchanging inputs and outputs between units (subsystems) of the system on the one hand, and between the system, through the agency of its units, and its environment on the other. There is thus a "flow" of such inputs and outputs as between all pairs of classes of units, whether the relation be internal or external. What I am calling the normative pattern governing the relationship is then to be conceived as regulating this flow. For stable interchange to go on there must on the one hand be flexibility for inputs and outputs to move, but there must also be ways of "channeling" this process to keep its variability within limits.

A prototypical case is the flow of transactions involving the exchange of things of "value," namely goods and services and money, which constitute a market process. The normative patterns on the other hand are the institutional patterns defining money itself, the norms of contract and of the aspects of property other than money, conceived as Durkheim did in the famous phrase about the noncontractual elements of contract. The equilibrium of a market system is dependent on the maintenance of limits, relative to a set of definable conditions, to the fluctuation in the rates of these flows. The stability of the *structure* of the market system in the present sense is on the other hand a matter of the stability of the normative pattern system, the institutions.

What, then, do we mean by the stability of an institutional complex? First, of course, is meant the stability of the normative pattern itself. The single term "norm," especially if it is equated with "rule," is probably too narrow because it seems to imply a level of simplicity which permits description in a single proposition; this would patently not be true of the institutions of property or contract. Secondly, stability implies a minimum level of commitment of acting units, *i.e.,* of dispositions to perform in accordance with the relevant expectations—rather than to evade or violate them—and to apply the relevant sanctions, positive or negative, to other units in response to performance, evasion or violation. Third, institutionalization implies acceptance of an empirical and mutually understood "definition of the situation" in a sense of understanding of what the system of reference *is;*[2] this can for example be ideologically distorted so as to make functioning impossible.[3]

Finally, institutionalization means some order of integration of the normative complex in question in the more general one governing the system as a whole, at the normative level itself. Thus the doctrine of "separate but equal" proved to be dubiously integrated with the rest of the American system of constitutional rights formulated on the basis of the constitutional right to "equal protection of the laws." It can thus be said that the 1954 decision of the Supreme Court was a step in institutional integration, or at least that this was the primary problem before the court.

Endogenous and Exogenous Sources of Change

The concept of stable equilibrium implies that through integrative mechanisms endogenous variations are kept within limits compatible with the maintenance of the main structural patterns, and through adaptive mechanisms fluctuations in the relations between system and environment are similarly kept within limits. If we look at what is meant by stable equilibrium from the perspective of the principle of inertia,[4] then it becomes a

---

[2] This definition is normative to acting units but existential to observers. Here the actor is placed in the role of an observer of his own situation of action, *i.e.,* is treated as potentially "rational."

[3] Thus it seems plausible to suggest that perhaps the most serious source of conflict in the UN at present lies in the ideological difference between the Western and the Communist powers as to what the UN itself, and the system of international order of which it is a guardian, in fact consist in. The slogans of imperialism and colonialism formulate the Communist view of everything not under their more-or-less direct control. If this is the "diagnosis" it is quite clear that the present organization is not "doing its job."

[4] The concept of inertia is here used in the sense of classical mechanics, namely to designate stability in rate and direction of process, not a state in which "nothing hap-

problem to account for alterations in this stable state through disturbances of sufficient magnitude to overcome the stabilizing or equilibrating forces or mechanisms. Once a disturbance fulfilling these criteria is present, then the problem is that of tracing its effects through the system, and defining the conditions under which new stable states can be predicted (or, retrospectively, accounted for).

Such changes may in principle be either endogenous or exogenous or both, but in approaching the problem it is essential to bear in mind that I am here dealing with the concept "social system" in a strict analytical sense. Therefore, changes originating in the personalities of the members of the social system, the behavioral organisms "underlying" these, or the cultural system as such are to be classed as exogenous, whereas common sense would have it that only the physical environment (including other organisms and societies), and perhaps the "supernatural," is truly exogenous.

The formal paradigm for the analysis of the general system of action which I with various associates have been using would suggest, first, that the immediately most important channels of exogenous influence on the social system are the culture and the personality systems and also that the modes of their influence are different. The direct influence of the cultural system in turn should involve in the first instance empirical knowledge, hence should lead into the field of the sociology of knowledge in that area. Important as this is, because of limitations of space I shall not deal directly with it here, but will confine myself to the boundary *vis-à-vis* the personality.

There is, however, a double reason why the boundary of the social system *vis-à-vis* the personality is particularly significant. In its most direct sense it is concerned with the "motivation" of the individual, in an analytical psychological sense, hence with his level of "gratification" and its negative, frustration. But *indirectly* the most critical point is that what is structurally the most critical component of social systems, what we call its institutionalized values, is institutionalized by way of its internalization in the personality of the individual. There is a sense in which the social system is "boxed in" between the cultural status of values and their significance to the integration of the individual personality.

The problem of analyzing the independent variability which may exist as between cultural values and personalities is beyond the scope of this paper; it may be presumed that problems such as those of charismatic innovation fall at least partly in this rubric. Given relative stability of this connection, however, we may suggest that there will be in the personality of the typical individual what may be called an integrate of value and motivational com-

---

pens." The *problem* then becomes that of accounting for change in rate or direction, including "slowing down." This of course runs counter to much of common sense in the field of human action.

mitments which can for heuristic purposes be assumed to be stable and that this in turn can be assumed to define the *orientation* component of the requisite role—expectations of the appropriate classes of individual actors. Furthermore, this should be true whether a society as a whole or a subsystem of it is under analysis. This assumption clearly implies that, for purposes of analyzing the particular process of change in question, the institutionalized values will be assumed to remain constant.

I am also assuming that the structure of normative patterns which defines the relations of the class of acting units under consideration to the objects in their situation is also given, initially, but that this is our primary independent variable; namely the problem is to account for processes of change in this normative structure, in institutions. This leaves the modalities of objects as the focus of initiation of change. I shall therefore postulate a change in the relation of a social system to its environment which in the first instance impinges on the definition of the situation for one or more classes of acting units within the system, and then has further repercussions which can put pressure for change on the normative institutional patterns. The type of pressure I have specifically in mind is in the direction of differentiation.

•

A Model of Differentiation

With these preliminaries in mind, let us now attempt to outline in general terms the main steps in a cycle of differentiation, and then apply the analysis to the case of differentiation between household and producing collectivity.

We may start with the postulation of a deficit of input at the goal-attainment boundary of the social system which is postulated as undergoing a process of differentiation, *e.g.,* the family household which also performs "occupational" functions. Looking at it from a functional point of view, it may be said that the "frustration" of its capacity to attain its goals, or fulfill its expectations, may focus at either of the functional levels which is important to it, namely its productive effectiveness or its effectiveness in performing what later come to be the "residual" family functions of socialization and regulation of the personalities of members, or of course some combination of the two. Secondly, it will of course concern the boundary between this and other subsystems of the society. In this case the important boundary conceptions are the markets for commodities and labor and the ideological "justifications" of the unit's position in the society, which may or may not take a prominently religious direction. But underlying this is the problem of input from the personality of the individual into the social system at the more general level; in the present case this is likely to be particularly important because familial and occupational roles are, for the personality of the adult, the most important foci of commitment to the performance of societal function. Third, there will be some balance between the two components of frustration just mentioned, namely with respect to the conditional components of facilities and rewards, and with respect to the normative components of expectation systems. The latter component is the indispensable condition of the process leading to differentiation.

The complexity involved in these three distinctions may seem formidable, but it may be argued that the difficulty is not so serious as it sounds. It is the last one which is the most crucial because of the importance of a normative component somewhere. The difference between the other two concerns that between exogenous and endogenous sources of change for the system in question; personalities in roles in the particular social system of reference operate "directly" on that system, not through its boundary interchanges with other social systems.

The most important point to be made here is that, *whatever its source,* if a disturbance impinges on the goal-attaining subsystem of a social system, its effects will, in the first instance, be propagated in two directions. One of these concerns the functional problem of access to facilities for the performance of primary functions, namely the kind of facilities available and the terms on which they are available. The other direction concerns the kind of integrative support which the unit receives within the system, the senses in which it can be said to have a "mandate" to "do a job." Back of that, in turn, and on a still higher level of control is the basic "legitimation" of its functioning. Support here may be defined as particularized to the specific unit or class of units. Legitimation on the other hand concerns more the functions than the particular unit and the normative more than the operative patterns.

These three problems fit into a hierarchy of control. The first is an adaptive problem and must be solved first if the groundwork of solution of the others is to be laid, and so on for the others. What is meant by "solution" in this case is provision of *opportunity* in a facilities sense for the higher level of functioning in question to be attained. Opportunity thus conceived is always double-barreled, in that it has a concrete resource aspect on the one hand, a normatively controlled "mechanism" or standard aspect on the other.

Another familiar sociological concept should be brought in here, namely "ascription." Ascription is essentially the *fusion* of intrinsically independent functions in the same structural unit. Looked at in this way differentiation is a process of "emancipation" from ascriptive ties. As such it is a process of gaining "freedom from" certain restraints. But it is also the process of fitting into a normative order which can subject the now independent units to a type of normative control compatible with the functional imperative of the larger system of which they are a part. In differentiating, however, the unit gains certain degrees of freedom of choice and action which were not open to it before the process of differentiation had taken place. Moreover, this should be the case whichever side of the division is taken as a point of reference.

•

The obverse of this emancipation from ascription to a relatively particularized source of income is the freedom to offer a much wider variety of services in exchange for income. The labor force, that is to say, may become much more highly differentiated, and a wider variety of specialized talents may find employment. A new set of conditions are of course introduced, because the more important specialized talents often involve prerequisites of training and experience which cannot be universally taken for granted.

These two are the relatively "conditional" factors from the point of view of the household. We may say that it cannot afford to let the process of differentiation take place unless certain minima in these respects are, if not guaranteed, made highly probable. These probabilities are, in turn, dependent on two further sets of considerations which involve the more ramified relationship systems in which the process takes place. These are considerations in the first place of the nature of the labor market in which the income earner has to offer his services; above all the extent to which he is protected against pressures to accept particularly disadvantageous terms. There are three main mechanisms involved in modern labor markets at the operative level, though others may operate in other ways. These are of course competition between potential employers, the self-protective measures of employee groups, e.g., through collective bargaining, and establishment and enforcement of a normative order by "higher" authority, e.g., public agencies. The effect of regulation of terms by any combination of these factors is to emancipate the unit from exposure to particular pressures exerted by any one source of supply, e.g., of income. Through such means as the monetary mechanisms and credit instruments, there is also time-extension, in that the employee is emancipated from the pressures of immediacy to a degree to which this may not be the case for the proprietor.

•

Let us now turn to the second context, that of support for the performance of function. This is the kind of context in which farming is regarded as a "way of life" rather than a "business." Typically occupational employment is justified by the higher level of efficiency of such organization in producing a higher standard of living, but this may be problematical when it involves ceasing to be "independent" and "working for one's own" rather than for an employer. On the other side there is the problem of "loss of function" of the family, with the implication that the differentiated family is not "doing a worthwhile job," but is coming to be a consumption unit alone —a question particularly coming to a head in the alleged concentration of the feminine role on "leisure" activities. We may follow through this context in terms of the problem of degrees of freedom, being careful to distinguish the two levels which above have been called support and legitimation.

The problem in which I am calling the context of support is the position of the family in locally significant "public opinion." The support of this unit is ascribed to the conception that acceptable status in the community is bound to proprietorship of an enterprise, with all its connotations about the place of property—that the employed person is in some sense a second class citizen. It seems to follow that, just as in the context of facilities available to differentiating units the relevant frame of reference or "reference group" was the market, both for labor and for consumers' goods, in that of "support" it is the local community, since both residential unit and employing unit for the typical adult must be comprised within this. In the undifferentiated case, the core structure of the local community in America consists in proprietary kinship units—in the first instance farm families, but the same structural patterns extend to small businesses and professional practices in market towns. In the differentiated case it is residential kinship units on the one hand, employing organizations on the other.

Since the basic "goals" of residential kinship units as such are in the nature of the case ascribed, namely as socialization of children and management of the personalities of members, the community gains in this respect an exceedingly important new range of freedom in the new levels and diversities of, in the above broad sense, "productive" achievement, which higher level organizations are capable of carrying out and which are beyond the capacities of kinship units. The typical family unit need no longer look to units of its own type of structure for these benefits, thus staying within the limits imposed by this structure, and members of the community can support the functions of the community *both* in the familial realm and in the productive without making their ascription to each other a condition.

This, however, is possible only if there are standards which regulate the terms on which the two categories of functions are related to each other. This, in part, concerns market relations; but a number of other things are also involved, such as obligations for contributing to the support of common community interests, both through taxation and through voluntary channels. There must be a new set of "rules of the game" according to which both sets of operating units can live in the same community without undue friction. One major focus of these balancing institutions lies in the field of stratification, above all perhaps because the larger scale of organization of producing units in the differentiated sense makes it impossible to preserve the basis of equality of kinship units of a family–farm community.

This leads over into the problem of legitimation which concerns the justifications or questioning of the basic pattern of organization of socially important functions in terms of the institutionalized values of the system. Here the problem is that of emancipating the formulas of legitimation from the organizational particularities of the less differentiated situation. These considerations clearly get over into the ideological realm. For differentiation to be legitimated it must no longer be believed that only proprietors are really "responsible" people, or that organizations which are not controlled by locally prestigeful kinship units are necessarily concerned only with "self-interest" and are not really "contributing." On the other side, the family which has "lost functions" can really be a "good family."

Perhaps the most important focus of this new legitimation is the new conception of the adequate, socially desirable *man,* particularly as organized about the balancing of the two differentiated spheres of performance and responsibility, in his occupational role on the one hand, in his family on the other. If this is the case, then clearly there are extremely important concomitant problems of change in the feminine role. The first stage of these probably concerns the ideological legitimation of a more differentiated femininity than before, namely that even in a family which has lost function it is justified for the woman to devote herself primarily to husband and children. A later phase involves various forms of community participation and occupational involvement.

These three seem to be the main contexts in which the direct impact of the impetus to structural change must work out if it is to result in the differentiation of a previously fused structure. For the sake of completeness, it should be mentioned that there will be certain other more indirect problem areas. One of these is that of the sheer content of consumption tastes which is involved in a change in the standard of living, and its relation to the occupational contribution of the income earner. A second is the problem of the relation of values, at various levels of specification, not only to the more immediate problems of the legitimation of the various classes of structural units in the system, but to that of the more generalized norms and standards which regulate their relations. Finally, the most indirect of all seems to lie in the field of what Durkheim called organic solidarity. I interpret this to mean the normative regulation of the adaptive processes and mechanisms. As I see it, this is the primary link between what I have called support on the one hand and the realistic play of "interests" of the various units on the other.

The above discussion has dealt, in far too great a hurry, with several different "functional" contexts in which some kind of reordering has to take place if a process of differentiation, as this has been defined, is to be completed and the new structure stabilized. It is of the essence of the present view that in each of these there is involved a complex balance of input–output relationships, such that too great a tipping in either direction with respect to any one such balance could make the difference between successful differentiation and its failure. The dismal complexity of the resulting picture is, however, somewhat mitigated by considerations of the hierarchy of control and hence of the fact that firm establishment of the "proper" patterns at the higher levels may make it possible to exercise control over rather wide ranges of variation at the lower.

•

The Consequences of Differentiation

. . . In conclusion, I should like to attempt to summarize certain of the primary conditions of successful differentiation which also constitute in a sense characterizations of the outcome in the relevant respects. First there is what I have called the *opportunity* factor. This is the aspect of the structure of the situation which is most directly relevant to the process of differentiation as such. The operation of the process of course presupposes a need or demand factor, the source of disturbance to which reference was made above. The implementation of the process of differentiation in turn implies a leadership factor in that some individual or group should take responsibility, not only for routine "management" but for reorganization. The entrepreneur of standard economic discussion is a prototypical example.

But for there to be genuine differentiation there must be a process by which facilities, previously ascribed to less differentiated units, are freed from this ascription and are made available through suitable adaptive mechanisms for the utilization of the higher-order new class of units which are emerging. The prototype of such facilities for the process considered above is that of labor services, freed from ascription to the household unit, but with their availability to the employing organization institutionally regulated in terms of the market system and the institutionalization of the contract of employment. The obverse is of course the accessibility, for the residual household units, of necessary facilities through the expenditure of money income on the markets for consumers' goods. Looked at then in structural terms, the opportunity factor is essentially the possibility of institutionalizing the mutual access to facilities, in this case through the market mechanisms. In another type of case, for instance, it may be the mechanisms of communication.

The second main context of structural reorganization concerns the way in which the two new and differentiated classes of units are related to each other in the wider system, in the first instance from the point of view of the structure of collectivities. I have suggested, for the case of the producing household, that what is primarily involved here is a restructuring of the local community. The latter can no longer be an aggregate of proprietary kinship units, only supplemented by a few structures articulating it with the wider society, but it comes to be organized about the relationships between "residential" units and "employing" units. It is evident that this entails articulating the most important *differentiated* roles of the same individual, in the first instance of course the typical adult male.

This may be called the restructuring of the ways in which the particular unit, collectivity and role, is included in higher-order collectivity structures in the society. Since in the nature of the case any initial collectivity unit (or role unit) is part of a society, it is not a question whether it should or should not be included; for example, the case of absorption of immigrant kin groups into a host society is a different problem from that now under consideration. The point is rather that there must be a restructuring of collectivities on the level immediately above that of the initial unit, with either the incorporation of both the old (or "residual") unit and the new in an already available higher-order unit, or the creation of a new category of such units, or both. The essential point is that there must be established a new collectivity structure within which both types of units perform essential functions and in the name of which both can draw the kind of "support" discussed above. The problem is of course particularly acute for the newly emerging unit or class of units.

The third context in which normative components of structure have to be reorganized as part of a process of differentiation is that of the more general complexes of institutionalized norms which apply not to one collectivity structure but to many. The prototype here for largescale and highly differentiated social systems is the system of legal norms, but it is not confined to that. Standards of performance or achievement, of technical adequacy, and the like are also involved.

In the case we have used for illustration, the standards in terms of which employing collectivities are legitimized are particularly important. Here it is important to recognize two different stages beyond that of the proprietary unit which was our original point of reference, namely that in which all productive roles are performed by household members. The next step has usually been the "family firm" in which the managerial and entrepreneurial roles were ascribed to kinship, but the "labor" roles were not. This of course is still very prominent in the "small business" sector of the American economy and also in some other fields. But beyond this is the case where the organization is cut entirely loose from kinship. The most important legal aspect of this development has been the generalization of the idea of the corporation and its legitimation in many different fields, quantitatively of course most conspicuously the economic.

At the role level, an important case is that of the standards of competence which become institutionalized as defining conditions of employment in certain classes of roles, behind which in turn lie levels of education. These, like legal norms, are independent of any particular employing collectivity or kinship group—in this sense both are universalistic. The rules of corporate organization define the kinds of things certain organized groups can do and the responsibilities they assume in organizing to do them; standards of education define the kinds of legitimate requirements of eligibility for certain types of employment which may be laid down, hence both the kinds of opportunities open to individuals of various classes and the ways in which access to such opportunity is limited.

It has been suggested above that a process of differentiation, with the meaning we have given that term, involves the establishment of a unit having primary functions of a higher order, seen in terms of the system in which it operates, than was the function of the unit from which it differentiates. If this is the case, then the norms governing the performance of that function, including the relations of its performers to other units in the social structure, must be of a higher order of generality than before. This is what we mean by saying that they are more universalistic; they define standards which cannot, in their relevance, be confined to the lower-order function and the units performing it. This criterion is directly involved with the emancipation of resources from ascription. Competence as a qualification for a role, in a sense which denies the relevance of kinship membership, is prototypical. Thus we may speak of an *upgrading* of the standards of normative control of the more differentiated system as compared with the less differentiated one.

This whole discussion has been based on the assumption that the underlying value-pattern of the system does not change as a part of the process of differentiation. It does not, however, follow that nothing changes at the level of values. It is an essential proposition of the conceptual scheme used here that every social system has a system of values as the highest-order component of its structure. Its values comprise the definition, from the point of view of its members—if it is institutionalized—of the desirable type of system at a level independent of internal structural differentiation or of particularities of situation. This "system" involves both a pattern type and an element of content, namely a definition of what kind of system the pattern applies to. In our case there are the values of households and of employing-productive units. In what I am calling "pattern" terms they may be the same, *e.g.,* both of them incorporating the general American pattern of "instrumental activism." But if these values are to be implemented in either type of system there must be specifications of the more general system to the type of function (not its particularities) and to the type of situation in which the unit operates.

Where differentiation has occurred, this means that the values of the new system, which includes both the new and the residual unit, must be different in the content component from that of the original unit, though not, under present assumptions, in the pattern component. The new values must be more extensive, in the special sense that they can legitimize the functions of both differentiated units under a single formula which permits each to do what it does and, equally essential, not to do what the other does. The difficulty of institutionalizing the more extensive values is evidenced by the widespread currency of what may be called romantic ideologies in this sense, the allegation that the "loss of function," which is an inevitable feature of what I call the residual unit after the differentiation has taken place, is a measure of failure to implement the value-pattern of the system. For example, the new dependence of households on occupational earnings from employing organizations is often interpreted as loss of a sense of responsibility for independent support. This to be sure is ideology, but as such is an index of incomplete institutionalization of restructured values.

The relation between the values of a higher-order social system and those of a differentiated subsystem may be said to be one of *specification* of the implications of the more generalized pattern of the more extensive system to the "level" of the subsystem, by taking account of the limitations imposed upon the latter by function and situation. In this sense a business firm may value "economic rationality" in a sense which comprises both productivity and solvency, with considerably less qualification for more extensive values than an undifferentiated family household can, and in a complementary sense the household can devote itself in economic contexts to "consumption."

The above is sufficient to indicate only a few highlights of a very complex problem area. In this paper I have dealt with only one aspect of the field of the theory of social change. I have had to do so very abstractly and with only a tiny bit of empirical illustration. It does, however, seem to me justified to draw the conclusion that the problems of this area are in principle soluble in empirical-theoretical terms. Above all, we have at our disposal a conceptual scheme which is sufficiently developed so that at least at the level of categorization and of problem statement it is approaching the type of closure—logical of course—which makes *systematic* analysis of interdependencies possible. We can define the main ranges of variability which are essential for empirical analysis, and the main mechanisms through which variations are propagated through the system. We can quantify to the point of designating deficits and surpluses of inputs and outputs, and here and there we can come close to specifying threshold values beyond which equilibrium will break down. . . .

CHAPTER 11

FRANCESCA CANCIAN

Functional Analysis
of Change

Functional analysis is frequently criticized as being of little use in describing and predicting change.[1] At the same time, many social scientists interested in investigating change hesitate to give up the functional approach. It has been fruitful in many empirical studies and crucial in many of the attempts to construct general theories of behavior.

Fortunately, a philosopher has come to aid of social scientists on this confused issue. Ernest Nagel[2] presents a formal definition of functional systems based on Merton's essay, "Manifest and Latent Functions."[3] Nagel does not explicitly consider the problem of functional analysis of change. His formal definition of a functional system, however, provides a basis for outlining several specific ways in which functional analysis can be used to study change and for concluding that most of the arguments about the static nature of such analysis are based on semantic confusion and unimaginative and incorrect methods.

The following discussion (1) summarizes Nagel's extensive formal definition of a functional system; (2) considers some of its methodological implications; (3) outlines the ways in which functional analysis, so defined,

---

From Francesca Cancian, "Functional Analysis of Change," *American Sociological Review,* XXV (1960), No. 6, pp. 818-826. Reprinted by permission of the author and the publisher.

[1] See, *e.g.,* Ralf Dahrendorf, "Out of Utopia," *American Journal of Sociology,* LXIV (1958), 115-127; Clifford Geertz, "Ritual and Social Change," *American Anthropologist,* LIX (1957), 32-54; Wayne Hield, "The Study of Change in Social Science," *British Journal of Sociology,* V (1954), 1-10; David Lockwood, "Some Remarks on 'The Social System,' " *British Journal of Sociology,* VII (1956), 134-146.

[2] Ernest Nagel, "A Formalization of Functionalism," in his *Logic without Metaphysics* (Glencoe, Ill.: The Free Press, 1956), pp. 247-283.

[3] Robert K. Merton, *Social Theory and Social Structure* (Glencoe, Ill.: The Free Press, 1957), pp. 19-84.

can deal with change; (4) answers some of the critics who charge that functional analysis cannot adequately treat change; and (5) presents an example of investigation of change by means of functional analysis.

A Definition of "Functional System"

To Nagel, functional analysis is distinguished by the use of a particular model, the model of a directively organized or functional system. A "model," here used in a very broad sense, is a set of general relationships. A model is useful if the relationships posited in it "fit" the data in the sense of parsimoniously yielding accurate and relevant predictions. The model of a functional system consists of a fairly complex set of properties or relationships. Two simpler models are described below for purposes of clarification and contrast.

The simplest and most general system model posits interdependence of elements within a certain boundary, that is, the interdependence has a specific referent. The model for such a *simple* system may be expressed as $x = f(y)$: one property is the function of another. This is the type of system implied by using "function" in the mathematical sense. Empirical examples are: the volume of gas at a constant temperature varies inversely with its pressure; the rate of suicide varies inversely with the strength of the collective conscience; presence of male initiation rites is associated with household composition.

These types of statements, using the model of a simple system, do not necessarily lead to predictions of either change or stability. Unless the state of part of the system at some future time is known, the future state of the system cannot be predicted. For example, to predict the suicide rate two years hence, one would have to know the strength of the collective conscience at that time.

Certain properties can be added to the definition of a simple system so that, by definition, predictions of change or stability can be made on the basis of present knowledge. In a *deterministic* system, as defined by Nagel,[4] the properties of the system at one time are a function of its properties at a certain previous time. Since it may be inconvenient to observe the whole set, one attempts to find the smallest number of properties or variables "such that the specific forms of *all* the properties . . . at any time are uniquely determined by these *n* properties at that time." [5] Nagel cites the mechanics of bodies, the several dimensions of which can be neglected, as an example of a deterministic system:

> Thus, in the case of a freely falling body, it suffices to know (in addition, of course, to the laws of motion) the position and momentum of the body at some

---

[4] *Op. cit.*, pp. 253-256.
[5] *Ibid.*, p. 255.

initial instant, in order to be able to calculate its position and momentum (and accordingly other properties of the body, such as its kinetic energy, which are definable in terms of these coordinates) at any other instant.[6]

If one knows the present values of certain key variables and the stability or rates of change of these variables, then one can predict the values of these variables, and many others, at any future time.

If one treats a social system as a deterministic system, certain types of statements may be made. For example, since a society is integrated at the community level and is beginning to develop irrigation, it can be predicted on the basis of laws of sociocultural development that it will develop cities and a national level of sociocultural integration within the next two centuries; since the present questionnaire responses of a small, task-oriented group show little agreement on role differentiation, it can be predicted on the basis of laws of progressive consensus on role differentiation that the responses will show more agreement after five meetings.

A deterministic system is a simple system—with the added restriction that the properties of the system at one time are a function of its properties at a previous time. A *functional* system is a deterministic system—with the added restriction that certain properties of the system are maintained despite potentially disruptive changes in the system or the environment or both.

A functional system, according to Nagel's definition, is made up of two types of variables: G's and "state coordinates." G is the property of the system that is maintained or is stable. State coordinates determine the presence or absence of G. The values of the state coordinates may vary to such an extent that the maintenance of G is threatened, but when one exceeds the "safe" limits for G, the other(s) compensates and G is maintained. Some of the state coordinates may lie outside the system boundary, that is, in the environment. Such a system of G and state coordinates may be called functional with respect to G and the state coordinates may be described as having the function of maintaining G.

For example, a small, task-oriented group could be treated as a functional system. Let G be the solution of the group's task or problem. Let the state coordinates be task-oriented activity and emotionally supportive activity. If these three variables can be usefully treated as a functional system, then: (1) problem solution is dependent on task-oriented activity and emotionally supportive activity; (2) at certain times, there will be such a preponderance of task-oriented activity that problem solution will be threatened because of decreased motivation or resentment over following others' suggestions—at these times emotionally supportive activity will increase and problem solution will no longer be threatened; (3) at certain

---

[6] *Ibid.*, p. 256.

times, there will be such a preponderance of emotionally supportive activity that problem solution will be threatened—at these times task-oriented activity will increase to maintain problem solution or G.

It should be noted that, by definition, more than one state of the system leads to maintenance of G. Thus, in the preceding example, eventual problem solution might result from both: initially high task-oriented activity and low supportive activity, followed by increased supportive activity; and initially low task-oriented activity and high supportive activity followed by increased task activity. In a functional system there is more than one combination of the values of certain parts of the system which will result in the same trait or will have the same consequences (maintenance of G). This is one way of stating the familiar notion of functional equivalents.

It should also be noted that stability of G is not *assumed* in a functional analysis. On the contrary, it is assumed that the environment or parts of the system or both are changing so much that it is impossible for G to persist unless there are specific mechanisms within the system to compensate for these changes. It is therefore inappropriate to use this system model if the environment and the system are treated as constant, or if there is no state of the system which threatens the maintenance of G.

The definition of "functional" as "fulfilling a basic need" does assume that there is no state of the system which threatens the maintenance of G. This definition is therefore inappropriate according to Nagel's concept of a functional system. Functional analysis, as here defined, does not assume that G (some need) is stable and then explain the existence of state coordinates in terms of their efficiency in fulfilling this need. Rather, functional analysis shows that G is or is not maintained because certain state coordinates do or do not compensate for each other's variation. An example of a *non*functional proposition is that religion and related institutions are maintained because of a need for the meaningfulness of life to be maintained, while a *functional* analysis would propose that the meaningfulness of life is maintained because of the interaction of religion and other institutions.

Thus far, no specific attention has been given to the limits on possible variation of the values of state coordinates. Three limits on the values of the variables determining G should be considered. First, there are limits dictated by physical reality. To return to our former example, the amount of task-oriented activity possible in a given time period is limited by the number of people in the group and the number of messages that can be communicated within that time. Second, within the limits of physical reality, there are limits determined by the definition of the system under consideration. If a property is used to define a system, one cannot analyze conditions under which this property disappears, unless a different definition is used. For example, if one wishes to study the relations among interaction, role differentiation, and cohesion *within social systems,* and a social system is defined by a certain amount of interaction, there cannot be less than this amount of interaction.

Within these two types of limits, there is a third which is the most relevant to this discussion. This is the limit beyond which compensation is impossible and G ceases to exist. In our previous example, it seems reasonable to assume that if either supportive activity or task-oriented activity increases or decreases beyond a certain point, no possible adjustment can result in maintenance of G or problem solution. Thus, if task-oriented activity exceeds certain limits, some of the group members may become so hostile or uninterested that no future supportive activity can regain their cooperation. Solution of the group's problem becomes impossible and the group can no longer be considered a functional system with respect to the G of problem solution.

This discussion of limits leads to a way of conceptualizing the potential stability of a given G in a given functional system. The persistence of G depends upon the amount of discrepancy between two ranges: the range of possible variation for each state coordinate and the range of variation that can be compensated for by variation in other state coordinates. G becomes less stable as the discrepancy between these two ranges increases.

In sum, a functional system is one that satisfies the following conditions: (1) the system can be analyzed into a set of interdependent variables or parts; (2) the values of some of these variables—state coordinates—determine whether or not a certain property G will occur in the system; (3) there are certain limits on the variation of the values of state coordinates, such that variation within the limits will be followed by a compensating variation of other state coordinates, resulting in the maintenance of G; (4) variation beyond these limits will not be followed by a compensating variation of other state coordinates and G will disappear.

This definition of functional systems is neither complete nor without problems of its own. However, it should suffice to show that there is no logical reason why a functional analysis cannot be useful in investigating change. There are several ways in which functional analysis can be so used. For example, the presence or absence of G can be predicted if one knows whether or not the state coordinates are exceeding the limits within which compensation is possible. Or, G itself can be a cycle or a rate of change. And there is no empirical reason why functional analysis cannot be used to investigate change if some phenomena fit the model of a functional system and if one can assume that they will continue to fit it in the future.

Before proceeding, it should be noted that Nagel's definition of functional analysis does not include all of the many meanings ascribed to the term function. Therefore, caution should be maintained in generalizing the finding that functional analysis, as conceived by Nagel, can be used to investigate change. Functional analysis has been so broadly defined that one sociologist concludes that the term is "synonymous with sociological analysis." [7] Nagel's definition elaborates and clarifies the type of "functional analysis" used, for example, by the sociologist Parsons,[8] the anthropologist Leach,[9] and the linguist Martinet.[10] This definition, of course, excludes all modes of analysis that do not meet the four criteria specified above. Semantic difficulty could be largely eliminated by clear definitions of the different types of "functional analysis" and consensus on terminology. In the meantime, the special definition presented here may help to avoid semantic confusion.

A Basic Methodological Rule

Nagel's formalization of functionalism provides a basis from which many useful methodological rules and terminological distinctions can be drawn, including some of those pointed out by Firth,[11] Levy,[12] Merton[13] and others. One rule, which has frequently been stated, is the importance of specifying the system and the G(s) in relation to which the state coordinates are functional. This rule is crucial to successful functional analysis of change (or stability) and deserves special attention. As Nagel points out in his comment on Merton's discussion of the ideological implications of functional analysis:

> Functional analyses in all domains, and not only in sociology, run a similar risk of dogmatic provincialism which characterizes some analyses in sociology, when the relational character of functional statements is ignored, and when it is forgotten that a system may exhibit a variety of G's or that a given item may be a member of a variety of systems.[14]

Specification of the system(s) and the G(s) under consideration is especially important when a plurality of systems and G's are involved. A subsystem may be functionally organized with respect to a G while the larger system is not. Or one may be interested in several G's and the conditions for maintaining some of the G's may preclude maintenance of others, that is,

---

[7] Kingsley Davis, "The Myth of Functional Analysis as a Special Method in Sociology and Anthropology," *American Sociological Review,* XXIV (1959), p. 757.

[8] Talcott Parsons and Neil J. Smelser, *Economy and Society* (Glencoe, Ill.: The Free Press, 1956).

[9] E. R. Leach, *Political Systems of Highland Burma* (Cambridge: Harvard University Press, 1951).

[10] André Martinet, "Function, Structure and Sound Change," *Word,* VIII (1952). 1-32.

[11] Raymond Firth, "Function," in W. L. Thomas, ed., *Current Anthropology* (Chicago: University of Chicago Press, 1956).

[12] Marion J. Levy, Jr., *The Structure of Society* (Princeton: Princeton University Press, 1952).

[13] *Loc. cit.*

[14] *Op. cit.,* p. 283.

the range of values of a state coordinate that maintains G_1 may cause G_2 to disappear.

The importance of these distinctions becomes more apparent if one considers the definition of such terms as "equilibrium" and "functional unity." Equilibrium means the maintenance of G. G can be a stable state, for example, corruption of city government, or allocation of reward according to evaluation of performance; or it can be a stable rate of change, for example, accelerating rate of technological innovation, or decreasing interpersonal communication in prepsychotics; or it can be a cycle or series of states, for example, change from a conservative power elite to an opportunistic elite and then again to a conservative elite, or change from feudalism to capitalism to communism. If only one G is being considered, equilibrium can be clearly defined. If a plurality of G's or subsystems or both is being considered and they are ranked on a scale, then the degree of stability of each G in each subsystem can be weighted and some general notion of the equilibrium of the total system can be defined. It is possible, however, that the G's and the subsystems cannot be ranked. In such a case, it would be meaningless to specify a general state of equilibrium if some G's in some subsystems are maintained while others are not. It would also be meaningless to discuss conditions of equilibrium for the system as a whole if the conditions for maintaining some G's preclude the maintenance of other G's.

A similar argument applies to the definition of the function of a phenomenon as "the contribution it makes to the total social life as the functioning of the total social system." [15]

> Such a view implies that a social system . . . has a certain kind of unity. . . . We may define it as a condition in which all parts of the social system work together with a sufficient degree of harmony or internal consistency, *i.e.*, without producing persistent conflicts which can neither be resolved nor regulated.[16]

To translate this statement by Radcliffe-Brown into our terminology, the postulate of functional unity means that the conditions for maintaining a specified set of G's in the system under consideration are not mutually exclusive or are mutually supportive. If no particular G's are specified, then "functional unity" would mean that no persistent properties conflict with each other. It seems very doubtful that functional unity, in this latter sense, characterizes many social systems. In addition, treating a social system as a functional unity without specifying the G's so unified results in a vague analysis and one that allows for no internal source of change. It is this use of functional unity that best merits Geertz's criticism of the adequacy of the functional approach in dealing with social change: "The emphasis on sys-

---

[15] A. R. Radcliffe-Brown, *Structure and Function in Primitive Society* (Glencoe, Ill.: The Free Press, 1952), p. 181.

[16] *Loc. cit.*

tems in balance, on social homeostasis, and on timeless structural pictures, leads to a bias in favor of 'well-integrated' societies in a stable equilibrium and to a tendency to emphasize the functional aspects of a people's usages and customs rather than their dysfunctional implications." [17]

Methods of Using Functional Analysis to Investigate Change

On the basis of the foregoing discussion, a more precise delineation of the resources and limitations of functional analysis in investigating change can be made. The definition of different types of system change itself raises complex problems which cannot be discussed here. However, one set of definitions is important to the problem of the functional analysis of change, namely, the distinction between change *of* and *within* the system.[18]

Change *within* the system refers to change that does not alter the system's basic structure. In a functional system, this means changes in state coordinates for which compensation is possible. G and the relationship between state coordinates remain the same. Change *of* the system is any change that alters the system's basic structure. In a functional system, this includes disappearance of G, the appearance of new state coordinates or the disappearance of old ones, and change in the range of variation of state coordinates for which compensation is possible.

The ways in which change is incorporated in functional analysis now may be specified. Their justification lies in the definition of functional systems and in the consequent possibility of ordering systems hierarchically and of treating (sub)systems as state coordinates maintaining G's in a more inclusive system.

(1) *Disappearance of G can be predicted as the result of failure to meet conditions of equilibrium.* Disappearance of G means change *of* the system. State coordinates exceed the limits within which compensation is possible and the functional system breaks down.

(2) *If G is defined as a stable rate of change or a moving equilibrium, a stable rate of change can be predicted as the result of fulfillment of the conditions of equilibrium.* In this case, state coordinates do not exceed the limits within which compensation is possible and G—a steady rate of change—is maintained.

(3) *Compensating changes in the values of state coordinates can be predicted as the result of an "initial" variation in other state coordinates that threaten the maintenance of G.* This is change *within* the structure of the system and it must, by definition, be possible in a functional system.

(4) *Systems can be treated as subsystems, that is, as state coordinates maintaining a G in a more inclusive system. Compensating changes in sub-*

---

[17] Geertz, *op. cit.*, p. 32.
[18] This distinction is discussed by Parsons and Smelser, *op. cit.*, pp. 247-248.

systems can be predicted as the result of an "initial" variation in other sub-systems that threaten the maintenance of G. In this case, change *of* a sub-system is change *within* a more inclusive system. In other words, what is a G from the point of reference of the subsystem is a state coordinate from the point of reference of the more inclusive system. Thus, the disappearance of G, as depicted in (1) above, could be treated as the variation of a state coordinate in a more inclusive system.

These four methods can be used under the following conditions: first, if it can be assumed that a set of phenomena form a functional system; second, if information about an "initial" change in a state coordinate can be obtained; and, third, if there is information about whether this change is within or outside of the limits governing the possibility of compensation. If one is interested in predicting when an "initial" change will occur and whether or not it will be confined to such limits, he might use the model of a deterministic system (if x occurs at one time, then y will occur at some future time) or of a simple system (if x then y). These two models may also be used to predict the ramifications of the disappearance of G.

Criticisms and Examples

If functional analysis can be used to investigate change in these various ways, why has it seldom been so used, and why have certain critics adamantly asserted its inherent static bias? There are several cases, in fact, in which these methods of analyzing change have been employed, as the examples presented below indicate. Both the critics and proponents of functional analysis, however, often fail to see the potential of this model, and the critics frequently misconstrue the aims of the analyses which they attack.

Functionalists themselves have often invited severe criticism. The concepts of moving equilibrium and of hierarchically ordered systems are rarely used, eliminating in most instances two of the four ways of studying change functionally. Many investigators do not attempt to formulate their analyses in terms of state coordinates—variables that are essential to the maintenance of some G and that can vary only within certain limits if G is to be maintained. In this case, none of the four methods of analyzing change can be used. There is no predictive power for change *or stability* in the statement, "the function of x is to maintain G," unless it implies that G will cease to exist if x and its functional equivalents are terminated or if certain limits are exceeded.

Failure to state functional studies in precise form, along with lack of specification of G, the state coordinates, and the system under consideration, results in inadequate analysis of both change and stability. If a functional analysis has been refined to the point where it provides an adequate explanation of stability, then it will always imply certain predictions about change; if the conditions of equilibrium are specified, the prediction can be made that change will occur when these conditions are not met.

However, lack of precision characterizes functionalists and nonfunctionalists alike, and is often unavoidable in exploratory studies. In any case, most of the critics who claim that a static bias inheres in functionalism stress neither the necessity of precise analysis nor the use of moving equilibriums and hierarchically ordered systems. Instead, they focus their attack on the defining attribute of functional systems, that is, the maintenance of a certain state of the system (G) or equilibrium.

Among anthropologists, one of the strongest criticisms has been made by E. R. Leach in the theoretical sections of his book, *Political Systems of Highland Burma*.[19] Like many other anthropologists, he assumes that functional analysis is inherently static and, *also,* that adequate descriptions of societies must be made in functional terms. Thus Leach states: "In practical field work situations the anthropologist must always treat the material of observation *as if* it were part of an overall equilibrium, otherwise description becomes almost impossible." [20] But elsewhere he writes: "While conceptual models of society are necessarily models of equilibrium systems, real societies can never be in equilibrium." [21] Firth seems to agree with this view when he comments that "the necessary equilibrium of the model as a construct means that essentially it is debarred from providing in itself a dynamic analysis." [22] Given these two assumptions, Leach appears to infer— validly—that functional analyses have been extremely inadequate in investigating change, and that major alterations in methodology will have to be made before the situation improves.

But both assumptions are invalid. The first, the assumption that social and cultural systems *must* be treated as if they were in equilibrium, ignores a possibility noted above. Functional system models may be preferable, but a simple or deterministic system model may also be used. The applicability of a functional model cannot be assumed a priori. The model should be applied in cases where it seems useful to treat specific states or parts of the system as G's and state coordinates. If the G's and state coordinates cannot be specified, the analysis will result in a great deal of confusion (and possibly some very productive hints for further research).

Secondly, an equilibrated or functional system need not be static unless "change *within* the system" is subsumed under the term "static." Moving equilibria may be used. Or systems and subsystems may be differentiated with subsystems treated as state coordinates and therefore, by definition, as changing. In addition, *using* the model of a functional system does not

---

[19] *Loc. cit.*
[20] *Ibid.,* p. 285 (emphasis in original).
[21] *Ibid.,* p. 4.
[22] Raymond Firth, Foreword in Leach, *ibid.,* p. vi.

imply that the system *is* in equilibrium, that G is being maintained. Specification of the conditions necessary to maintain G may explain why G is not being maintained. Thus Leach's criticism, at least in part, seems to be based on false premises.

If the criticisms in the theoretical sections of Leach's study are misleading, elsewhere in the volume Leach himself refutes the proposition that functional analyses are necessarily static. In the following brief (and incomplete) outline of his examination of cyclical political change in Kachin society an attempt is made to translate Leach's presentation into our terminology (G's, state coordinates).

Leach isolates certain political systems, among them the democratic (*gumlao*) and aristocratic (*gumsa*), and treats them as subsystems of Kachin society. Certain basic norms of this society are interpreted as the G of the larger system, and the different political subsystems as state coordinates. Leach also treats each political subsystem as itself a functional system. He specifies the conditions of equilibrium in each of the subsystems, and demonstrates that these conditions cannot be met for long periods of time if the basic norms of Kachin society are to be maintained. The result is a cyclical set of changes of the political systems *within* the larger Kachin social system. Political subsystems (state coordinates) change, but the basic norms (G) are maintained.

> A *gumsa* political state tends to develop features which lead to rebellion, resulting, for a time, in a *gumlao* order. But a *gumlao* community, unless it happens to be centered around a fixed territorial centre . . . , usually lacks the means to hold its component lineages together in a status of equality. It will then either disintegrate altogether through fission, or else status difference between lineage groups will bring the system back into the *gumsa* pattern.[23]

Leach shows how an aristocratic political system prospers and is maintained until it begins to undermine the Kachin norms concerning obligations towards one's wife's family. At this point, either the aristocratic system or Kachin society must disintegrate since one type of marriage system is essential to the aristocratic political system while a conflicting marriage system is "the crucial distinguishing principle of modern Kachin social structure." [24] Leach's evidence indicates that Kachin society is a functional system with respect to this marriage system. When the marriage system is threatened by the aristocratic system, the latter distintegrates, becomes democratic, and the marriage system is maintained. A similar reversal of the political order occurs when a democratic political system reaches the point of conflicting with the basic Kachin norm of higher status for the wife's family than for the husband's family. Thus, despite his criticism of structural–functional

---

[23] *Ibid.*, p. 204.
[24] *Ibid.*, p. 249.

analysis, Leach's presentation of cyclical change in Kachin society can be seen as a demonstration of the dynamic potential of such analysis.

The criticisms made by some sociologists are much more sweeping than those voiced by Leach, and seem to call for the abandonment of functional analysis rather than its refinement. Critics such as Dahrendorf and Hield appear to start with two assumptions: first, that functional systems must be static; second, that the G's used in functional analysis must be the values and norms that characterize the majority of the members of the group, often including those of the social scientists themselves. For example, Dahrendorf attacks "the sense of complacency with—if not justification of —the status quo, which by intention or default pervades the structure-functional school of social thought." [25] He also asserts that analyses of this "school" cannot deal with change, and since he rejects "the entirely spurious distinction between 'change within' and 'change of societies,' " [26] he charges in effect that no type of change can be incorporated into a functional analysis. The discussion above should suffice to disprove this charge.

Hield makes similar criticisms: "The 'structural functional' orientation is a set of methodological tools for the study of social control, deviance, and 're-equilibration.' " [27] Again: "Where deviance presents itself, the theoretical concern is with the processes involved in restoring or re-equilibrating a condition of equilibrium or social control." [28] And: "The study of change has thus been obscured by the formulation of theoretic constructs stressing order and stability." [29]

These criticisms have a certain validity *if* functional analysis is limited to the definition of G's in terms of a static system of shared values. The several examples presented above show the different possible definitions of G and thus of equilibrium. G may be a moving equilibrium, a state of conflict, a set of values characterizing a deviant group, or it may have nothing to do with values as, for example, in the case of an annual increase of gross national product.

These critics, then, incorrectly define equilibrium or G because they identify the inherent properties of functional analysis with the particular way such analysis has been used by many social scientists. More specifically, they attack the approach exemplified by Talcott Parsons and assume that this approach exhausts the analytic potentialities of functionalism.

Parsons has devoted a considerable part of his work to answering the Hobbesian problem of order. He defines the social system in terms of shared values: "Analytically considered, the structure of social systems as treated within the frame of reference of action, *consists* in institutionalized

---

[25] Dahrendorf, *op. cit.*, p. 122.

[26] *Ibid.*, p. 126.

[27] Hield, *op. cit.*, p. 2.

[28] *Ibid.*, p. 3.

[29] *Ibid.*, p. 10.

patterns of normative culture." [30] Parsons assumes the stability of values to "provide a reference point for the orderly analysis of a whole range of problems of variation which can be treated as arising from sources *other* than processes of structural change in the system." [31] If shared values define the system, it is difficult to treat major conflict and deviance in the area of values as part of the system. And if one assumes stability of values, major structural change *of* the system is excluded, by definition.

Thus Parsons' explicit strategy is to hold constant values and the basic structure of the system. It is extremely difficult validly to criticize a theorist's strategy, since its usefulness can be tested only by comparing prolonged research using one strategy with similar research using another and by assessing the results. Some kind of strategy is necessary and something must be held constant. Parsons, like Leach, treats certain aspects of the larger system as G's and then analyzes changes in subsystems or state coordinates. "Structural change in subsystems [state coordinates] is an inescapable part of equilibrating process in larger systems. . . ." [32]

---

[30] Talcott Parsons, "An Outline of the Social System" (Cambridge, Mass.: 1958), p. 19, mimeographed (emphasis in original).

[31] *Ibid.,* p. 25 (emphasis in original).

[32] *Ibid.,* p. 199.

CHAPTER 12

RALF DAHRENDORF

Toward a Theory of
Social Conflict[1]

I

After an interval of almost fifty years, a theme has reappeared in sociology which has determined the origin of that discipline more than any other subject area. From Marx and Comte to Simmel and Sorel, social conflict, especially revolution, was one of the central themes in social research. The same is true of many early Anglo-Saxon sociologists (although in their work the problem of revolution has been characteristically somewhat neglected), for example, the Webbs in England and Sumner in the United States. However, when Talcott Parsons in 1937 established a certain convergence in the sociological theories of Alfred Marshall, Émile Durkheim, Vilfredo Pareto, and Max Weber,[2] he no longer had in mind an analysis of social conflict; his was an attempt to solve the problem of integration of socalled social systems by an organon of interrelated categories. The new question was now "What holds societies together?"—no longer, "What drives them on?" The influence of the Parsonian posing of the question on more recent sociology (and by no means only on American sociology) can hardly be overrated. Thus, it is possible that the revival of the study of social conflict in the last decades appears to many not so much a continuation of traditional research paths as a new thematic discovery—an instance of dialectic irony in the development of science.

At this time, approaches to a systematic study of social conflict are still

From Ralf Dahrendorf, "Toward a Theory of Social Conflict," *The Journal of Conflict Resolution,* XI (1958), No. 2, pp. 170-183. Reprinted by permission of the author and the publisher.

[1] This paper was translated by Anatol Rapoport, Mental Health Research Unit, University of Michigan.

[2] Cf. Talcott Parsons, *The Structure of Social Action* (New York, 1937; 2nd ed., Glencoe, Ill.: The Free Press, 1949).

relatively isolated, compared to the innumerable works on social stratification or on the structure and function of specific institutions, organizations, and societies. Still, the thesis of a revival of the study of social conflict can be justified with regard to the works of Aron, Philip, Brinton, Kerr, Coser, Brinkmann, Geiger, Gluckman and others,[3] as well as an attempt to determine a systematic locus and a specific framework for a theory of conflict in sociological analysis.

Types and Varieties of Social Conflict

To begin with a commonplace observation, the problem of conflict is no less complex than that of integration of societies. We now know that the attempt to reduce all actually occurring conflicts among social groups to a common principle, say that of classes, is sterile. It leads either to empty generalizations (such as "Every society experiences social conflicts") or to empirically unjustifiable oversimplifications (such as "The history of all societies so far has been a history of class struggles"). It seems advisable, first, to sort out and to classify the problems which are conceived under the general heading of "social conflict." Even a superficial reflection leads to the distinction of a series of types.

There are wars, and there are conflicts among political parties—evidently two different kinds of struggle. With regard to a given society, A, one could say there are *exogenous* conflicts brought upon or into A from the outside, and there are *endogenous* conflicts generated within A. Of these two categories—which, at least analytically, can be relatively precisely distinguished—there are again several types. Let us confine our attention for the moment—for reasons which will presently be given—to endogenous conflicts. Then further subdivisions are directly perceived: slaves versus freemen in Rome, Negroes versus whites in the United States, Protestants versus Catholics in the Netherlands, Flemings versus Walloons in Belgium, Conservatives versus Labourites in England, unions versus employers in many countries. All these are opposing groups in wellknown conflicts. Perhaps each of these examples does not fall into a separate category; but certainly they cannot all be subsumed under a single type of social conflict. Whatever criterion one

3 Raymond Aron, "Social Structure and the Ruling Class," in *Class, Status, and Power*, ed., Reinhard Bendix and Seymour Martin Lipset (Glencoe, Ill.: The Free Press, 1954); André Philip, *Le Socialisme trahi* (Paris, 1957); Crane Brinton, *The Anatomy of Revolution* (2nd ed.; New York: Alfred A. Knopf, 1952); Clark Kerr, "Industrial Conflict and Its Mediation," *American Journal of Sociology*, XL (1954); Lewis Coser, *The Functions of Social Conflict* (Glencoe, Ill.: The Free Press, 1956); idem, "Social Conflict and Social Change," *British Journal of Sociology*, VIII (1957); Carl Brinkmann, *Soziologische Theorie der Revolution* (Tübingen, 1948); Theodor Geiger, *Klassengesellschaft in Schmelztiegel* (Köln-Hagen, 1949); Max Gluckman, *Custom and Conflict in Africa* (Glencoe, Ill.: The Free Press, 1957).

chooses for classification—for example, the objects of contention, or the structural origin of the conflicting groups, or the forms of conflict—several distinct types result.

The Limits and Goals of a Theory of Social Conflict

An ideal sociology cannot, in principle, exclude any of these categories and types of conflict from analysis. Nevertheless, the types mentioned do not all have the same importance for sociological analysis. A brief recollection of the intent of a sociological theory of conflict reveals that the contribution of sociology to the understanding of conflict (as well as the contribution of conflict to the social process) is in specific instances greater in some cases than in others.

The intent of a sociological theory of conflict is to overcome the predominantly arbitrary nature of unexplained historical events by deriving these events from elements of their social structures, in other words, to explain certain processes by prognostic connections. Certainly, it is important to describe the conflict between workers and employers purely as such; but it is more important to produce a proof that such a conflict is based on certain social structural arrangements, and hence is bound to arise wherever such structural arrangements are given. Thus it is the task of sociology to derive conflicts from specific social structures, and not to relegate these conflicts to psychological variables ("aggressiveness") or to descriptive-historical ones (the influx of Negroes into the United States) or to chance.

In the sense of strict sociological analysis, conflicts can be considered explained if they can be shown to arise from the structure of social positions, independently of the orientation of populations and of historical *dei ex machina*. This is necessarily a very abstract formulation; instead of elaborating it, it may be advisable to illustrate its meaning by the following treatment of a form of social conflict. First, however, let us draw a consequence of this formulation which will help to make our problem more precise.

Since the recognition of the inadequacy of the Marxist-Leninist theory of imperialism, the explanation of exogenous conflicts on the basis of the structure of a given society is once again an open problem, the treatment of which has scarcely begun. It seems, moreover, that the explanation of exogenous conflicts[4] by the tools of sociological structure analysis is possible only in a metaphorical sense—namely, only where entire societies (or less comprehensive "social systems") are taken to be the units of a new structure, that is, where C is analyzed in terms of the structure of its elements A and B without consideration of the inner structure of A and B. On these

---

[4] We recall here that a conflict which, from the point of view of Society A, appears as exogenous is represented from another point of view as a conflict between two societies or systems, A and B.

grounds it seems sensible to exclude exogenous conflict for the time being from a theory of social conflicts.

On the other hand, the abovementioned examples of endogenous conflict, if considered from the point of view of their structural significance, fall into two groups. On the one hand, they point to conflicts which arise only in specific societies on the basis of special historical conditions (Negroes or whites in the United States, Protestants versus Catholics in the Netherlands; Flemings versus Walloons in Belgium); on the other hand, however, there are conflicts which can be understood as expressions of general structural features of societies, or of societies in the same stage of development (Conservatives versus Labourites in England; unions versus employers' associations). Certainly in both cases an analysis leading to generalization is possible: a theory of minority or religious conflict is as meaningful as that of class conflict. Nevertheless, their respective weights within a general theory of society are evidently distinguishable. It is not surprising that the "classical" theory of conflict—I mean here primarily the class theory of conflict—has, above all, called attention to such social frictions which can be derived from the structure of societies independently of structurally incidental historical data.

The following approaches toward a theory of conflict also relate themselves to conflicts based on structure. So far, we are by no means considering a general theory of social conflict, although I would undertake to defend the assertion that we are dealing here with one of the most important, if not the most important, type of social conflict. However important as problems of social conflict St. Bartholomew's Night, Crystal Night and Little Rock may be, the French Revolution, the British General Strike of 1926 and the events in East Berlin on June 17, 1953, seem to me more germane for structural analysis. To put it less dramatically, the sociological theory of conflict would do well to confine itself for the time being to an explanation of the frictions between the rulers and the ruled in given organizations.

II

The explanation of motion requires two separate attacks. We must know the point of departure and the direction of motion or, better yet, the moving force. No theory of social change or of conflict can forego the description of the structural entity which undergoes change or within which conflicts occur. Such a description is offered by the integration theory of society. However, it is erroneous to assume that a description of how the elements of a structure are put together into a stable whole offers, as such, a point of departure for a structural analysis of conflict and change. So far, the claim of the socalled "structural–functional" theory of modern sociology to the status of a general theory of society is demonstrably unjustified.

Toward a Critique of a Structural–Functional Theory

This critique has been led in recent times repeatedly, most effectively by David Lockwood.[5] It is based on a relatively simple argument. As long as we orient our analysis toward the question as to how the elements of a society are combined into a coordinated functioning whole, then the representation of society as a social system is the last point of reference. We are therefore faced with the task of determining certain associations, institutions, or processes within this balanced whole, that is—in Merton's definition—of determining the intentional or unintentional consequences of these associations for the functioning and the preservation of the system. In this way, we come to contentions such as "the educational system functions as a mechanism of assigning social positions," or "religion functions as an agent of integrating dominant values." The majority of sociological investigations in the last years moves in this area of analysis.

However, such an approach leads to difficulties, if we put a question of a different sort. What was the function of the English trade unions in the General Strike of 1926? What was the function of the construction worker in Stalin Allee on June 17, 1953? Without doubt, it can be argued in many cases that militant trade unions or opposition political groups and parties also contribute to the functioning of the existing system.[6] But even where this was the case—and in the two cases cited it would be difficult to establish this—such a conclusion would say little about the role of the group in question. Moreover, it is clear that the intentional as well as the unintentional effects of such oppositional groups contribute toward an abolition or destruction of the existing system. The structural–functional position has a comfortable label for such cases; they are "dysfunctional" organizations, institutions or processes. But this designation again tells us less than nothing. It not only fails to explain the place of these things in the process but actually hinders such explanation by a terminology which seems to be congruent with the system but which, upon closer examination, reveals itself as a residual category. Whatever does not fit is conjured out of the world by word magic.

In every science, residual categories are a fruitful point of departure for new developments. It seems to me that a careful analysis of problems which the term "dysfunction" hides in the structural–functional theory automatically puts us on the trace of a meaningful sociological theory of con-

---

[5] David Lockwood, "Some Notes on 'The Social System,'" *British Journal of Sociology*, VII (1956), No. 2. Although Lockwood's argument leads to the same conclusion, it proceeds somewhat differently (cf. my *Social Classes and the Class Conflict*, pp. 159 ff.).

[6] This aspect of social conflict is, in fact central in the analysis of Lewis Coser (continuing that of Simmel) in his work on the functions of social conflict (cf. n. 3).

flict. At the same time, it offers a remarkable vantage point associated with an attempt of a scientific analysis of society.

Two Models of Society

If we extrapolate the analytical approaches of the structural–functional theory somewhat beyond their boundaries, and investigate their implicit postulates, we can construct a model of society which lies at the base of this theory and determines its perspectives. The essential elements of this societal model are these:

1. Every society is a relatively persisting configuration of elements.[7]
2. Every society is a well-integrated configuration of elements.
3. Every element in a society contributes to its functioning.
4. Every society rests on the consensus of its members.

It should be clear that a theory based on this model does not lend itself to the explanation, not even the description, of the phenomena of social conflict and change. For this purpose, one needs a model which takes the diametrically opposite position on all the four points above:

1. Every society is subjected at every moment to change; social change is ubiquitous.
2. Every society experiences at every moment social conflict; social conflict is ubiquitous.
3. Every element in a society contributes to its change.
4. Every society rests on constraint of some of its members by others.

The remarkable nature of our vantage point becomes evident when we examine the two groups of postulates with respect to their truth content, that is, if we ask ourselves which of the two models promises greater utility for cognition of reality. It appears that the juxtaposed pairs of postulates are in no way mutually exclusive with respect to social reality. It is impossible to decide by empirical investigation which of the two models is more nearly correct; the postulates are not hypotheses. Moreover, it seems meaningful to say that both models are in a certain sense valid and analytically fruitful. Stability and change, integration and conflict, function and "dysfunction," consensus and constraint are, it would seem, two equally valid

---

[7] There is much controversy over this implication of the structural–functional approach. Most functionalists deny that they make such an assumption. Indeed, assertions to the contrary are found in the works of Parsons, Merton, and others. Nevertheless, it can be shown that these assertions are, from the point of view of structural–functional theory, mere declarations. The notion of equilibrium and the concept of a system would have little sense if they did not make the assumption of stability of societies. However, two limitations are to be observed: (1) we have to do here (also in the implications which follow) not with a metaphysical postulate but rather with an assumption made for the purpose of analysis; and (2) stability does not mean statics in the sense of complete absence of processes within the "system."

aspects of every imaginable society. They are dialectically separated and are exhaustive only in combination as a description of the social problems. Possibly a more general theory of society may be thought of which lifts the equivalidity of both models, the coexistence of the uncombinable, onto a higher level of generality. As long as we do not have such a theory, we must content ourselves with the finding that society presents a double aspect to the sociological understanding, each side no better, no more valid, than the other. It follows that the criticism of the structural–functional theory for the analysis of conflict is directed only against a claim of generality of this theory, but leaves untouched its competence with respect to the problem of integration. It follows, on the other hand, also that the theory of conflict and change is not a general theory. Comparisons between natural and social sciences always carry the danger of misunderstanding. However, it may be maintained, without attributing to this analogy more than a logical meaning, that the situation of the sociologists is not unlike that of the physicists with respect to the theory of light. Just as the physicists can solve certain problems only by assuming the wave character of light and others, on the contrary, only by assuming a corpuscular or quantum theory, so there are problems of sociology which can be adequately attacked only with an integration theory and others which require a conflict theory for a meaningful analysis. Both theories can work extensively with the same categories, but they emphasize different aspects. While the integration theory likens a society to an ellipse, a rounded entity which encloses all of its elements, conflict theory sees society rather as a hyperbola, which, it is true, has the same foci, but is open in many directions and appears as a tension field of the determining forces.

The Tasks of a Theory of Social Conflict

The double aspect of society and the dialectics of the two types of sociological theory are in themselves a most fruitful object of reflection. Nevertheless, another problem seems to be more urgent. The theory of social integration has recently developed to a flourishing state as the structural–functional approach in ethnology and sociology. Our theory of conflict, however, is still in a very rudimentary state. It is an approach based on postulating ubiquitous social change and social conflict, the "dysfunctionality" of all the elements of social structure, and the constraining character of social unity. Our considerations put us in a position to formulate some requirements of such a theory:

1. It should be a scientific theory (as is the theory of social integration), that is, it should be formulated with reference to a plausible and demonstrable explanation of empirical phenomena.

2. The elements of the theory should not contradict the conflict model of society.

3. The categories employed should, whenever possible, agree with those of the integration theory or at least correspond to them.

4. A conflict theory should enable us to derive social conflicts from structural arrangements and thus show these conflicts systematically generated.

5. It should account both for the multiplicity of forms of conflict and for their degrees of intensity.

The last goal of a social theory is the explanation of social change. The integration theory gives us a tool for determining the point of departure of the process. To find the locus of the forces which drive the process and social change is the task of a theory of conflict. It must develop a model which makes understandable the structural origin of social conflict. This seems possible only if we understand conflicts as struggles among social groups, that is, if we make our task precise to the extent that it reduces to the structural analysis of conflicting groups. Under this supposition three questions come especially to the forefront, which conflict theory must answer:

1. How do conflicting groups arise from the structure of society?

2. What forms can the struggles among such groups assume?

3. How does the conflict among such groups effect a change in the social structures?

III

Wherever men live together and lay foundations of forms of social organization, there are positions whose occupants have powers of command in certain contexts and over certain positions, and there are other positions whose occupants are subjected to such commands. The distinction between "up" and "down"—or, as the English say, "Them" and "Us"—is one of the fundamental experiences of most men in society, and, moreover, it appears that this distinction is intimately connected with unequal distribution of power. The main thesis of the following attempt to construct a model for the structural analysis of conflict is that we should seek the structural origin of social conflict in the dominance relations which prevail within certain units of social organization. For these units I will use Max Weber's concept of "imperatively coordinated group." The thesis is not new; it is found (however often with important modifications) in the formulation of many social scientists before and after Marx. But we shall make no attempt to trace the history of this thesis.

Authority and Authority Structures

The concepts of power and authority are very complex ones. Whoever uses them is likely to be accused of lack of precision and of clarity to the extent that he tries to define them "exhaustively." Is the influence of a father on his children, the influence of an industrial combine on the government, or the influence of a demagogue on his followers an instance of an authority relation? Here, as in most other cases, it is basically not a question of a definition, but rather a question of an "operational definition," as it is often called today—a method of determination which allows us to identify as such the state of affairs when we are actually confronted with it. However, for the purpose of analysis and identification, Weber's determination of authority is sufficient: "The likelihood that a command of a certain content will be obeyed by given persons." [8] This determination contains the following elements:

1. Authority denotes a relation of supra- and subordination.

2. The supraordinated side prescribes to the subordinated one certain behavior in the form of a command or a prohibition.

3. The supraordinated side has the right to make such prescriptions; authority is a legitimate relation of supra- and subordination; authority is not based on personal or situational chance effects, but rather on an expectation associated with social position.

4. The right of authority is limited to certain contents and to specific persons.

5. Failure to obey the prescriptions is sanctioned; a legal system (or a system of quasilegal customs) guards the effectiveness of authority.

This determination of authority makes possible the identification of a cabinet minister, an employer, and a party secretary as occupants of authority positions—in contrast to an industrial syndicate or a demagogue, neither of which satisfies condition three above.

It is not the intention of our "definition" of authority to solve all analytical and empirical problems of this category. In fact, the very first step of our model leads us deep into these problems; in each imperatively coordinated group, two aggregates can be distinguished—those which have only general ("civil") basic rights, and those which have authority rights over the former. In contrast to prestige and income, a continuum of gradual transition cannot be constructed for the distribution of authority. Rather, there is a clear dichotomy. Every position in an imperatively coordinated group can be recognized as belonging to one who dominates or one who is dominated. Sometimes, in view of the bureaucratic largescale organization of modern societies—under the influence of the state—this assumption may at first sight seem problematic. However, a sharper analysis leaves no doubt that here also the split into the dominating and dominated is valid, even though in reality a considerable measure of differentiation is discernible among those in the dominating group.

---

[8] Max Weber, "Wirtschaft und Gesellschaft," in *Grundriss der Sozialökonomik,* III (3rd ed.; Tübingen, 1947), 28.

The Conflict-Theory Model

The dichotomy of social roles within imperatively coordinated groups,[9] the division into positive and negative dominance roles, is a fact of social structure. If and insofar as social conflicts can be referred to this factual situation, they are structurally explained. The model of analysis of social conflict which is developed against a background of an assumption of such a dichotomy involves the following steps:

1. In every imperatively coordinated group, the carriers of positive and negative dominance roles determine two quasigroups with opposite latent interests. We call them "quasigroups" because we have to do here with mere aggregates, not organized units; we speak of "latent interests," because the opposition of outlook need not be conscious on this level; it may exist only in the form of expectations associated with certain positions. The opposition of interests has here a quite formal meaning, namely, the expectation that an interest in the preservation of the status quo is associated with the positive dominance roles and an interest in the change of the status quo is associated with the negative dominance roles.

2. The bearers of positive and negative dominance roles, that is, the members of the opposing quasigroups, organize themselves into groups with manifest interests, unless certain empirically variable conditions (the condition of organization) intervene. Interest groups, in contrast to quasigroups, are organized entities, such as parties and trade unions; the manifest interests are formulated programs and ideologies.

3. Interest groups which originate in this manner are in constant conflict over the preservation or change of the status quo. The form and the intensity of the conflict are determined by empirically variable conditions (the conditions of conflict).

4. The conflict among interest groups in the sense of this model leads to changes in the structure of their social relations, through changes in the dominance relations. The kind, the speed, and the depth of this development depend on empirically variable conditions (the conditions of structural change).

The intent of such a model is to delimit a problem area, to identify the factors pertinent to it, to put them into order—that is, to propose fruitful questions—and at the same time to fix precisely their analytical focus. We have delimited our problem area by viewing social conflict as a conflict among groups which emerge from the authority structure of social organizations. We have identified pertinent factors in the conditions of organization,

---

[9] In what follows, I shall designate the roles to which the expectation of the exercise of authority is attached as "positive dominance roles" and, conversely, the roles without authority privileges as "negative dominance roles."

of conflict, and of change. Their order, however, can be expressed on the basis of the model in three functions: interest groups (for example, parties) are a function of conditions of organization if an imperatively coordinated group is given; specific forms of conflict (*e.g.,* parliamentary debates) are a function of the conditions of conflict if the interest groups are given; specific forms of change (*e.g.,* revolutions) are a function of the conditions of change if the conflict among interest groups is given. Thus the task of the theory of conflict turns out to be to identify the three sets of conditions and to determine as sharply as possible their respective weight—ideally, by quantitative measure.[10] The following remarks are hardly more than a tentative indication of the sorts of variables in question.

Empirical Conditions of Social Conflict

As far as the conditions of organization are concerned, three groups of factors come to mind. First, we have certain effective social conditions: for example, the possibility of communication among the members of the quasigroup and a certain method of recruitment into the quasigroups. Next, there are certain political conditions which must be fulfilled if interest groups are to emerge. Here, above all, a guarantee of freedom of coalition is important. Finally, certain technical conditions must be fulfilled: an organization must have material means, a founder, a leader, and an ideology.

Under conditions of conflict, two kinds are immediately conspicuous: the degree of social mobility of individuals (or of families) and the presence of effective mechanisms for regulating social conflicts. If we imagine a continuum of intensity of social conflict among interest groups, ranging from democratic debate to civil war, we may conjecture that the presence or absence of social mobility and of regulating mechanisms has considerable influence on the position of specific given conflicts on this continuum. Here, as with the other conditions, the determination of the exact weights of the factors is a task of empirical investigation.

Finally, a third group of conditions or variables determines the form and the extent of social structural changes which arise from the conflict of interest groups. Probably a relatively intimate connection exists between the intensity of the conflict and the change, that is, also between the conditions of conflict and of the structural changes. However, additional factors come into play, such as the capacity of the rulers to stay in power and the pressure potential of the dominated interest group. The sociology of revolutions and especially the unwritten sociology of uncompleted revolutions should contribute considerably to making these factors precise.

---

[10] By this remark is meant (1) a mathematical formulation of the functions, (2) a development of measurement scales for each of the conditions, and (3) the adjustment of the combined scales to groups of conditions.

It need hardly be re-emphasized that these unsystematic observations can, as such, hardly lay a foundation of a theory of conflict. Nevertheless, we put ourselves in a position to ask meaningful questions both on the theoretical level and with respect to empirical problems. Each of the conditions mentioned offers a fruitful object of theoretically oriented investigations. And in the empirical sphere, the systematic association of factors in such an investigation redirects our questions from a haphazard search for *ad hoc* relations in the world of coincidences to a meaningful study of specific interdependencies, whose locus and meaning are fixed by a general perspective. By the nature of the subject, our exposition up to this point had to remain somewhat abstract in form.

In spite of the tentative nature of the above-mentioned frame of reference, it is nevertheless possible to test its resolving power on an empirical problem.

•

IV

The Problem of the Totalitarian State

Since June 17, 1953, and with greater certainty since the events in Hungary and Poland in the autumn of 1956, we know that social conflict (and social change!) has by no means disappeared in the totalitarian states. Conflict theory raises this knowledge to the status of law. The state, that is, society in its political aspect, is an imperatively coordinated group. There are in it mere citizens (voters) and occupants of positions equipped with command opportunities. Therefore, political conflict is a structural fact of society under every imaginable condition. This conflict can assume mild or severe forms; it can even disappear for limited periods from the field of vision of a superficial observer; but it cannot be abolished. Now one of the aspects of a totalitarian state is an attempt to suppress the opposition, that is, to suppress social conflict. The question then arises, against the background of conflict theory: How do social frictions become manifest under such circumstances? We can analyze totalitarian states from the point of view of conditions of organization of interest groups—that of conflict and of structural change—and hope to arrive in this way at meaningful explanations of historical events and to testable predictions. Again it is possible here to make only a few indications.

Let us begin—for reasons which will soon become evident—with the conditions of conflict. The intensity of social conflicts depends on the measure of social mobility and on the presence of mechanisms for regulating the conflicts. Both mobility and regulation can be present in totalitarian states. One could argue that the regular "purges" in Communist states—that is, a replacement of the bearers of authority—function as a guarantee of stability (in the sense of alleviating social conflicts). In the same way, the systematic requirement of discussion with the aim of deciding the political "platforms" within and outside the state party may be an effective mechanism of regulation. Still, there seems to be an inherent tendency in most totalitarian states to isolate socially the leadership layer and to prevent discussions, that is, to disregard the mechanisms for regulating conflicts. Where this is the case, social conflicts threaten to increase in potential intensity and to take on a revolutionary character.

From the point of view of conditions of structural change, this means that political conflicts in totalitarian states aim more and more at sudden replacement of the ruling class. The important variable which determines the probability of realizing a radical change is the resistance of the rulers to the pressures making for change. Perhaps it is meaningful to make the empirical generalization that this resistance does increase to a certain degree with increasing pressure, but then gives way to a relatively speedy dissolution and so promotes change.

Central for the analysis of conflicts in totalitarian states, however, is our third set of conditions (first, as listed in the theory): the condition of organization. It follows in a way from the "definition" of a totalitarian state that there are no conditions in it for the organization of opposing interest groups. More specifically, although the social and technical conditions are often present, the political conditions are lacking;[11] there is no freedom of coalition. At this point, the resistance of the German eastern zone government to free elections becomes clear, as does the general threat of violent, possibly revolutionary conflict in totalitarian states. When—as expressly in Hungary or virtually on June 17, 1953 in Berlin—an opportunity for organization occurs to latent conflict groups, the total edifice of the totalitarian state collapses. Moreover, it seems very probable that this possibility can become realized at any moment in every totalitarian state.[12] In modern totalitarian societies founded on ideological state parties, there is a constant danger from the point of view of the rulers that a permitted organization, even the state party itself, may become the root of an opposition movement and of revolutionary conflict.

Our analysis will be broken off at the point where it promises testable results. It was not the intent of this discussion to treat exhaustively some empirical problem. Rather, we wanted to show that conflict theory puts us in a position to formulate more sharply urgent problems of empirical investiga-

---

[11] For certain technical conditions of organization, this is valid only within limits. Thus the liquidation of potential leaders of the opposition is a central component of totalitarian authority. In a way, both the East German and the Hungarian events can be taken as corroborations of the effectiveness of this policy.

[12] Relevant here is the wellknown slight decrease of pressure which seems to precede every revolution. Insofar, for example, as a certain relaxation of police control makes possible only an *ad hoc* organization, the emergence of open conflict becomes acute.

tion, to bring within our grasp unexplained events, to see what is known from additional points of view, and to transform tentative questions into a systematic search—that is, to do precisely what a scientific theory should accomplish. . . . In spite of all progress, the theory of social conflict is still more a challenge to the sociologist than a result of his researches.

CHAPTER 13

LEWIS A. COSER

Social Conflict and the
Theory of Social Change

This paper attempts to examine some of the functions of social conflict in the process of social change. I shall first deal with some functions of conflict *within* social systems, more specifically with its relation to institutional rigidities, technical progress and productivity, and will then concern ourselves with the relation between social conflict and the change *of* social systems.

A central observation of George Sorel in his *Reflections on Violence* which has not as yet been accorded sufficient attention by sociologists may serve us as a convenient springboard. Sorel wrote:

We are today faced with a new and unforseen fact—a middle class which seeks to weaken its own strength. The race of bold captains who made the greatness of modern industry disappears to make way for an ultracivilized aristocracy which asks to be allowed to live in peace.

The threatening decadence may be avoided if the proletariat hold on with obstinacy to revolutionary ideas. *The antagonistic classes influence each other in a partly indirect but decisive manner.* Everything may be saved if the proletariat, by their use of violence, restore to the middle class something of its former energy.[1]

Sorel's specific doctrine of class struggle is not of immediate concern here. What is important for us is the idea that conflict (which Sorel calls violence, using the word in a very special sense) prevents the ossification of the social system by exerting pressure for innovation and creativity. Though Sorel's call to action was addressed to the working class and its interests, he conceived it to be of general importance for the total social system; to his mind the gradual disappearance of class conflict might well lead to the decadence

---

[1] George Sorel, *Reflections on Violence,* ch. 2, par. 11.

of European culture. A social system, he felt, was in need of conflict if only to renew its energies and revitalize its creative forces.

This conception seems to be more generally applicable than to class struggle alone. Conflict within and between groups in a society can prevent accommodations and habitual relations from progressively impoverishing creativity. The clash of values and interests, the tension between what is and what some groups feel ought to be, the conflict between vested interests and new strata and groups demanding their share of power, wealth and status, have been productive of vitality; note for example the contrast between the 'frozen world' of the Middle Ages and the burst of creativity that accompanied the thaw that set in with Renaissance civilization.

Conflict not only generates new norms, new institutions, it may be said to be stimulating directly in the economic and technological realm. Economic historians often have pointed out that much technological improvement has resulted from the conflict activity of trade unions through the raising of wage levels. A rise in wages usually has led to a substitution of capital investment for labour and hence to an increase in the volume of investment. Thus the extreme mechanization of coal-mining in the United States has been partly explained by the existence of militant unionism in the American coalfields.[2] A recent investigation by Sidney C. Sufrin[3] points to the effects of union pressure, 'goading management into technical improvement and increased capital investment'. Very much the same point was made recently by the conservative British *Economist* which reproached British unions for their 'modernation' which it declared in part responsible for the stagnation and low productivity of British capitalism; it compared their policy unfavourably with the more aggressive policies of American unions whose constant pressure for higher wages has kept the American economy dynamic.[4]

This point raises the question of the adequacy and relevancy of the 'human relations' approach in industrial research and management practice. The 'human relations' approach stresses the 'collective purpose of the total organization' of the factory, and either denies or attempts to reduce conflicts of interests in industry.[5] But a successful reduction of industrial conflict may have unanticipated dysfunctional consequences for it may destroy an important stimulus for technological innovation.

---

[2] Cf. McAlister Coleman, *Men and Coal*, N.Y., Farrar and Rinehart, 1943.

[3] *Union Wages and Labor's Earnings*, Syracuse, Syracuse Univ. Press, 1951.

[4] Quoted by Will Herberg, 'When Social Scientists View Labor,' *Commentary*, Dec. 1951, XII, 6, pp. 590-6. See also Seymour Melman, *Dynamic Factors in Industrial Productivity*, Oxford, Blackwell, 1956, on the effects of rising wage levels on productivity.

[5] See the criticism of the Mayo approach by Daniel Bell, 'Adjusting Men to Machines,' *Commentary*, Jan. 1947, pp. 79-88; C. Wright Mills, 'The Contribution of Sociology to the Study of Industrial Relations,' *Proceedings of the Industrial Relations Research Association*, 1948, pp. 199-222.

It often has been observed that the effects of technological change have weighed most heavily upon the worker.[6] Both informal and formal organization of workers represent in part an attempt to mitigate the insecurities attendant upon the impact of unpredictable introduction of change in the factory. But by organizing in unions workers gain a feeling of security through the effective conduct of institutionalized conflict with management and thus exert pressure on management to increase their returns by the invention of further cost-reducing devices. The search for mutual adjustment, understanding and 'unity' between groups who find themselves in different life situations and have different life chances calls forth the danger that Sorel warns of, namely that the further development of technology would be seriously impaired.

The emergence of invention and of technological change in modern Western society, with its institutionalization of science as an instrument for making and remaking the world, was made possible with the gradual emergence of a pluralistic and hence conflict-charged structure of human relations. In the unitary order of the medieval guild system, 'no one was permitted to harm others by methods which enabled him to produce more quickly and more cheaply than they. Technical progress took on the appearance of disloyalty. The ideal was stable conditions in a stable industry.'[7]

In the modern Western world, just as in the medieval world, vested interests exert pressure for the maintenance of established routines; yet the modern Western institutional structure allows room for freedom of conflict. The structure no longer being unitary, vested interests find it difficult to resist the continuous stream of change-producing inventions. Invention, as well as its application and utilization, is furthered through the ever-renewed challenge to vested interests, as well as by the conflicts between the vested interests themselves.

Once old forms of traditional and unitary integration broke down, the clash of conflicting interests and values, now no longer constrained by the rigidity of the medieval structure, pressed for new forms of unification and integration. Thus deliberate control and rationalized regulation of 'spontaneous' processes was required in military and political, as well as in economic institutions. Bureaucratic forms of organization with their emphasis on calculable, methodical and disciplined behaviour arose at roughly the same period in which the unitary medieval structure broke down. But with the rise of bureaucratic types of organization peculiar new resistances to change made their appearance. The need for reliance on predictability exercises

---

[6] See, e.g., R. K. Merton, 'The Machine, The Workers and The Engineer,' *Social Theory and Social Structure,* Glencoe, Ill., 1949, pp. 317-28; Georges Friedmann, *Industrial Society,* Glencoe, Ill., 1956.

[7] Henri Pirenne, *Economic and Social History of Medieval Europe,* London, Routledge and Kegan Paul, 1949, p. 186.

pressure towards the rejection of innovation which is perceived as interference with routine.[8] Conflicts involving a 'trial through battle' are unpredictable in their outcome, and therefore unwelcome to the bureaucracy which must strive towards an ever-widening extension of the area of predictability and calculability of results. But social arrangements which have become habitual and totally patterned are subject to the blight of ritualism. If attention is focused exclusively on the habitual clues, 'people may be unfitted by being fit in an unfit fitness',[9] so that their habitual training becomes an incapacity to adjust to new conditions. A group or a system which no longer is challenged is no longer capable of a creative response. It may subsist, wedded to the eternal yesterday of precedent and tradition, but it is no longer capable of renewal.[10]

Conflict within and between bureaucratic structures provides means for avoiding the ossification and ritualism which threatens their form of organization. Conflict, though apparently dysfunctional for highly rationalized systems, may actually have important latent functional consequences. By attacking and overcoming the resistance to innovation and change that seems to be an 'occupational psychosis' always threatening the bureaucratic office holder, it can help to insure that the system do not stifle in the deadening routine of habituation and that in the planning activity itself creativity and invention can be applied.

We have so far discussed change within systems, but changes of systems are of perhaps even more crucial importance for sociological inquiry. Here the sociology of Karl Marx serves us well. Writes Marx in a polemic against Proudhon:

> Feudal production also had two antagonistic elements, which were equally designated by the names of *good side* and *bad side* of feudalism, without regard being had to the fact that it is always the evil side which finishes by overcoming the good side. It is the bad side that produces the movement which makes history, by constituting the struggle. If at the epoch of the reign of feudalism the economists, enthusiastic over the virtues of chivalry, the delightful harmony between rights and duties, the patriarchal life of the towns, the prosperous state of domestic industry in the country, of the development of industry organized in corporations, guilds and fellowships, in fine of all which constitutes the beautiful side of feudalism, had proposed to themselves the problem of eliminating all which cast a shadow upon this lovely picture— serfdom, privilege, anarchy—what would have been the result? All the elements which constituted the struggle would have been annihilated, and the

---

[8] For the pathology of bureaucracy, see R. K. Merton, 'Bureaucratic Structure and Personality,' *Social Theory and Social Structure,* op. cit., pp. 151-60.

[9] Kenneth Burke, *Permanence and Change,* N.Y., New Republic, 1936, p. 18.

[10] This is, of course, a central thesis of Arnold Toynbee's monumental *A Study of History,* Oxford University Press, 1946.

development of the bourgeoisie would have been stifled in the germ. They would have set themselves the absurd problem of eliminating history.[11]

According to Marx, conflict leads not only to ever-changing relations within the existing social structure, but the total social system undergoes transformation through conflict.

During the feudal period, the relations between serf and lord (between burgher and gentry), underwent many changes both in law and in fact. Yet conflict finally led to a breakdown of all feudal relations and hence to the rise of a new social system governed by different patterns of social relations.

It is Marx's contention that the negative element, the opposition, conditions the change when conflict between the sub-groups of a system becomes so sharpened that at a certain point this system breaks down. Each social system contains elements of strain and of potential conflict; if in the analysis of the social structure of a system these elements are ignored, if the adjustment of patterned relations is the only focus of attention, then it is not possible to anticipate basic social change. Exclusive attention to wont and use, to the customary and habitual bars access to an understanding of possible latent elements of strain which under certain conditions eventuate in overt conflict and possibly in a basic change of the social structure. This attention should be focused, in Marx's view, on what evades and resists the patterned normative structure and on the elements pointing to new and alternative patterns emerging from the existing structure. What is diagnosed as disease from the point of view of the institutionalized pattern may, in fact, says Marx, be the first birth pang of a new one to come; not wont and use but the break of wont and use is focal. The 'matters-of-fact' of a 'given state of affairs' when viewed in the light of Marx's approach, become limited, transitory; they are regarded as containing the germs of a process that leads beyond them.

Yet, not all social systems contain the same degree of conflict and strain. The sources and incidence of conflicting behaviour in each particular system vary according to the type of structure, the patterns of social mobility, of ascribing and achieving status and of allocating scarce power and wealth, as well as the degree to which a specific form of distribution of power, resources and status is accepted by the component actors within the different sub-systems. But if, within any social structure, there exists an excess of claimants over opportunities for adequate reward, there arises strain and conflict.

The distinction between changes *of* systems and changes *within* systems is, of course, a relative one. There is always some sort of continuity between

---

[11] Karl Marx, *The Poverty of Philosophy*, Chicago, Charles H. Kerr & Co., 1910, p. 132.

a past and a present, or a present and a future social system; societies do not die the way biological organisms do, for it is difficult to assign precise points of birth or death to societies as we do with biological organisms. One may claim that all that can be observed is a change of the organization of social relations; but from one perspective such change may be considered re-establishment of equilibrium while from another it may be seen as the formation of a new system.

At what point the shift is large enough to warrant the conclusion that a change *of* the system has taken place, is hard to determine. Only if one deals with extreme instances are ideal types—such as feudalism, capitalism, etc.—easily applied. A system based on serfdom, for example, may undergo considerable change within—*vide* the effects of the Black Death on the social structure of medieval society; and even an abolition of serfdom may not necessarily be said to mark the end of an old and the emergence of a new system, *vide* nineteenth-century Russia.

If 'it is necessary to distinguish clearly between the processes *within* the system and processes of change *of* the system', as Professor Parsons has pointed out,[12] an attempt should be made to establish a heuristic criterion for this distinction. We propose to talk of a change *of* system when all major structural relations, its basic institutions and its prevailing value system have been drastically altered. (In cases where such a change takes place abruptly, as, for example, the Russian Revolution, there should be no difficulty. It is well to remember, however, that transformations of social systems do not always consist in an abrupt and simultaneous change of all basic institutions. Institutions may change gradually, by mutual adjustment, and it is only over a period of time that the observer will be able to claim that the social system has undergone a basic transformation in its structural relations.) In concrete historical reality, no clear-cut distinctions exist. Change *of* system may be the result (or the sum total) of previous changes *within* the system. This does not however detract from the usefulness of the theoretical distinction.

It is precisely Marx's contention that the change from feudalism to a different type of social system can be understood only through an investigation of the stresses and strains *within* the feudal system. Whether given forms of conflict will lead to changes in the social system or to breakdown and to formation of a new system will depend on the rigidity and resistance to change, or inversely on the elasticity of the control mechanisms of the system.

It is apparent, however, that the rigidity of the system and the intensity of conflict within it are not independent of each other. Rigid systems which suppress the incidence of conflict exert pressure towards the emergence or

---

12 Talcott Parsons, *The Social System,* London, Tavistock Publications: 1951, p. 481.

radical cleavages and violent forms of conflict. More elastic systems, which allow the open and direct expression of conflict within them and which adjust to the shifting balance of power which these conflicts both indicate and bring about, are less likely to be menaced by basic and explosive alignments within their midst.

In what follows the distinction between strains, conflicts and disturbances within a system which lead to a re-establishment of equilibrium, and conflicts which lead to the establishment of new systems and new types of equilibria, will be examined. Such an examination will be most profitably begun by considering what Thorstein Veblen[13] has called 'Vested Interests'.

Any social system implies an allocation of power, as well as wealth and status positions among individual actors and component subgroups. As has been pointed out, there is never complete concordance between what individuals and groups within a system consider their just due and the system of allocation. Conflict ensues in the effort of various frustrated groups and individuals to increase their share of gratification. Their demands will encounter the resistance of those who previously had established a 'vested interest' in a given form of distribution of honour, wealth and power.

However, mere 'frustration' will not lead to a questioning of the legitimacy of the position of the vested interests, and hence to conflict. Levels of aspiration as well as feelings of deprivation are relative to institutionalized expectations and are established through comparison.[14] When social systems have institutionalized goals and values to govern the conduct of component actors, but limit access to these goals for certain members of the society, 'departures from institutional requirements' are to be expected.[15] Similarly, if certain groups within a social system compare their share in power, wealth and status honour with that of other groups *and* question the legitimacy of this distribution, discontent is likely to ensue. If there exist no institutionalized provisions for the expression of such discontents, departures from what is required by the norms of the social system may occur. These may be limited to 'innovation' or they may consist in the rejection of the institutionalized goals. Such 'rebellion' 'involves a genuine transvaluation, where the direct or vicarious experience of frustration leads to full denunciation of previously prized values'.[16] Thus it will be well to distinguish between those departures from the norms of a society which consist in mere 'deviation'

---

[13] See especially *The Vested Interests and the State of the Industrial Arts*, N.Y., 1919.

[14] See Robert K. Merton and Alice S. Kitt, 'Contributions to the Theory of Reference Group Behaviour' for a development of the concept of 'relative deprivation' (originally suggested by Stouffer *et al.* in *The American Soldier*) and its incorporation into the framework of a theory of reference groups.

[15] This whole process is exhaustively discussed by Merton in his paper on 'Social Structure and Anomie,' *Social Theory,* op. cit.

[16] Ibid., p. 145.

and those which involve the formation of distinctive patterns and new value systems.

What factors lead groups and individuals to question at a certain point the legitimacy of the system of distribution of rewards, lies largely outside the scope of the present inquiry. The intervening factors can be sought in the ideological, technological, economic or any other realm. It is obvious, moreover, that conflict may be a result just as much as a source of change. A new invention, the introduction of a new cultural trait through diffusion, the development of new methods of production or distribution, etc., will have a differential impact within a social system. Some strata will feel it to be detrimental to their material or ideal interests, while others will feel their position strengthened through its introduction. Such disturbances in the equilibrium of the system lead to conditions in which groups or individual actors no longer do willingly what they have to do and do willingly what they are not supposed to do. Change, no matter what its source, breeds strain and conflict.

Yet, it may be well to repeat that mere 'frustration' and the ensuing strains and tensions do not necessarily lead to group conflict. Individuals under stress may relieve their tension through 'acting out' in special safety-valve institutions in as far as they are provided for in the social system; or they may 'act out' in a deviant manner, which may have serious dysfunctional consequences for the system, and bring about change in this way. This, however, does not reduce the frustration from which escape has been sought since it does not attack their source.

If, on the other hand, the strain leads to the emergence of specific new patterns of behaviour of whole groups of individuals, social change which reduces the sources of their frustration may come about. This may happen in two ways: if the social system is flexible enough to adjust to conflict situations we will deal with change *within* the system. If, on the other hand, the social system is not able to readjust itself and allows the accumulation of conflict, the 'aggressive' groups, imbued with a new system of values which threatens to split the general consensus of the society and imbued with an ideology which 'objectifies' their claims, may become powerful enough to overcome the resistance of vested interests and bring about the breakdown of the system and the emergence of a new distribution of social values.

In his *Poverty of Philosophy*, Marx was led to consider the conditions under which economic classes constitute themselves:

> Economic conditions have first transformed the mass of the population into workers. The domination of capital created for this mass a common situation and common interest. This mass was thus already a class as against capital, but not for itself. It is the struggle . . . that the mass gathers together and

constitutes itself as a class for itself. The interests which it defends become class interests.[17]

With this remarkable distinction between class *in itself* and class *for itself* (which unfortunately he didn't elaborate upon in later writings though it informs all of them—if not the writings of most latter-day 'marxists'), Marx illuminates a most important aspect of group formation: group belongingness is established by an objective conflict situation—in this case a conflict of interests; but only by experiencing this antagonism, that is, by becoming aware of it and by acting it out, does the group (or class) establish its identity.

When changes in the equilibrium of a society lead to the formation of new groupings or to the strengthening of existing groupings that set themselves the goal of overcoming resistance of vested interests through conflict, changes in structural relations, as distinct from simple 'maladjustment', can be expected.

It is the sense of common purpose arising in and through conflict that is peculiar to the behaviour of individuals who meet the challenge of new conditions by a group-forming and value-forming response. Strains which result in no such formations of new conflict groups or strengthening of old ones may contribute to bringing about change, but a type of change that fails to reduce the sources of strain since by definition tension-release behaviour does not involve purposive action. Conflict through group action, on the other hand, is likely to result in a 'deviancy' which may be the prelude of new patterns and reward systems apt to reduce the sources of frustration.

If the tensions that need outlets are continually reproduced within the structure, abreaction through tension-release mechanisms may preserve the system but at the risk of ever-renewed further accumulation of tension. Such accumulation eventuates easily in the irruption of destructive unrealistic conflict. If feelings of dissatisfaction, instead of being suppressed or diverted are allowed expression against 'vested interests', and in this way to lead to the formation of new groupings within the society, the emergence of genuine transvaluations is likely to occur.

Whether the emergence of such new groupings or the strengthening of old ones with the attendant increase in self-confidence and self-esteem on the part of the participants will lead to a change *of* or *within* the system will depend on the degree of cohesion that the system itself has attained. A well-integrated society will tolerate and even welcome group conflict; only a weakly integrated one must fear it.

---

[17] Karl Marx, *The Poverty of Philosophy,* op. cit., pp. 188-9.

CHAPTER 14

C. WRIGHT MILLS

The Sources of Societal Power

Personal Milieu and Social Structure

I need to make clear a simple and very much overlooked distinction which, to my mind, is the single most important distinction available in the sociological sciences. It is the distinction between personal milieu and social structure. And we may think of it in this way:

> When a handful of men do not have work and do not seek jobs, we may look for the causes in their immediate situations and character. But when twelve million men are unemployed, then we cannot believe that all of them suddenly "got lazy" and turned out to be "no good." Economists call this "structural unemployment"—meaning, for one thing, that the men involved cannot personally control their job chances. Now, what individual men are usually aware of, and what they usually try to do, are limited by the horizon of their specific milieu. Most men do not transcend the boundaries of their jobs and families and local communities. In other milieux which they encounter they are and they remain visitors. That is why "great changes" are out of their control, for great changes, by definition, are those whose causes lie outside the ordinary milieu of ordinary men but which nevertheless affect their conduct and their outlook. And that is why in periods full of such changes many ordinary men feel that they are "powerless," which in all sober fact they are. Mass unemployment, for example, does not originate in one factory or in one town, nor is it due to anything that one factory or one town does or fails to do. Moreover, there is little or nothing that one man, one factory, or one town can do about it when it sweeps over their personal mileu.

From C. Wright Mills, "The Power Elite: Military, Economic and Political," in Arthur Kornhauser, ed., *Problems of Power in American Democracy* (Detroit: Wayne State University Press, 1957), pp. 154-167. Reprinted by permission of the publisher.

But the great historical changes—do not their causes lie somewhere? And cannot we trace them? Yes they do, and yes we can. Simply to tag them, we call them structural changes, and we define them by realizing in our definition that they are changes which transcend the milieux of most men. They transcend these personal milieux not only because they effect a great range of milieux, but because, by their nature, the structural principles of change have to do with the unintended, hence the unexpected consequences of what men, seated in and limited by various milieux, may be trying to do or trying to ward off.

But not all men are ordinary in the sense of being limited by narrow milieux. Some have access to many more milieux than do others, and some in addition are so placed in the social structure that they can look down, so to speak, upon the milieux of many ordinary men.

This is the most important general meaning that I wish to give the term "elite." This is *the* position of the elite.

The elite are those who command the leading institutions, and whose commanding positions so place them in their social structure that they transcend, to a greater or to a lesser extent, the ordinary milieux of ordinary men and women.

The Development of the Means of Power

From even the most superficial examination of the history of Western society, we learn that the power of any decision-maker is first of all limited by the level of technique, by the *means* of power and violence and organization that prevail in a given society. In this connection, we also learn that there is a rather straight line running upward through the history of the West, that the means of oppression and exploitation, of violence and destruction, as well as the means of production and reconstruction, have been progressively enlarged and increasingly centralized.

As the institutional means of power and the means of communication that tie them together have become steadily more efficient, those in command of these enlarged and centralized structures have come into command of instruments of rule quite unsurpassed in the history of mankind. And we are not yet at the climax of their development. We can no longer lean upon or take soft comfort from the historical ups and downs of ruling groups of previous epochs. In that sense, Hegel is correct: we learn from history that we cannot learn from it.

For every epoch and for every social structure, we must work out an answer to the question of the power of the elite. And the major questions about the American elite today—about its composition and its unity, and its power—must now be faced with due attention to the awesome means of power that are now available to them. Caesar could do less with Rome than Napoleon with France; Napoleon less with France than Lenin with

Russia; and Lenin less with Russia than Hitler with Germany. But what was Caesar's power at its peak compared with the power of the changing inner circle of Soviet Russia or of Eisenhower's temporary administration? The men of either circle can cause great cities to be wiped out in a single night and in a few weeks turn continents into thermonuclear wastelands. That the facilities of power are enormously enlarged and decisively centralized means that the decisions of small groups are now more consequential.

Within the American society, major national power now resides in the economic, the political, and the military domains. . . . Within each of these big three, the typical institutional unit has become enlarged, has become administrative, and, in the power of its decisions, has become centralized. Behind these developments, within each of them, there is a giant and fabulous technology; for as institutions, they have incorporated this technology and guide it, even as it shapes and paces their developments.

The economy—once a great scatter of small productive units in autonomous balance—has become dominated by two or three hundred giant corporations, administratively and politically interrelated, which together hold the keys to economic decisions.

The political order, once a decentralized set of several dozen states with a weak spinal cord, has become a centralized, executive establishment, which has taken up into itself many powers previously scattered, and now enters into each and every cranny of the social structure.

The military order, once a slim establishment in a context of distrust fed by state militia, has become the largest and most expensive feature of government, and, although well versed in smiling public relations, now has all the grim and clumsy efficiency of a sprawling bureaucratic domain.

In each of these institutional areas, the means of power at the disposal of centralized decision-making units have increased enormously and their central executive powers enhanced, while below each of their centers, modern administrative routines are elaborated and tightened up.

As each of these domains becomes enlarged and centralized, the consequences of its activities become greater, and its traffic with the others increases. The decisions of a handful of corporations bear upon military and political as well as upon economic developments around the world. The decisions of the military establishment rest upon and grievously affect political life as well as the very level of economic activity. The decisions made within the political domain determine economic activities and military programs. There is no longer, on the one hand, an economy, and, on the other, a political order containing a military establishment unimportant to politics and to money-making. There is a political economy, linked in a thousand ways with military institutions and decisions. On each side of the world-split running through central Europe and around the Asiatic rimlands, there is ever increasing the interlocking of economic, military, and political structures. And if there is government intervention in the corporate economy, so is there corporate intervention in the governmental process. In the structural sense, this triangle of power is the source of the interlocking directorate that is most important for the historical structure of the present.

The fact of the interlocking is clearly revealed at each of the points of crisis of modern capitalist society—slump, war and boom. In each, men of decision are led to an awareness of the interdependence of the major institutional orders. In the nineteenth century, when the scale of all institutions was smaller, their liberal integration was achieved in the automatic economy, by an autonomous balance of market forces, and in the automatic political domain, by bargaining and voting. It was then assumed that out of the oscillations and frictions that followed the circumscribed decisions then possible, a new equilibrium would in due course emerge. That can no longer be assumed, and it is not assumed by the men at the top of each of the three dominant hierarchies.

For given the scope of their consequences, decisions in any one of these ramify into the others, and hence top decisions become coordinated decisions. They become decisions with the total context of the nation, and indeed of the world, in mind. In their calculated risks, men of decision must anticipate longrange consequences, lest they be fatally overwhelmed by new and unforeseen problems.

At the pinnacle of each of the three enlarged and centralized domains, there have arisen the men of the higher circles, who make up the economic, the political and the military elites. At the top of the economy, among the corporate rich, there are the corporation executives; at the top of the political order, above the middle levels of the Congress, there are the members of the political directorate; and at the top of the military establishment, the elite of soldier-statesmen cluster in and around the Joint Chiefs of Staff and the upper echelon. And as each of these domains has coincided with the others, and as decisions tend to become total in their consequence, the leading men in each of the three domains of power—the warlords, the corporation chieftains, the political directorate—tend to come together, to form the power elite of America.

The Formation of the Power Elite

If the power to decide such national issues as are decided were shared in an absolutely equal way, there would be no power elite; in fact, there would be no gradation of power, but only a radical homogeneity. At the opposite extreme as well, if the power to decide issues were absolutely monopolized by one small group, there would be no gradation of power; there would simply be this small group in command, and below it, the undifferentiated, dominated mass. American society today represents neither the one nor the other of these extremes, but a conception of them is nonetheless useful. It makes us realize more clearly the question of the structure of power in the United States and the position of the power elite within it.

To say that there are obviously gradations of power and of opportunities to decide within modern society, is not to say that the powerful are united, that they fully know what they do, or that they are consciously joined in conspiracy. Such issues are best faced if we become, in the first instance, more concerned with the structural position of the high and mighty and with the consequences of their decisions, than with the extent of their awareness or the purity of their motives.

The formation of the power elite, as we may now know it, occurred during World War II and its aftermath. In the course of the organization of the nation for that war, and the consequent stabilization of the warlike posture, certain types of man have been selected and formed, and, in the course of these institutional and psychological developments, new opportunities and intentions have arisen among them.

Like the tempo of American life in general, the longterm trends of the power structure have been speeded up since World War II, and certain newer trends within and between the dominant institutions have also set in to shape the power elite:

(1) Insofar as the structural clue to the power elite today lies in the political order, that clue is the decline of politics as a genuine and public debate of alternative decisions—with nationally responsible and policy-coherent parties and with autonomous organizations connecting the lower and middle levels of power with the top levels of decision. America is now in considerable part more a formal political democracy than a democratic social structure, and even the formal political mechanics are weak.

The longtime trend of business and government to become more intricately and deeply involved with each other has, in this epoch, reached a point of explicitness not before evident. Now, in a hundred ways, they are difficult to see as two distinct worlds. And it is in terms of the executive agencies of the state that the rapprochement has proceeded most decisively. The growth of the executive branch of the government, with its agencies that patrol the complex economy, does not mean merely the "enlargement of government" as some sort of autonomous bureaucracy: it has meant the ascendancy of the corporation's man as a political outsider.

If during the New Deal the corporate chieftains joined the political directorate, since World War II they have come to dominate it. Long interlocked with government, now they moved into quite full direction of the economy of the war effort and of the postwar era. And this shift of the corporation executives into the political directorate has accelerated the longterm relegation of the professional politicians in the Congress to the middle levels of power.

(2) Insofar as the structural clue to the power elite today lies in the enlarged and military state, that clue is that, with the military ascendancy,

the warlords have, for the first time, become of decisive political relevance and have gained decisive political power. The military structure of America is now in considerable part a political structure. For the seemingly permanent military threat places a premium on the military and upon their control of men, material, money, and power. Virtually all political and economic actions are now judged in terms of military definitions of reality: the higher warlords have ascended to a firm position within the power elite. . . .

In some part at least this fact has come about by virtue of one simple historical fact, pivotal for the years since 1939: the focus of elite attention has been shifted from domestic problems, centered in the thirties around slump, to international problems, centered in the forties and fifties around war.

Since the governing apparatus of the United States has by long historic usage been adapted to and shaped by domestic clash and balance, it has not, from any angle, had suitable agencies and traditions for the handling of international problems. And such formal democratic mechanics as had arisen in the century and a half of national development prior to 1941 had not been extended to the US handling of international affairs. It is, in considerable part, in this vacuum that the power elite has grown.

(3) Insofar as the structural clue to the power elite today lies in the economic order, that clue is the fact that the economy is at once a permanent war economy and a private corporation economy. American capitalism is now in considerable part a military capitalism, and the most important relation of the big corporation to the state rests on the coincidence of interests between military and corporate needs, as defined by warlords and corporate rich. Within the elite as a whole, this coincidence of interest between the high military and the corporate chieftains strengthens both of them and further subordinates the role of the merely political men. Not politicians, but corporate executives, sit with the military and plan the organization of war effort.

The Uneasy Coincidence of the Three Powers

The shape and meaning of the power elite today can be understood only when these three sets of structural trends are seen at the point of their coincidence: the military capitalism of private corporations exists in a weakened and formal democratic system containing an already quite politicized military order. Accordingly, at the top of this structure, the power elite has taken its shape from the coincidence of interest between those who control the major means of production and those who control the newly enlarged means of violence; from the decline of the professional politician and the rise to explicit political command of the corporate chieftains and the professional warlords; from the absence of any genuine civil service of skill and integrity, independent of vested interests.

The power elite is composed of political, economic, and military men, but these instituted elites are frequently in some tension; they only come together on certain coinciding points and only on certain occasions of "crisis." In the long peace of the nineteenth century, the military were not in the high councils of state, not of the political directorate—and neither were the economic men; they made raids upon the state but they did not join its directorate. During the thirties, the political man was ascendant, and now the military and the corporate men are in top positions.

Of the three types of circles that compose the power elite today, it is the military that have benefited the most in their enhanced power, although the corporate have also become more explicitly and, in fact, more decisively entrenched in the more public decision-making circles. It is the professional politician that has lost the most, so much that, in examining the events and decisions, one is tempted to speak of a political vacuum in which the corporate rich and the high warlord, in their coinciding interests, rule.

But we must always be historically specific and we must always be open to complexities: (1) the simple Marxian view makes the big economic man the real holder of power; (2) the simple liberal view makes the big political man the chief of the power system; and (3) there are some who would view the warlords as virtual dictators. These are each an oversimplified view. And it is to avoid them that we use the term "power elite" rather than, for example, "ruling class."

"Ruling class," we feel, is a badly loaded phrase. "Class" is an economic term; "rule," a political one. The phrase, "ruling class" thus contains the theory that an economic class rules politically. That shortcut theory may or may not at times be true, but we do not want to carry that one rather simple theory about in the terms that we use to define our problems; we wish to state the theories explicitly, using terms of more precise and unilateral meaning. More specifically, the phrase "ruling class," in its common political connotations, does not allow enough autonomy to the political order and its agents, and it says nothing about the military as such. It should be clear by now that we do not accept as adequate the simple view that high economic men unilaterally make all decisions of national consequence. We hold that such a simple view of "economic determinism" must be elaborated by "political determinism" and by "military determinism"; that the higher agents of each of these three domains now often have a noticeable degree of autonomy; and that only in the often intricate ways of coalition do they make up and carry through the most important decisions. Those are the major reasons we prefer "power elite" to "ruling class" as a characterizing phrase for the higher circles, when we consider them in terms of power.

Insofar as the power elite has come to wide public attention, it has done so in terms of the "military clique," and, in fact, the power elite does take its current shape from the entrance into it in a decisive way of the military. Their presence and their ideology are its major legitimations, whenever the power elite feels the need to provide any. But what is called the "Washington military clique" is not composed merely of military men, and it does not prevail merely in Washington. Its members exist all over the country, and it is a coalition of generals in the roles of corporation executives, of politicians masquerading as admirals, of corporation executives acting like politicians, of civil servants who become majors, of vice-admirals who are also the assistants to a Cabinet officer, who is himself, by the way, really a member of an important managerial clique.

Neither the idea of a "ruling class" nor of a simple monolithic rise of "bureaucratic politicians," nor of a "military clique" is the correct view. The power elite today involves the often uneasy coincidence of economic, military and political power. . . .

CHAPTER 15

JULIAN H. STEWARD

A Neo-Evolutionist
Approach

In biology the theory of evolution today is more powerfully established than ever. In cosmology it has become the primary generator of man's thinking about the universe. But the idea of evolution in the cultural history of mankind itself has had a frustrating career of ups and downs. It was warmly embraced in Darwin's time, left for dead at the turn of the century, and is just now coming back to life and vigor. Today, a completely new approach to the question has once more given us hope of achieving an understanding of the development of human cultures in evolutionary terms.

The Nineteenth-Century Evolutionists

Before considering these new attempts to explain the evolutionary processes operating in human affairs, we need to review the attempts that failed. By the latter part of the nineteenth century, Darwin's theory of biological evolution had profoundly changed scientists' views of human history. Once it was conceded that all forms of life, including man, had evolved from lower forms, it necessarily followed that at some point in evolution man's ancestors had been completely without culture. Human culture must therefore have started from simple beginnings and grown more complex. The nineteenth-century school of cultural evolutionists—mainly British—reasoned that man had progressed from a condition of simple, amoral savagery to a civilized state, whose ultimate achievement was the Victorian Englishman, living in an industrial society and political democracy, believing in the Empire, and belonging to the Church of England. The evolutionists assumed that the universe was designed to produce man and civilization,

From Julian H. Steward, "Cultural Evolution," *Scientific American*, CXCIV (1956), No. 5, pp. 70-80. Copyright © 1956 by Scientific American, Inc., and reprinted by permission. All rights reserved.

that cultural evolution everywhere must be governed by the same principles and follow the same line, and that all mankind would progress toward a civilization like that of Europe.

Among the leading proponents of this theory were Edward B. Tylor, the Englishman who has been called the father of anthropology; Lewis H. Morgan, an American banker and lawyer who devoted many years to studying the Iroquois Indians; Edward Westermarck, a Finnish philosopher famed for his studies of the family; John Ferguson McLennan, a Scottish lawyer who concerned himself with the development of social organization; and James Frazer, the Scottish anthropologist, historian of religion and author of *The Golden Bough*. Their general point of view was developed by Morgan in his book *Ancient Society,* in which he declared: "It can now be asserted upon convincing evidence that savagery preceded barbarism in all the tribes of mankind, as barbarism is known to have preceded civilization." Morgan divided man's cultural development into stages of "savagery," "barbarism," and "civilization"—each of which was ushered in by a single invention.

These nineteenth-century scholars were highly competent men, and some of their insights were extraordinarily acute. But their scheme was erected on such flimsy theoretical foundations and such faulty observation that the entire structure collapsed as soon as it was seriously tested. Their principal undoing was, of course, the notion that progress (*i.e.,* toward the goal of European civilization) was the guiding principle in human development. In this they were following the thought of the biological evolutionists, who traced a progression from the simplest forms of life to *Homo sapiens*. Few students of evolution today, however, would argue that the universe has any design making progress inevitable, in either the biological or the cultural realm. Certainly there is nothing in the evolutionary process which preordained the particular developments that have occurred on our planet.

●

The Facts

When, at the turn of the century, anthropologists began to study primitive cultures in detail, they found that the cultural evolutionists' information had been as wrong as their theoretical assumptions. Morgan had lumped together in the stage of middle barbarism the Pueblo Indians, who were simple farmers, and the peoples of Mexico, who had cities, empires, monumental architecture, metallurgy, astronomy, mathematics, phonetic writing, and other accomplishments unknown to the Pueblo. Field research rapidly disclosed that one tribe after another had quite the wrong cultural characteristics to fit the evolutionary niche assigned it by Morgan. Eventually the general scheme of evolution postulated by the nineteenth-century theorists fell apart completely. . . . Another blow to the evolutionists' theory was the discovery that customs had spread or diffused from one group to another over the world: that is to say, each society owed much of its culture to borrowing from its neighbors, so it could not be said that societies had evolved independently along a single inevitable line. . . .

When the evolutionary hypothesis was demolished, however, no alternative hypothesis appeared. The twentieth-century anthropologists threw out the evolutionists' insights along with their schemes. Studies of culture lost a unifying theory and lapsed into a methodology of shreds and patches. Anthropology became fervently devoted to collecting facts. But it had to give some order to its data, and it fell back on classification—a phase in science which has been called the "natural history stage."

The "culture elements" used as the classification criteria included such items as the bow and arrow, the domesticated dog, techniques and forms of basketry, the spear and spear thrower, head-hunting, polyandrous marriage, feather headgear, the penis sheath, initiation ceremonies for boys, tie-dyeing techniques for coloring textiles, the blowgun, use of a stick to scratch the head during periods of religious taboo, irrigation agriculture, shamanistic use of a sweat bath, transportation of the head of state on a litter, proving one's fortitude by submitting to ant bites, speaking to one's mother-in-law through a third party, making an arrowhead with side notches, marrying one's mother's brother's daughter. Students of the development of culture sought to learn the origin of such customs, their distribution, and how they were combined in the "culture content" of each society.

Eventually this approach led to an attempt to find an overall pattern in each society's way of life—a view which is well expressed in Ruth Benedict's *Patterns of Culture*. She contrasted, for example, the placid, smoothly functioning, nonaggressive behavior of the Pueblo Indians with the somewhat frenzied, warlike behavior of certain Plains Indians, aptly drawing on Greek mythology to designate the first as an Apollonian pattern and the second as Dionysian. The implication is that the pattern is formed by the ethos, value system or world view. During the past decade and a half it has become popular to translate pattern into more psychological terms. But description of a culture in terms either of elements, ethos or personality-type does not explain how it originated. Those who seek to understand how cultures evolved must look for longer-range causes and explanations.

Multilinear Evolution

One must keep in mind Herbert Spencer's distinction between man as a biological organism and his functioning on the superorganic or cultural level, which has distinctive qualities. We must distinguish man's needs and capacity for culture—his superior brain and ability to speak and use tools —from the particular cultures he has evolved. A specific invention is not explained by saying that man is creative. Cultural activities meet various biological needs, but the existence of the latter does not explain the character of the former. . . . Thanks to his jaw and tongue structure and to the speech and auditory centers of his brain, man is capable of speech, but these facts do not explain the origin of a single one of the thousands of languages that have developed in the world. . . .

The failure to distinguish the biological basis of all cultural development from the explanation of particular forms of culture accounts for a good deal of the controversy and confusion about "free will" and "determinism" in human behavior. The biological evolutionist George Gaylord Simpson considers that, because man has purposes and makes plans, he may exercise conscious control over cultural evolution. On the other hand, the cultural evolutionist Leslie A. White takes the deterministic position that culture develops according to its own laws. Simpson is correct in making a biological statement, that is, in describing man's capacity. White is correct in making a cultural statement, that is, in describing the origin of any particular culture.

All men, it is true, have the biological basis for making rational solutions, and specific features of culture may develop from the application of reason. But since circumstances differ (e.g., in the conditions for hunting), solutions take many forms.

•

The facts now accumulated indicate that human culture evolved along a number of different lines; we must think of cultural evolution not as unilinear but as multilinear. This is the new basis upon which evolutionists today are seeking to build an understanding of the development of human cultures. It is an empirical approach—an attempt to learn how the factors in each given type of situation shaped the development of a particular type of society.

Multilinear evolution is not merely a way of explaining the past. It is applicable to changes occurring today as well—for example, among peasants, small farmers, wage workers on plantations and in mines and factories, primitive tribes. These several types of societies evolved, and their customs are being changed by economic or political factors introduced from the modern industrial world. Studies of such societies should obviously have practical value in guiding programs of technical aid for these peoples.

Hunters

To illustrate the empirical approach, let us consider very briefly several different types of societies, using the ways in which they made their living as the frame of reference. The first example is the form of society consisting of a patrilineal band of hunters. This type of organization was found among many primitive tribes all over the world, including the Bushmen of the deserts in South Africa, the Negritos of the tropical rain forest in the

Congo, the aborigines of the steppes and deserts in Australia, the now extinct aboriginal islanders in Tasmania, the Indians of the cold pampas on the islands of Tierra del Fuego, and Shoshoni Indians of the mountains in Southern California. Although their climates and environments differed greatly, all of these tribes had one important thing in common: they hunted cooperatively for sparsely scattered, nonmigratory game. In each case the cooperating band usually consisted of about fifty or sixty persons who occupied an area of some 400 square miles and claimed exclusive hunting rights to it. Since men could hunt more efficiently in familiar terrain, they remained throughout life in the territory of their birth. The band consequently consisted of persons related through the male line of descent, and it was required that wives be taken from other bands. In sum, the cultural effects of this line of evolution were band localization, descent in the male line, marriage outside the group, residence of the wife with the husband's band and control by the band of the food resources within its territory.

•

Early Civilizations

Farming was one of the major factors leading to dense populations which were the basis for another line of evolution that covered a considerable span of the early prehistory and history of China, Mesopotamia, Egypt, the north coast of Peru, probably the Indus Valley, and possibly the Valley of Mexico. This line had three stages. In the first period, primitive groups apparently began to cultivate food plants along the moist banks of the rivers or in the higher terrain where rainfall was sufficient for crops. They occupied small but permanent villages. The second stage in some of these areas started when the people learned to divert the river waters by means of canals to irrigate large tracts of land. Intensive farming made possible a larger population and freed the farmers from the need to spend all their time on basic food production. Part of the new-found time was put into enlarging the system of canals and ditches and part into developing crafts. This period brought the invention of loom weaving, metallurgy, the wheel, mathematics, the calendar, writing, monumental and religious architecture, and extremely fine art products. It was also marked by the beginnings of urban centers.

When the irrigation works expanded so that the canals served many communities, a coordinating and managerial control became necessary. This need was met by a ruling class or a bureaucracy, whose authority had mainly religious sanctions, for men looked to the gods for the rainfall on which their agriculture depended. Centralization of authority over a large territory marked the emergence of a state.

That a state developed in these irrigation centers by no means signifies that all states originated in this way. Many different lines of cultural evolution could have led from kinship groups up to multicommunity states. For example, feudal Europe and Japan developed small states very different from the theocratic irrigation states.

The irrigation state reached its florescence in Mesopotamia between 3000 and 4000 B.C., in Egypt a little later, in China about 1500 or 2000 B.C., in northern Peru between 500 B.C. and 500 A.D., in the Valley of Mexico a little later than in Peru. Then, in each case, a third stage of expansion followed. When the theocratic states had reached the limits of available water and production had leveled off, they began to raid and conquer their neighbors to exact tribute. The states grew into empires. The empire was not only larger than the state, but differed qualitatively in the ways it regimented and controlled its large and diversified population. Laws were codified; a bureaucracy was developed; a powerful military establishment, rather than the priesthood, was made the basis of authority. The militaristic empires began with the Sumerian Dynasty in Mesopotamia, the pyramid-building Early Dynasty in Egypt, the Chou periods in China, the Toltec and Aztec periods in Mexico, and the Tiahuanacan period in the Andes.

Since the wealth of these empires was based on forced tribute rather than on increased production, they contained the seeds of their own undoing. Excessive taxation, regimentation of civil life and imposition of the imperial religious cult over the local ones led the subject peoples eventually to rebel. The great empires were destroyed; the irrigation works were neglected; production declined; the population decreased. A "dark age" ensued. But in each center the process of empire building later began anew, and the cycle was repeated. Cyclical conquests succeeded one another in Mesopotamia, Egypt and China for nearly 2,000 years. Peru had gone through at least two cycles and was at the peak of the Inca Empire when the Spaniards came. Mexico also probably had experienced two cycles prior to the Spanish Conquest.

Our final example of a specific line of evolution is taken from more recent times. When the colonists in America pre-empted the Indians' lands, some of the Indian clans formed a new type of organization. The Ute, Western Shoshoni and Northern Paiute Indians, who had lived by hunting and gathering in small groups of wandering families, united in aggressive bands. With horses stolen from the white settlers, they raided the colonists' livestock and occasionally their settlements.

Similar predatory bands developed among some of the mounted Apaches, who had formerly lived in semipermanent encampments consisting of extended kinship groups. Many of these bands were the scourge of the Southwest for years. Some of the Apaches, on the other hand, yielded to the blandishments of the U. S. Government and settled peacefully on reservations; as a result, there were Apache peace factions who rallied around chiefs such as Cochise, and predatory factions that followed belligerent leaders such as Geronimo.

The predatory bands of North America were broken up by the U. S. Army within a few years. But this type of evolution, although transitory, was not unique. In the pampas of South America similar raiding bands arose after the Indians obtained horses. On an infinitely larger scale and making a far greater impression on history were the Mongol hordes of Asia. The armies of Genghis Khan and his successors were essentially huge mounted bands that raided entire continents.

Biology and Culture

Human evolution, then, is not merely a matter of biology, but of the interaction of man's physical and cultural characteristics, each influencing the other. Man is capable of devising rational solutions to life, especially in the realm of technical problems, and also of transmitting learned solutions to his offspring and other members of his society. His capacity for speech gives him the ability to package vastly complicated ideas into sound symbols and to pass on most of what he has learned. This human potential has resulted in the accumulation and social transmission of an incalculable number of learned modes of behavior. . . .

The biological requirements for cultural evolution were an erect posture, specialized hands, a mouth structure permitting speech, stereoscopic vision and areas in the brain for the functions of speech and association. Since culture speeded the development of these requirements, it would be difficult to say which came first.

The first step toward human culture may have come when manlike animals began to substitute tools for body parts. It has been suggested, for example, that there may have been an intimate relation between the development of a flint weapon held in the hand and the receding of the ape-like jaw and protruding canine teeth. An ape, somewhat like a dog, deals with objects by means of its mouth. When the hands, assisted by tools, took over this task, the prognathous jaw began to recede. There were other consequences of this development. The brain centers that register the experiences of the hands grew larger, and this in turn gave the hands greater sensitivity and skill. The reduction of the jaw, especially the elimination of the "simian shelf," gave the tongue freer movement and thus helped create the potentiality for speech.

Darwin called attention to the fact that man is in effect a domesticated animal; as such he depends upon culture and cannot well survive in a state of nature. Man's self-domestication furthered his biological evolution in those characteristics that make culture possible. Until perhaps 25,000 years ago he steadily developed a progressively larger brain, a more erect posture, a more vertical face and better developed speech, auditory and associational centers in the brain. His physical evolution is unquestionably still going on, but there is no clear evidence that recent changes have increased his inherent potential for cultural activities. However, the rate of his cultural development became independent of his biological evolution. In addition to devising tools as substitutes for body parts in the struggle for survival, he evolved wholly new kinds of tools which served other purposes: stone scrapers for preparing skin clothing, baskets for gathering wild foods, axes for building houses and canoes. As cultural experience accumulated, the innovations multiplied, and old inventions were used in new ways. During the last 25,000 years the rate of culture change has accelerated.

The many kinds of human culture today are understandable only as particular lines of evolution. Even if men of the future develop an I.Q. that is incredibly high by modern standards, their specific behavior will nonetheless be determined not by their reason or psychological characteristics, but by their special line of cultural evolution, that is, by the fundamental processes that shape cultures in particular ways.

1964 POSTSCRIPT

This paper follows "Cultural Evolution" in the *Scientific American* fairly closely, except that research since 1956 has modified its factual basis while the many symposiums on evolution in celebration of the 100th anniversary of the publication of Darwin's *Origin of the Species* in 1859 have suggested refinements of its conceptual approach. Attention is called to modifications indicated in "Some Mechanisms of Sociocultural Evolution" by Julian H. Steward and Demitri B. Shimkin in *Evolution and Man's Progress,* Hudson Hoagland and Ralph W. Burhoe, eds. (New York: Columbia University Press, 1962), pp. 67-87, which has a fairly complete bibliography of recent publications on cultural evolution.

The most important factual modification of the original article results from evidence on the role of irrigation in the development of the early civilizations of Mesoamerica, Peru, the Near East, and China. These civilizations reached their culminations in arid areas and had large irrigation systems, but the hypothesis that the managerial controls required for expanding irrigation works during their developmental periods led to their final integration as irrigation or hydraulic states must be modified. In all cases, increased agricultural productivity, population expansion, and growth of urban centers or "containers of civilization" where the rulers and various nonfarming specialists lived were factors in the development of states and empires; but it is still unclear how, in the absence or weakness of militarism, the great rural and urban populations were brought under centralized theocratic control.

A conceptual refinement of neo-evolution is that, since cultures cannot be classified in a taxonomy analogous to that of biology, it is futile and misleading to attempt to discuss evolutionary transformations of whole cultures. Although all components of a culture—economics, technology, society, humanistic features, language, and others—may be described in their interrelatedness as they characterize a society at a given point in time, these components change, or evolve, in different ways. Man's understanding of and technological control over his physical universe tends to be largely cumulative. Languages, from a genetic point of view, divide and subdivide so that the larger and more remotely related linguistic stocks cross-cut many kinds of societies and technological systems. Such stylistic features as art and architecture develop according to their own rationale, except that very unlike styles may serve similar functions in sociopolitical and religious structures. Finally, sociopolitical and economic systems evolve through a series of transformations which are only partly related to the other components of culture.

Recent work on cultural evolution has paid special attention to sociocultural transformations and has sought, by means of an empirical method, technological, ecological, or other causes of the many lines of evolution. Such evolution does not negate the possibility that historical factors, such as diffusion or migration, have introduced single key features of culture or whole cultures in particular cases.

CHAPTER 16

A. L. KROEBER

Diffusionism

Diffusionism is the name currently given several theories of the development of culture which specially emphasize the factor of diffusion.

Diffusion is the process, usually but not necessarily gradual, by which elements or systems of culture are spread; by which an invention or a new institution adopted in one place is adopted in neighboring areas, and in some cases continues to be adopted in adjacent ones, until it may spread over the whole earth.

Diffusion is obviously allied to tradition in that both pass cultural material on from one group to another. As usually understood, however, tradition refers to the transmission of cultural content from one generation to another of the same population; diffusion, from one population to another. Tradition therefore operates essentially in terms of time, diffusion in terms of space, although the spread through space may be rapid or slow and therefore involves a time factor also.

Both tradition and diffusion are conservative factors in culture history as contrasted with the creative one of invention, which in its broadest sense is denotive of the origination of new culture material or new cultural organization. Tradition conserves material or organization through time lapses within a greater or smaller population. Diffusion conserves it from the point of view of human culture as a whole. This aspect of diffusion has been largely underemphasized because attention has been given to the mechanism of the spread of culture per se, or because diffusions have been studied less from an interest in them than as a means by which historical events may be reconstructed or origins determined. Such interests are legitimate, but do not exhaust the significance of diffusion. It is obvious that new cultural material which does not diffuse beyond the people among whom it originates stands little chance of permanent preservation. It is likely to

From A. L. Kroeber, "Diffusionism," in Edwin R. A. Seligman and Alvin Johnson, eds., *The Encyclopedia of the Social Sciences,* III (1937), 139-142. Copyright 1937 by the Macmillan Company, and reprinted by permission of the publisher.

perish with the particular culture to which it remains attached, or even to be squeezed out of existence by new growths within this culture. Diffusion is then a process concerned with growth as well as preservation, whereas tradition as such affects only preservation. But neither in itself produces new culture content.

•

The mechanisms of diffusion are several: migration and colonization, that is, ethnic movements; conquest; missionization; commerce; revolution; and gradual infiltration, ranging from the conscious to the unconscious, or infiltration which comes into social consciousness only after it is an accomplished fact. The older anthropologists and the less subtle among historians have relied chiefly upon the first and grosser of these mechanisms. Ethnologists, archaeologists, and culture historians, on the other hand, recognizing more and more that these simple mechanisms are inadequate to explain the phenomena they are confronting, have increasingly discerned the importance of infiltration, and have tended to emphasize it as in the long run the most important phase of diffusion. They seem to have shown that the main streams of culture permeation often run surprisingly independently of migrations and political and military events. In extreme instances this has led to an underemphasis upon these more obvious factors, or even to impatience at their recognition. They can indeed be disturbing elements in the task of unraveling the full story of cultural events, which is normally both intricate and largely below the level of historic consciousness.

Both the culture area and the age-and-area concepts presuppose and rest upon diffusion, mainly of the infiltrating kind and as a normal process. But however normal the tendency of culture material to diffuse, it is clear that the actual spread of such material has not gone on irresistibly nor in any mechanically calculable manner, else all but extremely remote populations would long since have assimilated to nearly the same culture. Among the checks or limitations to diffusion—other than the self-evident ones of lack or scantiness of communications—are the factors of resistance and displacement. Resistance is due to the presence in the recipient cultures of material and systems which are, or are felt to be, irreconcilable with the invading traits or system and therefore tend to block them, checking their further diffusion. Frequently it is the presence of cultural habits functionally analogous to the new elements which results in a block. Coffee is unlikely to invade rapidly or successfully a nation addicted to tea drinking. Christianity and Islam, which are both monotheistic, Messianic, and scriptural, have diffused into the territory of each other very much less, except by violence, than they have diffused into countries of a different type of religion. Sometimes the factors that defeat or facilitate diffusion are far more subtle or intricate than in these examples, and yet are at least approximately determinable.

Displacement affects not the process of diffusion but its results. If repre-

sentative government gains at the expense of monarchy, the distribution of
the latter shrinks and the products of an earlier diffusion of the idea of
kingship begin to be obliterated, until perhaps the institution remains only
in scattered survivals. From such territorially discrete survivals the history
of the growth and decay, or diffusion and shrinkage, of monarchy could
perhaps be inferred even in the absence of documentary data, as among
primitive or nonliterate peoples. On the other hand, such sporadic occurrences might . . . also be due to wholly independent origins, to parallel
inventions of kingship. Convergent processes may also be the cause. Monarchy may arise in one place as a product of military defense, in another
theocratically, and yet the two institutions may assimilate quite closely, although independently, with the lapse of time. It is even possible that each
might then undergo diffusion until they met, and their coalesced areas
would then look as if they were the result of a single origin and diffusion.
Considerations of this sort make the unraveling of historically undocu-
mented culture data a difficult and delicate task, calling for intensive knowledge, reliable analysis, and a critically conservative judgment. Most of the
controversies of anthropology have revolved about problems of precisely
this order. The diffusionist schools, in the opinion of the others, have tried
to hack their way through this intricate Gordian knot.

On the other hand, the diffusionists have developed more clearly than
before the important concept of degeneration, not only of whole cultures
but of culture elements, and have provided some extremely suggestive examples. Their tendency has been to operate almost exclusively with rare
and unique inventions and very widespread diffusions, tempered at need
with degenerations. But this oversimplification of mechanisms should not
lead to overdistrust of the concept of cultural degeneration.

There are two schools of diffusionism, the German-Austrian and the
British. The former posits some seven or eight original *Kulturkreise*. These
are not, as the name might seem to imply, geographical spheres or areas of
culture, but are culture types or blocks of cultural material, each of which
at one time in the past is assumed to have existed as a discrete, internally
uniform culture, presumably of independent origin, in one part of the world
and then to have diffused essentially as a unit. These several culture blocks
originated successively in time as well as progressively in degree of advancement or complexity; and, through each spreading more or less over
the whole planet, have become represented in all cultures in an interpenetration or overlay of varying proportions. The task of culture history is the
segregation of any given culture into the elements derived from the several
Kulturkreise.

The *Kulturkreislehre* was first conceived by Foy and Graebner, promul-
gated chiefly by the latter, supported for Africa by Ankermann, and attacked by Father Schmidt. The latter, however, soon became a convert and
has since, with his associate Koppers and others, modified and amplified

the hypothesis, depriving it of its original rigor and lack of specific placing in time and space by tying the scheme in wherever possible with linguistics, archaeology, and history. The term *Kulturkreis* is being abandoned and the phrase *kulturgeschichtliche Methode* substituted, which is unfortunate in its implication that the study of culture history, at any rate among non-literate cultures, must be carried on through acceptance of the special assumptions of this school. Probably not far from half of the ethnologists of Austria and Germany either profess adherence to or have been influenced by the views of this school.

The British school originated a few years later with G. Elliot Smith, Perry, and Rivers, whose respective roles might be roughly characterized as inspirer, protagonist, and moderator. This school also has undergone some modifications and is best represented in its recent form by Smith's *Human History*. In contrast with the German school, it is monogenetic. Primitive culture is conceived as essentially stagnant, inclined to retrogression as much as to progress. It is contended that at one time and place in human history, namely, in Egypt around 3000 B.C., an unusual constellation of events produced a cultural spurt leading to the rapid development of agriculture, metallurgy, political organization and kingship, priesthood, concern with the after life and mummification, writing, and other cultural institutions. From this center of origination, this great cultural complex was carried in whole or in part, with secondary embellishments and degenerations, to Mesopotamia and the Mediterranean world, to India, Oceania, Mexico, and Peru and in fragmentary form even to remote peoples who remained otherwise primitive. The remainder of culture history is essentially the story of the minor modifications of this one great culture, until the Greeks began to dissolve and replace it by civilization.

The British school has won about the same degree of adherence at home as the German; and likewise has tended to label as evolutionists and antidiffusionists all students who showed themselves unsympathetic to its full tenets. It is perhaps significant that both schools have made practically no converts from each other nor outside their countries of origin. Scandinavia, France, and the United States have held almost unanimously aloof.

The methodological weaknesses of both diffusionist schools may be summarized as follows. Granted a certain modest empirical beginning, they very early took a long a priori leap, and since then have been forced to depend largely on selected evidence or construals of evidence to maintain the position thus taken, genuinely inductive inquiry being relegated to the background. The basic schemes are too simple to seem adequate to most culture historians and anthropologists. The mechanisms used, with their primary insistence on diffusion, are also too simple.

The virtues of the schools are in part associated with this overemphasis on diffusion, whose strength they have at any rate shown, thus helping to clear the ground of the older school of evolutionism or naïvely psychological theories of stages of progress. They have also made probable the specific connection between a number of geographically separate culture elements or complexes, and they have drawn fresh attention to culture history as a study of universal human interrelations. The future will probably characterize their theories as overshootings of a newly discerned and legitimate mark.

CHAPTER 17

AMITAI ETZIONI

Toward a Theory of Societal Guidance

In an endeavor to develop a macrosociology, we focus on one central question: Under what conditions are societal processes more guided by the participants as against the conditions under which they are more "ongoing"? The higher the capacity to guide, the freer members of a society are of its history; the lower, the more they are subject to patterns they did not mold. We refer to societal units that have a relatively high capacity to guide their own processes as "active" and to those that have a relatively low capacity as "passive."

The degree to which an actor is active is affected by his cybernetic capacities, his relative power, and his capacity to build consensus. Each of these factors has both an internal and an external dimension: how much he knows about himself and about others, how much he can mobilize power over members *and* over non-members, and to what degree he can gain the support of subunits and of external units. Since for many purposes it is useful to treat cybernetic and power capacities together, we shall refer to them jointly as his ability to *control*. When his skill in building consensus is also taken into account, we refer to his ability to *guide*. Since we see the subunits and other units as having in principle the same capacities as the actor under study, his activation obviously cannot be optimized by maximizing his control capacities but by improving his combination of control and consensus-building, that is, his guidance mechanisms.

We turn now to explore the factors which affect the societal capacity to guide. Our approach is at first analytic in that each factor is examined as if all the others were held constant; in the last section we take a more synthesizing and historical view of actors that are becoming generally more active on all major dimensions. In the analytic section we compare briefly both societies and subsocieties. The societies we focus on are encapsulated

The American Journal of Sociology, Vol. 73, No. 2, Sept. 1967, pp. 173-187.

in a state that serves as their chief organizational tool for both control and consensus-building. Similarly, the subsocietal actors are collectivities that have organizational "arms," such as a working class that has labor parties and trade unions. Societies without states and collectivities which are not organized are treated mainly for comparative purposes.

I. Control Factors

A. Cybernetic Capacities

Societal units differ significantly in their capacity to collect, process, and use knowledge. This holds not only for corporations that compete for a market but also for political parties (Kennedy is believed to have used the social sciences more effectively than Nixon in the 1960 presidential campaign), federal agencies (the U.S. Air Force is thought to be more active in this respect than the U.S. Navy and the U.S. Army), and civic organizations (the National Association for the Advancement of Colored People's capacity to use information seems to have increased between 1955 and 1965).

The input of knowledge into a societal unit follows, we suggest, the same basic patterns of other inputs; that is, it might be blocked—and hence partially or completely lost for action purposes—at each stage of the process. The varying capacities of societal units for collecting information ("raw material" input) seem to be associated with economic affluence but not in a one-to-one relationship. If we were to order countries (or other societal units) by their average income per capita and then score their capacity to collect information, let us say, in terms of expenditure on research, we expect that the most affluent units would have a much higher capacity than the next affluent ones, while the remaining units would have few such capacities at all. Three powerful federal agencies in the United States, the Department of Defense, the National Aeronautics and Space Administration, and the Atomic Energy Commission, spent more of the federal research and development (R & D) funds than the other thirty-odd agencies combined, or 90.8 per cent of the available funds: Defense, 61 per cent; NASA, 20.3 percent; AEC, 9.5 per cent. Three affluent states out of fifty gained more than 50 per cent of these R & D funds: California, 38.5 per cent; New York, 9.3 per cent; Massachusetts, 4.6 per cent.[1] Societal units' spending on information has much accelerated in the last generations as compared to

---

[1] Data on states' receipt of federal funds for R & D are from the *Statistical Abstracts of the United States: 1966*, p. 546, Table 779. Data on agency expenditures of R & D funds are from *Statistical Abstracts of the United States: 1966*, p. 544, Table 776. Figures exclude expenditures on R & D plants. All data are for fiscal year 1963.

earlier ones.[2] In short, patterns of inter-unit distribution of information seem significantly more inegalitarian than are those of the distribution of economic assets.

The ratio of investment in *collecting* over *processing* information is an indicator of the sophistication of the cybernetic overlayer and the knowledge strategy to which the particular unit subscribes. The United States and Great Britain, it seems, tend to invest relatively highly in collection; France, at least until recently, has stressed processing. A societal unit that emphasizes the collection of information disproportionately will, we expect, have a fragmented view of itself and its environment; it will have many "bits" but no picture, like survey data before tabulation. Such inadequate processing, we suggest, will tend to be associated with drifting (or passivity), because information that is not sufficiently processed is, in effect, not available for societal guidance.

On the other hand, a unit that overemphasizes *processing* is expected to have an "unempirical" view of itself and its environment, because it will tend to draw more conclusions from the available information than are warranted; it is similar to acting on the basis of a poorly validated theory. Thus, overprocessing is expected to be associated with hyperactivity, as the actor assumes he knows more than he does. Master plans used to guide economic development are typically hyperactive in their assumptions. Finally, societal units whose collection and processing are relatively balanced (not in absolute amounts but in terms of intrinsic needs of the guidance mechanisms) are expected to have comparatively more effective controlling overlayers, all other things being equal, and to be active without being hyperactive.

Information that has been processed might still be wasted as far as the societal unit is concerned if it is not *systematically introduced into the unit's decision-making and implementation overlayer* where the main societal "consumption" of information takes place. Two major variables seem useful for characterizing the different arrangements societal units have for interaction between the knowledge-producing and the decision-making units; one concerns the relative degree of autonomy of production, the other, the effectiveness of communications of the "product." It is widely believed that

---

[2] Thus, for instance, the United States' total federal expenditure on R & D in 1965 was approximately $14.8 billion; in 1955, $3.3 billion; in 1945, $1.6 billion. Data refer to fiscal years. They include R & D plant. See National Science Foundation, *Federal Funds for Research, Development and Other Scientific Activities: Fiscal Years 1965, 1966 and 1967,* Vol. XV, p. 4, Table 2. "90 to 95 per cent of all the behavioral scientists who ever lived are still alive" (Robert K. Merton, "The Mosaic of Behavioral Sciences," in Bernard Berelson [ed.], *The Behavioral Sciences Today* [New York: Harper & Row, 1964], p. 249).

structural differentiation between the producers and consumers of information is necessary; fusion of the two kinds of units—for instance, in the management of a corporation—is viewed as dysfunctional both for production of knowledge and for decision-making. For societal units whose knowledge and decision-making units are differentiated, various modes and forms of articulation and communication exist whose relative effectiveness remains to be explored.

Within this context, one issue is of special significance for the study of societal guidance: *The effects of the relative investments in production of transforming versus "stable" knowledge.* Knowledge tied to transformation is concerned with exploring potential challenges to the basic assumptions of a system. Production of "stable" knowledge elaborates and respecifies, even revises, secondary assumptions within the basic framework of a knowledge system, but the framework itself is taken for granted. Decision-making elites, we suggest, tend to prefer the production of "stable" to transforming knowledge and seek closure on basic knowledge assumptions. One reason for this preference is that basic assumptions cannot be selected and reviewed on wholly empirical grounds. Hence, once consensus has been reached on the basic assumptions of a world view, a self-view, a strategic doctrine, it is expensive politically, economically, and psychologically for the elites to allow these assumptions to be questioned, which is necessary if they are to be transformed. They hence tend to become *tabooed* assumptions, and the elites attempt to guide knowledge production toward elaboration, additions, and revisions within their limits. The more the ability to transform this basic framework is reduced, the lower the capacity for societal self-transformation. While societal units which do not transform do survive as long as the range of tolerance of their basic knowledge and societal pattern allows for sufficient adaptation to environmental changes, such adaptation tends to become increasingly costly, and more so the more rapidly these changes occur.

A comparison of corporations which have shifted to a new line of products, restructured their internal organizations, and found new markets when their old markets were gradually lost with those which kept modifying their basic lines but not changing them although their profits greatly declined, suggests that the transforming corporations maintained R & D units which were exempt from the tabooed assumptions *and* were expected sporadically to review these assumptions. That is, part of their institutionalized role was to engage in "search" behavior precisely where the decision-making elites would otherwise settle for "satisfying" solutions.[3]

---

[3] On these solutions and the tendency to "settle," see Herbert A. Simon, "A Behavioral Model of Rational Choice," *Quarterly Journal of Economics,* LXIX (1955), 99-118.

The societal parallel of this cybernetic arrangement is not difficult to point out. The intellectual community acts as a large-scale, societal R & D unit, as a critical examiner of tabooed assumptions. Under what economic, political, and sociological conditions intellectuals can fulfil this function and what, if any, functional alternatives exist are questions social scientists have much feeling about—but there is surprisingly little systematic research.[4]

These questions can be studied for any society and any societal unit. As the input of knowledge becomes a major *guided* societal activity (about three-quarters of the expenditure on R & D in the United States is federal) and as the ratio of this input as compared to other societal inputs increases both in relative expenditure and in sociopolitical significance, the macrosociological study of the organization of knowledge production and consumption becomes an unavoidable part of studies of societal change and guidance. Typically, earlier studies of a society stressed the size of its population, territory, and gross national product; the present approach adds the number of Ph.D.'s a society's educational system "turns out," the size of its professional manpower, and its investment in R & D as indicators of a major *societal* variable. Sociology of knowledge traditionally focused on the social conditions under which true statements are made;[5] macrosociology of knowledge focuses on the societal conditions under which knowledge is made available for societal purposes, adding a whole new field of inquiry to the study of societies.[6]

B. *Societal Decision-Making*

At the head of the societal controlling overlayers are decision-making elites—the sociopolitical equivalent of the electronic centers. The elites choose between alternative policies, issue signals to the performing units (i.e., to the underlayer), and respond to signals fed back to the head from the performing units. (The body of the overlayer is made up of communication networks which tie elites to other member units and to a power hierarchy.) Sociologists have studied elites by asking how "closed" versus

---

[4] For one of the few sociological studies, see Lewis Coser, *Men of Ideas* (New York: Free Press, 1965).

[5] For an overview of this sociology of knowledge, see Robert K. Merton, *Social Theory and Social Structure* (rev. ed.; New York: Free Press, 1957), pp. 456-88.

[6] For studies of this field, see Viscount Hailsham, Q.C., *Science and Politics* (London: Faber & Faber, 1963); Price, *op. cit.*; Jerome A. Wiesner, *Where Government and Science Meet* (New York: McGraw-Hill Book Co., 1965); Bernard Barber, *Science and the Social Order* (Glencoe, Ill.: Free Press, 1952); Norman Kaplan (ed.), *Science and Society* (Chicago: Rand McNally & Co., 1965); Norman W. Storer, *The Social System of Science* (New York: Holt, Rinehart & Winston, 1966).

"open" they are to members of various societal units, how dispersed control is among them, and how they relate to each other. But these are not cybernetic considerations. They belong under the headings of consensus formation (e.g., closed and widely open elites are believed less effective for consensus formation than relatively open ones) and power relations (e.g., decentralization is believed more effective than monopolization of control by one elite or its fragmentation among several). Cybernetic aspects of elites have been studied largely by non-sociologists and have not been systematically related to societal analysis.[7] The cybernetic study of elites concerns the consequences of differences in the procedures used by the various decision-making elites, the strategies employed, and the communication networks which lead from the elites to the performing units and back.

In seeking to explain the action or change of a societal unit, most sociologists are more inclined to explore "background" conditions (e.g., the level of economic resources the unit commands; the educational opportunities of elite members) than to study the decision-making procedures the elites follow. There is a widely held assumption that such "background" factors constitute the basic substructure which both sets the main limits of variability of societal action and change (e.g., poor countries lack the capital needed to develop) and specifies the factors which determine what decisions will be made among whatever options are left open (e.g., because of the revolution of rising expectations, democratic elites cannot limit much the availability of consumer goods). Differences in decision-making procedures are considered either "dependent" variables or trivial. In contrast, the theory of societal guidance suggests that societal actors have more autonomy. "Background" factors are viewed as setting a broad frame; which course is followed within its limits is affected by cybernetic factors, among which decision-making procedures are a significant element. An effective elite, for instance, might defer consumption increase in a poor country despite rising expectations and tip the scales in favor of stable development.

Actually, many of the undeveloped nations are not overpopulated or poor in resources but poor in control capacities, among which the quality of their elites ranks high in importance. For instance, in 1930 the level of economic development of Canada and Argentina was similar, on several key indicators.[8] Canada since then has continued to develop, while Argentina remains underdeveloped. A typical "background"-condition approach would stress the presence of the Protestant element in one country and its absence in the other, as well as the differences in the Catholic stock in the two countries (in Argentina it is more that of southern Spain and

---

[7] See Amitai Etzioni, *The Active Society* (New York: The Free Press, 1968), Chapter 8.

[8] See El Desarrollo Economico de la Argentina, E-CN. 12-429-Add. 4 (1958), pp. 3-5.

Italy, in Canada that of the French). One would expect, in line with Weber's analysis, these differences to correlate with attitudes favorable to capitalism.

Adding to this Weberian thesis, a theory of societal guidance would call attention to the difference between the responsive-democratic government of Canada and the authoritarian leadership of Argentina. True, this difference in leadership is in part due to differences in societal structure; Canada, for example, would not "tolerate" a Peron. But unless a one-to-one relationship between background factors and elite conduct is assumed, and elite conduct is viewed as having no significant independent effect on background factors, the analysis of the guiding quality of the elites has to be included as an integral part of societal theories. It suffices to contrast the development of each country under different governments following different decision-making procedures (e.g., Peron and Illia in Argentina) to illustrate the value of systematically including these factors. . . .Obviously the more assets a societal unit has and the more mobilized these are for societal action, the more advantages it can derive from their effective use. For passive units, which barely guide their own processes, "background" factors are of much importance; for units that react more creatively to environmental as well as to internal challenges, the quality of decision-making increases in significance.

Cybernetic factors other than the input of information and decision-making include various attributes of societal goals, such as the clarity of their formulation and the degree of compatibility of a unit's various goals. Also relevant is the quality of the communication networks that lead from the decision-making elites to the performance units and back, including the number and intensity of gaps, "noise" on the line, etc. As our purpose here is not to provide a list of these factors but to illustrate the main categories, we turn now to a third element of control, power.

C. Power: Its Sources and Its Mobilization

Societal assets and power. Societal structures are not just patterns of interaction of actors, patterns of expectations and symbols, but are also patterns of allocation of societal assets, of the possessions of a societal unit. These can be classified analytically as coercive, utilitarian, and normative, concerning, respectively, the distribution of the capacity to employ means of violence, material objects and services, and symbols (especially values). A measure of the assets a societal unit or subunit possesses is *not* in itself an indication of its power but only of its power *potential*. Assets may be used to generate more assets, may be consumed or stored, *or* may be used to overcome the resistance of other actors, which is what is meant by societal power. (This does not mean necessarily to force other actors; their resistance may be overcome, for instance, by offering a payoff.) In exploring the relations between assets and power, it is essential not to shift the frame of reference in mid-analysis. Conversion of assets into power at one point in time might lead to more assets at a later point; in the first point in time, however, the generation of power entails a "loss" of assets.

A central proposition of the theory of societal guidance is that the relationship between assets and power is a "loose" one—that is, the amount of assets allocated to a societal unit in a given structure provides a poor indicator of how much societal power the unit will generate. The amount of power generated seems to be much affected by the *intra*-unit allocation of the assets among alternative usages. A unit poor in assets can in principle command more power than a much more affluent one, if the poor unit assigns more of its assets to power "production." (With half the gross national product, the U.S.S.R. maintains a defense budget similar to that of the United States.)

The fraction of the assets possessed by a unit that is converted into power is itself influenced by the societal context and not freely set by the societal actor (e.g., that Negro Americans are less politically active than Jewish Americans is in part due to differences in educational opportunities). We suggest, however, that the intra-unit assignment of assets to power is a relatively more malleable attribute than the amount of assets the unit possessed (at any given point in time). It is here that an important element of voluntarism enters the social structure. A comparison of colonial societies in the years immediately preceding the "takeoff" of national independence movements with those immediately after they won their independence seems to show that the "takeoff" involved more change in the distribution of assets, in their relative use for generating societal power, than in the size of the assets base itself. Similarly, the American civil rights movement, which between 1953 and 1965 transformed segments of the Negro Americans from a passive to an active grouping, entailed much more of a change in the mobilization of power than in the amount of assets this grouping commanded.[9] The possession of assets rose slowly in comparison to the rise in political power.

Mobilization. Each societal unit has at any given point in time a *level of activation* which we define as the amount of assets available for collective action as compared to its total assets. For example, the percentage of the gross national product spent by the government, the percentage of the labor force employed by it, and the percentage of the knowledge-producers who work for it are crude indicators of national activation level. *Mobilization* refers to an upward change in the level of activation, to an increase in the fraction of the total assets possessed by a unit made available for collective action by that unit. (Demobilization refers to a reduction in that level.)

---

[9] For the premobilization state see James Q. Wilson, *Negro Politics* (New York: Free Press, 1965), esp. pp. 3-7.

The level of activation of most societal units most of the time is very low; if all their assets are taken into account, usually less than 15 per cent are available for collective action. Hence, relatively small percentage changes in the level of mobilization may increase the action capacity of a unit to a large extent. Major societal transformations, such as sociopolitical revolutions and the gaining of national independence, usually involve relatively high mobilization. The secret of the power of social movements lies in part in the relatively high mobilization which the asceticism and the intense commitment of the members allow for.

Aside from the asset base a collectivity commands and the amount of power it is mobilizing, the *kind* of power generated also affects the action capacity of the unit. To employ power is, by definition, to overcome resistance, but in society, as in nature, each application of power generates a counterpower, a resistance of its own (the result of the alienation of those who were made to suspend their preferences in favor of those of the power-wielders). While all power applications have this effect, some generate more alienation than others.

We suggest that when different power relationships are compared, if the means of control used are coercive, all other things being equal, resistance will tend to be high; if utilitarian, lower; and if normative, even smaller.[10] Most power-wielders may prefer to use the less alienating kinds, but there are limitations on their capacity to mobilize these kinds as well as on their understanding of the dynamics involved, with the consequence that they may opt to use a more alienating kind of power[11] even where this is not otherwise necessary.

The societal-guidance approach thus adds to the exploration of the asset base of a unit the degree to which it is mobilized for collective action and which kinds of power are mobilized. These added factors, in turn, determine to a considerable degree how alienating societal control will be and whether relations between the elites and the other units will be those of open conflict, encapsulated conflict, or co-operation.

II. Consensus Formation

So far guidance of change has been explored from a "downward" view, from the controlling overlayer to the controlled underlayer; even the discussion of the concepts of communication feedback and subject resistance has been from the viewpoint of a controlling agent. The main difference, though, between societal guidance and electronic cybernetics is that in the

---

[10] I suggested elsewhere that this classification is exhaustive and explored the possibilities of mixed kinds and the indicators involved. See my *A Comparative Analysis of Complex Organizations* (New York: Free Press, 1961), pp. 4-6.

[11] *Ibid.*, pp. 3-22.

societal realm we must systematically take into account that the controlled units have some of the controlling capacities themselves; they input knowledge, make decisions, pursue goals, and exercise power. Hence the capacity of any one unit to act is determined only in part by its ability to control the others. It is similarly affected by the degree to which the goals it has chosen to pursue and the means it employs are compatible with those preferred by other units—that is, the degree of consensus.

Consensus, the congruence of preferences of the units concerned, is viewed by typical sociological theories as largely given (or changing under the impact of ongoing processes); voluntaristic theories tend to view it as open to manipulation by charismatic leadership and/or mass media. From the viewpoint of a theory of societal guidance, consensus is the result of a process in which given preferences *and* guided efforts affect each other, the outcome of which tends to be in continual flux. Consensus needs to be continuously revised as new groups rise and the relations among old ones, as well as their preferences, change. A consensus that becomes institutionalized and loses the capacity to adapt and transform is hence likely to become increasingly inauthentic, representing yesterday's society but unresponsive to the contemporary, changing one. In the following discussion, unless specifically so indicated, the consensus referred to is dynamic, authentic, and responsive.

There is a trade-off curve between control and consensus; that is, for any given level of activation, the more consensus, the less need for control, and the less consensus, the more need for control if the same level of realization of goals is to be maintained. Which "mix" is used, though, is not without consequences; it affects the levels of alienation and resistance and hence the future capacity to act. Of course, when both consensus *and* control are higher, more change can be guided than when both are lower, without an increase in alienation. The additional consensus absorbs the additional alienation which the additional control would otherwise have generated by allowing greater reliance on the less alienating kinds of power or by achieving action in unison without that power being exercised. . . .

III. A Synthesizing View: The Active Society

A. A Typology of Societies

We turn now to illustrate a synthesizing perspective on social processes that may be attained once our understanding of the various components of societal guidance is more advanced; at the present stage, little more than a brief illustration can be provided. Using control and consensus formation as two dimensions of a property space, we characterize, in an ideal-typical manner, a society which is high on both as comparatively active, low on both as passive, high on control but low on consensus as overmanaged, and low on control but high on consensus as drifting.

The *passive society* is approximated by those primitive societies whose polities are highly undeveloped, especially "segmental" tribes.[12] Their low level of societal self-control is obvious. Consensus seems to be not only largely static but also hardly mobilizable for most *societal* goals. Typically, there is little machiney to form consensus if additional consensus were necessary, let us say, because of an external challenge. Hence, while "background" consensus may be quite high, the consensus-*formation* capacity is low. One indicator of this low capacity is that, when primitive societies do act, coercion often plays a rather central role in overcoming internal resistance.[13]

The *active society* maintains a level of control that is not lower and is possibly even higher than that of overmanaged societies, and it forms at least as much consensus as drifting societies. This is possible because the active society commands both more effective control and more effective consensus-formation mechanisms since it can rely more heavily on the less alienating kinds of power, especially on the normative one. Also, a high level of consensus formation can be achieved only at a high level of activation, because only under this condition can a large number and variety of goals (the various subsocieties and the society as a unit are committed to) be realized. This realization cannot be achieved by mere increase of societal control, as effective control requires the support of those subject to it. And, if the level of control is to be raised without at the same time raising alienation, a high capacity to form consensus is required. Thus, high control and high consensus, high activation and low alienation, are mutually reinforcing.

Finally, the active society has the highest capacity of the four ideal types for self-transformation, which is the most effective mechanism to avoid widespread alienation, because it makes it possible for the rise of radically different goals and subsocieties to be accommodated by the same system since it changes its basic pattern. If the societal pattern is responsive to these changing goals of the members, the membership will tend to be committed rather than alienated, and the society will be active.

The active society is a utopia in that it exists nowhere but is a not a utopia in the sense that it is not possible for a society to become one, for its functional requirements do not appear to violate any sociological law. Social-movement societies, such as Israel in 1948, approximate such an active society. A main difference between a social-movement society and the active one is that the latter stabilizes some social-movement features such as high consensus formation and intense commitment, rather than merely passing through such a phase.

---

12 M. Fortes and E. E. Evans-Pritchard (eds.), *African Political Systems* (London: Oxford University Press, 1950), pp. 197-296.

13 Max Gluckman, *Order and Rebellion in Tribal Africa* (New York: Free Press, 1963), pp. 39-40.

For an active society to be possible, consensus formation must be in part upward, allowing for the authentic expression of the members' preferences and for a real, and not "co-opted," participation. It is a central proposition of the theory of societal guidance that downward mobilization of consensus cannot effectively replace the upward elements; commitment achieved through mobilization of the sources of information and mass propaganda is short-lived and not nearly as effective as authentic, upward consensus formation, even while its spell lasts. The tenor of most of the literature on the subject assumes the opposite position, but we are not aware of any body of evidence which would allow this rather central question to be settled.

The *overmanaged*, high-control, low-consensus type is approximated by the totalitarian societies. Typically, they have inadequate consensus-formation structures, and those they have are mainly of the built-in variety. Societal action is initially oriented to goals which assume a very high capacity to act, but those are later scaled down, as consensus mechanisms do not allow discovering beforehand where and how much resistance will be encountered in the various subsocieties as various societal changes are attempted. Typically, too, use of the most alienating kind of power, coercion, is high. (While the use of normative power is also high, its being "mixed" with coercive power undermines its effectiveness.[14])

Whether or not overmanaged societies are transformable and what kinds of societies they will become if they are, are two widely debated questions. The discussion is between those who see democratization as taking place and those who argue that the totalitarian societies are ultra-stable.[15] This dichotomy seems not to exhaust the possibilities. Democratization seems unlikely, because democracies are themselves no longer well adapted since their present control and consensus mechanisms are insufficient for the higher level of activation needed and because there is no legitimation of democracy and no democratic experience in the history of most contemporary totalitarian societies. On the other hand, it seems hard to maintain that totalitarian societies are not transformable in view of the far-reaching societal changes in the U.S.S.R. since 1917.

The direction of any such change might be toward an active society whose level of control is relatively closer to that of totalitarian societies than that of the democratic ones; whose less segregated consensus-formation structure is closer to the totalitarian built-in one than the democratic

---

[14] For additional discussion of the difference between "pure" application of normative power and its "mixing" with other kinds of power, see my *A Comparative Analysis* . . . , pp. 55 ff.

[15] The transformation view is presented by Gabriel Almond, *The American People and Foreign Policy* (New York: Frederick A. Praeger, Publishers, 1960), p. xvi; the opposite one by Philip E. Mosely, "Soviet Foreign Policy since the Twenty-second Party Congress," *Modern Age*, VI (Fall, 1962), 343-52.

segregated one, and whose social-movement character can draw for legitimation on the most charismatic period of the totalitarian societies. The sharpest transition would be from reliance on force and propaganda as central means of compliance to a focus on education and utilitarian power; such a transformation, as drastic as it is, is more limited than a shift to a relatively pure utilitarian focus characteristic of capitalistic democracies. In fact, this seems to be a direction of change already evidenced in the U.S.S.R.

Drifting societies are approximated by capitalist democracies. Their most important relevant feature is that they tend to act to introduce significant structural changes only when the need to act is "overdue," in a "crisis," only when broad consensus can be mobilized *before* action is taken. Further, the action taken often does not remove the lag, as the changes introduced are an accommodation of the more conservative to the more change-oriented subsocieties. The second major reason capitalist democracies are drifting societies is that the more powerful subsocieties draw societal assets for their own consumption and power either by neutralizing the societal controls which might have prevented such a deflection or by slanting these controls to serve their subsocietal interests. In either case, as far as the society at large is concerned, it is ineffectual in guiding its processes and change.

B. Consensus, Equality, and Activation

Here an additional concept must be introduced to tie the analysis of consensus formation to the study of assets and alienation, the concept of equality. Equality is used here to refer to an allocative pattern indicated by a distribution profile that approximates a straight line; that is, groupings of the population that are equal in size possess equal amounts of assets. No society is completely egalitarian, but there are obviously significant differences in the degrees of inequality. These, in turn, are associated, though, of course, not on a one-to-one basis, with differences in power. When consensus is formed, it reflects the power relations among the members; the policy agreed upon tends to be closer to that preferred by the more powerful subsocieties. It is as though the weaker members say to themselves that they had better go along with a suggested policy, in which their concurrence is traded for some concessions, for fear that otherwise the powerful would impose a policy even more removed from their preferences. The amount of alienation that remains in the weaker units, however, is related to the measure of inequality. Consensus which leaves little alienation can be formed only under conditions of fairly high equality.

While this cannot be demonstrated here, we suggest that there is a secular historical trend toward a reduction in inequality among the subsocieties (e.g., classes, regions) making up the capitalistic democracies, although so far this reduction has been limited. (The trend is fairly obvious as far as political rights and status symbols are concerned; it is less clear with regard to economic well-being.) Continuation and acceleration of such a trend, if they were to take place, would move democratic societies in an active direction by allowing the formation of more consensus with less alienating undertones and more facing of societal problems as they arise. A major force which propels the transition from a drifting toward an active society is the mobilization of the weaker collectivities; this is triggered by the spread of education, changes in employment opportunities, and other factors that generate imbalanced status sets, as well as by the priming effect of some elites, especially intellectual ones. Since this statement is rather central to our conception of societal change as far as the transition of Western societies into the postmodern (see below for definition) period is concerned, the assumptions implied should be briefly outlined.

As we see it, transformation of capitalist democracies is not propelled by *conflict* among *classes* but by *interaction* among *organized collectivities*. Thus, the collectivities involved may be ethnic groups or regional communities and not just classes, and the relationship among the subsocieties might be of coalition, limited adversary, etc., and not necessarily all-out conflict. Above all, the units of action are not the collectivities per se but that part of each which has been mobliized by organizations. Thus, history is not affected by the working class as such, which is a passive unit, but by labor unions, labor parties, social-protest movements that mobilize a segment of the working class. (The same could be said about the civil rights movement and Negro Americans, national-independence movements and colonial people, etc.)

Collectivities are bases of potential power, but generally only a small fraction of these potentialities are actualized for purposes of societal action and change. The capacity of any collectivity to influence the pattern of societal change, its actual societal power, depends as much on its capacity to mobilize—that is, *on the outcome of the internal struggle between mobilizers and the immobilized*—as on the collectivity's potential power base.

It may be said that the capacity to mobilize is itself determined by the distribution of assets *among* the collectivities, that the more powerful units hold down the capacity to mobilize of the weaker societal units. While this is a valid observation, it is also true that the mobilization of any collectivity reduces the capacity of other collectivities to hold it down. For each point in time, hence, it is necessary to study not only the power potential of a societal actor but also his mobilization capacity, which affects his actual power at this point in time. The dynamic analysis then proceeds by comparing changes in potential and actual power over time and the effects of changes in the power of some actors over that of the others. A study of societal change which focuses largely on the stratification relations among collectivities (as Marx tended to do), not to mention one which excludes power analysis altogether, provides at best a fragmental theory of societal change.

What does all this imply for the transformation of capitalistic democracies? In these societies, most members of most collectivities have a formal right to participate in the political process, an egalitarian political institutional status unmatched in their societal positions. An increasing number are also gaining an education, which has a mobilizing effect.[16] For historical reasons which need not be explored here, campus groups, professionals, clergy, middle-class members of ethnic minorities, all of which command mobilizing skills, are allowed to exercise them and serve as mobilizers of the weaker collectivities, within the limits set by various constraints. And, as at the same time weaker collectivities are becoming increasingly mobilizable and the number of mobilizers is increasing, the total effect is increased societal power of the heretofore weaker (and underprivileged) collectivities. The effect of the mobilization of weaker collectivities, which is only in part neutralized by countermobilization of more powerful collectivities, is to transform the society in the direction of a relatively more egalitarian and active one. Whether such transformation will sooner or later lead to a showdown between the powerful and the mobilizing collectivities, or whether the mobilization will run out of steam on its own, or whether the scales will be tipped for an active society—that is, whether a structural *transformation* will take place—are questions our study of societal guidance points to but cannot at present answer.

We can conclude, however, that at least at the present both overmanaged and drifting societies seem to be leaning in the direction of an active society, rather than either of these two less active societies becoming the prevalent type. The new means of communication and of knowledge technology seem to be working in this direction in both kinds of societies; continued mobilization of the weaker collectivities in capitalist societies and increased pluralism in totalitarian societies may also be supportive of such a transformation. The new cybernetic capacities that are increasingly available to societies since 1945 offer a new range of societal options and hence mark a period that may be referred to as the post-modern one. And 1945 also marks the opening of the atomic age and hence suggests that a major issue for macrosociology, not touched upon here, is that of changing, not the systems' structures, but their boundaries. Answering the question as to which conditions favor and which block the rise of active societies and the transforma-

---

[16] For a review of several studies which show correlations between education and political activation, see Lester W. Milbrath, *Political Participation* (Chicago: Rand McNally & Co., 1965), pp. 42-154.

tion of an anarchic world into a communal one seems to us to require a macrosociology on top of prevailing "universal" theories; a theory of societal guidance may provide a systematic sociological framework for such an approach. It may also provide an avenue to carry the sociologists' contributions to these societal transformations.

CHAPTER 18

DAVID C. McCLELLAND

Business Drive and
National Achievement

What accounts for the rise in civilization? Not external resources (*i.e.,* markets, minerals, trade routes, or factories), but the entrepreneurial spirit which exploits those resources—a spirit found most often among businessmen.

Who is ultimately responsible for the pace of economic growth in poor countries today? Not the economic planners or the politicians, but the executives whose drive (or lack of it) will determine whether the goals of the planners are fulfilled.

Why is Russia developing so rapidly that—if it continues its present rate of growth—it will catch up economically with the most advanced country in the world, the United States, in 25 or 30 years? Not, as the USSR claims, because of the superiority of its Communist system, but because—by hook or by crook—it has managed to develop a stronger spirit of entrepreneurship among executives than we have today in the US.

How can foreign aid be most efficiently used to help poor countries develop rapidly? Not by simply handing money over to their politicians or budget makers, but by using it in ways that will select, encourage, and develop those of their business executives who have a vigorous entrepreneurial spirit or a strong drive for achievement. In other words: *invest in a man, not just in a plan.*

What may be astonishing about some of these remarks is that they come from a college professor and not from the National Association of Manufacturers. They are not the defensive drum rattlings of an embattled capitalist, but are my conclusions, based on nearly 15 years of research, as a strictly academic psychologist, into the human motive that appears to be largely

From David C. McClelland, "Business Drive and National Achievement," *Harvard Business Review,* XL (1962), No. 4. Reprinted by permission of the author and the publisher.

responsible for economic growth—research which has recently been sum-marized in my book, entitled *The Achieving Society*.[1]

Since I am an egghead from way back, nothing surprises me more than finding myself rescuing the businessman from the academic trash heap, dust-ing him off, and trying to give him the intellectual respectability that he has had a hard time maintaining for the last 50 years or so. For the fact is that the businessman has taken a beating, not just from the Marxists, who pictured him as a greedy capitalist, and the social critics, who held him responsible for the Great Depression of the 1930's, but even from himself, deep in his heart.

•

But now the research I have done has come to the businessman's rescue by showing that everyone has been wrong, that it is *not* profit per se that makes the businessman tick but a strong desire for achievement, for doing a good job. Profit is simply one measure among several of how well the job has been done, but it is not necessarily the goal itself.

The Achievement Goal

But what exactly does the psychologist mean by the "desire for achieve-ment"? How does he measure it in individuals or in nations? How does he know that it is so important for economic growth? Is it more important for businessmen to have this desire than it is for politicians, bishops, or generals? These are the kinds of questions which are answered at great length and with as much scientific precision as possible in my book. Here we must be content with the general outline of the argument, and develop it particularly as it applies to businessmen.

To begin with, psychologists try to find out what a man spends his time thinking and daydreaming about when he is not under pressure to think about anything in particular. What do his thoughts turn to when he is by himself or not engaged in a special job? Does he think about his family and friends, about relaxing and watching television, about getting his superior off his back? Or does he spend his time thinking and planning how he can "sell" a partic-ular customer, cut production costs, or invent a better steam trap or tooth-paste tube?

If a man spends his time thinking about doing things better, the psychol-ogist says he has a concern for achievement. In other words, he cares about achievement or he would not spend so much time thinking about it. If he spends his time thinking about family and friends, he has a concern for affiliation; if he speculates about who is boss, he has a concern for power, and so on. What differs in my approach from the one used by many psycholo-

---

[1] David C. McClelland, *The Achieving Society* (Princeton, N.J.: D. Van Nostrand Co., 1961).

gists is that my colleagues and I have not found it too helpful simply to *ask* a person about his motives, interests, and attitudes. Often he himself does not know very clearly what his basic concerns are—even more often he may be ashamed and cover some of them up. So what we do is to try and get a sample of his normal waking thoughts by asking him just to tell a few stories about some pictures.

Stories within Stories

Let us take a look at some typical stories written by US business executives. These men were asked to look briefly at a picture—in this case, a man at a worktable with a small family photograph at one side—and to spend about five minutes writing out a story suggested by the picture. Here is a very characteristic story:

> The engineer is at work on Saturday when it is quiet and he has taken time to do a little daydreaming. He is the father of the two children in the picture —the husband of the woman shown. He has a happy home life and is dreaming about some pleasant outing they have had. He is also looking forward to a repeat of the incident which is now giving him pleasure to think about. He plans on the following day, Sunday, to use the afternoon to take his family for a short trip.

Obviously, no achievement-related thoughts have come to the author's mind as he thinks about the scene in the picture. Instead, it suggests spending time pleasantly with his family. His thoughts run along *affiliative* lines. He thinks readily about interpersonal relationships and having fun with other people. This, as a matter of fact, is the most characteristic reaction to this particular picture. But now consider another story:

> A successful industrial designer is at his "work bench" toying with a new idea. He is "talking it out" with his family in the picture. Someone in the family dropped a comment about a shortcoming in a household gadget, and the designer has just "seen" a commercial use of the idea. He has picked up ideas from his family—he is "telling" his family what a good idea it is, and "confidentially" he is going to take them on a big vacation because "their" idea was so good. The idea will be successful, and family pride and mutual admiration will be strengthened.

The author of this story maintains a strong interest in the family and in affiliative relationships, but has added an achievement theme. The family actually has helped him innovate—get a new idea that will be successful and obviously help him get ahead. Stories which contain references to good new ideas, such as a new product, an invention, or a unique accomplishment of any sort, are scored as reflecting a concern for achievement in the person who writes them. In sum, this man's mind tends to run most easily along the lines of accomplishing something or other. Finally, consider a third story:

> The man is an engineer at a drafting board. The picture is of his family. He has a problem and is concentrating on it. It is merely an everyday occurrence—a problem which requires thought. How can he get that bridge to take the stress of possible high winds? He wants to arrive at a good solution of the problem by himself. He will discuss the problem with a few other engineers and make a decision which will be a correct one—he has the earmarks of competence.

The man who wrote this story—an assistant to a vice president, as a matter of fact—notices the family photograph, but that is all. His thoughts tend to focus on the problem that the engineer has to solve. In the scant five minutes allowed, he even thinks of a precise problem—how to build a bridge that will take the stress of possible high winds. He notes that the engineer wants to find a good solution by himself, that he goes and gets help from other experts and finally makes a correct decision. These all represent different aspects of a complete achievement sequence—defining the problem, wanting to solve it, thinking of means of solving it, thinking of difficulties that get in the way of solving it (either in one's self or in the environment), thinking of people who might help in solving it, and anticipating what would happen if one succeeded or failed.

Each of these different ideas about achievement gets a score of $+1$ in our scoring system so that the man in the last incident gets a score of $+4$ on the scale of concern or need for achievement (conventionally abbreviated to n achievement). Similarly, the first man gets a score of -1 for his story since it is completely unrelated to achievement, and the second man a score of $+2$ because there are two ideas in it which are scorable as related to achievement.

Each man usually writes six such stories and gets a score for the whole test. The coding of the stories for "achievement imagery" is so objective that two expert scorers working independently rarely disagree. In fact, it has recently been programed for a high-speed computer that does the scoring rapidly, with complete objectivity and fairly high accuracy. What the score for an individual represents is the frequency with which he tends to think spontaneously in achievement terms when that is not clearly expected of him (since the instructions for the test urge him to relax and to think freely and rapidly).

Thinking Makes It So

What are people good for who think like this all the time? It doesn't take much imagination to guess that they might make particularly good business executives. People who spend a lot of their time thinking about getting ahead, inventing new gadgets, defining problems that need to be solved, considering alternative means of solving them, and calling in experts for help should also be people who in real life *do* a lot of these things or at the very best are readier to do them when the occasion arises.

I recognize, of course, that this is an assumption that requires proof. But, as matters turned out, our research produced strong factual support. . . . In three countries representing different levels and types of economic development managers or executives scored considerably higher on the average in achievement thinking than did professionals or specialists of comparable education and background. Take two democratic countries:

> In the United States the comparison was between matched pairs of unit managers and specialists of the same position level, age, educational background, and length of service in the General Electric Company. The managers spent more of their time in the test writing about achievement than the specialists did.
> The same was true of middle-level executives from various companies in Italy when contrasted with students of law, medicine, and theology who were roughly of the same intelligence level and social background.

In other words, it takes a concern for achievement to be a manager in a foreign country like Italy, for instance, just as it does in the United States. It is worth noting in passing, however, that the level of achievement thinking among Italian managers is significantly lower than it is among American managers—which, as will be shown later, quite probably has something to do with the lower level and rate of economic development in Italy.

What about a Communist country? The figures for Poland are interesting, because (1) the level of concern for achievement is about what it is in the United States and (2) even in businesses owned and operated by the state, as in Poland, managers tend to have a higher concern for achievement than do other professionals.

Another even more striking result, . . . is the fact that there is *no real difference* between the average *n* achievement score of managers working for the US government (9.3) and those in US private business generally (8.90). Apparently, a manager working for the Bureau of Ships in the Department of the Navy spends as much time thinking about achievement as his counterpart in Ford or Sears, Roebuck; government service does not weaken his entrepreneurial spirit. Whether he is able to be as effective as he might be in private business is another matter, not touched on here.

Careful quantitative studies of the prevalence of achievement concern among various types of executives also yield results in line with what one would expect. Thus, sales managers score higher than other types of managers do.

In general, more successful managers tend to score higher than do less successful managers (except in government service where promotion depends more on seniority). The picture is clear in small companies, where the president tends to score higher than his associates. In large companies, the picture is a little more complicated. Men in the lowest salary brackets (earning less than $20,000 a year) definitely have the lowest average *n* achievement scores, while those in the next bracket up ($20,000 to $25,000 a year) have the highest average *n* achievement level. Apparently an achievement concern helps one get out of the ranks of the lowest paid into a higher income bracket. But from there on, the trend fades. Men in the highest income brackets have a somewhat lower average concern for achievement, and apparently turn their thoughts to less achievement-oriented concerns. Possibly these men are doing well enough to relax a little.

•

Achieving Nations

If the theory underlying the experiments with determining *n* achievement in individuals is correct, then what is true for groups of individuals might well prove true for nations. Does a high achievement concern herald a nation's rise? Let's take a look at the facts.

Naturally, tests of individual businessmen in particular countries would not prove very much about the influence of achievement concern on the nation's success. However, we figured that, by coding popular literature of past and present, we could get a rough estimate of the strength of the concern for achievement in a given country at a given time period. So we took samples from various time periods of a wide variety of the most popular imaginative literature we could find—poems, songs, plays—and scored them for *n* achievement just as we had scored the simple stories written by individuals.

When we plotted the number of achievement ideas per hundred lines sampled in a given time period against economic indexes for the same time period, we got two curves that showed a very interesting relationship to each other. Normally, we found, a high level of concern for achievement is followed some 50 years or so later by a rapid rate of economic growth and prosperity. Such was certainly the case in ancient Greece and in Spain in the late Middle Ages. Furthermore, in both cases a decline in achievement concern was followed very soon after by a decline in economic welfare. The relationship between the two curves is shown most dramatically in Figure 20-1, which plots the data for the 300-year time span from Tudor times to the Industrial Revolution in England:

There were two waves of economic growth in this time period, one smaller one around 1600 and a much larger one around 1800 at the beginning of the Industrial Revolution. Each wave was preceded by a wave of concern for achievement reflected in popular literature, a smaller one prior to the growth spurt around 1600 and a larger one prior to the Industrial Revolution.

What clearer evidence could one ask for? What people are concerned about determines what they do, and what they do determines the outcome of history!

Present Confirms Past

In modern nations, too, the picture is very much the same. Children's stories used in public school textbooks proved to be the most standardized form of popular literature that we could get from a large number of different countries. As a matter of fact, the simple imaginative stories that every country uses to teach its children to read are very similar in format to the stories produced by individuals when we test them as described earlier, particularly if one concentrates as we did on second-, third-, and fourth-grade readers, where normally political influences are quite unimportant. The stories could be coded quite easily by the standard n achievement scoring system.

Growth rates had to be estimated from the only figures available that could be trusted on such a wide variety of countries—namely, the figures showing electric power consumption—but there is ample evidence to show that electricity consumed is probably the best single available index of gross national income in modern times.

The n scores, when compared with the subsequent rates of economic growth for various countries, confirm the findings of the historical studies to a surprising extent. The higher the n achievement level in the children's readers around 1925, the more rapid the subsequent rate of economic growth. (For 22 countries, the correlation was actually a substantial .53.) Furthermore, the higher the n achievement level in a country's children's readers around 1950, the more rapid its rate of growth between 1952-1958. In fact, of 20 countries above average in n achievement in 1950, 13 (or 65 per cent) showed a rapid rate of economic growth in 1952-1958. Whereas, of 19 low in n achievement, only 5 (or 26 per cent) achieved a rapid rate of growth.

Prediction Possibilities

How meaningful are these findings, especially when one realizes the crudity of the data? In a certain sense, the cruder one admits the data to be, the more remarkable the findings appear. After all, the data suggest that one could have got a pretty good line on the economic future of various countries by studying its stories for children in 1925—regardless of a major depression, a World War, and a host of other political and economic factors.

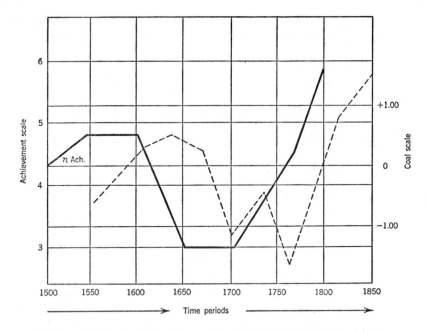

Achievement thinking (n. Ach.) = Mean number of achievement images per 100 lines.
Rate of industrial growth = Rate of gain in coal imports at London, as deviations from average trend (standard deviation units).

FIGURE 18-1. How achievement thinking expressed in English literature predicts the rate of industrial growth fifty years later.

Is it possible that we have stumbled on a way of predicting the future course of history? And from such an almost laughable source—stories for children—rather than the serious pronouncements of statesmen, generals, and economists? How is it possible?

The best interpretation of such findings would appear to run something as follows. The stories tell us what is on the minds of significant elites in the country, what these influential persons tend to think about most naturally, when they are "off guard," so to speak, and not under any particular pressure to think one thing or another. In this sense, the stories are exactly analogous to the ones written for us by individuals. If you ask a man whether he is interested in achievement, the chances are that he will tell you that of course he is. Similarly, if you were to ask a country's leaders whether they wanted their nation to forge ahead, they would find it unpatriotic to say no. But, regardless of what such leaders say in public, the stories in the children's readers of many nations will show whether their peoples' thoughts turn naturally to achievement or to matters other than achievement.

Here is an illustration. Take a simple story theme like one in which some children are building a boat. Such themes are frequently borrowed by one culture from another and appear in several different readers, but the way they are embroidered may be quite different and quite revealing. For example:

> In Country A, an *achievement*-oriented country, the emphasis is on making the boat, on constructing something that will work and not sink or tip over in a strong wind.
>
> In Country B, the emphasis may be on *affiliation,* on the fun that the children have in playing together to sail their boat. Here little may be said about the details of constructing a seaworthy craft and much about the personal interaction of the children.
>
> In Country C, the story may center on *power,* and describe how the children were organized to produce the boat. One boy might set himself up as a leader, coordinating the work of the other children and telling them what to do.

Apparently, what comes most readily to the minds of these authors—whether concepts of achievement, affiliation, or power—reflects sufficiently well what is on the minds of key people in the country. And not only will these concepts seem natural and pleasing to the readers of these stories but will determine what they spend their time doing in the years to come. Thus, if the stories stress achievement, it means that an entrepreneurial spirit is abroad in the land. It indicates that many key people are thinking in achievement terms even when they do not need to.

In a nation, a strong achievement orientation affects particularly the business or economic sector of the population. And if the entrepreneurial types are strongly motivated to do well, they apparently succeed in getting the economy moving at a faster rate. So the children's stories are a symptom of the quality or "drive" of the entrepreneurial sector of an economy.

Rising and Falling Nations

With this in mind it is interesting to look at scores for particular countries —if only to make a better guess as to where to invest one's money! A generation ago, the North European countries, particularly Sweden and England, were very high in *n* achievement, but both have fallen in the 1950's to well below average. Is it just a coincidence that one hears reports of stagnation or "maturity" in both economies? Are England's present difficulties the fault of outside circumstances, or do these difficulties stem from the fact that its citizens have lost their achievement drive? For some reason, the Central European countries—France, Germany, and Russia—were all low in achievement concern in 1925, but by the 1950's all had increased sharply.

The case of Russia is particularly critical for us. How does the United States stand in achievement motivation as compared to the USSR? According to a historical study, achievement concern in the United States increased regularly from 1800 to around 1890 but has decreased more or less regularly since, although there is a possibility that the decline has leveled off in the past 30 years. We are still above average and, in fact, were at approximately the same level as Russia in 1950, although we were probably on the way down while they were certainly on the way up.

From the point of view of this analysis, the argument as to whether a socialist or a free enterprise system is the better way of stimulating an economy has been based on a false premise all along. Americans claimed that the success of their economy resulted, naturally, from the free enterprise system. Then, when the Soviet Union scored successes in outer space and in other fields, the Russians immediately claimed these great economic and technological achievements stemmed from the superiority of their system.

Both contentions may well be wrong. Economic success and technological development depend on achievement motivation, and the rapid rate of Russian economic growth is due to an increase in her achievement concern just as ours was a generation or so earlier. There are other issues involved in comparing the two social systems, of course, but so far as this particular issue is concerned it has been misunderstood by both sides.

Need for Acceptance

There is one final question that must be answered before we move on. Is it possible that achievement motivation will be aroused in *any* nation which comes in contact with modern technology and vividly sees the opportunity for a better life? Can't achievement motivation be "borrowed" or assimilated from one nation to another? Are there not good illustrations of countries in which need for achievement has risen as they see more and more clearly the possibilities of growing and developing into modern, economically advanced nations? Are we just describing the "revolution of rising expectations" in fancy psychological jargon?

Opportunity is part of the story, of course. It does arouse people to act, but it arouses precisely those who have some need for achievement *already*. The soil must be ready for the seeds, if they are to grow. After all, many countries have been in touch with Western technology for generations—for example, the Islamic nations around the Mediterranean; yet they have been very slow to respond to the possibilities of a better life clearly presented to them all this time.

Consider, for example, a nation like Nigeria, which provides a good illustration of how opportunity and motivation must interact. Nigeria is essentially a federation of three regions, each of which is dominated by a different cultural group. Only one of these groups—the Yoruba—is known to be very high in need for achievement. In fact, long before the Yoruba had much contact with the West, this tribe was noted for its skill and interest in trade and native financial transactions. An indication of the validity of the achievement theory is shown by the fact that the Yoruba tribe, when exposed to new opportunities, produced a much stronger and more successful economic response than did the other tribes—as would be predicted. The regional bank operated by the Yoruba is in a much sounder position, for example, than the other two regional banks in Nigeria.

Opportunity challenges those who are achievement-oriented. Like two other groups high in *n* achievement, American Jews and American Catholics between the ages of 35 and 45, . . . the Yoruba reacted vigorously to develop economic opportunities as they became available. Exposure to economic and technological opportunities did not produce as vigorous a response from groups lower in *n* achievement in Nigeria any more than a similar exposure has done through the years to similar low *n* achievement groups in the United States.

What Can We Do?

Is it inevitable that the achievement concern shown by US citizens should continue to decline? Must we fade out in time as all other civilizations have in the past? Not if we understand what is happening and take steps to change it. Not if we move decisively and quickly to influence the sources of achievement concern in individuals and in our nation.

What are those sources? Clearly, not race or climate—those traditional external explanations of the superior energies of some nations. For Russia's *n* achievement level has increased decisively since 1925, while Sweden's and England's have dropped. Certainly there have been no equally decisive changes in the gene pools or the climates of those nations in that time period.

In fact, external factors are usually unimportant, though occasionally they may play a role, as they have in helping to create generally high levels of *n* achievement in immigrant countries like the United States, Canada, and Australia. Such nations tended to attract immigrants higher in *n* achievement, because:

1. They drew their population initially from countries that were higher in achievement concern than those from which the Latin American countries drew.

2. They provided a haven for many persecuted religious minorities whose achievement concern was very strong.

3. They did not provide as many opportunities for getting rich quick as did Mexico and Peru, for example, with their plentiful supplies of gold and silver.

In short, countries like the United States were lucky. The barrier to migration was so formidable that primarily those with high *n* achievement climbed it.

Historians have sometimes claimed that it was the great frontier in the United States that provided the challenge and stimulus to development. Nonsense. Great frontiers have existed and still exist in many South American countries without eliciting a similar response. It was the achievement-oriented immigrants to America who regarded the frontier as a challenge to be over-come. It was not the frontier that made them achievement-oriented. Opportunities, like new frontiers, always exist, but it takes a certain kind of person to see them and believe he can exploit them.

While our distance from Europe, our tolerance for religious minorities, our good fortune in drawing immigrants initially from countries high in n achievement tended to ensure that we got more citizens with high achievement motivation, our later restrictive immigration policies have drastically reduced our chances of continuing to receive such people. These policies continue to give preference to immigrants from the North European countries, whose achievement drive has dropped significantly, and to restrict immigration from other countries where the n achievement has been rising sharply. It would be a tragic irony of history if in an endeavor to protect ourselves, we managed to shut off the supply of that entrepreneurial spirit that made our country great!

Sources of Achievement

Where does strong achievement motivation come from? Values, beliefs, ideology—these are the really important sources of a strong concern for achievement in a country. Studies of the family have shown, for instance, that for a boy three factors are important in producing high n achievement—parents' high standards of achievement, warmth and encouragement, and a father who is not dominating and authoritarian. Here is a typical study that reveals this fact:

> A group of boys were blindfolded and asked to stack irregularly shaped blocks on top of each other with their left hands, at home in front of their parents. Separately, the mothers and fathers were asked how high they thought their sons could stack the blocks. Both parents of a boy with high n achievement estimated that their boys should do better; they expected more of him than did the parents of a boy with low n achievement. They also encouraged him more and gave him more affection and reward while he was actually doing the task. Finally, the fathers of boys with high n achievement directed the behavior of their sons much less when they were actually stacking the blocks; that is, they told them less often to move their hands this way or that, to try harder, to stop jiggling the table, and so forth than did the fathers of boys with low n achievement.

Other studies have shown that fathers must be respected by their sons; but after the boy is capable of achieving something for himself, his father must stop directing every step he takes if the boy is to develop a strong concern for achievement.

In a sense, however, these family studies only push the question further back. Where did the parents get their standards? Why do some emphasize achievement and affectionately reward self-reliance? Because, very simply, they themselves believe in achievement for their family or for their political, social, or religious group. For one reason or another they are caught up in some great wave of achievement ideology.

One of the paradoxes of history is that often the achievement concern was not itself initially directed toward business or economics. For instance, the two great waves of achievement concern in the history of England shown in Figure 20-1 were each associated with waves of Protestant reform or revival, whose explicit aims were not secular but strictly religious. The Methodists, for example, in the second wave of the English Protestant revival, stressed religious perfection in this life; yet even John Wesley recognized with some puzzlement that devout Methodists tended to get rich, a fact which he considered a handicap in attaining religious perfection.

But now we can understand what happened. The strong concern for Christian perfection in this world tended to produce an achievement orientation in Methodist parents and their sons that turned the boys toward business because, as we have shown above, an achievement concern is most easily satisfied in business. In our day, it is the secular religions of nationalism and communism that have placed the highest emphasis on achievement and tended to create higher levels of n achievement in underdeveloped and Communist countries. Communism lays the same claims to superiority as a means of salvation that Christianity once did. However wrong we may feel it to be, we must recognize that it tends to create a strong atmosphere of achievement that has important consequences for economic growth.

The Achievement Challenge

If we are to compete successfully with Russia in the economic sphere, we must develop an achievement ideology at least as strong as hers. If we are to help poor countries develop rapidly and become self-reliant, we must recognize that the first order of priority lies in fostering the entrepreneurial spirit in those countries, not in simply providing them with material capital or in meeting their physical needs.

Oddly enough, a businessman knows this about his own company. He knows that in the final analysis it is the spirit in the company that counts most—the entrepreneurial drive of the executives, the feeling of all that they are working together to achieve a common goal; it is not "hardware" that counts in the long run—the size and slickness of the plant or the money in the bank. These assets will melt away like snow in a hot sun without the proper achievement orientation in the company. Knowing this, the wise executive acts accordingly. He is concerned to keep the achievement orientation of the company alive by talking about its aims, by setting moderate but realizable goals for himself and his associates, by assigning personal responsibility, by making sure that people know how well they are doing, by selecting executives with high n achievement or by developing it in those who need it.

What is true for a business is also true for a country, but this is not widely recognized. And we must realize that it is important to foster the achieving spirit not only at home but abroad if we are to be effective as a nation. American foreign policy is currently based on two main strategies: (a) the provision of political freedom and (b) material aid. Both are excellent goals, but they are not enough. How long would a company last if its chief goals were freedom from interference by others and freedom from want? It needs positive, specific goals such as a more effective marketing program, or a strict cost reduction program; something dynamic is necessary to keep a company —and a country—alive and growing.

Over and over again we have failed to learn the lesson that political freedom without a strong drive for progress is empty and impossible to maintain for long. China was politically free under Chiang Kai-shek, but it lacked the dynamic of a really self-sacrificing achievement effort until it was taken over by the Communists. Unless we learn our lesson and find ways of stimulating that drive for achievement under freedom in poor countries, the Communists will go on providing it all around the world. We can go on building dikes to maintain freedom and impoverishing ourselves to feed and arm the people behind those dikes, but only if we develop the entrepreneurial spirit in those countries will we have a sound foreign policy. Only then can they look after their own dikes and become economically self-sufficient.

Compare India and China, for example. Despite newspaper reports to the contrary, economic experts assure us that China is developing much more rapidly economically today than is India. Why? Is it because the West has given less material help to India than the Communist world has to China? Probably not. Is it because there is less political freedom in India than in China? Certainly not. Yet if the keystones of our foreign aid policy are the ensuring of political freedom and the granting of economic aid, these measures are clearly not doing very well as far as developing India is concerned. Russia has apparently exported something more important to China—namely, an achievement dynamic that has galvanized the whole country. There is absolutely no evidence that this dynamic needs to be associated with regimentation and lack of personal freedom as it is in China, for the United States had this dynamic once, still has quite a lot of it, and could export it more effectively—if we really tried.

●

If there is one thing that all this research has taught me, it is that men can shape their own destiny, that external difficulties and pressures are not nearly so important in shaping history as some people have argued. It is how people respond to those challenges that matters, and how they respond depends on how strong their concern for achievement is. So the question of what happens to our civilization or to our business community depends quite literally on how much time tens of thousands or even millions of us spend thinking about achievement, about setting moderate achievable goals, taking calculated risks, assuming personal responsibility, and finding out how well we have done our job. The answer is up to us.

PART III

SPHERES OF CHANGE

The Modern Society

Introduction

With all due respect for the differences among societies, it can be said that they all do seem to change from a traditional to a modern type. Once all societies were "traditional"; probably one day they will all be "modern." It cannot be denied that, for the past three centuries or so, a number of nations have been the forerunners of modernization, the first to reach a new type of social structure which many other countries now seem bent on acquiring. This part of the volume is devoted to the examination of the emergence of modern society, not on the general societal level—this was discussed earlier, for instance in the work of Toennies—but in one social sphere after another.

In the most general terms, the transition from traditional to modern society involves: (1) a demographic revolution, in which both the death rate and the birth rate sharply decline; (2) a decrease in the size, scope, and pervasiveness of the family; (3) an opening of the stratification system to much higher rates of mobility; (4) a transition from a tribal or feudal structure to a bureaucracy of the democratic or totalitarian type; (5) a decline in the influence of religion; (6) the separation of education from family and community life, the lengthening and enrichment of the educational process, the development of schools and universities and, more recently, the enormous spread of education, from a monopoly of the few to a property of the many; (7) the growth of a "mass culture" nourished by mass education and the development of mass media of communication; (8) the emergence of a "market economy," and, even more important, of industrialization. (Economic institutions, not discussed in this section, are extensively reviewed in the next.)

But even as these revolutionary changes go on, as traditional societies become modern, important changes are taking place within modern society itself. These may be in line with the major modernization trends, or they may be smaller cross- and counter-currents in the major streams of history.

For instance, Kingsley Davis' discussion of the demographic aspects of modernization points to the radical decline in the death rate which, in

Western societies, was followed by a drastic decline in the birth rate. The "population explosion," which occurs when the decline in the birth rate lags way behind the decline in the death rate, has been a crucial problem for countries now in the process of modernization (discussed in the next part of the volume). Western countries, however, did not suffer from this problem, because they began with a more favorable population–resources ratio, so that resources increases always outweighed population increases; moreover, in later periods, the birth rate declined. Some of them—France, for instance —were even concerned with the opposite problem, the birth rate declining more rapidly than the death rate. This trend, had it continued, would have led to the slow extinction of Western society. Actually, however, after World War II, a cross-current set in, when an upsurge of the birth rate led to a population increase in Western countries. Of course premodernization birth rates were not regained; the major demographic trend of modernization was somewhat offset but not reversed.

In comparison with primitive or traditional society, the importance of the family in modern society has largely declined. With modernization, the nuclear family has been disconnected from the extended one, and kinship ties have been greatly weakened. The family is no longer the unit of production nor the major agency of education. The significance of familial values, too, has been greatly reduced. Still, as can be seen from Burgess' discussion, this has not led toward the extinction of the family. The economic and educational functions of the family have declined, but its importance as a source of companionship and emotional security in a mobile and competitive society has, if anything, increased.

In traditional societies, most people die in the social positions in which they are born. People tend to accept their positions as God-given and do not attempt to change them. Some channels of vertical mobility exist in most traditional societies—for instance, the Church in medieval society— but, as a rule, society is stratified into castes or estates, with fairly rigid social, cultural, economic, and often legal barriers. Modernization involves the opening up of the stratification system. In modern societies, many people die in higher, some in lower, statuses than they were born into; a large proportion of any social group moves upward or downward; and the social groups themselves change their place in the social structure. In the United States, for instance, ethnic groups have moved up the ladder as assimilation progressed, and newer groups have entered at the bottom. Barber's discussion centers around changes within two premodern systems of stratification approximating the "closed" type and around changes within two modern systems of stratification approximating the "open" type. It also deals with the revolutionary changes experienced in the transition from the first to the second type. As we see from these discussions, modernization involves a major trend toward the opening up of the class structure.

The picture is less clearcut so far as the changes within modern society are concerned. Some observers claim that, in the United States for instance, mobility has been diminishing—among other reasons, because largescale immigration has ceased and the economy has not been expanding at the previous rate. Barber, however, points out that what may seem a reversal of the trend is merely a consolidation of its achievements; several social processes are presently going on which serve to "strengthen the American open-class stratification system." But though the channels of mobility are still opening up, this of course is not to suggest that the opening of these channels can continue at anything like its initial pace. According to this view, the major trend that set in with modernization was not reversed or even stopped, but did slow down to some extent.

The degree of mobility directly affects the dynamics of politics. As Mosca points out, in each society there is a ruling minority and a majority that is being ruled. However, the structure of this ruling class as well as the criteria of recruitment into it change with the changes in its predominant societal function. One change that occurred in premodern times was the shift from military skills, first to land-ownership and then to wealth, as criteria of access to the ruling class. While wealth may still facilitate recruitment to the ruling class (or political elite) even in modern times, one of the main characteristics of modernization in the political sphere is that access to the political elite has become open to wider and wider strata of the population. In addition, the potential political power of nonpoliticians has increased enormously. This is true in modern democratic as well as nondemocratic countries, where it becomes evident from the constant flow of communication oriented toward the population at large to sustain its commitment to the regime.

Another major aspect of modernization in the political sphere has been the emergence of the modern state, whose boundaries mostly correspond to those of national identification. Scattered and loosely related smaller units have become integrated into largescale, tightly-knit political entities. The trend of modernization has been one of an ever-increasing concentration of power in the hands of a state that carries out and regulates more and more functions. This is closely connected with a drastic change in the mode of organization of the political structure: the transition from feudalism to bureaucracy. Political bureaucracy, Mosca suggests, first came into being with absolutism, but since then it has been enormously developed and elaborated, and has evolved into the democratic and totalitarian bureaucratic states.

There seems to be no reversal of these trends with the further developments within modern society. However, they do appear to have mostly exhausted themselves. Thus, the scope of political participation has been widened so far that there is little room for further expansion other than on the racial front. Similarly, the process of bureaucratization can no longer proceed at the same rate. As far as the process of state planning and regulation is concerned, there seems to be a movement in opposite directions in the two major sub-types of modern societies: while totalitarian societies, especially those whose industrialization is advanced, seem to somewhat reduce the very pronounced dominance of the state, democratic societies, especially those of the welfare type, seem slowly to increase the comparatively limited role of government; though even at its most extreme, the power of the government in democratic societies is much smaller than in totalitarian ones.

With the advent of modern society, religion retreated so far so fast that it was expected to dissappear. The influence religion had exerted in various social spheres rapidly declined; the proportion of religious people in society diminished; the intensity of religious feelings decreased. The main value system of modern society, the major focus of identification, became secular, of the national-historical type. But, as Herberg points out, over the last decades, especially in the United States, these trends of modernization were largely stopped and to a degree reversed. The number of Americans affiliated with religious bodies has been growing; militant anti-religiousness has practically disappeared; the scope of religion's influence in society has been broadened. This is usually referred to as a "religious revival," although, as Herberg suggested, present-day religion has become largely man-centered, a way of "belonging" socially, and a way of attaining peace of mind. It has little in common with the religion of yesteryear. One can hardly expect society to return to the religious state of premodern times, but on the other hand, within modern society, the trend toward more and more secularization has been arrested and to some degree reversed. It has become increasingly clear that religion is not about to disappear.

One of the unique features of modern society is its vast system of formal education. In this sphere, modernization has meant the vesting of education in specialized institutions, schools of all types. As can be seen from Drucker's discussion, in recent years this kind of education has vastly expanded. Today, more students study more subjects for more years in more schools than ever before. There has been an enormous increase in high school and college attendance in the United States; the educational revolution in Russia has been even more explosive.

The fact that education is no longer exclusive to an elite but has been opened to the masses, as well as the general trend in American society to emphasize adjustment to the group over achievement in work (see Riesman's discussion, Part V), resulted in a certain relaxation of academic standards in many schools and colleges. This trend was reversed to some extent during the late fifties, especially after Russia's achievements in space threw into dramatic relief the importance of high standards of education for a nation's stature. While education can never again become the refined leisure activity of a cultured minority, techniques are being developed to combine mass education with high standards. A combination of screening through high tuition fees in combination with fellowships, honor programs, tutoring, specialized schools, and other devices were to make it easier for education to aim both for quantity and for quality. In the late sixties and early seventies this orientation changed again, toward greater analysis in "open admission," schooling for minorities, community colleges, and above all, a broad based and deep questioning of the value of schooling vs. education by other means (as the Keniston article later in this section indicates).

In the sphere of culture, some of the problems and patterns of modern education are repeated on the adult level. Like education, culture in today's sense was once confined to a minority. With the development of mass education and of mass media of communication, there came into being what has been widely called "mass culture," passive submission to undemanding entertainment. While mass culture certainly is an advance in comparison to previous periods, when the majority of the population had little if any access to any culture whatever, it is often held to block the way for the masses to attain higher levels of culture and, indeed, to endanger the very existence of a higher culture.

The general pattern of the changes, then, seems to suggest that the processes of modernization, at least in some Western countries and especially in the United States, have been more or less "completed," that in a sense the dramatic changes of modernization have exhausted themselves. Many trends have been slowed down or halted; and in some areas, in which modernization has been "overdone," some limited "correcting" crosscurrents have set in. Obviously no society can maintain itself if its birth rate falls below its death rate for a long period. The decline in the educational, economic, and other functions of the family has been compensated for by an ascent of its "companionship" function. Though many people desire absolute equality, it is questionable whether this can ever be attained. At any rate, the trend toward the opening up of channels of mobility, if not reversed or halted, has slowed down. The revival of religion may suggest that there are certain basic questions—especially concerning the creation of the universe and the meaning of death—that no secular ideology can answer satisfactorily. In education and culture there has been no reversal of the trend of encompassing larger and larger numbers; rather a balancing trend has set in, consisting of the attempt to combine quantity and quality. In politics, the trend of bureaucratization has slowed down. The movement toward higher concentration of functions in the hands of the state continues in democratic countries, but is increasingly out of favor with both large segments of the public and the political leadership. It has, to a limited extent, been reversed in totalitarian ones.

In general, old (traditional) structures have been replaced by new (modern) ones, after which some further changes on a smaller scale have modified this trend. In other words, since the old equilibrium was disrupted and a new one came into being, further changes have tended to re-store balance where disproportionate changes made for excessive strains. These changes may be viewed as re-equilibrating processes but not as processes pushing for return to the old traditional equilibrium.

While some people may evaluate the slowing down and the occasional reversals of the larger trends as consolidating the gains of modernization, others may view them as "reactionary." In any case, we do not wish to imply that a perfect balance has been reached, making for permanent stability. But for the near future, modern societies seem comparatively sta-ble, and—barring a major nuclear disaster—unlikely to change rapidly on a large scale.

Kenneth Keniston reviews the alternative positions which have been taken in regard to the societal scope and significance of recent "counter" culture developments and social change movements. He sees on the one side those who view the "uprisings" of the late sixties and early seventies, as temporary setbacks of a trend which still is chiefly one of ever more and better mo-dernity, a position he questions. On the other side, he identifies a position which leads to seeing every wave as the forbinger of a revolutionary storm, disregarding the possibilities that such swellings will subside. Keniston's own stance is a synthesis of these two approaches in which the ongoing modern forces of super-technology and hyper-economy as well as those newer trends primarily oriented to an improvement in the quality of life, and a more humane and just society, can find a place.

In introducing Unger.

from '78 Etzioni ... traditional societies position & destiny,
mostly people die in one born to. Rigid castes or estates,
fairly rigid social, cultural, economic, legal barriers.

182 Etzioni

Have people thought of modern societies as stable (despite
changes associated with their emergence & Marx's
notion capitalism = change) -- i.e. become now
established ... "for the near future, modern societies
seem comparatively stable, and - barring a major
nuclear disaster - unlikely to change rapidly
on a large scale "

Framework of exercise ...

CHAPTER 19

KINGSLEY DAVIS

The Demographic Transition

The Revolutionary Decline in Mortality

The most significant and farreaching modern population trend is the worldwide decline in the death rate. This was not only the *first* major change to be observed in the evolution of the modern demographic cycle, but also the one that has triggered most of the changes, for it was upon mortality that the technological and economic revolution of modern times had its first and main demographic impact.

As early as the eighteenth century in northwestern Europe, the death rate was noticeably undergoing a gradual though fluctuating retreat. The drop became faster and steadier in the nineteenth century, but did not reach its most precipitous fall until early in the present century. (*See* Table 22-1.) A notion of how drastic the reduction was is seen in the fact that in five west European countries, the number of people surviving *to age 60* out of each 1,000 born was greater in the 1940's than the number surviving *to age fifteen* in the 1840's (763 as against 674). Or, to put it another way, in the 1840's, in these five countries on the average, half the population was dead by age 44½, whereas in the 1940's half had not died until age 73½.[1] Among eleven Western countries for which long series of life-tables are available, seven had their most rapid short-run gains in life-expectancy after 1915, three had their most rapid gains between 1900 and 1915, and one fell into the first period with respect to males and into the second period with respect to females. None of the eleven countries had its most rapid extension of life-expectancy prior to 1900.

From Kingsley Davis, "Social Demography," *The Voice of America Forum Lectures,* Behavioral Science Series 17, pp. 3-12. Reprinted by permission of the author and the publisher. This paper was originally prepared for use in the Voice of America's program titled "Forum—The Arts and Sciences in Mid-Century America."

[1] Derived from George J. Stolnitz, "A Century of International Mortality Trends: I," *Population Studies,* IX (1955), 29. The countries are Belgium, England and Wales, France, Netherlands, and Sweden.

The gains in life-expectancy in the Western industrial nations, though unprecedented at the time, are now being eclipsed by faster improvement in the underdeveloped countries. Most of these enjoyed a gradual lowering of mortality prior to World War I, but the fall was not generally remarkable until after that conflict. Since then the drop in the death rate has accelerated in a spectacular way, until it has become faster than anything ever experienced by the industrial nations. For seventeen underdeveloped countries for which fairly reliable death rates are obtainable, for example, the decline in the average crude death rate in 1940-1959, as against 1920-1939, was 37 per cent.[2] This is nearly three times the drop found in the four Scandinavian countries between the same periods (*See* Table 22-1), and it is greater than any preceding drop in those four countries as between two successive twenty-year periods.

Causes of the Decline in Mortality

The more gradual drop in death rates in the industrializing Western nations arose from a basically different set of causes from those currently operating in backward lands. In northwestern Europe and among the northwest-European peoples overseas, the mortality gains were comparatively slow because they depended on self-generated economic and scientific advance. Until late in the nineteenth century the main factor was economic—improvement in commerce, agriculture, and manufacturing—which provided a higher level of living, better housing, education, sanitation, etc. The quickening of the pace of death control around 1900 was due to the fact that, along with continued economic improvement, discoveries in scientific medicine and public health were at last beginning to yield fruit in the massive saving of lives. However, the scientific discoveries had to be slowly invented and applied.

In today's underdeveloped countries, on the other hand, the spectacular declines of mortality are being made by importing the latest medical discoveries from the most industrialized countries, usually with the help of medical personnel and funds from the latter nations. Modern techniques, applied on a mass basis under government sponsorship, have achieved almost miraculous results in the control of infectious diseases and other ailments among backward peoples. These results do not depend on economic development within the areas in question, because funds and personnel can be brought in from outside. They do not depend on scientific discoveries

---

[2] The countries used in the analysis were Barbados, Ceylon, Costa Rica, Cyprus, El Salvador, Fiji Islands, Jamaica, Malaya, Mauritius, Mexico, Panama, Philippines, Puerto Rico, Surinam, Taiwan, Thailand, and Trinidad-Tobago. These countries are still, for the most part, very underdeveloped economically.

within the areas in question, because the research is done in the laboratories of America, Australia, and Europe. This is why the extremely fast drop in the death rate in the world's backward areas is occurring at a more primitive stage of economic development than it did in the Western industrial nations. As noted above, the most rapid death-rate declines in the latter countries came after 1900, a time when these countries were already industrialized and when their birth rates had already started down. In the backward lands today, death rates are being brought down at a faster clip among peoples who in some cases are scarcely removed from savagery and in other cases are overwhelmingly agrarian.

The speed of the drop in the death rate of nonindustrial countries can be seen by comparison with Japan, the latest country to industrialize. One would expect that, owing to the recency of Japan's industrialization, rapid economic improvement *plus* twentieth-century medical advance would enable her to reduce her mortality faster than the older industrial nations did at a similar stage of development. And this is true. Her average death rate in 1940-1959 (despite her war losses) was 37 per cent lower than her average rate in 1920-1939. This, it will be recalled, is exactly the percentage reduction made by our seventeen underdeveloped countries between the two twenty-year periods! The fact that countries like El Salvador, Fiji, and Mauritius can make gains in lengthening life as fast as a rapidly industrializing country shows that such gains are now independent of local economic development.

Demographic Consequences of Death Control

The first, most obvious result of the dramatic lowering of mortality was rapid population growth. Again, however, the story in the underdeveloped countries of today differs from what it was earlier in the currently advanced nations. Since the death rate fell first among the industrializing West European peoples, these peoples experienced a remarkable colonization of new regions and continents. The same social and economic advances that were giving them control over deaths were giving them dominance over more backward races. But another consequence of their falling mortality was a drop in their birth rates. The latter began to turn down noticeably in the 1870's, long before the death rate had reached its present low level and before it had exhibited its fastest drop. The reason was that since the gains in saving lives were made primarily in infancy and early childhood, parents were having to contend with larger numbers of living children than they had ever had to contend with before, precisely at a time when, with industrialization and urbanization, large broods were more of a handicap. Accordingly, people reduced their procreation, partly by postponing marriage and partly by practicing abortion or contraception within marriage. Eventually, from about 1900 to 1932 (depending on the particular country) the birth rate in the industrial nations fell even faster than the death rate, thus decreasing the speed of population growth.

In the 1930's, then, it looked as though the industrial nations had passed through a cycle of rapid population growth and were heading for a normal condition of virtual demographic stability. It was naïvely believed that this might be the transition through which the whole world would move in an orderly fashion.

But two things happened to change this outlook: first, the birth rate went up again in the industrial nations themselves; second, the death rate went down faster in the underdeveloped nations than it had done previously among the advanced European peoples and at a more primitive stage of economic and social development. As a consequence of the way death control was being brought to backward regions, their birth rates were not dropping; and this, with the extremely rapid fall in mortality, gave them the fastest rates of population growth ever experienced by whole nations. The total result, since 1940, has been an increase in the world's population so unprecedented and unpredicted that it has been appropriately called a "population explosion." With more than 2.9 billion today, humanity is multiplying at better than 2 per cent per year. This rate, if continued, will double the population every 35 years.

Most of the world's increase is occurring in precisely the areas least able to accommodate increased numbers, the poorer and more underdeveloped regions. Between 1920 and 1960, for example, the increase in the world's underdeveloped regions amounts to 70.5 per cent, as compared to 41.1 per cent in the industrialized regions.

Social and Economic Consequences

Rapid population growth is impeding economic development in the underdeveloped regions by causing the gains in national income to be used to maintain swelling numbers of people at the old level of living, rather than to improve the level of living itself. Furthermore, when mortality is reduced rapidly without any reduction in the high birth rate the resulting population is abnormally young. Costa Rica, whose death rate dropped 50 per cent during the last thirty years, has 105 children aged 0-14 for each hundred adults aged 20-59; whereas Belgium has only 41. Such young populations mean a heavy child-dependency ratio, added to the burden of total population increase. An underdeveloped country tends to compensate by starting children to work at an early age, a practice that lowers the productivity of labor because education is cut short. The entry of large numbers of youth into the labor market each year tends to bring largescale unemployment and political instability. Costa Rica, for example, has one-fourth as many youths in the five-year age span fifteen to nineteen as she has adults in the forty-year age span 20-59; whereas Belgium has a little more than one-tenth as many.

It seems that the agrarian nations must make a choice between rapid population growth and rapid economic progress. If they decide to cut their population growth, it will presumably be by way of reducing the birth rate. . . . There is every indication from field studies that peasant women do not like having a large number of children, especially when most of them remain alive. All such studies show that on the average women prefer only two, three, or four children, not five to fifteen. Peasant men, however, since the burden of children does not fall directly on them, are less resistant to having large numbers of children except when hard-pressed economically. Actually, as long as the costs of children impinge directly on the parents, the economic incentive to limit offspring is mounting, because the aspirations of the people in peasant lands are running ahead of the actual economic growth. Insofar as the costs fall on the joint family (as in certain traditional social systems) or on the government (as in the welfare state), the potential parent can reproduce without economic penalty. No state has yet seen fit, however, to relieve parents of all the economic costs of reproduction, much less the noneconomic costs in terms of energy and inconvenience.

As the aspirations of the agrarian peoples rise while their economic growth falters, the burden of unusually large families will tend to force parents to reduce their reproduction. If they are encouraged in this by educational measures, by the availability of birth control devices, measures, and by a system that holds parents responsible for their children, the lag of the birth rate behind the declining death rate will be less than otherwise, and the alternative of increasing the death rate will more likely be avoided.

But even if the birth rate around the world is reduced, the question still remains, "Will it be reduced enough to match the low mortality?" Such a depressed birth rate would entail a heavy sacrifice. The sacrifice is commonly thought to consist in the abandonment of traditional values extolling large families; yet it must be emphasized that under conditions of high mortality—the normal situation during nearly all of human history—families were *not* large despite the high birth rate. There were, to be sure, large *households* in many societies, but this was due to living arrangements of kinsmen, not to the high birth rate. There was also a wider *range* in the number of living children than there is today, since couples varied sharply in their biological fecundity and in their capacity to keep their infants alive. The price of adjusting fertility to low mortality is therefore not small numbers of living children, for this has been the normal situation of mankind. Rather, what would be sacrificed is the *chance* of having a sizable family and the *proportion of life* spent with children. If the incidence of death falls so low that most couples need have only two children to replace the population, and if the average lifetime is extended to 83 years, each parent will spend only about a fourth of his adulthood with a child of his own under age fifteen in the household, and only about a tenth of it with a child under five. In view of the love for children, which cannot be unquestionably attributed to culture, one can question whether people will make such a sacrifice.

Perhaps an even greater cost of really low fertility is its effect on the age structure. Although lessening the child-dependency burden, it would enormously expand the old-age-dependency problem. Already, in countries where the birth rate has long been rather low, the population has become topheavy with oldsters. France, for example, now has 33 persons aged 60 or over for each 100 aged 20-59. In the future, as life-expectancy is continually lengthened, a rate of reproduction low enough just to replace the population will yield a higher ratio of elderly. For instance, the life-expectancy of white females in the north central region of the United States is now 73 years. If the whole population reached this figure and maintained it indefinitely, and if the birth rate constantly matched the death rate, the United States would have 45 persons aged 60, and 48 under fifteen, for each hundred aged 20 through 59. If we imagine future mortality improving by an orderly continuance of the fall in age-specific rates observed between 1900 and 1950, until the life-expectancy at birth reaches 83 years, a birth rate that just sustained the population would produce an age structure with 60 persons aged 60-plus, and 38 children under fifteen, for each hundred aged 20-59. This would be nearly double the old-age-dependency ratio in France, which thinks it has too old a population now.

Partly because the price is so high, no nation has yet reduced its reproductive effort sufficiently to match regularly a low modern death rate. Although such a reduction is not inconceivable (especially under radically new institutional arrangements), it should not be complacently assumed to be inevitable or probable or to entail no cost.

National Population Policies

. . . Numerous governments have tried to influence demographic behavior, but the particular nations concerned and the nature of their efforts have shifted markedly. During the 1930's the industrial nations became worried about their low birth rates, and some of them—notably Sweden, Germany, Italy, and France—adopted policies designed to stimulate reproduction. Although the more radical measures for this purpose have now been abandoned, family-allowance legislation and other measures favorable to reproduction are now common, being found in nations as diverse as Russia, Canada, Belgium, and Britain.

This governmental effort to raise the birth rate was based on fallacious reasoning. The birth rates of the 1930's were low, to be sure, but it was a mistake to assume that they would stay that way unless measures were taken. The subsequent baby-boom in industrial countries, especially after World War II, was not the result of the depression-born pronatalist policies, for it occurred in countries that had no such policies. It was mainly a result of prosperity and full employment permitting couples to get married and to have children. Although in most European countries the baby-boom has subsided in recent years, it has remained at such a high level in the new-world industrial countries (Canada, U.S.A., Australia, New Zealand) that, with a continued influx of immigrants, they are still experiencing very fast rates of population growth, their combined population being expected to increase by 22 per cent from 1960 to 1975. In both the old-world and the new-world industrial countries, rising levels of living are added to population growth to create ever more congestion. Escape from the nuisances created by crowding—noise, smog, traffic—cannot be found, because there is not enough space. In the United Kingdom, for example, there are 62 motor vehicles per square mile of land; in the United States there are 22 and in France 25. For this reason, even in the most prosperous countries, voices are beginning to be heard which urge the official encouragement of birth control.

So far, however, the only industrial country that has really carried out an anti-natalist policy is Japan. There the government's permissiveness with respect to abortion and its sponsorship of birth control clinics and family-planning education have helped reduce the crude birth rate 26 per cent below its lowest wartime bottom (1945) and 50 per cent below its postwar peak (1947). This is probably the sharpest birth-rate decline ever experienced by a large nation.

Some of the underdeveloped countries, worried by rapid population growth in the face of poverty and chronic overcrowding, have adopted policies designed to diminish births. The most successful of these has been Puerto Rico, where the birth rate, though still high, has steadily declined since the postwar peak in 1947. Red China vigorously pursued such a policy for awhile and still takes certain measures that lessen reproduction, such as the de-emphasis on the family and the use of women in the labor force. India is strengthening her nationwide anti-natalist policy, and countries such as Mauritius, Bermuda, El Salvador, Haiti, and the Federation of the West Indies are considering a similar policy.

The limitation of population growth, however, is not easy. The reduction of mortality in underdeveloped countries has been so fast and so unconnected with fundamental economic and social change in those countries, that parents cannot be expected yet to limit their offspring by their own efforts. In trying to hasten such an adjustment, no government can succeed by appealing to patriotism or to enlightened awareness of the population problem. It has to influence behavior by altering the conditions. In general, the alterations consist in increasing the effectiveness and availability of contraceptives and/or abortion and sterilization, increasing the participation of women in the labor force (making them not only personally ambitious but also economically independent), allowing the costs of children to fall on the parents themselves rather than upon the joint family or the state, and raising the parents' aspirations for their children's future. These are conservative measures. If they do not succeed, some governments may eventually consider radical means.

There is, of course, the possibility that the world's present climatic population increase will be stopped by a rise in mortality rather than a drop in fertility. The death rate can rise faster and higher than the birth rate, wiping out whole populations in a matter of days or weeks. . . .

Table **19–1**

Average Crude Death Rate in Four Scandinavian Countries, 1740 to 1958[a]

Period	Average Annual Deaths per 1000 Inhabitants[b]	Per Cent Drop from Prior Period[c]
1740-1759	29.1	——
1760-1779	28.1	3.6
1780-1799	26.2	7.2
1800-1819	25.8	1.6
1820-1839	23.0	12.1
1840-1859	21.4	7.4
1860-1879	20.9	2.3
1880-1899	18.0	15.6
1900-1919	15.4	17.2
1920-1939	11.7	31.3
1940-1959	10.2	13.3

[a] The countries are Denmark, Finland, Norway, Sweden.

[b] Average rates for the eighteenth century calculated from H. Gille, "Demographic History of the Northern European Countries in the Eighteenth Century," *Population Studies*, III (1949), 65.

[c] Crude death rates do not afford an accurate basis for comparing the force of mortality from one time to another, because they are influenced by the age structure independently of mortality. The effect of changes in the age structure is particularly important when birth rates are declining rapidly. However, since the alterations in the crude rate from one twenty-year period to the next are not markedly distorted in this way, the percentage changes give a fair index of the rate of change with time.

CHAPTER 20

ERNEST W. BURGESS

The Family in
a Changing Society

Never before in human history has any society been composed of so many divergent types of families. Families differ by section of the country, by communities within the city, by ethnic and religious groups, by economic and social classes, and by vocations. They are different according to the family life-cycle and by number and role of family members. They vary by the locus of authority within the family and by widely different styles of life. There are families of the Hopi Indian (primitive maternal), of the old Amish of Pennsylvania (patriarchal), of the Ozark mountaineers (kinship control), of the Italian immigrant (semipatriarchal), the rooming-house (emancipated), the lower middle class (patricentric), the apartment house (egalitarian), and the suburban (matricentric).

Unity in Diversity

With due recognition of all the diversity among American families, it is still possible and desirable to posit a concept of *the* American family. In a sense this is an ideal construction, in that it attempts to concentrate attention upon what is distinctive about families in the United States in comparison with those of other countries. These differential characteristics are largely in terms of process rather than of structure, and represent relative rather than absolute differences from families in other cultures. Chief among these distinctive trends are the following:

1. *Modifiability and adaptability* in response to conditions of rapid social change;

From Ernest W. Burgess, *The American Journal of Sociology*, LIII (1948), No. 6, pp. 417-422. Copyright 1958 by University of Chicago Press, and reprinted by permission of the author and the University of Chicago Press.

2. *Urbanization,* not merely in the sense that the proportion of families living in cities is increasing, but that rural as well as urban families are adopting the urban way of life;

3. *Secularization,* with the declining control of religion and with the increasing role of material comforts, labor-saving devices and other mechanical contrivances, like the automobile, the radio, and television;

4. *Instability,* as evidenced by the continuing increase in divorce, reaching in 1945 the proportion of one for every three marriages;

5. *Specialization,* on the functions of the giving and receiving of affection, bearing and rearing of children, and personality development, which followed the loss of extrinsic functions, such as economic production, education, religious training, and protection;

6. The *trend to companionship,* with emphasis upon consensus, common interests, democratic relations, and the personal happiness of family members.

•

The Family and Society

With all the variations among American families, it is apparent that they are all in greater or lesser degree in a process of change toward an emerging type of family that is perhaps most aptly described as the "companionship" form. This term emphasizes the point that the essential bonds in the family are now found more and more in the interpersonal relationship of its members, as compared with those of law, custom, public opinion, and duty in the older institutional forms of the family.

Not that companionship, affection, and happiness are absent from the institutional family. They exist there in greater or lesser degree, but they are not its primary aims. The central objectives of the institutional family are children, status, and the fulfillment of a social and economic function in society.

The distinctive characteristics of the American family, as of the family in any society, are a resultant of (1) survivals from earlier forms of the family, developing under prior or different economic and social conditions; (2) the existing social and economic situation; and (3) the prevailing and evolving ideology of the society.

Survivals

The American family has had a rich and varied historical heritage, with strands going back to all European countries and to the religious ideologies of the Catholic, Jewish, and Protestant faiths. What is distinctive in the American family, however, has resulted from its role, first, in the early rural situation of the pioneer period and, second, in the modern urban environment.

The growth of democracy in the family proceeded in interaction with the development of democracy in society. Pioneer conditions promoted the emancipation both of women and of youth from subordination to the family and to the community. Arrangements for marriage passed from the supervision of parents into the control of young people.

The rural family of the United States before World War I, however, had progressed toward, but had not achieved, democratic relations among its members. Control was centered in the father and husband as the head of the farm economy, with strict discipline and with familistic objectives still tending to be dominant over its members. Children were appraised in terms of their value for farm activities, and land tenure and farm operations were closely interrelated with family organization and objectives.

The Evolving Urban Environment

The modern city, growing up around the factory and serving as a trade center for a wide area, provided the necessary conditions for the development of the distinctive characteristics of the American family. It still further promoted the equality of family members and their democratic interrelationships, initiated and fostered to a certain degree by the rural pioneer environment. In the urban community the family lost the extrinsic functions which it had possessed from time immemorial and which continued, although in steadily diminishing degrees, in the rural family. The urban family ceased to be, to any appreciable extent, a unity of economic production. This change made possible a relaxation of authority and regimentation by the family head. Then, too, the actual or potential employment of wife and children outside the home signified their economic independence and created a new basis for family relations. In the city the members of the family tended to engage in recreational activities separately, in their appropriate sex and age groups. Each generation witnessed a decline of parental control over children.

This increased freedom and individualization of family members and their release from the strict supervision of the rural neighborhood was naturally reflected in the instability of the family. The divorce rate has averaged a 3 per cent increase each year after the Civil War.

Urbanization involves much more than the concentration and growth of population. It includes commercialization of activities, particularly recreational; specialization of vocations and interests; the development of new devices of communication—telephone, telegraph, motion picture, radio, the daily newspaper, and magazines of mass circulation. All these still further promote the urbanization and secularization of families residing not only in cities but even in remote rural settlements.

The Ideology of American Society

Democracy, freedom and opportunity for self-expression are central concepts in the American ideology. The frontier situation favored their expression in the social, economic and political life of the people. As they found articulation in the American creed, they reinforced existing tendencies toward democracy and companionship within the family.

Urban life in its economic aspects provided less opportunity than did the rural environment for the exemplification of the American ideology. For example, the development of big business and enormous industries decreased the opportunities for the husband and father to run his own business. But the city greatly increased the economic freedom and independence of the wife and children by providing employment outside the home. The social conditions of the modern city led to the emancipation of family members from the institutional controls of the rural family. The urban family tended to become an affectional and cultural group, united by the interpersonal relations of its members.

The Family in Process

The paradox between the unity and the diversity of the American family can be understood in large part by the conception of the family in process. This means, first of all, that it is in transition from earlier and existing divergent forms to an emergent generic type and, second, that it is in experimentation and is developing a variety of patterns corresponding to the subcultures in American society.

The Family in Transition

Much of what is termed the "instability" of the American family arises from the shift to the democratic companionship type from the old-time rural family of this country and the transplanted old-world family forms of immigrant groups.

Many of the current problems within the family are to be explained by the resulting conflicting conceptions in expectations and roles of husbands and wives and of parents and children. The husband may expect his wife to be a devoted household slave like his mother, while she aspires to a career or to social or civic activities outside the home. Immigrant parents attempt to enforce old-world standards of behavior upon their children, who are determined to be American in appearance, behavior, and ideas.

The Family in Experimentation

The changes taking place in the family have constituted a vast experiment in democracy. Hundreds of thousands of husbands and wives, parents and children, have participated in it. Couples have refused to follow the pattern of the marriages of their parents and are engaged in working out new designs of family living more-or-less of their own devising. This behavior has been fully in accord with the ideals and practices of democracy and has exemplified the American ideology of individual initiative and opportunity for self-expression.

This experiment in family formation, while apparently proceeding by individual couples, has been essentially collectivistic rather than pluralistic behavior. Each couple has naturally cherished the illusion that it was acting on its own. To be sure, individual initiative and risk-taking were involved.[1] Many individual ventures have ended in disaster. But actually it has been a collective experiment in the sense that the couples were acting under the stimulus of current criticisms of family life and were attempting to realize in their marriage the new conceptions of family living disseminated by the current literature, presented by the marriages of friends, or developed in discussion by groups of young people.

Adaptability versus Stability

In the past, stability has been the great value exemplified by the family and expected of it by society. This was true because the family was the basic institution in a static society. American society, however, is not static but dynamic. The virtue of its institutions do not inhere in their rigid stability, but in their adaptability to a rapid tempo of social change.

The findings of two recent studies underscore the significance of adaptability for the American family. Angell began his study of the family in the depression with the hypothesis that its degree of integration would determine its success or failure in adjustment to this crisis.[2] He found, however, that he needed to introduce the concept of adaptability to explain why certain families, highly integrated and stable before the depression, failed and why some moderately integrated families succeeded, in adjusting to the crisis. A restudy of these cases indicated that adaptability was more significant than integration in enabling families to adjust to the depression.

---

[1] *See* Floyd Dell, *Love in Greenwich Village* (New York: Doubleday, Doran & Co., 1926).

[2] Robert C. Angell, *The Family Encounters the Depression* (New York: Charles Scribner's Sons, 1936).

Another study[3] arrived at a similar conclusion. In predicting success and failure in marriage, data were secured from couples during the engagement period. Certain couples with low prediction scores were later found to be well adjusted in their marriage. The explanation seemed to lie in the adaptability of one or both members of the couple, which enabled them to meet and solve successfully difficult problems as they developed in the marriage.

Adaptability as a personal characteristic has three components. One is psychogenic, and represents the degree of flexibility in the emotional reaction of a person to a shift from an accustomed to a different situation. The second component is the tendency of the person, as culturally or educationally determined, to act in an appropriate way when entering a new situation. The third component of adaptability is the possession of knowledge and skills which make for successful adjustments to a new condition.

Successful marriage in modern society, with its divergent personalities, diversity of cultural backgrounds, and changing conditions, depends more and more upon the adaptability of husbands and wives and parents and children. The crucial matter, then, becomes the question of the adaptability of the family as a group, which may be something different from the adaptability of its members.

The growing adaptability of the companionship family makes for its stability in the long run. But it is a stability of a different kind from that of family organization in the past, which was in large part due to the external social pressures of public opinion, the mores, and law. The stability of the companionship family arises from the strength of the interpersonal relations of its members, as manifested in affection, rapport, common interests and objectives.

Flexibility of personality is not sufficient to ensure adaptability of the family to a changing society. Its members should also be culturally and educationally oriented to the necessity for making adjustments. For example, the prospects of successful marriage would be greatly improved if husbands on entering wedded life were as predisposed in attitudes as are wives to be adjustable in the marital relation. Finally, adaptability in marriage and family living demands knowledge and skills on the part of family members. These are no longer transmitted adequately by tradition in the family. They can be acquired, of course, the hard way, by experience. They can best be obtained through education and counseling based upon the findings of social science research.

---

[3] *See* E. W. Burgess and Paul Wallin, "Engagement and Marriage," chapter on "Adaptability" (unpublished manuscript).

The Family and Social Science

The instability of the American family as evidenced by its rising divorce rate is, in general, incidental to the trial-and-error method by which divorced persons ultimately find happiness in a successful remarriage.[4] But trial and error is a wasteful procedure. It involves tragic losses both to husbands and wives and to their children. So far as possible, it should be replaced by a more rational and less risk-taking planning.

The solution, however, does not lie fundamentally in legislation. Laws, within limits, may be helpful as in the ensuring of economic and social security, the improvement of housing and nutrition, in the exemptions from income taxes for wives and children, and in family allowances for children.

State and federal governments have taken steps to undergird the economic basis of the family and are likely to be called upon for further aid. But assistance to young people entering marriage and to the family in attaining its cultural objectives is coming from other institutions and agencies.

The school and the church have for some time shown a growing interest in assuming responsibility for education for marriage and family life. This is most marked in colleges and universities, a large majority of which, upon demand of the student body, now offer one or more courses in the family, family relations, marriage and the family, and preparation for marriage. High schools are experimenting with different types of courses in human relations and in family relations or with the introduction of family-life education material in existing courses. Churches, through Sunday school classes, young peoples' societies, young married couples' clubs, and Sunday evening forums, have promoted programs in family-life education. Community programs have been organized under the auspices of the Y.M.C.A., the Y.W.C.A., settlements, social centers, associations for family living, parent–child study associations, and other agencies.

Marriage and family counseling are developing under both older and newer auspices. The public still turns to the minister, the physician, and the lawyer for assistance upon spiritual, physical, and legal aspects of marriage. Theological, medical, and law schools are beginning to realize their responsibilities for training their students for this activity. The family social caseworkers, particularly those with psychiatric training, are at present the persons best trained professionally for marriage and family counseling. The identification in the public mind of family-service societies with relief-giving has largely limited this service to dependent families, although in some cities special provision has been made to extend marriage and family counseling on a fee basis to middle-class clientele.

---

[4] Harvey J. Locke, "Predicting Marital Adjustment by Comparing a Divorced and a Happily Married Group," *American Sociological Review*, XII (1947), 187-191.

Beginning with the Institute of Family Relations in Los Angeles, established in 1930, and the Marriage Council of Philadelphia two years later, marriage-counseling centers under the independent auspices are now functioning in an increasing number of our largest cities, in some smaller communities, and in a growing number of colleges and universities.

The growing disposition of young people is, as we have seen, to make their own plans for marriage and family living. They are, at the same time, interested in the resources available in education, in counseling, and in the findings of research in the psychological and social sciences. Leaders in the family-life educational and counseling movement are also looking to research to provide the knowledge which they may use in giving more efficient service.

. . . This paper attempts to state the role of research in relation to the solution of the problems of the family in our modern society. Its role is to provide the knowledge which an increasing number of young people are desirous of using in planning marriage and parenthood.

The outstanding evidence of this attitude and expectation is the reliance upon science of upper- and middle-class parents in the rearing of children. Their diet is determined upon the advice of a pediatrician, and their rearing is guided by the latest book on child psychology. This is a wide and significant departure from the older policy of bringing up the child according to methods carried down by tradition in the family.

A second illustration is the growing interest of young people in the factors making for the wise selection of a mate and for success or failure in marriage, as derived from psychological and sociological studies.

A third significant fact is the widespread public interest in A. C. Kinsey's book, *Sexual Behavior in the Human Male*, containing the first report of sex behavior of 5,300 male Americans, based upon a very complete schedule and a carefully organized interview.

These are but three of the indications of the receptivity of intelligent young people to the findings of the psychological and social sciences and of their willingness to utilize them in planning for marriage and parenthood. In short, these activities are being taken out of the realm of the mores and are being transferred to the domain of science.

The findings of research do not, in and of themselves, provide the data for a design for marriage and family life. It is, however, the function of social science research to collect and to analyze the fund of experience of young people in their various experiments in achieving happiness in marriage and family life. Therefore, these findings of research should be made available to them through books, magazines, and newspapers; through motion pictures and radio; and through marriage counseling and programs of family-life education. . . .

CHAPTER 21

BERNARD BARBER

Change and Stratification Systems

Change and the Stratification Systems in Feudal and Early Modern France and England

The long history of France and England from feudal times in the eleventh century to early modern times in the eighteenth century cannot, of course, be described in any simple terms. There were changes over this long period in every aspect of these societies and in the European world which was their setting. Yet there is a sense in which it is possible to say that both France and England remained relatively constant during this time. Though all the different social changes that occurred did change their stratification systems in some measure, nevertheless these systems maintained the same basic structural type and processes through some six or seven hundred years. Our first case or cases, then, are intended as examples of changes in stratification systems that are changes *within type,* not changes *of type.* Such changes within type are often important, of course, but sociologically they are different from changes of type.

Essentially, during the feudal and early modern periods, France and England had stratification systems that were nearer to the caste than to the open-class type. That is to say, on the whole the predominant institutional norms disapproved of social mobility, and in fact there was relatively little mobility. But . . . there was an important admixture of open-class norms that gave the stratification systems of these societies a somewhat more mixed character. In addition, there was always a steady, though relatively small, stream of actual social mobility in France and England during the feudal and early modern periods. . . .

Though there was always a small amount of mobility during this period, most of it gradual, the relative importance of the different processes of mobility changed somewhat. In the feudal period, of course, the achievement of knighthood was an important process of mobility. In the early feudal period, up to about the year 1100, knighthood could often be achieved through deeds of prowess on the field of battle. This was a time when French and English society was relatively disorganized, subject to continual petty and private warfare among the knightly class, and when people lived in fear of unlawful violence. Knightly skill was highly valued, but the training and equipment necessary to obtain and practice this skill were so expensive that they were usually available only to members of the upper classes. As Coulborn has put it, the would-be knight "needed special training from the age of twelve, a horse specially bred for fighting, and expensive armor." [1] Where a wealthy knight was willing to pay for the equipment of a good warrior whom he desired as his vassal and military support, however, this avenue of mobility remained open. With the rise of the centralized feudal states in the twelfth and thirteenth centuries, individual knights had fewer occasions for engaging in their own petty private wars. After the middle of the twelfth century in France, says Painter, "a noble who wished to follow the traditional occupation of his class was obliged to do so under the authority of a feudal prince or feudal monarch." [2] The knight was no longer, so to speak, a small entrepreneur, but a kind of employee or retainer of the great princes. During the twelfth century also, says Bloch in his account of French feudal society, "the right to be dubbed a knight was transformed into an hereditary privilege." [3] But some mobility into the knightly class through skill and valor on the actual field of battle still occurred, though there was less of it than in the more violent, more disorganized earlier period of feudal society.

But if the emergence of the centralized feudal state made individual mobility through military prowess less common, it enlarged the scope of other processes of social mobility. A man could now more often rise through service in the administrative and legal bureaucracies of the great princes and monarchs. Or men who had accumulated wealth in urban commerce could buy land and a patent of nobility. Kings and great princes were always in need of more money to strengthen their positions. From the time of the thirteenth century and the reign of St. Louis onwards, there is evidence of the granting of letters of ennoblement by the royal court. The king still sometimes used his right of making knights to reward some act or career

---

[1] Rushton Coulborn, ed., *Feudalism in History* (Princeton University Press, 1956), p. 9.

[2] Sidney Painter, *French Chivalry: Chivalric Ideas and Practices in Mediaeval France,* (Baltimore: Johns Hopkins Press, 1940), p. 17.

[3] Marc Bloch, *La Société Féodale* (2 vols.; Paris: Editions Albin Michel, 1939, 1940), Vol. II, p. 59.

of military bravery or administrative service. But often also he used this right merely to obtain funds. By about 1300 there were French royal commissioners traveling about selling nobility to wealthy merchants, as well as freedom to some of the royal serfs. To be sure, this selling of nobility, though it fluctuated in amount, was always kept under control, in both the feudal and early modern periods. This door into the nobility was never open more than a relatively small way. Bloch is correct when he says, "In truth, the period that extends from 1250 to about 1400 was, on the continent, one in which there was a most rigid hierarchization of the social strata." [4] With only slight qualification, the same could have been said not only of England in the same period, but of both France and England for the next four hundred years as well. . . .

Although there was some change of balance among the processes of mobility during this long period, there was no basic change either in the structure of influence or in the predominant ideological conception of the nature of society and of the stratification system. The structure of influence rested fundamentally on landholding and associated rights, and the land remained in the hands of the nobles or was bought up by those who wished to become nobles. There was some change in the relative predominance of the king and court as against the rest of the nobles during this long period, of course. The rise of the centralized state in the feudal period marked an increase in the influence of the king. But by the seventeenth and eighteenth centuries—a little earlier in England, a little later in France—the king's influence in society relative to that of the rest of the nobles had declined somewhat. Always, however, predominant influence remained with the landholding noble class as a whole, whatever the changes in the relative share of influence possessed by the king as premier noble.

This enduring structure of influence was supported by an equally enduring ideological conception, the organic conception of society in which a predominant value was placed upon the roles of the noble warriors, noble rulers, and noble clergymen. . . . No counter-ideology gained any strength among the nonnoble, middle-class people in France or England. The middle-class elements—the merchants, the lesser gentry, and the well-to-do yeomanry—wished, as individuals, to change their own class position in society; they wished to rise into the nobility. But they did not give their allegiance to any ideology that recommended a change in the caste type of stratification system itself.

One sphere in which there was considerable change during the feudal and early modern periods in France and England was the domestic "style of life" of the noble class. This change did not, however, have any fundamental effect on the stratification system. In the early feudal period, in the eleventh century, for example, the standard of living even for the knightly class was low. A petty

---

[4] *Ibid.*, p. 66.

noble had to be content with coarse woolen clothes, an abundance of simple food, and a two-room wooden house surrounded by a moat and palisade. A great lord might have enough serf labor at his command to build a high artificial mound on which to erect his large and fine residence. He might also have servile artisans to produce clothes and armor of reasonably good quality. But even the greatest lords in the eleventh century did not have fine stone castles, silken garments, or spices for their food. By the end of the eleventh century, however, the French noble class became enriched from several sources. The conquest of Spain, the Holy Land, England, and Sicily brought not only wealth in the form of gold but also new skills, new foods, and new fabrics.

After the Conquest, this new domestic "style of life" spread to England. Also, in the twelfth century, there began to be more and larger towns and commercial fairs in France and England. From both the towns and the fairs the nobles received money rents from the merchants and also new goods of all kinds to make their standard of living better. The greatest of the lords were now extremely wealthy and could command great resources of labor and whatever goods were on the market. Such men built themselves fine stone castles, wore costly silks imported from the East and rare furs brought from the north of Europe, drank good wines for the first time, and added rarities like sugar and spices to their tables. . . .

And from the sixteenth century onwards, with the opening up of the Western world and the continuing slow economic advance in Europe, the noble standard of living improved still further. But none of the change in this area of society, although over the period of six hundred years or more it was considerable and important in other respects, such as the economic, resulted in basic change in the caste type of stratification system in France and England.

Perhaps if the caste system had not had admixtures of open-class elements, there might sooner have occurred a basic change in its character, either through revolution or incrementally. Perhaps if there had not been opportunities for social mobility, opportunities for men to rise in the church, in the service of the state, or by purchasing land and titles with the money accumulated in commerce, there might sooner have occurred a basic change in the stratification system. But these opportunities were continuously available in France and England, and they served to dissolve social strains and personal resentments that might otherwise have supported ideologies and movements opposed to the existing society and its stratification system. It is, of course, often said that "the rising bourgeoisie" did constitute a group suffering from such social strains and personal resentments and that they did, consequently, form an inherently revolutionary element in French and English society. But . . . there is good evidence that although some individual members of the bourgeoisie did rise in every century of the feudal and early modern periods, the bourgeois group as a whole was not at all self-consciously or otherwise revolutionary. A bourgeois, as we have seen, was in basic agreement with the caste norms and ideologies. Fundamentally, what he wanted was either to pass on his class position to his children or to move himself or his children into the noble class. He did not believe in equality for all, at least not here on earth, though he might, if he was a firmly believing Christian, look forward to it in Heaven. If the successful bourgeois had any deviant sentiments about the virtues of earthly universalism, they were soon driven out by his rise into a noble social class where such sentiments no longer suited his own social interests.

How, then, did the change from a basically caste type of stratification system to a basically open-class one occur in modern France and England? We cannot, of course, give a very satisfactory answer. In France, it was the Revolution and the social changes in every aspect of society which the Revolution involved that ushered in the change to an open-class stratification system. But there is no consensus among historians on what the causes of the Revolution were. Almost every conceivable social factor has been defined by some historian as the essential cause. Until there is a good deal more historical research and the kind of theory of change in societies as a whole considered at the beginning of this chapter, a satisfactory account of the origins and development of the French Revolution will be lacking. Nor can we do much better in explaining the fundamental changes in the stratification system that occurred in England. Although the historical evidence has not yet been collected to prove the point firmly, it does seem that the admixture of open-class elements *may have been* a little larger in England than in France and that these elements *may have been* sufficient to obviate a revolutionary solution to the necessity for social change. Moreover, the example of the social costs of the Revolution in France probably had an important influence in keeping the changes in England on the whole on peaceful paths. There was some violence in England too in the late eighteenth and early nineteenth centuries, but by and large England moved into an open-class stratification system peaceably.

How precisely can we assign an historical date to the change from the caste to the open-class type of stratification system in France and England? Not very precisely, because we do not have the evidence with regard to changes in the balance of institutional norms and in the actual amounts of mobility which would be the best indicators of the fundamental social transformation. In France we know that the basic legal changes took place during the Revolution. How soon these were effective in producing changes in stratificational norms and in amounts of mobility we do not know. A great deal of change in these respects took place during the Revolution itself, and this change was enlarged and consolidated in the early-middle nineteenth century. In England, where changes in all respects were more gradual, less violent, more unplanned, it is perhaps even harder to set a definite date for the transformation of the stratification system. Probably there, as in France, the change did not occur until sometime during the early-middle nineteenth century. In both societies, of course, there persisted an admixture of caste elements after the establishment of a basically open-class type. In all complex societies there is some mixture of institutional elements and social processes. The sociologist must always keep this fact in mind, since the mixture is often the source of fundamental social change.

•

Change and the Stratification System in Russia

Social change occurs not only at varying rates of speed, but as the result of varying amounts of social planning. In this, our third case, we have an example of a society where the change from a basically caste type of stratification system to an open-class one has been brought about by revolution and by overall state social planning.

•

In legal terms, prerevolutionary Russia was, like eighteenth-century France, an "estate" society. The law defined special rights and duties for each of the three estates: the clergy, hereditary nobility, and a third estate consisting of peasants and town-dwelling merchants and workers. In terms of social stratification, prerevolutionary Russia was, again like eighteenth-century France, basically of the caste type, but with a much larger admixture of open-class elements. Indeed, since Russia had begun to industrialize, and this with increasing speed in the twentieth century, the admixture of open-class elements was large enough that some scholars have argued that Russia was already more nearly an open-class than a caste society. Certainly there was a small but increasing number of industrialists, merchants, and skilled workers; moreover, many upper-class intellectuals were ardently devoted to universalistic values and ideologies. Hence the appeal of various democratic, constitutional, socialist, and Marxist social philosophies. Many of the mobile bourgeois, however, did not approve in principle of social mobility for all but, like their eighteenth-century proto-types in France, wanted only to move into the hereditary noble class themselves. Just how much actual social mobility and institutionalized approval existed in prerevolutionary Russia, we do not know. We can only venture the estimate that these open-class elements were probably somewhat subordinate to the basically caste type of stratification system. This is not to imply, of course, that over the longer run there would not have occurred inevitably a slow and gradual increase in the open-class elements, eventuating in a basically open-class society.

But social change in Russia was not to take place gradually or peaceably. A violent revolution initiated, and social planning has carried to completion, basic changes in every part of Russian society: in the organization of production, in the property system, in the political and legal systems, in education, in science, in the family, in religion, and, not least of all, in values and ideologies. Just how the revolution was begun or the social transformation completed is not, like many great historical events, entirely clear even to those who have studied the history and sociology of Russian society most intensively. However, the fundamental importance of Marxist-Leninist theory and of Communist Party organization in initiating and consolidating the revolution is unmistakable. In the beginning, in fact, Marxist-Leninist theory gave the revolution a utopian cast. It proclaimed that such fundamental social structures as the stratification system, the state bureaucracy, and the family would ultimately be unnecessary. Eventually, however, though basic changes in these and other structures were made, the Russians have had to recede from their utopian views or at least announce the postponement of the realization into the indefinite future.

Even in a revolution, basic social changes do not occur overnight, nor sometimes even in a single generation. The deaths and destruction, the expropriation of property, and the social disfranchisement of the formerly privileged classes did, in the period of revolutionary violence and immediately thereafter, cause a great increase in both upward and downward social mobility in Russia. But as Lenin recognized in his "Testament," there is a limit to the extent to which "new" men can immediately take the place of the "old" social groups. It takes time especially to train technical specialists; it also takes time to allow "new" men to gain the necessary experience even in positions that require no special technical training. Lenin and the other revolutionary leaders were compelled, therefore, to allow many of the former middle- and upper-class industrial, civil-service, and free-professional experts to remain in their old positions. Looking to the future, however, the Communists began to train their own experts. During the 1920's, special privileges in education were given to industrial workers and their children. This facilitated the social mobility of these "proletarian" groups. Undoubtedly, though, some of the children of those members of the old upper classes who had been retained in high positions were able to profit from their family advantages and maintain unchanged the social class position in which they were born. That is the consequence, or "price," of preserving some stable continuity in a society even though it has undergone a fundamental social revolution.

Probably the period of maximum social mobility and of the most rapid increase in open-class norms and ideologies occurred in Russia in the late twenties, the thirties, and the forties, the period in which there was the greatest proportionate expansion of Russia's industrial, governmental, military, scientific, and educational systems. The absolute number of middle- and higher-ranking positions in Soviet society was vastly increased in this period, and probably the proportion of these positions relative to the lower ones was also somewhat increased. These increases created a vast expansion of the opportunities for social mobility of both large and small degree. Along with the expansion resulting from industrialization, the recurrent "purges" of prerevolutionary groups from the higher-ranking positions also enlarged the opportunities for social mobility during the thirties and forties.

By now, Soviet society has settled down with an open-class stratification system very much like that of the other industrialized countries of Europe and in the United States. . . . The educational system is now as much one of the key elements in the process of mobility in Russia, as it is in other open-class industrial societies that require and provide opportunities for individual achievement. . . . Actual access to what is formally a universally available education system is influenced by social class position in Russia as it is in other open-class societies. The settling down of Russian society probably has lessened, relative to the thirties and forties and earlier, the amount of social mobility that now occurs. Nevertheless, there is still a considerable amount of social mobility. . . . Probably a fairly large minority of the population remains in the class into which it was born; another large minority moves up or down in relatively small degree; and a small minority moves up or down in the class structure in large degree. Until we have better comparative evidence for Russia and other industrial countries which will reveal subtle differences in the amount and processes of mobility, the safest estimate of the Russian stratification system is that it consists of norms, structure, and processes basically similar to those of other open-class industrial societies in Europe and the United States. That is the estimate supported by all the good evidence now in hand.

•

Change and the Stratification System in Great Britain

It has often been said that during and since the end of World War II Great Britain has gone through a "social revolution." Great social changes have indeed occurred during the last fifteen years in many different parts of the society, and these have been important to nearly every member of the society. But are these changes "revolutionary"? In some sense, perhaps they are. But not in the sense of involving fundamental changes *of type* in any of the major social institutions. The changes have been planned and carried through by means of long-established democratic political techniques. They have been agreed to, on the whole, by the adherents of both of the major political parties. In short, they have been built on long-standing social consensus. In this . . . case, then, we shall consider recent changes in the stratification system of Great Britain as examples of changes within a stable and institutionalized open-class system.

As we have suggested earlier in this chapter, Great Britain may have had a predominantly open-class type of stratification since at least the early-middle part of the nineteenth century. All during that century, and continuing up to the present, a series of incremental changes have tended to make the stratification system approximate ever more nearly the open-class type. Social change has often not come as fast or as easily as many Britons wished; there have always been many people to criticize the persistence of caste elements in British society. But the general direction of change in the stratification system has been constant. And in this perspective especially, the post-World War II changes in Britain represent another large increment of a long trend of change within the open-class type of stratification system. During the last one hundred and fifty years, for example, the availability of education, both as to amount and quality, has been spreading in Britain. The recent increases in scholarships, the improvement of schools for the poorer groups, and the "opening up" of the "public schools" and of Oxford and Cambridge, then, are social changes that build upon earlier and similar changes in the educational system. Further, the diminution of family advantages for the maintenance of high social class position through the levying of progressive income and inheritance taxes is also not new to Britain, though these instruments of an open-class society have been applied with increased force in the postwar period. Finally, if the political influence of the lower classes reached a peak in Britain after the war through the Labour Party and the Labour Government, this too was a development founded on a long history of slowly increasing political influence among the lower classes.

A long series of peaceable, slow, and interrelated social changes have made the stratification system of Great Britain approach ever more nearly, though not absolutely achieve, the open-class type. There seems to have occurred a general "flattening" of the class structure, that is, there has been a trend toward relatively fewer people in the upper and lower classes. The proportion of people in that broad range of the class structure ideologically defined as "the middle classes" has been increasing. Differences of evaluation and of the associated social privileges still exist, but they are less obvious than formerly because more subtly graded and more subtly expressed. The rise in the standard of living of the lower and lower-middle classes— their better food, better education, better health, better housing, and better clothes—has not only increased their chances for social mobility, but has eliminated some of the most striking of the former symbols of their social class inferiority.

•

. . . There seem to be on all sides stronger sentiments of approval of social mobility; equality of opportunity for individual achievement in all socially valued roles is now a more common ideal in all social classes. Great Britain, then, is not now a classless society; nor has she undergone a major social revolution such as that of 1789 in France or of 1917 in Russia. She has, rather, taken somewhat longer steps than at other times in the past down a path of change toward a more nearly open-class type of stratification system—a path she has been following for a long time.

Change and the Stratification System in the United States

Our . . . final case is the United States. . . . The United States is an example of a society in which the changes of the stratification system are changes *within type*. . . . Just how much change there has been in the American open-class stratification system, we cannot precisely say. Nor can we be absolutely sure about the general direction of the change that has occurred within that type. The social changes taking place recently may, as some Americans have thought, be in the direction of a somewhat less open-class society. But it seems more likely that these changes have generally strengthened the conditions necessary for an open-class stratification system and made that system a little bit more realizable in practice. For example, there is no evidence that Americans now approve any less of social mobility than they ever have in the past. Indeed, there seems to be a persistence of open-class sentiments and aspirations, even in the face of widespread social depression or individual "failure" . . . and an equally persistent amount of social mobility. Even the Negroes, with regard to whom the caste elements in American society have always been strongest, have recently won a set of social improvements, among which not the least is the weakening of the prejudices against them among their white fellow Americans.

Certainly we can point to a number of social processes and social changes that have probably served to strengthen the American open-class stratification system. Education and educational opportunity, though still not equal for all, are changing in the direction of greater availability and equality. Political and other forms of social influence are becoming somewhat less unequally distributed among the social classes. The development of labor union organizations and their participation in national and local politics has been one of the basic sources of the reduction of political and social inequality among the classes. As in England, the American tax system serves to diminish the differential advantages provided by accumulated family wealth; this system has recently become an even more effective instrument of this open-class function. Science and technology have continually been creating in American society new opportunities for entrepreneurial ability and new jobs requiring valued social and technical knowledge and skill. And these in turn provide continuing opportunities for social mobility. In general, conservative or reactionary inequalitarian ideologies and movements have either been lacking or strikingly unsuccessful in their appeals for support. Other social changes have at least not weakened, and sometimes they have actively strengthened, the set of conditions required for enlarging the realization of an open-class type of stratification system in the United States.

To many people, the account given above of social change and the

American stratification system will seem excessively optimistic. But perhaps it will seem so only because Americans have tended to have utopian expectations with regard to their stratification system and have been impatient of any hindrance to completely free social mobility. . . . Such mobility does not occur. Therefore Americans can be optimistic without being utopian. Optimism, of course, does not mean that they should be complacent. Because the stratification system is a system in process, continuous social action of many different kinds is required either to maintain it in the state Americans desire or to improve it. They must therefore pay constant attention to the social arrangements and policies that foster the kind of stratification system and change they want. Increasingly, as social science develops, social change can be planned and foreseen. The choice for Americans now is not between an open-class and a caste type of stratification system; it is among degrees of approximation to the open-class system and to the American ideals. Perhaps this is also true now for societies all around the world.

CHAPTER 22

GAETANO MOSCA

The Varying Structure of the Ruling Class

The Concept of the Ruling Class

In all societies—from societies that are very meagerly developed and have barely attained the dawnings of civilization, down to the most advanced and powerful societies—two classes of people appear, a class that rules and a class that is ruled. The first class, always the less numerous, performs all the political functions, monopolizes power, and enjoys the advantages that power brings. The second, the more numerous class, is directed and controlled by the first, in a manner that is now more-or-less legal, now more-or-less arbitrary and violent; it supplies the first class, in appearance at least, with material means of subsistence and with the instrumentalities that are essential to the vitality of the political organism.

In practical life we all recognize the existence of this ruling class. We all know that, in our own country, whichever it may be, the management of public affairs is in the hands of a minority of influential persons, to which, willingly or unwillingly, the majority defers. We know that the same thing goes on in neighboring countries, and in fact we should be hard put to it to conceive of a real world otherwise organized—a world in which all men would be directly subject to a single person without relationships of superiority or subordination, or in which all men would share equally in the direction of political affairs. If we reason otherwise in theory, that is due partly to inveterate habits that we follow in our thinking and partly to the exaggerated importance that we attach to two political facts that loom far larger in appearance than they are in reality.

The first of these facts—and one has only to open one's eyes to see it—

is that in every political organism there is one individual who is chief among the leaders of the ruling class as a whole and stands, as we say, at the helm of the state. That person is not always the person who holds supreme power according to law. At times, alongside of the hereditary king or emperor, there is a prime minister or a major-domo who wields an actual power that is greater than the sovereign's. At other times, in place of the elected president, the influential politician who has procured the president's election will govern. Under special circumstances, there may be, instead of a single person, two or three who discharge the functions of supreme control.

The second fact, too, is readily discernible. Whatever the type of political organization, pressures arising from the discontent of the masses who are governed, from the passions by which they are swayed, exert a certain amount of influence on the policies of the ruling, political class.

But the man who is at the head of the state would certainly not be able to govern without the support of a numerous class to enforce respect for his orders and to have them carried out; and granting that he can make one individual, or indeed many individuals, in the ruling class feel the weight of his power, he certainly cannot be at odds with the class as a whole or do away with it. Even if that were possible, he would at once be forced to create another class, without the support of which action on his part would be completely paralyzed. On the other hand, granting that the discontent of the masses might succeed in deposing a ruling class, inevitably, as we shall later show, there would have to be another organized minority within the masses themselves to discharge the functions of a ruling class. Otherwise all organization and the whole social structure would be destroyed.

From the point of view of scientific research the real superiority of the concept of the ruling, or political, class lies in the fact that the varying structure of ruling classes has a preponderant importance in determining the political type, and also the level of civilization, of the different peoples.

. . . We think it may be desirable . . . to reply at this point to an objection which might very readily be made to our point of view. If it is easy to understand that a single individual cannot command a group without finding within the group a minority to support him, it is rather difficult to grant, as a constant and natural fact, that minorities rule majorities, rather than majorities minorities. But that is one of the points—so numerous in all the other sciences—where the first impression one has of things is contrary to what they are in reality. In reality the dominion of an organized minority, obeying a single impulse, over the unorganized majority, is inevitable. The power of any minority is irresistible as against each single individual in the majority, who stands alone before the totality of the organized minority. At the same time, the minority is organized for the very reason that it is a minority. A hundred men acting uniformly in concert, with a common understanding, will triumph over a thousand men who are not in accord and can therefore be dealt with one by one. Meanwhile, it will be easier for the former to act in concert and have a mutual understanding, simply because they are a hundred and not a thousand. It follows that the larger the political community, the smaller will the proportion of the governing minority to the governed majority be and the more difficult will it be for the majority to organize for reaction against the minority.

However, in addition to the great advantage accruing to them from the fact of being organized, ruling minorities are usually so constituted that the individuals who make them up are distinguished from the mass of the governed by qualities that give them a certain material, intellectual or even moral superiority; or else they are the heirs of individuals who possessed such qualities. In other words, members of a ruling minority regularly have some attribute, real or apparent, which is highly esteemed and very influential in the society in which they live.

From the Warriors to the Wealthy

In primitive societies that are still in the early stages of organization, military valor is the quality that most readily opens access to the ruling or political class. In societies of advanced civilization, war is the exceptional condition. It may be regarded as virtually normal in societies that are in the initial stages of their development; and the individuals who show the greatest ability in war easily gain supremacy over their fellows, the bravest becoming chiefs. The fact is constant, but the forms it may assume in one set of circumstances or another vary considerably.

As a rule, the dominance of a warrior class over a peaceful multitude is attributed to a superposition of races, to the conquest of a relatively unwarlike group by an aggressive one. Sometimes that is actually the case: we have examples in India after the Aryan invasions, in the Roman Empire after the Germanic invasions and in Mexico after the Aztec conquest. But more often, under certain social conditions, we note the rise of a warlike ruling class in places where there is absolutely no trace of a foreign conquest. As long as a horde lives exclusively by the chase, all individuals can easily become warriors. There will of course be leaders who will rule over the tribe, but we will not find a warrior class rising to exploit, and at the same time to protect, another class that is devoted to peaceful pursuits. As the tribe emerges from the hunting stage and enters the agricultural and pastoral stage, then, along with an enormous increase in population and a greater stability in the means of exerting social influence, a more-or-less cleancut division into two classes will take place, one class being devoted exclusively to agriculture, the other class to war. In this event, it is inevitable that the warrior class should little by little acquire such ascendancy over the other as to be able to oppress it with impunity.

Poland offers a characteristic example of the gradual metamorphosis of a warrior class into an absolutely dominant class. Originally the Poles had the same organization by rural villages as prevailed among all the Slavic peoples. There was no distinction between fighters and farmers—in other words, between nobles and peasants. But after the Poles came to settle on the broad plains that are watered by the Vistula and the Niemen, agriculture began to develop among them. However, the necessity of fighting with warlike neighbors continued, so that the tribal chiefs, or voivodes, gathered about themselves a certain number of picked men whose special occupation was the bearing of arms. These warriors were distributed among the various rural communities. They were exempt from agricultural duties, yet they received their share of the produce of the soil along with the other members of the community. In early days their position was not considered very desirable, and country dwellers sometimes waived exemption from agricultural labor in order to avoid going to war. But gradually as this order of things grew stabilized, as one class became habituated to the practice of arms and military organization while the other hardened to the use of the plow and the spade, the warriors became nobles and masters, and the peasants, once companions and brothers, became villeins and serfs. Little by little, the warrior lords increased their demands, to the point where the share they took as members of the community came to include the community's whole produce, minus what was absolutely necessary for subsistence on the part of the cultivators; and when the latter tried to escape such abuses, they were constrained by force to stay bound to the soil, their situation taking on all the characteristics of serfdom pure and simple.

In the course of this evolution, around the year 1333, King Casimir the Great tried vainly to curb the overbearing insolence of the warriors. When peasants came to complain of the nobles, he contented himself with asking whether they had no sticks and stones. Some generations later, in 1537, the nobility forced all tradesmen in the cities to sell such real estate as they owned, and landed property became a prerogative of nobles only. At the same time the nobility exerted pressure upon the king to open negotiations with Rome, to the end that thenceforward only nobles should be admitted to holy orders in Poland. That barred townsmen and peasants almost completely from honorific positions, and stripped them of any social importance whatever.

•

Everywhere—in Russia and Poland, in India and medieval Europe—the ruling warrior classes acquire almost exclusive ownership of the land. Land, as we have seen, is the chief source of production and wealth in countries that are not very far advanced in civilization. But as civilization progresses, revenue from land increases proportionately. With the growth of population there is, at least in certain periods, an increase in rent, in the Ricardian sense of the term, largely because great centers of consumption arise, such at all times have been the great capitals and other large cities, ancient and modern. Eventually, if other circumstances permit, a very important social transformation occurs. Wealth rather than military valor comes to be the characteristic feature of the dominant class: the people who rule are the rich rather than the brave.

The condition that in the main is required for this transformation is that social organization shall have concentrated and become perfected to such an extent that the protection offered by public authority is considerably more effective than the protection offered by private force. In other words, private property must be so well protected by the practical and real efficacy of the laws as to render the power of the proprietor himself superfluous. This comes about through a series of gradual alterations in the social structure whereby a type of political organization, which we shall call the "feudal state," is transformed into an essentially different type, which we shall term the "bureaucratic state." We are to discuss these types at some length hereafter, but we may say at once that the evolution here referred to is as a rule greatly facilitated by progress in pacific manners and customs and by certain moral habits which societies contract as civilization advances.

Once this transformation has taken place, wealth produces political power, just as political power has been producing wealth. In a society already somewhat mature—where, therefore, individual power is curbed by the collective power—if the powerful are as a rule the rich, to be rich is to become powerful. And in truth, when fighting with the mailed fist is prohibited whereas fighting with pounds and pence is sanctioned, the better posts are inevitably won by those who are better supplied with pounds and pence.

There are, to be sure, states of a very high level of civilization which in theory are organized on the basis of moral principles of such a character that they seem to preclude this overbearing assertiveness on the part of wealth. But this is a case—and there are many such—where theoretical principles can have no more than a limited application in real life. In the United States all powers flow directly or indirectly from popular elections, and suffrage is equal for all men and women in all the states of the union. What is more, democracy prevails not only in institutions, but to a certain extent also in morals. The rich ordinarily feel a certain aversion to entering public life, and the poor a certain aversion to choosing the rich for elective office. But that does not prevent a rich man from being more influential than a poor man, since he can use pressure upon the politicians who control public administration. It does not prevent elections from being carried on to the music of clinking dollars. It does not prevent whole legislatures and considerable numbers of national congressmen from feeling the influence of powerful corporations and great financiers.

•

In all countries of the world, those other agencies for exerting social influence—personal publicity, good education, specialized training, high rank in church, public administration, and army—are always readier of access to the rich than to the poor. The rich invariably have a considerably shorter road to travel than the poor, to say nothing of the fact that the stretch of road that the rich are spared is often the roughest and most difficult.

•

The Ruling Class in Periods of Renovation and Crystallization

. . . As soon as there is a shift in the balance of political forces—when, that is, a need is felt that capacities different from the old should assert themselves in the management of the state, when the old capacities therefore lose some of their importance or changes in their distribution occur— then the manner in which the ruling class is constituted changes also. If a new source of wealth develops in a society, if the practical importance of knowledge grows, if an old religion declines or a new one is born, if a new current of ideas spreads, then, simultaneously, farreaching dislocations occur in the ruling class. One might say, indeed, that the whole history of civilized mankind comes down to a conflict between the tendency of dominant elements to monopolize political power and transmit possession of it by inheritance, and the tendency toward a dislocation of old forces and an insurgence of new forces; and this conflict produces an unending ferment of endosmosis and exosmosis between the upper classes and certain portions of the lower. Ruling classes decline inevitably when they cease to find scope for the capacities through which they rose to power, when they can no longer render the social services which they once rendered, or when their talents and the services they render lose in importance in the social environment in which they live. So the Roman aristocracy declined when it was no longer the exclusive source of higher officers for the army, of administrators for the commonwealth, of governors for the provinces. So the Venetian aristocracy declined when its nobles ceased to command the galleys and no longer passed the greater part of their lives in sailing the seas and in trading and fighting.

In inorganic nature we have the example of our air, in which a tendency to immobility produced by the force of inertia is continuously in conflict with a tendency to shift about as the result of inequalities in the distribution of heat. The two tendencies, prevailing by turn in various regions on our planet, produce now calm, now wind and storm. In much the same way in human societies, there prevails now the tendency that produces closed, stationary, crystallized ruling classes, now the tendency that results in a more or less rapid renovation of ruling classes.

The oriental societies which we consider stationary have in reality not always been so, for otherwise, as we have already pointed out, they could not have made the advances in civilization of which they have left irrefutable evidence. It is much more accurate to say that we came to know them at a time when their political forces and their political classes were in a period of crystallization. The same thing occurs in what we commonly call "aging" societies, where religious beliefs, scientific knowledge, methods of producing and distributing wealth have for centuries undergone no radical alteration and have not been disturbed in their everyday course by infiltrations of foreign elements, material or intellectual. In such societies political forces are always the same, and the class that holds possession of them holds a power that is undisputed. Power is therefore perpetuated in certain families, and the inclination to immobility becomes general through all the various strata in that society.

So in India we see the caste system become thoroughly entrenched after the suppression of Buddhism. The Greeks found hereditary castes in ancient Egypt, but we know that in the periods of greatness and renaissance in Egyptian civilization political office and social status were not hereditary. We possess an Egyptian document that summarizes the life of a high army officer who lived during the period of the expulsion of the Hyksos. He had begun his career as a simple soldier. Other documents show cases in which the same individual served successively in the army, civil administration, and priesthood.

The best known and perhaps the most important example of a society tending toward crystallization is the period in Roman history that used to be called the Low Empire. There, after several centuries of almost complete social immobility, a division between two classes grew sharper and sharper, the one made up of great landowners and high officials, the other made up of slaves, farmers and urban plebeians. What is even more striking, public office and social position became hereditary by custom before they became hereditary by law, and the trend was rapidly generalized during the period mentioned.

On the other hand it may happen in the history of a nation that commerce with foreign peoples, forced emigrations, discoveries, wars, create new poverty and new wealth, disseminate knowledge of things that were previously unknown, or cause infiltrations of new moral, intellectual and religious currents. Or again—as a result of such infiltrations, or through a slow process of inner growth, or from both causes—it may happen that a new learning arises, or that certain elements of an old, long forgotten learning return to favor, so that new ideas and new beliefs come to the fore and upset the intellectual habits on which the obedience of the masses has been founded. The ruling class may also be vanquished and destroyed in whole or in part by foreign invasions, or, when the circumstances just mentioned arise, it may be driven from power by the advent of new social elements who are strong in fresh political forces. Then, naturally, there comes a period of renovation, or, if one prefer, of revolution, during which individual energies have free play and certain individuals, more passionate, more energetic, more intrepid or merely shrewder than others, force their way from the bottom of the social ladder to the topmost rungs.

Once such a movement has set in, it cannot be stopped immediately. The example of individuals who have started from nowhere and reached prominent positions fires new ambitions, new greeds, new energies; and this molecular rejuvenation of the ruling class continues vigorously until a long period of social stability slows it down again. We need hardly mention examples of nations in such periods of renovation. In our age that would be superfluous. Rapid restocking of ruling classes is a frequent and very striking phenomenon in countries that have been recently colonized. When social life begins in such environments, there is no ready-made ruling class, and while such a class is in process of formation, admittance to it is gained very easily. Monopolization of land and other agencies of production is, if not quite impossible, at any rate more difficult than elsewhere. That is why, at least during a certain period, the Greek colonies offered a wide outlet for all Greek energy and enterprise. That is why, in the United States, where the colonizing of new lands continued through the whole nineteenth century and new industries were continually springing up, examples of men who started with nothing and have attained fame and wealth are still frequent—all of which helps to foster in the people of that country the illusion that democracy is a fact.

Suppose now that a society gradually passes from its feverish state to calm. Since the human being's psychological tendencies are always the same, those who belong to the ruling class will begin to acquire a group spirit. They will become more and more exclusive and learn better and better the art of monopolizing to their advantage the qualities and capacities that are essential to acquiring power and holding it. Then, at last, the force that is essentially conservative appears—the force of habit. Many people become resigned to a lowly station, while the members of certain privileged families or classes grow convinced that they have almost an absolute right to high station and command.

•

From Feudalism to Bureaucracy

Before we proceed any further, it might be wise to linger briefly on the two types into which, in our opinion, all political organisms may be classified, the feudal and the bureaucratic.

This classification, it should be noted, is not based upon essential, unchanging criteria. It is not our view that there is any psychological law peculiar to either one of the two types and therefore alien to the other. It seems to us, rather, that the two types are just different manifestations, different phases, of a single constant tendency whereby human societies become less simple, or, if one will, more complicated in political organization, as they grow in size and are perfected in civilization. Level of civilization is, on the whole, more important in this regard than size, since, in actual fact a liter-

ally huge state may once have been feudally organized. At bottom, therefore, a bureaucratic state is just a feudal state that has advanced and developed in organization and so grown more complex; and a feudal state may
derive from a once bureaucratized society that has decayed in civilization
and reverted to a simpler, more primitive form of political organization,
perhaps falling to pieces in the process.

By "feudal state" we mean that type of political organization in which all
the executive functions of society—the economic, the judicial, the administrative, the military—are exercised simultaneously by the same individuals,
while at the same time the state is made up of small social aggregates, each
of which possesses all the organs that are required for self-sufficiency. The
Europe of the Middle Ages offers the most familiar example of this type of
organization—that is why we have chosen to designate it by the term "feudal"; but as one reads the histories of other peoples or scans the accounts of
travelers of our own day, one readily perceives that the type is widespread.

•

In the bureaucratic state, not all the executive functions need to be concentrated in the bureaucracy and exercised by it. One might even declare
that so far in history that has never been the case. The main characteristic
of this type of social organization lies, we believe, in the fact that, wherever
it exists, the central power conscripts a considerable portion of the social
wealth by taxation, and uses it first to maintain a military establishment and
then to support a more-or-less extensive number of public services. The
greater the number of officials who perform public duties and receive their
salaries from the central government or from its local agencies, the more
bureaucratic a society becomes.

•

Feudalism introduced . . . the political supremacy of an exclusively
warrior class. . . . Another characteristic of the feudal system was the centralization of all administrative functions and all social influence in the
local military leader, who at the same time was master of the land—virtually the one instrument for the production of wealth which still existed.

Feudalism, finally, created a new type of sovereignty that was intermediate between the central, coordinating organ of the state and the individual.
Once their position had become hereditary, the more important local leaders bound lesser leaders to themselves by subgrants of land, and these lesser
chiefs were tied by oaths of feudal homage and fidelity to the man who
made the grant. They had, therefore, no direct relations with the head of
the feudal confederation as a whole, the king. In fact, they felt obliged to
fight the king if the leader to whom they were directly bound was at war
with him. This, certainly, was the main cause of the long resistance which
the feudal system offered to the continuous efforts of the central power to
destroy it.

. . . Down to the fourteenth century, the memory of the old unity of all civilized and Christian peoples, guided in religious matters by the Roman pontiff, who little by little gained recognition as supreme hierarch of the universal church, and in temporal matters by the successor of the ancient Roman emperor, lingered alive and vigorous in the intellectual classes, the clergy and the doctors of the law. Unless such memories had been very much alive, we should be at a loss to explain the attempt to restore the Empire that took place under Charlemagne and Pope Leo III in the year 800, or another somewhat more successful attempt that was made by Otto I of Saxony in 962.

A name and an idea may exercise a great moral influence, but they are not enough to restore a centralized, coordinated political system once that system has fallen to pieces. In order to effect such a restoration, they have to have a material organization at their disposal, and in order to have such an organization the agencies required for establishing it must be available. Such agencies Charlemagne's successors and the Germanic emperors lacked. They had neither a sound financial organization nor a regular bureaucracy nor, finally, a standing army that was capable of enforcing obedience to imperial edicts.

In Charlemagne's day, the old Germanic band still furnished a fairly well-disciplined militia for the Frankish armies, and the local lords were not yet omnipotent. For the same reason the emperors of the House of Saxony, and the first two emperors of the House of Franconia, could count on the cooperation of the German military class, which was not yet solidly grouped about a few leaders. Imperial and regal power attained its maximum efficiency in Germany under Henry III of Franconia. That emperor managed for some time to keep a few of the principal duchies unfilled, or to have them occupied by relatives of the reigning house. He held the duchy of Franconia and, for a time, the duchy of Swabia under his personal dominion and further retained the exclusive right to name the holders of the great ecclesiastical fiefs, bishoprics and abbacies, which were not hereditary and which covered almost half of the territory of Germany. Henry III died an untimely death. Henry IV at that moment was a minor, and he was personally weak. His struggles with the papacy permitted the higher German nobility to regain the ground it had lost.

But the moment the feudal system had taken a strong hold in Germany, the military base of the empire became shaky. Then the struggle between the Empire and the Church gave the local sovereignties the support of a great moral force in their clash with imperial authority. The effort to reestablish the worldwide political unity of Christian peoples, which Charlemagne had made and which Otto I of Saxony had repeated, may be considered a complete and final failure with the death of Frederick II of Hohenstaufen.

But the state of semibarbarism which characterized the darkest period of the Middle Ages in central and western Europe was not to be eternal. Civilization was to rise again. The process of reabsorbing local powers into the central organ of the state had, therefore, to start anew under a different form; and, in fact, what the representative of the ancient Roman Empire had been unable to do became the task of the various national monarchies.

Meantime, from about the year 1000 on, another sort of local sovereignty had begun to rise alongside of the fief: the medieval town, the commune. The commune was a federation of guilds, neighborhood organizations and trade corporations—all the various associations of people who were neither nobles nor subject vassals—which were organized in the more troublous periods of feudal anarchy, in order that those who belonged to them might enjoy a certain measure of personal security through mutual defense. The communes became powerful first in northern Italy, then in Germany and Flanders and in those countries they were among the greatest obstacles to the growth of the power of the . . . emperors. They achieved more modest positions in France, England, the Iberian kingdoms and southern Italy. In those countries they supported the crown against feudalism.

In general, the national monarchies claimed historical connections with the old barbarian monarchies which the invading Germans had set up on the ruins of the ancient Roman Empire. But after the period of political dissolution that occurred under Charlemagne's first successors, they began to take shape again following geographic and linguistic lines rather than historic traditions. The France of St. Louis, for instance, did not correspond to the old territory of the Franks. In one direction it embraced ancient Septimania, which the Visigoths had formerly controlled. In the other it withdrew from Flanders, Franconia and the Rhineland, which were all Germanic territories and were eventually attracted into the orbit of the Holy Roman Empire.

Furthermore, though his title might derive officially from the titles with which the old barbarian kings had adorned their persons, the national king was at first only the head, and sometimes the nominal head, of a federation of great barons—first among them, but first among peers. Hugh Capet and Philip Augustus were looked upon in just that way in France. King John of England appears in that guise in the text of the Magna Charta, and so do the kings of Aragon in the oath which they were obliged to take before the Cortes. As is well known, the barons of Aragon, in council assembled, invited the new king to swear that he would keep all the old agreements. Before enumerating them, they repeated a declaration: "We, who one by one are your equals and all united are more than your equals, name you our king on the following conditions." And when the conditions had been read, they concluded: "And otherwise not."

More than six centuries of struggle and slow but constant ferment were needed for the feudal king to develop into the absolute king, the feudal hierarchy into a regular bureaucracy, and the army made up of the nobles in arms and their vassals into a regular standing army. During those six hundred years, there were periods when feudalism was able to take advantage of critical moments that country and crown chanced to be passing through and regain some of its lost ground. But in the end victory rested with centralized monarchy. The kings little by little succeeded in gathering into their hands assemblages of material agencies that were greater than the feudal nobility could match. They also made shrewd use of the support of the communes and of powerful and constant moral forces, such as the widespread belief that reigning dynasties had been divinely appointed to rule, or a theory of the doctors of law that the king, like the ancient Roman Emperor, was the sovereign will that created law and the sovereign power that enforced it.

The process by which feudal monarchy evolved into an absolute bureaucratic monarchy might be called typical or normal, since it was followed in France and in a number of other countries in Europe. Nevertheless, there were other processes which led, or might have led, to the same results. The commune of Milan, for instance, in the valley of the Po, developed first into a signoria, or tyranny, and then into a duchy. In the first half of the fifteenth century it subjected many other communes and acquired a fairly extensive territory. It might easily have become a modern national kingdom. Elsewhere great feudatories enlarged their domains and transformed them into kingdoms. That was the case with the margraves of Brandenburg, who became kings of Prussia and then emperors of Germany, and with the dukes of Savoy, who became kings of Sardinia and finally of Italy.

Economic causes seem to have exercised very little influence on the transformation of the feudal state into the bureaucratic state, and that evolution certainly is one of the events that have most profoundly modified the history of the world. Systems of economic production did not undergo any very radical changes between the fourteenth century and the seventeenth, especially if we compare them with the changes that took place after bureaucratic absolutism was founded. On the other hand, between the end of the fifteenth century and the second half of the seventeenth—in other words, during the period when the feudal system was losing ground every day and was being permanently tamed—a farreaching revolution was taking place in military art and organization, owing to improvements in firearms and their wider and wider use. The baronial castle could easily and rapidly be battered down as soon as cannon became common weapons. The heavy cavalry had been made up of nobles, the only ones who could find time for long training and money for the expensive knightly equipment. But cavalry ceased to be the arm that decided battles, once the arquebus had been perfected and the infantry had generally adopted it.

•

The absolute bureaucratic state may be regarded as permanently established and fully developed in France at the beginning of the personal reign of Louis XIV—in 1661, that is. At the same time, or soon after, the strengthening of central authority and the absorption of local sovereignties became more or less completely generalized throughout Europe. The few states, such as Poland or Venice, that would not, or could not, move with the times and transform their constitutions, lost power and cohesion, and disappeared before the end of the eighteenth century.

Thus the origins of absolute monarchy are relatively recent. Inside it, and under its wing, new ruling forces, new intellectual, moral and economic conditions, rapidly grew up, so that in less than a century and a half its transformation into the modern representative state became inevitable. The rapidity of that evolution strikes us as one of the most interesting phenomena in history.

CHAPTER 23

WILL HERBERG

Religious Revival in
the United States

The Contemporary Upswing in Religion

No one who attempts to see the contemporary religious situation in the United States in perspective can fail to be struck by the extraordinary pervasiveness of religious identification among present-day Americans. Almost everybody in the United States today locates himself in one or another of the three great religious communities. . . .

In the quarter of a century between 1926 and 1959, the population of continental United States increased 28.6 per cent; membership of religious bodies increased 59.8 per cent: in other words, church membership grew more than twice as fast as population. Protestants increased 63.7 per cent, Catholics 53.9 per cent, Jews 22.5 per cent. Among Protestants, however, the increase varied considerably as between denominations: Baptist increase was well over 100 per cent, some "holiness" sects grew even more rapidly, while the figure for the Episcopal Church was only 36.7 per cent, for the Methodist Church 32.2 per cent, for the Northern Presbyterians 22.4 per cent, and for the Congregationalists 21.1 per cent.[1] In general, it may be said that "practically all major types of American religion have staged what is popularly called a 'comeback.' "[2]

In 1950 total church membership was reckoned at 85,319,000, or about 57 per cent of the total population. In 1958 it was 109,557,741, or about 63

From Will Herberg, *Protestant—Catholic—Jew* (New York: Doubleday and Company, Inc., 1955). Copyright © 1955 by Will Herberg, and reprinted by permission of the author and Doubleday and Company, Inc., pp. 46-53, 256-272.

[1] "Trends of Church Membership in the Larger Religious Bodies," *Information Service,* issued by the National Council of the Churches of Christ in the United States of America, March 8, 1952.

[2] Herbert W. Schneider, *Religion in 20th Century America* (Cambridge: Harvard University Press, 1952), p. 16.

per cent, marking an all-time high in the nation's history.[3] Indeed, all available information tends to show that the proportion of the American people religiously affiliated as church members has been consistently growing from the early days of the republic. In his address to the Evanston Assembly of the World Council of Churches, President Eisenhower pointed out that "Contrary to what many people think, the percentage of our population belonging to churches steadily increases. In a hundred years, that percentage has multiplied more than three times." [4]

President Eisenhower was here probably understating the case. Comparisons are difficult, and figures even approximately accurate are not available for earlier times, but it seems to be generally agreed that church membership in the United States at the opening of the nineteenth century was not much more than 10 or 15 per cent of the population; [5] through the century it grew at a varying rate, reflecting many factors, but above all the success of the evangelical movement in bringing religion to the frontier and the vast influx of Roman Catholic immigrants with a high proportion of church membership. At the opening of the present century, church membership stood at something like 36 per cent of the population; in 1926, when the Census of Religious Bodies established a new basis of calculation, it was about 46 per cent; in 1958, 63 per cent.[6] The trend is obvious, despite the lack of precision of the particular figures.

It is not easy to understand just what these figures reveal beyond a steady increase through a century and a half. Church membership does not mean the same today as it meant in the eighteenth or early nineteenth century, when something of the older sense of personal conversion and commitment still remained. Further, such factors as recent population trends and the increased mobility conferred by the automobile cannot be ignored in any serious effort to estimate the reasons for the growing proportion of Americans in the churches. There is also the significant fact that considerably more Americans regard themselves as church members than the statistics of church affiliation would indicate. Asked, "Do you happen at the present time to be an active member of a church or of a religious group?", 73 per cent of Americans over eighteen answered in the affirmative: of those identifying themselves as Catholics, 87 per cent said "yes"; of those identifying themselves as Protestants, 75 per cent; and of those identifying

---

[3] *Yearbook of American Churches,* Benson Y. Landis, ed., issued annually by the National Council of the Churches of Christ in the United States of America, New York, edition for 1960, pp. 258, 279.

[4] *The New York Times,* August 20, 1954.

[5] Cf. Winfred E. Garrison, "Characteristics of American Organized Religion," *The Annals of the American Academy of Political and Social Science,* Vol. 256, March 1948, p. 20.

[6] *Yearbook of American Churches, op. cit.,* edition for 1955, pp. 288-289; edition for 1960, pp. 278-279.

themselves as Jews, 50 per cent.[7] The overall total of 73 per cent is considerably higher than the percentage indicated in church membership statistics: 57 per cent in 1950 and 63 per cent in 1958. It would seem that many more people in the United States regard themselves as members, even "active" members, of a church than are listed on the actual membership rolls of the churches. The fact of the matter seems to be that: "In America, there is no sharp division between those within the religious fold and those outside, as there tends to be in Europe. It is extremely difficult, in fact, to determine just how many members the churches have, since no clear boundary marks off members from those who participate without formal membership." [8]

About 70 to 75 per cent of the American people, it may be safely estimated, regard themselves as members of churches; [9] another 20 or 25 per cent locate themselves in one or another religious community without a consciousness of actual church membership; they constitute a "fringe of sympathetic bystanders," [10] so to speak. Only about 5 per cent of the American people consider themselves outside the religious fold altogether.

•

That public opinion is markedly more favorable to religion today than it has been for a long time is recognized by all observers. "A hostile attitude toward religion as such," Schneider notes, "gets less of a hearing today than a century ago, or even half a century ago." [11] . . . It is probably true that "in no other modern industrial state does organized religion play a greater role" than it does in the United States.[12]

With institutional growth and enhanced public status has come a notable increase in the self-assurance of the spokesmen of religion, who no longer feel themselves defending a losing cause against a hostile world. . . . Spokesmen of religion are now beginning to speak with the confidence of those who feel that things are going their way and that they are assured of a respectful hearing. Indeed, there have lately arisen voices among the "irreligious" minority who profess to see their "freedom *from* religion" threatened by the increasingly proreligious climate of our culture and the new aggressiveness of the churches.[13] It is a far cry indeed from the 1920's, when religion and the churches were in retreat, faith was taken as a sign of intellectual backwardness or imbecility, and the initiative had passed to the "emanci-

---

[7] "Who Belongs to What Church?" *The Catholic Digest,* January 1953.

[8] Robin M. Williams, Jr., *American Society: a Sociological Interpretation* (New York: Alfred A. Knopf, 1951), p. 325.

[9] *See* Jerald C. Brauer, *Protestantism in America* (Philadelphia: Westminster Press, 1953), p. 286.

[10] *American Society, op. cit.,* p. 325.

[11] *Religion in 20th Century America, op. cit.,* p. 32.

[12] *American Society, op. cit.,* p. 304.

[13] *See e.g., Religion in 20th Century America, op. cit.,* p. 33.

pated" debunkers of the superstitions of the "Babbitts" and the "Bible Belt." That age has disappeared almost without a trace, and the generation that has arisen since finds it well-nigh impossible to imagine what those days were like, so remote from our consciousness have they become.

Particularly significant as reflecting a reversal of trend is the new intellectual prestige of religion on all levels of cultural life. On one level, this means the extraordinarily high proportion of socalled "religious books" on the best-seller lists; on another, the remarkable vogue in intellectual circles of the more sophisticated religious and theological writing of our time. Kierkegaard (rediscovered in this generation), Tillich, Maritain, Reinhold Niebuhr, Buber, Berdyaev, Simone Weil—these writers have standing and prestige with the intellectual elite of today in a way that no religious writers have had for many decades. Religious ideas, concepts, and teachings have become familiar in the pages of the "vanguard" journals of literature, politics and art.

•

The Triple Melting Pot

The outstanding feature of the religious situation in America today is the pervasiveness of religious self-identification along the tripartite scheme of Protestant, Catholic, Jew. From the "land of immigrants," America has . . . become the "triple melting pot," restructured in three great communities with religious labels, defining three great "communions" or "faiths." This transformation has been greatly furthered by what may be called the dialectic of "third generation interest": the third generation, coming into its own with the cessation of mass immigration, tries to recover its "heritage," so as to give itself some sort of "name" or context of self-identification and social location, in the larger society. "What the son wishes to forget"—so runs "Hansen's Law"—"the grandson wishes to remember." But what he can "remember" is obviously not his grandfather's foreign language, or even his grandfather's foreign culture; it is rather his grandfather's *religion.* America does not demand of him the abandonment of the ancestral religion as it does of the ancestral language and culture. This religion he now "remembers" in a form suitably "Americanized," and yet in a curious way also "retraditionalized." Within this comprehensive framework of basic sociological change operate those inner factors making for a "return to religion" which so many observers have noted in recent years—the collapse of all secular securities in the historical crisis of our time, the quest for a recovery of meaning in life, the new search for inwardness and personal authenticity amid the collectivistic heteronomies of the present-day world.

Self-identification in religious terms, almost universal in the America of today, obviously makes for religious belonging in a more directly institutional way. It engenders a sense of adherence to a church or denomination and impels one to institutional affiliation. These tendencies are reinforced by the pressures of other-directed adjustment to peer-group behavior, which today increasingly requires religious identification and association with some church. Thus a pattern of religious conformism develops, most pronounced, perhaps, among the younger, "modern-minded" inhabitants of suburbia, but rapidly spreading to all sections of the American people.

The picture that emerges is one in which religion is accepted as a normal part of the American way of life. Not to be—that is, not to identify oneself and be identified as—either a Protestant, a Catholic, or a Jew is somehow not to be an American. It may imply being foreign, as is the case when one professes oneself a Buddhist, a Muslim, or anything but a Protestant, Catholic, or Jew, even when one's Americanness is otherwise beyond question. Or it may imply being obscurely "un-American," as is the case with those who declare themselves atheists, agnostics, or even "humanists." . . . Americanness today entails religious identification as Protestant, Catholic, or Jew in a way and to a degree quite unprecedented in our history. To be a Protestant, a Catholic, or a Jew is today the alternative way of being an American.

●

The Religion of "Belonging"

The ultimate ambiguity of the present religious situation in this country is obvious on the face of it. Every manifestation of contemporary American religion reveals diverse sides, of varying significance from the standpoint of Jewish-Christian faith. No realistic estimate of the present religious situation is possible unless this fundamental ambiguity is recognized.

The new status of religion as a basic form of American "belonging," along with other factors tending in the same direction, has led to the virtual disappearance of anti-religious prejudice, once by no means uncommon in our national life. The old-time "village atheist" is a thing of the past, a folk curiosity like the town crier; Clarence Darrow, the last of the "village atheists" on a national scale, has left no successors. The present generation can hardly understand the vast excitement stirred up in their day by the "atheists" and "iconoclasts," who vied for public attention less than half a century ago, or imagine the brash militancy of the "rationalist" movements and publications now almost all extinct. Religion has become part of the ethos of American life to such a degree that overt anti-religion is all but inconceivable.

The same factors that have led to the virtual disappearance of overt anti-religion have also made for a new openness to religion and what religion might have to say about the urgent problems of life and thought. In many ways the contemporary mind is more ready to listen to the word of faith than Americans have been for decades.

Yet it is only too evident that the religiousness characteristic of America today is very often a religiousness without religion, a religiousness with almost any kind of content or none, a way of sociability or "belonging" rather than a way of reorienting life to God. It is thus frequently a religiousness without serious commitment, without real inner conviction, without genuine existential decision. What should reach down to the core of existence, shattering and renewing, merely skims the surface of life, and yet succeeds in generating the sincere feeling of being religious. Religion thus becomes a kind of protection the self throws up against the radical demand of faith.

Where the other-directed adjustment of peer-group conformity operates, the discrepancy becomes even more obvious. The other-directed man or woman is eminently religious in the sense of being religiously identified and affiliated, since being religious and joining a church or synagogue is, under contemporary American conditions, a fundamental way of "adjusting" or "belonging." But what can the other-directed man or woman make of the prophets and the prophetic faith of the Bible, in which the religion of the church he joins is at least officially grounded? The very notion of being "singled out," of standing "over against" the world, is deeply repugnant to one for whom wellbeing means conformity and adjustment. Religion is valued as conferring a sense of sociability and "belonging," a sense of being really and truly *of* the world and society, a sense of reassurance; how can the other-directed man then help but feel acutely uncomfortable with a kind of religion—for that is what biblical faith is—which is a declaration of permanent resistance to the heteronomous claims of society, community, culture and cult? The other-directed man generally protects himself against this profoundly disturbing aspect of biblical faith by refusing to understand it; indeed, insofar as he is other-directed, he really cannot understand it. The religion he avows is still formally the Christian or Jewish faith rooted in the prophetic tradition; it is, however, so transformed as it passes through the prism of the other-directed mind that it emerges as something quite different, in many ways, its opposite.

•

"The 'unknown God' of Americans seems to be faith itself." [14] What Americans believe in when they are religious is . . . religion itself. Of course, religious Americans speak of God and Christ, but what they seem to regard as really redemptive is primarily religion, the "positive" attitude of *believing*. It is this faith in faith, this religion that makes religion its own object, that is the outstanding characteristic of contemporary American religiosity.

[14] Reinhold Niebuhr, "Religiosity and the Christian Faith," *Christianity and Crisis,* XIV (1955), No. 24.

•

Religion Becomes Man-Centered

Prosperity, success, and advancement in business are the obvious ends for which religion, or rather the religious attitude of "believing," is held to be useful. There is ordinarily no criticism of the ends themselves in terms of the ultimate loyalties of a God-centered faith, nor is there much concern about what the religion or the faith is all about, since it is not the content of the belief but the attitude of believing that is felt to be operative.

Almost as much as worldly success, religion is expected to produce a kind of spiritual euphoria, the comfortable feeling that one is all right with God. Roy Eckardt calls this the cult of "divine-human chumminess" in which God is envisioned as the "Man Upstairs," a "Friendly Neighbor," who is always ready to give you the pat on the back you need when you happen to feel blue. "Fellowship with the Lord is, so to say, an extra emotional jag that keeps [us] happy. The 'gospel' makes [us] 'feel real good.' " [15] Again, all sense of the ambiguity and precariousness of human life, all sense of awe before the divine majesty, all sense of judgment before the divine holiness, is shut out; God is, in Jane Russell's inimitable phrase, a "livin' Doll." What relation has this kind of god to the biblical God who confronts sinful man as an enemy before he comes out to meet repentant man as a savior? Is this he of whom we are told, "It is a fearful thing to fall into the hands of the living God" (*Heb.* 10.31)? The measure of how far contemporary American religiosity falls short of the authentic tradition of Jewish-Christian faith is to be found in the chasm that separates Jane Russell's "livin' Doll" from the living god of scripture.

The cultural enrichment that is looked for in religion varies greatly with the community, the denomination, and the outlook and status of the church members. Liturgy is valued as aesthetically and emotionally "rewarding," sermons are praised as "interesting" and "enjoyable," discussions of the world relations of the church are welcomed as "educational," even theology is approved of as "thought-provoking." On another level, the "old-time religion" is cherished by certain segments of the population because it so obviously enriches their cultural life.

But in the last analysis, it is "peace of mind" that most Americans expect of religion. "Peace of mind" is today easily the most popular gospel that goes under the name of religion; in one way or another it invades and permeates all other forms of contemporary religiosity. It works in well with the drift toward other-direction characteristic of large sections of American so-

---

[15] Roy Eckhardt, "The New Look in American Piety," *The Christian Century,* November 17, 1954.

ciety, since both see in adjustment the supreme good in life. What is desired
and what is promised is the conquest of insecurity and anxiety, the overcoming of inner conflict, the shedding of guilt and fear, the translation of
the self to the painless paradise of "normality" and "adjustment"! Religion,
in short, is a spiritual anodyne designed to allay the pains and vexations of
existence.

●

The burden of the criticism of American religion from the point of view
of Jewish-Christian faith is that contemporary religion is so naïvely, so in-
nocently *man-centered*. Not god, but man—man in his individual and corporate being—is the beginning and end of the spiritual system of much of
present-day American religiosity. In this kind of religion there is no sense
of transcendence, no sense of the nothingness of man and his works before a holy god; in this kind of religion the values of life, and life itself, are
not submitted to Almighty God to judge, to shatter, and to reconstruct; on
the contrary, life, and the values of life, are given an ultimate sanction by
being identified with the divine. In this kind of religion it is not man who
serves god, but god who is mobilized and made to serve man and his purposes—whether these purposes be economic prosperity, free enterprise, social reform, democracy, happiness, security, or "peace of mind." . . . The
American is a religious man, and in many cases personally humble and
conscientious. But religion as he understands it is not something that makes
for humility or the uneasy conscience: it is something that reassures him
about the essential rightness of everything American, his nation, his culture, and himself; something that validates his goals and his ideals instead
of calling them into question; something that enhances his self-regard instead of challenging it; something that feeds his self-sufficiency instead of
shattering it; something that offers him salvation on easy terms instead of
demanding repentance and a "broken heart." Because it does all these
things, his religion, however sincere and well-meant, is ultimately vitiated
by a strong and pervasive idolatrous element.

●

Yet we must not see the picture as all of one piece. Within the general
framework of a secularized religion embracing the great mass of American
people, there are signs of deeper and more authentic stirrings of faith. Duncan Norton-Taylor, in his comments on the new religiousness of businessmen, may not be altogether wrong in noting that "particularly among the
younger men, there *is* a groping for a spiritual base." [16] Norman Thomas,
though recognizing that the "return to religion," which is "one of the significant phenomena of our confused and troubled times," is a "phenomenon
of many and contradictory aspects," nevertheless finds it, in part at least,

---

[16] Duncan Norton-Taylor, "Businessmen on Their Knees," *Fortune*, October, 1953.

"definitely characterized by an awareness of, or search after God." [17] Certainly among the younger people, particularly among the more sensitive young men and women on the campuses of this country, and in the suburban communities that are in so many ways really continuous with the campus, there are unmistakable indications of an interest in and concern with religion that goes far beyond the demands of mere social "belonging." [18] These stirrings are there; they are not always easily identified as religion on the one hand, or easily distinguishable from the more conventional types of religiousness on the other; but they constitute a force whose range and power should not be too readily dismissed. Only the future can tell what these deeper stirrings of faith amount to and what consequences they hold for the American religion of tomorrow. . . .

---

[17] Norman Thomas, "Religion and Civilization," *The Atlantic Monthly,* August, 1947.
[18] Will Herberg, "The Religious Stirring on the Campus," *Commentary,* XIII (1952), No. 2.

CHAPTER 24

PETER F. DRUCKER

The Educational Revolution

An abundant and increasing supply of highly educated people has become the absolute prerequisite of social and economic development in our world. It is rapidly becoming a condition of national survival. What matters is not that there are so many more individuals around who have been exposed to long years of formal schooling—though this is quite recent. The essential new fact is that a developed society and economy are less than fully effective if anyone is educated to less than the limit of his potential. The uneducated is fast becoming an economic liability and unproductive. Society must be an "educated society" today to progress, to grow, even to survive.

A sudden, sharp change has occurred in the meaning and impact of knowledge for society. Because we now can organize men of high skill and knowledge for joint work through the exercise of responsible judgment, the highly educated man has become the central resource of today's society, the supply of such men the true measure of its economic, its military, and even its political potential.

This is a complete reversal of man's history within the last fifty years or so. Until the twentieth century, no society could afford more than a handful of educated people; for throughout the ages, to be educated meant to be unproductive.

•

It has always been axiomatic that the man of even a little education would forsake the hoe and the potter's wheel and would stop working with his hands. After all, our word "school"—and its equivalent in all European languages—derives from a Greek word meaning "leisure."

To support more educated people than the barest minimum required gross exploitation of the "producers," if not strict rules to keep them at work

---

and away from education. The short burst of education in the Athens of Pericles rested on a great expansion of slavery, the intellectual and artistic splendor of the Italian Renaissance on a sharp debasement of the economic and social position of peasant and artisan.

Idealists tried to break this "iron law" by combining manual work and education; the tradition goes back to the Rule of St. Benedict with its mixture of farmwork and study. It found its best expression in the mid-nineteenth century, in Emerson's New England farmer who supposedly read Homer in the original Greek while guiding a plow. But this, of course, never worked. The Benedictines—imperiling their salvation, to the lasting benefit of mankind—very soon left farming to villeins and serfs and concentrated on study. Long before Emerson's death, those New England farmers who cared for the plow had left both Homer and New England for the rich soils of the Midwest, while those few who had cared for Homer had left farming altogether to become lawyers, preachers, teachers or politicians. The "iron law" was indeed inescapable as long as manual labor was the really productive labor.

Thomas Jefferson believed in higher education and in equality as much as any American. He considered the founding of the University of Virginia and the authorship of the Declaration of Independence, rather than the Presidency, his greatest achievements. Yet in his educational master plan he proposed to limit access to higher education to a handful of geniuses. It was obvious that only a few could be spared from manual labor.

Today the dearth of educated people in the formerly colonial areas appears such a handicap as by itself to be adequate condemnation of colonialism and proof of the "wickedness" of the imperialists. But education did not come first in the scale of social needs even fifty years ago; flood control and land boundaries, equitable taxation and improved agriculture, railroads and incorruptible magistrates, all ranked much higher. If the colonial powers were then criticized on the score of education, it was for forcing it on too many, for destroying thereby the native culture, and for creating an unemployable, overeducated proletariat. The educated person was then still a luxury rather than a necessity and education a preparation for dignified leisure rather than for productive work.

In my own childhood forty years ago, schools still assumed that education was for "nonwork." They preached that the educated man should not despise the honest worker, as schools had preached since the days of Seneca in the first century.

The Scale of the Explosion

Thirty years ago, only one out of every eight Americans at work had been to high school. Today four out of every five of the young people of high school age in the United States attend high school. Twenty years hence, when today's middleaged will have retired, practically every working American will be a high school graduate. We have already passed the halfway mark.

Even greater has been the jump in college and university attendance. Thirty years ago, it was still an almost negligible 4 per cent or less of the appropriate age group. Today the figure is around 35 per cent for the nation; this takes in groups such as the southern Negro or the southern "poor white," for whom going to college is still all but unknown. In the metropolitan areas of the country—even in such predominantly working-class cities as Detroit—the figure is nearly 50 per cent. It will, barring catastrophe, be that high for the nation as a whole in another fifteen years. By then two out of every three young Americans in the metropolitan areas will, regardless almost of income, race, or sex, be exposed to higher education.

In the American work force of thirty years ago, there were at most three college graduates for every hundred men and women at work. There are eighteen today; the figure will be thirty-five, twenty years hence—even if, contrary to all expectations, going to college becomes no more general than it is already among the two-thirds of our people who live in metropolitan areas.

On top of all this, adult education is booming. Fifty years ago, only those adults went back to school who had been unable to get a formal education as children. Adult education was for the educationally underprivileged— the immigrant from southern Europe who wanted to learn English, or the man who had gone to work at age fourteen and wanted to improve himself. In England adult education was the "Workers Educational Alliance" or the "Home University Library," both offering standard school subjects to workers and clerks. The German *Volkshochschule* served the same purpose.

Adult education during the last fifteen years has been growing faster in this country than college enrollment. And now, increasingly, it means advanced education for the already highly educated. It is almost routine for the experienced and successful physician to go back to school for advanced training every two or three years. Refresher courses are increasingly demanded of our teachers. Some fifty universities—in addition to a dozen large companies and professional management associations—offer advanced management courses to successful men in the middle and upper ranks of business, who usually already have college if not advanced degrees. Yet before World War II only two such programs existed, both new and both struggling to get students.

The educational revolution has been even more explosive in Soviet Russia. Thirty years ago, basic literacy was confined to a small minority and had probably fallen even below the low standards of czarist Russia. The educational push hardly began until the mid-thirties. Today, because of Russia's larger population, the proportion of young people in secondary or higher education is still quite a bit lower than in this country, but the absolute numbers are fast approaching ours.

In the total population of the Soviet Union, educated people must still be a small group. Few if any of the top people in the Soviet Union have had more than elementary formal schooling; certainly of those over forty in the Soviet Union, even high school graduates are still only a tiny fraction. But in Russia, too, it has become evident that education is the capital resource of a modern, industrial society. We know now that the Russian achievement does not rest on the Communist tenets of "socialist ownership of productive resources," the "dictatorship of the proletariat," "collectivization of agriculture," or "national planning." Every one of them has been as much an impediment as a help, a source of weakness fully as much as a source of strength. The achievement rests squarely upon the tremendous concentration of resources, time, and effort on producing an educated society.

The two outstanding success stories among small nations, Switzerland and Mexico, have nothing in common save extraordinary educational development. Switzerland is the one European country where secondary education, in the last thirty years, has become almost universal. Mexico is the only country in the world that, since the mid-thirties, has spent no money on defense but has instead made education the first charge on its national income. And is it entirely coincidence that the major countries in the Free World that have found the going the roughest since World War II, Great Britain and France, are also the countries in which the educational revolution has advanced the least, in which the supply of educated people, though of high quality, is today still not much larger proportionately than it was in 1930 or even in 1913? In England the supply may well be smaller, considering the steady emigration of so many of the highly educated young people.

We are undergoing the educational revolution because the work of knowledge is no longer unproductive in terms of goods and services. In the new organization, it becomes the specifically productive work. The man who works exclusively or primarily with his hands is the one who is increasingly unproductive. Productive work in today's society and economy is work that applies vision, knowledge, and concepts—work that is based on the mind rather than on the hand.

There will therefore be no permanent oversupply of educated people. On the contrary, the more there are, the greater should be the demand for them. Educated people are the "capital" of a developed society. The immediate impact of, say, using physicians instead of barbers is to uncover needs, opportunities, and areas of ignorance, leading to the need both for more physicians and for more medical and biological research. The same process can be seen in every other field—and with particular force in the economic field of production and distribution. Every engineer, every chemist, every accountant, every market analyst immediately creates the opportunity and the need for more men who can apply knowledge and concepts, both in his own field and all around it.

This may sound obvious. But it is so new that it is not yet recognized. Our accountants, for instance, still base their terms and measurements on the eighteenth-century tenet that manual labor creates all value. They still call it "productive labor"; the work of men of knowledge is "nonproductive labor" or "overhead," a term reeking of moral disapproval. When economists talk of "capital" they rarely include "knowledge." Yet this is the only real capital today. The development of educated people is the most important capital formation, their number, quality, and utilization the most meaningful index of the wealth-producing capacity of a country.

The Impact on Society

What is today called "automation," that is, the rapid substitution of work by knowledge and concept for work by human hands, is a first impact of the educated society. It is a moot question whether the essence of automation lies in specific machinery and technical ideas, or whether it lies rather in basic concepts about the nature of work.

But there can be little doubt that the driving force in automation is the fact that people who have been exposed to formal schooling for twelve or sixteen years have expectations in respect to work and jobs which manual work, no matter how well paid, does not fulfill. They increasingly demand jobs in which they can apply knowledge, concepts, and system. They increasingly refuse to accept jobs in which they cannot apply what they have learned, namely, to work with their minds. They may be satisfied with a job of little skill—and there are a good many semiskilled knowledge jobs— but they expect work that draws on mental rather than manual faculties.

In the United States, where most of the young people in the metropolitan areas go at least to high school, the assembly line is already obsolete. The labor necessary to run it is becoming scarce. Young people with a high school education do not want to work as human machine tools. Moreover, to use people with that degree of education for the semiskilled and unskilled manual jobs of the assembly line would be a gross waste of valuable, expensive, and scarce resources.

Tomorrow everybody—or practically everybody—will have had the education of the upper class of yesterday and will expect equivalent opportunities. Yet only a small minority can get ahead, no matter what work they choose. This is why we face the problem of making every kind of job meaningful and capable of satisfying an educated man. This is why the new organization must create an effective relationship of function, rank, rewards, and responsibility, not only for its professionals, but for all those employed in knowledge jobs.

•

The educational revolution has had an equal impact on the world economy. Educational capacity, as much as natural resources or industrial plants, is becoming a crucial factor in international trade, economic development, and economic competition. Educational development, above all, has become a central problem of the poor countries.

Many of these underdeveloped countries spend today a larger proportion of their national income on education than does the United States. Yet where we complain that one-fifth of our young people still do not finish high school, many of these countries can barely keep one-fifth of their young people in elementary school. They cannot finance the cost of a literate society, let alone that of an educated society.

This educational inequality is a serious international and interracial problem. Its inevitable result is to make inequality greater, to make the rich richer and the poor poorer. Even greater is the danger that it will push poor, underdeveloped countries into the totalitarian camp; for a totalitarian tyranny, so it appears to them, can raise enough money for the rapid development of education even in the poorest. (This is a delusion. Practically all the poor underdeveloped countries are much poorer than Russia was in 1917 and much further behind in education. They are unlikely therefore to repeat her performance in education even by faithfully copying every Russian tenet and action. But this may be found out only when it is too late.)

Here, it would seem, is a highly promising area for international aid and cooperation. There is need and opportunity for financial aid to help the underdeveloped countries pay for the rapid expansion of education. There is need for systematic cooperative effort in training and developing people, especially future teachers. There is need and opportunity to help think through the purposes, the structure and the methods of education needed in those countries. Above all, there is need for the developed countries, and especially for the United States, to accept a national policy of assisting underdeveloped countries in building education.

•

"The Battle of Waterloo," it is said, "was won on the playing fields of Eton." Perhaps, but no one asserts that it was won in Eton's classrooms. "The Prussian schoolmaster," another saying goes, "defeated France in the War of 1870 that created imperial Germany." But long ago this was exposed as empty boast; the credit belongs to the German railway and the German armaments designers.

With the launching of Russia's Sputnik, however, the old pleasantry became a grim fact. The higher education of a country controls its military, its technological and its economic potential. In an age of superpowers and absolute weapons, higher education may indeed be the only area in which a country can still be ahead, can still gain decisive advantage.

The greatest impact of the educational revolution is therefore on international power and politics. It has made the supply of highly educated people a decisive factor in the competition between powers—for leadership and perhaps even for survival. . . .

CHAPTER 25

KENNETH KENISTON

A Second Look
at the Uncommitted

No issue today divides the public or the intellectual community so deeply as does the "counterculture," the "new culture," "Consciousness III"—which I will call the new youthful opposition.

However fashionable it has become to laud or lambaste the dissenting young, serious issues lie hidden behind current polemics. For the debate about the oppositional young ultimately involves a debate about the nature of man and society and requires that we examine our basic assumptions about both. I suspect that this debate, which crosscuts and confounds the traditional distinctions between conservatives and liberals, may well define the basic terms of intellectual inquiry, controversy, and creativity during the decades ahead.

The emergence of a youthful opposition is an instance of a historic event that was predicted by no one twenty years ago. The many diverse theorists who share what I will call "liberal" assumptions failed in the 1950s and early 1960s to anticipate the emergence of the youthful revolt; these theorists even predicted that such a revolt would become progressively *less* likely as affluence and higher education spread. To understand the theoretical importance of the current debate about the meaning of the youthful opposition of some of the widely shared theoretical assumptions of liberal thinkers therefore requires a closer examination.

The "Liberal" Analysis

Liberal theories of man have usually started with the malleability or plasticity of human nature. . . . Given this implicit or explicit assumption of human plasticity, psychology concentrated on the processes by which human beings are influenced, shaped, and molded. . . .

Reprinted from *Social Policy* (July/August) 1971, Vol. 2, No. 2.

But if liberal psychology emphasized human plasticity and the techniques by which human conviction and behavior can be molded and modified, liberal social theories in sociology, politics, and economics as a rule stressed equilibrium, stability, and the mechanisms of social control. The basic model of human society was the model of the "social system," constantly seeking to reach "dynamic equilibrium." The major theoretical effort of liberal sociologists went into explaining precisely *how* this equilibrium, harmony, lack of conflict, or absence of revolution had been guaranteed.

Political theorists emphasized the stabilizing effects of competing interest groups, each with "veto power" over the others. The importance of pluralistic tolerance, of "democratic consensus," and of "liberal personality" was extensively studied. Still others examined how social conflicts are routinized —channeled into institutional forms that minimize social disruption and encourage compromise and reconciliation.

For their part, some economists emphasized the "countervailing powers" that prevent the domination of the economy by any one set of monopolistic interests. Even Keynesianism can be seen as an effort to define the means whereby a stable economy might be guaranteed. Experts on labor relations scrutinized the way highly organized trade unions and the institutions of collective bargaining minimized class struggle, thus promoting peaceful "conflict resolution." In virtually all areas of scholarly endeavor, then, the major theoretical emphasis was on explaining that stability which was considered the goal and norm of societal existence.

The liberal assumptions of human plasticity and sociopolitical equilibrium were joined explicitly in the theory of socialization and acculturation. Malleable man was said to be related to stable society through a series of special socializing institutions like the family and the education system, whose primary function was to "integrate" the individual into society. Specifically, the chief job of families and schools—increasingly schools in technological society—was to teach children the social roles and cultural values necessary for adult life in that society.

Liberal social theorists did not naively confuse stability with stasis. A society in a state of basic equilibrium might still be a society that was changing rapidly: the equilibrium could be "dynamic." Social change created social strains and psychological stresses; but if all went well, it did not finally upset the basic social equilibrium. Between social strain and social disequilibrium stood a series of "mechanisms of social control," ranging from the police force to the practice of psychotherapy, which served to reduce societal tension by resocializing or isolating deviant individuals and by encapsulating or co-opting deviant social movements. The ideal kind of social change was seen as incremental—slow, quantitative, gradual, and nonrevolutionary. Indeed, some social changes, e.g., rising economic prosperity or increasing education, were believed to increase the stability of the societies in which they occurred. Increasing prosperity meant that more human needs could be met by society; prolonging education provided more individuals with a lengthier and more thorough socialization experience.

Nor were liberal social theorists ignorant of the fact that revolution, social convulsions, and dramatic upheavals abound in history. But convulsive social upheavals were almost always seen as symptoms of a breakdown of the system of social control, and as regressive or destructive in their consequences. "Meaningful social change" was thought most likely to occur through "gradualism" and "piecemeal social reform."

There is no inevitable reason why functional failures—e.g., breakdown in mechanisms of social control—should be deemed undesirable. Had Nazi Germany with all its mechanisms of social control, from the Gestapo on down, failed from a functional point of view, we might well have deemed this failure ideal from a broader ethical or political point of view.

In a similar way, liberal social thinkers generally interpreted individual deviance from dominant social norms and values as the unfortunate result of "failures of socialization," usually in the early years of life. . . .

But in practice, liberal social theories have tended to identify functional "failure" with undesirable moral failures. The collapse of the French Revolution into Bonapartism or of the Russian Revolution into Stalinism was cited to demonstrate the general undesirability of revolutions and to confirm the implication that social change involving naked conflict was the undesirable result of a "breakdown" in the system of social control.

In looking to the future, liberal theorists, naturally enough, foresaw more of what their theories led them to view as normal, desirable, and inevitable: more industrial productivity, more technologization, more piecemeal reform, more higher education, more stability, and more effective management.

Admittedly, problems were anticipated—for example, the problem of avoiding political apathy when most major social and ideological problems had been solved. Most liberal writers urged that new ways be found to involve the young in the political future of their nation, and most deplored the "privatism" of the "silent generation" of the 1950s. Other problems were also foreseen: the problems of mass culture, of the lonely crowd, of the use of leisure time, of the organization man, of rapid job obsolescence, and so on. But compared with the old problems of scarcity, economic depression, class warfare, and ideological conflict, these new problems seemed minor. It was persuasively argued by writers like Daniel Bell, Seymour Martin Lipset, and Edward Shils that the age of ideology was over and that the remaining problems of Western civilization could be defined as largely instrumental—as problems of "how," not of "what." As a result, it was believed that these problems would eventually yield to scientific knowledge, professional expertise, and technical know-how.

Theories like these attempted to explain—indeed they *did* explain—the relative domestic stability of the Western democracies in the 1950s, along with the general acceptance, acquiescence, or apathy of educated youth. But in retrospect, they were too airtight and too historically parochial. We can now see that they took a particular historical moment—one that today seems abnormal in its tranquility—and constructed theories that elevated this particular moment into the natural state of affairs. And among other things, this liberal system of ideas—it would be fair to call it an ideology— effectively prevented us from anticipating, much less understanding, the increasingly wide-scale dissent among a growing minority of the young during the 1960s.

It is easy to caricature, criticize, and mock liberal social thought; but it will be the work of a generation to develop a view of the world that does a better job. In the meantime, we had best admit that we are all, to varying degrees, products of these liberal theoretical bases.

Yet in its treatment of the relation of youth to society, liberal social thought, like Marxism, predicted precisely the opposite of what has actually happened. And that fact alone should impel us to question and redefine the basic assumptions from which liberalism began.The emergence of a youthful opposition, then, demands new theories not only of youthfulness but of human nature, of society, and of their relationship.

Two new analyses of the youthful opposition are emerging that have theoretical depth and scope: they properly attempt to understand the new opposition in terms of a broader theory of man and society. The first theory, which is an adaptation of liberal theories, asserts, in essence, that the youth movement in the industrialized nations is historically a counterrevolutionary movement, a reaction against the more basic forces involved in the growth of a new technological society. The second theory counters by claiming that the dissenting young are true revolutionaries, a historical vanguard that is defining a new and better society. It is worth examining each theory in greater detail.

Youth as a Counterrevolutionary Force

Consider first the "counterrevolutionary" theory of youth. The most thoughtful proponents of this view are men like Zbigniew Brzezinski, Lewis Feuer, and, in very different ways, Raymond Aron, Daniel Bell, Alvin Toffler, Bruno Bettelheim, and Herman Kahn. These thinkers differ on a great many key issues, and it does each an injustice to group them together without also underlining their differences; but they are usually in essential agreement on several major points.

First, they agree that we are in the midst of a major social transformation that is taking us out of an industrial society into the postindustrial, technological, postmodern, superindustrial, or, in Brzezinski's terms, "technetronic" society of the future. The new society will be highly rationalized. It will be characterized by high productivity, automation, increased leisure time, more individual choices, better social planning, greater opportunities for the expression of individual interests, rapid rates of social change, more rational administration, and the demand for enormously high levels of education among those who occupy positions of leadership. It will be a society of complex, large-scale organizations, global communications, and a basically technical approach to the solution of human problems. In this society, power will lie increasingly not with those who possess economic capital, but with those who possess educational "capital." In the technetronic society, the "knowledge industry," centered above all in the professoriate and the universities, will be the central industry of society and the central motor of historical change.

The second assumption common to the counterrevolutionary theories of youth is that periods of basic historical transition are inevitably marked by social disturbances. The introduction of factories in Europe and America in the nineteenth century was marked by growing class conflict and the Luddite movement, which led displaced agricultural workers to try to destroy the factories that were depriving them of work. Today, the transition into the technetronic age is marked by an equally violent revulsion on the part of those whose skills and values are made obsolete by the new social revolution.

Specifically, a postindustrial society imposes what Daniel Bell terms a heavy "organizational harness" upon the young: it requires them to study for many years, to acquire highly specialized technical skills, to stay in school, and to postpone gratification well into biological adulthood. Equally important, this new society renders obsolete a large number of traditional values, skills, and outlooks. A technetronic society needs, above all, skilled executives, systems analysts, computer programmers, trained administrators, and high-level scientists. Those who possess these skills are in the forefront of historic change: their talents are needed; their outlooks are valued. But those identified with "traditional" fields like the humanities and the social sciences find that their values and skills are becoming increasingly unnecessary, irrelevant, and obsolete; they are today's neo-Luddites. The ideals of romanticism, expressiveness, and traditional humanism may dominate the contemporary youth culture, but they do not dominate the social structure —the specific institutions that are changing our lives. One consequence, then, is what Bell terms the disjuncture between the culture—specifically, the adversary culture of intellectuals and many students—and the dominant social structure of large-scale organization, technology, mass communications, and electronics.

The conclusion that the revolt of the young is essentially counterrevolutionary follows from the first two points. According to this theory, the humanistic young are rebelling because of their latent awareness of their own obsolescence. The "organizational harness" around their necks is too tight and heavy for them to endure. An ever-larger group of young men and women feel that they have no place in the modern world, for they lack salable skills, basic character, styles, and value orientations that are adapted to the emergent postindustrial society. They are, as Bruno Bettelheim puts it, "obsolete youth." They rebel in a blind, mindless, and generally destructive way against rationalism, intellect, technology, organization, discipline, hierarchy, and all of the requisites of a postindustrial society. Sensing their historical obsolescence, they lash out like the Luddites against the computers and managers that are consigning them to the dustbin of history. It is predictable that they will end with bombing, terrorism, and anarchy; for the obsolete young are desperately pitting themselves against historic forces they cannot stop. But students of engineering, business administration, and so on—students in the fields most rewarded in the technetronic society—do not protest or rebel; instead, it is the obsolescent humanist and social scientist who lead the counterculture.

Although theorists differ as to precisely *which* unconscious forces are expressed in student dissent, the logic of the counterrevolutionary argument makes a recourse to psychologism almost mandatory. For if the manifest issues of student unrest are seen as pseudo-issues, disguises, and rationalizations, then we are forced into the realm of the not-conscious in our attempt to locate the "real" motives behind the youthful opposition. And in today's post-Freudian age, such explanations are likely to involve recourse to concepts like unconscious Oedipal feelings, adolescent rebellion, castration anxiety, and the "acting out" of feelings that originate in the early family.

As a result, the counterrevolutionary view of youth is associated with an interpretation of psychoanalysis that sees Oedipal urges as driving forces for student rebellion. To be sure, theorists do not agree about the exact nature of the Oedipal forces that are acted out. Some, like Feuer, see a simple reenactment of the jealous child's hatred of his powerful father; others see a blind striking out against surrogates for a father who was not powerful *enough* to inoculate his son against excessive castration anxieties; another psychoanalyst has pointed to insufficient parental responsiveness as a causative factor in radicalism; early family permissiveness or failure to set limits has also been blamed. But whatever the precise irrational forces behind the youthful revolt are said to be, the counterrevolutionary theory, by denying the validity of the youth movement's own explanations of its acts, is forced to hypothesize unconscious motivations as the "real" motives behind the revolt.

A final conclusion follows from this argument: no matter how destructive the revolt of the young may be in the short run, that revolt is historically foredoomed to failure in the long run. The technetronic society, the postindustrial world, the superindustrial state—these forces are unstoppable. The liberal democratic state is being basically transformed; but the rantings and rampagings of the young, devoted to obsolescent ideas of self-expression, anarchism, romanticism, direct democracy, liberation, and the expansion of consciousness, cannot stop this transformation. The revolt of the young may indeed be, in Daniel Bell's phrase, the emergent "class conflict" of postin-dustrial society. But the logic of Bell's analysis suggests that students are a neo-Luddite, counterrevolutionary class and that their counterrevolution will fail. Increasingly, power will be held by those who have more success-fully acquired the capital dispensed by the knowledge industry. The counter-culture is, in Brzezinski's words, the "death rattle" of the historically obsolete.

The counterrevolutionary theory of the youth revolt is a reformulation of liberal theory, modified to make room for the convulsions of the last decade. Within any social equilibrium theory, there must be room for the possibility that the system will temporarily get "out of balance." The as-sumption of thinkers like Brzezinski is that we have entered a period of imbalance accompanying the transition from an industrial to a technetronic society. In this transitional period, traditional mechanisms of social control, older forms of integration between social structure and culture, and previous forms of socialization have ceased to function adequately. But in the future, it is assumed, equilibrium can once again be regained. Upon arrival in the technetronic society, the postindustrial society, or the world of the year 2000, the temporary storm squalls on the weather front between industrial and postindustrial society will have dissipated, and we will once again be in a state of relative social equilibrium. If we can only wait out the transition, maintaining and repairing our basic institutions, we can build a new equilib-rium—one that will grind under the youthful opposition just as triumphant industrialism destroyed the Luddites. Meanwhile, we must fight to preserve decency, civilization, rationality, and higher education from the depreda-tions of the mindless young.

Youth as a Revolutionary Force

The second major theory holds that the dissenting young are historically a revolutionary force. This theory views the counterculture as a regenera-tive culture and interprets the forces that oppose it as ultimately counter-revolutionary. This view is expressed in different forms in the works of Theodore Roszak and Charles Reich, in the writings of members of the counterculture like Tom Hayden and Abbie Hoffman, and, most convinc-ingly of all, by Philip Slater. Let us consider the basic assumptions of the revolutionary view of the youth culture.

First, this theory also accepts the notion that industrialized societies are in a period of major cultural, institutional, and historical transition. But it alleges that the thrust of the liberal democratic state has exhausted itself. What is variously termed "corporate liberalism," the "Establishment," or the "welfare-warfare state" is seen as fundamentally bankrupt. Admittedly, industrial states have produced unprecedented wealth. But they have not been able to distribute it equitably, nor have they found ways to include large minorities in the mainstream of society. Furthermore, their basic assumptions have led directly to disastrous "neo-imperialistic" wars like the American involvement in Southeast Asia. Corporate liberalism has produced a highly manipulated society in which "real" human needs and interests are neglected in the pursuit of political power, the merchandising of products, or the extension of overseas markets. Large-scale organizations have dehumanized their members, depriving men of participation in the decisions that affect their lives. The electronic revolution merely provides the rulers of the corporate state with more effective means of manipulating the populace. In brief, corporate liberalism, though once historically necessary, has today reached the end of its tether.

The second assumption of this theory is that the economic successes and moral failures of liberal industrial societies today make possible and necessary a new kind of consciousness, new values, new aspirations, and new life-styles—in short, a new culture. The old industrial state was founded upon the assumption of scarcity. It was organized to reduce poverty, to increase production, to provide plenitude. But today it has largely succeeded in this goal, and as a result a new generation has been born in affluence and freed from the repressed character structure of the scarcity culture. In an era of abundance, the niggardly, inhibited psychology of saving, scrupulosity, and repression is no longer necessary. Alienated relationships between people who view each other as commodities are no longer inevitable. The "objective consciousness" of the scientist or technician is becoming obsolete. In brief, the material successes and moral failures of corporate liberalism permit and require the emergence of a new and truly revolutionary generation with a new consciousness, a postscarcity outlook, and a new vision of the possibilities of human liberation.

It follows from this analysis that the new oppositional culture is not an atavistic and irrational reaction against the old culture but a logical outgrowth of it—an expression of its latent possibilities, a rational effort to remedy its failings, in some sense its logical fulfillment. If the central goal of the old culture was to overcome want and if that goal has been largely achieved, then the counterculture stands on the shoulders of the old culture, fulfilling, renewing, and expressing that culture's latent hopes. Far from being historical reactionaries, the counterculturists are the historical vanguard. Their alleged anarchism and anti-intellectualism are but efforts to express the desire for human liberation whose roots lie in the postponed dreams of the old culture. As the British philosopher Stuart Hampshire has recently suggested, the dissenting young are not against reason, but only against a constricted definition of reason as a quantitative calculus that ignores human values, feelings, and needs.

The revolutionary theory of youth also entails a definite view of the psychology of young rebels and revolutionaries. It asks that we take them completely at their word when they state the reasons for their protests, disruptions, dropouts, or rejections. The dissenting young are seen as miraculously healthy products of the irrational, dangerous, and unjust world they inherited. Their motives are noble, idealistic, and pure; and their statements of their goals are to be taken at face value. They are not animated by their childhood pasts, but by a vision (which they may, however, find difficult to articulate) of a freer, more peaceful, more liberated, and more just society. As for the Oedipus complex, to discuss the psychological motives of the members of the youthful opposition at all is seen as a typically "liberal" way of distracting attention from the real issues. Thus, even if the dissenting young behave in an undemocratic, dogmatic, or violent way, one "understands" their behavior by discussing the undemocratic, dogmatic, and violent society to which they are objecting.

This view of the psychology of the youthful opposition follows logically from the assumption that the young are in the historical vanguard. For in general, historical vanguards must be endowed with extraordinary wisdom and prescience, and with a special freedom from that gnawingly irrational attachment to the personal or historic past that plagues most "non-vanguard" groups. In the view of one theorist, "radical man" is the highest possible form of human development. Another political theorist has argued that only rebellion can attest to human freedom, and that among today's young, only those who rebel are truly free. The argument that the youthful revolt arises from psychopathology is here countered by its opposite—by the claim that the new opposition springs from the extraordinary insight, maturity, high consciousness, and "positive mental health" of its members.

Finally, as is by definition true of any historical vanguard, the triumph of this vanguard is seen as ultimately inevitable. With rising abundance, new recruits to the counterculture are being created daily. It is the old, then, who are obsolete, not the young. The locomotive of history, so to speak, has the youth movement sitting on the front bumper, scattering its opponents in a relentless rush into the future. Eventually the opponents of progressive change will be defeated or will die of old age; only then will the truly liberating potentials of the postscarcity era be actualized in society.

In many respects the theory of the youth movement as revolutionary is embryonic and incomplete. The counterrevolutionary theory builds upon the highly developed resources of liberal social thought. But the "revolutionary" view, rejecting both liberalism and Marxism, presents us more with a vision of what the counterculture might be at its best than with a complex or thorough social analysis. Only in the work of Philip Slater do we have the beginnings of a critical examination of liberal theory, a task so enormous that it is obviously beyond the capabilities of any one man, much less one book. Most other writers who view the counterculture as revolutionary limit themselves to a vision that is more literary than descriptive and that makes little attempt to connect the emergence of the counterculture to the structural changes emphasized by writers like Bell, Brzezinski, or Kahn.

In this sense, the revolutionary theory of the new opposition remains more of a promise than a fulfillment.

Limits of the Two Theories

My presentation of two polar theories obviously does scant justice to the complexity of the specific theorists who have seriously considered the counterculture. There is no unity, much less membership in a "school," either among those who oppose or among those who support the youthful opposition. Among its critics, for example, Feuer and Bettelheim concentrate on the psychopathology that allegedly animates its members, while Brzezinski and Kahn focus on the structural or social conditions that make the youthful opposition obsolete. Similarly, there is an enormous difference between the romantic eulogy of "Consciousness III" presented by Reich and the more careful social-psychological analysis offered by Slater in his *The Pursuit of Loneliness*.

But no matter how oversimplified this account of the revolutionary and the counterrevolutionary theories may be, if either interpretation of youthful dissent were fundamentally adequate, this discussion could end. It therefore behooves us to examine each of these theories critically.

We should first acknowledge that each of the theories has highly persuasive points. Those who view the new opposition as historically counterrevolutionary are correct in underlining the increasing importance of technology, complex social organizations, and education in the most industrialized nations. They have pointed accurately to the new role of a highly educated and technologically trained elite. And they seem to help us explain why youthful dissenters are virtually absent among potential engineers, computer specialists, and business administrators, but drawn disproportionately from the ranks of social scientists and humanists.

Above all, however, the opponents of the youthful opposition are accurate in their criticism of that opposition. They rightly argue that the counterculture almost completely neglects the institutional side of modern life. Thus the call for liberation, for the expansion of consciousness, and for the expression of impulse has not been matched by the creation, or even by the definition, of institutions through which these purposes could be achieved and sustained in anything like a modern technological society. Furthermore, in its cultural wing, the new opposition has often been callous toward continuing injustice, oppression, and poverty in America and abroad. In its political wing, the counterculture has been vulnerable to despair, to apocalyptic but transient fantasies of instant revolution, to superficial Marxism, and to a romance with violence. Finally, the youthful opposition as a whole has never adequately confronted or understood its own derivative relationship to the dominant society. Perhaps as a result, it has too often been a caricature rather than a critique of the consumption-oriented, manipulative, technocratic, violent, electronic society it nominally opposes. In pointing to the weakness of the counterculture, its critics seem to me largely correct.

Yet there is a deep plausibility, as well, in the theory that the youthful opposition is, in historical terms, a revolutionary movement. In particular, the "revolutionary" theorists accurately capture the growing feeling of frustration and the increasing sense of the exhaustion of the old order that obsesses growing numbers of the educated young in industrialized nations. Furthermore, they correctly recognize the irony in the fact that the most prosperous and educated societies in world history have generated the most massive youthful opposition in world history. And in seeking to explain this unexpected opposition, the revolutionary theory understands well its relationship to the "systemic" failings of corporate liberalism—its failure to include large minorities in the general prosperity; its exploitative or destructive relationship to the developing nations; its use of advanced technology to manipulate the citizens in whose interest it allegedly governs; its neglect of basic human needs, values, and aspirations in a social calculus that sees men and women as merely "inputs" or "outputs" in complex organizations.

The strengths of each theory, however, are largely negative: in essence, each is at its best in pointing to the flaws of the culture or the social system defended by the other. But judged for its positive contribution, each theory tends to have parallel weaknesses: each disregards the facts at odds with its own central thesis. In order to do this, each operates at a different level of analysis: the counterrevolutionary theory at the level of social institutions, the revolutionary theory at the level of culture. As a consequence, each theory neglects precisely what the other theory correctly stresses.

The counterrevolutionary theory of the new opposition starts from an analysis of social institutions, modes of production, and the formal organization of human roles and relationships. Despite its emphasis upon the psychopathology of the new rebels, it is fundamentally a sociological theory of institutional changes and technological transformations. It stresses the importance of applied science, the growth of new educational institutions, and the power of the new elite that dominates the "knowledge industry." In defining the future, it emphasizes the further development of rational-bureaucratic institutions and the revolutionary impact of new electronic technology upon social organization, communication, and knowledge. But it tends to forget consciousness and culture, treating ideas, symbols, values, ideologies, aspirations, fantasies, and dreams largely as reflections of technological, economic, and social forces.[1]

---

[1] Daniel Bell is a notable exception in his emphasis on the autonomy of the adversary culture.

Theorists who argue that the new opposition is historically revolutionary operate at a quite different level of analysis. For them, the two key concepts are culture and consciousness. What matter most are feelings, aspirations, ideologies, and world views. Charles Reich's recent analysis of three kinds of consciousness is explicit in asserting that institutions are secondary and, in the last analysis, unimportant. Most other revolutionary theorists also start from an analysis of a "new consciousness" to argue that the decisive revolution is a cultural revolution. How men view the world, how they organize their experience symbolically, what their views are—these are seen as historical determinants. Institutional changes are said to follow changes in human aspirations and consciousness.

Daniel Bell has written of the disjuncture of social structure and culture in modern society. We need not accept his entire analysis to agree that this disjuncture is reflected in theories about youthful dissent. For on closer examination, those theories turn out to be talking either about social structure *or* culture, but rarely about both. The key weakness of the counterrevolutionary theory is its neglect of consciousness and culture, its assumption that social-structural, technological, and material factors will be decisive in determining the future. The parallel weakness of the revolutionary view of youthful dissent is its disregard of the way organized systems of production, technology, education, communication, and "social control" influence, shape, and may yet co-opt or destroy the youthful opposition. In fact, then, these two theories are not as contradictory as they seem: in many ways, they are simply talking about two different aspects of the modern world.

A second limitation of both theories is their assumption that the trends they define are historically inevitable. In this respect, both theories are eschatological as well as explanatory. The postindustrial or technetronic view assumes the future inevitability of a postindustrial, technetronic, technocratic society. Given this assumption, it follows logically that anyone who opposes the technetronic society is historically counterrevolutionary. Brzezinski, for example, writes:

> The Luddites were threatened by economic obsolescence and reacted against it. Today the militant leaders of the [student] reaction, as well as their ideologues, frequently come from those branches of learning which are more sensitive to the threat of social irrelevance. Their political activism is thus only a reaction to the more basic fear that the times are against them, that a new world is emerging without either their assistance or their leadership.

Brzezinski's claim that the youth revolt constitutes a counterrevolutionary force clearly rests on the assumption that the technetronic society is inevitable.

Exactly the same assumption of historical inevitability is made by supporters of the counterculture. Reich is very explicit about this:

> [The revolution] will originate with the individual and with culture, and it

will change the political structure only as its final act. It will not require violence to succeed, and it cannot be successfully resisted by violence. It is now spreading with amazing rapidity. . . . It is both necessary and inevitable, and in time it will include not only youth, but all people in Amercia.

Given Reich's assumption that history is on the side of the counterculture, it follows automatically that those who oppose it are actually counterrevolutionary.

But this claim that the future is in fact predetermined by blind historical forces is open to major question. In retrospect, most previous claims about the historical inevitability of this or that trend have turned out to have been mere expressions of the wishes of those who made these claims. It makes equal or better sense to believe that "History" is on the side neither of the technetronic revolution nor of the counterculture. In fact, we may deny that history is on anyone's side, arguing that it is simply made by human beings, acting individually and in concert, influenced by the institutions in which they live *and* by their consciousness and culture.

If we reject the assumption of historical inevitability, both the counterrevolutionary and the revolutionary theories must be understood in part as efforts to justify a set of special interests by attributing historical inevitability to them, and perhaps ultimately as exercises in the use of prophecy to convince others of the truth of the prophecy and thereby to make the prophecy self-fulfilling. Andrew Greeley has compared Charles Reich with the ancient Hebrew prophets; the similarities are vivid. Although the more academic prose of Brzezinski, Feuer, or Bettelheim does not lend itself so readily to comparisons with the Old Testament, the same prophetic tendencies are there as well. But in either case, the claim that God and His modern-day equivalents, History, Technology, and Culture, are on our side is best understood as a claim that men make to rally support and persist despite adversity.

What both theories fail to comprehend is the extent to which the emergence of a new youthful opposition requires us to embark upon a critical reexamination of concepts of man, society, and their interrelationship that we have heretofore taken largely for granted. This inability to come to grips with the theoretical challenge posed by the new opposition is seen clearly in the respective attitudes of the two groups of theorists toward education. Neo-liberals who see student dissent as largely counterrevolutionary are committed to a view of education as socialization either to the role requirements of industrial society or to the core values of Western civilization. In light of this view, it follows that a postindustrial society characterized by prolonged higher education should be a society in which youthful dissent is rare. The eruption of wide-scale disaffection among the most educated products of the most industrialized societies thus requires neo-liberal theories to posit wide-scale "deviant socialization" or else to argue that higher education is failing to "do its job." In fact, however, extensive evidence concerning the backgrounds of young dissenters provides little support for the "deviant socialization" interpretation of the new opposition. And paradoxically, those institutions of higher education that liberals have traditionally seen as doing the "best job" seem to be the breeding grounds for the greatest disaffection.

Those who view youthful disaffection as a revolutionary phenomenon are faced with the same dilemma. They tend to see higher education as a way of "integrating" or "co-opting" youth into the existing society. It therefore comes as a surprise that higher education seems to promote disaffection and to be closely related to the emergence of a youthful counterculture. But those who view the youth movement as revolutionary have so far failed to offer any adequate explanation of why many young men and women in so many nations have escaped the net of socialization. The fact that theorists of neither persuasion can explain the contemporary correlation between higher education and dissent indicates the need for a critical analysis of our prevailing assumptions concerning human malleability, social equilibrium, and socialization.

What follows is not an attempt to provide this critical reanalysis, or even to outline it. Rather, it is an agenda, or, more precisely, some items on an agenda that, if accomplished, might move us toward a better understanding of the meaning of the new opposition and of contemporary society. In brief, the work I believe needs to be done falls into three broad categories. First, there must be a critical reanalysis and reformulation of the theoretical assumptions on the basis of which we attempt to understand man and society. Second, we must begin to come to terms with the characteristics of modern society and modern man in their own right, not in terms of strained analogies to the past. Third, a revised theoretical framework and a better understanding of contemporary man in society should help define a new political agenda.

Plasticity, Equilibrium, and Socialization

The first assumption to be reanalyzed critically is the assumption of virtually limitless human malleability and susceptibility to influence. Without denying that men can adapt to most surroundings, that they often conform to the pressures of their peers, or that they internalize social norms and cultural concepts, we need to rediscover and emphasize those elements in "human nature" that make men less than totally plastic.

Here the concepts of development defined by Freud and Piaget point to a psychological approach that clearly contradicts the almost exclusively environmental view of psychological change that has dominated liberal thought. Critically interpreted, the work of Freud and Piaget may help us understand man not merely as an adjusting and adapting animal, but as a creature whose growth has both important societal prerequisites and a dynamic of its own. We can then think of man as possessing a "human nature" that can be "violated" by social expectations; we may then be better able to see man as possessing innate potentials for autonomy and integration that may at times lead him into conflict with his society. And we will also, of course, need to explore in detail the ways in which these developmental potentials may be actualized or frustrated by any given social or historical context.

Furthermore, the role of conflict in human development needs to be reexamined. Liberal psychology has tended to minimize the catalytic importance of conflict in growth: conflict has been seen as neurotic, undesirable, and productive of regression. But there is much current evidence that individuals who attain high levels of complexity in feeling, thinking, and judging do so *as a result of* conflict, not in its absence. Students of cognitive development, like observers of personality development, find that disequilibrium, tension, and imbalance tend to produce growth. If this be true, then the absence of psychological conflict or tension may be as pathological as an overabundance of conflict, and the liberal view of the ideal man as smoothly socialized and conflict-free may need to be discarded.

Turning to broader theories of society, a comparable critical reexamination of basic assumptions seems in order. Above all, the utility of the equilibrium model of society must be examined. Increasingly, critical sociologists have begun to suggest that a "conflict" model of society and of social change may be more suited to the facts of contemporary history than a theory of societal balance. Just as we should appreciate the catalytic role of conflict in human development, so should we acknowledge the critical importance of conflict in social change. Both human and social development, I believe, are best viewed as dialectic processes, involving force, counterforce, and potential resolution: thesis, antithesis, and potential synthesis. At a societal level, such a view would require us to start from change, struggle, revolution, and transformation as the basic and "natural" state of affairs rather than view them as unfortunate exceptions that require special explanation.

This view of society would put social change in the first chapter, not in the last chapter as one of the unexplained problems of our theory. It would see conflict among individuals, groups, and historical forces as a necessary and vital component of historical change, not as a result of a "failure" of the "mechanisms of social control." It would also entail that any given "resolution" of conflicting historical forces should, in turn, generate new antithetical forces that would oppose that resolution, thus continuing the dialectic of change. A sociology based on the theory of conflict would especially attempt to understand the processes by which new conflicts are generated out of apparent equilibrium, rather than focus solely on how equilibrium is maintained.

Such a view of society obviously moves us away from liberalism and toward Marxism. But Marxism, too, must be examined critically. Just as we today should reject the nineteenth-century biology and physics upon which Freud based his psychological determinism and many of his specific views of personality, so we need not continue to accept the nineteenth-century economism and millenarianism of Marx's thought. Marx's view that the critical historical conflict was class conflict, although it reflected the facts of the mid-nineteenth century, may less clearly reflect the realities of the late-twentieth century. And the nineteenth-century optimism that led Marx to believe that historical conflict would ultimately be progressively resolved, like his millennial view of the classless state as the end of historical conflict, seems today unwarranted. We must question whether the historical dialectic in fact "stopped" at the end point defined by Marx or whether it continues today in ways that Marx could not have foreseen. And finally, we must acknowledge that groups Marx defined as progressive may have become reactionary in the century since his work.

If we abandon the notion of society as a stable and homogeneous entity, then the process by which individuals and their societies interrelate becomes vastly more complex. For if every society contains within it important internal conflicts, then growing children are exposed not to a stable, self-consistent set of social expectations and cultural values, but to social and cultural contradictions. Intrapsychic conflicts and social contradictions will thus be mutually related, although never in a simple one-to-one fashion. Furthermore, in times of rapid historical change, the societal conflicts to which one generation is exposed will differ from those of the previous generation; partly for this reason, individuals of different historical generations will typically differ from each other in basic personality.

Contradiction Within the Knowledge Sector

The second related theoretical task is to understand in detail the special characteristics of modern personality and modern society. Even if a critical analysis of the basic assumptions of liberal thought were completed, the substance of a more adequate account of what is unique about our own era would still be lacking. Here, once again, I can only indicate the general lines of thought that seem most likely to be worth pursuing.

If we start from a dialectical view of historical change, but admit that Marx's juxtaposition of a revolutionary proletariat and a reactionary bourgeoisie did not necessarily mark the last stage in the dialectic, then we must entertain seriously the possibility that the conflicts about which Marx wrote have been largely resolved and that new conflicts have today begun to emerge. In the period before and after the Second World War, the dominant class conflicts of the nineteenth and early twentieth centuries were increasingly resolved, reconciled, or synthesized in the liberal-democratic-capitalist or socialist states in Western Europe, America, and, after the war, Japan. These new industrial states proved themselves immensely productive economically and immensely inventive technologically. Older problems of mass poverty increasingly disappeared, and the proportion of workers involved in primary and secondary production dwindled to a decreasing minority. First in America, and then increasingly in Western Europe and Japan, the middle class grew to be the largest class, the working class became increasingly prosperous, and both classes became more and more committed to the preservation of the existing society. Especially during the years of the cold war, a domestic equilibrium was reached in the liberal democracies, and this equilibrium provided the empirical ground upon which liberal social thought grew and by which it seemed confirmed. To be sure, like all historical syntheses this one was far from complete: large minorities were excluded from the general prosperity; problems of poverty amid affluence continued; subtle forms of imperialism replaced the earlier forms; and so on. Yet all things considered, the decades from 1945 to 1965 were remarkable for the absence of basic social conflict in all the highly industrialized non-Communist nations.

The successes of the emergent technological society, however, were purchased at an enormous moral and ecological price. Increases in national productivity were not enough to include in the mainstream of affluence those whose poverty was "structural" rather than merely economic. Racism persisted in America despite a century's public commitment to end it. Effective political power remained in the hands of a small minority of the population. It is therefore incorrect to say that the traditional economic, social, and political conflicts of industrial societies were totally "resolved." It is more accurate to say that, for the first time in history, the day could be foreseen when with the techniques at hand they *might* be resolved.

Meanwhile, there grew a new generation that took for granted the accomplishments of corporate liberalism, expressing neither gratitude nor admiration for technological achievements. To this new generation, what were instead important were, first of all, the inabilities of a society dedicated to the elimination of social evils to fulfill its own promises and, second, the surfacing of a set of cultural and psychological goals that had previously, and apparently even reasonably, been deferred for the sake of technological advance, on the assumption that social and human progress would follow. But such progress proved neither automatic nor universal, and this failure has defined one aspect of the emergent aspirations of the new youthful opposition.

To understand the new conflicts in corporate liberal society, I believe we must, above all, examine the increasingly central role of the "knowledge sector" in the most industrial nations. This sector includes not only universities, scientific laboratories, research institutes, and the world of creative artists but a much broader set of enterprises including corporate research and development, the communications industry, data analysis and data processing, the major higher professions, advertising, merchandising, administrative science and personnel management, entertainment, systems analysis, and so on. So defined, the knowledge sector is clearly that sector of contemporary industrialized societies which has grown most rapidly in size and power. Often exploited, yet more often manipulating; immensely powerful, yet vastly vulnerable; an interest group, but one that possesses unprecedented power, the knowledge sector in modern society must be recognized as new and *sui generis*. Most contemporary efforts to define the role of this sector fail because they see it in analogies borrowed from the past—rather as if we tried to understand the capitalist-worker relationship as simply a form of the feudal bond between lord and vassal. One of the major theoretical tasks ahead is the careful definition and explication of the relationship between this new sector and the remainder of society.[2]

In the last decade, it has become clear that the neutral, "value-free," objective self-definition of the knowledge sector masks an important ideology, an ideology increasingly recognized and challenged by the new opposition. This ideology can be termed "technism," that is, a set of pseudoscientific assumptions about the nature and resolution of human and social problems. Most highly articulated in various forms of system analysis, technism insists that the highest rationality involves measurement and consigns the incommensurable (feelings, values, "intangibles") to a lesser order of rationality and reality.

Paradoxically, however, it is from within the knowledge sector that today there also emerges the most astringent critique of technism. Institutions of higher education, once predicted to become the central institutions of postindustrial society, have indeed become the prime exemplars of a technist approach to problems of government, business, and social planning; but they have also become the prime generators of the antitechnist, romantic, expressive, moralistic, anarchic humanism of the new opposition. Rejecting technism, this opposition stresses all those factors in human life and social experience that do not fit the technist equations. If "value-free," objective technism is the dominant voice of the dominant knowledge sector, then expressive, subjective anarchism is the subversive voice. Theodore Roszak's eulogy of the counterculture is illustrative, for Roszak abhors above all what he calls "objective consciousness"—the technist consciousness of the scientist or program analyst. The new opposition can thus be seen as the ideological reflection of an emergent contradiction *within* the knowledge sector, as the new antithesis of the knowledge sector's technism, as embodying a counteremphasis on feelings, on "creative disorder," on the non-quantifiable, the subjective, and the qualitative. Increasingly this contradic-

---

[2] See Richard Flacks, "Young Intelligentsia in Revolt," *Trans-Action*, June 1970.

tion between "objective" technism and "subjective" anarchism defines the key ideological polarity of our time.

The intimate relationship between the knowledge sector and the new opposition is also apparent when we examine the social origins of the members of the opposition. For the core of the counterculture consists not of the children of the working class or the lower middle class, but of the children of the knowledge sector. I have elsewhere argued that the new opposition is not monolithic, and that we must distinguish its "political" from its "cultural" wing. Available evidence suggests that members of the political wing tend to be recruited disproportionately from among the children of professors, social workers, ministers, scientists, lawyers, and artists. These young men and women are the ones most concerned with institutional, social, and political change, and are also most likely to express solidarity with the basic values of their parents. Recruits to the cultural, expressive, aesthetic, or "hippie" wing of the counterculture, in contrast, tend to be drawn to a much greater degree from the families of media executives, entertainers, advertising men, merchandisers, scientific administrators, and personnel managers. These young men and women are more concerned with the expansion of consciousness, the development of alternate life-styles, and the pursuit of communal ways of living. As a rule, they reject not only the conventional values and institutions of American society but also the values and life-styles of their parents. The parents of the "politicals" are thus the more established members of the knowledge sector, whereas the parents of the "culturals" are the "newly arrived," whose membership in the knowledge sector is more tenuous and ambivalent. If we accept the analogy between knowledge in technological society and capital in industrial society, the parents of the political wing of the opposition are more often the holders of "old money" whereas the parents of the cultural wing are more often *nouveaux riches.*

The knowledge sector is generating its own opposition through a variety of processes, including the ambivalences of the parents of youthful dissenters toward the very knowledge sector in which they are employed. But no process is of greater importance than the impact of higher education upon its recruits. Higher education bears a paradoxical relationship to the knowledge sector. On the one hand, higher education is essential for the maintenance and growth of the knowledge sector; but on the other hand, higher education provides many of the catalysts that push students to develop a critical perspective that leads them to become part of the youthful opposition and thus to oppose the dominant ideology of the knowledge sector. . . .

Once a student has acquired the ability to approach even one subject critically, it is hard to prevent him from applying the same critical orientation to other areas of life and society. Given the discovery that there are many distinct perspectives on "truth" in natural science, engineering, or literature, the student is more likely to become a relativist in moral, ideological matters as well. Taught to challenge traditional belief in a narrow academic arena, at least some students will move quickly to challenge traditional moral codes in society. What can be thought of as a "critical consciousness"—a mind-set disposed to question, examine, probe, and challenge—tends to generalize from the area where it was first learned to other areas, and finally to all of life. The result is, increasingly, an across-the-board relativization of knowledge, a pervasive individualization of morality, a greatly increased autonomy from authority and tradition.

Precisely because a technological society cannot rely exclusively on a narrowly technical system of higher education, it must foster a high degree of critical consciousness among its most educated products; and this critical consciousness is readily turned against the dominant assumptions and practices of the technological society. In a way not often acknowledged by educators, but increasingly sensed by the general public, higher education today is "subversive" in that it is helping to create youths who challenge many of the basic assumptions of their society.

Increasingly, higher education conspires with the mass media and the juxtaposition of cultures within modern societies to create millions of young men and women who are unwilling to accept the existing social order uncritically. Higher education is a key process by which the contradictions of technological society are being generated.

These notes on contemporary society are obviously incomplete, sketchy, and doubtless often wrong. They should indicate, however, my conviction that in analyzing contemporary technological societies, we do well to start from one of the central points emphasized by the "counterrevolutionary" theorists, namely, the ascendency of the knowledge sector. But an analysis of the meaning of this sector leads, I believe, not to the conclusion that it will inevitably triumph, but rather to the realization that the knowledge sector is riven through with basic contradictions, and that it is generating its own critics on a mass scale.

A New Politics?

The connection between social theory and political action is exceedingly complex. No matter how refined, precise, and detailed a theory, it does not necessarily or automatically lead to a political agenda. Yet, on the other hand, political action in the absence of social theory tends to be haphazard, trial-and-error, and empirical in the worse sense. Such is the case with much of what today passes as "radical politics": lacking any grounding in critcal social theory, it tends to consist in *ad hoc* reactions of moral indignation, to lack any long-range direction, to fritter away the best energies of its members in internecine battles, or to adopt programs inspired by a pop-Marxist analysis of guerilla warfare in some far-off ex-colonial nation.

Several general political implications follow from this line of reasoning. For one, it follows that visions of immediate social or political revolution are based on a flawed social and historical analysis. The processes of socio-historical change in which we are living are long-term, secular processes that will take at least a generation to work themselves out. In the meantime, fantasies of instant revolution, apocalyptic spasms of activity followed by despair, and romantic reenactments of nineteenth-century Russian terrorism are counterproductive. Those who seek basic change in American society must be willing to stick with the effort for decades, and to try to lead humane and decent lives themselves even in the absence of revolution.

Another corollary of the views outlined here concerns the need to support a particular kind of higher education. Those who bitterly oppose the new opposition are already eager to limit higher education to technical education, eliminating or deemphasizing its critical component. This strategy, if successful, could well reduce the numbers of those who possess that critical consciousness which seems vital for membership in the new opposition. It is therefore important for all who sympathize with the opposition to seek to extend higher education that is truly critical. The current radical attack upon higher education is, I think, misguided when it fails to discriminate between technical and critical education. Higher education in the broad sense not only has been but should continue to be the nursery for the new opposition.

Finally, the proposition that social forces that begin as progressive generally end as reactionary obviously applies to the youthful opposition itself. As the youthful opposition ceases to be youthful, it must constantly guard against further evolution into a reactionary force. Already we can envision how this could occur: the collectivism of the counterculture could readily become an insistence upon the abrogation of individual rights; the tribalism of Consciousness III could well portend a society of coercive group membership; the counterculture's opposition to technism could degenerate into a mindless hatred of reason, science, intellect, reflection, and accuracy. Today the youthful opposition is so weak politically that none of these dangers seems socially or politically important. But should the opposition gain in strength, its own reactionary potentials might well unfold.

In essence, then, a politics consistent with the goals of the agenda items I have discussed must be one that rejects both the "value-free" technism of corporate liberalism and the subjective anarchism of the counterculture, attempting instead the painful and slow work of creating a synthesis of the institutions of technological society with the culture of oppositional youth. That synthesis must ultimately entail the creation of a culture in which the concept of liberation is not merely a facile slogan but a commitment to the hard work of creating institutions within which genuine human relatedness may be attained. That synthesis must attempt to combine new-culture participation with old-culture competence, Consciousness III enthusiasm with Consciousness II professionalism, and all of this in ways that have hardly begun to be imagined, much less tried. It must involve an effort to turn modern technology around so that it facilitates man's liberation instead of encouraging his manipulation, so that it makes wars less possible rather than more likely, so that it helps men understand each other rather than oppose one another.

It is, of course, easy to call for a synthesis in general terms; it will be difficult to achieve it in practice. Nor do I believe that such a synthesis, whether theoretical or political, is inevitable. We are indeed at a historical juncture, a turning point, a cultural and institutional crisis. And the youth revolt, the counterculture, the new opposition—these define one pole, one catalyst, one ingredient in that crisis. But what happens in the next decades is not predetermined by the blind forces of History. It will largely depend on the intelligence, goodwill, and staying power of countless individuals who are willing to work together toward a society in which men and women attain new freedom not only from the external coercions of hunger, injustice, and tyranny but from the inner coercions of greed, power-lust, and envy.

PART **IV**

MODERNIZATION

Introduction

Many contemporary societies are still predominantly traditional, in the sense that their demographic, economic, educational, religious, and political structure is much like that which existed centuries ago before modernization set in. Still, even these societies, in addition to having their own internal dynamics, are affected by contacts with other modern societies. Most of them, therefore, have already started on the way toward modernization, though they differ considerably in the point and time of departure, the stage they have reached, the pace, orderliness, and the path their development follows, as well as in the end result for which they strive.

Selections in this part examine modernization mainly from the viewpoint of contemporary traditional or transitional societies. Though some of the generalizations suggested below would apply to all modernization processes, including those of the first traditional societies to modernize, they mostly concern modernization in the contemporary world.

Smelser draws on a differentiation model of the kind presented above by Parsons, to provide an analytical framework for the study of modernization. He analyzes the process by which the major social functions gain structural independence. Previously, the same social units served a large variety of functions. With modernization, special social units evolve for the separate performance of each set of functions. Once the family was the unit in which, among other things, work, religious devotion, and education were carried out. Now work is delegated to the factory and the office, religious services to the church, and formal education to the school. Each of these units has its own authority structure, its own sets of norms prescribing the appropriate forms of behavior, and its own systems of rewards and sanctions to induce conformity and discourage deviation.

Thus differentiation is not just a type of technical specialization, but is profoundly connected with the whole social process of modernization. The crucial link between differentiation and modernization lies in the fact that for every social function there is a distinct set of structural conditions under which it is optimally served. While production can be carried out in the family, it is maximized when delegated to a unit of its own, where actors are detached, calculative, and limited in their orientation to the specific tasks at hand. Education requires an asymmetric relationship in which the students are more involved with the teacher than the teacher with the students. That is to say, to allow for communication of values and voluntary discipline, the students must identify with the teacher; the teacher, on the other hand, must combine an emotional commitment to his work and to students in general with a somewhat detached orientation to each individual student, so as to ensure the objectivity of his judgment. Such an asymmetrical relationship is easier to maintain in the school than in the family. Similar points could be made about other structural differentiations. The total effect of differentiation is that the various societal functions—especially the economy, science, and administration, which "suffered" most from the fusion into the particularistic, diffuse, affective family—are now being served by units "designed" to fit their needs and hence are served more effectively.

The transition is not always smooth; modernization cannot come about without the disruption of the old patterns. Frequently it is accompanied by *anomie,* expressed for instance in outbursts of violence or mass hysteria. It becomes necessary for the new system to find ways of relating the newly differentiated units so as to provide new mechanisms to integrate society. The frequent rise of religious sects and the ascent of radical political movements are indicative of the need for reintegration. Nationalism as an ideology serves this need.

Each of the subsequent selections deals with one major facet of modernization and confronts the twofold problem of developing specialized sectors and relating them in a new fashion. These articles cast light on some of the central problems of modernization, but obviously do not exhaust their analysis. The student interested in developing nations will find a rich literature on almost every subject discussed here.

Rostow's key contribution to the analysis of economic development is the concept of "takeoff." The term, by now used in political science and sociology as well, is borrowed from the field of aeronautics: an airplane must gain a certain amount of speed before it has enough momentum to take off and continue to higher altitudes and greater speeds on its own. Similarly in the process of economic development: up to a certain level, growing investments in—and increased outputs of—an economy are absorbed by the population growth and by increased consumption. Only after the increase of production rises above that of consumption can a flow of investment allow the economy to grow continuously, on its own, without the aid of capital investment from the outside and without additional changes in the consumption, saving, and investment habits of the population. Rostow suggests that this transition, or takeoff point, occurs within a fairly limited period—a generation or less—and that it is likely to result from the development of particular economic sectors.

If Smelser's work is part of the modern theoretical work employing the differentiation model, Rostow is a neo-evolutionist reviving an earlier tradition. He expects societies to follow a sequence of similar stages and to move in the same general direction—toward the attainment of high productive ability. To what use societies put this ability is a different question altogether. Some use much of their newly gained capacities to buy a large military machinery, increase national status, and for purposes of territorial expansion; others are more inclined to use their new resources to increase the citizen's standard of living, while still others reinvest much of their yield to make future national income even higher.

The most crucial aspect of modernization is industrialization. Industrialization may be perceived as part of the general process of differentiation, in that its advent implies the growing structural independence of the production and exchange function. Industrialization is also the base for economic takeoff in that increased production and exchange make it possible for output to exceed consumption. While industrialization is primarily a technological and economic process, it is closely related to the dynamics of other social spheres. The two selections dealing with industrialization—those of Moore and Bendix—emphasize the noneconomic aspects of industrialization, primarily its effect on value systems and motivational complexes. Industrialization tends to lead to a separation of labor and management. If industrialization is to proceed, each group must develop the value orientations enabling it to play its part. Moore deals with the changes in the values, habits, and outlooks of workers that are required to sustain their motivation to participate, while Bendix discusses the changing ideologies of management by means of which it justifies its own role in the process.

As Moore points out, there is at least an initial period in which the members of a traditional society have fixed economic needs that are more-or-less satisfied by the traditional economy. The prospects of a higher standard of living leave these people largely indifferent. An incentive such as increased wages is largely ineffective so long as the additional purchasing power so established has no social meaning. It seems, though, that following education and the development of new commitments and tastes, the economic demands of these workers can be expected to increase. It is more difficult to induce them to attain the kind of self-discipline without which it is impossible to build up a modern economy. Long training, regular performances, punctuality, precision, and so on are all patterns of behavior new to the members of these societies and impose a high strain on their motivation. It remains to be seen whether a sufficient number of workers in all or even most transitional societies will develop such patterns or whether they will in practice prefer a lower standard of living as an unavoidable consequence of a less demanding work life.

Though dealing with industrialization in Europe, Bendix's analysis casts light on a process which at present is especially relevant to newly developing areas. Bendix studies the changes in management's conception of its relations with workers, the justifications devised for the new modes of subordination. These ideologies as well as the relationships they deal with, are, as Bendix emphasizes, affected by many elements of the social structure: the degree of interclass tensions and conflicts; the availability of mechanisms of peaceful adjustments on the political level; cultural traditions of the managerial groups, and many other factors. The different development of the same authority relationship in various societies, and the many factors affecting this development, discussed by Bendix, illustrate the fact that societies change as systems and that hence the study of industrialization requires the study of modernization in general.

S. N. Eisenstadt focuses his study of modernization on the socio-political framework, rather than on the inadequate economic, technical, or demographic developments so often stressed by others. He sees crises of modernization in societies such as Indonesia, Pakistan, Burma and Sudan, as the result of a rise in the political power and mobilization of component social groups, without a parallel development of over-arching, society wide, normative and regulatory political mechanisms. The societies which have undergone breakdowns in modernizations also reveal a common pattern of "sharp dissociation" between instrumental and expressive elites, suggesting that much of whatever integrative power is available, is not being mobilized in support of the system. The result is an odd mixture of commitment to modernization in a narrow rationalistic sense with the pursuit of utopian social and political ideals, a self contradicting course which weakens both developments.

Joseph Gusfield asks, in effect, how much change does modernization require. He questions the assumption that traditional culture, institutions and values are impediments to change and obstacles to modernization. "Tradition" is a more specific and ambiguous phenomenon than usually realized. Traditional culture is not a uniform consistent body of norms and values nor is traditional society a homogeneous social structure. Some elements may be favorable to modernity, others not. The old is not necessarily replaced by the new. The range of alternatives may simply be increased. Modernizing forces do not necessarily weaken tradition. On the contrary, in India, modern communications and educational facilities have actually reinforced and speeded up the process of Sanskritization. And, tradition can be an important source of political legitimation, as Mahatma Gandhi so well demonstrated.

The Alex Inkeles' excerpt reports the major findings of his cross-national study of the qualities characteristic of modern man and the dynamics responsible for his particular personality type. Unlike many of the other essays in this volume and section, Inkeles is not only more attentive to social-psychological forces (vs. structural ones) but is relatively free of sociological relativism. He recognizes that there is a particular constellation of attitudes, values and modes of behavior which is found up and down the occupational ladder in all six—very different societies studied. This unique syndrome Inkeles calls the "modern personality." Its traits include openness to new experience, independence from parental authority and taking an active part in civic affairs. Education is the most powerful factor in producing the modern personality but occupational experience in large-scale organizations, especially factories, also nourishes the growth of modern attitudes. Thus "late socialization" experiences are shown to be capable of great potency in bringing about personality changes, a finding sure to cheer those who are optimistic about the possibility of reshaping and transforming societies. Inkeles closes on the finding that contrary to widely held and firmly entrenched assumptions, migration and exposure to modern institutions do not lead to psychic distress. Does modernization perhaps provide a satisfaction of some universal basic human needs?

CHAPTER 26

NEIL J. SMELSER

Toward a Theory of Modernization

A thorough analysis of the social changes accompanying economic development would require an ambitious theoretical scheme and a vast quantity of comparative data. Because I lack both ingredients—and the space to use them if I possessed them—I shall restrict this exploratory statement in two ways: (1) Methodologically, I shall deal only with ideal-type constructs in the Weberian sense; I shall omit discussion of any individual cases of development, as well as discussion of the comparative applicability of particular historical generalizations. (2) Substantively, I shall consider only modifications of the social structure; I shall omit discussion of factor-allocation, savings and investment, inflation, balance of payments, foreign aid, size of population, and rate of population change, even though these variables naturally affect and are affected by structural changes. These restrictions call for brief comment.

Max Weber defined an ideal-type construct as a "one-sided accentuation . . . by the synthesis of a great many diffuse, discrete, more or less present and occasionally absent *concrete individual* phenomena, which are arranged . . . into a unified *analytical* construct. In its conceptual purity, this mental construct cannot be found anywhere in reality." [1] The analyst utilizes such ideal constructs to unravel and explain a variety of actual historical situations. Weber mentioned explicitly two kinds of ideal-type constructs—first, "historically unique configurations" such as "rational bourgeois capitalism," "medieval Christianity," etc. and second, statements concerning

From Neil J. Smelser, "Mechanisms of Change and Adjustment of Changes," in Wilbert E. Moore and Bert F. Hoselitz, eds., *The Impact of Industry* (Paris: International Social Science Council, in press). Reprinted by permission of the author and the publisher.

[1] Max Weber, *The Methodology of the Social Sciences* (Glencoe, Ill.: The Free Press, 1949), pp. 90, 93.

historical evolution, such as the Marxist laws of capitalist development.[2] While the second type presupposes some version of the first, I shall concentrate on the dynamic constructs.

Economic development generally refers to the "growth of output per head of population." [3] For purposes of analyzing the relationships between economic growth and the social structure, it is possible to isolate the effects of several interrelated technical, economic, and ecological processes frequently accompanying development: (1) In the realm of technology, the change *from* simple and traditionalized techniques *toward* the application of scientific knowledge. (2) In agriculture, the evolution *from* subsistence farming *toward* commercial production of agricultural goods. This means specialization in cash crops, purchase of nonagricultural products in the market, and frequently agricultural wage-labor. (3) In industry, the transition *from* the use of human and animal power *toward* industrialization proper or "men aggregated at power-driven machines working for monetary return with the products of the manufacturing process, entering into a market based on a network of exchange relations." [4] (4) In ecological arrangements, the movement *from* the farm and village *toward* urban centers. These several processes often occur simultaneously; this is not, however, necessarily the case. Certain technological improvements—*e.g.,* the use of improved seeds—can be introduced without automatically and instantaneously producing organizational changes; agriculture may be commercialized without accompanying industrialization, as in many colonial countries; industrialization may occur in villages; and cities may proliferate in the absence of significant industrialization. Furthermore, the specific social consequences of technological advance, commercialized agriculture, the factory, and the city, respectively, are not in any sense reducible to each other.

Despite such differences, all four processes tend to affect the social structure in similar ways. All give rise to the following ideal-type structural changes which ramify throughout society: (1) Structural differentiation, or the establishment of more specialized and more autonomous social units. I shall illustrate this process in several different spheres—economy, family, religion, and stratification. (2) Integration, which changes its character as the old social order is made obsolete by the process of differentiation. The state, the law, political groupings, and other associations are particularly salient in this integration. (3) Social disturbances—mass hysteria, outbursts of violence, religious and political movements, etc.—which reflect the uneven march of differentiation and integration.

---

[2] *Ibid.,* pp. 93, 101-103.

[3] W. A. Lewis, *The Theory of Economic Growth* (London: George Allen & Unwin, 1955), p. 1.

[4] N. Nash, "Some Notes on Village Industrialization in South and East Asia," *Economic Development and Cultural Change,* III (1954), No. 3, p. 271.

Obviously, the implications of technological advance, agricultural re-organization, industrialization, and urbanization differ from society to so-ciety, as do the resulting structural realignments. Some of the sources of variation in these ideal patterns of pressure and change follow:

(1) Variations in premodern conditions. Is the society's value-system congenial or antipathetic to industrial values? How well integrated is the society? How "backward" is it? What is its level of wealth? How is the wealth distributed? Is the country "young and empty" or "old and crowded?" Is the country politically dependent, recently independent, or altogether autonomous? Such pre-existing conditions shape the impact of the forces of economic development.

(2) Variations in the impetus to change. Do pressures to modernize come from the internal implications of a value-system, from a desire for national security and prestige, from a desire for material prosperity, or from a combination of these? Is political coercion used to form a labor force? Or are the pressures economic, as in the case of population pressure on the land or loss of handicraft markets to cheap imported products? Or do eco-nomic and political pressures combine, as in the case of a tax on peasants payable only in money? Or are the pressures social, as in the case of the desire to escape burdensome aspects of the old order? Such differences in-fluence the adjustment to modernization greatly.

(3) Variations in the path toward modernization. Does the sequence be-gin with light consumer industries? Or is there an attempt to introduce heavy, capital-intensive industries first? What is the role of government in shaping the pattern of investment? What is the rate of accumulation of tech-nological knowledge and skills? What is the general tempo of industrializa-tion? All these affect the nature of structural change and the degree of dis-comfort created by this change.

(4) Variations in the advanced stages of modernization. What is the emergent distribution of industries in developed economies? What are the emergent relations between state and economy, religion and economy, state and religion, etc.? While all advanced industrialized societies have their "in-dustrialization" in common, unique national differences remain. For in-stance, social class differs in its social significance in the United States and the United Kingdom, even though both are highly developed countries.

(5) Variations in the content and timing of dramatic events during mod-ernization. What is the significance of wars, revolutions, rapid migrations, natural catastrophes, etc. for the course of economic and social develop-ment?

Because of these sources of variation, it is virtually impossible to discover hard and fast empirical generalizations concerning the evolution of social structures during economic and social development. My purpose, therefore, in this paper, is not to search for such generalizations, but rather to outline certain ideal-type directions of structural change which modernization involves. On the basis of these ideal types we may classify, describe and analyze varying national experiences. Factors such as those just described determine in part the distinctive national response to these universal aspects of modernization, but this in no way detracts from their "universality." While I shall base my remarks on the vast literature of economic development, I can in no sense attempt an exhaustive comparative study.

Structural Differentiation in Periods of Development

The concept of structural differentiation can be used to analyze what is frequently referred to as the "marked break in established patterns of social and economic life" in periods of development.[5] Simply defined, differentiation refers to the evolution from a multi-functional role structure to several more specialized structures. The following are typical examples: (1) In the transition from domestic to factory industry, the division of labor increases, and the economic activities previously lodged in the family move to the firm. (2) With the rise of a formal educational system, the training functions previously performed by the family and church are established in a more specialized unit—the school. (3) The modern political party has a more complex structure than tribal factions and is less likely to be fettered with kinship loyalties, competition for religious leadership, etc. Formally defined, then, structural differentiation is a process whereby *"one* social role or organization . . . differentiates into *two or more* roles or organizations which function more effectively in the new historical circumstances. The new social units are structurally distinct from each other, but taken together are functionally equivalent to the original unit." [6]

Differentiation concerns only changes in role-structure. We should not, therefore, confuse differentiation with two closely related concepts: (1) The cause or motivation for entering the differentiated role. Wage-labor, for instance, may result from a desire for economic improvement, from political coercion, or indeed from a desire to fulfill traditional obligations (*e.g.*, to use wages to supply a dowry). These "reasons" should be kept conceptually distinct from differentiation itself. (2) The integration of differentiated roles. As differentiated wage-labor begins to appear, for instance, there also appear legal norms, labor exchanges, trade unions, and so on, which regulate—with varying degrees of success—the relations between labor and management. Such readjustments, even though they sometimes produce a new social unit, should be considered separately from role-specialization in other functions.

---

[5] S. Kuznets, "International Differences in Income Levels," in S. Kuznets, W. E. Moore, and J. J. Spengler, eds., *Economic Growth: Brazil, India, Japan* (Durham, N.C.: Duke University Press, 1955), p. 23.

[6] N. J. Smelser, *Social Change in the Industrial Revolution* (Chicago: University of Chicago Press, 1959), p. 2.

Let us now inquire into the process of differentiation in several different social realms.

Differentiation of Economic Activities

Typically, in underdeveloped countries, production is located in kinship units. Subsistence farming predominates; other industry is supplementary but still attached to kin and village. In some cases occupational position is determined largely by an extended group such as the caste.

Similarly, exchange and consumption are deeply embedded in family and village. In subsistence agriculture there is a limited amount of independent exchange outside the family; this means that production and consumption occur in the same social context. Exchange systems proper are still lodged in kinship and community (*e.g.,* reciprocal exchange), in stratification systems (*e.g.,* redistribution according to caste membership), and in political systems (*e.g.,* taxes, tributes, payments in kind, forced labor). Under such conditions market systems are underdeveloped, and the independent power of money to command the movement of goods and services is minimal.

As the economy develops, several kinds of economic activity are removed from this family-community complex. In agriculture, the introduction of money crops marks a differentiation between the social contexts of production and consumption. Agricultural wage-labor sometimes undermines the family production unit. In industry it is possible to identify several levels of differentiation. Household industry, the simplest form, parallels subsistence agriculture in that it supplies "the worker's own needs, unconnected with trade." "Handicraft production" splits production and consumption, though frequently consumption takes place in the local community. "Cottage industry," on the other hand, frequently involves a differentiation between consumption and community, since production is "for the market, for an unknown consumer, sold to a wholesaler who accumulates a stock." [7] Finally, manufacturing and factory systems segregate the worker from his capital and frequently from his family.

Similar differentiations appear simultaneously in the exchange system. Goods and services, previously exchanged on a noneconomic basis, are pulled more and more into the market. Money now commands the movement of more and more goods and services and thus begins to supplant—and sometimes undermine—the religious, political, familial, or caste sanctions which previously had governed economic activity. Such is the setting for the institutionalization of relatively autonomous economic systems which show

---

[7] These "levels," which represent points on the continuum from structural fusion to structural differentiation, are taken from J. H. Boeke, *The Structure of the Netherlands Indian Economy* (New York: International Secretariat, Institute of Pacific Relations, 1942), p. 90.

a greater emphasis on values such as universalism, functional specificity, and rationality.

Empirically we may classify underdeveloped economies according to how far they have moved along this line of differentiation. Migratory labor, for instance, may be a kind of compromise between full membership in a wage-labor force and attachment to an old community life; cottage industry introduces extended markets but retains the family-production fusion; the hiring of families in factories maintains a version of family production; the expenditure of wages on traditional items such as dowries also shows this half-entry into the more differentiated industrial-urban structure. The reasons for these partial cases of differentiation may lie in resistances on the part of the populace to give up traditional modes, in the economics of demand for handmade products, in systems of racial discrimination against native labor, or elsewhere. In any case, the concept of structural differentiation provides a yardstick to indicate the distance which the economic structure has evolved toward modernization.

Differentiation of Family Activities

One implication of the removal of economic activities from the kinship nexus is that the family loses some of its previous functions and thereby itself becomes a more specialized agency. The family ceases to be an economic unit of production; one or more members now leave the household to seek employment in the labor market. The family's activities become more concentrated on emotional gratification and socialization. While many halfway houses such as family hiring and migratory systems persist, the tendency is toward the segregation of family functions and economic functions.

Several related processes accompany this differentiation of the family from its other involvements: (1) Apprenticeship within the family declines. (2) Pressures develop against the intervention of family favoritism in the recruitment of labor and management. These pressures often lie in the demands of economic rationality. The intervention often persists, however, especially at the managerial levels, and in some cases (*e.g.*, Japan) family ties continue as a major basis for labor recruitment. (3) The direct control of elders and collateral kinsmen over the nuclear family weakens. This marks, in structural terms, the differentiation of the nuclear family from the extended family. (4) One aspect of this loss of control is the growth of personal choice, love, and related criteria as the basis for courtship and marriage. Structurally this is the differentiation of courtship from extended kinship. (5) One result of this complex of processes is the changing status of women, who become generally less subordinated economically, politically, and socially to their husbands than under earlier conditions.

In such ways structural differentiation undermines the old modes of integration in society. The controls of extended family and village begin to dissolve in the enlarged and complicated social setting which differentiation creates. New integrative problems are posed by this growing obsolescence. We shall inquire presently into some of the lines of integration.

Differentiation of Value Systems

The concept of differentiation can also elucidate the delicate problem of the role of values in economic development. It is clear that values affect development significantly, though in many different ways. Max Weber's analysis of Protestantism is an illustration of the force of religious values in encouraging development. In addition, secular nationalism plays an important role in the industrial "takeoff."

> . . . with the world organized as it is, nationalism is a *sine qua non* of industrialization, because it provides people with an overriding, easily acquired, secular motivation for making painful changes. National strength or prestige becomes the supreme goal, industrialization the chief means. The costs, inconveniences, sacrifices, and loss of traditional values can be justified in terms of this transcending, collective ambition. The new collective entity, the nation-state, that sponsors and grows from this aspiration is equal to the exigencies of industrial complexity; it draws directly the allegiance of every citizen, organizing the population as one community; it controls the passage of persons, goods, and news across the borders; it regulates economic and social life in detail. To the degree that the obstacles to industrialization are strong, nationalism must be intense to overcome them.[8]

In fact, nationalism seems in many cases to be the very instrument designed to smash those traditional religious systems—such as the classical Chinese or Indian—which Weber himself found to be less permissive than Protestantism for economic modernization. Yet nationalism too, like many traditionalistic religious systems, may hinder economic advancement by "reaffirmation of traditionally honored ways of acting and thinking," [9] by fostering anti-colonial attitudes after they are no longer relevant, and, more indirectly, by encouraging passive expectations of "readymade prosperity." [10] It seems possible to distinguish between these contrasting forces of "stimulus" and "drag" that value-systems have on economic development by using the logic of differentiation. . . .

In the early phases of modernization, many traditional attachments must

---

[8] K. Davis, "Social and Demographic Aspects of Economic Development in India," in *Economic Growth: Brazil, India, Japan, op. cit.,* p. 294.

[9] B. F. Hoselitz, "Non-Economic Barriers to Economic Development," *Economic Development and Cultural Change,* I (1952), No. 1, p. 9.

[10] J. van der Kroef, "Economic Development in Indonesia: Some Social and Cultural Impediments," *Economic Development and Cultural Change,* IV (1955), No. 2, pp. 116-133.

be modified in order to set up more differentiated institutional structures. Because these established commitments and methods of integration are deeply rooted in the organization of traditional society, a very generalized and powerful commitment is required, in the nature of the case, to "pry" individuals from these attachments. The values of ascetic and this-worldly religious beliefs, xenophobic national aspirations, and political ideologies such as socialism provide such a lever. Sometimes these various types of values combine into a single system of legitimacy. In any case, all three have an "ultimacy" of commitment in the name of which a wide range of sacrifices can be demanded and procured.

The very success of these value-systems, however, breeds the conditions for their own weakening. In a perceptive statement, Weber noted that by the beginning of the twentieth century, when the capitalistic system was already highly developed, it no longer needed the impetus of ascetic Protestantism. Capitalism had, by virtue of its conquest of much of Western society, solidly established an institutional base and a secular value-system of its own—"economic rationality." These secular economic values no longer needed the "ultimate" justification required in the newer, unsteadier days of economic revolution.

Such lines of differentiation, we might add, constitute the secularization of religious values. In this process, other institutional spheres—economic, political, scientific, etc.—come to be established more nearly on their own. The values governing these spheres are no longer sanctioned directly by religious beliefs, but by an autonomous rationality. Insofar as such rationalities replace religious sanctions in these spheres, secularization occurs.

Similarly, nationalistic and related value-systems undergo a process of secularization as differentiation proceeds. As a society moves toward more and more complex social organization, the encompassing demands of nationalistic commitment give way to more autonomous systems of rationality. The Soviet Union, for instance, as its social structure grows more differentiated, seems to be introducing more "independent" market mechanisms, "freer" social scientific investigation in some spheres, and so on. These measures are not, moreover, directly sanctioned by an appeal to nationalistic or communistic values. Finally, it seems a reasonable historical generalization that in the early stages of development nationalism is heady, muscular, and aggressive; as the society evolves to an advanced state, however, nationalism tends to settle into a more remote and complacent condition, rising to fury only in times of national crisis.

Thus the paradoxical element in the role of religious or nationalistic belief-systems; insofar as they encourage the breakup of old patterns, they may stimulate economic modernization; insofar as they resist their own subsequent secularization, however, the very same value-systems may become a drag on economic advance and structural change.

Differentiation of Systems of Stratification

In analyzing systems of stratification, we concentrate on two kinds of issues:

(1) To what extent are ascribed qualities subject to ranking? Some ascription exists in all societies, since the infant in the nuclear family always and everywhere begins with the status of his parents. The degree to which this ascribed ranking extends beyond the family to race, ethnic membership, etc. varies from society to society. In our own ideology we minimize the ascriptive elements of class and ethnic membership, but in practice these matter greatly, especially for Negroes.

(2) To what extent do ascribed qualities determine membership in occupational, political, religious, and other positions in society? In theory, again, the American egalitarian ideology places a premium on the maximum separation of such positions from ascribed categories, but in fact family membership, minority group membership, etc. impinge on the ultimate "placing" of persons. In many nonindustrialized societies this link between ascription and position is much closer. Such criteria as these reveal the degree of "openness," or social mobility, in a system.

Under conditions of economic modernization, structural differentiation increases along both these dimensions:

(1) Other evaluative standards intrude on ascribed memberships. For instance, McKim Marriott has noted that in the village of Paril in India:

> . . . Personal wealth, influence, and morality have surpassed the traditional caste-and-order alignment of kind groups as the effective bases of ranking. Since such new bases of ranking can no longer be clearly tied to any inclusive system of large solidary groupings, judgments must be made according to the characteristics of individual or family units. This individualization of judgments leads to greater dissensus (*sic*).[11]

Of course, castes, ethnic groups, and traditional religious groupings do not necessarily decline in importance *in every respect* during periods of modernization. As political interest groups or reference groups for diffuse loyalty, they may even increase in salience. As the sole bases of ranking, however, ascriptive standards become more differentiated from economic, political, and other standards.

(2) Individual mobility through the occupational hierarchies increases. This signifies the differentiation of the adult's functional position from his point of origin. In addition, individual mobility is frequently substituted

---

[11] McKim Marriott, "Social Change in an Indian Village," Chapter 35, this book; J. S. Coleman, *Nigeria: Background to Nationalism* (Berkeley and Los Angeles: University of California Press, 1958), pp. 70-73.

for collective mobility. Individuals, not whole castes or tribes, compete for higher standing in society. This phenomenon of increasing individual mobility seems to be one of the universal consequences of industrialization. After assembling extensive empirical evidence on patterns of mobility in industrialized nations, Lipset and Bendix concluded that "the overall pattern of [individual] social mobility appears to be much the same in the industrial societies of various Western countries." [12] Patterns of class symbolization and class ideology may, however, continue to differ among industrialized countries.

The Integration of Differentiated Activities

One of Emile Durkheim's remarkable insights concerned the role of integrative mechanisms under conditions of growing social heterogeneity. Launching his attack against the utilitarian view that the division of labor would flourish best without regulation, Durkheim demonstrated that one of the concomitants of a growing division of labor is an *increase* in mechanisms to coordinate and solidify the interaction among individuals with increasingly diversified interests.[13] Durkheim found this integration mainly in the legal structure, but one can locate similar kinds of integrative forces elsewhere in society.

Differentiation alone, therefore, is not sufficient for modernization. Development proceeds as a contrapuntal interplay between differentiation (which is divisive of established society) and integration (which unites differentiated structures on a new basis). Paradoxically, however, the process of integration itself produces more *differentiated* structures—e.g., trade unions, associations, political parties, and a mushrooming state apparatus. Let us illustrate this complex process of integration in several institutional spheres.

Economy and Family

Under a simple kind of economic organization—subsistence agriculture or household industry—there is little differentiation between economic roles and family roles. All reside in the kinship structure. The *integration* of these diverse but unspecialized activities also rests in the local family and community structures and in the religious traditions which fortify both of these.

---

[12] S. M. Lipset and R. Bendix, *Social Mobility in Industrial Society* (Berkeley and Los Angeles: University of California Press, 1959), pp. 13 ff.

[13] Émile Durkheim, *The Division of Labor in Society* (Glencoe, Ill.: The Free Press, 1949), chs. 3-8. A recent formulation of the relationship between differentiation and integration may be found in R. F. Bales, *Interaction Process Analysis* (Cambridge, Mass.: Addison-Wesley Press, 1950).

Under conditions of differentiation, the social setting for production is separated from that for consumption, and productive roles of family members are isolated geographically, temporally, and structurally from their distinctively familial roles. Such differentiation immediately creates integrative problems. How is information concerning employment opportunities to be conveyed to workpeople? How are the interests of families to be integrated with the interests of firms? How are families to be protected from market fluctuation? Whereas such integrative exigencies were faced by kinsmen, neighbors, and local largesse in premodern settings, modernization gives birth to dozens of institutions and organizations geared to these new integrative problems—labor recruitment agencies and exchanges; labor unions; government regulation of labor allocation; welfare and relief arrangements; cooperative societies; savings institutions. All these involve agencies which specialize in integration.

Community

If industrialization occurs only in villages or if villages are "built around" paternalistic industrial enterprises, many ties of community and kinship can be maintained under industrial conditions. Urbanization, however, frequently creates more anonymity. As a result, one finds frequently in expanding cities a growth of voluntary associations—churches and chapels, unions, schools, halls, athletic clubs, bars, shops, mutual aid groups, etc. In some cases this growth of integrative groupings may be retarded because of the back-and-forth movement of migratory workers, who "come to the city for their differentiation" and "return to the village for their integration." In cities themselves the original criterion for associating may be common tribe, caste, or village; this criterion may persist or give way gradually to more "functional" groupings based on economic or political interests.

Political Structure

In a typical premodern setting, political integration is closely fused with kinship position, tribal membership, control of the land or control of the unknown. Political forms include chieftainships, kingships, councils of elders, powerful landlords, powerful magicians and oracles, etc.

As social systems grow more complex, political systems are modified accordingly. Fortes and Evans-Pritchard have specified three types of native African political systems, which can be listed according to their degree of differentiation from kinship lineages: (1) small societies in which the largest political unit embraces only those united by kinship; thus political authority is coterminous with kinship relations; (2) societies in which the political framework is the integrative core for a number of kinship lineages; (3) societies with an "administrative organization" of a more formal nature.

Such systems move toward greater differentiation as population grows and economic and cultural heterogeneity increases.[14] In colonial and recently-freed African societies, political systems have evolved much further, with the appearance of parties, congresses, pressure groups, and even "parliamentary" systems.[15] In describing the Indian village, Marriott speaks of the "wider integration of local groups with outside groups." [16] Sometimes this wider political integration, like community integration, is based on an extension and modification of an old integrative principle. Harrison has argued that modern developments in India have changed the significance of caste from the "traditional village extension of the joint family" to "regional alliances of kindred local units." This modification has led to the formation of "new caste lobbies" which constitute some of the strongest and most explosive political forces in modern India.[17] We shall mention some of the possible political consequences of this persistence of old integrative forms later.

These examples illustrate how differentiation in society impinges on the integrative sphere. The resulting integrative structures coordinate and solidify—with varying success—the social structure which the forces of differentiation threaten to fragment. In many cases the integrative associations and parties display tremendous instability—labor unions turn into political or nationalistic parties; religious sects become political clubs; football clubs become religious sects, and so on.[18] The resultant fluidity points up the extremely pressing needs for reintegration under conditions of rapid, irregular, and disruptive processes of differentiation. The initial response is a kind of trial-and-error floundering for many kinds of integration at once.

We have sketched some structural consequences of modernization and integration. These changes are not, it should be remembered, a simple function of "industrialization." Some of the most farreaching structural changes have occurred in countries which have scarcely experienced the beginnings of industrialization. For instance, colonialism—or related forms of economic dominance—creates not only an extensive differentiation of cash products and wage labor but also a vulnerability to world price fluctuations in commodities. Hence many of the structural changes described above—and the resulting social disturbances to be described presently—

---

[14] M. Fortes and E. E. Evans-Pritchard, eds., *African Political Systems* (London: Oxford University Press, 1940), pp. 1-25.

[15] D. Apter, *The Gold Coast in Transition* (Princeton: Princeton University Press, 1956); T. Hodgkin, *Nationalism in Colonial Africa* (New York: New York University Press, 1957), pp. 115-139; G. A. Almond and J. S. Coleman, *The Politics of Developing Areas* (Princeton: Princeton University Press, 1960).

[16] "Social Change in an Indian Village," *loc. cit.*

[17] S. E. Harrison, *India: The Most Dangerous Decades* (Princeton: Princeton University Press, 1960), pp. 100 ff.

[18] *Nationalism in Colonial Africa, op. cit.,* pp. 85 ff.

characterize both societies which are industrializing and some that are still "preindustrial."

Discontinuities in Differentiation and Integration: Social Disturbances

The structural changes associated with modernization are disruptive to the social order for the following reasons:

(1) Differentiation demands the creation of new activities, norms, rewards and sanctions—money, political position, prestige based on occupation, and so on. These often conflict with old modes of social action, which are frequently dominated by traditional religious, tribal, and kinship systems. These traditional standards are among the most intransigent of obstacles to modernization, and when they are threatened, serious dissatisfaction and opposition arise.

(2) Structural change is, above all, *uneven* in periods of modernization. In colonial societies, for instance, the European powers frequently revolutionized the economic, political, and educational frameworks, but simultaneously encouraged or imposed a conservatism in traditional religious, class, and family systems.

> . . . the basic problem in these [colonial] societies was the expectation that the native population would accept certain broad, modern institutional settings . . . and would perform within them various roles—especially economic and administrative roles—while at the same time, they were denied some of the basic rewards inherent in these settings . . . they were expected to act on the basis of a motivational system derived from a different social structure which the colonial powers and indigenous rulers tried to maintain.[19]

Under noncolonial conditions of modernization similar discontinuities appear. Within the economy itself, rapid industrialization, no matter how coordinated, bites unevenly into the established social and economic structure. And throughout the society, the differentiation occasioned by agricultural, industrial and urban changes always proceeds in a seesaw relationship with integration; the two forces continuously breed lags and bottlenecks. The faster the tempo of modernization, the more severe are the discontinuities. This unevenness creates *anomie* in the classical sense, for it generates disharmony between life experiences and the normative framework by which these experiences are regulated.

(3) Dissatisfactions arising from conflict with traditional ways and those arising from *anomie* sometimes aggravate one another when they come into contact. *Anomie* may be relieved in part by new integrative devices such as unions, associations, clubs, and government regulations. Such innovations

---

[19] S. N. Eisenstadt, "Sociological Aspects of Political Development in Underdeveloped Countries," *Economic Development and Cultural Change*, V (1957), No. 4, p. 298.

are often opposed, however, by traditional vested interests because the new forms of integration compete with the older undifferentiated systems of solidarity. The new result is a three-way tug-of-war among the forces of tradition, the forces of differentiation, and the new forces of integration. Such conditions create virtually unlimited potentialities for group conflict.

Three classic responses to these discontinuities are anxiety, hostility, and fantasy. These responses, if and when they become collective, crystallize into a variety of social movements—peaceful agitation, political violence, millenarianism, nationalism, revolution, underground subversion, etc. There is plausible—though not entirely convincing—evidence that those drawn most readily into such movements are those suffering most severely the pains of displacements created by structural change. For example,

[Nationalism appeared] as a permanent force in Southeast Asia at the moment when the peasants were forced to give up subsistence farming for the cultivation of cash crops or when (as in highly colonized Java) subsistence farming ceased to yield a subsistence. The introduction of a money economy and the withering away of the village as the unit of life accompanied this development and finally established the period of economic dependence.[20]

Other theoretical and empirical evidence suggests that social movements appeal most to those who have been dislodged from old social ties by differentiation but who have not been integrated into the new social order.

Many belief-systems associated with these movements envision the grand and almost instantaneous integration of society. In many cases the beliefs are highly emotional and unconcerned with realistic policies. In nationalistic colonial movements, for instance, "the political symbols were intended to develop new, ultimate, common values and basic loyalties, rather than relate to current policy issues within the colonial society." [21] Furthermore, such belief-systems reflect the ambivalence resulting from the conflict between traditionalism and modernization. Nationalists alternate between xenophobia and xenophilia; they predict that they will "outmodernize" the West in the future and simultaneously "restore" the true values of the ancient civilization; they argue for egalitarian and hierarchical principles of social organization at the same time.[22] Nationalistic and related ideologies unite these contradictory tendencies in a society under one large symbol; then, if these ideologies are successful, they are often used as a means to modernize and thus erase those kinds of social discontinuity which gave rise to the original nationalistic outburst.

---

[20] E. H. Jacoby, *Agrarian Unrest in Southeast Asia* (New York: Columbia University Press, 1949), p. 246.

[21] "Sociological Aspects of Political Development," *op. cit.*, p. 294.

[22] M. Matossian, "Ideologies of Delayed Industrialization," *Economic Development and Cultural Change*, VI (1957), No. 3, pp. 217-228.

Naturally not all the cases of early modernization produce violent nationalistic or other social movements. When such movements do arise, furthermore, they take many different forms. I shall merely list what seem to be the five most decisive factors in the genesis and molding of social disturbances:

(1) The scope and intensity of the social dislocation created by structural changes. "The greater the tempo of these changes . . . the greater the problems of acute malintegration the society has to face." [23]

(2) The structural complexity of the society at the time when modernization begins. In the least developed societies, where "the language of politics is at the same time the language of religion," protest movements more or less immediately take on a religious cast. In Africa, for instance, utopian religious movements seem to have relatively greater appeal in the less developed regions, whereas the more secular types of political protest such as trade union movements and party agitations have tended to cluster in the more developed areas. The secularization of protest increases, of course, as modernization and differentiation proceed.

(3) The access of disturbed groups to channels of influencing social policy. If dislocated groups have access to those responsible for introducing reforms, agitation tends to be relatively peaceful and orderly. If this access is blocked, either because of the isolation of the groups or the intransigence of the ruling authorities, demands for reform tend to take more violent, utopian, and bizarre forms. Hence the tendency for fantasy and unorganized violence to cluster among the disinherited, the colonized, and the socially isolated migrants.

(4) The overlap of interests and lines of cleavage. In many colonial societies, the social order broke more-or-less imperfectly into three groupings: first, the Western representatives who held control of economic enterprises and political administration, and who frequently were allied with large local landowners; second, a large native population who—when drawn into the colonial economy—entered as tenant farmers, wage laborers, etc.; and third, a group of foreigners—Chinese, Indians, Syrians, Goans, Lebanese, etc.—who fitted "in between" the first two as traders, moneylenders, merchants, creditors, etc. This view is oversimplified, of course, but many colonial societies approximated this arrangement. The important structural feature of such a system is that economic, political, and racial-ethnic memberships *coincide* with each other. Hence *any* kind of conflict is likely to assume racial overtones and arouse the more diffuse loyalties and prejudices of the warring parties. Many colonial outbursts did in fact follow racial lines. Insofar as such "earthquake faults" persist after inde-

---

[23] "Sociological Aspects of Political Development," *op. cit.*, p. 294; J. S. Coleman, "Nationalism in Tropical Africa," in L. W. Shannon, *Underdeveloped Areas* (New York: Harper & Row, 1957), pp. 42 ff.; *Nationalism in Colonial Africa, op. cit.*, p. 56.

pendence, these societies are likely to be plagued by similar outbursts. If, on the other hand, the various lines of cleavage crisscross, it is more nearly possible to insulate and manage specific economic and political grievances peacefully.

(5) The kind and extent of foreign infiltration and intervention on behalf of protest groups.

Structural Bases for the Role of Government

Many have argued on economic grounds for the presence of a strong, centralized government in rapidly modernizing societies. Governmental planning and activity are required, for instance, to direct saving and investment, to regulate incentives, to encourage entrepreneurship, to control trade and prices, and so on. To such arguments I should like to add several considerations arising out of the analysis of structural change in periods of rapid development:

(1) Undifferentiated institutional structures frequently constitute the primary social barriers to modernization. Individuals refuse to work for wages because of traditional kinship, village, tribal, and other ties. Invariably a certain amount of political pressure is required to pry individuals loose from these ties. The need for such pressure increases, of course, with the rate of modernization desired.

(2) The process of differentiation itself creates those conditions which demand a larger, more formal type of political administration. A further argument for the importance of government in periods of rapid and uneven modernization lies, then, in the need to accommodate the growing cultural, economic, and social heterogeneity, and to control the political repercussions from the constantly shifting distribution of power which accompanies extensive social reorganization.

(3) The apparent propensity for periods of early modernization to erupt into explosive outbursts creates delicate political problems for the leaders of developing nations. We might conclude this essay on the major social forces of modernization by suggesting what kinds of government are likely to be most effective in such troubled areas. First, political leaders will increase their effectiveness by open and vigorous commitment to utopian and xenophobic nationalism. This commitment serves as a powerful instrument for attaining three of their most important ends: (a) the enhancement of their own claim to legitimacy by endowing themselves with the mission for creating the nation-state; (b) the procurement of otherwise impossible sacrifices from a populace which may be committed to modernization in the abstract but which resists the concrete breaks with traditional ways; (c) the use of their claim to legitimacy to hold down protests and to prevent generalized symbols such as communism from spreading to all sorts of particular grievances. These same political leaders should not, however,

take their enthusiasm for this claim to legitimacy too literally. They should not rely on the strength of their nationalistic commitment to ignore or smother grievances altogether. They should play politics in the usual sense with aggrieved groups in order to give these groups an access to responsible political agencies and thereby reduce those conditions which give rise to counterclaims to legitimacy. One key to political stability would seem to be, therefore, the practice of flexible politics behind the façade of an inflexible commitment to a national mission.

•

In this essay I have attempted to sketch, in ideal-type terms, the ways in which economic and social development are related to the social structure. I have organized the discussion around three major categories—differentiation, which characterizes a social structure moving toward greater complexity; integration, which in certain respects balances the divisive character of differentiation; and social disturbances, which result from the discontinuities between differentiation and integration.

To this analysis must be added four qualifications: (1) I have not attempted to account for the determinants of economic development itself. In fact, the discussion of differentiation, integration, and social disturbance takes as given a certain attempt to develop economically. These three forces condition the *course* of development, however, once it has started. (2) For purposes of exposition I have presented the three major categories in a certain order—differentiation, integration, social disturbances. We should not assume from this, however, that any one of them assumes causal precedence in the analysis of social change. Rather they form an interactive system. Disturbances, for instance, may arise from discontinuities created by structural differentiation, but these very disturbances may shape the course of future processes of differentiation. Likewise, integrative developments may be set in motion by differentiation, but in their turn they may initiate new lines of differentiation. (3) Even though the forces of differentiation, integration, and disturbance are closely linked empirically, we should not "close" the "system" composed of the relationship among the three forces. Differentiation may arise from sources other than economic development; the requirement of integration may arise from conditions other than differentiation; and the sources of social disturbance are not exhausted by the discontinuities between differentiation and integration. (4) The "all-at-once" character of the transition from less differentiated to more differentiated societies should not be exaggerated. Empirically the process evolves gradually and influences the social structure selectively. The emphasis on various halfway arrangements and compromises throughout the essay illustrates this gradualness and irregularity.

CHAPTER 27

W. W. ROSTOW

The Takeoff into
Self-Sustained Growth

The purpose of this article is to explore the following hypothesis: that the process of economic growth can usefully be regarded as centering on a relatively brief time interval of two or three decades, when the economy and the society of which it is a part transform themselves in such ways that economic growth is, subsequently, more-or-less automatic. This decisive transformation is here called the takeoff.

The takeoff is defined as the interval during which the rate of investment increases in such a way that real output *per capita* rises, and this initial increase carries with it radical changes in production techniques and the disposition of income flows, which perpetuate the new scale of investment and perpetuate thereby the rising trend in *per capita* output. Initial changes in method require that some group in the society have the will and the authority to install and diffuse new production techniques; and a perpetuation of the growth process requires that such a leading group expand in authority and that the society as a whole respond to the impulses set up by the initial changes, including the potentialities for external economies. Initial changes in the scale and direction of finance flows are likely to imply a command over income flows by new groups or institutions; and a perpetuation of growth requires that a high proportion of the increment to real income during the takeoff period be returned to productive investment. The takeoff requires, therefore, a society prepared to respond actively to new possibilities for productive enterprise; and it is likely to require political, social, and institutional changes which will both perpetuate an initial increase in the scale of investment and result in the regular acceptance and absorption of innovations.

From W. W. Rostow, "The Takeoff into Self-Sustained Growth," *The Economic Journal*, LXVI (1956), No. 261, pp. 25-48. Reprinted by permission of the author and the Royal Economic Society, London.

In short, this article is an effort to clarify the economics of industrial revolution where an industrial revolution is conceived of narrowly with respect to time and broadly with respect to changes in production functions.

Three Stages in the Growth Process

The historian examining the story of a particular national economy is inevitably impressed by the long-period continuity of events. Like other forms of history, economic history is a seamless web. The cotton-textile developments in Britain of the 1780's and 1790's have a history stretching back for a half century at least; the United States of the 1840's and 1850's had been preparing itself for industrialization since the 1790's, at the latest; Russia's remarkable development during the two pre-1914 decades goes back to 1861 for its foundations, if not to the Napoleonic Wars or to Peter the Great; the remarkable economic spurt of Meiji Japan is incomprehensible outside the context of economic developments in the latter half of the Tokugawa era; and so on. . . . From the perspective of the economic historian, the isolation of a takeoff period is, then, a distinctly arbitrary process. It is to be judged, like such other arbitrary exercises as the isolation of business cycles and secular trends, on whether it illuminates more of the economic process than it conceals; and it should be used, if accepted, as a way of giving a rough framework of order to the inordinately complicated biological problem of growth, rather than as an exact model of reality.

There is difficulty in this set of conceptions for the statistical analyst of economic development as well as for the historian. At first sight, the data mobilized, for example, by Clark, Kuznets, Buchanan and Ellis exhibit a continuum of degrees of development both within countries over time and as among countries at a given period of time, with no *prima facie* case for a clearly marked watershed in the growth process.[1] In part, this statistical result arises from the fact that historical data on national product and its components are only rarely available for an economy until after it has passed into a stage of more-or-less regular growth; that is, after the takeoff. In part, it arises from the fact that, by and large, these authors are more concerned with different levels of *per capita* output (or welfare)—and the structural characteristics that accompany them—than with the growth

---

[1] Colin Clark, *The Conditions of Economic Progress* (2nd ed.; London, 1951); Simon Kuznets, "International Differences in Capital Formation and Financing," mimeographed, Conference on Capital Formation and Economic Growth, November 1953 (New York: National Bureau of Economic Research, 1953); Norman Buchanan and Howard Ellis, *Approaches to Economic Development* (New York: Twentieth Century Fund, 1955). *See also* the United Nations data presented as a frontispiece to H. F. Williamson and John A. Buttrick, *Economic Development* (New York: Prentice-Hall, 1954).

process itself. The data they mobilize do not come to grips with the inner determinants of growth. The question raised here is not how or why levels of output *per capita* have differed, but rather how it has come about that particular economies have moved from stagnation, to slow, piecemeal advance, to a situation where growth was the normal economic condition. Our criterion here is not the absolute level of output *per capita,* but its rate of change.

In this argument, the sequence of economic development is taken to consist of three periods: a long period (up to a century or, conceivably, more) when the preconditions for takeoff are established; the takeoff itself, defined within two or three decades; and a long period when growth becomes normal and relatively automatic. These three divisions would not, of course, exclude the possibility of growth giving way to secular stagnation or decline in the long term. It would exclude from the concept of a growing economy, however, one which experiences a brief spurt of expansion which is not subsequently sustained; for example, the United States industrial boom of the War of 1812, or the ill-fated spurts of certain Latin American economies in the early stages of their modern history.

Takeoffs have occurred in two quite different types of societies; therefore, the process of establishing preconditions for takeoff has varied. In the first and most general case, the achievement of preconditions for takeoff required major change in political and social structure and, even, in effective cultural values. . . . In the second case, takeoff was delayed not by political, social, and cultural obstacles, but by the high (and even expanding) levels of welfare that could be achieved by exploiting land and natural resources. In this second case, takeoff was initiated by a more narrowly economic process, as, for example, in the northern United States, Australia and perhaps Sweden. . . . As one would expect in the essentially biological field of economic growth, history offers mixed as well as pure cases.

In the first case the process of establishing preconditions for takeoff might be generalized in impressionistic terms as follows:

We start with a reasonably stable and traditional society, containing an economy mainly agricultural, using more-or-less unchanging production methods, saving, and investing productively little more than is required to meet depreciation. Usually from outside the society, but sometimes out of its own dynamics, comes the idea that economic progress is possible; and this idea spreads within the established elite, or (more usually) in some disadvantaged group whose lack of status does not prevent the exercise of some economic initiative. More often than not, the economic motives for seeking economic progress converge with some noneconomic motive, such as the desire for increased social power and prestige, national pride, political ambition, and so on. Education, for some at least, broadens and changes to suit the needs of modern economic activity. New enterprising men come forward willing to mobilize savings and to take risks in pursuit of profit, notably in commerce. The commercial markets for agricultural products, domestic handicrafts, and consumption-goods imports widen. Institutions for mobilizing capital appear, or expand from primitive levels in the scale, surety, and time horizon for loans. Basic capital is expanded, notably in transport and communications, often to bring to market raw materials in which other nations have an economic interest, often financed by foreign capital. And here and there modern manufacturing enterprise appears, usually in substitution for imports.

Since public health measures are enormously productive in their early stages of application, and, as innovations go, meet relatively low resistance in most cultures, the death rate may fall and the population begin to rise, putting pressure on the food supply and the institutional structure of agriculture, creating thereby an economic depressant or stimulus (or both in turn), depending on the society's response.

The rate of productive investment may rise up to 5 per cent of national income; but this is unlikely to do much more than keep ahead of the population increase. And, in general, all this activity proceeds on a limited basis, within an economy and a society still mainly characterized by traditional low-productivity techniques and by old values and institutions which developed in conjunction with them. The rural proportion of the population is likely to stand at 75 per cent or over.

In the second case, of naturally wealthy nations, with a highly favorable balance between population and natural resources and with a population deriving by emigration from reasonably acquisitive cultures, the story of establishing the preconditions differs mainly in that there is no major problem of overcoming traditional values inappropriate to economic growth and the inert or resistant institutions which incorporate them; there is less difficulty in developing an elite effective in the investment process; and there is no population problem.[2] Technically, much the same slow-moving process of change occurs at high (and, perhaps, even expanding) levels of *per capita* output and with an extensive growth of population and output still based on rich land and other natural resources. Takeoff fails to occur mainly because the comparative advantage of exploiting productive land and other natural resources delays the time when self-reinforcing industrial growth can profitably get under way.

The beginning of takeoff can usually be traced to a particular sharp stimulus. The stimulus may take the form of a political revolution which affects directly the balance of social power and effective values, the character of economic institutions, the distribution of income, the pattern of investment outlays and the proportion of potential innovations actually applied; that is, it operates through the propensities. It may come about through a tech-

---

[2] Even in these cases, there have often been significant political and social restraints which had to be reduced or eliminated before takeoff could occur; for example, in Canada, the Argentine and the American South.

nological (including transport) innovation, which sets in motion a chain of secondary expansion in modern sectors and has powerful potential external economy effects which the society exploits. It may take the form of a newly favorable international environment, such as the opening of British and French markets to Swedish timber in the 1860's or a sharp relative rise in export prices and/or large new capital imports, as in the case of the United States from the late 1840's, Canada and Russia from the mid-1890's; but it may also come as a challenge posed by an unfavorable shift in the international environment, such as a sharp fall in terms of trade (or a wartime blockage of foreign trade) requiring the rapid development of manufactured import substitutes, as in the case of the Argentine and Australia in the 1930's and during the Second World War. . . .

What is essential here is not the form of stimulus but the fact that the prior development of the society and its economy result in a positive sustained, and self-reinforcing, response to it: the result is not a once-over change in production functions or in the volume of investment, but a higher proportion of potential innovations accepted in a more-or-less regular flow and a higher rate of investment.

In short, the forces which have yielded marginal bursts of activity now expand and become quantitatively significant as rapid-moving trends. New industries expand at high rates, yielding profits which are substantially reinvested in new capacity; and their expansion induces a more general expansion of the modern sectors of the economy where a high rate of ploughback prevails. The institutions for mobilizing savings (including the fiscal and sometimes the capital-levy activities of government) increase in scope and efficiency. New techniques spread in agriculture as well as in industry, as increasing numbers of persons are prepared to accept them and the deep changes they bring to ways of life. A new class of businessmen (usually private, sometimes public servants) emerges and acquires control over the key decisions determining the use of savings. New possibilities for export develop and are exploited; new import requirements emerge. The economy exploits hitherto unused backlogs in technique and natural resources. Although there are a few notable exceptions, all this momentum historically attracted substantial foreign capital.

The use of aggregative national-income terms evidently reveals little of the process which is occurring. It is nevertheless useful to regard as a necessary but not sufficient condition for the takeoff the fact that the proportion of net investment to national income (or net national product) rises from (say) 5 per cent to over 10 per cent, definitely outstripping the likely population pressure (since under the assumed takeoff circumstances the capital –output ratio is low), and yielding a distinct rise in real output *per capita*. Whether real consumption *per capita* rises depends on the pattern of income distribution and population pressure, as well as on the magnitude, character, and productivity of investment itself.

As indicated in Table 31-1, I believe it possible to identify at least tentatively such takeoff periods for a number of countries which have passed into the stage of growth.

The third stage is, of course, the long, fluctuating story of sustained economic progress. Overall capital per head increases as the economy matures. The structure of the economy changes increasingly. The initial key industries, which sparked the takeoff, decelerate as diminishing returns operate on the original set of industrial tricks and the original band of pioneering entrepreneurs give way to less single-minded industrial leaders in those sectors; but the average rate of growth is maintained by a succession of new, rapidly growing sectors, with a new set of pioneering leaders. The proportion of the population in rural pursuits declines. The economy finds its (changing) place in the international economy. The society makes such terms as it will with the requirements for maximizing modern and efficient production, balancing off, as it will, the new values against those retarding values which persist with deeper roots or adapting the latter in such ways as to support rather than retard the growth process. This sociological calculus interweaves with basic resource endowments to determine the pace of deceleration.

Table 27-1

Some Tentative, Approximate Takeoff Dates

Country	Takeoff	Country	Takeoff
Great Britain	1783-1802	Russia	1890-1914
France	1830-1860	Canada	1896-1914
Belgium	1833-1860	Argentine[c]	1935-
United States[a]	1843-1860	Turkey[d]	1937-
Germany	1850-1873	India[e]	1952-
Sweden	1868-1890	China[e]	1952-
Japan[b]	1878-1900		

[a] The American takeoff is here viewed as the upshot of two different periods of expansion: the first, that of the 1840's, marked by railway and manufacturing development, mainly confined to the East—this occurred while the West and South digested the extensive agricultural expansion of the previous decade; the second the great railway push into the Middle West during the 1850's marked by a heavy inflow of foreign capital. By the opening of the Civil War the American economy of North and West, with real momentum in its heavy-industry sector, is judged to have taken off.

b Lacking adequate data, there is some question about the timing of the Japanese takeoff. Some part of the post-1868 period was certainly, by the present set of definitions, devoted to firming up the preconditions for takeoff. By 1914 the Japanese economy had certainly taken off. The question is whether the period from about 1878 to the Sino-Japanese War in the mid-1890's is to be regarded as the completion of the preconditions or as takeoff. On present evidence, I incline to the latter view.

[c] In one sense the Argentine economy began its takeoff during the First World War. But by and large, down to the pit of the post-1929 depression, the growth of its modern sector, stimulated during the war, tended to slacken; and, like a good part of the Western World, the Argentine sought during the 1920's to return to a pre-1914 normalcy. It was not until the mid-1930's that a sustained takeoff was inaugurated, which by and large can now be judged to have been successful despite the structural vicissitudes of that economy.

[d] Against the background of industrialization measures inaugurated in the mid-1930's, the Turkish economy has exhibited remarkable momentum in the past five years, founded in the increase in agricultural income and productivity. It still remains to be seen whether these two surges, conducted under quite different national policies, will constitute a transition to self-sustaining growth, and whether Turkey can overcome its current structural problems.

[e] As noted in the text it is still too soon (for quite different reasons) to judge either the Indian or Chinese Communist takeoff efforts successful.

It is with the problems and vicissitudes of such growing economies of the third stage (and especially with cyclical fluctuations and the threat of chronic unemployment) that the bulk of modern theoretical economics is concerned, including much recent work on the formal properties of growth models. The student of history and of contemporary underdeveloped areas is more likely to be concerned with the economics of the first two stages; that is, the economics of the preconditions and the takeoff. If we are to have a serious theory of economic growth or (more likely) some useful theories about economic growth, they must obviously seek to embrace these two early stages—and notably the economics of the takeoff. The balance of this article is designed to mobilize, tentatively and in a preliminary way, what an economic historian can contribute to the economics of takeoff.

The Takeoff Defined and Isolated

There are several problems of choice involved in defining the takeoff with precision. We might begin with one arbitrary definition and consider briefly the two major alternatives.

For the present purposes the takeoff is defined as requiring all three of the following related conditions:

(*a*) a rise in the rate of productive investment from (say) 5 per cent or less to over 10 per cent of national income (or net national product);

(*b*) the development of one or more substantial manufacturing[3] sectors, with a high rate of growth;

(*c*) the existence or quick emergence of a political, social and institutional framework which exploits the impulses to expansion in the modern sector and the potential external economy effects of the takeoff and gives to growth an on-going character.

The third condition implies a considerable capability to mobilize capital from domestic sources. Some takeoffs have occurred with virtually no capital imports, *e.g.,* Britain and Japan. Some takeoffs have had a high component of foreign capital, *e.g.,* the United States, Russia and Canada. But some countries have imported large quantities of foreign capital for long periods, which undoubtedly contributed to creating the preconditions for takeoff, without actually initiating takeoff, *e.g.,* the Argentine before 1914, Venezuela down to recent years, the Congo currently. In short, whatever the role of capital imports, the preconditions for takeoff include an initial ability to mobilize domestic savings productively, as well as a structure which subsequently permits a high marginal rate of savings.

This definition is designed to isolate the early stage when industrialization

---

[3] In this context "manufacturing" is taken to include the processing of agricultural products or raw materials by modern methods, *e.g.,* timber in Sweden, meat in Australia, dairy products in Denmark. The dual requirement of a "manufacturing" sector is that its processes set in motion a chain of further modern sector requirements and that its expansion provide the potentiality of external economy effects.

takes hold rather than the later stage when industrialization becomes a more massive and statistically more impressive phenomenon. In Britain, for example, there is no doubt that it was between 1815 and 1850 that industrialization fully took hold. If the criterion chosen for takeoff was the period of most rapid overall industrial growth, or the period when largescale industry matured, all our takeoff dates would have to be set forward: Britain, for example, to 1819-1848, the United States to 1868-1893, Sweden to 1890-1920, Japan to 1900-1920, Russia to 1928-1940. The earlier dating is chosen here because it is believed, on present (often inadequate) evidence, that the decisive transformations (including a decisive shift in the investment rate) occur in the first industrial phases; and later industrial maturity can be directly traced back to foundations laid in these first phases.

This definition is also designed to rule out from the takeoff the quite substantial economic progress which can occur in an economy before a truly self-reinforcing growth process gets under way. British economic expansion between (say) 1750 and 1783, Russian economic expansion between (say) 1861 and 1890, Canadian economic expansion between 1867 and the mid-1890's—such periods, for which there is an equivalent in the economic history of almost every growing economy—were marked by extremely important, even decisive, developments. The transport network expanded, and with it both internal and external commerce; new institutions for mobilizing savings were developed; a class of commercial and even industrial entrepreneurs began to emerge; industrial enterprise on a limited scale (or in limited sectors) grew. And yet, however essential these pretakeoff periods were for later development, their scale and momentum were insufficient to transform the economy radically or, in some cases, to outstrip population growth and to yield an increase in *per capita* output.

With a sense of the considerable violence done to economic history, I am here seeking to isolate a period when the scale of productive economic activity reaches a critical level and produces changes which lead to a massive and progressive structural transformation in economies and the societies of which they are a part, better viewed as changes in kind than merely in degree.

•

The Inner Structure of the Takeoff

Following the definition of takeoff . . . we must consider not merely how a rise in the investment rate is brought about, from both supply and demand perspectives, but how rapidly growing manufacturing sectors emerged and imparted their primary and secondary growth impulses to the economy.

Perhaps the most important thing to be said about the behavior of these variables in historical cases of takeoff is that they have assumed many different forms. There is no single pattern. The rate and productivity of investment can rise, and the consequences of this rise can be diffused into a self-reinforcing general growth process by many different technical and economic routes, under the aegis of many different political, social and cultural settings, driven along by a wide variety of human motivations.

The purpose of the following paragraphs is to suggest briefly, and by way of illustration only, certain elements of both uniformity and variety in the variables whose movement has determined the inner structure of the takeoff.

The Supply of Loanable Funds

By and large, the loanable funds required to finance the takeoff have come from two types of sources: from shifts in the control over income flows, including income-distribution changes and capital imports and from the ploughback of profits in rapidly expanding particular sectors.

The notion of economic development occurring as the result of income shifts from those who will spend less productively to those who will spend more productively is one of the oldest and most fundamental notions in economics.

Historically, income shifts conducive to economic development have assumed many forms. In Meiji Japan and also in Tsarist Russia, the substitution of government bonds for the great landholders' claim on the flow of rent payments led to a highly Smithian redistribution of income into the hands of those with higher propensities to seek material advance and to accept innovations. In both cases, the real value of the government bonds exchanged for land depreciated; and, in general, the feudal landlords emerged with a less attractive arrangement than had first appeared to be offered. Aside from the confiscation effect, two positive impulses arose from land reform: the state itself used the flow of payments from peasants, now diverted from landlords' hands, for activity which encouraged economic development; and a certain number of the more enterprising former landlords directly invested in commerce and industry. In contemporary India and China, we can observe quite different degrees of income transfer by this route. India is relying to only a very limited extent on the elimination of large incomes unproductively spent by large landlords, although this element figures in a small way in its program. Communist China has systematically transferred all nongovernmental pools of capital into the hands of the State, in a series of undisguised or barely disguised capital levies; and it is drawing heavily for capital resources on the mass of middle and poor peasants who remain.

In addition to confiscatory and taxation devices, which can operate effectively when the State is spending more productively than the taxed individuals, inflation has been important to several takeoffs. In Britain of the late

1790's, the United States of the 1850's, Japan of the 1870's there is no doubt that capital formation was aided by price inflation, which shifted resources away from consumption to profits.

The shift of income flows into more productive hands has, of course, been aided historically not only by government fiscal measures but also by banks and capital markets. Virtually without exception, the takeoff periods have been marked by the extension of banking institutions which expanded the supply of working capital; and in most cases also by an expansion in the range of longrange financing done by a central, formally organized, capital market.

Although these familiar capital-supply functions of the State and private institutions have been important to the takeoff, it is likely to prove the case, on close examination, that a necessary condition for takeoff was the existence of one or more rapidly growing sectors whose entrepreneurs (private or public) ploughed back into new capacity a very high proportion of profits. Put another way, the demand side of the investment process, rather than the supply of loanable funds, may be the decisive element in the takeoff—as opposed to the period of creating the preconditions, or of sustaining growth once it is under way. The distinction is, historically, sometimes difficult to make, notably when the state simultaneously acts both to mobilize supplies of finance and to undertake major entrepreneurial acts. There are, nevertheless, periods in economic history when quite substantial improvements in the machinery of capital supply do not, in themselves, initiate a takeoff, but fall within the period when the preconditions are created: e.g., British banking developments in the century before 1783, Russian banking developments before 1890, etc.

One extremely important version of the ploughback process has taken place through foreign trade. Developing economies have created from their natural resources major export industries; and the rapid expansion in exports has been used to finance the import of capital equipment and to service the foreign debt during the takeoff. United States, Russian, and Canadian grain fulfilled this function, Swedish timber and pulp, Japanese silk, etc. Currently, Chinese exports to the Communist Bloc, wrung at great administrative and human cost from the agricultural sector, play this decisive role. It should be noted that the development of such export sectors has not in itself guaranteed accelerated capital formation. Enlarged foreign-exchange proceeds have been used in many familiar cases to finance hoards (as in the famous case of Indian bullion imports) or unproductive consumption outlays.

It should be noted that one possible mechanism for inducing a high rate of ploughback into productive investment is a rapid expansion in the effective demand for domestically manufactured consumers' goods, which would direct into the hands of vigorous entrepreneurs an increasing proportion of income flows under circumstances which would lead them to expand their own capacity and to increase their requirements for industrial raw materials, semi-manufactured products and manufactured components.

A final element in the supply of loanable funds is, of course, capital imports. Foreign capital has played a major role in the takeoff stage of many economies: *e.g.,* the United States, Russia, Sweden, Canada. The cases of Britain and Japan indicate, however, that it cannot be regarded as an essential condition. Foreign capital was notably useful when the construction of railways or other large overhead capital items with a long period of gestation, played an important role in the takeoff. After all, whatever its strategic role, the proportion of investment required for growth which goes into industry is relatively small compared to that required for utilities, transport and the housing of enlarged urban populations. And foreign capital can be mightily useful in helping carry the burden of these overhead items either directly or indirectly.

What can we say, in general, then, about the supply of finance during the takeoff period? First, as a precondition, it appears necessary that the community's surplus above the mass-consumption level does not flow into the hands of those who will sterilize it by hoarding, luxury consumption or low-productivity investment outlays. Second, as a precondition, it appears necessary that institutions be developed which provide cheap and adequate working capital. Third, as a necessary condition, it appears that one or more sectors of the economy must grow rapidly, inducing a more general industrialization process, and that the entrepreneurs in such sectors plough back a substantial proportion of their profits in further productive investment, one possible and recurrent version of the ploughback process being the investment of proceeds from a rapidly growing export sector.

The devices, confiscatory and fiscal, for ensuring the first and second preconditions have been historically various. And, as indicated below, the types of leading manufacturing sectors which have served to initiate the takeoff have varied greatly. Finally, foreign capital flows have, in significant cases, proved extremely important to the takeoff, notably when lumpy overhead capital construction of long gestation period was required; but takeoffs have also occurred based almost wholly on domestic sources of finance.

The Sources of Entrepreneurship

It is evident that the takeoff requires the existence and the successful activity of some group in the society which accepts borrowers' risk, when such risk is so defined as to include the propensity to accept innovations. As noted above, the problem of entrepreneurship in the takeoff has not been profound in a limited group of wealthy agricultural nations whose populations derived by emigration mainly from northwestern Europe. There the problem of takeoff was primarily economic; and when economic incentives for industrialization emerged, commercial and banking groups moved over easily into industrial entrepreneurship. In many other countries, however, the development of adequate entrepreneurship was a more searching social process.

Under some human motivation or other, a group must come to perceive it to be both possible and good to undertake acts of capital investment; and, for their efforts to be tolerably successful, they must act with approximate rationality in selecting the directions toward which their enterprise is directed. They must produce not only growth, but tolerably balanced growth. We cannot quite say that it is necessary for them to act as if they were trying to maximize profit; for the criteria for private profit maximization do not necessarily converge with the criteria for an optimum rate and pattern of growth in various sectors. But in a growing economy, over periods longer than the business cycle, economic history is reasonably tolerant of deviations from rationality, in the sense that excess capacity is finally put to productive use. Leaving aside the question of ultimate human motivation, and assuming that the major overhead items are generated, if necessary, by some form of state initiative (including subsidy), we can say as a first approximation that some group must successfully emerge which behaves as if it were moved by the profit motive, in a dynamic economy with changing production functions; although, risk being the slippery variable, it is under such assumptions that Keynes' dictum should be borne in mind: "If human nature felt no temptation to take a chance, no satisfaction (profit apart) in constructing a factory, a railway, a mine or a farm, there might not be much investment merely as a result of cold calculation." [4]

In this connection, it is increasingly conventional for economists to pay their respects to the Protestant ethic.[5] The historian should not be ungrateful for this light on the gray horizon of formal growth models. But the known cases of economic growth which theory must seek to explain take us beyond the orbit of Protestantism. In a world where Samurai, Parsees, Jews, North Italians, Turks, Russian and Chinese civil servants (as well as Huguenots, Scotsmen and British Northcountrymen) have played the role of a leading elite in economic growth, John Calvin should not be made to bear quite this weight. More fundamentally, allusion to a positive scale of religious or other values conducive to profit-maximizing activities is an insufficient sociological basis for this important phenomenon. What appears to be required for the emergence of such elites is not merely an appropriate value system, but two further conditions: first, the new elite must feel itself denied the conventional routes to prestige and power by the tradi-

---

[4] John M. Keynes, *The General Theory of Employment, Interest and Money* (New York: Harcourt, Brace and Company, 1936), p. 150.

[5] *See, for example,* N. Kaldor, "Economic Growth and Cyclical Fluctuations," *Economic Journal,* March 1954, p. 67.

tional less acquisitive society of which it is a part; second, the traditional society must be sufficiently flexible (or weak) to permit its members to seek material advance (or political power) as a route upward alternative to conformity.

Although an elite entrepreneurial class appears to be required for takeoff, with significant power over aggregate income flows and industrial investment decisions, most takeoffs have been preceded or accompanied by radical change in agricultural techniques and market organization. By and large, the agricultural entrepreneur has been the individual landowning farmer. A requirement for takeoff is, therefore, a class of farmers willing and able to respond to the possibilities opened up for them by new techniques, landholding arrangements, transport facilities, and forms of market and credit organization. A small, purposeful elite can go a long way in initiating economic growth; but, especially in agriculture (and to some extent in the industrial working force), a wider-based revolution in outlook must come about.[6]

Whatever further empirical research may reveal about the motives which have led men to undertake the constructive enterpreneurial acts of the takeoff period, this much appears sure: these motives have varied greatly from one society to another; and they have rarely, if ever, been motives of an unmixed material character.

Leading Sectors in the Takeoff

. . . The overall rate of growth of an economy must be regarded in the first instance as the consequence of differing growth rates in particular sectors of the economy, such sectoral growth rates being in part derived from certain overall demand parameters (*e.g.*, population, consumers' income, tastes, etc.), in part from the primary and secondary effects of changing supply factors, when these are effectively exploited.

On this view the sectors of an economy may be grouped in three categories:

---

[6] Like the population question, agriculture is mainly excluded from this analysis, which considers the takeoff rather than the whole development process. Nevertheless, it should be noted that, as a matter of history, agricultural revolutions have generally preceded or accompanied the takeoff. In theory we can envisage a takeoff which did not require a radical improvement in agricultural productivity: if, for example, the growth and productivity of the industrial sector permitted a withering away of traditional agriculture and a substitution for it of imports. In fact, agricultural revolutions have been required to permit rapidly growing (and urbanizing) populations to be fed without exhausting foreign exchange resources in food imports or creating excessive hunger in the rural sector; and as noted at several points in this argument, agricultural revolutions have in fact played an essential and positive role, not merely by both releasing workers to the cities, and feeding them, but also by earning foreign exchange for general capital-formation purposes.

(*a*) *Primary growth sectors,* where possibilities for innovation or for the exploitation of newly profitable or hitherto unexplored resources yield a high growth rate and set in motion expansionary forces elsewhere in the economy;

(*b*) *Supplementary growth sectors,* where rapid advance occurs in direct response to—or as a requirement of—advance in the primary growth sectors, *e.g.,* coal, iron and engineering in relation to railroads. These sectors may have to be tracked many stages back into the economy, as the Leontief input–output models would suggest;

(*c*) *Derived growth sectors,* where advance occurs in some fairly steady relation to the growth of total real income, population, industrial production or some other overall, modestly increasing parameter. Food output in relation to population, housing in relation to family formation are classic derived relations of this order.

Very roughly speaking, primary and supplementary growth sectors derive their high momentum essentially from the introduction and diffusion of changes in the cost-supply environment (in turn, of course, partially influenced by demand changes); while the derived-growth sectors are linked essentially to changes in demand (while subject also to continuing changes in production functions of a less dramatic character).

At any period of time, it appears to be true even in a mature and growing economy that forward momentum is maintained as the result of rapid expansion in a limited number of primary sectors, whose expansion has significant external economy and other secondary effects. From this perspective, the behavior of sectors during the takeoff is merely a special version of the growth process in general; or, put another way, growth proceeds by repeating endlessly, in different patterns, with different leading sectors, the experience of the takeoff. Like the takeoff, longterm growth requires that the society not only generate vast quantities of capital for depreciation and maintenance, for housing and for a balanced complement of utilities and other overheads, but also a sequence of highly productive primary sectors, growing rapidly, based on new production functions. Only thus has the aggregate marginal capital–output ratio been kept low.

•

What can we say, then, in general about these leading sectors? Historically, they have ranged from cotton textiles, through heavy-industry complexes based on railroads and military end products, to timber, pulp, dairy products and finally a wide variety of consumers' goods. There is, clearly, no one sectoral sequence for takeoff, no single sector which constitutes the magic key. There is no need for a growing society to recapitulate the structural sequence and pattern of Britain, the United States or Russia. Four basic factors must be present:

(1) There must be enlarged effective demand for the product or products of sectors which yield a foundation for a rapid rate of growth in output. Histori-

cally, this has been brought about initially by the transfer of income from consumption or hoarding to productive investment; by capital imports; by a sharp increase in the productivity of current investment inputs, yielding an increase in consumers' real income expended on domestic manufactures; or by a combination of these routes.

(2) There must be an introduction into these sectors of new production functions as well as an expansion of capacity.

(3) The society must be capable of generating capital initially required to detonate the takeoff in these key sectors; and especially, there must be a high rate of ploughback by the (private or state) entrepreneurs controlling capacity and technique in these sectors and in the supplementary growth sectors they stimulated to expand.

(4) Finally, the leading sector or sectors must be such that their expansion and technical transformation induce a chain of Leontief input–output requirements for increased capacity and the potentiality for new production functions in other sectors, to which the society, in fact, progressively responds.

Conclusion

This hypothesis is, then, a return to a rather old-fashioned way of looking at economic development. The takeoff is defined as an industrial revolution, tied directly to radical changes in methods of production, having their decisive consequence over a relatively short period of time.

This view would not deny the role of longer, slower changes in the whole process of economic growth. On the contrary, takeoff requires a massive set of preconditions going to the heart of a society's economic organization and its effective scale of values. Moreover, for the takeoff to be successful, it must lead on progressively to sustained growth; and this implies further deep and often slow-moving changes in the economy and the society as a whole.

What this argument does assert is that the rapid growth of one or more new manufacturing sectors is a powerful and essential engine of economic transformation. Its power derives from the multiplicity of its forms of impact, when a society is prepared to respond positively to this impact. Growth in such sectors, with new production functions of high productivity, in itself tends to raise output per head; it places incomes in the hands of men who will not merely save a high proportion of an expanding income but who will plough it into highly productive investment; it sets up a chain of effective demand for other manufactured products; it sets up a requirement for enlarged urban areas, whose capital costs may be high, but whose population and market organization help to make industrialization an ongoing process; and, finally, it opens up a range of external economy effects which, in the end, help to produce new leading sectors when the initial impulse of the takeoff's leading sectors begins to wane.

We can observe in history and in the contemporary world important changes in production functions in nonmanufacturing sectors which have powerful effects on whole societies. If natural resources are rich enough, or new agricultural tricks are productive enough, such changes can even outstrip population growth and yield a rise in real output per head. Moreover, they may be a necessary prior condition for takeoff or a necessary concomitant of takeoff. Nothing in this analysis should be read as deprecating the importance of productivity changes in agriculture to the whole process of economic growth. But in the end takeoff requires that a society find a way to apply effectively to its own peculiar resources what D. H. Robertson once called the tricks of manufacture; and continued growth requires that it so organize itself as to continue to apply them in an unending flow, of changing composition. Only thus, as we have all been correctly taught, can that old demon, diminishing returns, be held at bay.

CHAPTER 28

WILBERT E. MOORE

Motivational Aspects
of Development

In the literature on economic development a certain notable division between optimists and pessimists is apparent. This division is highly predictive of disciplinary origin. Economists—representatives of the "dismal science"—are customarily optimistic about economic growth and its social consequences. Anthropologists and sociologists are customarily pessimistic about the possibilities of economic growth and particularly about its consequences. Although possibly these fields attract different personality types —the manic and the depressed—it seems more likely that conventional theory and habits of thought explain the difference.

Some Contrasting Theory

Theory of Motives and Consequences

Traditional economic theory has not been strongly concerned with attitudes and motives. Human attitudes and motives are simply assumed to be appropriate to rational choice of means effective for maximizing satisfactions, as economically defined and measured. Human wants are thought to be essentially unlimited, and human nature pretty much the same wherever encountered. A monetary market system coordinates the factors of production and allocates rewards, and financial incentives are assumed to be effective in allocating labor. The movement of labor between sectors of the economy is regarded as a function of its differential marginal productivity, which is principally determined by relative states of capitalization, technique, and, possibly, enterprise.

From Wilbert E. Moore, "Labor Attitudes toward Industrialization in Underdeveloped Countries," *The American Economic Review*, XLV (1955), No. 2, pp. 156-165. Reprinted by permission of the author and the American Economic Association.

Given these assumptions, such hints of pessimism that economists have about economic growth in underdeveloped areas could be expected to center on questions of capital, market organization, and entrepreneurial activity, but not on the willingness of potential workers to work. And since the economist has a normal prejudice toward the view that improvements in levels of production and consumption are consistent with universal human aspirations, he is certainly inclined to optimism about the consequences of economic growth.

Anthropological and sociological theory stands in sharp contrast to this set of views. Attitudes and motives are of more central concern as variables, related to differential positions within any social system. The person is viewed as having been socialized in ways appropriate to differential social roles, to hold values appropriate to group activity and its survival, and to behave in ways that are "irrational" and "nonrational" as judged on economic grounds. Wants are thus viewed as limited and relative to social position. The social system is viewed as strongly resistant to change, in part because of secondary and tertiary consequences of changes in a complex functional network. If these considerations are important within societies, they are even more marked between them. To contrast with the economist's "similarity of human nature" assumption, the anthropologist or sociologist offers "cultural relativity." He is likely to emphasize differences in values and aspirations in space and time, and to be extremely reluctant to assume that Western experience can be used as a guide to behavior in Dahomey, Nepal, or even Peru.

Given these assumptions, such hints of optimism that anthropologists or sociologists have about economic growth in undeveloped areas could be expected to center on the adaptability of economic incentives and organization to traditional attitudes and patterns, and especially on the willingness of potential workers to work. And since the anthropologist-sociologist has a normal prejudice toward the view that bread or all purchasable goods and services are not enough to satisfy human values, he is certainly inclined to pessimism about the consequences of economic change.

These contrasts are, of course, moderately unfair to both professional groups. Many economists, and especially those who have studied labor mobility, the operation of labor markets, and worker behavior, have expressed strong misgivings about the assumptions of traditional theory. Many anthropologists and sociologists, and especially those who have studied the actual impact of modern economic forms in undeveloped areas, have noted the stresses and tensions in traditional systems and the considerable success of the new employment alternatives in recruiting labor.

Theory of Organized Cooperation

The literature on economic development has included very little material on another aspect of theory, on which our two professional groups tend to disagree. There are differing views on the nature of business and industrial organization as related to the attitudes or motives of participants.

Traditional economic theory has little to say on this subject, since labor is viewed as allocated by market mechanisms and the relation between employer and employee the same in principle as any other economic contract. The productive efficiency of the division of labor has received consistent attention, but the problems associated with the authoritative coordination of labor implicit in factory organization remain relatively unexplored. Only in Marxist economic theory and, more recently, in attempts to construct alternative theories of the labor movement and management–union relations, have variables such as power and group loyalties been considered.

Traditional anthropological and sociological theory also has little to say on business or industrial organization, partly because of a concentration on the structure of society generally, partly because economic organization was thought to be the proper province of economists. Only in Weberian sociological theory and, more recently, in attempts to treat "the factory as a social system" have variables such as the authority of office, communication systems, and "informal organization" been considered.

Despite the recent and still somewhat peripheral attention given industrial organization in the disciplines we have been comparing, some differences between the disciplines can be detected. There is a notable tendency for the economist to emphasize—and exaggerate—individual, competitive aspirations, and an equally notable tendency for the anthropologist or sociologist to emphasize—and exaggerate—group cooperative aspirations. If the economist's model of behavior tends to be the prize fight, the sociologist's model tends to be the quilting bee.

Some Empirical Evidence

Faced with such contrasting views of economic behavior and its motivational sources, the analyst may be forgiven some confusion and permitted to seek refuge in the data. Unfortunately, evidence has not been collected or analyzed in ways that permit a clear resolution of theoretical disputes. It is possible, however, to get some leverage on the issues by reference to the reported experience in the recruitment and utilization of labor in undeveloped areas.[1]

Apathy and Opposition

A considerable body of evidence runs contrary to the notions that human wants are unlimited, that financial incentives will transfer labor from non-

---

[1] This section represents a selective summary of a rather extensive discussion, with citations to the literature, in Wilbert E. Moore, *Industrialization and Labor* (Ithaca: Cornell University Press, 1951).

industrial to industrial pursuits, and thus that the potential worker may be viewed as welcoming release from traditional restraints. Some of this evidence can be interpreted in terms of "rational conduct," but not in terms of economic maximization. The potential worker in undeveloped areas is typically required to give up traditional forms of organization and reciprocal obligations that have combined to afford him security, both material and affective. The kinship system in any nonindustrial society is likely to provide a major barrier to individual mobility, because it is a social security system, because it is the focus of positive values and advantages, and because extended kin obligations are likely to reduce the effective appeal of individual rewards. With an extended kinship system, if the individual faces adversity, his kinsmen are obliged to come to his aid. If he prospers, he is obliged to share his good fortune with great-uncles and second cousins once removed. Industrialization breaks up such units by geographical separation and, more importantly, by social separation.

The other side of the coin (an inappropriate metaphor in its connotations) is the lack of appreciation of the new status system. This may take the form of a relatively low and highly particular appeal of wages, often commented on with reference to "native" laborers, but also commented on by preclassical writers in economic theory with reference to workers in the early stages of the Industrial Revolution. The principle bears extension, however. New occupations simply do not fit traditional standards of prestige, or are valued negatively because they involve manual labor and merit placement irrespective of age, kinship position, caste, or other forms of "ascribed" status. To the extent that the potential worker operates as an independent producer, the change to wage labor involves some loss of "freedom," even if it offers higher rewards. To the extent that the potential worker operates as the equivalent of a craftsman, the change to factory employment is likely to involve a loss of socially recognized skills, of "workmanship," in the division of labor and its subordination to machine processes.

It would be hard to deny that a considerable part of this apathy and opposition is "reasonable," but equally hard to deny that its explanation lies partly in social standards and values that are badly served by wage incentives and by industrial forms of labor allocation.

The Force of Circumstances

If wages have a limited appeal to nonindustrial populations and new employments are negatively valued, it is not surprising that workers are more commonly "pushed" than "pulled" into modern forms of economic activity. Much of the "push" is in fact the largely unintentional consequence of external intervention. The successful attempt to reduce mortality has the effect of deteriorating man–land ratios, thus increasing agricultural underemployment and causing the landless and impoverished rural dweller to seek and accept other means of livelihood. The introduction of cheap manufactured goods may well displace the handicraft worker and make available an additional pool of workers, either directly or through increased dependency on agriculture. Even the trader may be displaced by largescale distribution, or simply by more efficient organization of established markets.

The coercion of hunger does not exhaust the available pressures. Direct political coercion also has an extensive record, ranging from forced labor to the indirect coercion of taxation—a system which has been widely used as a device in colonial Africa.

Not all of the sources of pressure on the potential worker are so clearly external in origin. Any society exhibits some degree of tension and strain, some evidence of dissatisfaction. The presence of new alternatives may allow the deviant who seeks to evade the sanctions of the traditional order to escape from unwanted and oppressive controls.

Again it would be hard to deny that the attitudes implicit in these types of behavior are reasonable and again equally hard to deny that they do not correspond to notions of high sensitivity to slight differences in incentives and opportunity.

The Efficacy of Positive Inducements

Not all of the empirical evidence involves such negative attitudes toward industrial labor. Wages do have an appeal, particularly if they can be used for goods and services that form part of traditional patterns of consumption and traditional modes of relationship. The transitional forms are many, and often oddly at variance with Western conceptions of market operation. The African from the native reserve who works long enough in the mines to pay his hut tax is presumably not highly integrated into a market system. He becomes slightly more integrated when he uses wages to buy cattle for use as a bride price, but this still has a distinctly exotic flavor. His behavior fits our standard conceptions better when he proves interested in all sorts of commercialized goods and services, but of course by then he is likely to have little in common with the values of the preindustrial community.

In some places other inducements to work seem to have operated, although not necessarily in the absence of financial incentives or contrary to their economically expected effect. Patriotic motives and other collective goals have formed the basis of appeals to workers in most industrial societies, with what effect it is difficult to say precisely. Certainly it is likely that a sense of voluntary participation in a worthwhile common enterprise offers some source of satisfaction to workers, although the standard forms of productive organization are not well adapted to making the use of such appeals very convincing. Here, it may be noted, is a possible positive role for union-type organization. Certainly the communists have attempted to involve workers in undeveloped areas in the organized building of the new, as well as the destroying of the old forms of social allegiance and power.

Toward a Tenable Theory

The discussion to this point implies the rejection of two extreme theoretical positions, both of which constitute alternatives available in the literature. The one extreme may be attributed to economics, although by no means all economists would subscribe. To traditional economists, labor attitudes are simply unproblematical, as they are adequately subsumed under the assumptions of maximizing want satisfactions. The other extreme may be attributed to anthropology, in the same unrepresentative sense. To the anthropologist, labor attitudes are so problematical, because they are so conditioned by variable cultures, that no other general statement about them is possible.

The attempt to formulate here the elements of a low-order theory rests upon the assumption that it is possible to give a general characterization to the undeveloped areas, to specify some of the crucial characteristics of modern economic organization, and to indicate some of the labor attitudes which are significant for transition from one to the other.

The Nature of Undeveloped Areas

Although it is true that cultures differ, and in many ways, it is possible at a higher level of generalization to detect common and essential functions in the organization of society. Every society has provisions and rules for reproduction, socialization of the young, production and allocation of goods and services, adjustment to the nonhuman environment, maintenance of order. It is also possible to detect some common bases in cognitive orientations and values. All societies encourage some material aspirations (although not necessarily expanding and competitive), some rational, technical orientation to the use of the environment (although not necessarily innovative), and some positive value on health and length of life.

There are internal sources of tension and strain in all societies. The model of the perfectly integrated society is a useful analytical fiction for many purposes, but ought not to be confused with primitive or agrarian societies. The sources of strain include, at least, uncertainties in socialization from generation to generation, chance innovations, and competing role demands given scarcities of time, treasure, and energy (or affective loyalty).

All undeveloped areas have already been disrupted in some form and degree by the "external" influence of Western patterns. The consequences of this interference may or may not be favorable to continuous economic development, but this will depend in some measure on the strategy adopted in view of the situation, as well as on the probable effects of influences so far.

One negative generalization is also negative in its implications for labor attitudes toward industrialization. Mobility on the basis of individual performance is generally not markedly present in undeveloped areas, and does not generally form a part of the positive value system. Whether for the individual or for the system as a whole, continuity and not change is likely to be the major value.

The Nature of Modern Economic Organization

It is now commonly recognized that modern economic enterprise depends upon a complex institutional structure. For purposes of simplification, this may be partially summarized as a monetary-market mechanism for allocation of the factors of production and for achieving distribution of goods and services. For the nonhuman factors of production, this involves at least transferable property rights and rational cost accounting. For the human factors of production, this involves a wage system for putting into the hands of the specialized worker a medium for commanding the necessary and appropriate goods and services for himself and his dependents.

Although part of the division of labor will be coordinated by impersonal market mechanisms, the fixed capital and economies of scale in the productive unit characteristic of industrial organization imply also administrative coordination and the development of scales of authority.

If labor is to be rationally allocated and optimally utilized, it appears essential to select on the basis of technical competence, to coordinate on the basis of relationships specific to the interdependent tasks, and to tie rewards to types of activities. These rewards need not be exclusively financial and indeed rarely will be. All of the rewards imply a system of social ranking closely related to position in the productive system.

The Nature of the Transition

Whether one looks at undeveloped areas or the most highly industrialized ones, a fundamental theoretical point is evident. That point is the great complexity of human motivation. Men will work for as many reasons as there are values to be served by such activity and will refuse to work where that serves his values. The fact that industrial systems emphasize values that are commanded in a market and incentives that provide monetary claims on a market should not blind us to the diversity of ends or the diversity of means for their satisfaction.

The effectiveness of wage incentives is relative to the availability of goods and services in the market that form part of the effective wants of workers.

This is essentially a common-sense static principle. But it is quite limiting, and failure to recognize it accounts for some of the exasperation of observers of "irrational" natives. The worker in an undeveloped area is typically not accustomed to expect, or even to aspire to, any considerable raising of ceilings on his consumption and social position. And there are many wants typically not satisfiable by market mechanisms. So we have both limited demand and limited supply.

To translate this principle into dynamic terms, the available evidence indicates that we should expect an increase in demand through knowledge, education, and the development of new values, and in supply through the addition of goods newly available because of industrialization and the movement of services into the market.

This view of market-oriented attitudes can be broadened, with considerable benefit to its theoretical importance.

The effectiveness of the appeal of new employment alternatives is relative to the availability of need-satisfying rewards. This principle will still apply if material or even financial wellbeing is held constant. The potential rewards include prestige and esteem within an acceptable system of social valuation. This also is a common-sense static principle and is also limiting. The traditional system of social valuation will not typically include the new activities, and the latter compete or conflict with the former. Both change and choice tend to be devalued. If some relationship between wages and markets has been established, higher wage levels can be used as a principal lever on conservative traditions, and this has been their historic role. The private employer is unlikely to act "correctly" in this matter, and this may be a major area for governmental policy in economic development.

Over time, we should expect an increase in aspiration and the addition of values associated with status mobility, merit evaluation, and a realistic sense of choice and initiative. We should also expect new systems of social organization and stratification to which these aspirations and values are appropriate.

Economic growth, insofar as it is affected by labor attitudes, is likely to be radically retarded or contained by any one of several vicious circles. There is considerable evidence of a reciprocal relationship between low wages and low productivity, whether the connection works through mere physical energy or through more subtle frustration and apathy. The failure to detect and utilize convertible craft skills, the assumption that initially unskilled local labor is incapable of training, and the adoption of the "color bar" as an extreme and open manifestation of these practices, constitute waste in the short run and possible failure of continued development in the long run.

It appears evident that neither the available skills nor the appropriate attitudes can be assumed to be adequate among the potential workers in undeveloped areas. Growth seems to have been most rapid and most probably continuous in the future where considerable resources have been devoted to formal education and where education and in-service training have been most closely geared to the skill demands of an industrial economy. Now, clearly, education in many colonial areas has encouraged anything but the development of mechanical and technical skills, and the opportunities for use of any such skills have not been made available to natives. That the new native leaders tend to be political agitators rather than economic administrators is scarcely surprising in view of colonial political and economic policies.

The development of positive labor attitudes toward industrialization would probably be enhanced by the fostering of a sense of social participation, as well as by the expansion of individual opportunity and the provision of amenities and security at least equivalent to those available in traditional organization. A sense of social participation has been consistently neglected even in advanced industrial societies. We do not know how flexible industrial organization may be made. But if economic development entails a revolutionary change in the organization of society, as it does, there is at least some theoretical reason for supposing that workers as well as managers or government officials might welcome positive participation in partial compensation for their uprooting.

In view of the complex richness of human motivation, the idea that economic and noneconomic incentives are necessarily competitive for a limited supply is untenable. Both may be increased simultaneously and continuously within very high limits. . . .

CHAPTER 29

REINHARD BENDIX

Industrialization, Ideologies, and Social Structure

Changes in Ideology

At the inception of industrialization in England, an ideology of tradition-alism prevailed; John Stuart Mill called it the "theory of dependence." According to this view the laboring poor are children, who must be governed, who should not be allowed to think for themselves, who must perform their assigned tasks obediently and with alacrity, who must show deference to their superiors, and who—if they only conduct themselves virtuously—will be protected by their betters against the vicissitudes of life. This interpretation of authority is self-confirming and self-serving. But it sets up the presumption that the dependence of the poor and the responsibility of the rich are the valid moral rules of the social order. In the course of industrial development, these ideas were gradually modified. As the responsibility of the rich was increasingly rejected by the advocates of *laissez-faire,* the dependence of the poor was turned from an inevitable into a self-imposed fate. As it was "demonstrated" that the rich cannot care for the poor without decreasing the national wealth, it was also asserted that by abstinence and exertion the poor can better their lot. The same virtues which in the eighteenth century were extolled so that the lowly will not aspire above their station were praised by the middle of the nineteenth century because they enable a man to raise himself by his own efforts.

In England, and even more in America, this praise of effort led toward the end of the nineteenth century to an apotheosis of the struggle for existence. The militant language of an ethics of the jungle was applied to the relations between employers and workers. Riches and poverty merely re-

From Reinhard Bendix, "Industrialization, Ideologies, and Social Structure," *American Sociological Review,* XXIV (1959), No. 5, pp. 616-623. Reprinted by permission of the author and the American Sociological Association.

flect differences of ability and effort. The employer's success is evidence of his fitness for survival, and as such justifies his absolute authority over the enterprise. This assertion of authority has a clearcut meaning only as long as most managerial functions are in the hands of one man. The idea becomes ambiguous as the use of expertise in the management of enterprises increases and the managerial function becomes subdivided and specialized. Yet the idea of the employer's absolute authority over his enterprise coincided with the "scientific management" movement which sought to give him expert advice on what to do with that authority. It may be suggested, therefore, that the doctrines of Social Darwinism gradually lost their appeal, in part because changes in industrial organization gave rise to a changing imagery of men in industry. From the Gilded Age to the 1920's, workers and managers were self-evident failures or successes in a struggle for survival, in which they were the recalcitrant objects or the exasperated originators of managerial commands. Today they have become individuals-in-groups whose skills must be improved and allocated systematically, and whose productivity must be maximized by appropriate attention to their psychological makeup. Thus, over the past two hundred years, managerial ideologies in Anglo-American civilization have changed from the "theory of dependence" to *laissez-faire,* to Social Darwinism, and finally to the "human relations" approach.

In the Russian development we also find the assertion of paternal authority and of childlike dependence, and in much the same terms as in England. But in Russia this ideology of traditionalism was a very different thing from what it was in England, because of the Tsar's assertion of supreme authority over all the people. This authority remained intact regardless of how many privileges the Tsar granted to the landlords and regardless of how rarely he interfered in fact with the use and abuse of these privileges. Ideologically, the Tsar maintained his pre-eminence through repeated assertions concerning his paternal care and responsibility for all of "his" people. Through repeated petitions and sporadic revolts, the people used this Tsarist claim in order to obtain redress for their grievances against landlords and employers. Finally, because of the early centralization of authority under the Muscovite rulers, the whole distribution of wealth and rank among the aristocracy turned upon the competition for favors at the Court and hence reinforced the Tsar's supremacy.

During the second half of the nineteenth century this pattern of Tsarist autocracy had farreaching consequences. The dislocations incident to the emancipation of the serfs (1861) and the development of industry brought in their train assertions of absolute authority by the employers, efforts of the workers to organize themselves, and sporadic attempts of the government to regulate the relationship between them. Although ostensibly acting on an equitable basis, the government in fact supported the employers against the workers. Much of this is again broadly familiar from the English experience; but Russia's historical legacies prevented the shift in ideology which has been described for England. As long as Tsarist autocracy remained intact, neither the rejection of responsibility by the Tsar and the ruling strata nor the demand for the self-dependence of the workers developed. Instead, the Tsar and his officials continued to espouse the ideology of traditionalism. Quite consistently, Tsarist officials sought to superintend both employers and workers in order to mitigate or suppress the struggles between them. That is, the officials aided *and* curbed the employers' exercise of authority, as well as the workers' efforts to formulate grievances and organize protest movements.

Tsarist autocracy was overthrown in the Russian revolutions of 1905 and 1917. Although vast differences were brought about by the revolutions, the managerial ideology of Tsarism lived on in a modified form. In theory, Tsarist officials had regarded employers and workers as equally subject to the will of the Tsar; loyal submission to that will was the mark of good citizenship. In theory, Lenin believed that all workers were equal participants in the management of industry and government; their loyal submission to the Communist party represented their best interest and expressed their sovereign will. The logic of Lenin's as of the Tsarist position is that under a sovereign authority the same person or organization can and should perform both subordinate and superordinate functions. For example, Soviet labor unions approach the ideal of workers' control of industry when they are called upon to participate in the management of industry. But they also function in a managerial capacity when they inculcate labor discipline among their members under the authoritative direction of the Communist Party.

Ideologically, this position is defended on the ground that the party represents the historical interests of the proletariat against the shortrun interests of individuals and factions. In this orientation one can still see survivals of Tsarist autocracy, since all wisdom and responsibility reside in a small group or indeed in one man who, like the Tsar, knows better than private persons what is the good of all, and cannot but wish the wellbeing of the people. But there is also an important difference. The leaders of the Russian revolution were faced with the task of developing self-discipline and initiative among workers if a suitable industrial workforce was to become available. They proceeded to inculcate these qualities by the direct or indirect subordination of everyone to the discipline of the Communist Party. This policy continued the Tsarist tradition by making all matters the object of organizational manipulation rather than of personal striving; but it also represented a break with the past in that it was no longer restricted to personal submission.

Historical Significance of Ideological Change

What are the historical implications of this analysis of managerial ideologies? Ruling groups everywhere, including the rulers of developing industrial societies, justify their good fortune as well as the ill fortune of those subject to their authority. Their self-serving arguments may not appear as a promising field of research; in fact, the whole development of industrialization has been accompanied by an intellectual rejection of such ideologies as unworthy of consideration. Yet the fact is that all industrialization involves the organization of enterprises in which a few command and many obey; and the ideas developed by the few and the many may, I believe, be considered a symptom of changing class relations, and hence as a clue to an understanding of industrial societies.

Historically, ideologies of management became significant in the transition from a preindustrial to an industrial society. The authority exercised by employers was recognized as distinct from the authority of government. This was a novel experience even in Western Europe where there was precedent for such autonomy in other institutions, because the industrial entrepreneurs were "new men" rather than a ruling class buttressed by tradition. This was also the period during which the discipline of sociology originated. Under the impact of the French revolution, society came to be conceived in terms of forces that are independent from, as well as antagonistic to, the formal institutions of the body politic. Some early elaborations of this key idea enable us to see the historical significance of ideologies of management.

The authority of employers rests on the contractual acquisition of property, which the eighteenth-century philosophers made the conceptual basis of the social order. In Rousseau's view, that order can be and ought to be based on a general will which presupposes that the individual acts for the whole community. In such a society, as George Herbert Mead has pointed out, ". . . the citizen can give laws only to the extent that his volitions are an expression of the rights which he recognizes in others . . . [and] which the others recognize in him. . . ." [1] This approach provides a model for a society based on consent, so that the power of rule-making is exercised by all and for all. This foundation of society upon a "general will" was directly related to the institution of property. As Mead has stated,

> If one wills to possess that which is his own so that he has absolute control over it as property, he does so on the assumption that everyone else will possess his own property and exercise absolute control over it. That is, the in-

---

[1] George Herbert Mead, *Movements of Thought in the Nineteenth Century* (Chicago: University of Chicago Press, 1936), p. 21.

dividual wills his control over his property only insofar as he wills the same
sort of control for everyone else over property.[2]

Thus, the idea of a reciprocal recognition of rights specifically presupposed
the equality of citizens as property-owners.

This implication gave pause to some eighteenth- and nineteenth-century
philosophers. They noted that the reciprocity of rights among property own-
ers based on freedom of contract does not apply to the relations between
employers and workers. As early as 1807 the German philosopher Hegel
formulated the problematic nature of this relationship in a manner which
anticipates the modern psychology of the self, just as Rousseau's "general
will" anticipates the sociological analysis of interaction. Hegel maintains
that men come to a recognition of themselves through a process whereby
each accepts the self-recognition of the other and is in turn accepted by
him. That is, each man's sense of identity depends upon his acceptance of
the identity of others and upon their acceptance of himself. In Hegel's view,
this reciprocity is lacking in the relation between master and servant. The
master does not act toward himself as he acts toward the servant; and the
servant does not do toward others what his servitude makes him do against
himself. In this way the mutuality of recognition is destroyed, and the relations
between master and servant become one-sided and unequal.[3]

In Western Europe, this inequality of the employment-relationship coincided with the ideological and institutional decline of traditional subordination. Yet while the old justifications of subordination crumbled, and new
aspirations were awakened among the masses of the people, their experience of inequality continued. According to De Tocqueville, this problem
had a differential impact upon masters and servants. In the secret persuasion of his mind the master continues to think of himself as superior; but
he no longer recognizes any paternal responsibilities toward the servant.
Still, he wants his servants to be content with their servile condition. In effect,
the master wishes to enjoy the age-old privileges without acknowledging
their concomitant obligations; and the servant rebels against his subordination, which is no longer a divine obligation and is not yet perceived as a
contractual obligation.

Then it is that [in] the dwelling of every citizen . . . a secret and internal
warfare is going on between powers ever rivals and suspicious of each other:
the master is ill-natured and weak, the servant ill-natured and intractable; the

2 *Ibid.*, p. 17.
8 Georg Friedrich Wilhelm Hegel, *Phänomenologie des Geistes* (Leipzig: Felix
Meiner, 1928), pp. 143, 147. My paraphrasing attempts to convey Hegel's meaning
without use of his language. The relevant passages are readily accessible in C. J.
Friedrich, ed., *The Philosophy of Hegel* (New York: Modern Library, 1953), pp.
399-410.

one constantly attempts to evade by unfair restrictions his obligation to protect and to remunerate, the other his obligation to obey. The reins of domestic government dangle between them, to be snatched at by one or the other. The lines that divide authority from oppression, liberty from license, and right from might are to their eyes so jumbled together and confused that no one knows exactly what he is or what he may be or what he ought to be. Such a condition is not democracy, but revolution.[4]

In the nineteenth century men like Hegel, De Tocqueville, and Lorenz von Stein pointed out that the spread of egalitarian ideas was causing a transition in the relations between masters and servants. This transition may be called a crisis of aspirations. . . . As a consequence, most European countries witnessed the rise of a "fourth estate" which struggled against existing legal liabilities and for basic civil rights, above all the right to suffrage. In a parliamentary debate on Chartism, Disraeli remarked that this struggle was invested with a degree of sentiment usually absent from merely economic or political contests. To the extent that such complex movements can be characterized by a common denominator this sentiment referred, I think, to the workers' quest for a public recognition of their equal status as citizens. Where this and other civil rights became accepted, such recognition compensated for the continued social and economic subordination of the workers and thus assuaged the crisis of aspirations. Moreover, the political utilization of these civil rights could lead to a recognition of basic social rights which today is embodied in the institutions of social welfare characteristic of many Western democracies. The initial crisis of aspirations continued, on the other hand, where civil rights were rejected or where their acceptance was postponed for too long, leading either to an eventual revolutionary upheaval as in Tsarist Russia, or to a more-or-less damaging exacerbation of class-relations as in Italy and France.

My hypothesis is that the break with the traditional subordination of the people gave rise to a generic problem of many industrial societies. The question of nineteenth-century Europe concerned the terms on which a society undergoing industrialization will incorporate its newly recruited industrial work force within the economic and political community of the nation. Ideologies of management are significant because they contribute to each country's answer to this question. In England the workers were invited to become their own masters, if they did not wish to obey; in Russia they were told that their subordination was less onerous than it seemed, because their own superiors were also servants of the almighty Tsar.

---

[4] Alexis de Tocqueville, *Democracy in America* (New York: Vintage Books, 1945), Vol. II, p. 195. Some phrases in the preceding paragraph are also taken from this chapter of De Tocqueville's work.

•

Ideologies, Industrial Bureaucracy, and Totalitarianism

Since the eighteenth century Anglo-American and Russian civilizations have witnessed a growing managerial concern with the attitudes as well as the productivity of workers. It is possible to relate this change of ideology to a large number of the developments which comprise the transition from an early to a mature industrial society. The changing structure of industrial organizations was only one of these developments. Yet the bureaucratization of economic enterprises is of special importance for any attempt to "interpret the difference of fact and ideology between a totalitarian and nontotalitarian form of subordination in economic enterprises." [5] Bureaucratization is also especially suitable for a comparative study of authority relations in industry, since it involves processes that are directly comparable in two such different civilizations as England and Russia. This choice of focus deliberately eschews a comprehensive theory of society in favor of selecting a problem which, if suitable for comparative analysis, will also lead to an analysis of social structures. For, if comparable groups in different societies confront and over time resolve a common problem, then a comparative analysis of their divergent resolutions will reveal the divergence of social structures in a process of change.[6]

Problems of a systematic management of labor come to the fore where the increasing complexity of economic enterprises makes their operation more and more dependent upon an *ethic of work performance*. This ethic involves a degree of steady intensity of work, reasonable accuracy, and a compliance with general rules and specific orders that falls somewhere between blind obedience and unpredictable caprice. Where personal supervision is replaced by impersonal rules, the efficiency of an organization will vary with the degree to which these attributes of work-performance are realized, and this realization is part of the ongoing bureaucratization of economic enterprises. That is to say, management subjects the conditions of employment to an impersonal systematization, while the employees seek to modify the implementation of the rules as their personal interests and their commitment (or lack of commitment) to the goals of the organization dictate. As everyone knows, there is no more effective means of organizational sabotage than a letter-perfect compliance with all the rules and a consistent refusal of the employees to use their own judgment. . . . In the

---

[5] Reinhard Bendix, *Work and Authority in Industry* (New York: John Wiley & Sons, 1956), p. xx.

[6] Here I am indebted to the work of Max Weber, although more to what he did in his own studies than to what he wrote about them in his methodology. *See* my *Max Weber, An Intellectual Portrait* (New York: Doubleday, 1960), Ch. 8.

literature on organizations, the exercise of discretion by subordinates is known by a number of terms: Veblen called it the "withdrawal of efficiency"; Max Weber referred to it as the bureaucratic tendency toward secrecy; Herbert Simon might call it the "zone of nonacceptance." I have suggested the phrase "strategies of independence" so as to get away from the negative connotations of the other terms, since the exercise of discretion may serve to achieve, as well as to subvert, the goals of an organization.

Now, the great difference between totalitarian and nontotalitarian forms of subordination consists in the managerial handling of this generic attribute of all authority relations. The historical legacies of some Western countries have encouraged management to presuppose the existence of a common universe of discourse between superiors and subordinates, and this presupposition is related to the successful resolution of the crisis of aspirations. From the evangelism and the tough-minded *laissez-faire* approach of eighteenth-century England to the latest refinement of the "human relations" approach, managerial appeals have been addressed to the good faith of subordinates in order to enlist their cooperation. Whether such good faith existed is less important than that such appeals were made, though it is probable that in England and the United States large masses of workers in one way or another accepted managerial authority as legitimate even if they were indifferent to, or rejected, the managerial appeals themselves. In Russia, on the other hand, historical legacies did *not* encourage management (under the tsars) to presuppose the existence of a common universe of discourse between superiors and subordinates. From the time of Peter the Great to the period of rapid industrial growth in the last decades preceding World War I, managerial appeals were addressed to the workers' duty of obedience toward all those in positions of authority. Whether or not the workers actually developed a sense of duty, the appeals presupposed that they had not. Accordingly, officials and managers did not rely on the good faith among their subordinates, but attempted instead to eliminate the subordinates' strategies of independence.

This managerial refusal to accept the tacit evasion of rules and norms or the uncontrolled exercise of judgment is related to a specific type of bureaucratization which constitutes the fundamental principle of totalitarian government. In such a regime the will of the highest party authorities is absolute in the interest of their substantive objectives. The party may disregard not only all formal procedures by which laws are validated, but also its own previous rulings; and where norms may be changed at a moment's notice, the rule of law is destroyed. Totalitarianism also does away with the principle of a single line of authority. Instead of relying on an enactment of laws and on the supervision of their execution from the top, totalitarian regimes use the hierarchy of the party in order to expedite and control at each step the execution of orders through the regular administrative channels. This may be seen as the major device by which such regimes seek to prevent officials from escaping inspection, while compelling them to use their expertise in an intensified effort to implement the orders of the regime. A totalitarian government is based, therefore, on two interlocking hierarchies of authority. The work of every factory, of every governmental office, of every unit of the army or the secret police, as well as every cultural or social organization, is programmed, coordinated, and supervised by some agency of government. But it is also propagandized, expedited, criticized, spied upon, and incorporated in special campaigns by an agency of the totalitarian party, which is separately responsible to the higher party authorities.

The rationale of this principle of a double government can be stated within the framework of Max Weber's analysis of bureaucracy. An ideally functioning bureaucracy in his sense is the most efficient method of solving largescale organizational tasks. But this is true only *if* these tasks involve a more-or-less stable orientation toward norms which seek to maintain the rule of law and to achieve an equitable administration of affairs. These conditions are absent where tasks are assigned by an omnipotent *and* revolutionary authority. Under the simulated combat conditions of a totalitarian regime, the norms that govern conduct do not stay put for any length of time, although each norm in turn will be the basis of an unremitting drive for prodigies of achievement. In response, subordinates will tend to use their devices of concealment for the sake of systematic, if tacit, strategies of independence. They will do so not only for reasons of convenience, but because the demands made upon them by the regime are "irrational" from the viewpoint of expert knowledge and systematic procedure. The party, on the other hand, seeks to prevent the types of concealment that make such collective strategies possible by putting every worker and official under maximum pressure to utilize their expertise to the fullest extent. This is the rationale of a double hierarchy of government, which places a party functionary at the side of every work unit in order to prevent concealment and to apply pressure. The two hierarchies would be required, even if all key positions in government and industry were filled by party functionaries. For a functionary turned worker or official would still be responsible for "overfulfilling" the plan, while the new party functionary would still be charged with keeping that official under pressure and surveillance.

In this way totalitarianism replaces the old system of stratification by a new one based on criteria of activism and party orthodoxy. The ethic of work performance on which this regime relies is not the product of century-long growth as in the West, but of material incentives and of a political supervision that seeks to prevent evasion from below as well as from above. For example, the collective "bargaining" agreements of Soviet industry are in fact declarations of loyalty in which individuals and groups pledge themselves publicly to an overfulfillment of the plan, while the subsequent organization of public confessionals, the manipulation of status differences between activists and others, the principle of collective leadership, and further devices seek to maximize performance and prevent the "withdrawal of efficiency." The individual subordinate is surrounded almost literally. Aside from ordinary incentives, he is controlled by his superior and by the party agitator who stands at the side of his superior; but he is also controlled "from below" in the sense that the social pressures of his peer group are manipulated by party agitators and their agents. This institutionalization of suspicion and the consequent elimination of privacy are justified on the ground that the party "represents" the masses, spearheads the drive for Russian industrialization, and leads the cause of world communism. . . .

CHAPTER 30

S. N. EISENSTADT

Breakdowns of
Political Modernization

The optimism which guided much of the concern with and many of the studies of underdeveloped areas or new nations, and which assumed that these countries were advancing—even if slowly and intermittently—towards full-fledged modernization and continuous growth, has lately given way to a much more cautious and even pessimistic view. This pessimism has been mainly due to the fact that in many new nations, where initially modern frameworks were established in different institutional fields, especially in the political one, the progress towards modernization was not only slow, but also these constitutional regimes faltered, giving way, in their place, to various autocratic and authoritarian or semi-authoritarian regimes. Indonesia, Pakistan, Burma, and Sudan are perhaps the most important recent examples of this trend.[1] The purpose of this paper is to analyze the nature of the social processes in these countries which led to these changes, to what may be called breakdowns in their political modernization.

Patterns of Breakdowns of Modernization

The significant characteristic of the developments in these countries is not that the "take off" from a traditional setting to modernity did not fully

---

Reprinted from S. N. Eisenstadt: BREAKDOWNS OF MODERNIZATION in *Economic Development and Cultural Change*, Vol. XII, No. 4, July 1964, pp. 345-367.

[1] On Indonesia see: H. Feith, *The Decline of Constitutional Democracy in Indonesia* (Ithaca: Cornell University Press, 1962); W. A. Hannah, *Bung Karno's Indonesia* (New York: American Universities Field Staff, 1961); and G. Y. Pauker, "Indonesia, Internal Developments of External Expansion," *Asian Survey*, XIV, No. 2 (February 1963), 69-76.

On Burma: E. R. Leach, "L'avenir Politique de la Birmanie," Bull Sedeis, Futuribles, Paris, November 1962; L. W. Pye, *Politics, Personality, and Nation Building* (New Haven: Yale University Press, 1962); L. Walinsky, *Economic Development in Burma, 1951-1960* (New York: Twentieth Century Fund, 1962); and John H. Badgley, "Burma, materialize within them. In almost all these countries attempts were made to establish modern political and social frameworks and institutions, and many aspects or characteristics of such institutions—be they constitutions, modern bureaucratic administrations, political parties, or modern economic enterprises—were initially established. Similarly, many important indices of modernization—be they socio-demographic indices like urbanization, literacy or exposure to mass media, some diversification of the occupational structure, or structural indices like weakening of traditional frameworks, growing differentiation, the development of some modern forms of political organization like interest groups and parties—could be found, to some extent at least, continuously expanding in these societies. And yet, all these developments did not give rise to the development, especially in the political field, of viable modern institutional systems capable of absorbing continuously changing, diversified problems and demands. Many such institutional frameworks which were established in the initial period of modernization became disorganized and unable to function, giving place to the less differentiated, usually more autocratic or authoritarian regimes.

In other words, there developed in these societies several important indices of economic modernization—some changes in the relative product shares by major sectors of the economy and in per capita real income—and of political modernization. Among these the most important were, first, the development of a highly differentiated political structure in terms of specific political roles and institutions, of the centralization of the polity, and of development of specific political goals and orientations. Second, political modernization here, as in general, was characterized by a growing extension of the scope of the central legal, administrative, and political activities and their permeation into all spheres and regions of the society. Third, it was characterized by the weakening of traditional elites and traditional legitimation of rulers and by the establishment of some sort of ideological and often also institutional accountability of the rulers to the ruled, who are the holders of the potential political power. The formal expression of this process is the system of elections as it has evolved, in different ways, in most modern political systems.

Moreover, in all these spheres in the societies there also developed an-

---

the Nexus of Socialism and Two Political Traditions," *Asian Survey*, III, No. 2 (February 1963), 89-96.

On Pakistan: K. B. Sayeed, *Pakistan, the Formative Phase* (Karachi: Pakistan Publishing House, 1960); K. J. Newman, "Pakistan's Preventive Autocracy and Its Causes," *Pacific Affairs*, XXXII, No. 1 (March 1959), 18-34; K. B. Sayeed, "The Collapse of Parliamentary Democracy in Pakistan," *Middle East Journal*, XIII, No. 4 (1959), 389-406; R. Wheeler, "Pakistan, New Constitution, Old Issues," *Asian Survey*, III, No. 2 (February 1963), 107-16; H. Tinker, *India and Pakistan* (New York: Praeger, 1962); L. F. R. Williams, "Problems of Constitution Building in Pakistan," *Asian Review* (n. s.), LVIII (July 1962), 151-60; and K. Callard, *Pakistan, a Political Study* (New York: Macmillan, 1957).

other crucial aspect of modernization—namely, the structural propensity to continuous change. Hence, they all faced the most crucial test of modernization, i.e., the ability to maintain "sustained" growth in the major institutional spheres and to develop an institutional structure capable of absorbing such changes with relatively few eruptions and breakdowns.

But it was exactly here that the major problems of the countries studied arose. Despite the development of the various socio-demographic and structural indices of modernization, they did not develop within them a viable institutional structure which was able to deal with the problems generated by the socio-demographic and structural changes, and at least in the political field, they changed to less differentiated, less flexible, institutional frameworks which were able to cope with a smaller range of problems. In some of these cases, like Pakistan and perhaps Sudan, these "reversals" in the political field did not undermine the possibilities of some economic growth and may even have facilitated it. In others, like Indonesia and seemingly also Burma, the breakdown of the constitutional regime was paralleled by economic stagnation.

But although most of these societies have by now "reverted," as it were, to a level of social and especially political institutions which can be—as we shall see—seen as less flexible or differentiated than that at which they presumably started in their initial stages of modernization, yet in almost none of them did there take place a complete reversal to truly traditional types of central social institutions.

This is manifest in several interconnected ways. Although in many cases the new autocratic or authoritarian elites behaved as if in the "traditional" (whether colonial, as in Pakistan, or "pre-colonial" regal, as in Burma) manner, or attempted to utilize traditional symbols and attitudes, they were not able or perhaps even willing to revert entirely to a traditional, premodern political structure. Some external, but still important, symbols of modernity—such as universal suffrage (even if suspended), some modern legal frameworks, were, officially at least, maintained. What is even more important is that these new rulers of elites portrayed their own legitimation in secularized, modern terms and symbols—in terms or symbols of social movements or of legal rationality and efficiency, rather than in terms of purely traditional values. This is true even in those cases, as that of Pakistan, where the emphasis on some aspects of the Islamic tradition has been relatively strong, or where, as in Indonesia, the search for new symbols or ideology was strongly couched in traditional terms.

Whatever accountability the new rulers of these societies evinced towards their subjects was not usually couched in terms of the older "religious" mandate of the ruler, but mainly in terms of more modern values in which, in principle, at least, the citizens participated or shared with the rulers. Whatever the limitations on political activities these regimes may have attempted to establish, they did not abandon the idea of the citizen as distinct from the older (traditional and colonial) idea of a subject. Similarly, however anti-Western or anti-capitalist the ideologies of these regimes were, they did not entirely negate modernity. Rather, they attempted to discover or rediscover some synthesis between what they thought might be the "basic"—those undiluted by accidents of history or by materialistic orientations—values and elements of both their own tradition and those of modernity. Such attempts or formulations may have been pure utopian expressions of pious intentions without the ability or will to pay any institutional price demanded for their implementations.

Again, however actually stagnant or inefficient many of the institutional frameworks of these societies may have been before or become after the changes in their regimes, they have but rarely set themselves actively against the expansion of all of the social aspects or processes of modernization, such as education, economic development and industrialization, or rural development. Thus we do not have here cases of non-development of modernization, or a lack of "take off" to modernization, but rather of breakdown of some (especially political) modern institutions—even if in the cases mentioned above, this breakdown took place in relatively early phases of modernization. . . .

The "external" story of all these cases is, on the face of it, relatively simple and straightforward and, in most of these cases, similar in very broad outlines, despite the great differences in detail and setting. One basic characteristic of this story is the development of continuous internal warfare and conflict between different groups within the society, the development of extreme antagonism and cleavages without the possibility of finding any continuous and viable *modus vivendi* between them. These conflicts, the details of which have, of course, greatly varied from case to case, were also usually closely connected with continuous economic crises and, very often, with growing uncontrolable inflation. These crises, in their turn, were often fed by these very continuous conflicts and by the lack of consensus and of any clear policy of how to deal with them.

Conflicts or economic problems of what may seem as initially alarming magnitudes did probably exist and have been resolved, even if only partially, in other modern or modernizing countries. What is, therefore, of crucial importance is the fact that in the countries under consideration, these conflicts were not resolved or regulated. As a result, they spiralled into a continuous series of vicious circles which undermined the stability and continuity of the emerging modern frameworks.

Political and Symbolic Processes Connected with the Breakdown of Modernization

In order to be able to explain why, in the countries studied here, these conflicts were not solved, we might attempt first to analyze the nature of some of the major developments in these societies, [especially] in the political sphere. The most general trend that developed in this sphere in these societies was a marked discrepancy between the demands of different groups—parties, cliques, bureaucracy, army, regional groups—and the responses and ability of the central rulers to deal with these demands. The levels of these demands were either higher or much lower (i.e., more or less articulated) than the level of aggregation and policy making within the central institutions.[2] In most of these cases, the demands of most social groups oscillated continuously between highly articulated types of political demands, as manifest in the formation of varied interest groups and of social movements with a high level of political intensity, on the one hand, and on the other the more primitive, less articulated types, demands typified by direct pressures on the bureaucracy, as manifested in petitioning the local potentates (or bureaucracy) and central rulers and infrequent mob outbreaks.

The power position of the various groups making these varied demands has greatly increased as a result of the processes of modernization. They could no longer be suppressed and neglected, but at the same time no ways of integrating them in some orderly way were found. There developed but few middle range institutional frameworks within which these varied types of political demands could become regulated and translated into concrete policy demands and policies. The leadership of the parties or of the varied movements was not able to aggregate these varied interests and political orientations in some relatively ordered way or to develop adequate policies to deal with the different demands of the major groups and with major problems to which these demands were related. The formal institutions appropriate for such aggregation and policy formation existed in these societies in the form of central executive, administrative, and legislative organs, on the one hand, and of various parties on the other, but they were not able to perform effectively such aggregation or policy formulation.

Nevertheless, there existed within these political systems some organs—such as organs of bureaucratic administration and of local government or traditional communal units—which were able to deal with less articulated types of demands. Following the overthrow of these regimes, they became again very important foci of political processes and aggregation, as they often were in the colonial or even pre-colonial times. But during the preceding period, even their functioning was not very efficient, because they were subordinate to the more differentiated but ineffective agencies and were caught up in the various uncertainties which developed within these agen-

---

[2] The terms "articulation," "aggregation," etc., are used here mostly as in G. Almond and J. Coleman, eds., *The Politics of the Developing Areas* (Princeton: Princeton University Press, 1960). The various case studies presented in this book contain excellent background material and analysis for the problems discussed here.

cies. Hence, these organs—and especially the bureaucracy—became very often both inefficient and corrupt.

Thus, the most important characteristic of the political situation in these countries has not been the mere existence of numerous conflicts or of different levels of articulation of demands, or even the lack of full coordination between these different levels—a situation which can be easily found in relatively stable traditional regimes. But in the societies studied here, because of the push to modernization, these different levels of political demands and activities were not, as in many premodern regimes, kept in relatively segregated, even if interlocked, compartments, but were brought into relatively common frameworks of political process and decision making. At the same time, within this framework adequate mechanisms and principles of aggregating them or of regulating the conflicts attendant on their development did not develop. In other words, the new values that many people wanted to realize in these societies demanded a relatively high level of coordination of individuals' behavior, and no structure of power and organization linking these individuals and the new, more articulated, demands and activities has been created—even the older structure might have broken down.

A similar picture emerges if we examine the nature and scope of what may be called eruptions and movements of protest that have developed in these societies. In terms of the contents of the symbols that have been developed or taken over by these movements, they were not necessarily different from the whole range of such symbols that had developed during different periods or stages of modernization in European, Asian, and African countries. They ranged from nationalistic, anticolonial, traditionalistic, ethnic symbols through symbols of social protest or economic deprivation up to various symbols of cultural renovation coined in anti-Western terms or in terms of religious and communal rivival. They were probably—but not always and not necessarily—more extreme in the intensity of their protest than those that could be found in other, more sedate movements. But beyond this, some other more crucial characteristics of these movements and symbols stand out. First was the relative closeness, separateness, and segregation of these different movements. Second was their sectarian nature, on the one hand, and their intermittency and alteration between brief periods of highly intensive eruptions and long periods of stagnation and inactivity, on the other. Third, within many such sectarian and mutually hostile movements there often developed a coalescence of different, seemingly conflicting values or social orientations—such as those of traditionalism and economic development or of traditionalism and democracy. These different orientations were not usually organized or coordinated in a way which would make them meaningful, not only in terms of the momentary situation, but also in terms of some continuous activity, policy formulation, and implementation.

This was an important indicator of the lack of predisposition on the part of these various movements to become incorporated or transposed into wider frameworks, parties, or informal organs of public opinion, and of the lack of adaptation to such wider regulative frameworks. This lack of predisposition on the part of the movements was often matched by the lack of ability on the part of the ruling institutions to absorb these various symbols and orientations into their own frameworks. As a result of these characteristics, the movements of protest and of opposition in these countries oscillated between apathy, withdrawal of the interest of wider groups and strata from the central insitutions, on the one hand, and very intensive outbursts which made extreme demands on these institutions, demands for total, immediate change of the regime or of the place of any given group within this regime, on the other hand. . . .

This inadequate development of new integrative mechanisms has been manifest in several aspects of institutional developments and of crystallization of symbols in these societies. One of the most important indications of this situation could be found in the development, in all institutional spheres but perhaps especially in the political one, of a sharp dissociation between what has been called solidarity makers, on the one hand, and the instrumentally task-oriented leaders and administrators, on the other hand.

This distinction is not necessarily identical with that between politicians and administrators, and it may well cut across them, although, obviously, the politicians may be more prone to become "solidarity makers" while the government official may be more prone to an instrumentally oriented leader. Rather, it applies to two basic aspects or facets which are inherent in any political (and social) system, although they may greatly vary in their exact structural location in different political structures. Truly enough, in some of the new states one of these types—especially the relatively modern, efficient administrator—might have been almost entirely lacking; but in most of the cases, cadres developed of relatively skilled people who were able to organize various administrative agencies, to develop new economic enterprises and some mechanisms or organs of organizational activity, and to attempt to establish some policies based on these rules. Many such groups or cadres came from the colonial administration; others developed as a result of economic development or programs of educational expansion.

But in most of the cases studied, the rules, injunctions, and policies developed by these cadres, leaders, or organizations were not legitimized or upheld by new common symbols and by those leaders or groups who upheld and developed these new symbols. The new symbols which were developed or upheld in these countries did not seem valid or relevant to the more mundane problems with which the rules developed by the "instrumental" cadres dealt. While some discrepancy between such different orientations is probably inherent in any political system, its extent was, in the cases discussed here, much more acute and extreme. This discrepancy could be found in all the countries studied here. Thus, for instance, in Indonesia we find that the sets of symbols and value orientations continuously developed by Sukarno and by the major parties were not only incapable of addressing themselves to the manifold problems of modernization, but negated, as it were, their existence and significance, although at the same time these problems were besetting the body politic. In Burma the mixture of symbols of Buddhism and socialism developed by U Nu, especially after the first military take-over, dealt only with the most marginal of concrete problems besetting Burmese political lfie. In Pakistan, the constitutional debates about the nature of the state in general and the Islamic state in particular did not greatly help the solution of the many acute administrative, economic, and political problems besetting this state in the first stages of its development. . . .

A similar situation can be discerned in the processes of development of the new central symbols in relation to those partial groups or sectors of the society. The various separate particularistic "primordial" symbols of local, ethnic, caste, or class groups were not incorporated into the new center of the society, and their reformation on a new level of common identification did not take place. Hence, these symbols tended to become points of structural separateness and impediments for the development of a new civil order.

It was not the mere persistence of these symbols that was of crucial importance, but rather the fact that they were not incorporated into the more central symbolic framework which had to be oriented towards the more differentiated and variegated problems that developed in these societies as a result of the continuous process of modernization and the growing interaction between the different groups within them. Or, in other words, no new ideology or value and symbol system developed at the center which could provide some minimal acceptable meaning and framework of answers to the varied problems stemming from the new social situation.

•

If we attempt to summarize the description of the situations in the countries analyzed above, two aspects seem to stand out. First, in all the cases analyzed here, there tended to develop, in almost all the institutional spheres, a situation of growing interaction between different groups and strata, of their being drawn together into new common frameworks, of growing differentiation, and at the same time of lack of adequate mechanisms to deal with the problems attendant on such internal differentiation, and on the growing interaction between the various groups. This coming together of different groups into common social frameworks may have been intermittent and unequally distributed between different groups and strata of the population. But from all these points of view, it is extremely doubtful whether it differed greatly from developments in other modernizing or modern societies at similar levels of modernization which were more successful in establishing relatively stable institutional frameworks.

The crucial problem of these societies has not been a relatively small extent of modernization, but rather the lack of development of new institutional settings, the lack of regulative mechanisms and normative injunctions upheld within strategic areas of the social structure and capable of dealing with the various problems arising in all these spheres. This situation could be described in Durkheim's terms as the non-development and non-institutionalization of the precontractual elements of contracts in the society. The number of "contracts," i.e., of different spheres of interaction—be they in the field of labor relations, industrial relations, or administrative practice— in which new contractual and administrative arrangements developed was very great. But adequate frameworks for the application of normative injunctions to specific situations did not develop, and many contractual arrangements were not upheld by commonly shared values and orientations. Again, in Durkheim's terms, in all these cases there took place a failure to establish and institutionalize new levels of solidarity, to make the transition from mechanic to organic solidarity or from a level of low organic solidarity to a higher one, even though the older frameworks of solidarity were undermined by the growing differentiation and interaction between different groups and strata.

Explaining the Breakdown of Political Modernization

The preceding discussion attempted to provide an analytic description of the developments in these societies. It does not, by itself, explain the reasons for the lack of development of the adequate integrative mechanisms in these societies. We shall attempt now to analyze some of these reasons.

This lack was not due to the lack of attempts by the rulers or the aspirants to elite positions to develop such mechanisms and policies, or to the lack of demands by various groups in the society for the development of some far-reaching social and economic policies. Manifold policies which aimed at the establishment of some regulative principles in the body politic and at the implementation of various collective goals were developed and implemented by the political elites—very often in response to various demands on behalf of wider groups in the society. But these policies and the demands to which they responded did not contribute to the establishment of relatively stable coordination in the society.

In order to be able to understand the reasons for these developments, it is necessary to put them into the wider context of the social and political orientation of the broader social strata and of the interaction between them and the elites. All these societies were characterized by the development within them of continuous processes of social mobilization. But the structure of these processes of social mobilization assumed here some special characteristics. The most important of these characteristics was that the wider social groups and strata—be they rural or urban groups, ecological or professional units—evinced a very high degree of social and cultural "closeness" and self-centeredness, however great their dependence on other groups might have become.

The most important aspect of this closeness was the predominance of a purely "adaptive" attitude to the wider social setting with but little active solidary orientation to it or identification with it. This adaptive orientation could be manifest in two different, seemingly opposing but often coalescing ways. The first such way, most frequently found among various "traditional" lower- and sometimes also middle-rural and urban groups, is characterized by a relatively passive attitude to the wider social settings, by a great extent of rigidity in their conception of society in general and of their own place within it, in particular. These characteristics had many repercussions on the structure and activities of these groups when they were pushed into new, modernized, and differentiated urban, industrial, and semi-industrial settings. They resulted in the perpetuation of previous "traditional" types of relationships, i.e., of paternalistic arrangements in industrial settings and relations in dealing with officials, politicians, or leaders of the church, in the lack of readiness to undertake responsibility or initiative in the new settings, and in general in great passivity and in small ranges of interests.

The second major way in which this adaptive attitude to the wider social setting could be manifest was that of what may be called exaggerated, unlimited "openness" and "flexibility" and attempts to obtain within this new setting many various benefits, emoluments, and positions without any consideration of actual possibilities or of other groups in the societies.

There were only relatively few groups within these societies which evinced somewhat greater and more realistic internal and external flexibility. Most important among them were some economic business communities or new professional groups, some relatively differentiated rural leadership, and some reformative religious groups. But these were, in most of the societies studied here, weak and above all relatively segregated both from the central institutions of the societies and from wider social strata.

The most important structural outcome of these tendencies was that even though new types of specialized and differentiated social organizations, trade unions, or professional organizations were created both among the elite and among the broader groups of society which were drawn into new frameworks, this did not result in the creation of a viable new differentiated institutional structure. These groups were unable to function effectively because they had to work under what may be called "false" premises, i.e., some of the prerequisites for their effective functioning did not develop in these settings. They very often exhibited characteristics of "delinquent

communities," as they have been called by a student of French "retarda-
tion" or "traditionalism," i.e., communities not oriented to the attainment
of their manifest goals (be they economic growth, community development,
or the like), but to the maintenance of the vested status and interest positions of their members within the existing settings.[4]

Morever, even if there tended to develop within some institutional
spheres—be it in education, in the field of economic enterprises, or in the
professions—either through diffusion, or through the development of specially active groups, some more stable, differentiated groups and organizations, their ability to develop and maintain their organization and activities
within the wider setting was very restricted. Very often they succumbed to
the pressures of the environment, becoming disorganized.

These structural characteristics may also to some extent explain the
nature of political activities and orientations that develop within these societies among broader groups and especially the fact of monolithic aspirations, i.e., attempts to direct and control all social developments and all
avenues of social and occupational mobility within them and to monopolize
all positions of power and allocations of prestige. . . . Political self-per-
ception and self-legitimation of the political leaders were also to no small
extent focused on the procurement through the new political frameworks of
many benefits—to the collectivity as such, to the major (articulate) strata,
and especially to those strata which were, as it were, deprived from sharing
in these benefits in the former period.

As a result, the policies undertaken by the rulers in these societies have
been characterized by continuous oscillation between the attempts at controlling all the major power positions and groups in the society and monopolizing the positions of effective control, on the one hand, and a continuous
giving in to the demands of various groups, on the other hand. In general,
the various more restrictive policies in all these fields could be found in the
more "traditional" countries like Pakistan or Sudan, while the policies of
"giving in" to exaggerated demands of various groups could be found especially in the more modern countries like Indonesia and Burma, although
both tendencies could be found, in some measure, in all these countries.

Needless to say, many such policies—especially the more repressive and
regimentating ones—can be found also in many other "new" and older nations; and for each concrete policy undertaken in Indonesia, Burma, or
Pakistan, there could also be found an equivalent in a more stable regime.
But the most important characteristic of these policies as they developed in
the countries analyzed here has been not any specific detail, but rather the
continuous oscillation between the repressive orientation, on the one hand,

---

[4] J. R. Pitts, "Continuity and Change in Bourgeois France," in *In Search of France*
(Cambridge: Harvard University, Center for International Affairs, 1963), esp. pp.
254-59.

and the giving in to the various demands of many groups on the other, or the lack of development of any stable or continuous criteria of priorities.

Thus, extremely important parallels in the orientations and activities of the new elites and of large parts of the broader groups and strata within these societies can be found. Both were characterized by maintaining and developing within the new modern institutional frameworks relatively rigid and restricted social, cultural, and political orientations conceived in terms of the preceding social structure or in terms of "flexible" but unattainable goals. Hence, there tended to develop in these cases a vicious circle of pressures on existing resources, pressures which were strongly linked to the rigidity of aspirations of these groups and were often reinforced by the policies and activities of the rulers which ultimately necessarily tended to deplete these resources. A very general result of the policies developed in such situations was to reduce available resources and to squander them. Such squandering of resources took place often because of "symbolic" or ideological reasons, and because of the attempts of the rulers to attest, in this way, to their legitimation. It usually minimized the range of maneuvering ability available to the rulers. At the same time, because of lack of any clear principles of regulation or priorities, they tended to exacerbate the level of conflict between various groups as the aspirations of them all rose while the total output of the economy remained static or even decreased. . . .

•

The problem of why in Turkey, Japan, Mexico, and Russia there emerged in the initial stages of modernization elites with orientations to change and ability to implement relatively effective policies, while they did not develop in these initial phases in Indonesia, Pakistan, or Burma, or why elites with similar differences tended to develop also in later stages of modernization, is an extremely difficult one and constitutes one of the most baffling problems in comparative sociological analysis. There are but few available indications to deal with this problem. Very tentatively, it may perhaps be suggested that to some extent it has to do with the placement of these elites in the preceding social structure, with the extent of their internal cohesiveness, and of the internal transformation of their own value orientation.

In most of the countries analyzed here, the new elites were mostly composed of intellectuals, and in many cases they constituted the only initially available modern elite. They had but very few internal social and ideological contacts or identifications (even if ambivalent ones) with either the bearers of pre-existing traditions or with the wider groups of the society. The modernizing orientations of these elites were focused more on the political than on the economic sphere. Surprisingly enough, they were also very often less focused on the cultural sphere, in the sense of redefinition and reformation of their own basic internal value-orientation. Consequently, they were not able to establish a strong internal cohesiveness and strong ideological and value identifications and connections with other potentially modernized groups and strata.

On the other hand, the elites in Turkey, Japan, and Mexico or some of the more cohesive elites in countries of later stages of modernization, however great the differences between them, had yet some contrary characteristics in common. They were not usually composed only of intellectual groups entirely alienated from the pre-existing elites and from some of the broader groups of the society, but were to some extent placed in secondary elite position in the preceding structure and had somewhat closer relations with many active, broader groups. In the ideological and value spheres, they aimed at the development of a new, more flexible set of symbols and collective identity which, while not negating the traditions, would also provide some new meaning for the new processes of change. Hence, they tended, on the one hand, to be more cohesive, while at the same time to effect some internal value transformation within the broader groups and strata.

•

The development of processes of social mobilization without adequate integration, of rifts between the "instrumental" and "solidarity making" leaders, and within the symbolic and ideological realms of a society, did develop in all the countries in which some breakdowns of modernization and especially of political modernization took place. They developed, as we have seen, in different phases of stages of modernization in the various new states enumerated above.

One common outcome of these processes is implicit in most of the preceding analysis—namely, the "reversal" of these regimes to what may be called a lower, less flexible level of political and social differentiation, as seen in the scope of problems with which they are capable of dealing. But, on the other hand, as has already been pointed out above, most of these less differentiated regimes have to some extent retained some of the symbols, goals, and institutional arrangements of modernity, even if they attempted to develop new ideologies and symbols.

This combination has necessarily created a potential contradiction which could develop in principle into several different directions. One such possible outcome was the institutionalization of a relatively modern system, a somewhat lower level of differentiation, albeit with some possibilities of limited institutional absorption of change, conducive to some economic growth. The other possibility is that of development of stagnative regimes with but very little capacity for absorption of change and which may either become relatively stable or develop a system of vicious circles of eruptions, blockages, and violence. But the analysis of the conditions which may lead to any of these directions is beyond the province of this paper.

CHAPTER 31

JOSEPH R. GUSFIELD

Tradition and Modernity: Misplaced Polarities in the Study of Social Change

"Tradition" and "modernity" are widely used as polar opposites in a linear theory of social change.[1] A significant assumption in this model of change is that existing institutions and values, the content of tradition, are impediments to changes and are obstacles to modernization. It is with this assumption that our paper is concerned. We wish to call attention to the manifold variations in the relation between traditional forms and new institutions and values, variations whose possibilities are either denied or hidden by the polarity of the traditional-modern model of social change. We want, further, to explore the uses of tradition and modernity as explicit ideologies operating in the context of politics in new nations. Our materials are largely drawn from modern India, although we shall refer to other Asian and African countries as well.

The concepts of economic development and of economic modernization have now been generalized to many areas of national life by social scientists. There is now a discussion of communication development, educational development, and, most widely used, of political development.[2]

Reprinted from *The American Journal of Sociology*, Vol. 72, No. 4, Jan. 1967, pp. 351-362.

[1] There is a wide literature analyzing concepts of tradition and modernity or development. Leading efforts to conceptualize these societal types are W. W. Rostov, *The Stages of Economic Growth* (Cambridge: Cambridge University Press, 1960); Gabriel Almond and James Coleman, *The Politics of Developing Areas* (Princeton, N.J.: Princeton University Press, 1960), chap. i; Daniel Lerner, *The Passing of Traditional Society* (Glencoe, Ill.: Free Press, 1958), chaps. ii, iii.

[2] See the various volumes published by Princeton University Press under the series title "Studies in Political Development." Also see A. F. K. Organski, *The Stages of Political Development* (New York: Alfred A. Knopf, Inc., 1965).

At the same time that the concept of development has become generalized, a large number of specific studies of new nations have made us aware of the wide variety of outcomes and possibilities for change and continuity. These have led to a more critical appreciation of the many possible interrelations between new and old aspects of social, economic, and political life. The new that tradition and innovation are necessarily in conflict has begun to seem overly abstract and unreal.

In the study of economic growth we have come to be aware that Weber's conception of traditional versus rational economic behavior is a great distortion of the realities of many concrete situations. In the study of political alternatives and possibilities we have become sensitive to the reifying effect of unilinear theories. They make Anglo-American political forms either inevitable or necessarily superior outcomes of political processes in new nations.

In exploring the concepts of tradition and modernity we shall discuss the assumptions of conflict between them. These assumptions are inconsistent with recent studies which will reveal a wide range of possible alternatives and show that "tradition" is a more specific and ambiguous phenomenon than usually realized.

We will examine some assumptions of this theory and indicate the difficulties in its use. . . .

Fallacy: Traditional Culture Is a Consistent Body of Norms and Values

In elaborating the distinction and interaction between the "great tradition" of urban centers and the "little tradition" of village communities, anthropologists have called our attention to the diversity and the existence of alternatives in what has been supposed to be a uniform body of rules and values. We must avoid accepting the written and intellectualized versions of a culture as the only form of a common set of beliefs and behavior patterns. [But] even within the literate forms of a tradition, inconsistency and opposition are marked; Hindu philosophical and religious teaching is consistent with a number of diverse orientations to life. The doctrine of the four *ashramas*, for example, conceives of the good life as one in which men pursue different values at different stages in the life cycle.[3]

The importance of this diversity is that it provides legitimizing principles for a wide set of alternative forms of behavior. This point has been rather convincingly made in the recent discussion of economic development and cultural values in India.[4] Neither the behavior of popular religion nor teach-

---

[3] For a description of the doctrine of Ashramas, see K. M. Sen, *Hinduism* (London: Penguin Books, 1961), chap. iii.

[4] Milton Singer, "Cultural Values in India's Economic Development," *Annals*, CCCV (May, 1956), 81-91.

ings of the scriptures are devoid of moral bases for materialistic motivations or for disciplined and rational pursuit of wealth. Everyone need not be a *sadhu* (holy man) at all times.

Fallacy: Traditional Society Is a Homogeneous Social Structure

Like other societies, Indian society has institutionalized different styles of life in different groups, both within and without the caste system. Such divisions of labor make it possible for specific communal and status groups to be the bearers of traditions which differ from the dominant streams yet enable valued social functions to be performed. While Weber referred to "the Protestant ethic," the specific sects who carried the ethic were by no means typical of all Protestant groups. The role of foreign and pariah peoples has often been commented upon as a source of economic growth, innovation, and entrepreneurial behavior.[5] The Jews in Europe, the Muslims in West Africa, the Chinese in Indonesia, and the East Indians in East Africa are examples of groups whose marginality has rendered them able to engage in the impersonality of market behavior and to remain aloof from the status consumption demands of the indigenous population. In India, the Parsees and the Jains have been potent carriers of economic innovation and the development of large-scale industrial production.

Generalizations about the anti-economic character of the Hindu traditions lose sight of the provision for specific groups which are ethically capable of carrying a logic of economic growth and change. Within the caste system of Hinduism, the untouchables have been able to perform tabooed occupations necessary to the economy. Other castes have developed traditions of business and commerce which, although dishonored in Hindu "tradition," are permissible and even obligatory for the Marwari, the Chettiar, and the Baniya. It is their very legitimation within existing structure that permits their acceptance and implementation of innovating economic behavior.

Fallacy: Old Traditions Are Displaced by New Changes

The capacity of old and new cultures and structures to exist without conflict and even with mutual adaptations is a frequent phenomenon of social change; the old is not necessarily *replaced* by the new. The acceptance of a new product, a new religion, a new mode of decision-making does not necessarily lead to the disappearance of the older form. New forms may

---

[5] Sheldon Stryker, "Social Structure and Prejudice," *Social Problems,* VI (1959), 340-54; Bert Hoselitz, "Main Concepts in the Analysis of the Social Implications of Technical Change," in B. Hoselitz and W. Moore, *Industrialization and Society* (New York: UNESCO, 1963), pp. 11-29, especially pp. 24-28.

only increase the range of alternatives. Both magic and medicine can exist side by side, used alternatively by the same people.

The syncretism of inconsistent elements has long been noted in the acceptance of religious usages and beliefs. Paganism and Catholicism have often achieved a mutual tolerance into a new form of ritualism drawn from each in Spanish-speaking countries.[6] The "great tradition" of the urban world in India has by no means pushed aside the "little tradition" of the village as they made contact. Interaction has led to a fusion and mutual penetration. We have become increasingly aware that the outcome of modernizing processes and traditional forms is often an admixture in which each derives a degree of support from the other, rather than a clash of opposites.

Fallacy: Traditional and Modern Forms Are Always in Conflict

The abstraction of a "traditional society" as a type separate from a specific historical and cultural setting ignores the diversity of content in specific traditions which influence the acceptance, rejection, or fusion of modernist forms. Japan is unlike the Western societies in the ways in which "feudalism" and industrial development have been fused to promote economic growth.[7] Commitment to emperor and to family, a collectivistic orientation, and a high degree of vertical immobility have been factors supporting social and economic change in the Japanese context while they appear to have been factors producing resistance in the individualistic culture of the West. Traditional structures can supply skills, and traditional values can supply sources of legitimation which are capable of being utilized in pursit of new goals and with new processes.

Anthropologists have made the same point in connection with problems of selective culture change. One traditional culture may possess values more clearly congruent with modernization than another; another may cling more tenaciously to its old ways than another. Ottenberg's study of tribes in West Africa found them able to accept and utilize the British culture in Nigeria to a much greater extent than was true of the other major Nigerian tribes. The Ibo's system of voluntary associations, coupled with their values of individualism and achievement, adapted them well to the kinds of opportunities and demands which British colonialism brought. In contrast, the Masai

---

[6] For one account of such syncretisms, see Robert Redfield, *The Folk Culture of Yucatan* (Chicago: University of Chicago Press, 1941), chap. ix.

[7] For some analyses of this phenomenon in Japan, see Reinhard Bendix, *Nation-Building and Citizenship* (New York: John Wiley & Sons, 1965), chap. vi; Robert Scalapino, "Ideology and Modernization: The Japanese Case," in D. Apter (ed.), *Ideology and Discontent* (New York: Free Press, 1965), pp. 93-127; Everett Hagen, *On the Theory of Social Change* (Homewood, Ill.: Dorsey Press, 1962), chap. xiv.

in East Afria are a notorious case of resistance to culture change, fiercely upholding existing ways with very little accommodation.[8]

Fallacy: Tradition and Modernity Are Mutually Exclusive Systems

A given institution or cultural system contains several aspects or dimensions. Each dimension does not function in the same way in response to new influences on a society. Tradition and modernity are frequently mutually reinforcing, rather than systems in conflict.

Earlier theories of economic growth viewed extended family systems and caste structure as impediments to economic growth.[9] We now recognize, however, that such relations are complex and can vary from one context to another. Caste as an unalloyed impediment to economic growth has been much exaggerated through failing to balance its role in the division of labor and in caste mobility (one dimension) against its tendencies toward status demands as limitations on desire to accumulate capital (a second dimension). Efforts on the part of castes to become mobile, to attempt improvements in their material as well as their ritual position are by no means new to Indian life. The expanded scope of regional castes, the development of caste associations, and the importance of castes in politics are not impediments to economic growth. They enable credit facility, occupational sponsorship and training, and political influence to be made available on a basis of segmental, traditional loyalties. This brings an element of trust and obligation into an economic context where suspicion and distrust are otherwise frequently the rule between persons unconnected by other ties than the "purely" economic.

Studies of the impact of industrialization on family life in preindustrial and primitive societies similarly indicate the compatibility of extended family forms with industrialism.[10] In the context of Indian economic growth, the large extended families of the Tatas, Birlas, and Dalmias are among the most striking instances of major industrial organizations growing out of and supported by traditional family units. Berna's study of entrepreneurship in

---

[8] Simon Ottenberg, "Ibo Receptivity to Change," in M. Herskovits and W. Bascom, *Continuity and Change in African Culture* (Chicago: University of Chicago Press, 1959), pp. 130-43; Harold Schneider, "Pakot Resistance to Change," *ibid.*, pp. 144-67.

[9] For a generalized statement of this view, stressing an open system of social mobility as a prerequisite for economic growth, see Kingsley Davis, "The Role of Class Mobility in Economic Development," *Population Review*, VI (July, 1962), 67-73.

[10] William Goode, "Industrialization and Family Change," in Hoselitz and Moore, *op. cit.*, chap. xii; Jean Comhaire, "Economic Change and the Extended Family," *Annals*, CCCV (May, 1956), 45-52; Manning Nash, *Machine Age Maya* (Glencoe, Ill.: Free Press, 1958).

Madras provides additional information, among small businesses, of the extended family as a major source of savings and capital accumulation.[11]

The role of traditional values in the form of segmental loyalties and principles of legitimate authority are of great importance in understanding the possibilities for the occurrence of unified and stable polities at a national level. The contemporary Indian political process utilizes caste, village, and religious community as basic segmental groups through which the individual and the family are drawn into modern political institutions. Primary ties of kinship and clan are in process of fusion to centralized structures of national, participative politics.

The "stuff" of much modern politics in India is itself drawn from the pre-existing struggles between caste, religion, region, and economic groupings. We have become aware that much of what appears to be ideological and economic conflict in Indian politics is actuated and bolstered by struggles for social and economic position among the various caste groups.

Fallacy: Modernizing Processes Weaken Traditions

This discussion of Indian education suggests that new institutions and values may, and often do, fuse and interprenetrate the old. In his influential paper on caste mobility, M. N. Srinivas has shown that, while higher social levels appear to be "westernizing" their life styles, when lower and middle levels seek mobility they do so by becoming more devotedly Hinduistic, following more Brahminical styles, and otherwise Sanskritizing their behavior.[12] The fluidity introduced by political competition under independence and democracy becomes harnessed to a more traditional orientation.

The technological consequences of increased transportation, communication, literacy, and horizontal mobility, in furthering the spread of ideas, also intensifies the spread and influence of the "great tradition" into more and more communities and across various social levels. Pilgrimages to distant shrines become easier and enable the conception of a unified, national religion to take firmer root. Caste groups can now be formed on regional and even national lines, buttressed by associational life and written journals. The spread of community development and of educational facilities brings in its wake new, semiurban personnel who carry the Sanskritic traditions fully as much, if not more so, than they do the westernizing influences. The communities of the "little tradition" are, in fact, more open to such traditional winds of change than to wholly new movements. The holy men and

---

[11] James Berna, "Patterns of Entrepreneurship in South India," *Economic Development and Cultural Change*, VII (April, 1959), 343-62.

[12] "Sanskritization and Westernization" in M. N. Srinivas: *Caste in Modern India* (Bombay: Asia Publishing House, 1962).

the wandering players who carry religious messages and dramas drawn from the Hindu great traditions are more likely to effect attention than the movies.[13]

Tradition, Ideology, and Nationhood

Tradition is not something waiting out there, always over one's shoulder. It is rather plucked, created, and shaped to present needs and aspirations in a given historical situation. Men refer to aspects of the past as tradition in grounding their present actions in some legitimating principle. In this fashion, tradition becomes an ideology, a program of action in which it functions as a goal or as a justificatory base. The concern for tradition as an explicit policy is not an automatic response to change but is itself a movement capable of analysis.

The desire to be modern and the desire to preserve tradition operate as significant movements in the new nations and developing economies. It is our basic point here that these desires, functioning as ideologies, are not always in conflict; that the quest for modernity depends upon and often finds support in the ideological upsurge of traditionalism. In this process, tradition may be changed, stretched, and modified, but a unified and nationalized society makes great use of the traditional in its search for a consensual base to political authority and economic development.

Many observers have noted the phenomenon of the revival of indigenous tradition as a phase of nationalistic and independence movements, especially where intellectuals had come to look to some other country as a basic source of new values.[14] Such reactions have set in among Russian intellectuals against France in the nineteenth century, among the Indonesians against the Dutch, among the Japanese against Europe; and against the British among the Indians both during and after the struggle for independence. The Indian intellectuals, westernized and European in cultural orientation, underwent a renaissance of traditional Hinduism as one aspect of the struggle against colonial dominion. Despite their general commitment to modernization (often against the British post-Sepoy rebellion policy of maintaining native custom), a recrudescence of Indian national identity was partially fostered by explicit adoption of customs and styles which were both traditional and closer to popular behavior. It was this ideology which

---

[13] John Gumperz, "Religion as a Form of Communication in North India," *Journal of Asian Studies,* XXIII (June, 1964), 89-98.

[14] John Kautsky, *Political Change in Underdeveloped Areas* (New York: John Wiley & Sons, 1962), pp. 53-54; Heimsath, *op. cit.,* chap. xii; Mary Mattosian, "Ideologies of Delayed Industrialization," *Economic Development and Cultural Change* (April, 1958), pp. 217-28.

Gandhi gave to the movement, even as he sought the abolition of many features of that tradition.

The issue of the nationalist movement is not abated in its victory. For the new elites of newly independent nations, the issue is not so much that of overcoming tradition but of finding ways of synthesizing and blending tradition and modernity.

Those who depict the elites in India as cut off from roots in an indigenous civilization ignore the ways in which Hinduism and Indian family life exert strong pulls as continuing aspects of Indian life, even where highly westernized. Almost always the Indian intellectual speaks a regional language as his mother tongue, is steeped in classic Sanskrit literature, and is deeply tied to an extended family. Parental arrangement is still the very dominant mode of marital selection, and he is often married to a highly traditional wife.

Independence, even within the westernized circles, has given continuing support to a movement toward the recapturing of Hindu folklore and the furtherance of tradition as a source of national unity in a common culture. What Indian book or journal does not have its section that links modern thought or institutions to analogues in Hindu scripture? How often is the romanticization of the village and the rejection of the city not found among vigorous exponents of political democracy and economic change? This ideological construction of Indian tradition is offered as a "great tradition," and this Indian populism is found among intellectual and urbanized elites as it is in the provincial and peasant villages.

Nationalism is deeply committed to both horns of the dilemma of tradition and modernity. The effort to define a national heritage in the form of a set of continuing traditions is also a way of coping with the wide gap that separates elite and mass, city and village, region and region in the Indian context. It is a complement to the modernizing processes which are involved in the aspiration toward a unified nation. A common culture that cuts across the segmental and primordial loyalties is a basis for national identity and consensus. Without it, the modernization based on nationhood lacks a foundation for legitimating central authority. . . .

The synthesis of tradition and modernity is evident in Gandhian influence. Was Gandhi a traditionalist or a modernizer? Asking the question poses the immense difficulty in separating the various streams in reform and social change blowing over the Indian subcontinent. Certainly his genius lay in uniting disparities, in utilizing the traditional authority of the holy man for social reforms and for political union. His leadership of the independence movement gave India a common experience which has been one of the crucial legacies of the independence movement to its present national existence and to the authority of the Congress Party.

The Gandhianism of the neo-Gandhians, such as Vinoba Bhave and Jayaprakash Narayan, represents an important ideological development in the search for political institutions which will cope with the problems of nationhood within indigenous cultural forms. But Gandhian Socialism represents only one form in which this drive toward a synthesis is manifest. The recent movement toward the development of local autonomy and participation in India rests both on the growing political power of village communities and the ideological force which has recreated a tradition of Indian village democracy. In the various proposals for a system of Panchayati Raj (movement toward greater local power in economic decisions at the village level), Indian government and politics are wrestling with the problem of creating a consensus for developmental policies which will have the legitimating support in tradition, even if the tradition is newly discovered.

The Mediating Elites

Elsewhere we have analyzed the growing political power of new, less westernized, and more localistic political elites and subelites in India.[15] Such people, with sources of power in state and region, mediate between the westernized elites and the mass of the Indian society in ways which bring a greater degree of traditional commitments and styles, of caste and other primordial ties, into the political and cultural arena.

The very process of political egalitarianism and modernization contains the seeds of new ideologies of tradition. Literacy in Indian not only stimulates a common cultural content but has also led to ideologies of regionalism, extolling the virtues of regional languages and cultures. While such movements impede the development of an all-India culture consensus, they are neither antimodern nor specifically anti-India. They do, however, presage the decline of that form of national elite that has been associated with colonial cultural influences. India appears to be approaching and entering a phase in which modernization will be directed and implemented by persons whose loyalties and ideologies are considerably more traditionalized than has been true in the past decades. . . .

•

To conclude, the all too common practice of pitting tradition and modernity against each other as paired opposites tends to overlook the mixtures and blends which reality displays. Above all, it becomes an ideology of antitraditionalism, denying the necessary and usable ways in which the past serves as support, especially in the sphere of values and political legitimation, to the present and the future.

---

[15] J. Gusfield, "Political Community and Group Interests in Modern India," *Pacific Affairs*, XXXVI (Summer, 1965).

CHAPTER 32

ALEX INKELES

Making Men Modern: On the
Causes and Consequences
of Individual Change in
Six Developing Countries

The Project on the Social and Cultural Aspects of Economic Development at Harvard's Center for International Affairs interviewed 6,000 men from six developing countries to study the impact on the individual of his exposure to and participation in the process of national and economic modernization. To a striking degree, the same syndrome of attitudes, values, and ways of acting—such as openness to new experience, independence

This paper was presented at the Dallas meeting of the American Association for the Advancement of Science in the section on "Comparative Sociology and Contemporary Social Issues," December 29, 1968. My chief collaborators from the early days of the project were Howard Schuman and Edward Ryan, who served, respectively, as field directors for Pakistan and Nigeria, and David H. Smith, who was my assistant in Chile and later was assistant director of the project in Cambridge. The field work and later analysis were greatly facilitated by the work of our local collaborators in all six of the countries. We owe particular debt to Juan César and Carlotta Garcia, Perla Gibaja, and Amar Singh who were field directors for Chile, Argentina, and India, respectively, and to Olatude Oloko who was assistant field director in Nigeria. In its different aspects, stages, and settings, the research has been supported by the Rockefeller Foundation, the Ford Foundation, the National Science Foundation, and the National Institute of Mental Health. The Cultural Affairs Division of the Department of State provided local currencies to support our field work in India, Israel, and Pakistan, and the Office of Scientific Research of the U.S. Air Force supported technical exploration in problems of translation and computer analysis undertaken in Cambridge. All these organizations gave their support through the Center for International Affairs of Harvard University, which is the sponsor and institutional home of our project on the social and cultural aspects of economic development.

from parental authority, and taking an active part in civic affairs—defines the modern man in each of the six countries and in all the occupational groups of cultivator, craftsman, and industrial worker. Education is the most powerful factor in making men modern, but occupational experience in large-scale organizations, and especially in factory work, makes a significant contribution in "schooling" men in modern attitudes and in teaching them to act like modern men. Those who come from very traditional backgrounds and receive little formal schooling can, under the right circumstances, still become modern in adult life. Modern men in developing countries not only have modern attitudes, but they can be shown to behave differently. Despite popular impressions to the contrary, exposure to the influence of migration and modern institutions does not lead to psychic distress.

Since 1962 a group of my colleagues and I at Harvard University have been working to understand the impact on the individual of his participation in the process of modernization. In the pursuit of this goal we devised a complex and comprehensive questionnaire touching on a wide variety of life situations and intended to measure a substantial segment of the range of attitudes, values, and behaviors we conceive as particularly relevant to understanding the individual's participation in the roles typical for a modern industrial society.[1] This questionnaire we then administered to some 6,000 young men in six developing countries: Argentina, Chile, India, Israel, Nigeria, and East Pakistan. All three of the continents containing the overwhelming majority of developing nations are represented. The sampled countries cover the range from the newest nations which have only recently won their independence to those with a long history of self-governance; from those only now emerging from tribal life to those with ancient high cultures, and from those furthest removed from, to those most intimately linked to, the European cultural and industrial social order. The men interviewed were selected to represent points on a presumed continuum of exposure to modernizing influences, the main groups being the cultivator of the land still rooted in his traditional rural community; the migrant from the countryside just arrived in the city but not yet integrated into urban industrial life; the urban but nonindustrial worker still pursuing a more or less traditional occupation, such as barber or carpenter, but now doing so in the urban environment even though outside the context of a modern large-scale organization; and the experienced industrial worker engaged in production using inanimate power and machinery within the context of a more or less

---

[1] Some sixty-eight of the questions are listed, in abbreviated form, in table 1 of Smith and Inkeles 1966. A complete copy of the questionnaire may be obtained by ordering Document 9133 from the Chief, Auxiliary Publication Project, photoduplication Service, Library of Congress, Washington, D.C. remitting $13.50 for microfilm or $117.50 for photocopies.

modern productive enterprise. To these we have added sets of secondary school and university students who enjoy the presumed benefits of advanced education. Within and across these sample groups we exercised numerous controls in the selection of subjects and in the analysis of our data, both to understand the influence and to prevent the uncontrolled effects of socio-cultural and biosocial factors such as age, sex, education, social origins, ethnic membership, past life experience, and the like.

Our interview included almost 300 entries. Some 160 of these elicited attitudes, values, opinions, and reports on the behavior of others and one-self, touching on almost every major aspect of daily life. The questionnaire included various tests of verbal ability, literacy, political information, intel-ligence, and psychic adjustment. In some cases it took four hours of interviewing to complete—a demanding experience for both interviewer and interviewee.

We completed our field work near the end of 1964, and since that time have been engaged in processing and then later analyzing the very sub-stantial body of data we collected. At this time our analysis is sufficiently far advanced so that we can discern the main outlines of some of the con-clusions we must draw. To present these within the rigorous limits of the time and space currently allotted for scholarly communications requires imposing a telegraphic style and forgoing the presentation of detailed evi-dence to support my arguments. Each of my conclusions will address itself to one of the main issues to which our research was directed. Each issue is presented in the form of a question to which I will assay an answer. The four main issues dealt with here should not be understood as being the only ones to which we addressed ourselves; neither should it be assumed that our data provide answers only to these questions.

1. *How far is there an empirically identifiable modern man, and what are his outstanding characteristics?*—Many social scientists have a conception of the modern man, but few have submitted this conception to an empirical test to ascertain whether this type really exists in nature and to determine how often he appears on the scene. Important exceptions may be found in the work of Kahl (1968), Dawson (1967), and Doob (1967). We too have our model of the modern man, a complex one including three components which we refer to as the analytic, the topical, and the behavioral models, all of which, we assumed, might well tap one general underlying common dimension of individual modernity.[2]

We believe our evidence (presented in some detail in Smith and Inkeles 1966) shows unmistakably that there is a set of personal qualities which

---

[2] This model has been sketched in a preliminary way in Inkeles 1966. A fuller ac-count is presented in Inkeles, forthcoming in Faunce and Garfinkel.

reliably cohere as a syndrome and which identify a type of man who may validly be described as fitting a reasonable theoretical conception of the modern man. Central to this syndrome are: (1) openness to new experience, both with people and with new ways of doing things such as attempting to control births; (2) the assertion of increasing independence from the authority of traditional figures like parents and priests and a shift of allegiance to leaders of government, public affairs, trade unions, cooperatives, and the like; (3) belief in the efficacy of science and medicine, and a general abandonment of passivity and fatalism in the face of life's difficulties; and (4) ambition for oneself and one's children to achieve high occupational and educational goals. Men who manifest these characteristics (5) like people to be on time and show an interest in carefully planning their affairs in advance. It is also part of this syndrome to (6) show strong interest and take an active part in civic and community affairs and local politics; and (7) to strive energetically to keep up with the news, and within this effort to prefer news of national and international import over items dealing with sports, religion, or purely local affairs.

This syndrome of modernity coheres empirically to meet the generally accepted standards for scale construction with reliabilities ranging from .754 to .873 in the six countries.[3] Looking at the range of items which enters into the scale, one can see that it has a compelling face validity. In addition, the empirical outcome accords well with our original theoretical model and, indeed, with those of numerous other students of the problem. Evidently the modern man is not just a construct in the mind of sociological theorists. He exists and he can be identified with fair reliability within any population which can take our test.[4]

To discover that there are indeed men in the world who fit our model of a modern man is comforting, but perhaps not startling. After all, we can probably somewhere find an example of almost any kind of man one might care to delineate. It is important to emphasize, therefore, that men manifesting the syndrome of attitudes, values, and ways of acting we have designated "modern" are not freaks. They are not even rare. On the contrary, there are

---

[3] Reference is to the reliabilities of the long form of the scale (OM-2) containing 159 items. Reliabilities for some of the various short forms were sometimes lower but were generally in the same range. See Smith and Inkeles 1966, p. 367.

[4] On the basis of our experience with the longer versions of the questionnaire, we have been able to devise several short forms which permit rapid identification of the more modern and more traditional men in any population. Details on the construction and content of these short forms are given in Smith and Inkeles 1966. One of these short forms (OM-12) which has proved a highly reliable instrument is currently being used in more than twenty pure- and applied-research programs in over a dozen developing countries.

very substantial numbers of them in all six of the countries we have studied.[5]

Furthermore, we consider it to be of the utmost significance that the qualities which serve empirically to define a modern man do not differ substantially from occupation to occupation, or more critically, from culture to culture. In constructing our standard scales of modernity we utilized a pool of 119 attitude items.[6] In each country these items were then ranked according to the size of the item-to-scale correlation, and the subset of items having the highest correlations was then selected as defining the modern man for the given country. Using this "coherence" method to construct the national modernity scales, we might have found a totally different set of items defining the syndrome of modernity in each of our six national samples. Indeed, if we used only the twenty items ranking highest in the item-to-scale correlations for each country, we could theoretically have come out with six totally different syndromes, one for each country, no one overlapping in the least with any other. The actual outcome of the analysis was totally different. The probability that even one item would come out in the top fifty in all six countries is approximately five in a thousand. We actually had ten items which were in the top fifty in all six countries, sixteen more in the top fifty in five countries, thirteen more which were in this set in four of the six countries. The probability that the same thirty-nine items would by chance be in the top fifty in four of the six countries is so infinitesimal as to make our results notable indeed.

This means that what defines man as modern in one country also defines him as modern in another. It argues for the actual psychic unity of man-

---

[5] Of course, when you use a scale score to designate a "type" of man, the number of men who fit your typology depends entirely on your decision as to a cutting point on both the items and on the scale as a whole. For example, in one form of our modernity scale (IM-6) a representative subset of thirty-three items is scored so that only by affirming the most decidedly modern position at the end of the theoretical continum of alternative answers does a man get a point toward his modernity score. On this strict test, getting as many as half the answers "right" would qualify 37 percent of our Nigerian sample as "modern." If we set a higher standard, and reserve the term modern for men who get two-thirds or more of the answers "right," then only 6 percent qualify. Raising the standard still higher to require that a man get three-fourths or more of the answers "correct" reduces the pool of modern men to 2 percent of the sample. The comparable proportions qualifying as modern by this standard in our Pakistani sample are much lower, being 14 percent; 2 percent, and 0 percent, respectively. Changing the scoring standard for the individual questions would, obviously, also affect the proportions classified as modern.

[6] These included *all* questions which in our opinion measured attitudes and could be unambiguously scored as having a "modern" and a "traditional" answer. Queries which did not meet these criteria were excluded from consideration. This meant mainly background questions, information-testing items, behavioral measures, adjustment measures, and the like. For details see Smith and Inkeles 1966.

kind in a structural sense and the potential psychic unity of mankind in the factual sense. In speaking of the unity of mankind in terms of psychic structure, I mean that the nature of the human personality, its inner "rules" of organization, is evidently basically similar everywhere. That is, the association of the elements or components of personality do not—and I think in substantial degree *cannot*—vary randomly or even relatively freely. There is evidently a system of inner, or what might be called structural, constraints in the organization of the human personality which increase the probability that those individuals—whatever their culture—who have certain personality traits will also more likely have others which "go with" some particular basic personality system. So far as the future is concerned, moreover, I believe that this structural unity provides the essential basis for greater factual psychic unity of mankind. Such a factual unity, not merely of structure but of *content*, can be attained insofar as the forces which tend to shape men in syndromes such as that defining the modern man become more widely and uniformly diffused throughout the world. This point requires that we consider the second issue to which our research addressed itself.

2. *What are the influences which make a man modern? Can any significant changes be brought about in men who are already past the formative early years and have already reached adulthood as relatively traditional men?*—Education has often been identified as perhaps the most important of the influences moving men away from traditionalism toward modernity in developing countries. Our evidence does not challenge this well-established conclusion. Both in zero-order correlations[7] and in the more complex multivariate regression analysis, the amount of formal schooling a man has had emerges as the single most powerful variable in determining his score on our measures. On the average, for every additional year a man spent in school he gains somewhere between two and three additional points on a scale of modernity scored from zero to 100.

Our modernity test is not mainly a test of what is usually learned in school, such as geography or arithmetic, but is rather a test of attitudes and values touching on basic aspects of a man's orientation to nature, to time, to fate, to politics, to women, and to God. If attending school brings about such substantial changes in these fundamental personal orientations, the school must be teaching a good deal more than is apparent in its syllabus on reading, writing, arithmetic, and even geography. The school is evidently also an important training ground for inculcating values. It teaches ways of orienting oneself toward others, and of conducting oneself, which could have

---

[7] The correlation (Pearsonian) between education and the overall measure of modernization ranges from 0.34 in Pakistan to 0.65 in India. The size of these coefficients is substantially affected by the educational "spread" in each sample. That spread is largest in India, with the cases rather evenly distributed from zero to thirteen years of education.

important bearing on the performance of one's adult roles in the structure of modern society. These effects of the school, I believe, reside not mainly in its formal, explicit, self-conscious pedagogic activity, but rather are inherent in the school as an *organization*. The modernizing effects follow not from the school's curriculum, but rather from its informal, implicit, and often unconscious program for dealing with its young charges.[8] The properties of the rational organization as a hidden pursuader—or, as I prefer to put it, as a silent and unobserved teacher—become most apparent when we consider the role of occupational experience in shaping the modern man.

We selected work in factories as the special focus of our attention in seeking to assess the effects of occupational experience in reshaping individuals according to the model of the modern man. Just as we view the school as communicating lessons beyond reading and arithmetic, so we thought of the factory as training men in more than the minimal lessons of technology and the skills necessary to industrial production. We conceived of the factory as an organization serving as a general school in attitudes, values, and ways of behaving which are more adaptive for life in a modern society. We reasoned that work in a factory should increase a man's sense of efficacy, make him less fearful of innovation, and impress on him the value of education as a general qualification for competence and advancement. Furthermore, we assumed that in subtle ways work in a factory might even deepen a man's mastery of arithmetic and broaden his knowledge of geography without the benefit of the formal lessons usually presented in the classroom. Indeed, the slogan for our project became, "The factory can be a school—a school for modernization."

Although our most sanguine hopes for the educational effects of the factory were not wholly fulfilled, the nature of a man's occupational experience does emerge as one of the strongest of the many types of variables we tested and is a quite respectable competitor to education in explaining a person's modernity. The correlation between time spent in factories and individual modernization scores is generally about 0.20.[9] With the effects of education controlled, the factory workers generally score eight to ten points higher on the modernization scale than do the cultivators.[10] There is little

---

[8] In much of the current discussion of the effectiveness and ineffectiveness of our schools, this aspect of the school's impact has been generally neglected. For an important exception see Dreeben 1968.

[9] However, in India it was only 0.08. We believe this to be not a condition peculiar to India, but to our industrial sample there. Everywhere else we sampled from fifty to more than 100 factories, including all types and sizes of industry, but in India our sample was limited to eleven factories, mostly large, and two of these were not truly industrial; they processed minerals.

[10] Keep in mind that the test has a theoretical range from zero to 100, and an observed range in our samples almost as great. With samples of our size, differences so large are significant at well above the .01 level. This test of significance and many of the other statistics presented in this report require that one meet certain conditions,

reason to interpret this difference as due to selection effects since separate controls show that new workers are not self- or preselected from the village on grounds of already being "modern" in personality or attitude. Nevertheless, we can apply a really stringent test by making our comparisons exclusively within the industrial labor force, pitting men with few years, of industrial experience against those with many, for example, five or more. When this is done, factory experience continues to show a substantial impact on individual modernization, the gain generally being about one point per year on the overall measure of modernization (OM).

It is notable that even when we restrict ourselves to tests of verbal fluency and to tests of geographical and political information, the more experienced workers show comparable advantages over the less experienced. To choose but one of many available examples, in Chile among men of rural origin and low education (one to five years)—and therefore suffering a double disadvantage in background—the proportion who could correctly locate Moscow as being the Soviet Russian capital rose from a mere 8 percent among the newly recruited industrial workers to 39 percent among those with middle experience and to 52 percent among the men who had eight years or more in the factory. Even among those with the double advantage of higher education (six to seven years) and urban origins, the proportion correctly identifying Moscow decidedly rose along with increasing industrial experience, the percentages being 68, 81, and 92 for the three levels of industrial experience, respectively. Summary evidence from all six countries is presented in table 32–1. It should be clear from these data that the factory is serving as a school even in those subjects generally considered the exclusive preserve of the classroom.[11]

To cite these modernizing effects of the factory is not to minimize the greater absolute impact of schooling. Using a gross occupational categorization which pits cultivators against industrial workers, we find that the classroom still leads the workshop as a school of modernization in the ratio of 3:2. Using the stricter test which utilizes factory workers only, grouped by length of industrial experience, it turns out that every additional year in school produces three times as much increment in one's modernization score

---

such as random sampling, which our data do not meet. Nevertheless, we present such statistics in order to provide a rough guide or standard of judgment, in the belief that to do so is preferable to leaving the reader without any criterion by which to evaluate one figure as against another. The reader must be cautioned, however, not to interpret any single statistic too literally. Conclusions should be drawn not from single figures but from the whole array of evidence across the six countries.

11 It will be noted that the pattern manifested in the other five countries is not shown in Israel. There the new workers are as well informed as the experienced. We attribute this not so much to the qualities of Israeli industry as to the nature of Israeli society. In that small, mobile, and urbanized environment, information tends to be rapidly and more or less evenly diffused throughout the nation and to all classes.

Table **32–1**

Percentage of Industrial Workers among Low[a] Educated Giving Correct Answers on Information Tests
(by Country and Months of Factory Experience)

Question	Argentina		Chile	
	3	*90*	*2*	*96*
Identify electrical apparatus[b]	37	63*	33	62***
Identify movie camera	60	69*	6	8
Cite 3 or more city problems	5	18	15	32***
Identify international leader[c]	26	67**	47	85***
Identify local leader	33	51	27	81***
Identify Moscow	36	60*	17	67***
Name 3 or more newspapers[d]	12	21	81	92
Approximate *N* cases.	40	70	90	130

* t-test score significant at the .05 level.
** Significance at the .01 level.
*** Significance at the .001 level or better.
[a] Data for high education groups on these seven questions in each country provide an additional 42 tests of which 33 were in accord with the conclusion that men with more factory experience score higher on information tests, 7 were inconclusive, and 2 contradictory.

as does a year in the factory, that is, the ratio goes to 3:1. The school seems clearly to be the more efficient training ground for individual modernization. Nevertheless, we should keep in mind that the school has the pupil full time, and it produces no incidental by-products other than its pupils. By contrast, the main business of the factory is to manufacture goods, and the changes it brings about in men—not insubstantial, as we have seen— are produced at virtually zero marginal cost. These personality changes in men are therefore a kind of windfall profit to a society undergoing the modernization process. Indeed, on this basis we may quite legitimately reverse the thrust of the argument, no longer asking why the school does so much better than the factory, but rather demanding to know why the school, with its full time control over the pupil's formal learning, does not perform a lot *better* than it does relative to the factory.

Our experience with the factory enables us to answer the secondary question posed for this section. Since men generally enter the factory as more or less matured adults, the effects observed to follow upon work in it clearly are late socialization effects. Our results indicate that substantial changes can be made in a man's personality or character, at least in the sense of attitudes, values, and basic orientations, long after what are usually considered the most important formative years. The experience of factory work is, of course, not the only form which this late socialization takes. It may come in the form of travel or migration, by exposure to the media of mass

India		Israel		Nigeria		East Pakistan	
				Country and Average Months Experience			
2	*72*	*3*	*84*	*3*	*48*	*1*	*48*
44	76***	80	88	91	91	50	70**
29	51**	84	88	68	70	9	37***
0	1	24	25	30	22	52	52*
1	31***	80	81	11	17	2	26**
15	52***	67	92	70	78	52	79*
1	16***	86	86	11	17	2	2
6	28**	75	61	81	91	20	44**
75	130	25	100	60	25	65	120

ᵇ In Pakistan, India, and Nigeria a picture of a radio was shown; in Argentina, Chile, and Israel, a picture of a tape recorder was used instead.

ᶜ Respondents were asked to identify Lyndon Johnson in Chile, Argentina and Israel; John F. Kennedy in Pakistan and India; Charles de Gaulle in Nigeria.

ᵈ In Argentina "name books" was substituted for "name newspapers."

Table **32–2**

Variance in Scores of Individual Modernization (OM-3) Accounted for by Early and Late Socialization Influences in Six Developing Countries (%)

Variable	Argentina	Chile	India	Israel	Nigeria	Pakistan
Early Socialization	28.8	26.0	52.4	22.1	23.0	22.2
Late Socialization	31.6	34.4	31.4	22.4	28.2	28.3

communication, or through later life in the city for men who grew up in the countryside.[12] We therefore combined our explanatory variables into two main sets, one representing *early* socialization experience—as in formal schooling—and the other reflecting *late* socialization experiences—as in one's adult occupation. We may observe (from table 2) that the late socialization experiences stake out a very respectable place for themselves in the competition to account for the observed variance in individual modernization scores.[13] In five countries the set of late socialization variables ex-

[12] The distinctive effectiveness of each of these potentially modernizing experiences, and others, will be assessed in the general report of our project in preparation under the authorship of Alex Inkeles and David H. Smith, to be titled *Becoming Modern.*

[13] In this regression analysis we utilized as the dependent variable a long form of

plained as much or more of the variance in modernization scores as did the combined early socialization variables, each set explaining between one-fourth and one-third of the variance.

In India the early socialization variables were decidely more powerful—accounting for 52 percent as against 31 percent of the variance explained by the late socialization variables. But in absolute terms, the late experiences are still doing well.[14] All in all, we take this to be impressive evidence for the possibility of bringing about substantial and extensive changes in the postadolescent personality as a result of socialization in adult roles.

3. *Are there any behavioral consequences arising from the attitudinal modernization of the individual? Do modern men act differently from the traditional man?*—Many people who hear of our research into individual modernization respond to it by acknowledging that we may have discovered what modern man *says*, but they are more interested in knowing what he *does*. This view overlooks the fact that taking a stand on a value question is also an action, and one which is often a very significant one for the respondent.[15] Our critics' comment also tends implicitly to underestimate the importance of a climate of expressed opinion as an influence on the action of others. And it probably assumes too arbitrarily that men use speech mainly to mislead rather than to express their true intentions. Nevertheless, the question is a legitimate one, and we addressed ourselves to it in our re-

---

the modernity scale OM-3, not as described in Smith and Inkeles 1966. Using seven principal predictor variables selected on theoretical and empirical grounds, we obtained multiple correlation coefficients of from about .57 to .76 in our six countries. We could thus account for between 32.5 percent and 59.0 percent of variance in the modernity scale scores. We then grouped the predictor variables in two sets. The set of early socialization variables included ethnicity, father's education, and own formal education. Late socialization variables included occupational type, consumer goods possessed (as a measure of standard of living), a measure of mass media exposure, and age. Each set was then used alone to ascertain what portion of the variance it could explain, as indicated in table 32–2. A discussion of the rationale for selecting these particular variables and grouping them so, as well as details of the linear multiple regression analysis, will be presented in a later publication by David H. Smith and Alex Inkeles.

[14] An alternative approach to estimating the relative contribution of the two sets of variables is to consider the decrement in the total variance explained when either set is withdrawn from the total pool of predictors. When this was done, the late socialization variables again emerged as more powerful everywhere except in India. The following set of figures presents, first, the decrement in the total variance explained resulting from withdrawal of the early socialization variables, and second, the decrement resulting from withdrawal of the late socialization variables from the total predictor pool: Argentina .127/.155; Chile .100/.184; India .276/.066; Israel .101/.104; Nigeria .068/.120; East Pakistan .070/.131. The fact that these decrements are so much smaller than the proportion of variance explained by each set alone indicates that to some extent the sets overlap, and when one set is dropped the other "takes over" for it in explaining some part of the variance.

[15] For example, it is an act of substantial civic courage for a young man in a tradi-

search. Although this part of our analysis is least advanced, we can offer some tentative conclusions on the basis of preliminary analysis.

We have the definite impression that the men we delineate as modern not only *talk* differently, they *act* differently. To explore this relationship we constructed a scale of modernization based exclusively on attitudinal questions, rigorously excluding those dealing with action rather than belief or feeling.[16] This measure of attitudinal modernity we then related to the behavioral measures in our survey. In all six countries we found action intimately related to attitude. At any given educational level, the man who was rated as modern on the attitudinal measure was also more likely to have joined voluntary organizations, to receive news from newspapers every day, to have talked to or written to an official about some public issue, and to have discussed politics with his wife. In many cases the proportion who claimed to have taken those actions was twice and even three times greater among those at the top as compared with those at the bottom of the scale of attitudinal modernity. Table 32–3 presents the relevant evidence. We should note, furthermore, that the items included in table 32–3 are illustrative of a larger group of about thirty individual questions and a dozen scales selected on theoretical grounds as appropriate tests of the relation between expressed attitudes and reported behavior. The items used for illustration were not arbitrarily selected as the only ones supporting our assumptions.[17]

The particular behaviors we cited above are all "self-reported." The

---

tional village to tell our interviewer he would be more inclined to follow the local coop leader than the village elders, or that he considers himself more a Nigerian than an Ife, or whatever is the local tribal basis of solidarity.

[16] In the project identification system this scale is designated OM-1. It includes only seventy-nine items selected from the larger pool by a panel of expert judges on the grounds that (*a*) they dealt only with attitudes, not information, political orientation, or action, and (*b*) they clearly were appropriate to test the original theoretical conception of modernity as more or less "officially" defined by the project staff.

[17] This assertion is supported by consideration of the relevant gamma statistics on the relationship of attitudinal modernity (OM scores) and information tests. For this purpose low- and high-education groups were tested separately (except in Pakistan), hence the number of gamma statistics obtained is twice the number of items used. The average gamma statistics shown below are based on three-part tables which included middle as well as low and high OM. Separate results are given for items and for scales, since the scales show the combined effects of groups of items and hence are not truly "independent" additional tests of the hypothesis under scrutiny.

Tests	*Country*					
	Argentina	*Chile*	*India*	*Israel*	*Nigeria*	*Pakistan*
Based on items:						
Average gamma	201	232	342	244	205	303
Number of tests	60	62	58	52	46	29
Based on scales:						
Average gamma	305	296	449	313	276	339
Number of tests	24	24	24	28	24	10

Table **32–3**

Percentage of High Educated[a] Engaging in Various Forms
of Modern Behavior   (by Country and Modernity Score)

Form of Behavior	Country and Modernity Score[b]			
	Argentina		Chile	
	Low	High	Low	High
Joined 2 or more organizations	26	48	50	61
Voted often	54	54	44	57
Talked politics with wife	40	57*	29	61***
Contacted official about public issue	2	9	4	17**
Read newspapers daily	40	77***	31	53**
High on geographic information scale	44	78***	23	60***
High on political information scale	22	56***	18	37***
High on consumer information scale	10	21**	7	39***
High on opposites test	50	76	36	63***
Approximate N cases.[c]	50	150	60	160

* t-test based on the extremes of the continuum on each form of behavior significant
at the .05 level.
** Significance at the .01 level.
*** Significance at the .001 level or better. All other t-tests of the relation were
below the .01 level.
[a] In each country the total sample was divided at the median into a "high" and "low"
educated group. The average number of years of education for the high group was:
Argentina: 7.6; Chile: 6.6; India: 10.2; Israel: 8.6; Nigeria: 8.5; and Pakistan: 4.8.

question inevitably arises as to whether then we are not merely testing attitudinal consistency—or merely consistency in response—rather than any
strict correspondence between modernity of *attitude* and modernity of *behavior*. The answer is partly given by considering the relation of attitudinal
modernity to our several tests of information. These questions did not deal
with "mere" attitudes, but obliged the respondent to prove objectively
whether he really knew something. Quite consistently the men who were
more modern on the attitude measures validated their status as modern men
by more often correctly identifying a movie camera, naming the office held
by Nehru, and locating the city of Moscow. Men with the same education
but with unequal modernity scores performed very differently on these tests,
with those more modern in attitude scoring high on the tests of information
two or more times as often as those classified as traditional in attitude.
The details are summarized in the lower part of table 32–3, which presents
summary scale results.

We conducted a further and more exact check on the extent to which
self-reported behavior is fact rather than fantasy by comparing what men

			Country and Modernity Score				
India		*Israel*		*Nigeria*		*East Pakistan*	
Low	High	Low	High	Low	High	Low	High
32	31	2	6	86	97	0	6
60	65	76	86	. .	. . . . .	. .	. . . . .
74	80	46	72**	50	65	65	83*
20	26	17	27	11	21	5	15
32	61**	36	81	63	84***	35	42
20	51***	29	75***	7	48***	9	53*
22	65***	36	72***	20	48***	7	39**
67	94*	29	53**	84	89	23	52***
59	86***	31	57***	59	71	47	78***
55	115	40	110	60	120	45	125

[b] The range of Overall Modernity Scores was split into "low"—bottom 25%, "middle"—middle 50%, and "high"—top 25% for each country's *entire* sample. Modernity scores are highly correlated with education. Since in this table only the high educated are represented, more men fall into the category of those with high as against low modernity scores.

[c] Ns are approximate due to the disqualification of part of the sample on certain questions, e.g. those legally under age could not be expected to "vote often."

claimed to do with objective tests of their actual performance. For example, we asked everyone whether or not he could read. Individuals certainly might have been tempted to exaggerate their qualifications. But later in the interview we administered a simple literacy test, asking our respondents to read a few lines from local newspaper stories we had graded for difficulty. In most settings less than 1 percent of the men who had claimed they could read failed the literacy test. They proved objectively to have been accurately and honestly reporting their reading ability. Similarly, men who claimed to use the mass media regularly were—as they should have been— better able to correctly identify individuals and places figuring prominently in world news. In Nigeria, for example, among experienced workers of low education, the proportion who could correctly identify de Gaulle as the president of the French Republic was 57 percent among those who claimed to pay only modest attention to the mass media, 83 percent among those who asserted they listened or read more often, and 93 percent among those who claimed to read a newspaper or listen to the radio almost every day. Many additional examples which test the internal consistency of attitude

Table **32–4**
Percent[a] among Low Educated[b] Whose Performance on a Test of Behavior Accords with Their Oral Claim (by Claim and Country)

Objective Behavior (%) and Claim	Country					
	Argentina	Chile	India	Israel	Nigeria	East Pakistan
Naming 3 newspapers among those who claim to read papers:						
Rarely/Never	[c]	73[d] (356) ***	13 (582) ***	68 (28)	59 (71) ***	38
Daily		98 (85)	60 (63)	90 (119)	85 (152)	45
Correctly identifying international leader among those claiming mainly interested in:						
Other news	43 (299) **	59 (414)	8 (668)	79 (216)	7 (276)	4 (459)
World news	73 (30)	76 (29)	12 (26)	84 (68)	8 (73)	10 (10)
Correctly identifying international leader who claim on total information media exposure they are:						
Low	14 (51) ***	45 (196) ***	1 (71) ***	73 (45)	4 (78) *	0 (85) **
High	79 (29)	79 (76)	18 (11)	84 (38)	17 (18)	10 (40)

Correctly identifying Washington who claim on total information media exposure they are:						
Low	14 (51)	43 (196)	3 (71)	64 (44)	3 (78)	2 (85)
High	72 (29)	70 (76)	7 (28)	90 (38)	28 (18)	3 (40)
(Low vs. High difference)	***	***		*	***	***
Who can read at least a little among those who claim they:						
Can read	c	c	99 (408)	99 (266)	99 (346)	74 (80)

* .05 level of significance reached in t-tests of the difference in the proportion manifesting a given behavior in the case of those falling at the extremes of the continuum on each "claim."

** .01 level of significance.

*** .001 level of significance.

a Percentages are a proportion of the cells' base N who manifested a given behavior. These cell Ns represent all those of low education who made the indicated behavioral claim, e.g., claimed to read a newspaper daily.

b The average number of years of education by country was Argentina: 4.5; Chile: 3.7; India: 1.0; Israel: 5.1; Nigeria: 6.2; and Pakistan: .2.

c Data unavailable for country.

d Includes "a few times a week" in "rarely or never" category.

and behavior are summarized in table 32–4.[18] Clearly, the men who claim to have the attributes we score as modern give a better account of themselves on objective tests of performance. We may conclude not only that modern is as modern does, but also that modern *does* as modern *speaks*.

4. *Is the consequence of the individual modernization inevitably personal disorganization and psychic strain; or can men go through this process of rapid sociocultural change without deleterious consequences?*—Few ideas have been more popular among the social philosophers of the nineteenth and twentieth centuries than the belief that industrialization is a kind of plague which disrupts social organization, destroys cultural cohesion, and uniformly produces personal demoralization and even disintegration. Much the same idea has been expressed by many anthropologists who fear—and often have witnessed—the destruction of indigenous cultures under the massive impact of their contact with the colossus represented by the European-based colonial empires. But neither the establishment of European industry in the nineteenth century, nor the culture crisis of small preliterate peoples overwhelmed by the tidal wave of colonial expansion may be adequate models for understanding the personal effects of industrialization and urbanization in developing nations.

To test the impact on personal adjustment resulting from contact with modernizing influences in our six developing countries, we administered the Psychosomatic Symptoms Test as part of our regular questionnaire. This

---

[18] For lack of space, table 32–4 shows the percentage whose behavior validated their oral "claim" only in the case of those falling at the extremes of the continuum on each "claim," and the *t*-tests are based on these same extremes. To leave no doubt that this outcome was not a fortuitous result of considering only the extremes, we note the gamma statistics for the full cross-tabulations including all steps in both the oral claim and the behavioral test. The five tests of the relation between claim and behavior applied in six countries yield a potential thirty tests, but some were inapplicable in certain instances. The procedure was repeated separately for the "low" and "high" educated, divided at the median in each country. For the low educated, where twenty-seven of the tests were applicable, the association of claim and behavior was in the expected direction in all cases, and the gammas ranged from 0.011 to 0.877, with a mean of 0.351 and a median of 0.334. For the high educated, the hypothesis could be tested in twenty-three full cross-tabulations. All but two of the associations were in the expected direction, the gammas ranging from −0.123 to 0.690, and over this range the mean gamma was 0.309 and the median 0.276.

[19] Variants of the test were used with the Yoruba as reported by Leighton et al. 1963, and the Zulu as reported by Scotch and Geiger 1963–64. Details on the form of the test as we used it and the results of our investigation were presented by Alex Inkeles and David Smith to the Eighth Congress of the International Anthropological Association at Tokyo-Kyoto in September 1968 under the title "The Fate of Personal Adjustment in the Process of Modernization," and will appear in the *International Journal of Comparative Sociology*, 1970.

test is widely acknowledged to be the best available instrument for cross-cultural assessment of psychic stress.[19] Using groups carefully matched on all other variables, we successively tested the effect of education, migration from the countryside to the city, factory employment, urban residence, and contact with the mass media as these modernizing experiences might affect scores on the Psychosomatic Symptoms Test. No one of these presumably deleterious influences consistently produced statistically significant evidence of psychic stress as judged by the test. Those who moved to the city as against those who continued in the village, those with many years as compared to those with few years of experience in the factory, those with much contact with the mass media as against those with little exposure to radio, newspaper, and movies, show about the same number of psychosomatic symptoms.

In each of six countries, we tested fourteen different matched groups, comparing whose who migrated with those who did not; men with more years in the factory with those with fewer, etc. Because some of these matches did not apply in certain countries, we were left with seventy-four more or less independent tests of the proposition that being more exposed to the experiences identified with the process of modernization produces more psychosomatic symptoms. Disregarding the size of the difference and considering only the sign of the correlation between exposure to modernization and psychosomatic symptoms as (+) or (—), it turns out that in thirty-four instances the results are in accord with the theory that modernization is psychologically upsetting, but in forty other matches the results are opposed to the theory. Very few of the differences in either direction, furthermore, were statistically significant. Indeed, the frequency of such statistically significant correlations was about what you would expect by chance. Of these significant differences, furthermore, only two supported the hypothesis while two contradicted it. This again suggests that only chance is at work here. We must conclude, therefore, that the theory which identifies contact with modernizing institutions and geographical and social mobility as certainly deleterious to psychic adjustment is not supported by the evidence. Indeed, it is cast in serious doubt. Whatever is producing the symptoms—and the test does everywhere yield a wide range of scores—it is something other than differential contact with the sources of modernization which is responsible.

Life does exact its toll. Those who have been long in the city and in industry but who have failed to rise in skill and earnings are somewhat more distressed. But this outcome can hardly be charged to the deleterious effects of contact with the modern world. Perhaps if we had studied the unemployed who came to the city with high hopes but failed to find work, we might have found them to have more psychosomatic symptoms. If we were faced with this finding, however, it would still be questionable whether the observed condition should be attributed to the effects of modernization. The fault would seem to lie equally in the inability of traditional agriculture to provide men with economic sustenance sufficient to hold them on the land.

We conclude, then, that modernizing institutions, per se, do not lead to greater psychic stress. We leave open the question whether the process of societal modernization in general increases social disorganization and then increases psychic tension for those experiencing such disorganization. But we are quite ready to affirm that extensive contact with the institutions introduced by modernization—such as the school, the city, the factory, and the mass media—is not in itself conducive to greater psychic stress.

Men change their societies. But the new social structures they have devised may in turn shape the men who live within the new social order. The idea that social structures influence the personal qualities of those who participate in them is, of course, as old as social science and may be found in the writings of the earliest social philosophers. Its most dramatic expression, relevant to us, was in the work of Marx, who enunciated the principle that men's consciousness is merely a reflection of their relation to the system of ownership of the means of production. The rigidity of Marx's determinism, and the counterdetermination of many people to preserve an image of man's spiritual independence and of the personal autonomy and integrity of the individual, generated profound resistance to these ideas. The idea that ownership or nonownership of the means of production determines consciousness is today not very compelling. To focus on ownership, however, is to concentrate on the impact of macrostructural forces in shaping men's attitudes and values at the expense of studying the significance of microstructural factors. Yet it may be that these microstructural features, such as are embedded in the locale and the nature of work, are prime sources of influences on men's attitudes and behavior.

In reviewing the results of our research on modernization, one must be struck by the exceptional stability with which variables such as education, factory experience, and urbanism maintain the absolute and relative strength of their impact on individual modernization despite the great variation in the culture of the men undergoing the experience and in the levels of development characterizing the countries in which they live.[20] This is not to deny the ability of the macrostructural elements of the social order to exert a determining influence on men's life condition and their response to it. But such macrostructural forces can account for only one part of the variance in individual social behavior, a part whose relative weight we have not yet measured with the required precision. When we attain that precision we may find some confirmation of popular theories, but we are also certain to discover some of them to be contradicted by the data—just as we have in our study of microstructural factors. The resolution of the competition be-

---

[20] This idea is more fully elaborated in Inkeles 1960.

tween these two theoretical perspectives cannot be attained by rhetoric. It requires systematic measurement and the confrontation of facts however far they are marshalled in the service of ideas. The facts *we* have gathered leave *us* in no doubt that microstructural forces have great power to shape attitudes, values, and behavior in regular ways at standard or constant rates within a wide variety of macrostructural settings.

PART V

Levels of Change

Introduction

Society may be viewed as a set of Chinese nesting boxes; smaller social units exist and function within larger ones, and these within still larger ones. While all these "boxes" ultimately have the same building stones, each has some characteristics of its own, or "emergent properties," as they are called. Some rely chiefly on formal, others mainly on informal communication; some may use force, others are forbidden to use it; and so on.

The following selections call attention to the comparative study of change on various social levels, a dimension of the study of change that has hardly been explored. They illustrate the importance of taking into account emergent properties.

The studies and work of Kurt Lewin and Elton Mayo have initiated a school often referred to as "group dynamics" or "human relations." Its influence is especially large in social psychology and education, as well as in the applied social sciences; it has been somewhat critically received by several leading sociologists.[1]

From the selection here presented, it might seem at first as if Lewin were dealing with modification in the behavior of individuals, more specifically with changes in their food habits. But it soon becomes clear that actually Lewin is interested in the dynamics of the social climate of small,

---

[1] The student interested in additional reading on this school might turn to Dorwin Cartwright and Alvin Zander, eds.. *Group Dynamics: Research and Theory* (2nd ed.; Chicago: Row, Peterson and Co., 1960); and to Warren B. Bennis, Kenneth D. Beme, Robert Chin, eds., *The Planning of Social Change* (New York: Holt, Rinehart & Winston, 1961). For a critical discussion of this school and arguments in its favor see various articles collected in Part II of Amitai Etzioni, ed., *Complex Organizations: A Sociological Reader* (New York: Holt, Rinehart & Winston, 1961).

face-to-face groups. As a result of several experimental studies, only one of which could be presented here, Lewin concluded that people are more reluctant to modify their behavior—and if they do, are less likely to persist in their new behavior—if they are approached as individuals, that they are more apt to change if they are approached as members of a group, so that their individual modification of behavior goes hand in hand with changes in the climate of the group and that these personal modifications are more likely to persist if they can be anchored in group support. As Lewin sees it, the individual, in need of his group's approval, tends to adjust his behavior to the group's standards. Hence it is easier for him to change when the group standards change as well.

The Lewin study serves to call attention to a major controversy within social science, of much importance to the study of social change: the relative flexibility, as against stability, of the personality. The orthodox Freudians are on the one extreme, often more extreme than the master himself. They view the basic personality as relatively stabilized in early childhood, hence determined largely by the parent–child relationship. As the person moves from group to group through his social life, he expresses his personality, but it hardly changes. At the other extreme are some students of Lewin, more extreme than the master himself, who view the personality as a kind of radar that constantly picks up clues from the immediate social environment and adjusts behavior to it. Hence the ability to change is almost unlimited.

Most social scientists take some kind of middle view, recognizing both the role of personality and that of social groups in determining behavior and viewing the two as factors affecting each other. But there are important differences among them, according to the relative weight they tend to attribute to the two factors. Since the evidence is far from clearcut, each student will have to decide for himself which interpretation is more satisfactory to him. The conclusions reached are, of course, of much consequence for one's view of such problems as the efficacy and limits of adult education, rehabilitation of criminals, and therapy of mental patients.

Moving to larger and more encompassing social units, Haire deals with collectivities which specialize in the service of specific goals, often referred to as complex organizations, while Park deals with the ethnic group, one kind of collectivity that has no such goals. Both Haire and Park work with neo-evolutionary models, but while Haire is ultimately concerned, as are most students of organizations, with the question of effectiveness, Park is interested in that of integration and elimination of social conflict. Haire deals with the growth of one unit, Park with the merger of two or more.

The special characteristics of complex organizations are that they tend to be large, bureaucratic, run from one center with an effort to enforce a disciplined service to a given set of goals. Many organizations, at least of the general type Haire discusses, include a large number of persons that only partially or indirectly accept the organizational goals. This creates problems of communication and morale, which become more pronounced the larger the organization grows. Here, Haire resorts to a biological model. When the organism evolves and becomes more complex and differentiated, it develops a specialized nervous system for the purpose of intrasystem communication and coordination. Similarly, when the organization grows, becomes more complex, and develops a specialization of functions, it too must face up to the increased problem of integration and must counter the growing communication blocks. This is why the organization, as it grows, must provide for an increased ratio of clerical personnel largely concerned with communication and for the disproportionate growth of staff in general, one of whose functions it is to provide information for coordination, control, and integration.

Park studies the relationships between ethnic or racial groups as they change under the impact of their mutual interaction. Reviewing a large variety of cultural contacts and group interaction, Park finds a specific pattern repeating itself, a set of stages often referred to as a "natural history." The stages, formulated slightly differently in various of Park's articles, are four: contact, competition, accommodation, and assimilation. Of much interest is Park's notion of the source of the forces that move intergroup relations along the course from contact to assimilation: they lie in these relations themselves. Each phase triggers certain processes that carry the relationship a step further. Contact between two groups leads to competition, which brings them to know each other more intimately, which results in accommodation, which creates the conditions for deeper interaction, which removes the barrier to assimilation. The central point is that, after the initial step, the process is one of increasingly harmonious relations, of declining differences. The harmonious relationship begins with the formation of economic, instrumental ties, proceeding to much deeper social, emotional, normative bonds.

Park had little doubt that all social groups follow these steps, in this order, and that eventually not just ethnic but racial groups too will assimilate (though in his earlier writings this position is somewhat more qualified). The key word is "eventually," which accompanies many of Park's statements and makes it practically impossible to validate or invalidate his assertions. Whether all intergroup relations really go through the same set of stages, in the same order, is a question that must be answered empirically. While the evidence is far from clear, a case at least equally strong could be made for the proposition that they follow different patterns which lead to different "end-states." Arnold Rose ties to his analysis of race relations, a parallel analysis of the more encompassing societal forces also in play. He sees as the major forces bringing about the rapid change in race relations since 1940, continuing industrialization and technological advance, high degree of mobility among the American people, economic prosperity, the organization and political education of minority groups, increased American awareness of anti-racist world opinion, Supreme Court support for civil rights and, to a lesser extent, support by other federal branches of government and Northern state governments, of efforts for more equal implementation of civil rights.

According to Rose, the main forces sustaining the subordination and segregation of Negroes are the inertial ones of tradition and the status quo. The single most important specific factor has been the counter-mobilization of racist opposition, e.g., White Citizens Councils and the resurgence of the K.K.K. There is no longer, however, any grounding in economic and political conditions for racist ideology; it is now merely the expression of a traditional psychology. Few sociologists would agree with all of Rose's analysis; yet more than any other selection we could have chosen to include given the limits of available space, Rose seems to us to have focused his inquiry on the proper analytic level. One may challenge his answers, but he has surely raised some crucial questions.

Riesman moves the discussion of change to a higher level, that of the study of societies. The study of units of this size and complexity confronts the contemporary sociologist with serious dilemmas. On the one hand, there is the danger of statements that are extremely difficult to document, on the other, of shying away from the study of societies altogether. Riesman approaches the subject in the manner of the classical sociologist, studying society and its course, leaving much of the detailed documentation to his colleagues and students.

Before the full meaning of Riesman's insight can be understood, it is important to realize that his discussion of the changes in the character structure of modern man is actually concerned with the changes in the character of society; like many an anthropologist, he learns about societal change by studying changes in the characters of its typical members.

Riesman's conclusion was probably the most oft-cited statement of sociology in the 1950's. He found that the behavior based on self-direction, on internalized sets of values, often referred to as the Protestant Ethic, is being replaced by behavior largely directed from the outside by the social environment. One might say that Riesman found that character can be explained neither by an orthodox Freudian nor by a strict Lewinian view, but that a shift has occurred from behavior approximating the one type to behavior approximating the other.

The normative issues Riesman's findings raise are evident, nor does Riesman avoid them. He does not think that the moral value of the inner-directed person and his way of life is "higher" than that of the other-directed. Both types have their appealing and appalling sides; the inner-directed person is likely to be self-reliant but rigid and intolerant; the other-directed person is flexible but spineless. Riesman closes by depicting a third personality type that emerges as a synthesis of the character struggle of the two, that of the autonomous man. The autonomous man is not compulsive either in following his milieu or in ignoring it. He relates to people through affection and to objects through creativity; he is both sociable and creative. At present the autonomous type is in the minority, but it may become a "saving remnant," laying the groundwork for a new society, Riesman's utopia.

It is important to note that these concepts were developed by Riesman in the early fifties. International developments and their repercussions on the national society have resulted in several major changes that could not have been foreseen on the basis of an analysis of American society alone. Using Riesman's terms, there seems to have occurred a heightening of other-directedness in some areas and a considerable revival of inner-directedness in others. The pressure of the global struggle with Communism brought first the McCarthy period, in which intellectual and political inner-directedness was highly penalized. In the late sixties and early seventies there has been some untightening, though some of the pressure of earlier periods has become institutionalized. In an effort to counter the impact of an international movement supporting radical social changes in other societies, and on the global level, America has largely curtailed the number, importance, and power of groups and individuals supporting such changes in its own society.

As mentioned above these changes in American society must be accounted for, at least in part, by relating them to changes on the next higher level of analysis—the international level. Basically, the global system differs from that of societies in that it has no implementation in a state. National societies are social groups that share not only values and social bonds, but also an integration supported by police forces, courts, and prisons. While the tendency of sociologists is to underplay the role of this feature of society, this is the major demarcation line that distinguishes it from other social collectives, *e.g.*, ethnic groups, private organizations, and international systems. The importance of such a framework of coercion lies in the fact that its potential or actual use is likely to limit the conflicts resulting from social change, thus both limiting the scope and pace of change and at the same time safeguarding, to a large extent, the continued peaceful adjustment of society to new needs and pressures. The international system is not only practically without an order-enforcing framework (despite the few instances of use of force by the United Nations to impose order, as in the Middle East and the Congo), but it also has far fewer common values, universal sentiments, and shared interests than the national system. The application of societal theories to international systems is most helpful when it is used to ask under what conditions integrative forces outweigh the conflict arousing ones and under what conditions community building can take place. This is the ultimate anchorage of macro-sociological analysis: viewing the world as one system.*

---

* For additional discussion, see Amitai Etzioni, *The Active Society* Free Press, New York, 1968; chapters 19 and 20.

CHAPTER 33

KURT LEWIN

Group Dynamics and Social Change

Promoting Change: Lecture versus Group Decision

A preliminary experiment in changing food habits[1] was conducted with six Red Cross groups of volunteers organized for home nursing. Groups ranged in size from thirteen to seventeen members. The objective was to increase the use of beef hearts, sweetbreads, and kidneys. If one considers the psychological forces which kept housewives from using these intestinals, one is tempted to think of rather deepseated aversions requiring something like psychoanalytical treatment. Doubtless a change in this respect is a much more difficult task than, for instance, the introduction of a new vegetable such as escarole. There were, however, only 45 minutes available.

In three of the groups attractive lectures were given which linked the problem of nutrition with the war effort, emphasized the vitamin and mineral value of the three meats, giving detailed explanations with the aid of charts. Both the health and economic aspects were stressed. The preparation of these meats was discussed in detail, as well as techniques for avoiding those characteristics to which aversions were oriented (odor, texture, appearance, etc.). Mimeographed recipes were distributed. The lecturer was able to arouse the interest of the groups by giving hints of her own methods for preparing these "delicious dishes" and her success with her own family.

For the other three groups Mr. Alex Bavelas developed the following

From Kurt Lewin, "Group Decision and Social Change," in Eleanor E. Maccoby, Theodore M. Newcomb, and Eugene L. Hartley, eds., *Readings in Social Psychology* (New York: Holt, Rinehart, and Winston, Inc., 1958). Reprinted by permission of the publisher.

[1] The studies on nutrition discussed in this article were conducted at the Child Welfare Research Station of the State University of Iowa for the Food Habits Committee of the National Research Council (Executive Secretary, Margaret Mead).

procedure of group decision. Again the problem of nutrition was linked with that of the war effort and general health. After a few minutes, a discussion was started to see whether housewives could be induced to participate in a program of change without attempting any high-pressure salesmanship. The group discussion about "housewives like themselves" led to an elaboration of the obstacles which a change in general and particularly change toward sweetbreads, beef hearts, and kidneys would encounter, such as the dislike of the husband, the smell during cooking, etc. The nutrition expert offered the same remedies and recipes for preparation which were presented in the lectures to the other groups. But in these groups preparation techniques were offered after the groups had become sufficiently involved to be interested in knowing whether certain obstacles could be removed.

In the earlier part of the meeting a census was taken on how many women had served any of these foods in the past. At the end of the meeting, the women were asked by a showing of hands who was willing to try one of these meats within the next week.

A follow-up showed that only 3 per cent of the women who heard the lectures served one of the meats never served before, whereas after group decision 32 per cent served one of them.

If one is to understand the basis of this striking difference, several factors may have to be considered.

Degree of Involvement

Lecturing is a procedure in which the audience is chiefly passive. The discussion, if conducted correctly, is likely to lead to a much higher degree of involvement. The procedure of group decision in this experiment follows a step-by-step method designed (a) to secure high involvement and (b) not to impede freedom of decision. The problem of food changes was discussed in regard to "housewives like yourselves" rather than in regard to themselves. This minimized resistance to considering the problems and possibilities in an objective, unprejudiced manner, in much the same way as such resistance has been minimized in interviews which use projective techniques, or in a sociodrama which uses an assumed situation of role-playing rather than a real situation.

Motivation and Decision

The prevalent theory in psychology assumes action to be the direct result of motivation. I am inclined to think that we will have to modify this theory. We will have to study the particular conditions under which a motivating constellation leads or does not lead to a decision or to an equivalent process through which a state of "considerations" (indecisiveness) is changed into a state where the individual has "made up his mind" and is ready for action, although he may not act at that moment.

The act of decision is one of those transitions. A change from a situation of undecided conflict to decision does not mean merely that the forces toward one alternative become stronger than those toward the other alternative. If this were the case, the resultant force should frequently be extremely small. A decision rather means that the potency of one alternative has become zero or is so decidedly diminished that the other alternative and the corresponding forces dominate the situation. This alternative itself might be a compromise. After the decision people may feel sorry and change their decision. We cannot speak of a real decision, however, before one alternative has become dominant so far as action is concerned. If the opposing forces in a conflict merely change so that the forces in one direction become slightly greater than in the other direction, a state of blockage or extremely inhibited action results rather than that clear onesided action which follows a real decision.

Lecturing may lead to a high degree of interest. It may affect the motivation of the listener. But it seldom brings about a definite decision on the part of the listener to take a certain action at a specific time. A lecture is not often conducive to decision.

Evidence from everyday experience and from some preliminary experiments by Bavelas in a factory indicate that even group discussions, although usually leading to a higher degree of involvement, as a rule do not lead to a decision. It is very important to emphasize this point. Although group discussion is in many respects different from lectures, it shows no fundamental difference on this point.

Of course, there is a great difference in asking for a decision after a lecture or after a discussion. Since discussion involves active participation of the audience and a chance to express motivations corresponding to different alternatives, the audience might be more ready "to make up its mind," that is, to make a decision after a group discussion than after a lecture. A group discussion gives the leader a better indication of where the audience stands and what particular obstacles have to be overcome.

In the experiment on hand, we are dealing with a group decision after discussion. The decision itself takes but a minute or two. (It was done through raising of hands as an answer to the question: Who would like to serve kidney, sweetbreads, beef hearts next week?) The act of decision, however, should be viewed as a very important process of giving dominance to one of the alternatives, serving or not serving. It has an effect of freezing this motivational constellation for action. We will return to this point later.

Individual versus Group

The experiment does not try to bring about a change of food habits by an approach to the individual as such. Nor does it use the "mass approach" characteristic of radio and newspaper propaganda. Closer scrutiny shows that both the mass approach and the individual approach place the individual in a quasiprivate, psychologically isolated situation with himself and his own ideas. Although he may, physically, be part of a group listening to a lecture, for example, he finds himself, psychologically speaking, in an "individual situation."

The present experiment approaches the individual as a member of a face-to-face group. We know, for instance, from experiments in level of aspiration[2] that goal setting is strongly dependent on group standards. Experience in leadership training and in many areas of re-education, such as re-education regarding alcoholism or delinquency,[3] indicates that it is easier to change the ideology and social practice of a small group handled together than of single individuals. One of the reasons why "group-carried changes" are more readily brought about seems to be the unwillingness of the individual to depart too far from group standards; he is likely to change only if the group changes. We will return to this problem.

One may try to link the greater effectiveness of group decision procedures to the fact that the lecture reaches the individual in a more individualistic fashion than group discussion. If a change of sentiment of the group becomes apparent during the discussion, the individual will be more ready to come along.

It should be stressed that in our case the decision which follows the group discussion does not have the character of a decision in regard to a group goal; it is rather a decision about individual goals in a group setting.

Expectation

The difference between the results of the lectures and the group decision may be due to the fact that only after group decision did the discussion leader mention that an inquiry would be made later as to whether a new food was introduced into the family diet.

Leader Personality

The difference in effectiveness may be due to differences in leader personality. The nutritionist and the housewife who did the lecturing were persons of recognized ability, experience, and success. Still, Mr. Bavelas, who led the discussion and subsequent decision, is an experienced group worker and doubtless of unusual ability in this field.

To determine which of these or other factors are important, a number of

---

[2] K. Lewin, "Behavior and Development as a Function of the Total Situation," in L. Carmichael, ed., *Manual of Child Psychology* (New York: John Wiley, 1946), pp. 791-844.

[3] K. Lewin and P. Grabbe, eds., "Problems of Re-education," *Journal of Social Issues*, I (1945), No. 3.

systematic variations have to be carried out. To determine, for instance, the role of the decision as such, one can compare the effect of group discussion with and without decision. To study the role of group involvement and the possibility of sensing the changing group sentiment, one could introduce decisions after both, lecture and discussion, and compare their effects.

•

Quasistationary Social Equilibriums and the Problem of Permanent Change

The Objective of Change

The objective of social change might concern the nutritional standard of consumption, the economic standard of living, the type of group relation, the output of a factory, the productivity of an educational team. It is important that a social standard to be changed does not have the nature of a "thing," but of a "process." A certain standard of consumption, for instance, means that a certain action—such as making certain decisions, buying, preparing and canning certain food in a family—occurs with a certain frequency within a given period. Similarly, a certain type of group relations means that within a given period certain friendly and hostile actions and reactions of a certain degree of severity occur between the members of two groups. Changing group relations or changing consumption means changing the level at which these multitudinous events proceed. In other words, the "level" of consumption, of friendliness, or of productivity is to be characterized as the aspect of an ongoing social process.

Any planned social change will have to consider a multitude of factors characteristic for the particular case. The change may require a more-or-less unique combination of educational and organizational measures; it may depend upon quite different treatments or ideology, expectation, and organization. Still, certain general formal principles always have to be considered.

The Conditions of a Stable Quasistationary Equilibrium

The study of the conditions for change begins appropriately with an analysis of the conditions for "no change," that is, for the state of equilibrium.

From what has been just discussed, it is clear that by a state of "no social change" we do not refer to a stationary, but to a quasistationary equilibrium; that is, to a state comparable to that of a river which flows with a given velocity in a given direction during a certain time interval. A social change is comparable to a change in the velocity or direction of that river.

A number of statements can be made in regard to the conditions of quasistationary equilibrium.

(1) The strength of forces which tend to lower that standard of social life should be equal and opposite to the strength of forces which tend to

raise its level. The resultant of forces on the line of equilibrium should therefore be zero.

(2) Since we have to assume that the strength of social forces always shows variations, a quasistationary equilibrium presupposes that the forces against raising the standard increase with the amount of raising and that the forces against lowering increase (or remain constant) with the amount of lowering. . . .

(3) It is possible to change the strength of the opposing forces without changing the level of social conduct. In this case the tension (degree of conflict) increases.

Two Basic Methods of Changing Levels of Conduct

For any type of social management, it is of great practical importance that levels of quasistationary equilibriums can be changed in either of two ways: by adding forces in the desired direction, or by diminishing opposing forces. If a change from the level L_1 to L_2 is brought about by increasing the forces toward L_2, the secondary effects should be different from the case where the same change of level is brought about by diminishing the opposing forces.

In both cases the equilibrium might change to the same new level. The secondary effect should, however, be quite different. In the first case, the process on the new level would be accompanied by a state of relatively high tension; in the second case, by a state of relatively low tension. Since increase of tension above a certain degree is likely to be paralleled by higher aggressiveness, higher emotionality, and lower constructiveness, it is clear that as a rule the second method will be preferable to the high pressure method.

The group decision procedure which is used here attempts to avoid high pressure methods and is sensitive to resistance to change. In an experiment by Bavelas on changing production in factory work, for instance, no attempt was made to set the new production goal by majority vote, because a majority vote forces some group members to produce more than they consider appropriate. These individuals are likely to have some inner resistance. Instead, a procedure was followed by which a goal was chosen on which everyone could agree fully.

It is possible that the success of group decision and particularly the permanency of the effect is, in part, due to the attempt to bring about a favorable decision by removing counterforces within the individuals, rather than by applying outside pressure.

•

Social Habits and Group Standards

Viewing a social stationary process as the result of a quasistationary equilibrium, one may expect that any added force will change the level of the process. The idea of "social habit" seems to imply that, in spite of the application of a force, the level of the social process will not change because of some type of "inner resistance" to change. To overcome this inner resistance, an additional force seems to be required, a force sufficient to "break the habit," to "unfreeze" the custom.

Many social habits are anchored in the relation between the individuals and certain group standards. An individual may differ in his personal level of conduct from the level which represents group standards by a certain amount. If the individual should try to diverge "too much" from group standards, he would find himself in increasing difficulties. He would be ridiculed, treated severely, and finally ousted from the group. Most individuals, therefore, stay pretty close to the standard of the groups they belong to or wish to belong to. In other words, the group level itself acquires value. It becomes a positive valence corresponding to a central force field with the force keeping the individual in line with the standards of the group.

Individual Procedures and Group Procedures of Changing Social Conduct

If the resistance to change depends partly on the value which the group standard has for the individual, the resistance to change should diminish if one diminishes the strength of the value of the group standard or changes the level perceived by the individual as having social value.

This second point is one of the reasons for the effectiveness of "group-carried" changes resulting from procedures which approach the individuals as part of face-to-face groups. Perhaps one might expect single individuals to be more pliable than groups of like-minded individuals. However, experience in leadership training, in changing of food habits, work production, criminality, alcoholism, prejudices, all indicate that it is usually easier to change individuals formed into a group than to change any one of them separately.[4] As long as group standards are unchanged, the individual will resist changes more strongly the further he is to depart from group standards. If the group standard itself is changed, the resistance which is due to the relation between individual and group standard is eliminated.

Changing as a Three-Step Procedure: Unfreezing, Moving, and Freezing of a Level

A change toward a higher level of group performance is frequently short-lived: after a "shot in the arm," group life soon returns to the previous level. This indicates that it does not suffice to define the objective of a planned change in group performance as the reaching of a different level. Perma-

---

4 "Problems of Re-education," *op. cit.*

nency of the new level, or permanency for a desired period, should be included in the objective. A successful change includes therefore three aspects: unfreezing (if necessary) the present level L_1, moving to the new level L_2, and freezing group life on the new level. Since any level is determined by a force field, permanency implies that the new force field is made relatively secure against change.

The "unfreezing" of the present level may involve quite different problems in different cases. Allport [5] has described the "catharsis" which seems to be necessary before prejudices can be removed. To break open the shell of complacency and self-righteousness, it is sometimes necessary to bring about deliberately an emotional stir-up.

Although in some cases the procedure is relatively easily executed, in others it requires skill and presupposes certain general conditions. Managers rushing into a factory to raise production by group decisions are likely to encounter failure. In social management as in medicine, there are no patent medicines and each case demands careful diagnosis. . . .

---

[5] G. W. Allport, "Catharsis and the Reduction of Prejudice" in "Problems of Reeducation," *op. cit.,* pp. 3-10.

CHAPTER 34

MASON HAIRE

Biological Models and Empirical Histories of the Growth of Organizations

The Biological Model

The biological model for social organizations—and here, particularly for industrial organizations—means taking as a model the living organism and the processes and principles that regulate and describe its growth and development. It means looking for lawful processes in organizational growth grounded in factors inside the firm and for the forces shaping it as it grows. It means restating, in specific terms, the interdependence of size, shape, and function in organizations. . . .

An outstanding characteristic of a social organization is simply that it is a special kind of aggregation of individuals. Many of the problems of organization seem to arise from two facets of this fact—first, that it is made up of individuals and, second, that it is an aggregation of them. From the first comes the problem of conflict between individual and organization and the organizational necessity of resisting the centrifugal force associated with individuals—each with his own goal and each tending to fly off from the path of the whole. From the second comes the pressure, as the size of the aggregation increases, to provide communication among the parts, integration of the parts into the whole, and the possibility of specialization of function.

It is in these last areas particularly—those growing out of the size of the aggregation—that the biological model seems most appropriate. Here, too, we have the problem of integrating the parts into a single functioning unit, of maintaining communication among them, and of developing and coor-

From Mason Haire, ed., *Modern Organization Theory* (New York: John Wiley & Sons, Inc., 1959). Reprinted by permission of the author and the publisher.

dinating specialized functions. If we look at the living organism for a moment, while we think of the problems of an organization, the relevance of the model may become clear.

The first step—the interdependence of size, shape, and function—can be seen particularly well in D'Arcy Thompson's example.[1] Taking the story of Jack the Giant Killer, Thompson points out that Jack had nothing to fear from the Giant. If he were, as he is pictured, ten times as large as a man and proportioned like one, Jack was perfectly safe. The Giant's mass would be 10^3, or a thousand times a man's, because he was ten times as big in every dimension. However, the cross-section of his leg bones would have increased only in two dimensions, and they would be 10^2, or a hundred times as big as a man's. A human bone simply will not support ten times its normal load, and the Giant, in walking, would break his legs and be helpless. He was trapped by a simple principle called the square-cube law which points out that, in normal spatial geometry, as volume increases by a cubic function, the surface enclosing it increases only by a square.

. . . We see here the force of gravity acting to put a limit on increase in size without a corresponding change in shape. The organism exists under the pressures of the environment, and a simple relationship drawn from the geometry of its shape expresses the factor through which the environmental pressure is exerted. A man cannot grow as big as a giant and still have the shape of a man. A deer cannot grow as big as an elephant and still look like a deer; it has to look (something) like an elephant to support the elephant's mass. The size cannot vary completely independently of the shape.

A similar application of the principle shows the interdependence of functions with size and shape. Small, unicellular organisms can take in oxygen directly through the skin, and one side is sufficiently near the other so that oxygen permeates the entire organism. As an organism gets bigger, however, the same square-cube law, operating with atmospheric pressure, demands a change in structure and shape. In a larger mass, oxygen no longer permeates throughout, and it is necessary to provide specialized veins and arteries to carry the blood through the whole system. At the same time, the skin surface has become inadequate—growing only by a square—to assimilate adequate oxygen. New folds of spongy tissue, maximizing surface in relation to mass, develop (as lungs), providing a specialized function and shape to accommodate a change in size.

In dealing with the growth of industrial organizations, it has been customary to see the specialized function of the chief executive as the limiting factor leading to diminishing returns with increase in size. Since the supply of this specialty is inelastic within a firm but infinitely elastic within an industry, a limit is seen to profitable expansion. It seems likely, however,

---

[1] Sir D'Arcy Thompson, *On Growth and Form* (2nd ed.; Cambridge, England: Cambridge University Press, 1952).

and empirical evidence seems to suggest, that the limitation also comes from other implications of the size-shape-function relationship. As the organization grows, its internal shape must change. Additional functions of coordination, control, and communication must be provided and supported by the same kind of force that previously supported an organization without these things. If the relationship were linear, there would be no problem. If each increment in size produced one increment (or one plus) in productive capacity and needed one increment of additional supportive function, there would be no limit. However, in the organism, the proportion of skeleton needed to support the mass grows faster than the mass itself and puts a limit on size as a function of the environmental forces playing on it. Similarly, it is suggested that, as the size of a firm increases, the skeletal structure (needed to support it against the forces tending to destroy it) grows faster than the size itself and hence comes to consume a disproportionate amount of the productive capacity of the organization. If this is so, it becomes important to identify the skeletal support of the firm, the forces it resists, and the rates at which the support must grow. Some empirical findings will be presented along these lines.

In the organismic examples used above, it was the force of gravity, and the closely related atmospheric pressure, which impressed modifications on a living form as its size changed. In organisms of other scales of size, other forces seem primarily determinative. In small insects, for example, where the ratio of wet weight to dry weight is high, it seems to be surface tension which determines modifications in form.[2] In still smaller microscopic organisms, it may be the shocks and jars associated with Brownian movement. What kind of force field can be the relevant one for social organisms? It is hard to hypothesize. However, knowing something of the forces operating on living organisms, we could study the modifications with growth and see the operation, for example, of gravity. In industrial organizations, we can study the history of growth and infer the operation of the forces from the direction of changes in shape and function as size changes. With adequate empirical histories, it should be possible to infer some of the characteristics of the force, even before it is possible to identify it.

•

Some kinds of clues seem to exist to help in this job. For one thing, in physical organisms, the form itself shows where the force tending to destroy the organism is strongest. A shelf bracket is thickest and strongest where the tendency for the loaded shelf to break from the wall is greatest. The bowstring arch of a bridge is shaped as it is, not for aesthetic reasons, but to provide maximum support where the weight associated with the size of the bridge tends to destroy it. In general, as physical objects get bigger but retain the same proportions, they get weaker, and a larger and larger propor-

---

[2] G. R. de Beer, *Growth* (London: Edward Arnold, 1924).

tion must go toward supporting their own mass. Consequently, with increase in size their forms are modified to resist the force associated with size. The appropriate modification is a clue to the force. The appropriate support for a physical structure is a perfect diagram of the forces tending to destroy it. Similarly, in the industrial organization, special attention to the modification of form as size increases may give us at least a clue to the strength of the force tending to destroy it, and to its point of application.

•

Empirical Histories of Firms

In order to see some of the phenomena of growth in industrial organizations, let us look at the histories of some actual firms. Four companies will be reported on here. These reports are the first results of a research project designed to study growth, and the sample is not necessarily representative of all of industry along any dimension. Several factors dictated the choice of companies. One of them was the simple availability of the firm and the cooperation of the management. To make accurate studies, it was necessary to take payroll records, telephone books, organizational charts, and similar data back to the beginning of the company; finally, sometimes we had to interview the oldest living inhabitants about the origins. These procedures were expensive both for the companies and for the research workers, but accurate data on size and assignment were seldom readily available. Another selective factor, associated with the first, was size. To encompass data of this kind in the early stages of investigation, it was necessary to use relatively small groups. The four firms reported here recently totaled about 2,000; 200; 275; and 300 employees; larger organizations will come later. Still another criterion was youth; in the first studies it seemed useful to try to get companies in which it was still possible to trace histories from the start. Finally, an attempt was made to choose firms where the growth was rapid and where technological advantage in the company materially reduced the pressure of competition on the firm's growth.

•

Internal Changes Associated with Growth

Physical models of organizations lead us to notice the relative proportions of parts as the size of the whole changes and to measure the proportion progressively assigned to such functions as communications and integration. A look at the internal changes in the organizations studied will give us some suggestions about these problems and will provide also some data on growth of functions which have been conspicuously lacking in discussion of organizations.

The relative proportions assigned to line and staff are shown in figures

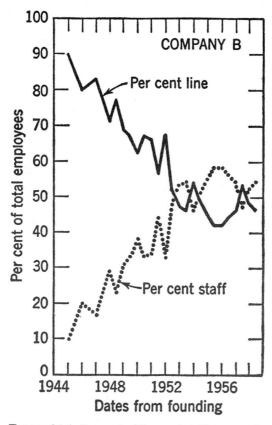

FIGURE 34-1. Per cent of line and staff personnel.

34-1 to 34-4. It was necessary to provide some definitions of line and staff to make these measures comparable from one firm to another. In industrial practice there seems to be no uniformity in the use of the terms. Here the distinction is made as follows: the "line" includes those who directly make and sell a product; the "staff" includes those who provide specialized support, advice, and help. In borderline cases, the proximity to the product and direct control over it were taken as determinative. For example, product planning, when intimately connected with the actual production organization, is here considered as line; product research is not. Similarly, a quality-control function may operate as part of the line, if it is immediately in the operation and stops production, modifies practice directly, and rejects output. In some instances, it serves a staff function when, for example, it is a more removed reportorial service comparable to the financial control afforded by bookkeeping practices.

Two patterns seem to appear. Two of the firms stabilize at about 50 per cent devoted to staff, and two at about 25 per cent. All four companies seem to show a relatively stable proportion in recent years. In all of them the initial proportion, of course, was virtually 100 per cent line. The average size of these companies in the first year of their operation was about eight people, a figure which neither requires nor leaves much room for functional specialization. Beyond this point, however, all four show a rapid shift toward a higher proportion of staff, and the first six to ten years in each firm showed a steep increase in the per cent of staff until the figures stabilized.

There seems to be less relation between absolute size and the steady state of the line-staff proportion than with age. The sizes varied considerably, but the age of six to ten years at the time of steadying gave a narrower range. The fact that three of the four companies are young, with their staff growth in the recent postwar years, suggests that it is perhaps more a function of the times than of growth in general. The fourth company, however, shows much the same pattern, though its main staff growth reached just into the depression thirties, suggesting that the particular times are not determinative.

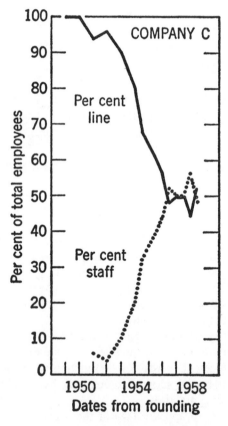

FIGURE 34-2. Per cent of line and staff personnel.

The rapid rise of the proportion of the whole allocated to staff function with early growth takes us back to the argument about the shelf bracket. The brace is strongest where the force tending to destroy it is greatest. If this is true in industrial organizations, the force tending to destroy is greatest at the point where it is shored up by increased staff. What can that force be? The two main functions of the staff are to provide information for control and coordination, and to provide expert assistance beyond the skill or training of line executives. The pressures which threaten to crack the organization as size increases must be in these areas.

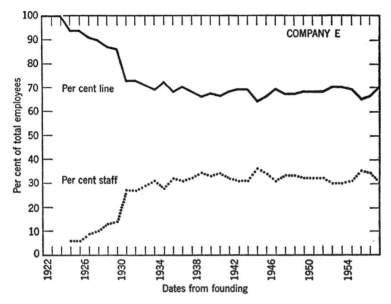

FIGURE 34-3. Per cent of line and staff personnel.

It seems fruitful to think of an organization as built on a module determined by the amount and kind of work one man can do. The best definition of a superior in the hierarchy is that he is responsible for more work than one man can do. As the job grows to be more than he can do, he is given subordinates to help him get it done. In this manner a new level is created in the organization. When the job of supervising these subordinates grows too big, he is given subsubordinates. In general, the vertical extent of the organization grows out of this simple module of the amount of line work one man can do or supervise. To be sure, this same pressure sometimes expands the organization horizontally—divisions are created for line specialties or, more often, to accommodate geographical distributions of the basic activities—but the real branch organization comes from another pressure. Levels are formed, in general, when a man has more than he can do of essentially the same kind of responsibility he has had. However, where a special expertise is required, usually somewhat different from the basic function, the horizontal extent is increased by the addition of branches. It is still the same module—what one man can do—but in a slightly different realm of competence. The specialized functions are of two rough types: control and coordination, as in the case of personnel function, financial control, quality control, and the like; and technical specialties such as research and development, advertising, legal counsel, and, perhaps, industrial relations.

These two pressures flowing from the amount of work one man can do seem to be at the base of the direction of growth of companies. Roughly, when it is more work of the same kind, we have vertical extension; when it is special competences, horizontal. Can these be said to be the pressures tending to destroy the organization? I think so. Whyte[3] gives a delightfully

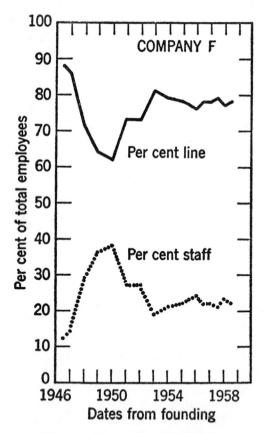

FIGURE 34-4. Per cent of line and staff personnel.

[3] W. F. Whyte, *Human Relations in the Restaurant Industry* (New York: McGraw-Hill, 1948).

succinct history of the growth and decline of a restaurant—the industry in which more organizations fail early than in any other. Here the one-man diner flourishes. The owner has been cook, counterman, and cashier, as well as greeter and purchasing agent. He expands and now must keep the cook cooking well, the waitresses efficient and happy, and the cashier honest. He has functions of public relations to supervise (but not to perform) as well as those of labor relations, purchasing, and the like. Very often, in the Shakespearian mold, the very qualities that lent him his worth in his individual operation lead him to fail, as he cannot effectively assume his new responsibilities. They are of two kinds: as supervisor, he must get the subordinates to help him get the work done and keep information flowing back and forth for control and coordination; as manager, he must have the specialized skills of the staff branches, often before he can afford to represent them in individuals.

In the cases reported here, it is the support for these supervisory and managerial tasks which grow most rapidly in the first six to ten years. Apparently the basic line function grows without much threat to the life of the social organism. The structure is strengthened most to provide support for control and coordination on the one hand, to extend assistance for policy-making and planning on the other. It seems reasonable to argue that the relative growth of staff to line provides a parallel to the shelf bracket or the bridge arch—the organization grows fastest where the force tending to destroy it is strongest; the shape of the support is a diagram of the forces acting against the structure.

Before we leave the staff-line relationship, one or two other points are worth noticing. It has been argued that, as the line grows by a linear function, the staff will grow geometrically.[4] This old wives' tale—which, like many pronouncements having to do with organization theory, is completely unsupported by empirical evidence—seems to be widely accepted. Only one study of the facts in the case has come to light. Baker and Davis[5] have shown that, in surveying about 200 companies, the line and staff both grow linearly. Unfortunately, Baker and Davis' data are also misleading on this point. They questioned companies at a point in time, to get a cross-sectional rather than a longitudinal result. Then, when they plot size of staff against size of total, they get a spurious growth curve. It is not a curve of growth representing the dynamics within an organization, but a set of static measurements arranged by size.

The four companies studied here, while differing considerably in their patterns of growth, all show both the points mentioned above. In the early

---

[4] R. C. Davis, *The Fundamentals of Top Management* (New York: Harper & Row, 1951).

[5] A. W. Baker and R. C. Davis, *Ratios of Staff to Line Employees and Stages of Differentiation of Staff Function* (Columbus, Ohio: Ohio State University, 1954), Monograph No. 72.

years, while the line grows linearly, the staff grows by some exponential function (though no single one seems to describe the curve well). Later, in another period of growth, they grow at quite similar rates. In terms of rough averages, during the period when the line first doubled, the staff grew about six times as large. When the line next doubled, the staff grew about five times; the next doubling of the line was accompanied by a tripling of the staff, and from then on they (approximately) each doubled. Early, the staff grows geometrically as the line grows linearly, but this relation tapers off to parallel growth.

Two other points might be noticed with regard to the staff before we leave it. One is the remarkable resistance of the staff to negative growth. The companies studied did not all grow uniformly larger. At times they cut the total personnel. In the total histories observed, there were nineteen such cases of layoffs, totaling 311 people from all firms. What proportion of these were line and what were staff? During the time in which 311 were laid off, there were actually 325 line workers furloughed; fourteen new staff people were hired during the very layoff period. Many reasons might be advanced for this. Staff people are specialists and harder to come by than line; it is simple economy to save them. Cutting down line and saving staff builds for the future. When business picks up again the line workers can be rehired to take places in the organization the staff has held intact. A more cynical interpretation might be that the staff plans and designs the layoffs, though line management makes the policy. No one ever plans to let himself go. Indeed, the process of laying off apparently required more staff to do it. Whatever the reason, it is clear that the staff is the place to take a job. It seems to have built-in tenure.

A second point which might be mentioned is the considerable regularity shown in the point of introduction of one staff function—personnel. The four companies had separate personnel people when their sizes were 177, 152, 138, and 248. Except for the last one, the figures are remarkably close together.

The Growth of Supervision and the Span of Control

Earlier we referred to the idea that the limiting condition leading to diminishing returns is based on the fact that the pyramidal shape of an organization always has a single individual at the apex and that this chief execu tive's function is inexpandable within the firm. This view of the function of the executive seems to be based on two notions: one, that there is a unit of decision-making potential of finite size, which can be stretched to cover only a certain amount of operation; and two, that there is a "span of control" which limits, more-or-less absolutely, the rate at which the pyramid can spread out beneath the top executive. The first notion—of an indivisible, inexpandable unit of decision-making—seems to leave out the possibility of decentralization, and the extreme of virtually autonomous organization within a single skin in the style, for example, of General Motors. While there may be an eventual upper limit on size associated with the operation of a factor of this kind, it does not seem to be limiting in the range of sizes which characterizes most of the industry. The second assumption, about the span of control, is even more tenuous. For one thing, even granting the reality of this span, it is not very sharply limiting. A figure of eight subordinates controlled by each superior occurs quite frequently in writings about span of control. In practice, a company with six levels of command below the vice-presidents is not out of the question. This would give us six levels of superiors with each man supervising eight subordinates. Such an organization would have a total payroll of 8^6, or about a quarter of a million; if we increase the span of control to ten, the same-shaped organization would give us a million employees. Surely this factor does not limit the size of industrial firms in the ranges with which we are familiar. Again, in practice, this kind of span of control does not seem to fit observed facts; Sears Roebuck is the classic example in which the number of subordinates reporting directly to policy-making levels has been increased well beyond the number usually discussed. Sears often has 50 subordinates reporting to a single man. To man a full organization of six levels, with 50 men reporting to each superior, would take 100 times the population of the United States.

The idea of the span of control in itself is an interesting one. It is often discussed as if there were some absolute answer to the question—"How many subordinates can a superior manage?"—as if the span were a kind of inflexible constant in social organizations, rather than a factor which itself is variable as a result of a number of such things as the training of the subordinates; the objectives of the group; the situation in which they find themselves; the communication facilities available to them; and the like. . . .

In dealing with principles of management, one often sees references to Graicunas' formulation of the limitations of authority.[6] Graicunas stresses the number of relationships with and between subordinates as their number increases. Using almost all possible relationships, he comes to a formula of

$$r = N \left(\frac{2^N}{2} + N - 1 \right)$$

where r is the number of relationships and N is the number of subordinates. With three subordinates, for example, we get a total of eighteen relationships, with four, 44. These surprising totals, however, are achieved only by taking a most elaborate view of human interactions. We must consider A's relationship with B in C's presence separately from his relationship with B alone and separately from his relationship with C in B's presence and in-

---

[6] L. Gulick and L. F. Urwick, *Papers on the Science of Administration* (New York. New York Institute of Public Administration, 1937).

clude B's relationship with C as well as C's with B. While all these relationships are logically contained in the system, it is not clear how they limit the span of control. Koontz and O'Donnell,[7] for example, say:

> An executive with four subordinates may well hesitate before adding a fifth member to the group when by doing so he increases the total possible relationships *for which he is responsible* [italics mine] by 127 per cent (from 44 to 100) in return for a 20 per cent increase in subordinate working capacity.

Surely this is just plain silly. Students must have been misled by the mathematical nicety Graicunas introduced in a previously foggy field. Making the superior responsible in any direct sense for all the relationships between and among his subordinates seems to extend unduly the functions of the executive. It would seem to me that these figures point again to the complexity of communication required to maintain contact within a growing organization, rather than to a limit on the realm of authority of the manager. . . .

When we look at the average number of line production workers supervised by first-line foremen, the simple ratio of one to eight does not stand up. In 1958, the four companies had an average of thirteen production workers reporting to each line foreman. The companies varied among themselves. Over their total life, the average number of men reporting to a supervisor were 19, 18, 7, and 13 for the four companies—a ratio of about 1 to 14 for

Table **34–1**

Average Number of Employees per Supervisor

Size of Company	Average Number Supervised
20-50	11.5
50-100	14
100-200	12
Over 200	21

Table **34–2**

Top and Middle Management as a Percentage of Total

Size of Firm	Per cent in Top and Middle Management
20-50	13.6
50-100	10.5
100-200	5.9
Over 200	4.1

[7] H. Koontz and C. O'Donnell, *Principles of Management* (New York: McGraw-Hill, 1955), p. 91.

all four companies for their total life span. The ratio of supervisors to supervised does not go up as the company grows. On the contrary, as the line increased, each supervisor was responsible for more men. To return to the argument from the shelf bracket, more supervision is not one of the supports against the destructive forces associated with size.

The ratio of top and middle management shows an even greater decline with increasing size. Table 39-2 shows the general relationship. When the firms are small the ratio is somewhat misleading, since there is an almost irreducible minimum of management no matter how small the total. Using a table similar to that given for first-line supervisors, the decreasing ratio is clear. Management grows in size as the total grows, but more slowly than the total, and it is an increasingly smaller part of the whole. The strength that management provides does not need to be increased more than proportionately as the company grows. Contrary to the argument that diminishing returns come from a pinch at the top, in the range of sizes studied here, the top seems perfectly adequate.

The Rise of the Clerical Function

Parkinson has made us all self-conscious about the clerical function in modern organization. To look at this, a special tabulation was kept in these four firms of all the people who were primarily paper handlers of one sort or another. The total number of clerical workers does increase as the company increases. In general, as the companies went from 40 to 80 employees, the clerical staff doubled, and the doubling of total size and clerks roughly continued. The table shows some variation, but not the alarming growth one

Table **34–3**

Clerical Workers as a Percentage of Total

Size of Company	Per cent of Clerks
20-50	12
50-100	15
100-200	12
Over 200	14

might expect. . . . As a company ages, the tendency to acquire a larger percentage of clerks appears. Part of this may be the staying power of the staff mentioned earlier. Or, in part, it may be a kind of agglutinative accretion, as when a line promotion requires a new secretary because there is no room for salary increase. In any case, the number and proportion of clerks tends to grow and grow.

The clerks have been treated separately from the staff for the present study because of the timeliness of the interest. They belong to the staff, however, and, as such, it is worthwhile considering their function for a moment. They are part of the general function of control, coordination, and communication which increases rapidly as the size increases. These functions are the responsibility of the line, but they are largely implemented by the staff. We saw that the staff increased by a factor of six when the line first doubled; the steady growth of the clerical function gives another clue to what is happening. The clerk's job is largely concerned with information —recording, duplicating, disseminating, keeping, and finding information —to support the integrative function.

In the biological organism, there is the same pressure for information in the interest of integration. Part of it is answered by the growth of the nervous system into a more complex network. Part of it is met by a simple increase in the speed of the transmission of the signal. For example, in a sea-urchin egg, without a proper nervous system, a signal barely moves along the membrane at a centimeter an hour; in the sponge it is already up to a centimeter a minute. A differentiated communication system—a nervous system—greatly improves the situation. In a jellyfish a signal goes 10 cm/sec, in a worm about ten times as fast. The arthropods step up the rate by another factor of ten; and finally the anthropoids—including man—again show a tenfold increase to something like 100 m/sec. Two things might be noticed; one, that in larger and more complex organisms there is a marked increase in transmissive capacity and hence in adaptive response; and, two, in very complex organisms two specialized branches develop— one for internal adjustments (the autonomic nervous system) and one for handling external information.[8]

In social organisms we cannot do much to speed the actual transmission of the nerve impulse, but we can and do develop, like the biological model, separate specialized functions for internal and external adjustments. Instead of increasing the actual transmission speed, there is one thing which we can do. It is a truism in communication engineering that it is always possible to trade band-width for time. If a message takes a channel of x frequencies to travel in y time, one can usually use $2x$ frequencies, and, by simultaneous transmission, achieve $\frac{1}{2}y$ time. This is essentially what happens in the combined staff-clerical function. Unable to speed up transmission, we duplicate messages and transmit simultaneously, achieving a measure of the desired speed.

. . . With the great deal of attention currently paid to the rise of the staff, it will perhaps make us happier with it if we realize its true role. The tendency to refer to staff as "nonproductive workers," "overhead personnel," or "burden personnel" expresses a frustration that is quite common, but it represents a bookkeeping fiction more than it does a factual reflection of the true organizational role of the function. . . .

---

[8] R. Redfield, *Levels of Integration in Biological and Social Sciences* (Lancaster, Pa.: Jacques Cattell Press, 1942), *Biological Symposia,* VIII, pp. 67-78.

CHAPTER 35

ROBERT E. PARK

The Race-Relations Cycle

The impression that emerges from the review of international and race relations is that the forces which have brought about the existing interpenetration of peoples are so vast and irresistible that the resulting changes assume the character of a cosmic process. New means of communication enforce new contacts and result in new forms of competition and of conflict. But out of this confusion and ferment, new and more intimate forms of association arise.

The changes which are taking place on the Pacific Coast—"the last asylum," in the language of Professor Ross, "of the native-born"—are part of the changes that are going on in every other part of the world. Everywhere there is competition and conflict; but everywhere the intimacies which participation in a common life enforces have created new accommodation, and relations which were merely formal or utilitarian have become personal and human.

In the relations of races there is a cycle of events which tends everywhere to repeat itself. Exploration invariably opens new regions for commercial exploitation; the missionary, as has frequently been said, becomes the advance agent of the trader. The exchange of commodities involves in the long run the competition of goods and of persons. The result is a new distribution of population and a new and wider division of labor.

The new economic organization, however, inevitably becomes the basis for a new political order. The relations of races and people are never for very long merely economic and utilitarian, and no efforts to conceive them in this way have ever been permanently successful. We have imported labor as if it were mere commodity, and sometimes we have been disappointed to find, as we invariably do, that the laborers were human like ourselves. In this way it comes about that race relations which were economic later be-

From Robert E. Park, *Race and Culture* (Glencoe, Ill.: The Free Press, 1950), pp. 149-151. Reprinted by permission of the publisher.

come political and cultural. The struggle for existence terminates in a struggle for status, for recognition, for position and prestige, within an existing political and moral order. Where such a political and moral order does not exist, war, which is the most elementary expression of political forces, creates one. For the ultimate effect of war has been, on the whole, to establish and extend law and order in regions where it did not previously exist.

The race relations cycle, which takes the form, to state it abstractly, of contacts, competition, accommodation, and eventual assimilation, is apparently progressive and irreversible. Customs regulations, immigration restrictions, and racial barriers may slacken the tempo of the movement, may perhaps halt it altogether for a time, but cannot change its direction; cannot at any rate, reverse it.

In our estimates of race relations we have not reckoned with the effects of personal intercourse and the friendships that inevitably grow up out of them. These friendships, particularly in a democratic society like our own, cut across and eventually undermine all the barriers of racial segregation and caste by which races seek to maintain their integrity.

It was the intimate and personal relations which grew up between the Negro slave and his white master that undermined and weakened the system of slavery from within, long before it was attacked from without. Evidence of this was the steady increase, in spite of public opinion and legislation to the contrary, of the number of free Negroes and emancipated slaves in the South. Men who believed the black man foreordained to be the servant of the white were unwilling to leave the servants they knew to the mercy of the system when they were no longer able to protect them.

In spite of the bitter antagonism that once existed toward the Chinese, the attitude of the Pacific Coast is now generally amiable, even indulgent, and this in spite of the nuisance of their *tong* wars and other racial eccentricities. The Chinese population is slowly declining in the United States, but San Francisco, at any rate, will miss its Chinese quarter when it goes.

There has never been the antagonism toward the Japanese in this country that there once was toward the Chinese. Even such antagonism as existed has always been qualified by a genuine admiration for the Japanese people as a whole. Now that the exclusion law seems finally to have put an end to Japanese immigration, there is already a disposition to relax the laws which made the permanent settlement of Orientals on the Pacific Coast untenable.

It does not follow that because the tendencies to the assimilation and eventual amalgamation of races exist, they should not be resisted and, if possible, altogether inhibited. On the other hand, it is vain to underestimate the character and force of the tendencies that are drawing the races and peoples about the Pacific into the ever-narrowing circle of a common life. Rising tides of color and Oriental exclusion laws are merely incidental evidences of these diminishing distances.

In the Hawaiian Islands, where all the races of the Pacific meet and mingle on more liberal terms than they do elsewhere, the native races are disappearing, and new peoples are coming into existence. Races and cultures die—it has always been so—but civilization lives on.

CHAPTER 36

ARNOLD ROSE

The American Negro Problem in the Context of Social Change

The "Negro protest" must be seen in the context of the Negro problem in the United States and of the forces of social change operating throughout the society. The protest movement is directed against a situation in American society, and it finds its strengths and its obstacles in that situation, which itself is in a condition of rapid flux.

Major Causes of Change

The major forces causing the rapid change in race relations since 1940 seem to have been continuing industrialization and technological advance, the high level of mobility among the American people, economic prosperity, the organization and political education of minority groups, an increased American awareness of world opinion, consistent support for civil rights on the part of the Supreme Court and a lesser support from the other branches of the federal government and the Northern state governments, and the propaganda and educational efforts for more equal implementation of civil rights. Some of these forces are likely to continue to exert the same pressure as in the recent past; others are likely to change in their influence, and new forces are likely to have increasing influence.

Industrialization and Technological Progress

Industrialization has created changes in race relations in several ways.

Reprinted from *The Annals of the American Academy of Political and Social Sciences,* Jan. 1965, pp. 1-16. (The American Academy of Political and Social Science, Philadelphia.)

First, it has eliminated cotton agriculture as the dominant source of Southern wealth. Racism grew up as an American ideology partly in response to the need to maintain a reliable and permanent work force in the difficult job of growing cotton. While American Negro slavery was older than extensive cotton agriculture, it took on major economic and political significance in connection with the rise of "King Cotton" after 1793, and the patterns of discrimination and prejudice that have persisted to the present day took their form originally in the cotton-growing areas. Cotton agriculture remained a dominant element in the economy of the Southern states until the 1930's, but then it lost its pre-eminence because of the diversification of agriculture and the rise of manufacturing. The continuation of racism after the displacement of cotton as "king" is an example of the sociological principle that ideologies continue after the conditions that gave rise to them cease to exist. Nevertheless, the decline of cotton agriculture permitted other forces to weaken racism.

Industrialization prompted a sizable move of people from rural areas into the cities, where they found factory jobs and entered service occupations. Urbanization has always been associated with the weakening of traditional social structures. The caste system governing the relations between whites and Negroes in the South had its birth in the rural areas and imposed its structure upon a relatively static rural society. When Negroes moved into the cities—and even in the South the majority of them now live in cities—the elaborate requirements of the caste system could hardly be maintained. Relationships in the city are too casual and too functional to require the constant manifestations of subordination on the part of Negroes that characterized the rural caste system. Segregation became more physical than symbolic, and behind the walls of segregated isolation, Negroes were better able to build resistance to subordination.

Industrialization also brought about emigration from the South. While the great migration of Negroes was to the Northern cities until about 1940, it became increasingly a westward migration after that. The migration was, of course, partly due to the lag in Southern industrialization, but even with that now being overcome, the especially strong discrimination against Negroes in the South has motivated their continued migration out of the region. The majority of Negroes, however, no longer live in the Deep and Upper South—the old Border states have realigned themselves largely with Northern states—and the outward migration must necessarily slow down. The main significance of the northward and westward migration for the Negroes was that it separated them from the full-bloom caste system of the South, even though they met other forms of discrimination and prejudice in the other regions of the country. In the North—which, for this purpose, includes the West also—they vote freely and have the almost full protection of the laws and the law-enforcement machinery. They, as well as the whites, get a better education in the North, and this has been a major factor in improving their status. Thus, Negroes have been much better able to improve their condition in the North, and they have used their improved condition—especially their vote—to help Negroes still living in the South.

Technological progress has been an important—though not the sole—factor which has contributed to the high level of prosperity since 1940. The prosperity and the almost full employment associated with it during the period 1940–1954 have been especially beneficial to Negroes. Measurements vary, but it has been estimated that the rise of average real income among Negroes since 1940 has been two to three times that among whites, though practically all of that improvement occurred before the economic recession of 1955. As the average income of Negroes is still significantly below that of the whites, the rapid improvement of their economic condition must be seen against the backdrop of great economic discrimination and poverty in the pre-1940 period. The prospects for further automation and the industrial use of nuclear energy will involve still higher productivity and a higher standard of living for employed workers in the future—and Negroes are no longer excluded from the general economic improvement, especially in the North. The rise in average family income among Negroes since 1935 has meant not only a fuller participation in the material benefits of the modern economy, but also a greater opportunity to obtain more education and other cultural benefits. It should also be remembered that continuing general prosperity among whites has tended to reduce one major source of frustration among whites, which sometimes contributes to scapegoating and race-baiting.

Technological change—especially in the form of automation—is having another effect—partly negative—on the position of Negroes in the United States. As a relatively unskilled element in the work population, the Negro is often the most rapidly displaced worker when changing technology requires an upgrading of skills. This process is aggravated by the fact that many Negroes are relative newcomers to the ranks of Northern industrial workers, and therefore have the lowest seniority and least protection from unionization. Hence, Negroes are the hardest hit by technological unemployment. Technological change and low seniority have, for all practical purposes, replaced discrimination as the main force in excluding Negroes from factory jobs in the North and West. Thus Negroes constitute a disproportionately large number of the "permanently unemployed," and their rate of becoming unemployed was about double that of white workers during the several recessions that have occurred since 1955. In July 1963, 11.2 per cent of the Negroes in the labor force were unemployed, compared to 5.1 per cent among whites. Occupational training for Negroes is crucial. If minority workers get new job training, they will cease to be subject to special handicaps and will substantially close the gap between them and the already skilled workers of the majority group, who now also need retraining.

Protest and Pressure Associations

The development of an educated elite and of a lively sense of group identification among Negroes has significantly impelled American race relations into a more equalitarian direction since the turn of the century. A wide range of protest and pressure associations have exerted their influence, sometimes with and sometimes without collaboration of liberal whites. Although this movement was quite highly developed by 1940, it has taken on some significant additional elements since then. The nonviolent resistance technique —as a means of achieving desegregation borrowed from Gandhi, who was himself influenced by Thoreau—was apparently first used in the United States in 1942, by the then newly organized Congress on Racial Equality (CORE) in Chicago. Applied first in selected Northern cities, it was gradually tried in the Border states and did not begin work in the South until about 1954. The technique caught nationwide attention in 1955 with the spontaneous and independent development of the Montgomery (Alabama) bus strike, led by the Reverend Martin Luther King. After the successful conclusion of this effort, King organized the Southern Christian Leadership Conference (SCLC) which worked for desegregation in other Southern cities. In 1960, the CORE technique of "sit-ins," used for years on an interracial basis, was adopted spontaneously by groups of Southern Negro college students and employed all over the South with considerable success. These students formed the Student Nonviolent Co-ordinating Committee (SNCC), and a sympathetic group of Northern students—both white and Negro—formed the Students for Integration (SFI) and the Northern Student Movement (NSM) to provide moral and physical aid to the Southern SNCC and to CORE. The NSM also conducts an educational program for culturally deprived Negro children in certain Northern cities.

The significance of all these organizations was not simply that the Gandhian technique of nonviolent resistance was successfully added to the repertory of those seeking equal rights for Negroes, but also that large sections of the Negro masses were now directly participating in the efforts for the improvement of their status. The new organizations, rivals to some extent among themselves, placed themselves in partial opposition to the older NAACP and Urban League because their more traditional techniques of legal action in the courts and negotiation with whites in positions of power did not lend themselves to direct, local participation. The competition was healthy, however, for while the Negro youth and some lower income persons joined the newer organizations, the growing Negro adult middle class was stimulated to give increasing support to the older organizations. In the summer of 1963, all these organizations—supported by significant segments of organized religion and labor—joined forces to promote a dramatic "March on Washington."

Violence as a technique for changing the pattern of race relations was also developed in the post-World War II period. Some of this was a purely spontaneous response to white violence and did not take an organized form, as in the case of the Jacksonville, Florida, Negroes in March 1964, who rioted and destroyed white property when a Negro woman was killed by a white man. But of greater significance was the acceptance of a philosophy of violence by a small number of fairly well-educated Negroes, such as the group led by James Lawson of the United African Nationalist Movement, and by small numbers of poorly educated Negroes in the Muslim Brotherhood, the African Nationalist Pioneer Movement, and other nationalist organizations.

While cold conflict with white America had been found among the Negro lower class ever since the Garvey movement of the 1920's, it was never so well organized as in the Black Muslim movement ("Temple of Islam") of the 1950's and 1960's. This disciplined organization, probably reaching a membership of 100,000 by 1960, had as its stated goal a segregated territory within the United States, and it espoused—vaguely, in order not to violate the law—future violence to attain this goal. In 1964, one of its leaders, Malcolm X of New York, broke off from the parent movement headed by Prophet Elijah Muhammed to head a movement promising more immediate violence.

These were the new organized power currents that developed among Negroes in the post-World War II era. While not all of them sought integration, all of them did seek equality. They suggested a heightened group identification and impatience among Negroes, and since they occurred at a time when desegregation was becoming a reality, they suggested that Negroes themselves—while hastening the demise of discrimination—might delay integration in its final stages. That is, group identification may become so strong that Negroes, like American Jews, may not want full integration.

Effects of World War II

As the Negro population was becoming more politically alert to the possibilities of changing race relations, the white population was becoming more aware of the need to change its traditional ways of associating with and thinking about Negroes. Perhaps the most important force here was the Second World War itself. It transformed the United States from an isolated and isolationist nation into a leading power with responsibilities in every part of the world. The American people had to see themselves as other people saw them, and they found the world's major criticism to be America's handling of its racial violence. Newspapers in every country reported on American discrimination and racial violence. A significant number of Americans became aware of this criticism, and it had a profound effect on their consciences. World reaction gained even greater significance as the colored nations of Asia and Africa, formerly under colonial rule, gained their independence. As the United States government partly realigned its foreign policy toward these new nations, it was obliged to encourage a more equalitarian treatment of nonwhite minorities at home. The formation of newly independent African nations after 1957 increased race-pride among American Negroes and strengthened their drive toward equality.

The Second World War and its aftermath brought unprecedented numbers of Americans in touch with other peoples. The Armed Services transported millions of Americans to Europe and Asia, and the tourist trade sent millions more to all parts of the world. Asiatics and Africans, especially students, began to visit the United States in significant numbers. A colored man on the downtown streets of New York City and Washington, D. C., was almost as likely to be a foreign as a native one, and even Southerners could no longer be sure whether the Negroes they saw in their cities were Americans or Africans. Perhaps more far-reaching was the change in the nation's mass media. Before 1940, newspapers, movies, and radio either ignored the Negro or stereotyped him unfavorably; after 1950, these media paid the Negro—foreign and native—a great deal of objective or favorable attention. Some social science research and certain novels made the Negro almost popular in some mainly intellectual white circles. With the rising living standards of the American Negro and his efforts to integrate himself into American life, white Americans generally were also much more likely to have direct contact with middle-class Negroes.

Federal Government Assistance

The more educated white Americans and those in closest contact with foreign opinion were most involved in the effort to eliminate discrimination and prejudice. This included the chief federal government officials. The United States Supreme Court led the way, perhaps because it was closer to the Constitution, which had been a thoroughly equalitarian document since 1868, and perhaps because it weighted foreign opinion along with domestic white opinion. The Supreme Court had generally sought to guarantee Negroes some legal protection, but it had equivocated until 1944 about the right to vote and about the equal use of public facilities. That year, a unanimous Court—in the case of Smith *v.* Allwright—declared unequivocally that the "white primary" was illegal, and that other such subterfuges to prevent Negroes from voting in the South were unconstitutional. Since then, the Court has consistently decided, with undivided opinions, that no branch of any government in the United States could practice any discrimination whatsoever on grounds of race or religion.

Perhaps the most important of these decisions was the one handed down on May 17, 1954, which held that it was unconstitutional for the public schools to segregate the races. This decision withdrew the last legal support from the Southern states' effort to segregate public facilities, such as parks, playgrounds, libraries, and bathing beaches, as well as schools. The "separate but equal" doctrine was dead. The decision also applied to privately owned transportation facilities directly engaged in interstate commerce, including rail and bus terminal waiting rooms and restaurants. Only a small proportion of the local governments affected took immediate steps to desegregate, but through various pressures, the elaborate caste system of the South began to be dismantled. After 1954, the federal courts adjudicated many cases that were brought in order to implement the historic decision wiping out "separate but equal" facilities, but it could go no further in principle, for it was now operating in complete accord with the Constitutional provisions for full equality.

The Executive branch of the federal government began to fulfill its responsibilities for enforcing equality during the 1930's. The Roosevelt administration (1933–1945) practiced equality in the administration of some of its programs and for the first time hired Negroes in other than custodial or honorary capacities. The main innovation of the Roosevelt era, however, was forced on the President by the combined pressure of all the Negro organizations during the war, namely, the establishment of a Fair Employment Practices Commission (FEPC) which had the task of preventing discrimination in employment by industries holding contracts with the federal government. The Truman administration (1945–1953) went further in eliminating discrimination in federal employment and in the operation of federal programs, although it lost the FEPC in 1946 through Congressional action. Its main achievements along these lines were the virtual abolition of discrimination and segregation in the armed services and the support and publicity given to the President's Civil Rights Commission. The Eisenhower administration (1953–1961) continued the existing nondiscriminatory policies and gave administrative support to the courts' rulings on school desegregation—even to the point of calling out federal troops to enforce school desegregation in Little Rock, Arkansas, in 1957. The Kennedy administration (1961–1963) pumped life into the government committee to enforce nondiscrimination in employment by industries with government contracts—thereby reviving in effect the FEPC for major manufacturing companies—and extended administrative support to the courts' rulings on nondiscrimination by the states and by agencies of interstate transportion. Most important was the 1961 ruling by the Interstate Commerce Commission that rail and bus terminals might not segregate passengers. Further Executive action was taken in late 1962: President Kennedy signed a long delayed Executive Order to restrict government guarantees on loans to builders who insisted on excluding Negroes, and the Attorney General began a policy of calling on the National Guard and federal troops to assist in enforcing court orders for school desegregation. In June 1963, the President responded to the crescendo of Negro protests against discrimination—stimulated by growing unemployment and by the observance of the centennial anniversary of the Emancipation Proclamation—by setting before Congress a comprehensive program of proposed legislation guaranteeing voting rights and desegregation of public schools and prohibiting private enterprises involved in interstate commerce to refuse to do business with Negroes. While the last-mentioned feature had been in the statutes of twenty-eight Northern states since shortly after the Supreme Court (1883) had declared unconstitutional the Civil Rights Act of 1875, Congress regarded it as a drastic innovation and showed a strong inclination to cut down a portion of the President's proposal. After the death of President Kennedy in November 1963, President Johnson gave even more effective support to the civil rights bill then before Congress, and the bill became law on July 2, 1964.

The Legislative branch has the greatest power but the least achievement, largely because of the presence within it of Southern congressmen. These are a minority but hold the balance of power between the conservatives and liberals—a position they exploit in order to prevent enactment of civil rights legislation—and they have a disproportionate share of congressional leadership positions because of their seniority. Until 1964, the Congress' main contribution to the equalization of the races was a negative one: it has not sought to reverse the actions of the Judicial and Executive branches—except for killing the FEPC in 1946. In 1957, Congress passed its first statute since the 1870's to enforce civil rights; it was a weak law, which gave federal authorities some power to restrain local polling officials from preventing voting by Negroes. In 1960 it passed a second statute which slightly strengthened this law. It is doubtful that these statutes helped the position of Negroes enough to offset the damage inflicted on other liberal legislation, such as the bill to provide federal aid for education, by the political bargaining that was required. Negroes would be among those helped by the enactment of many bills which Southern congressmen block by deals with the conservatives: scarcely a bill comes before Congress these days—except occasionally in the fields of defense and foreign policy—which does not have a "race angle." Pending legislation that enhances the civil rights of Negroes has usually been killed by the Southern congressional bloc, who extend support to non-Southern conservatives in their opposition to other socially progressive measures, in exchange for help in preventing the passage of civil rights bills. Until the mass civil rights' demonstration of mid-1963, there did not seem to be much hope for significant legislation from Congress.

Some of what Negro leaders want from the federal government can be provided by the Executive branch, and the votes of Negroes are more effective in the Presidential elections than in the Congressional races. It is doubtful, however, that civil rights groups will diminish their efforts to get federal legislation. The main effort in 1960–1961 was to modify certain procedural rules in the Congress so that substantive civil rights legislation would be easier to pass. By 1963, however, the pressure from an awakening Negro populace—aided by many whites—forced Negro leaders to seek more substantive legislation to outlaw discrimination in voting, education, employment, and business relations.

The Civil Rights Act of 1964, which passed both houses of Congress with overwhelming majorities, despite a Southern filibuster in the Senate and the opposition of the leading contender for the Republican nomination for President, was the most comprehensive legislation to be enacted since post-Civil War days. Its success was due to the active support of President Lyndon Johnson, to demonstrations by civil rights and religious organizations, and to recognition by the congressional leadership of both parties of the facts of social change and of the moral and international issues involved. The main provisions of the eleven titles of the Act were: Title 1 prohibits voting registrars from applying different standards to white and Negro voting applicants and permits the Attorney General to sue in federal courts to enforce this. Title 2 prohibits refusal of service on account of race in hotels, restaurants, gasoline stations, and places of amusement if their operations affect interstate commerce, and it permits the Attorney General to sue in federal courts to enforce this. Title 3 requires that Negroes have equal access to, and treatment in, publicly owned or operated facilities and permits the offended citizen or the Attorney General to sue to enforce this. Title 6 provides that no person shall be subjected to racial discrimination in any program receiving federal aid. Title 7 bars discrimination by employers or unions with twenty-five or more employees or members and places enforcement powers in the hands of both a new Commission and the Attorney General. Title 9 permits the federal courts and the Attorney General to intervene in any state suit in which racial discrimination may be involved. If these provisions of the law are enforced, they will wipe out the remnants of the American caste system insofar as law can do so. . . .

Forces Maintaining Segregation

Such have been the main forces promoting the equalization of Negroes in American society since 1940. The main forces maintaining the subordination and segregation of Negroes have been those of tradition and the *status quo*. In 1954, however, a new factor entered which has undoubtedly prevented change from being more rapid than it might otherwise have been. This was the organization of Southern white opposition, mainly in the White Citizens' Councils. There had been no significant organization aiming to hold the Negro in a subordinate position since the decline of the Ku

Klux Klan in the late 1920's. Minor and local organizations had made sporadic efforts, but the leading reactionary movements of the period between 1930 and 1954 avoided attacking the position of Negroes. The reaction to the rapid changes of the post-1940 period did not gain organized expression until 1954. Racists did not organize their resistance to changes in the caste system effectively until the very keystone of that system was endangered by the Supreme Court decision to desegregate the public schools. But the economic, political, and legal aspects of the caste system had already changed materially, and the pattern of social segregation had long been threatened before the proponents of the caste system organized themselves to protect it. For twenty-five years, the old racist ideology had found only occasional—and little heeded—spokesmen, and it was only after 1954 that it was again vigorously reasserted—and this at a time when the original source for this thinking had disappeared together with most of its material benefits. The ideology of racism was now no longer the response to a conflict between economic and political forces on the one hand and the idealism of the American creed and Constitution on the other, but merely an expression of a traditional psychology. . . .

Summary of Progress to 1964

In the dynamic situation created by these forces, any description of the position of Negroes written at any one moment is bound to be dated before it can be printed. The picture at the beginning of 1964 is here painted in broad strokes, necessarily superficial and incomplete. In 1940 Negroes were excluded from most occupations outside of agriculture and service; by 1960 some Negroes were to be found in nearly every occupation. Between 1940 and 1960 the proportion of white males in the labor force who had "white-collar jobs" rose from 30.3 to 41.2 per cent, while among nonwhite males the corresponding rise was from 5.0 to 16.0 per cent. At the same time the rise in skilled and semiskilled "blue-collar jobs" was from 34.3 to 38.6 per cent among white males and from 16.6 to 32.7 per cent among nonwhite males. Considerable employment discrimination remained in the South and even in the Border states, but it was greatly diminished in the Northern and Western states. This did not mean that Negroes were approaching occupational equality, for there was the heritage of inadequate training, low-skill orientations, poor general education, and low seniority. The training lag was the most serious, because union and company seniority rules often made it impossible for Negroes to obtain training for better jobs.

Politics

Negroes were voting without restriction in most areas of the Upper South, and in some cities of the Deep South. Between 1956 and 1960, while the increase in the total population voting was 8 per cent, the estimated increase in the number of Negroes voting was 16 per cent. The only state that almost systematically excluded Negroes from the polls—as they had been throughout the South in 1940—was Mississippi. Here, and in many rural areas of the other Deep Southern states, they were illegally prevented from voting by the whim of local polling officials and by threats of violence. The poll tax still existed in five states as a requirement for voting, although by the beginning of 1964 a Constitutional amendment was passed to make it illegal for federal elections. Several Southern states had literacy and "understanding" tests for all voting, but they were given to Negroes with discriminatory severity. Negroes occasionally ran for the minor local offices. In Atlanta a Negro was elected to the Georgia state legislature with the aid of white voters. The main changes in Southern politics resulting from Negro voting were the election of liberal Democrats in several states and the breaking of the barriers which hitherto had prevented conservatives from voting Republican. . . .

Social Relations

These changes in the economic and political spheres were occurring regularly and generally with little public attention or controversy. Changes in the area of social relations, however, were coming about in some areas but not in others, and at times received a great deal of notice. The movement of rural Negroes into the Northern and Southern cities was associated with housing segregation, and housing segregation brought the inevitable segregation of neighborhood facilities, over-crowding, high rents, run-down buildings, slums, and expansion into new neighborhoods attended by conflict with whites. This became the most serious aspect of the race problem, certainly in the North. The chief legal buttress for housing segregation had been the "restrictive covenant," a clause written into a deed for property preventing its resale to members of specified groups, mainly Negroes. In 1948, the United States Supreme Court decided that the racial restrictive covenant was unenforceable in the courts, thus wiping out the legal support for housing segregation and allowing it to rest on voluntary action.

The decision eased the situation for Negroes somewhat, and it was followed by various organized efforts to develop integrated housing in the North. Publicly subsidized housing was no longer segregated, and some privately sponsored integrated housing projects were developed. But the great masses of urban Negroes remained segregated, and there was some evidence that housing segregation was increasing in the South. Negroes themselves fought the housing restrictions generally only when there was insufficient space to live; only a few of them sought to break the pattern of segregation itself. By the end of the 1950's some Northern states passed statutes making it illegal to refuse to rent or sell housing to Negroes, and generally in the North the space pressures on Negroes eased considerably.

Late in 1962 the President issued an executive order which restricts the lending of money with government guarantees if the housing affected is not available for lease or purchase by minority groups. Political considerations limited the coverage of this order to only about a third of the 90 per cent of all housing units covered by such loans. A full withholding of government credit and guarantees would remove the strongest barrier to housing integration. Whether Negroes would move in large numbers to take advantage of it is more questionable. At this time, residential segregation is one of the most serious and least soluble aspects of the race problem, particularly in the Northern states.

Segregation of other public and privately owned but essentially public facilities remained the effect of housing segregation in the North. This has become known as "de facto" segregation, and there were several local efforts to mix children in the public schools despite the fact that their residences were largely segregated. Forced segregation of schools, playgrounds, restaurants, hotels, and other public and commercial establishments became exceptional in the North as the climate of opinion changed and the old "public accommodations" statutes of the Northern states once again became operative. Some cities began movements to upgrade Negro education—to compensate for cultural deprivation in the family and community—preparatory to initiating programs to end de facto school segregation. In the South, desegregation of these kinds of facilities began as a result of the court decisions and the organized movements already examined.

By 1961, school systems were formally desegregated in all the border states; in many scattered areas of the Upper South and in a few cities of the Deep South there was token desegregation. Violence had attended school desegregation in Dover, Delaware; Clinton and Nashville, Tennessee; Little Rock, Arkansas; and New Orleans, Louisiana. But it was accomplished peacefully and more thoroughly in the larger school systems of Washington, D.C.; St. Louis, Missouri; Dallas and Houston, Texas; and Atlanta, Georgia. By 1961 only Mississippi, Alabama, and South Carolina had none of their schools desegregated, and by 1963 even these had token desegregation in a few schools. There was only spotty and token desegregation in all of the Deep Southern states and some of the Upper South states, but over one-third of all Negro children living in school districts segregated by statute before 1955 were in desegregated schools by 1963. . . .

Interracial marriages were probably on the increase in the North, although they were still not frequent. In the South, interracial marriage continued to be illegal: this was the one type of law discriminating among the races still on the statute books of the Southern states; not even the Negro organizations have sought to challenge it, and hence the courts had no occasion to declare it unconstitutional. The probability is that the courts would declare it unconstitutional, for they had nullified a California statute barring marriage between whites and Orientals. But apparently the Negro leadership thought it unwise to challenge this last formal barrier of the caste system, at least until other forms of desegregation should be accomplished in greater degree. At the present writing (winter, 1964), there are two cases in the state courts challenging the constitutionality of the laws forbidding interracial marriage. . . .

Future Development

There could be no doubt that the races were moving rapidly toward equality and desegregation by 1964. In retrospect, the change of the preceding twenty years appeared as one of the most rapid in the history of human relations. Much of the old segregation and discrimination remained in the Deep South, and housing segregation with its concomitants was still found throughout the country, but the all-encompassing caste system had been broken everywhere. Prejudice as an attitude was still common, but racism as a comprehensive ideology was maintained by only a few. The change had been so rapid, and caste and racism so debilitated, that this author ventures to predict—if the present trends continue—the end of all legal segregation and discrimination within a decade, and the decline of informal segregation and discrimination to a mere shadow in two decades. The attitude of prejudice might remain indefinitely, but it will be on the minor order of Catholic-Protestant prejudice within three decades. These changes would not mean that there would be equality between the races within this time, for the heritage of past discriminations would still operate to give Negroes lower "life chances." But the dynamic social forces creating inequality will, if the present trends continue, be practically eliminated in three decades. As far as separation of the races without overt discrimination is concerned, this will come for a while to be more associated with Negro group identification than with white exclusionism. It would only be appropriate to guess that most sociologists would find these predictions "optimistic," but then, most sociologists found the predictions contained in *An American Dilemma* of twenty years ago optimistic, and most of these predictions have since come true.

But of particular significance for our analysis is the fact that Negroes *still* experience discrimination, insult, segregation, and the threat of violence, and in a sense have become more sensitive and less "adjusted" to these things. To them the current problems and current conflicts have much more significance than those of ten or twenty years ago. Schooled as they are by the American Creed, their standard of comparison for the present situation is not what existed in 1940, but what the Constitution and "the principles of democracy" say should be. Further, most American Negroes are aware of great changes going on in Africa, and in fact are inclined to exaggerate the "improvements" there resulting from the demise of old-fashioned colonialism. From their perspective, the changes occurring in the United States are much too slow; they want "freedom *now*," as the slogan goes. White Americans, who have in mind the United States Constitution and their country's role in a world whose population is two-thirds colored, might agree with them.

CHAPTER 37

DAVID RIESMAN

From "Inner-Directed" to "Other-Directed"

My purpose here is to trace a shift I believe to have occurred in very recent times in the character structure of modern man: a shift from the predominance of a type I have called "inner-directed," whose source of guidance in life is an internalized authority, to a type I have called "other-directed," dependent on external authorities. We shall further explore the relationship between these two types of character and the changing feelings in people as to their power to resist social pressures. For obviously, given the objectively identical social pressure, the individual's feeling and experience will depend upon his character, in which his previous life-experiences, especially those of mastery and submission, have been crystallized.

While our helplessness in the world is historically the condition of every advance in our mastery of it, the feeling of helplessness may today be so overpowering that regression, and not advance, ensues. But only when we have understood those forces that make for helplessness can we assay the probable outcome, and see what might be required for a new leap to security and freedom. . . . One requirement is a type of character structure that can tolerate freedom, even thrive on it; I call persons of such type "autonomous," since they are capable of conscious self-direction. The very conditions that produce other-direction on the part of the majority today, who are heteronomous—that is, who are guided by voices other than their own—may also produce a "saving remnant" who are increasingly autonomous and who find strength in the face of their minority position in the modern world of power.

From David Riesman, "The Saving Remnant," in J. W. Chase, ed., *The Years of the Modern* (New York: David McKay, 1949), pp. 115-147. Reprinted by permission of the author and the publisher.

The Inner-Directed Type

Throughout most of history, people have lived in the bosom of nature, and at her mercy. They have sought a kind of defensive power and command of nature through magic and animism, by which they attempted to personalize and to propitiate the environment. The Pueblo Indians of the American Southwest, for instance, still cope with fear of drought by preoccupation with word-perfect rituals of rain-making—and by very practical communal organization of the available water supply. These tribes quiet their anxiety over the weather by substituting for it anxiety over the ritual, which remains in their control. In such a society, as in the feudal past, people live on a relatively unawakened level, with limited life-expectations and limited potentialities for choice. An overall balance is struck between helplessness and power; institutions mediate this balance, and character structure builds upon it.

This balance altered radically in the West during the age that opens with the Renaissance and closes, to set an equally arbitrary date, with the virtual cutting off of immigration from Europe following World War I. During this period, men were forced to face a world of changed dimensions, changed social relations, and changed meanings. As a result, some felt increasingly helpless and alone; the Calvinist doctrines appealed to them because those doctrines stressed man's helplessness to secure grace, the "chosen" being predestined by a terrifying and inscrutable God. The practical Calvinist, however, did not merely wait for the day of judgment; he tried to force God's hand by a ritual. This ritual, unlike the Pueblo Indian's rain-making, was symbolized by hard work in the worldly processes of production—even though the ultimate aim was otherworldly. The result for many was success in mundane pursuits, which was regarded as a sign of election. Thus both hard work and its practical fruits assuaged the feeling of helplessness in the new conditions of life and led to the attainment of a new balance between power and weakness.

This period was the age of the early physical and industrial frontiers—the frontiers of expanding industry and trade, as well as expanding geographical frontiers. This age also enlarged the frontiers of intellectual and emotional discovery, excavating man's past and acquainting him with other cultures. To pioneer on a frontier—whether an external one, at the edge of a white settlement, or an internal one, at the edge of the known in science, art, or industry—requires a somewhat new type of character that is, to a degree, capable of self-piloting, a type that can act when the guidance of custom breaks down or when a choice must be made among several different sets of customs.

I call this type inner-directed, since the source of direction is internalized. By inner-direction, however, I do not mean genuine autonomy, but rather obedience to an internal psychic "gyroscope" which, installed in childhood, continues to pilot the person as he struggles to master the exigent demands of the frontier. This gyroscope is set going by the parents, or rather by their idealized image (the Freudian superego); or by heroes or great men of antiquity or revered elders taken as models. Driven by these internal voices, the inner-directed person is often ambitious—for fame, for goodness, for accomplishment in the world; and this is as true of the bold men of the Renaissance as of the hard, ascetic Puritans. By their own efforts at self-discipline and self-development, these men often helped to "produce" their own characters; the conquering of this internal frontier was accompanied and rewarded by mastery over others and over nature.

In all I have said, I speak primarily of the middle classes, for it was among them that inner-directed types arose; the lower classes moved more slowly out of feudalism. In time, as the doctrine of predestination became attenuated or forgotten, these middle classes developed an ideology of liberalism and individualism that proclaimed for all men the values of freedom and self-reliance compatible with characterological inner-direction. The inner-directed person came to *feel* free and to *feel* self-made: in his psychological innocence, he was not aware how many of "his" choices had been made for him already by his parents and his conditioning generally. He might have read the famous phrase of Heraclitus—"Character is fate"—to mean that he, as an individual, possessed his own fate, working in him through his own self-mastery; while we today would read the same sentence to mean that our own character is not truly ours, but is produced by our social environment, our "fate" of living in a particular place and time—a new, more sophisticated doctrine of predestination. Moreover, the inner-directed person, living in a time of expanding frontiers, could in fact achieve a small degree of the freedom that he felt. Many inner-directed persons achieved a measure of psychic autonomy and independence as theocratic controls declined in the eighteenth and nineteenth centuries.

•

Inner-direction was never very widespread, but rather represented the ideal model toward which people strove. We have evidence that many people of that era tried desperately to conduct themselves in the approved inner-directed way, but were unable to conform. Thus, in Vermont of the eighteenth and nineteenth centuries, many more people started diaries and account books—perfect symbols of inner-direction—than kept them up. Such people must have felt helpless in their efforts at self-mastery, particularly since they took as models those pre-eminent men, from George Washington to Andrew Carnegie, who then stood unshaken by disciples of Marx and Freud. Thus, in a very special sense, the feelings of potency were monopolized by those whose inner-direction was relatively stable and successful in the public mind, while a reservoir of hidden impotence existed. Yet for many of the unsuccessful, failure never seemed quite final, and so long as the future beckoned, or the belief in grace persisted, helplessness could be staved off.

The Other-Directed Type

Individual helplessness and collective power play leapfrog with each other throughout history. Today, the helplessness foreseen by a few thinkers, and sensed even in the earlier age of frontiers by many who failed, has become the common attribute of the mass of men. We turn now to discuss some of the factors responsible for this development: in economic and political life, in methods of childrearing, and in their consequences for character structure.

When immigration from Europe was cut off in 1924, a great symbol of hope in the Western world was destroyed. The "no help wanted" sign had been posted on the American frontier in 1890, but it was now hung out along our borders for all to see. Today, in the advanced industrial countries, there is only one frontier left—that of consumption—and this calls for very different types of talent and character.

The inner-directed type fitted the conditions of essentially open capitalism, which rewarded ability to envisage new possibilities for production, and zeal to realize those possibilities. To a degree, this is still the case. Nevertheless, we think that, on the whole, contemporary society, especially in America, no longer requires and rewards the old enterprise and the old zeal. This does not mean that the economic system itself is slowing down; total production may continue to rise; but it can be achieved by institutionalizing technological and organizational advance, in research departments, management counsel, and corporate planning staffs. The invention and adoption of new improvements can be routinized, built into the system, so to speak, rather than into the men who run the system. Therefore, the energies of management turn to industrial and public relations, to oiling the frictions not of machines but of men.

Likewise, with the growth of monopolistic competition, the way to get ahead is not so much to make a better mousetrap but rather to "package" an old mousetrap in a new way, and then to sell it by "selling" oneself first. People feel they must be able to adapt themselves to other people, both to manipulate them and to be manipulated by them. This requires the ability to manipulate oneself, to become "a good package," to use a phrase current among personnel men. These pressures are, of course, not confined to business, but operate also in the professions, in government, and in academic life.

As work becomes less meaningful and intense, however, leisure grows, and men who are discarded as workers are cultivated in the one role that still matters, that of consumer. This is not an easy role, and people become almost as preoccupied with getting the "best buys" as they once were with finding their proper "calling" in the production economy. They turn, then, to the mass media of communication for advice in how to consume; at the same time, these media help make them anxious lest they fail in the role of consumer. We speak here not merely of "keeping up with the Joneses"—this is part of an older pattern—but rather of the much more unsettling fear of missing those leisure-time experiences, including sex, love, art, friendship, food, travel, which people have been induced to feel they should have.

These changes in the nature of work and leisure have made themselves felt most strongly among the middle classes of the American big cities in the last 25 years or so. It is here that we find developing the character type that I call other-directed, a type whose source of direction is externalized. The clear goals and generalized judgments of the inner-directed types are not implanted in the other-directed person in childhood. Rather, he is taught, vaguely, to do the "best possible" in any given situation. As soon as he can play with other children, he is made sensitive to the judgments of this play group, looking to it for approval and direction as to what is best. Parents and other adults come to value the child in terms of his ability to live up to the group's expectations and to wrest popularity from it.

The adult never loses this dependence, but continues to live psychologically oriented to his contemporaries—to what might be called his "peer group." Of course, it matters very much who these others are: whether they are his immediate circle of the moment, or a higher circle he aspires to, or the anonymous circles of whose doings he learns from the mass media of communication. But the great psychological difference from inner-direction is that this modern type needs open approval and guidance from contemporaries. This new need for approval goes well beyond the human and opportunistic reasons that lead people in any age to care very much what others think of them. People in general want and need to be liked, but it is only the other-directed character type that makes others its chief source of direction and its chief area of sensitivity and concern.

These differences in the source looked to for direction lead to different modes of conformity in the two types. The inner-directed person will ordinarily have had an early choice made for him among the several available destinies of the middle-class child. What holds him on course is that he has internalized from his elders certain general aims and drives—the drive to work hard, or to save money, or to strive for rectitude or for fame. His conformity results from the fact that similar drives have been instilled into others of his social class. As against this, the other-directed person grows up in a much more amorphous social system, where alternative destinations cannot be clearly chosen at an early age. The "best possible" in a particular situation must always be learned from the others in that situation. His conformity to the others is thus not one of generalized drives, but of details—the minutiae of taste or speech or emotion which are momentarily "best." Hence he internalizes neither detailed habits nor generalized drives, but instead an awareness of and preoccupation with the *process* of securing direction from others.

We can find exemplars of the other-directed character in leisured urban circles of the past, where the preoccupations were those of consumption, not production, and where status depended on the opinion of influential others. What is new is the spread of such an outlook over large sectors of a middle class that was once inner-directed. Elements of this outlook, moreover, have now filtered down in America to many members of the lower-middle class.

It is my tentative conclusion that the feeling of helplessness of modern man results from both the vastly enhanced power of the social group and the incorporation of its authority into his very character. And the point at issue is not that the other-directed character is more opportunistic than the inner-directed—if anything, the contrary is true. Rather, the point is that the individual is psychologically dependent on others for clues to the meaning of life. He thus fails to resist authority or fears to exercise freedom of choice even where he might safely do so.

An illustration may clarify my meaning. I have sometimes asked university students why they come to class so regularly day after day, why they do not—as they are technically free to do—take two or three weeks off to do anything they like on their own. The students have answered that they must come to class or otherwise they will flunk, though the fact is that many students get ahead when they finally do break through the routines. It has become apparent that the students cling to such "rational" explanations because, in their feeling of helplessness, freedom is too much of a threat. They fail to see those loopholes of which they could take advantage for their own personal development; they feel safer if they are obeying an authoritative ritual in sympathetic company. Their attendance at class has much the same meaning as the Pueblo Indian's rain-making dance, only the student has less confidence that his "prayer" will be heard. For he has left "home" for good, and all of modern thought teaches him too much for comfort and too little for help. . . .

Some Factors in the Transition

Let us examine several further factors that have robbed the middle-class individual of his defenses against the pressure of the group. We shall deal in somewhat more detail with changes in the nature of private property of work and of leisure, all of which at one time functioned as defenses.

In the feudal era, the individual was attached to property, largely land, by feudal and family ties. The breakdown of feudalism meant helplessness for many peasants, who were thrown off the land; but for the middle class the result was a gradual gain in consciousness of strength. A new type of relationship between persons and property developed: the person was no longer attached to property, but attached property to himself by his own energetic actions. Property, including land, became freely alienable; at the same time, it was felt to be an individual, not a family, possession. And property was satisfying, substantial—an extended part of the self. Inside the shell of his possessions, the inner-directed person could resist psychological invasion.

Today, however, property is not much of a defense. Taxes and other state activities, inflation and the panicky desire for liquid assets, have made it factually friable. Moreover, the fears of property-holders outrun the actual dangers. Thus, even powerful groups in America feel more frightened of Communism than its actual power warrants. Property no longer represents the old security for those who hold it, and the fear that it may vanish any day makes it as much a source of anxiety as of strength. The rich no longer dare flaunt wealth, but tread softly, guided by considerations of "public relations." Wealthy students often act as if ashamed of their wealth; I have sometimes been tempted to point out that the rich are a minority and have rights, too.

The change in the meaning of work is even plainer. For the inner-directed person, work seemed self-justifying: the only problem was to find the work to which one felt called. As we have seen, the age of expanding frontiers provided the individual with an inexhaustible list of tasks. Work, like property, moreover, was considered a mode of relating oneself to physical objects, and only indirectly to people. Indeed, the work-hungry inner-directed types of this period sometimes found that they were cut off from family and friends, and often from humanity in general, by their assiduity and diligence. And work, like property, was a defense against psychological invasion, a "do not disturb" sign guarding the industrious man of the middle class.

Today the meaning of work is a very different one, psychologically, though in many professions and industries the older modes still persist. To an increasing degree, the self is no longer defined by its productive accomplishments but by its role in a "Friendship" system. As the "isolate" or "rate-buster" is punished and excluded from the work force in the shop, so the lone wolf is weeded out of management; up-to-date personnel men use deep-probing psychological tests to eliminate applicants, whatever their other gifts, who lack the other-directed personality needed for the job.

To be sure, out of anxiety, a lingering asceticism, and a need for an impressive agenda, the professional and business men and women of the big cities continue to work hard, or more accurately, to spend long hours in the company of their fellow "antagonistic cooperators"; "work" is seen as a network of personal relationships that must be constantly watched and oiled. Increasingly, both work and leisure call on the same sort of skills—sociability, sensitivity to others' feelings and wants, and the exercise of taste-preferences freed from direct considerations of economic advantage. Work in this case has a certain unreality for people, since it has almost floated free from any connection with technical crafts. The latter have been built into machines or can easily be taught; but people must still go to the office and find ways of keeping, or at least looking, busy. Thus in many circles work and leisure are no longer clearly distinguished, as we can see by observing a luncheon or a game of golf among competitors.

The feeling of powerlessness of the other-directed character is, then, the result in part of the lack of genuine commitment to work. His life is not engaged in a direct struggle for mastery over himself and nature; he has no long-term goals since the goals must constantly be changed. At the same time, he is in competition with others for the very values they tell him are worth pursuing; in a circular process, one of these values is the approval of the competing group itself. Hence he is apt to repress overt competitiveness, both out of anxiety to be liked and out of fear of retaliation. In this situation, he is likely to lose interest in the work itself. With loss of interest, he may even find himself little more than a dilettante, not quite sure that he is really able to accomplish anything.

•

When we turn from the sphere of work to the sphere of leisure, we see again that roles in which the individual could once find refuge from and defense against the group have become stylized roles, played according to the mandates and under the very eyes of the group. The individual in the age of inner-direction had little leisure; often he was so work-driven that he could not even use the leisure given him. On occasion, however, he could escape from the pressures and strains of the workaday world into a private hobby or into the resources of culture, either "highbrow" or popular. In either case, the stream of entertainment and communication was intermittent; to come into contact with it required effort. Leisure, therefore, by its very scarcity, provided a change of pace and role. Moreover, beyond these actual leisure roles stood a group of fantasy roles—roles of social ascent, of rebellion against work and inhibition, dreams of world-shaking achievement; the individual was protected against invasion at least of his right to these dreams.

Today, leisure is seldom enjoyed in solitude, nor is it often used for unequivocal escape. Hobbies of the older craft type seem to have declined, and a baseball game is perhaps the only performance where the mass audience can still judge competence. The torrent of words and images from radio, the movies, and the comics begins to pour on the child even before he can toddle; he starts very early to learn his lifelong role of consumer. The quantity of messages impinging on the child becomes increasingly "realistic"; instead of "Just-So Stories" and fairy tales, children are given "here and now" stories of real life, and escape into imaginative fantasy is therefore held at a minimum.

Likewise, movies, fiction, and radio for adults increasingly deal with "here and now" problems: how to handle one's relations with children, with the opposite sex, with office colleagues away from the office. Story writers for the better woman's magazines are instructed to deal with the intimate problems faced by the readers, and soap opera is one long game of Going to Jerusalem; when one problem sits down, another is left standing. Indeed, we might claim, there is no "escape" from leisure. Wherever we turn, in work or in popular culture, we are faced by our peers and the problems they present, including the pressure they put on us to "have fun." A kind of ascetic selflessness rules much of the greatly expanded leisure of the other-directed person—selflessness disguised by the craving for comfort, fun, and effortlessness, but ascetic nonetheless in its tense use of leisure for preparing oneself to meet the expectations of others.

Thus, the newly reached horizons of leisure and consumption made possible by our economic abundance have not been as exhilarating for the individual as the realized horizons of work and production proved to be for many in the age of expanding frontiers. . . .

I do not mean to imply that our society "produces" other-directed people because such people are in demand in an increasingly monopolistic, managerial economy. The relations between character and society are not that simple. Moreover, neither character nor society changes all at once. But it would take us too far afield to trace the many formative agencies in the shift, still far from complete, from inner-direction to other-direction in the middle classes.

Furthermore, I must guard against the implication that I think inner-direction is a way of life preferable to other-direction. Each type has its virtues and its vices: the inner-directed person tends to be rigid and intolerant of others; the other-directed person, in turn, is likely to be flexible and sensitive to others. Neither type is altogether comfortable in the world. But in different ways each finds the discomforts it needs psychologically in order, paradoxically, to feel comfortable. The inner-directed person finds the struggle to master himself and the environment quite appropriate; he feels comfortable climbing uphill. The other-directed person finds equally appropriate the malaise that he shares with many others. Engrossed in the activities that the culture provides, he can remain relatively unconscious of his anxiety and tonelessness. Moreover, the character type must always be judged in context. Many persons who are inner-directed and who, in an earlier age, would have gone through life in relative peace, today find themselves indignant at a big-city world in which they have not felt at home. Other-directed persons also may not feel at home, but home never had the same meaning for them. It would appear to the envious inner-directed observer that the other-directed manage their lives better in a mass society. Conversely, the other-directed may envy the seeming firmness of the inner-directed, and look longingly back on the security of nineteenth-century society, while failing to see that firmness was often merely stubbornness and security merely ignorance. . . .

The Saving Remnant

Nevertheless, even under modern conditions, and out of the very matrix of other-directed modes of conformity, some people strive toward an autonomous character. An autonomus person has no compulsive need to follow the other-direction of his culture and milieu—and no compulsive need to flout it, either. We know almost nothing about the factors that make for such positive results; it is easier to understand the sick than to understand why some stay well. It hardly helps to repeat our point that man's helplessness is the condition for his every advance, because this generalization tells us too little about individual cases. However, it seems that the helplessness of modern man in a world of power has been one element in the genesis of some of the extraordinary human achievements of our age. Some of these achievements are the physical and literary productions of men's hands and minds, but other achievements lie in the internal "productions" of men—their characters; it is of these that I speak here.

There were autonomous people of course, in the era of inner-direction, but they were made of sterner stuff; the barriers they encountered were the classic ones: family, religion, poverty. On the other hand, the person who seeks autonomy today in the upper socio-economic levels of the Western democracies is not faced with the barriers that normally restricted him in the past. The coercions against his independence are frequently invisible. An autonomous person of the middle class must work constantly to detach himself from shadowy entanglements with his culture—so difficult to break with because its demands appear so "reasonable," so trivial.

For our study of autonomy, we have drawn freely on Erich Fromm's concept of the "productive orientation" in *Man for Himself*. Fromm shows the orientation of a type of character that can relate itself to people through love, and to objects and the world generally through the creative gift. The struggle for a productive orientation becomes exigent at the very moment in history when solution of the problem of production itself, in the technical sense, is in sight.

All human beings, even the most productive, the most autonomous, are fated, in a sense, to die the death of Ivan Ilyitch, in Tolstoy's "The Death of Ivan Ilyitch," who becomes aware only on his deathbed of his underlived life and his unused potentialities for autonomy. All of us realize only a fraction of our potentialities. Always a matter of degree, always blended with residues of inner-direction or other-direction, autonomy is a process, not an achievement. Indeed, we may distinguish the autonomous by the fact that his character is never a finished product, but always a lifelong growth.

I speak of autonomy as an aspect of character structure, and not in terms of independence of overt behavior. The autonomous person may or may not conform in his behavior to the power-requirements of society; he can choose whether to conform or not. (The Bohemians and rebels are not usually autonomous; on the contrary, they are zealously tuned in to the signals of a defiant group that finds the meaning of life in a compulsive nonconformity to the majority group.) Yet the separation of "freedom in behavior" from "autonomy in character" cannot be complete. Autonomy requires self-awareness about the fact of choice, about possible ways of living. The autonomous person of today exists precisely because we have reached an awareness of the problem of choice that was not required among the Pueblos, or, for the most part, in the Middle Ages, or even in the period after the Reformation, when the concepts of God's will and of duty confined choice for many within fairly narrow bounds.

The very fluidity of modern democratic social systems, that, for the mass of people, results in anxiety and "escape from freedom," forces those who would become autonomous to find their own way. They must "choose themselves," in Sartre's phrase, out of their very alienation from traditional ties and inner-directed defenses which inhibited true choice in the past. However, I think Sartre mistaken in his Kantian notion that men can choose themselves under totalitarian conditions. Likewise, if the choices that matter are made for us by the social system, even if it is in appearance a democratic system, then our sense of freedom also will atrophy; most people need the opportunity for some freedom of behavior if they are to develop and confirm their autonomy of character. Nevertheless, the rare autonomous character we have been describing, the man of high, almost precarious, quality, must arise from that aloneness, that helplessness of modern man, that would overwhelm a lesser person. It is in this quality and in the mode of life he is groping to achieve, that he has made a contribution to the problem of living in a power-world.

•

If these conjectures are accurate, then it follows that, by a process of unconscious polarization which is going on in society, a few people are becoming more self-consciously autonomous than before, while many others are losing their social and characterological defenses against the group. The latter, though politically strong, are psychically weak, and the autonomous minority, by its very existence, threatens the whole shaky mode of adaptation of the majority.

Nevertheless, joy in life has its own dynamic. . . . Character structure is not completely fixed for the individual, so long as life lasts, or for the group. Men have some control over the fate by which their characters are made. By showing how life can be lived with vitality and happiness even in time of trouble, the autonomous people can become a social force, indeed a "saving remnant." By converting present helplessness into a condition of advance, they lay the basis of a new society, though they may not live to see it.

PART VI

PROCESSES OF CHANGE

Introduction

Every process has a beginning, a middle, and an end—which is hardly a revelation, but does provide a helpful way of organizing some insights concerning modes of change. The following discussions deal with the conditions under which social changes are initiated, spread from the initial sector or sectors to others (rarely do all parts of a society change simultaneously), and finally, in one way or another, terminated. With few exceptions, the statements made in this section, though they are illustrated by application to one specific kind of social change, are applicable to a variety of social processes on several levels and in different institutional spheres. In this sense they are general. On the other hand, they are limited in scope, since, unlike classical or contemporary theories, they do not provide broad analytical frameworks but just one or two elements of such constructions.

Underlying the analysis of most processes described in this section is the assumption that the various parts of any social system are interdependent, so that changes in one sector will be followed by strains which necessitate adjustive changes in other sectors if the social system is to maintain its viability. This seems to be the basic common denominator of the various viewpoints represented.

The beginning of social change is to a large degree a response to the presence of some degree of social disorganization, caused either internally or externally. This is just another way of saying that strains in a social system call for new adjustments. A well-integrated social system, in which needs are effectively fulfilled and men are largely satisfied, is rather rare. This is especially true of modern society, which tends to contain a comparatively high amount of social disorganization, because of its size and complexity and the rapid pace of change generated in part as a response to earlier disorganization. Hence, the central question for the student of modern society is not, "Is there social disorganization?" for which the answer is invariably, "Yes, there is," but rather, "What is its scope, what institutional areas are affected, how strategic are the affected areas, and is disorganization accelerating or subsiding?"

Phillip Hauser sees the core source of intra-societal contradictions and strains—which in turn are singularly important instigators of social change processes—not in the relations among classes or races, but among the various demographic layers of society. Society, especially contemporary society, is composed of layers which, like geological strata, reflect the accumulated deposits of time. Contemporary society, the chaotic or anachronistic society, is experiencing unprecedented strains and tensions due to what Hauser calls the social morphological revolution. The key elements of the social morphological revolution are the population explosion, the population implosion (concentration-urbanization), and population diversification (many races, nationalities, close contact), and the acceleration in the tempo of technological and social change.

The social morphological revolution is responsible for many human ecology problems having to do with housing, circulation of persons and goods, waste removal, air and water pollution, recreational facilities, urban design, etc.; as well as other personal, social and organizational problems, such as delinquency and crime, alcoholism, drug addiction and mental disorder, the youth revolt of "hippies" and "activists", unemployment, poverty, bigotry, inter-group conflict, family disorganization, labor-management conflict, the conservative-liberal debate, maladministration of criminal justice, paralysis in government, and so on. Many of these latter problems can be superficially traced to our society's emphasis on secondary rather than primary group ties, and on interpersonal relations defined by utility rather than emotion and sentiment, isolation of the conjugal or nuclear family from the extended kin network, the primacy of bureaucracy over informal organization, etc. In brief, the little community burgeoned into mass society. Hauser sees a need for greater planning and stronger efforts to bridge the gap between social research and social policy and action, as a way to bring the processes of a chaotic society back into order.

Viewing the initiation of processes of social change—either revolutions or reforms—largely as a response to social disorganization, caused either internally or externally, implies that change is the outcome of an interplay among a variety of factors. Some factors are mere background conditions, while others are more closely related to the initiation of change. In addition, there often is a definite event that actually precipitates a major social change. Discussing the role of such a precipitant, MacIver points out that it should not be viewed in isolation, as the sole generator of social change, but rather in conjunction with the entire system as it is being changed. Frequently, the precipitant appears to be the decisive factor in bringing about a drastic change, while in fact the system was "ripe," and the specific event only "triggered" rather than "caused" the transformation. However, the precipitant is not without importance, since it exerts an influence on the timing and concrete manifestation of the particular change and thus plays a not negligible role in altering the course of events.

Turning from the conditions and factors of change to change itself, we recognize that each process which involves a new pattern of behavior, new attitudes, new techniques, etc. might be referred to as an innovation. This is the case whatever the nature of the change, whether introduced violently or peacefully, abruptly or gradually, by a sudden occurrence or after long preparation. The term "innovation" suggests that deliberation has taken place, but actually, as Kallen points out, this is not necessarily the case.[2] While some innovators consciously plan their innovations, others may not seek to innovate at all and may not be aware of doing so. Innovation may be spontaneous or unconscious, unplanned, and even undesired; so long as a new pattern of human thought or action has emerged, an innovation has occurred.

Innovation and acceptance of innovation do not occur at random, but depend on the urgency of social needs, the degree of disorganization, as well as the flexibility of society and the degree to which change has been institutionalized. As a rule, the more dynamic a society, the more tolerant it is toward innovation. Whereas traditional societies actively suppress innovation, modern societies actively encourage it. But, as Kallen points out, even in modern society innovation encounters resistance, due to emotional investment in old patterns and distrust of new ones. Linton demonstrates that even in the same society not all innovations stand an equal chance of being accepted. In order to be accepted an innovation must be in line with a society's needs and interests, and it must be compatible with the society's existing framework. Modern society, for instance, is unlikely to pay attention to innovations in the field of magic, but is likely to encourage innovations in the field of science and technology. In fact, innovation in these areas is highly institutionalized. Universities, industries, and the military establish special research divisions and devote large amounts of resources to the search for new information and its application. Part of the education system, especially scientific training, is geared to the encouragement of innovations. Once an innovation is favorably judged, special divisions (*e.g.,* development units in corporations) are devoted to its implementation and to promoting its acceptance in society (marketing and advertising). In some cases, not only the new product but even the need for it is produced.

Acceptance of innovations is really nothing more than the receiving end of the diffusion of an innovation. The term diffusion has been used mostly to indicate the spread of items from one culture to another. But the term diffusion applies here also, and is used to refer to the spread of an item within a culture—from the innovator to a group, from one group to another. Crosscultural diffusion is discussed in Part II by Kroeber in his

---

[2] The terms "invention" and "discovery" as used by Linton cover roughly the same ground as the term "innovation" as discussed by Kallen.

analysis of the diffusionist approach. We included here an empirical study about intracultural diffusion. The article by Coleman, Menzel, and Katz traces the diffusion of a medical innovation—more specifically, a new drug —among physicians. Analysis of the data collected suggests, as the authors point out, that the physician's readiness to use a new drug, *i.e.*, his tendency to accept an innovation, is a function not only of his individual traits, but also of his relations with other physicians. The more integrated he is in the community of physicians, the sooner will he accept the new drug.

Like the concept of diffusion, the principle of accumulation deals with the spread of an innovation as the process of social change moves from the sector in which it was initiated to other sectors. Myrdal's central claim is that by the very fact that a process starts rolling, it gains additional momentum, that change in one sector triggers changes in others. The importance of this insight in the particular area Myrdal studied, that of race relations, lies in that there is a vicious circle in which discrimination makes for lower education, which makes for less employment opportunities, which makes for a lower standard of living, all of which, in turn increase (and "justify") discrimination, and so on. Myrdal's point is that if one could break into this circle at any one place, bring about an improvement in any one of the sectors, this in turn would bring about cumulative improvements. This raises some questions: Will any initial "push" do to start the process rolling, or must it have a certain magnitude? And, if the latter, how does one establish what it is? Are all factors equally potent in setting the cumulative process in motion or are some more potent than others? And finally, how far can the momentum thus gained carry a process such as desegregation?

Ogburn addresses himself to the same general problems of change in one sector expanding to other sectors. Ogburn's basic assumption, like that of the other authors in this section is, that the various parts of a sociocultural system or subsystem are interrelated, hence changes in one sector necessitate adaptive changes in others. But unlike the previous authors, he is concerned with the gap in time between the initial changes and the adaptive responses. This cultural (or social) lag makes for maladjustments in the society in which it occurs—the longer the lag, the greater the strain— so that eventually, if the lags occur in significant spheres, the society faces the possibility of complete or partial disintegration.

An altogether different question is whether there is one single sector or set of sectors that always leads and others that always lag, or whether different sectors lead in different processes of social change. Ogburn puts more stress on cases where material factors change first and cultural factors adapt, but he points out that it is also possible for nonmaterial factors to start the process of change.

Since the time period in which the change in one sector has already occurred but adaptive changes in other sectors have not yet taken place is, as

Ogburn points out, a period of maladjustment, the question is raised of whether many such strains could not be significantly reduced by adequate planning. On the other hand, it might be feared that planning, while reducing strain in one sphere, would increase strain in other spheres by entailing excessive restrictions on the individual.

Morton Kaplan's study is one of change of the system, a study of transformation and of its rules. When certain rules of equilibrium are transgressed, the present system ceases to exist, and a new system comes into being. This transformation does not occur at random, but follows certain patterns. One can delineate a universe of possible structures of a given system. Kaplan presents six such possible structures, as sufficient for the effective study of international relations. Once such a universe of possible structures has been etablished, one can safely state that, when a system which has one of these structures is strained to the breaking point, one of the five others will emerge. (The breakdown of the system into its elementary units must be one possibility in any such universe of structures.) The next question is then: "Which of the other structures is likely to emerge, and to what degree can this be predicted on the basis of our knowledge of the present structure, of the strains making for its disintegration, and of the interstructural rules of transformation?"

Though Kaplan studies rules of transformation on the level of international systems, there is no reason why his method cannot be applied to other social systems. Thus one could predict that if a modern democracy were to disintegrate, either anarchy would prevail or a totalitarian regime would emerge, which would be controlled either from the inside or, to varying degrees, from the outside (though there is always at least a logical possibility of the resurrection of the initial structure). One could then analyze the conditions under which each of the possible structures would emerge; *e.g.,* when is the fall of a democracy more likely to lead to anarchy, when to dictatorship.

The study of the rules of transformation adds an entirely new dimension to the exploration of social change. Many earlier studies analyzed change *in* a structure or *of* a structure, but had little to say about what new structure would emerge if an existing one were to disintegrate. While a notion of rules of transformation might be too stringent for sociological theory at this stage, it seems that movement in this direction constitutes one of the most promising lines of thought and research for the whole area of social change.

CHAPTER 38

PHILIP M. HAUSER

The Chaotic Society: Product of the Social Morphological Revolution

Contemporary society, whether observed globally, nationally, or locally, is realistically characterized as "the chaotic society" and best understood as "the anachronistic society." Contemporary society is realistically characterized as chaotic because of its manifest confusion and disorder—the essential elements of chaos. On the international scene, to draw upon a few examples, consider the situation in Vietnam, Czechoslovakia, the Middle East, and Nigeria. On the national level consider the United States, France, the United Kingdom, China, and almost any country in Asia, Latin America or Africa. On the local level, in the United States, consider New York, Chicago, Los Angeles, Detroit, Cleveland, Memphis, Miami, and over 100 other cities which have been wracked by violence.

Contemporary society can be best understood when it is viewed as an anachronistic society. To be sure, society at any time, at least during the period of recorded history, has been an anachronistic society. For throughout the millennia of the historical era, society, at any instant in time, comprised layers of culture which, like geological strata, reflected the passage and deposits of time. Confusion and disorder, or chaos, may be viewed in large part as the resultant of the dissonance and discord among the various cultural strata, each of which tends to persist beyond the set of conditions, physical and social, which generated it.

In some ways chaos in contemporary society differs from that in earlier societies only in degree. But there are a number of unique factors in contemporary chaos which make it more a difference in kind. First, contemporary society, as the most recent, contains the greatest number of cultural layers, and, therefore, the greatest potential for confusion and disorder.

Reprinted from *American Sociological Review*, Feb. 1969, Vol. 34, No. 1, pp. 1-18.

Second, contemporary society possesses cultural layers much more diverse than any predecessor society and, therefore, much greater dissonance. Third, contemporary society, unlike any predecessor, contains the means of its own destruction, the ultimate weapon, the explosive power of nuclear fusion.

It is my central thesis that contemporary society, the chaotic and anachronistic society, is experiencing unprecedented tensions and strains by reason of the social morphological revolution. The key to the understanding of contemporary society lies, therefore, in an understanding of the social morphological revolution. Moreover, it is a corollary thesis that comprehension of the social morphological revolution points to the directions social engineering must take for the reduction or elimination of the chaos that threatens the viability of contemporary society.

I am mindful of the fact that "the social morphological revolution" is not a familiar rubric to the sociological fraternity—nor to anyone else. It is a neologism, albeit with a legitimate and honorable ancestry, for which I must plead guilty. I offer two justifications for injecting this abominable rhetoric into the literature. First, I am convinced that it contains useful explanatory power that has not yet been fully exploited in macro-social considerations, or in empirical research, or in social engineering activities. Second, it is appropriate that the discipline of sociology possess a revolution of its own. After all, the agronomists have the "agricultural revolution"; economists, the "commercial" and "industrial" revolutions; natural scientists, the "scientific revolution"; engineers, the "technological revolution"; and demographers, the "vital revolution." Sociologists, even if they have not formally recognized it, have the "social morphological revolution," and perhaps it is in order formally to acknowledge and to christen it.

The Social Morphological Revolution

What is this social morphological revolution and what are its antecedents?

To answer the second of these questions first, I must repeat that its ancestry is legitimate and honorable. Durkheim[1], encapsulating earlier literature, provided in a focused way insight into the implications of the most abstract way of viewing a society, namely, by size and density of its population. In his consideration of the structure of the social order Durkheim[2] used the term "social morphology." Wirth[3] in his classical article "Urbanism as a Way of Life," drawing on Aristotle, Durkheim, Tonnies, Sumner, Willcox, Park, Burgess and others, explicitly dealt with the impact of size, density and heterogeneity of population of human behavior and on the social order.

---

[1] Emile Durkheim, *L'année Sociologique* 1897-98. Volume II.

[2] *The Rules of Sociological Method.* Glencoe: The Free Press, 1938.

[3] Louis Wirth, *Community Life and Social Policy.* Chicago: University of Chicago Press, 1956.

The social morphological revolution refers to the changes in the size, density and heterogeneity of population and to the impact of these changes on man and society. . . .

Elements

The social morphological revolution is the product of three developments, energized by, and in interaction with, a fourth. The three developments may be described in dramatic terms as the "population explosion," the "population implosion," and "population diversification." The fourth, and interrelated development, is the acceleration in the tempo of technological and social change.

The "population explosion" refers to the remarkable increase in the rate of world population growth, especially during the modern era. In the long view world population growth rates have increased from perhaps two percent per millennium during the Paleolithic Period to two percent per annum at the present time—a thousand-fold increase.[4]

In quick summary, it took most of the two to 2½ million years man, or a close relative, has occupied the earth to generate a world population of one billion persons—a number not achieved until about 1825. It required only 105 years more to reach a population of 2 billion, by 1930; and only 30 years more to reach a total population of 3 billion, by 1960.[5]

The population explosion is still under way and, in fact, has achieved a greater magnitude since the end of World War II with its extension to the two-thirds of mankind in the developing areas of the world—in Asia, Africa and Latin America. Despite growing efforts to dampen rates of population growth, and contrary to the wishful thinking of some family planners, the facts indicate continuing acceleration of world population. Certainly, short of the catastrophic, there is little prospect of significant reduction in world population growth between now and the end of this century. Present fertility and mortality trends would beget a world population of 7.5 billion by the year 2000, and even the relatively optimistic preferred projection of the United Nations gives a world total of 6.1 billion by the century's end.[6] Despite efforts to reduce fertility, then, the realistic prospect is that continuing mortality declines, as well as stubbornly high birth rates, will continue to produce explosive world population growth for at least the next two human generations.

The "population implosion" refers to the increasing concentration of the

---

[4] Fletcher Wellemeyer, and Frank Lorimer. "How many people have ever lived on earth." *Population Bulletin,* 18 (February 1962).

[5] United Nations. *The Determinants and Consequences of Population Trends.* New York: United Nations, 1953. *World Population Prospects.* New York: United Nations, 1966.

[6] Ibid., p. 15.

world's peoples on a small proportion of the earth's surface—the phenomenon of urbanization and metropolitanization. Again, in the long view, this is a relatively recent development. Permanent human settlement was not achieved until the Neolithic Period. Such permanent settlement had to await the great inventions, technological and social organizational, of the Neolithic Revolution—including domesticated plants and animals, the proliferation of the crafts, and forms of collective behavior and social organization. Clumpings of population large enough to be called towns or cities did not emerge until after about 3500 B.C., and mankind did not achieve the technological and social organizational development to permit cities of 100,000 or more until as recently as Greco-Roman civilization. With the collapse of the Roman Empire, the relatively large urban agglomerations in the Roman sphere of influence diminished in size to small towns providing services to rural hinterlands together with which they constituted almost autonomous subsistence economies.

With the emergence of Europe from the Dark Ages and the series of "revolutions"—the Agricultural Revolution, the Commercial Revolution, the Industrial Revolution, the Scientific Revolution, and the Technological Revolution—man achieved levels both of technological and social organizational development that permitted ever larger agglomerations of people and economic activities. In consequence, the proliferation of cities of 1,000,000 or more inhabitants became possible during the 19th century, and the emergence of metropolitan areas and megalopolis, the coalescence of metropolitan areas, during the second half of the 20th century. In 1800 only 2.4 percent of the world's people resided in places of 20,000 or more; and only 1.7 percent in places of 100,000 or more. By 1960, 27.1 percent were located in places of 20,000 or more, and 19.9 percent in places of 100,000 or more.[7]

The trend towards increased urban and metropolitan concentration of population is likely to continue. The reasons for this are to be found in the advantages of clumpings of population and economic activities. As Adam Smith noted, the greater the agglomeration, the greater is the division of labor possible; and this permits increased specialization, easier application of technology and the use of non-human energy, economies of scale, external economies, and the minimization of the frictions of space and communication. In brief, the population implosion is likely to continue because clumpings of people and economic activities constitute the most efficient producer and consumer units yet devised. Moreover, such population agglomerations generate a social milieu of excitement and lure which add to the forces making for larger aggregations. Projections of world urban population indicate that by the end of the century 42 percent of the world's peoples may be

---

[7] Kingsley Davis. "The origin and growth of urbanization in the world." *American Journal of Sociology,* Vol. 60, March 1955, p. 433. Gerald Breese. *Urbanization in Newly Developing Countries.* Englewood Cliffs: Prentice-Hall, 1966.

resident in places of 100,000 or more, as contrasted with 20 percent in 1960, 5.5 percent in 1900, and 1.7 percent in 1800.[8]

"Population diversification" alludes to the increasing heterogeneity of populations not only sharing the same geographic area but also, increasingly, the same life space—economic, social and political activity. And the "same geographic area" and "the same life space," with accelerating technological and social organizational developments, have expanded during the 20th century virtually to embrace the entire world. Population heterogeneity involves diversity in culture, language, religion, values, behavior, ethnicity and race. These characteristics are obviously not mutually exclusive categories, but they constitute foci of problems of communication, conflicts of interest, and frictions of interaction. Population diversification connotes not only the physical presence of a heterogeneous human aggregation but also social interaction among the diverse elements.

Finally, the accelerated tempo of technological and social change requires little elaboration. Suffice it to say that technological change has, in general, preceded and necessitated social change, and that the difference between rates of technological and social change and differential rates of social change have originated great cultural strains and dissonance.[9]

The four developments discussed are, needless to say, highly interrelated and constitute the important elements of the social morphological revolution. The population explosion has fed the population implosion. Both have fed population diversification. And the accelerated tempo of technological and social change has operated as both antecedents to, and consequences of, the other three developments. Each in its own way, and all four in concert, have precipitated severe problems: chronic and acute; physical, economic, social and political; domestic and international.

The social morphological revolution incorporates the vital revolution and is closely interrelated with the other revolutions—agricultural, commercial, scientific, technological, and industrial. It is both antecedent to, and consequent of, the other revolutions and, as such, should be, on the one hand, better understood when considered in relation to them and, on the other hand, should be helpful in explaining them.

The Social Morphological Revolution in the United States

The United States constitutes the world's most dramatic examples of all four of the developments described. These developments are reaching climactic proportions, have precipitated major crises, and constitute a framework for comprehending and dealing with America's urban difficulties. Virtually all of the urban problems which are increasingly and urgently requir-

---

[8] Ibid.
[9] William F. Ogburn. *Social Change*. New York: The Viking Press, Inc., 1922.

ing national attention, whether they be physical, personal, social, ethnic and racial, economic or governmental problems, may be viewed as frictions of the social morphological revolution which is still under way—frictions in the transition from an agrarian to an urban and metropolitan order.

The Population Explosion

In 1790, when the first Decennial Census of the United States was taken, the United States had a total population of less than 4 million persons. By 1960 the population of the nation numbered more than 180 million; during 1967 it reached 200 million.

The U.S. Bureau of the Census has from time to time made projections of U.S. population on varying assumptions about the future course of fertility and mortality. Such projections made in 1967 indicate that, despite the declining crude birth rate, the United States will continue to experience large absolute population increase in the decades which lie ahead. These projections show that by 1990, only 22 years hence, the population of the U.S. may reach a level of from 256 to 300 million. One of these projections, based on a fertility assumption that takes the current slump in the birth rate into account, would produce a population of 206 million by 1970, 232 million by 1980, and 267 million by 1990. The same projection gives a population of 308 million by the year 2000 and 374 million by 2015 (U.S. Bureau of the Census, 1957, 1962, 1967).

The Population Implosion

In 1790, 95 percent of the population of the United States lived in rural areas, on farms, or in places having fewer than 2500 persons. The 5 percent of the population which lived in cities were concentrated in 24 such places, only two of which (New York and Philadelphia) had populations of 25,000 or more. By 1850, population in urban places was still as low as 15 percent. By 1900, however, almost two-fifths of the population lived in cities. But it was not until as recently as 1920 that the U.S. became an urban nation in the sense that more than half of the population (51 percent) lived in cities. That many critical problems affect cities and urban populations should not be too surprising in light of the fact that, in 1970, the United States completed her first half century as an urban nation, a period shorter than a lifetime.

The speed of the population implosion becomes clear in an examination of developments since the turn of the century. In the first sixty years of this century the increase in urban population absorbed 92 percent of the total population growth in the nation. In the decade 1950 to 1960, the increase in urban population absorbed more than 100 percent of total national growth; that is, total rural population, including nonfarm as well as farm, actually diminished for the first time.

The increase in the population of metropolitan areas is equally dramatic. The increase in the population of the Standard Metropolitan Statistical Areas (SMSA's) absorbed 79 percent of total national growth between 1900 and 1960; and the 24 largest SMSA's, those with 1,000,000 or more, absorbed 43 percent in the first sixty years of this century.

The population implosion in this nation is still under way. If present trends continue the metropolitan population, between 1960 and 1985, will increase by some 58 percent, while the non-metropolitan population increases by less than 12 percent. By 1985, then, 71 percent of the people in this nation would reside in metropolitan areas as compared with 63 percent in 1960.

Population Diversification

The United States has been one of history's most dramatic examples of population diversification as well as of the population explosion and the population implosion. Although the original European settlers were predominantly from the United Kingdom, the infusion of African Negro population began during the seventeenth century and was followed by waves of diverse European stocks during the nineteenth and early twentieth centuries.

The Census of Population first counted "foreign born" whites in 1850. At that time they constituted 9.7 percent of the total population. Although successive waves of immigration were heavy, the foreign-born whites never exceeded 14.5 percent of the total, a level reached in 1890 and again in 1910; they have been a dwindling proportion of the total ever since. By reason of restrictions on immigration, the foreign-born will become a decreasing proportion of the population of the nation in the decades which lie ahead. [On the other hand,] the proportion of nonwhites, mainly Negroes, is likely to increase.

By reason of the "Negro Revolt," the most acute present manifestation of chaos in the United States, a closer examination of Negro population trends is required. In 1790, as recorded in the first census of the United States, there were fewer than 800,000 Negroes in the nation, but they made up about 20 percent of the total population. By that date they had already been resident in the colonies for 175 years, mainly as the property or indentured servants of their white masters.

Negro Americans remained about one-fifth of the total population until 1810. From then to 1930 they were an ever declining proportion of the total, as slave traffic ceased and white immigration continued. By 1930 the proportion of Negroes had diminished to less than one-tenth of the total. Since 1940, however, the Negro growth rate has been greater than that of the white population, and their proportion had risen to 11 percent by 1967.

In 1790, 91 percent of all Negroes lived in the South. The first large migratory flow of Negroes out of the South began during World War I, prompted by the need for wartime labor and the freeing of the Negro from the soil, with the diversification of agriculture and the onset of the delayed industrial revolution in the South. This migration of Negroes from the South was greatly increased during and after World War II. As a result, the proportion of total Negroes located in the North and West almost quadrupled between 1910 and 1960, increasing from 11 to 40 percent.

The migratory movement of Negroes from the South to the North and West effected not only a regional redistribution but also, significantly, an urban-rural redistribution. In 1910, before the out-migration of the Negro from the South began, 73 percent lived in rural areas. By 1960, within fifty years, the Negro had been transformed from 73 percent rural to 73 percent urban, and had become more urbanized than the white population.

The great urban concentration of Negro Americans is also revealed by their location in metropolitan areas. By 1910, only 29 percent of Negroes lived in the Standard Metropolitan Statistical Areas. By 1960, this concentration had increased to 65 percent.

Negro population changes, past and in prospect, have resulted in greatly increased sharing with whites of the same geographical local areas, accompanied by increased pressure for social contact and social interaction. The acute tensions which characterize white-black relationships in the United States today represent a compounding of the impact of the social morphological revolution. For within the framework of the general population explosion and implosion in the entire nation, there has occurred an even more dramatic population explosion and implosion among Afro-Americans. These developments have greatly exacerbated the problems in the population of Afro-Americans in urban and metropolitan areas over a relatively short period of time, and the contrast in background and life-styles between blacks and whites by reason of the disadvantaged position of blacks over the years, have combined to produce tensions that may well constitute the most serious domestic problem in the United States for some time to come.

Consequences of the Social Morphological Revolution

The combined effects of the population explosion, the population implosion, and population diversification have produced in the realm of the social the equivalent of a mutation in the realm of the genetic. The social morphological revolution has profoundly altered human nature and the social order. In broad overview the social morphological revolution has modified the human aggregation as a physical construct and as an economic mechanism; it has transformed human behavior and social organization, including the nature of government; it has generated and aggravated a host of problems —physical, personal, social, institutional, and governmental.

Examples of the physical problems are given by the problems relating to housing supply and quality, circulation of persons and goods, solid and human waste removal, air and water pollution, recreational facilities, urban design, and the management of natural resources.

Examples of personal, social and organizational problems are given by the incidence of delinquency and crime, alcoholism, drug addiction, and mental disorder. It is evident in the current revolt of youth, which at the extremes include the "hippie," who resolves his problems by retreat, and the "activist," who resolves his problems by beating his head against the doors of the Pentagon, or police clubs at the University of California at Berkeley and at other universities. It is revealed also in unemployment, poverty, racism, bigotry, inter-group conflict, family disorganization, differential morbidity and mortality, labor-management conflict, the conservative-liberal debate, the maladministration of criminal justice; and in corruption, malapportionment and inertia in government, and the fragmentation and paralysis of local government. It is further revealed by continuing resort to physical force as a means for the resolution of conflicts of interest. No matter how laudable the goals, when force is employed by labor and management, by students, by advocates of peace, by minority groups, or in most extreme form by nations at war, it is a mechanism incompatible with the continued viability of contemporary society. In fact, if society is to remain viable, when there is disorder, it has no alternative to the use of overwhelming collective force for restoration of order. Of course, upon the restoration of order, the causes of disorder must be investigated and removed, or tensions may mount and produce even greater disorder. The point is that contemporary society, by reason of unprecedented interdependence, is highly vulnerable and easily disrupted—a fact which is increasingly perceived and exploited by dissident persons and groups.

These types of problems may be viewed sociologically as consequences of the social morphological revolution which generated secondary group, as distinguished from primary group association; inter-personal relations based on utility from emotion and sentiment; the conjugal or nuclear, from the extended family; formal from informal social control; rational from traditional behavior; enacted from crescive institutions; and bureaucracy from small-scale and informal organization. Especially significant have been the changes in the elements and processes of the socialization of the child—the transformation of the helpless biological specimen, the infant, into a human being or member of society. In brief, the social morphological revolution transformed the "little community",[10] which has characterized predecessor societies, into the "mass society".[11]

It is my contention that the confusion and disorder of contemporary life may be better understood and dealt with as frictions in the transition still under way from the little community to the mass society; and that the chaos

---

[10] Robert Redfield. *The Little Community: Viewpoints for the Study of a Human Whole*. Chicago: University of Chicago Press, 1955.

[11] Karl Mannheim. *Man and Society in an Age of Reconstruction: Studies in Modern Social Structure* (trans. Edward Shils). London: K. Paul, Trench, Trubner, Ltd., 1940.

of contemporary society, in large part, is the product of dissonnance and conflict among the strata of culture which make up our social heritage. The problems or frictions are often visible manifestations of what my former teacher and colleague, William Fielding Ogburn, termed "cultural lag".[12]

Permit me to provide a few concrete examples of cultural lag in contemporary society—examples of special significance and impact. I do so, as a sociologist, to illustrate the use of the analytical framework provided by the social morphological revolution in the consideration of specific social problems.

Governance

Focusing on the United States, consider the example of cultural lag in our system of governance. Needless to say, confusion and disorder in government has a multiplier impact on other realms of chaos.

Consider some of the elements involved in the raging "conservative-liberal" debate. In the ongoing political context, the polemic centers on the role of government in the social and economic order. It is evident in the attitudes toward "big government," and, in general, in anachronistic political ideology. Three illustrations of "cultural lag" in ideology help to explain the paralysis which afflicts this nation in efforts to deal with the acute problems which beset us.

One is the inherited shibboleth that "that government is best which governs least." The doctrine made considerable sense when our first census was taken in 1790. At that time, 95 percent of the American people lived on farms or in towns having fewer than 2500 persons. What was there for government to do, compared with the situation in 1960, in which 70 percent of the American people lived in urban places and about 63 percent were residents of metropolitan areas? Can you visualize a United States today without a Social Security System, without a Public Health Service, without a Federal Reserve Board, without the Interstate Commerce Commission, and without the Civil Aeronautics Administration? The slogan "that government is best which governs least" is a good example of a cultural survival which has persisted beyond its time. . . .

Furthermore, consider the irony in the national political situation, in which by reason of seniority provisions for committee memberships and chairmanships in the Congress and the one-party system in the post-bellum South, this most underdeveloped region of the United States, which is still in the early stages of the social morphological revolution, maintains a vise-like grip on the national legislative process—a grip bolstered by the filibuster which permits tyranny by a minority.

---

[12] Ogburn, op. cit.

The rapidity with which this nation has become urbanized has produced serious malapportionment in the House of Representatives in the Congress, in state assemblies, and in municipal councils. For example, in 1960, there were 39 states with an urban population majority, but not a single state in the Union where the urban population controlled the state legislature. This condition accelerated Federal interventionism. For it was the insensitivity to urban problems, the problems of the mass society, by the malapportioned rural-dominated legislatures that drew the Federal government into such realms as public housing, urban renewal, highways and expressways, civil rights, mass transportation, and education. To the addicts of the outmoded slogans discussed above, these programs are viewed as the violation of "states rights." But it is an ironic thing that the most vociferous advocates of states rights have played a major role, by their ignoring of 20th century mass society needs, in bringing about the increased centralization of governmental functions.

A final example of cultural lag in the American system of governance is given by the chaos in local government. The framework for the structure of local government in the United States is the local governmental structure of 18th century England. The Constitutional fathers did not, and could not have been expected to, anticipate the emergence of population agglomerations of great size, density, and heterogeneity, which transcended not only municipal and township lines but also county and state boundaries. In consequence, our metropolitan clumpings of people and economic activities are characterized by governmental fragmentation which paralyzes local efforts to deal with metropolitan area-wide problems, such as those relating to air and water pollution, traffic congestion, crime, employment, housing, and education.

By reason of its implications for the socialization of the child, the consequences of governmental fragmentation for public education at the primary and secondary levels are especially worthy of attention. It may be argued that public school education is today converting this nation into a caste society, stratified by race and by economic status. I illustrate this with a neologism for which I apologize. I refer to the "pre-conception IQ," the IQ of the child before he is conceived. The child with a very high pre-conception IQ, high enough to select white-skinned parents who live in the suburbs, has by this astute act guaranteed unto himself an input for public school education two to ten times that of the child with a miserably low pre-conception IQ, stupid enough to select black-skinned parents in the inner-city slums. This is a way of saying that the child in the suburbs gets a first-class education, and the child in the inner city, black or white, gets a third or fourth rate education. As a result, education is no longer performing its historic mission in this nation in contributing to national unity and to the maintenance of an open society. On the contrary, the kind of education we now have in our slums and ghettos is recycling the present chaotic situation into perpetuity. Our metropolitan areas today have blacks who were born in the city, reared in the city, educated in the city, and who have not acquired the basic, the saleable or the citizenship skills prerequisite to their assuming the responsibilities and obligations as well as the rights of American citizenship. Quite apart from other factors operating, it is clear that the failure of local governmental structure to keep up with the social morphological revolution is a major element in this disastrous situation.

Racism

Without question, the most serious domestic problem which haunts the United States today is the Negro Revolt. There are only three considerations necessary to understand the "why" of this situation. First, the Afro-American has been on this continent for three and a half centuries. He involuntarily spent two and a half centuries in slavery; he spent a half century in the rural slum South under the unfulfilled promises of the Emancipation Proclamation; and he has spent an additional half century in the slum ghettos of metropolitan America, in the North and South.

Second, since World War II the entire world has been swept by what has felicitously been called "the revolution of rising expectations." This is the first generation in the history of man in which no peoples are left on the face of this earth who are willing to settle for second place in level of living and who do not insist on freedom and independence if not already achieved. This revolution of rising expectations has not bypassed Afro-Americans. In a fundamental sense the Negro Revolt is simply America's local manifestation of the revolution of rising expectations.

Third, there is a shorter-run and a more immediate consideration. With the Johnson administration and the success of previous Congresses in the passage of civil rights legislation, new vistas of opportunity and new expectations were aroused in the black community. It is an ironic thing that the Negro Revolt and the riots are not in spite of these advances but in a sense because of them. Blacks were led to believe that they were finally achieving full equality in the American scene. But what happened in reality? There was little to match the Federal leadership on the state front in terms of gubernatorial leadership, or on the local front in terms of mayoralty leadership, or in leadership in the private sector. Nothing substantial happened to change the reality of living in rat-infested slums and of unemployment rates two to three times that of whites. Little was done to change the character of the segregated communities in which the Negro lived, and little was done to change the character of the woefully deficient educational opportunities for the black child. As the gap between expectation and reality increased, so did frustration, alienation, and bitterness which have led to violence.

Underlying all three of these factors which account for the present restiveness, hostility, and violence of Afro-Americans is "white racism," the major cause of the present crisis. Racist doctrine may be understood as a negative and extreme form of ethnocentrism, the product of the isolated little community of relatively small size, density and cultural homogeneity. The persistence of racist attitudes and behavior constitutes another example of cultural lag—the survival of a little community into the mass society. A prejudicial attitude towards other human beings, whether in the positive form of ethnocentrism or its negative counterpart as hostility towards others on a categoric basis, is a cultural atavism—an anachronistic set of attitudes incompatible with the requirements of cooperative association in a mass society. In the context of large, dense and heterogeneous population agglomerations, racism necessarily spells trouble and conflict. It should not be too surprising that white racism is now breeding or exacerbating black racism, and, therefore, intensifying hostility and conflict. Furthermore, the paralysis of government in the United States, as described above, further compounds the crisis and offers little hope of any short-run resolution of tension and conflict. This nation, on its present course, may well be in for an indefinite period of guerilla warfare on the domestic as well as on the international front.

Other Examples of Cultural Lag

There are many other examples of cultural lag in American society. They include the constitutional right to bear arms—admittedly necessary in 18th century America but a dangerous anachronism in the last third of 20th century America. They include also the inalienable rights of labor to strike and of management to shut down and employ the lockout, often through trial by ordeal of the public. In twentieth century mass society, labor's right to strike and management's right to lockout may be described as the rights of labor and management to revert to the laws of the jungle—to resolve their conflicts of interest by means of brute force. The same can be said of the so-called right of the students to impose their views through the employment of force, or of any person or group who fails to resolve conflicts of interest in a mass society by an adjudicative or democratic procedure. . . .

Concluding Observations

Man is the only significant culture-building animal on earth. He not only adapts to environment, he creates it as well. He has created a world in which mankind itself is the crucial environment—a mankind characterized by large numbers, high densities and great heterogeneity. He is still learning how to live in this new world he has created. The product of the chief components of the social morphological revolution—the population explosion, the population implosion and population diversification—together with rapid technological and social change—is contemporary society, a chaotic society, an anachronistic society. It is a society characterized by dissonant cultural strata—by confusion and disorder. It is also a society which for the first time in human history possesses the capacity to destroy itself—globally as well as nation by nation.

In addition to the acceleration in the rate of technological and social change, and partly in response to it, society has acquired a greater capacity for social change. But, although the capability for social change has undoubtedly increased, adequate and effective mechanisms for the control of social change, for accommodation and adaptation to the changing social milieu, as well as to the changing material world, have yet to be evolved. Planning as a mechanism for rational decision-making is still in its infancy and has yet to develop an integrated approach with apposite administrative, economic and social planning, along with physical planning. Progress is being made in this respect, however. In this nation, for example, planning has become a respectable word now if modified by the term "city"; but when modified by such terms as "metropolitan," "regional," or "national," it is still considered a dangerous thought in some quarters. But planning, in ever broader contexts, will undoubtedly be a first step in the dissipation of confusion and the restoration of order. The question is whether mankind can muddle through without collective suicide before rational decision-making overtakes the confusion and disorder of our tottering transitional society.

I should make it clear that I recognize that disorder cannot, and should not, be entirely eliminated. For disorder betokens the need for change, often desirable, as well as necessary. Order as such is not by itself a discrete goal of high priority. Hitler, for example, achieved a high degree of order in his Third Reich; and Stalin, in his version of a communist society. The task is rather to welcome disorder, both in Durkheim's sense of helping to define the limits of order and as a symptom of needed change, but to control the levels of disorder, while effecting change, so that it does not threaten the viability of society.

In the United States, at the present time, "law and order" has become a political slogan with many overtones. But the disorder which afflicts American society by reason of the Negro Revolt and that of other minority groups, including the poor, points to the inadequacies of the slogan. The slogan is but a half-truth; and as Oliver Wendell Holmes once observed, "A half-truth is like a half-brick—it can be thrown a lot farther." The entire slogan, to meet the needs of our society, should be "law, justice, and order." For until justice is achieved by our minorities, we will not have order, unless we choose to make ourselves over into a repressive society. . . .

I conclude with a variation on my major theme. The chaotic society when understood as an anachronistic society can be transformed into a coeval or synchronous society. The first step in this direction lies, necessarily, in the comprehension of the nature and consequences of the social morphological revolution—which will be the product of research. More knowledge than we now possess is needed. But we have sufficient knowledge, even now, to state that the remediation of our chaotic society can be accomplished by bridging the gap between the social sciences, including sociology, and social policy and action.

CHAPTER 39

R. M. MacIVER

The Role of the Precipitant

Wherever, in the more practical or in the more theoretical type of investigation, we distinguish some factor that is introduced from the outside, or else emerges from within, so that it evokes a series of repercussions or reactions significantly changing the total situation, we may call such a factor a "precipitant." The search for precipitants in this sense is one of the favorite forms of the limited causal quest.

Often we envisage a situation as dependent on the balance of two opposing forces, or on the equilibrium of a number of forces. The balance or equilibrium is unstable, temporary, precarious. One of the simplest of cases would be where public opinion is nearly equally divided in favor of and against a particular policy. Some event, some accident, some act of leadership, may decisively turn the scales. In a larger sense, we may think of one set of forces making for the perpetuation of an established order and another making for change or revolution. The forces of change are held in leash by the resisting forces. Again, some event, a war, an invention, the rise of a new prophet, a local outbreak of the suppressed forces, may be conceived as destroying the pre-existing equilibrium. Some writers actually go so far as to interpret all change along similar lines. Thus the German legal philosopher Binding maintains that "the causation of a change is identical with a change in the balance between the restraining and the promoting conditions" and adds that "man is the cause of an effect insofar as he causes any superiority of the promoting over the deterring conditions." [1] But what right have we to assume that equally matched opposites meet in every situation until some precipitant overthrows their balanced neutrality? Why should change advance by a series of jumps and halts as disturbances successively interrupting states of equilibrium? The conception arbitrarily denies the reality of geniune causal *process*. It is more

From R. M. MacIver, *Social Causation* (New York: Ginn and Company, 1942), pp. 163-164, 169-172, 177-178. Reprinted by permission of the author and the publisher.
[1] Karl Binding, *Normen und ihre Übertretung* (Leipzig, 1914), Vol. II, pp. 472-510.

pertinent to inquire under what conditions and with what limitations the principle of precipitant and preceding equilibrium is justified.

•

As a device for interpreting social and economic changes, the concept of equilibrium and disturbance is less serviceable than the concept of equilibrium and precipitant. The former never introduces us to any vital source of change, it always minimizes change in favor of the *status quo*. But since, as we have seen, it is precisely the difference, the contrast, between social phenomena or social situations that we must seize upon if we are to make any effective advance in our causal inquiries, we cannot expect much enlightenment in that regard from a viewpoint that looks on change itself as the incidental and temporary interruption of a persistent order. It is quite otherwise when the change-provoking factors are thought of as precipitants. For now we need postulate no self-maintaining order, we are committed to no doctrine of permanence, to no distinction between primary and secondary causes. All that is implied is a condition of things that endures, for no matter how short a time, until some intrusive or explosive factor converts it into another condition of things. It may be that we are dealing with a relatively closed system, or a system that slowly changes, or with a mere moment of seeming inertia. Then something decisive occurs. A class order that has been dominant for centuries is overturned. A mode of production that has been long established is, in a relatively brief period, transformed into another. A political party that commanded a majority allegiance is suddenly overthrown. A leader, a general, a popular hero, falls from his eminence to oblivion or disrepute. In all such situations we usually conceive that some one factor has intervened, has emerged within or thrust itself into the total situation, in such a way as to bring about a state of disequilibrium, a change of direction, or a realignment of forces.

Innumerable changes occur that seem to conform to this pattern. But an immediate caution is necessary, for a danger besets this mode, as indeed all other modes, of isolating a factor as distinctively causal. It is the danger of attaching an undue weight or role to the designated factor. We omit for the present any consideration of the evidence required to assure us that a particular event, or some narrow conjuncture of events within a total changing situation, effectively disturbs or disrupts a pre-existing equilibrium. We will assume that the designated factor does function as precipitant. A single thrust may set a landslide moving. A spark may set a whole forest afire, with all its entailments. The mistake of a general may lose a war and thus have farreaching repercussions on a whole civilization. One invention may revolutionize an industry. "A grain of sand in a man's flesh, and empires rise and fall." These things are in the record. But there are empires that do not fall because an emperor dies, and there are wars that are not lost because a general makes a mistake, and the thrust sends the landslide moving only because the conditions are all prepared for it. The situation may be ripe for change, and for change only in the particular direction congenial to the complex of forces controlling it. The landslide would have happened sooner or later apart from the particular thrust, or from any thrust at all. The appeal or the manifesto that seemed to change the fortunes of political parties may merely accentuate or bring to light the till then inarticulate but deeper-working trends of public opinion. The storm may shake from the trees only the ripe fruit or the dead leaves.

•

On the other hand there are events, intrusive forces, interventions, discoveries, even accidents, that in the light of our best knowledge still appear decisive, changing the direction of the whole stream of human affairs. If, to take a much quoted example, the Persians had defeated the Greeks at Marathon, the history of civilization would doubtless have been a quite different story. And there are frequent instances in which a single event has a train of consequences so dependent upon it that we cannot assume they would have been brought about apart from this event. The act of an assassin at Sarajevo precipitated a world war. Who can say with assurance that this kind of war would have occurred, sooner or later, had there not been this event? And even if the absence of the particular precipitant should only have delayed such a war, who can affirm that it would not have followed an entirely different course, had it broken out at some different time?

It is apparent, then, that the role of the precipitant may vary enormously in significance and that in each instance we can assess its causal importance only if we understand the whole dynamic system into which it enters. The causal efficacy we impute to any factor must always be contingent not only on the other factors, but also on the dynamic interdependence of them all within the total situation. It is only as a temporary heuristic expedient that we can select any item as "cause" and speak of the rest as "conditions." . . .

While a particular complex of social attitudes may enter very significantly into the causal process, it is difficult to ever assign to a factor of this sort the salience and immediate causal decisiveness suggested by our term "precipitant." These qualities are more appropriately looked for in the *event,* the dated conjecture of forces that perceptibly disturbs or disrupts a pre-existing order or coherence. A war, a revolution, a bold stroke of policy, a drastic new law, a quarrel between leaders, the assassination of a ruler, are obvious examples of precipitant in this sense. Any of these may, under certain conditions, decisively disrupt the going system, and yet, any of them may reasonably be regarded, at the hour of its occurrence, as not inevitably the outcome or expression of the conditions or forces inherent in the particular system it disrupts. There is an element of conjuncture, if not a sheer chance, in the mode and time of the occurrence. The most indubitable type is that in which the decisive factor comes wholly or essentially from outside the affected system. A war, for example, might precipitate important changes in the economic employment of women, in the credit structure of a country, or even in an artistic style. The settlement of missionaries or of traders among a primitive people may initiate profound changes in the life of that people. Again, wherever a system is relatively closed, that is, when it rigorously clings to pre-established lines and resists all innovations or new adaptations, it is likely that significant change will await the impact of some definite precipitant and be more drastic or shattering when it occurs. A caste system, for example, is usually broken open only by some powerful intrusive factor, such as revolt, invasion, a new gospel appealing to the masses, or the introduction of an externally developed industrial technique.

CHAPTER 40

HORACE M. KALLEN

Innovation

The changes or novelties of rites, techniques, customs, manners, and mores which constitute innovation are usually thought of as purposive. The actualities of the social process, however, do not validate this connotation. The attribution of intent is always retrospective. But the causes of innovation are too complex to be covered by merely personal intent. Insofar as human existence is a process and not sheer repetition, the rise, the forms, the life cycles, and the influence of innovations are the vital theme of history and the social sciences. Innovation includes in its range the transformations in food, clothing, shelter, defense against enemies and disease, tools and technologies of production and consumption, forms of play and sport, rituals and liturgies of religion, precedents of law, inventions in science and thought, styles and attitudes in literature and the arts. Every social institution is a field of innovation, no matter how conservative its intent and how standardized its techniques and procedures. The limit to innovation comes only at the point where the identity of an establishment itself is menaced.

Within this limit innovations may be numerous and rapid; the very individuality of the institution may consist in them. This is the case among the various divisions of science. The essential of each of these is the process of deliberate innovation which goes by the name of scientific method. Scientific method is simply another name for the gathering, testing, and applying of innovations. How these innovations are reached is indifferent. Every innovation involves a certain contingency, a dimension of chance and luck; every innovation also begins as focal to some particular individual or very small group. Once a "scientific" mind has become aware of it, it is developed formally and tested experimentally, given its chance to succeed or fail. The

From Horace M. Kallen, "Innovation," in Edwin R. A. Seligman and Alvin Johnson, eds., *The Encyclopedia of the Social Sciences* (New York: Macmillan, 1937), Vol. 4. Copyright 1937 by the Macmillan Company, and reprinted by permission of the publisher.

work of breeders of animals, legumes, fruits; the invention and elaboration of machines; the transformations of the art of medicine in the last fifty years, insofar as these have anything deliberate in them, all rest on the presumption and use of scientific method. This is postulated wherever innovation is both deliberate and follows the gradients of social change. Where innovation is incongruous with those, it must either struggle for its survival, establishing itself by means of a process of give and take with its environment, or be imposed by *force majeure,* as when after a revolution or a war the victor imposes upon the defeated a new way of doing or thinking.

Innovation may be slow or rapid, manifold or simple, but it is ineluctable. In a sense, the mere lapse of time is innovating. Aging takes place in institutions and societies no less than in woods and wines. This autogenous transformation through invariant repetition seems, however, never to occur in isolation. It is crossed and modified by other processes which add novelties a priori. Such are inventions, wars, crises and catastrophes, migrations, exhaustion of materials, exhaustion of interest (*i.e.* boredom). Boredom is a psychic force of innovation which deserves more attention than it has received. The revulsion which it generates and the subsequent searching and seeking are no small part of the dynamics of fashion, gaming, sport, crusades, exploration, scientific investigations, and the like. All these involve contacts with changing environments, natural and human, osmosis or more violent impacts of cultures, and consequent innovations.

The optimal conditions for innovation are a certain flexibility and readiness in the organic pattern of a society itself. These develop as a rule more easily in new societies, where a fresh start is being made; they develop also during a crisis such as a war, a profound business depression, a natural catastrophe or a revolution. At such times, playing upon a ground of fear and uncertainty, is a feeling of the significance of the social adventure. Novelties are invited, projected, and perhaps installed and domesticated; experiments are made, and change may become a standard of public policy. Such was the case in Athens from the Persian wars through the Peloponnesian War, and in the United States while the frontier lasted; it is now the case in Soviet Russia. Where custom coheres too firmly and authority is unshaken, the situation is reversed. In primitive societies the new way must be assimilated to the ways of the fathers before it can be accepted. Theocracies require that it shall confirm before it can be confirmed by the divine authority which they wield. Military or bureaucratic establishments reject it if it does not conform to the customary patterns and rituals of conduct. So does the institution of the law. In all these cases, the variant is seen as a disorderly interruption of set routine and therefore a priori a heresy, a sedition and a danger. If its import is acknowledged and it is adopted, it is usually denatured of all qualities inharmonious with the established procedure. Apparently only a crisis, the feeling of danger at hand, can transform this habitual inertia into a readiness to try new tools and ways.

•

Innovators are not necessarily rebels, and the temper of innovation is not by any means the temper of revolt. Novelties, spontaneous deviations of the same energy, continually pour from the main stream of custom and convention. Thus the industrial revolution in England, the growth and diffusion of the factory system in the United States, in Germany, and in Japan, took place mainly in the context of the old mores and on the initiative and by the effort of persons who were on the whole champions of those mores. Now the mores are being transformed and displaced by what they allowed. Again, the impact of photography and the theory of color vision on the painter's art constituted a fecundation of method and a diversion of ideals. The impressionists began by affirming the novelty, and were forced into a defensive denying of the tradition. Socalled modern movements are innovations only because of reaction against the innovation which photography itself represented. The intent of the postimpressionist schools was conservative; their achievements were innovations.

Nevertheless, innovators are forced into a combative position. For their novelties enter a social organization most of whose establishments are going concerns and enter as competitors and deprecators of one or another. If they succeed in establishing themselves, they become embodied in the organic flow of the mores. They cause that flow to deviate to a slightly different gradient definable by what they represent. This is what the city life of the Renaissance did to Christian society in Europe, what the fusion of the scientific with the technological attitude did to the eighteenth century mind, and what the industrial system is doing to contemporary civilization. Of course there are programs of innovation whose dynamic is a reaction against the established order. Such programs sometimes function as precipitates of deep-lying emotions which are not disturbing enough to change the social order, but do nourish a formulated opposition to it. The opposition becomes organized into cults and movements whose rituals and programs then identify it as a sort of antibody in the social organism. So Methodism grew to maturity in the Episcopal milieu of England. The single tax movement in the United States is such a development, and such also are cults of diet (like vegetarianism), of dress (like nudism), of health and of other goods of life. They arise as variants and survive as orderly antagonists within the nexus of the social process.

Since all innovations animate readjustments in the distribution and organization of social forces they automatically evoke the antagonism of those who are disturbed. If the antagonism is pervasive and deep, the innovation perforce lapses. If, however, it satisfies a want or nullifies an annoyance, however illusorily, it gathers a following. . . .

Innovations are mostly resisted out of motives of self-interest and fear.

The new is quite usually synonymous with the unreasonable, the dangerous, the impossible. As William James pointed out long ago, rationality is a sentiment in which the feeling of familiarity is fused with that of congruity with our fundamental hopes and desires. Sometimes mere familiarity may become identical with this congruity. Thus people resist changing their dietary habits in spite of the fact that this change is required by health, the social setting, or religion; there are freethinking Jews who get indigestion at the very thought of pork and "liberated" Hindus who are upset by the idea of meat. Between love of food and love of God or country the difference is in degree, not in kind. All involve clinging to the habitual, familiar and secure. . . . Where innovations have finally established themselves and compel recognition, they are assimilated to the old order—or the old order is assimilated to them—by means of some formula. Thus in the United States, "trusts" were feared at their origin and laws were passed to constrain them. But they developed into the dominant controls of the economic process; the established order has had to count with them and acquiesce in them. The Supreme Court of the United States celebrated this necessity by the well known decision concerning "the rule of reason" (Standard Oil Co. versus United States, 221 U.S. 1 [1911]), which has resulted in the virtual nullification of the original intent to control the trusts rigorously. . . .

CHAPTER 41

RALPH LINTON

Discovery, Invention, and Their Cultural Setting

Discovery and Invention

Discovery and invention are the obvious starting points for any study of cultural growth and change, since it is only by these processes that new elements can be added to the total content of man's culture. Although developed cultural traits can be transmitted from one culture to another and most cultures owe the bulk of their content to this process, every culture element can ultimately be traced to a discovery or invention or to a more or less complex combination of various discoveries and inventions, which arose at a particular time and place.

We may define a discovery as any addition to knowledge, an invention as a new application of knowledge. To give a concrete example, on an individual rather than a social basis, when a small child pulls a cat's tail and gets scratched, this particular sequence of cause and effect is a discovery as far as the child is concerned. The observed fact that cats will scratch when their tails are pulled is an addition to his store of knowledge. If the child pulls the cat's tail when someone else is holding it, so that that person will get scratched, this is in the nature of an invention. The knowledge is employed in a new way to achieve a particular end. If the child is then spanked, he will have another discovery to his credit.

Since it is the application of knowledge, *i.e.,* invention, which is functionally important to culture, we will refer to all new active elements which are developed within the frame of a particular culture and society as inventions.

From Ralph Linton, *The Study of Man* (New York: Appleton-Century-Crofts, 1936), pp. 304, 306, 316-323, 341-343. Copyright 1936 by D. Appleton-Century Co., and reprinted by permission of the publishers.

Inventions—Classified

. . . There have been numerous attempts to classify inventions, none of them altogether successful and all depending for their utility upon the particular problem in which they are to be employed. There is the simple division of inventions into religious, social, and technological. This is useful for descriptive purposes, yet there are practical difficulties in drawing lines between even such elementary divisions. Almost every religious invention has numerous purely social aspects. The revelation, if such happens to be the starting point of the new cult, nearly always includes regulations for human relationships as well as for the relationship between believers and the supernatural. It may even include fairly complicated rules as to how the faithful should dress, what food they should eat, and how they should kill their meat. Moreover, such a classification is of little value for the study of the dynamics of culture. The classification most useful in this appears to be the simple one of *basic inventions* and *improving inventions*.

A basic invention may be defined as one which involves the application of a new principle or a new combination of principles. It is basic in the sense that it opens up new potentialities for progress and is destined, in the normal course of events, to become the foundation of a whole series of other inventions. The bow would be a good example of such an invention. It involved the use of a new principle and became the starting point for a whole series of improving inventions, such as those which culminated in the laminated bow, crossbow, and so on. A more modern example of such a basic invention would be the vacuum tube, whose potentialities for use are only beginning to be understood. An improving invention, as the name implies, is a modification of some pre-existing device, usually made with the intention of increasing its efficiency or rendering it available for some new use. Thus the modern hand telephone instrument is an improving invention superimposed upon the basic telephone invention. Although certain inventions are clearly basic and others as clearly improving, the assignment of many others rests upon the observer's judgment of when any modification is important enough to be said to involve a new principle. Perhaps the best test is a pragmatic one, classing any invention as basic when it becomes the starting point for a divergent line of inventions and improving when it does not.

•

Although a certain romantic interest attaches to basic inventions . . . , the bulk of cultural progress has probably been due to the less spectacular process of gradual improvement in pre-existing devices and the development of new applications for them. In fact, basic inventions seem to be valuable mainly as the starting point for series of improving inventions. Very few of them are efficient or satisfactory in the condition in which they first appear. Thus the first automobiles were little better than toys or scientific curiosities. They did not begin to play their present important role in our culture until they had been refined and perfected by literally hundreds of improving inventions.

A sufficient number of improving inventions can even transform an appliance into something quite different from the original and with totally different applications. Thus the wheel appears to have been, in its inception, a development of the roller and something employed exclusively in transportation. As the potentialities of the device were recognized, it was turned to other uses, as for drawing water for irrigation and for the manufacture of pottery. Still later came a realization of its potentialities for transforming direct into rotary motion and for transmitting power, until this transportation appliance became an integral part of thousands of devices which were in no way related to transportation. Again, the bow, beginning as a weapon, or more probably as a toy, not only underwent a series of modifications which perfected it for its original use but, through a divergent line of inventive evolution, became ancestral to the harp and ultimately to all stringed musical instruments. In both of these cases, the development of the new appliances rested upon a long series of improving inventions, no one of which seemed to be of tremendous importance in itself, but which, in the aggregate, produced something fundamentally different from the original appliance. For this reason it is extremely hazardous to class any appliance as the result of a . . . basic invention unless its actual history is known. The new principle which gives it its basic quality may have crept in little by little, entering by such gradual degrees that its point of first appearance can hardly be detected.

The Cultural Setting

Hitherto we have discussed . . . inventions from the point of view of their own qualities, but the picture would be quite misleading if we stopped there. There is a constant and intimate association between the inventor and his products and the cultural setting in which inventions are produced and must function. We have defined an invention as a new application of knowledge, a definition which at once implies that the knowledge must precede the invention. Although the knowledge incorporated into a new invention may derive in part from a fresh discovery, most of it always derives from the culture of the inventor's society. Every inventor, even the one who produces a basic invention, builds upon this accumulation of previously acquired knowledge, and every new thing must grow directly out of other things which have gone before. Thus no inventor reared in a culture which was ignorant of the wheel principle could conceivably produce even such simple appliances as the potter's wheel or lathe. The wheel would have to be invented first. The content of the culture within which the inventor operates thus imposes constant limitations upon the exercise of his inventive abilities. This applies not merely to mechanical inventions but to invention in all other fields as well. The mathematical genius can only carry on from the point which mathematical knowledge within his culture has already reached. Thus if Einstein had been born into a primitive tribe which was unable to count beyond three, lifelong application to mathematics probably would not have carried him beyond the development of a decimal system based on fingers and toes. Again, reformers who attempt to devise new systems for society or new religions can only build with the elements with which their culture has made them familiar. It is ridiculous to try to understand the form and content of such sects as Christianity and Mohammedanism until we know the cultural background from which they sprang.

•

Acceptance

New traits are accepted primarily on the basis of two qualities, utility and compatibility: in other words, on the basis of what they appear to be good for and how easily they can be fitted into the existing culture configuration. Both these qualities are, of course, relative to the receiving culture and are influenced by such a long series of factors that an outsider can hardly ascertain all of them. . . . Cultural change is mainly a matter of the replacement of old elements by new ones, and every culture normally includes adequate techniques for meeting all the conscious needs of the society's members. When a new trait presents itself, its acceptance depends not so much on whether it is better than the existing one as on whether it is enough better to make its acceptance worth the trouble. This in turn must depend upon the judgment of the group, their degree of conservatism, and how much change in existing habits the new appliance will entail. Even in . . . mechanical appliances, superiority cannot be judged simply in terms of increased output. There are pleasant and unpleasant forms of work, and even such a simple change as that from the use of adzes to axes for tree-felling entails a change in muscular habits which is unpleasant for the time being. . . .

Very much the same situation holds with regard to the problem of compatibility. The acceptance of any new culture element entails certain changes in the total culture configuration. Although the full extent of these changes can never be forecast, certain of them are usually obvious. If the new trait is of such a sort that its acceptance will conflict directly with important traits already present in the culture, it is almost certain to be rejected. One cannot conceive of techniques of mass production being accepted by a culture which had a pattern of uniqueness. There actually are societies which believe that no two objects should ever be the same and never make any two things exactly alike.

•

In the matter of compatibility, as in that of utility, there is a broad zone of uncertainty. There are new elements which may be recognized as slightly superior to existing ones and other elements which may be seen to be somewhat incompatible, but not enough so as to make their acceptance impossible. Very often the advantages and disadvantages are so evenly balanced that the acceptance of the new trait may seem desirable to certain members of the society and undesirable to others. The ultimate acceptance or rejection of elements which fall within this zone is controlled by still another series of variable factors about which we know very little. One of the most important of these is certainly the particular interests which dominate the life of the receiving group. A new trait which is in line with these interests will be given more serious consideration and has a better chance of adoption than one which is not. A slight gain along the line of these interests is felt to be more important than a larger one in some other line in which the group takes little interest. Thus the Hindus have always been highly receptive to new cults and new philosophic ideas as long as these did not come into too direct conflict with their existing patterns, but have shown an almost complete indifference to improved techniques of manufacture. The material world was felt to be of so little importance that minor advances in its control were not considered worth the trouble of changing established habits.

•

In our own civilization, invention itself has become a focus of interest as long as it confines itself to mechanical lines. Social and religious invention is still frowned upon, but this attitude may change as the necessity for advance in these fields becomes increasingly apparent. However, there has never been a time in history when individuals were afforded a better opportunity to add to the material aspects of a culture. In most societies the way of both the inventor and his inventions are hard, and surprisingly few inventions survive to be actually incorporated into culture. For every invention which has been successful in the cultural and social sense, there have probably been at least a thousand which have fallen by the wayside. Many of these have been successful in the practical sense, being actually more efficient than the appliances which were used before and continued to be used after. However, society rejected them, and if they have not been completely forgotten they survive simply as antiquarian curiosities. We know that the Alexandrian Greeks had a steam-engine which was effective enough for one to be installed on the Pharos and used to haul up fuel for the beacon. Leonardo da Vinci's notebooks provide a perfect mine of inventions, many of which show a surprising similarity to modern ones. Perfectly feasible repeating rifles and machine-guns were developed during the first hundred years that hand firearms were in use. All of these inventions failed to "take."

It seems that any invention which fails of acceptance by society within the first generation after it appears may be set down as a total loss. Even when, as in Europe, there are methods for recording it and preserving it as a latent element within the culture, it is rarely if ever revivified. The examples cited above had nothing to do with the modern inventions which they foreshadowed. The inventor works from his own knowledge and his own sense of needs and rarely pores over archives. The same things are invented again and again and rejected again and again until changes in the culture continuum have prepared a place for them. The process is slow and, from the point of view of the inventor, most discouraging. In the progressive enrichment of its culture, no society has ever employed even a tithe of its members' inventive ability. There are few cultures which can show more than a mere handful of traits which have been invented by members of the societies which bear them. All cultures have grown chiefly by borrowing. . . .

CHAPTER 42

JAMES COLEMAN, HERBERT MENZEL, and ELIHU KATZ

Social Processes in Physicians' Adoption of a New Drug

Over the past twenty years, the practice of medicine has undergone profound changes, not the least of which has been the accelerated rate of change itself. Again and again, new diagnostic techniques, new laboratory tests, new drugs, new forms of anesthesia, new surgical procedures, and new principles of patient management make their appearance. Most of these innovations are minor steps which alter the medical scene only by gradual accretion, if at all; many, indeed, are short-lived or quickly superseded; a few have been milestones in medical developments. Whatever the ultimate significance of a new practice may be, its immediate fate, once it has been launched from the laboratory or research clinic, rests in the hands of the practicing physician in the field.

The pathways by which a successful innovation in medical practice spreads through the profession have seldom been systematically investigated. The present study is a contribution toward that end. It concerns the fate of a single innovation in four cities, a new variant in a well-established family of drugs. Such a case study can hardly claim to represent the course of all types of medical innovation under all circumstances, but it does illuminate some important paths and processes through which medical innovations can make their way into the practice of physicians. One may add that drugs are peculiarly suitable as tracers of these paths, because they are

From James Coleman, Herbert Menzel, and Elihu Katz, "Social Processes in Physicians' Adoption of a New Drug," *The Journal of Chronic Diseases*, IX (1959), No. 1, pp. 1-19. Reprinted by permission of the authors and Pergamon Publishers.

physical objects with standardized names, their release dates are easily ascertainable, and pharmacists maintain exact prescription records.

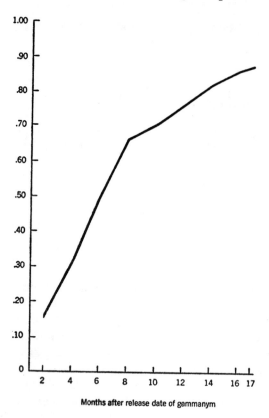

FIGURE 42-1. Cumulative proportion of doctors introducing gammanym over a sixteen-month period (N = 125).

The data of this study stem from two sources. In four Midwestern communities, interviews were conducted with 125 general practitioners, internists, and pediatricians, who generously contributed an average of 1½ hours of their time. They constituted 85 per cent of all practitioners of their specialties in these cities. In addition, data on the prescriptions written by these 125 physicians were obtained from almost all the pharmacies in these communities.[1] The prescription data covered a period of sixteen months

[1] Ninety-one additional interviews were held with practitioners of other specialties, but their prescription record was not examined. The communities had altogether 356 physicians in active private practice. The sample was designed to include all the general practitioners, internists, and pediatricians and a selected group of other specialists. The population of the four cities ranged from about 25,000 to just over 100,000.

beginning with the release date of a new drug which will here be called "gammanym." At this time, two older drugs of the same general type were in widespread use. They had appeared some years earlier and are here designated as "alphanym" and "betanym." The three medications belong to a well-established family of drugs which has widespread applicability in the hands of general practitioners and many specialists. By the end of the survey period, sixteen months after its release, gammanym had become at least a part of the standard medication of most practicing physicians; 87 per cent of the general practitioners, internists, and pediatricians in the sample under study had introduced it into their practice. But this change had been neither immediate nor all-encompassing. The overall rate of introduction of gammanym by these doctors is seen in Figure 42–1. This cumulative curve indicates for each stated date the percentage of doctors who had already prescribed the drug up to that time. As can be seen, more and more doctors introduced the drug during this sixteen-month period until almost 90 per cent had used it; then the curve finally leveled off.

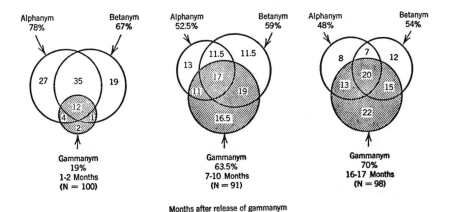

FIGURE 42-2. Overlapping use of alphanym, betanym, and gammanym during three time intervals.

To be sure, the rapid rise in the use of gammanym did not mean that its predecessors, alphanym and betanym, were dropped from use. The degree of overlapping use of two or three of the drugs by the same doctor is pictorially represented in Figure 42–2, for three time intervals, representing the beginning, middle, and end of the period studied. Thus, for example, as late as sixteen and seventeen months after the release of gammanym, only 22 per cent of the doctors were prescribing gammanym exclusively, while 15 per cent were prescribing both betanym and gammanym, 13 per cent were prescribing both alphanym and gammanym, and 20 per cent were writing prescriptions for all three drugs during these same two months (more accurately, during the six sampling days representing these two months). The introduction of gammanym meant for most doctors an addition to whatever drugs of this type they were already using, rather than a substitution. Only slowly, if at all, did some of the doctors stop using the older drugs.

Drug Adoption and Individual Characteristics of Physicians

This, then, describes the overall course of the acceptance of gammanym in these four communities, from the time it first arrived on the drugstore shelves to the time when it appeared on prescription slips of most of the doctors in town. But what exactly happened during this period? Through what paths and processes did the new drug find its way into the prescribing habits of the local physician? As one essential step in answering these questions, it is necessary to examine and compare the doctors who introduced the new drug quickly with those who prescribed it only after most of their colleagues had done so. By ascertaining the backgrounds, types of practice, and other characteristics of these doctors, we can begin to sketch a picture of the "innovator" among the local practicing physicians.

Let us first look at specialty differences. Pediatricians introduced gammanym into their practices more quickly than internists, and internists introduced it more quickly than general practitioners. The average pediatrician first prescribed the drug 6.6 months after its release, the average internist 8.2 months, and the average general practitioner 9.0 months after release. This result is somewhat surprising in view of the general impression that internists are the pace setters. But the contradiction is only apparent and results from the different prescription volume of the different specialties. The pediatricians' average number of prescriptions for alphanym, betanym, and gammanym combined was 13.6 per three-day sampling period; for internists it was 2.7; and for general practitioners 3.6. When doctors with roughly the same volume of prescriptions are compared, the contradiction disappears. Internists then introduce the new drug more rapidly than pediatricians or general practitioners.

Less surprising is the finding that doctors who expose themselves frequently to the primary sources of information were much more likely to be innovators than those who do not. . . . The rate of gammanym introduction was more rapid among those who receive many journals, among those who attend many out-of-town specialty meetings, and among those who conscientiously attend conferences in their own hospitals than among those who do not. It is difficult to assess to what extent this is due to an actual effect of these means of communication on the doctor's prescription habits. Quite possibly it means merely that doctors who are sensitive to new developments read more and go to more meetings. What we do know is that the relationship of drug introduction to journal reading and meeting attendance is independent of the doctor's specialty. . . . In fact, reading and attendance . . . have a considerably stronger relationship to early use of gammanym than does the doctor's specialty. It appears that the innovator is less characterized by his specialty than by voluntary activities like attendance at meetings and reading journals which bring him into closer contact with events in the profession.

But this is not equally true for *all* information-getting activities. There are some potential sources of influence or information, exposure to which shows no relationship to early use of gammanym. . . . Doctors who read many pharmaceutical house organs, those who attend many nonspecialty meetings (American Medical Association, state and regional medical societies, etc.), and those who attend county medical society meetings regularly were little or no quicker to introduce the drug than their colleagues who attend those media less regularly. These media apparently attract a fairly representative audience of doctors among whom sensitivity to new developments is not more prevalent than among physicians in general.

Drug Adoption and Physicians' Contacts with Colleagues

The media discussed so far have been the relatively obvious channels through which innovations may be diffused to local doctors. But doctors were also found to be affected in their drug adoptions in some less obvious ways. One path which might not have been anticipated is the office arrangement of the doctor. By simply dividing doctors into those who share offices with one or several colleagues and those who have an office alone, we find a considerable difference. The doctors who share offices introduced the drug an average of 2.3 months sooner than their colleagues who practice alone.

It is useful to ask just what social and psychologic processes may produce this effect. Two hypotheses seem quite reasonable. First, being in close professional contact with colleagues keeps a doctor well informed, so that he is saved the difficulty of finding out for himself about each new development. He has surrogates to carry part of the burden of finding out about new developments, for, as soon as any of his office partners seriously considers trying a new therapy or even just finding out about a new development, he will discuss it with him.

A second interpretation of the results, however, seems equally reasonable. Introducing a new technique into his practice is always somewhat dangerous for the physician. He has no firsthand knowledge of possible ill effects, yet he must shoulder the blame if ill effects should occur. Because of this, the doctor needs all the reassurance he can get from his fellows to lessen the uncertainty which he faces. The doctor who shares an office with others can, in a sense, depend upon their support and use it for reassurance, while the doctor who practices alone must make the bold step without this added support. It is difficult to determine which of these two interpretations is most valid without knowing whether the primary barrier to drug innovation among doctors who are alone is lack of information or lack of assurance.

But for whatever reason office-sharing leads to earlier use of new drugs, it is apparent that a doctor's social location in the community of his local colleagues affects his drug use by giving him access to information, by providing him with assurance, or in some other way. This leads to a more general question. What about the dozens of other relations that a doctor may have with his colleagues, beside that of office partnership? What, for example, might be the importance of his contact with colleagues in the hospital during leisure hours? Would it affect his use of new practices and products? In order to answer questions like these, one must know the relations among the doctors of the community, that is, one must know the social structure of the medical community which these relations make up. To uncover the most important facets of this structure, three questions were asked of each doctor in the interview: (1) "When you need information or *advice* about questions of therapy, where do you usually turn?" (2) "Who are the three or four physicians with whom you most often find yourself *discussing* cases or therapy in the course of an ordinary week—last week, for instance?" (3) "Would you tell me who are your three *friends* whom you see most often socially?" In answer to each of these questions, three names of other doctors were requested. The replies to the three questions yielded three cross-sections of the structure of the medical communities, much like a biologist's sections of a plant fiber along several axes. Figure 42–3 presents, as an illustration, one of these cross-sections for one of the four cities covered in the survey. This particular diagram pictures that city's

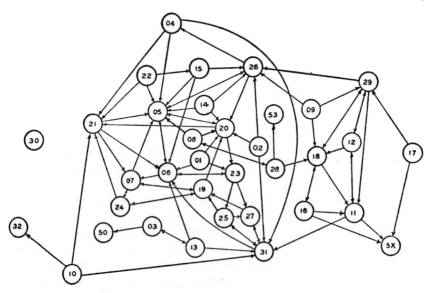

FIGURE 42-3. Discussion network in City D.

structure of discussion partnerships, that is, a sectioning according to the replies to the second question above. In this sociogram, as such a diagram is called, each circle represents a physician, who is identified by a code number. An arrow pointing from Circle 04 to Circle 05 means that Dr. 04 named Dr. 05 as one of his most frequent partners in the discussion of cases. The double-headed arrow connecting Circle 05 and Circle 06 means that Dr. 05 and Dr. 06 each named the other as a frequent partner in the discussion of cases. The fact that seven different arrows point to Circle 31 (near bottom) means that seven different colleagues named Dr. 31 as a frequent discussion partner; in other words, Dr. 31 is quite popular as a discussion partner.

Our general question now becomes: How does this social structure of the community of physicians in a city facilitate or inhibit the diffusion of a new drug? This is an immensely complex question to answer—as complex as the social structures themselves. But it is possible to break the structure and the question into simpler components and to investigate them one by one. Perhaps the simplest question that can be asked in this connection is what is the difference in the rate of drug adoptions between doctors who have contact with many and with few colleagues? This question is a direct parallel to the earlier question about the difference in the rate of drug adoption between doctors who have office partners and those who have none. One can ask more specifically: What is the difference in the rate of drug adoptions between doctors who are named as advisors (or as discussion partners, or as friends) by many of their colleagues and those who are not named by any? One may call the first group socially integrated and the second group socially isolated.

We have pointed out that doctors with office partners introduced gammanym more quickly than those who practice alone. This leads to the hypothesis that the well-integrated doctors would be quicker to introduce this new drug than their more isolated colleagues. This is indeed what is found to be true, and it is true for each of the three cross-sections of the social structure which are under examination here. . . . The effect is quite strong in the predicted direction. Doctors highly integrated into each of the structures[2] were much quicker to introduce the new drug than the more isolated doctors. The average doctor among those most frequently named as advisors introduced the new drug 3.1 months before the average of those who are never named as advisors. The corresponding mean difference between those integrated and isolated as discussion partners is 4.1 months and between those integrated and isolated as friends is 4.3 months. The importance of these factors can be gauged from the fact that no other factor examined in the entire study yielded a mean difference of more than four

---

[2] *I.e.,* those named four times or more as advisors or three times or more as discussion partners or friends.

months, with the single exception of total volume of prescriptions for this general type of medicine. These results suggest that the networks of informal relations among doctors were highly effective as chains of information and influence in the diffusion of this innovation.

Yet, one might reasonably object, is it not likely that these differences in integration and isolation merely reflect different individual characteristics among these doctors and that it is really these personality differences, and not the contacts with other doctors, which account for the striking results found? This is especially plausible in the case of the advisorship network. After all, the doctors who are often designated as advisors may very well be chosen by their colleagues precisely because they are aware of new medications. In that case, their early introductions of new drugs would be a cause rather than a consequence of their high integration. Yet, contrary to this interpretation, the effect of the advisorship network is smaller, not larger, than that of the networks of discussion partners and friends. It is the friendship network which yields the largest difference (4.3 months) between the average adoption times of the integrated and isolated doctors. Since an "integrated" doctor here means one named by many colleagues as a "friend . . . seen most often socially," it is very unlikely that his integration is a result of some professional habit which is accompanied by early introduction of new drugs. It is much more likely that early introduction of the new drug was conditioned by the doctors' informal contacts with one another, through the network of friendships, and through the more strictly professional relationships as well.

Two Processes of Diffusion

But even stronger evidence for this claim can be found in another place. If the socially integrated doctors tended to introduce the drug early merely because of some personality characteristic, the use of the new drug should have spread among these integrated doctors in very much the same way as among the isolates, except earlier. If, on the other hand, it is true that the socially integrated doctors owe their early introduction of gammanym to the networks of contacts which surround them, then the use of the new drug should not only spread *earlier* among them than among the isolates, but the very *nature of the process* of diffusion should then be different. At the extremes, there would be these two processes of diffusion: (1) Among the isolated doctors, it would be an individual process. The effective stimuli—such as detail men, medical journals, advertising from drug houses, and so on—remain fairly constant throughout the diffusion period. The number of doctors introducing the new drug each month would remain a constant percentage of those who have not already adopted the drug. A typical graph for this process would look like the lower curve of Figure 42–4. (2) Among the integrated doctors, it would be an interpersonal or "snowball" process. If, for example, one pioneer introduces the new drug and converts a col-

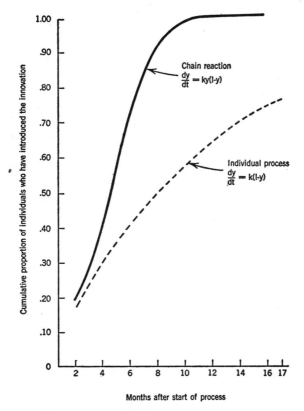

FIGURE 42-4. Comparison of a model of chain-reaction innovation with a model of individual innovation.

league to it during the first month, then these two doctors will convert two others during the second month; during the third month, there would be four doctors making new converts; and so on. The number of doctors introducing the new drug each month would not remain a constant percentage of those yet to be converted, but would gain headway in proportion to those who have already been converted. A typical graph for this process would look like the upper curve in Figure 42-4.

The difference in the shape of the two theoretical curves shown in Figure 42-4 corresponds closely to the differences between the empirical curves obtained for the doctors termed "socially integrated" and "socially isolated" according to the criteria mentioned earlier.[3] In each instance, the curves start

---

[3] The empirical curves referred to here may be inspected in the original article from which this text is excerpted. More concise numerical documentation will be found in our "The Diffusion of an Innovation among Physicians," *Sociometry,* XX (1957), 253-270. A detailed examination of the correspondences and contrasts will be found in our forthcoming *Medical Innovation—A Case Study* (New York: Bobbs-Merrill Company).

out with roughly the same proportion of users in the first two months and then diverge sharply. The curves for the integrated doctors continue steeply upward to their ceiling, indicating at least in part a person-to-person process. The curves for the isolated doctors become gradually less steep, as would be expected in the case of an individual diffusion process. (None of the empirical curves, to be sure, fit the extremes shown in Figure 42–4 exactly.)

No such contrast appears when doctors are categorized according to specialty, number of journals received, specialty meetings attended, or similar individual characteristics. In each instance, one group of doctors adopted the drug faster than the other, as has already been pointed out; but the difference in adoption rates between the two groups appears from the very beginning and does not change systematically as time progresses. In graphic representation, the corresponding upper and lower curves diverge from the beginning and have essentially the same shape. This is as expected, if the doctors represented by these upper and lower curves differ in individual receptivity to or awareness of innovations, but not in their location in effective networks of interpersonal relations.

While these results constitute only a case study of the diffusion of one new product among the doctors of four cities, they have important implications. They suggest that a doctor's tendency to innovate is not only a function of something about him as an individual, but also—and more strongly —a function of his social location among other doctors. The social and professional contacts a doctor has with his colleagues evidently serve important functions in the diffusion of a new practice which are not duplicated by journals, meetings, detail men, or drug house advertisements.

But this result leaves much unsaid. What is it about the social networks that affects the innovating behavior of men within them? Is it merely transmission of information, or do these networks provide the doctor in an unclear situation with the security of numbers? And what are the various stages of the diffusion process as the new drug changes from one used by a small minority into one used by almost the whole community? These are the questions to be considered now.

The Question of Simultaneous Adoptions by Doctors Who Associate with One Another

How can some of these more complex questions about the stages of diffusion be examined? One way, though certainly not the only way, is to examine pairs of doctors who maintain some specified form of contact with one another. Each doctor, it will be recalled, had been asked three questions about his relations to his colleagues. (To whom did he turn for *advice?* With whom did he most often *discuss cases?* What *friends* did he see most often socially?) A doctor and any colleague whom he named in reply to any of these questions constitute a pair of related doctors.

If the networks of doctor-to-doctor contacts are effective, then pairs of related doctors should be more alike in their behavior than pairs assorted at random. More specifically, if a chain-reaction process of drug introduction is at work, then, it seems, adjacent links in the chain—that is, pairs of related doctors—should introduce the drug at about the same time, ideally, during the very same months. If, on the other hand, the use of gammanym was not transmitted through these networks, then the interval between the gammanym adoption dates of doctors and their advisors, doctors and their discussion partners, and doctors and their friends would be no shorter than those of any two doctors picked at random.

Actually, the average intervals between the dates of gammanym adoption of each doctor and those whom he had named as his advisors, discussion partners, or friends were almost identical to the average intervals for pairs picked at random. This meant the rejection of our original hypothesis that pairs of doctors in contact would introduce the drug more nearly simultaneously than pairs of doctors assorted at random. There was, on the other hand, the earlier evidence that the doctor's integration was important to his introduction of gammanym. This dictated a more intensive look at the behavior of pairs of doctors. Accordingly, we raised the question of whether the networks, though ineffective for the *whole* period studied, may have been effective for the *early* period, immediately after the drug was marketed. This, indeed, proved to be the case.

The Stages of Social Diffusion

In order to describe this tendency more precisely, an *index of simultaneity* has been devised, constructed separately for each month. As applied here, it measures how closely the drug introduction of doctors during a given month followed the introductions by any associates who had adopted the drug during the same month or earlier. This index would have a value of $+1$ if each doctor had introduced the drug during the same month as his discussion partner (or friend or advisor); it would be zero if the introduction dates of the two doctors in a pair were as far apart as expected by chance.[4] In Figure 42–5, the values of this index are plotted. Separate curves are plotted for pairs of friends, pairs of discussion partners, and advisor-advisee pairs. Comparing the three structures, it appears that the discussion network and the advisor network are much alike in their effects. Both are most effective during the earliest period. Both are somewhat more effective than the friendship network during these early periods. The friendship network, on the other hand, appears to have its maximum

---

[4] For further details on the index of simultaneity and the model of randomness used therein, *see* our "The Diffusion of an Innovation among Physicians," *Sociometry*, XX (1957), 253-270.

effectiveness later, about five months after gammanym appeared on the market. Finally, after about six months, none of the networks any longer show an effect.

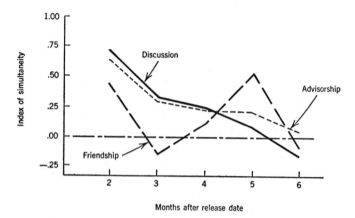

FIGURE 42-5. Index of pair simultaneity for three networks at different times.

These findings, which show different effectiveness of the social networks at different times after the drug's release, have several implications which will be examined shortly. But first, the very structure of the networks has its own implication. Whatever effect these networks have should operate first in the more dense parts of the structure, where a number of lines of social relationship converge and should only then spread out to the more open parts of the structure, that is, to the relatively isolated doctors. It has already been shown that the more isolated doctors, on the average, introduced gammanym considerably later than the socially more integrated doctors. We propose, however, that, when more isolated doctors did introduce the drug early, it was not with the help of the social networks. While the networks were operative as channels of influence early for the integrated doctors, they were operative only later for the more isolated ones. This is what seems to have occurred. Figure 42–6 plots the index of simultaneity separately for more and less integrated doctors. (The graphs show weighted averages for all three networks; separately the numbers of cases would be so small as to produce erratic trends.)

The peak of effectiveness of doctor-to-doctor contacts for the well-integrated doctors appeared in the earliest month for which it can be plotted (the second month), after which effectiveness sharply declined. For the relatively isolated doctors, by contrast, the networks were not so effective at first as were those for the integrated doctors, but they maintained their effectiveness longer. Thus it appears that the networks of relations were effective not only for the more integrated doctors, but also for those relatively isolated doctors who introduced the drug during the first five months of the drug's availability.

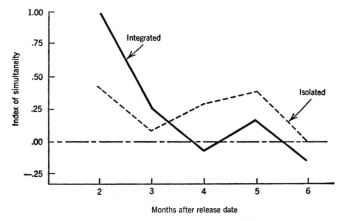

FIGURE 42-6. Index of pair-simultaneity at different times for doctors differing in integration.

To summarize the results so far, it appears that social influence in the process of drug adoption occurred in several stages. First, it operated only among the doctors who are most integrated into the community of their colleagues through ties of a professional nature (as advisors or as discussion partners). Then it spread through the friendship network to doctors who are closely tied to the medical community through their friendship relations. By this time, social influence had also become operative in the more diffuse parts of the social structure, that is, among the relatively isolated doctors. Finally, there came a phase during which an occasional doctor still introduced gammanym, but in complete independence of the time at which his associates introduced it; the networks now showed *no* effect. For the integrated doctors, this phase began four or five months after the drug's release. For the isolated doctors, it began about six months after the drug's release. By this time, the social structure seems to have exhausted its effect. Doctors who introduced gammanym into their practices after this time apparently responded exclusively to influences outside the social networks, such as the professional journals, detail men, drug house advertisements, and so on. They did not, it appears, depend upon their personal relations with other doctors for information and influence. The channels of influence between doctors had operated most powerfully during the first few months after the release of the new drug. Such influence as any doctor had upon his immediate associates by his introduction of the drug occurred very soon after the drug became available. Why is this?

The Role of Contacts with Colleagues in Clearcut and Ambiguous Situations

One answer is that it is only in the early months after a drug's appearance that a doctor needs the support and judgment of his colleagues. It is chiefly when the drug is new that the doctor who is to adopt it needs his colleagues to confirm his judgment and to share the feeling of responsibility in case the decision to adopt the drug should be wrong. At this time, familiarity with the new drug is minimal and the doctor is in an uncertain situation. Several sociopsychological experiments have shown that it is precisely in situations which are objectively unclear, situations in which the individual's own senses and other objective resources cannot tell him what is right and what is wrong, that he needs and uses social validation of his judgments most fully. The first months following the release of a new drug appear to present just this kind of situation. To be sure, the particular drug innovation with which this research has dealt was not a dramatic one. Presumably the effects shown here would be much stronger in the case of a more radical innovation. It is nevertheless suggested that the reason for the greater effectiveness of contacts with gammanym users during the earliest months after the release of the drug was due to the greater uncertainty about the drug that prevailed at that time. It is proposed that a doctor will be influenced more by what his colleagues say and do in uncertain situations than in clearcut situations.

This hypothesis also implies that the necessity for support and validation of judgments by colleagues would be much greater in decisions about some medical conditions than about others. It would be great where the physiology of the illness is not well understood and the treatment is subject to much trial and error. It would be small in conditions which are well understood and in which the action of the medication is well known. It is possible, in fact, to test this implication with certain data of this study. This time the data do not refer to the time of introduction of a new drug, but rather to the habitual use or nonuse of certain classes of modern drugs for two specified conditions. These were respiratory infections and mild-to-moderate cases of essential hypertension. Respiratory infections allow few alternatives of treatment, and their success or failure becomes quickly apparent. They present a clearcut situation. Hypertension, on the other hand, allows many kinds of treatment, and their success can be gauged only slowly and with difficulty. Hypertension presents an uncertain situation.

The implication of the general hypothesis is therefore that pairs of related doctors should be more alike (compared to chance expectations) in their treatment of hypertension than in their treatment of respiratory infections. In order to test this hypothesis, the doctors were classified first according to whether or not they named a broad-spectrum antibiotic as "the antibiotic or sulfonamide [they] most commonly used in infectious conditions of the respiratory tract." They were also classified according to whether or not they included Rauwolfia serpentina drugs in their "usual treatment for essential hypertension in mild or moderate cases." Finally, the Rauwolfia users were divided according to whether they preferred reserpine or other Rauwolfia preparations. With respect to the first classification, a doctor and his friend were considered alike if both or neither named a broad-spectrum drug; with respect to the second, doctors were considered alike if both or neither included Rauwolfia drugs; and, with respect to the third, they were considered alike if both or neither preferred reserpine to other Rauwolfia drugs.

Table 42–1 gives the results in terms of an index of homogeneity. This index would be +1 if all pairs were alike; it would be zero if pairs of related doctors were no more often alike than expected by chance; and it is

Table **42–1**

Homogeneity of Pairs of Related Doctors in Treatment of Respiratory Infections and Hypertension[a]

	Advisor-Advisee Pairs	Discussion Pairs	Friendship Pairs
Respiratory infections (broad-spectrum versus other antibiotics)	−0.056	−0.016	0.029
Hypertension (Rauwolfia included or not)	0.054	0.095	0.109
Hypertension (reserpine versus non-reserpine)	0.280	0.410	0.233
N (number of pairs)	(253)	(258)	(211)
	(165)	(151)	(121)
	(111)	(97)	(71)

[a] These data refer to all 216 interviewed physicians, not only to the 125 whose prescription record was examined. Cf. footnote 1.

negative if pairs of related doctors are less often alike than expected by chance.[5] The results confirm the hypothesis: in all three networks, pairs are homogeneous beyond chance expectations in hypertension treatment but hardly at all in the treatment of respiratory infections. This finding, like that of the simultaneity of gammanym adoptions by pairs of doctors in the early months, presumably arises from the need for social support and social validation in situations where authoritative objective validation is scant.

[5] For details, *see loc. cit.*

Summary

Two hundred and sixteen physicians in four cities were interviewed, and the prescription records of 125 general practitioners, internists, and pediatricians among them were searched, in order to study how the use of a new drug termed "gammanym" spread through these communities of physicians. The main findings are:

(1) Gammanym was introduced earlier by doctors with a large volume of prescriptions for this general type of drug, by those who exposed themselves frequently to certain media of information, and by those who shared their offices with one or several partners.

(2) Doctors who maintained a variety of contacts with a large number of colleagues, the socially integrated doctors, typically introduced the new drug into their practices months before their relatively isolated colleagues. The degree of a doctor's integration was measured by the number of his colleagues who named him, in response to certain interview questions, as an advisor, frequent discussion partner, or frequently visited friend.

(3) Among the integrated doctors, the use of the new drug spread at an accelerating rate, indicating an interpersonal process of diffusion, while among the isolated doctors use of the new drug spread at a constant rate, indicating largely individual responses to constant stimuli outside the community of doctors.

(4) The hypothesis that a doctor and his friend, a doctor and his advisor, and a doctor and his discussion partner would tend to introduce the new drug at about the same time was not borne out for the period as a whole.

(5) During the early months following the drug's release, however, doctors who introduced the drug tended to follow closely upon any associates who had adopted it earlier.

(6) This phenomenon was strongest during the very earliest months in the case of pairs of discussion partners and advisor-advisee pairs. In the case of pairs of friends, it reached its peak about two months later. In all three cases, the phenomenon occurred among the relatively isolated doctors as well as among the integrated doctors, but it reached its peak much later in the case of the isolated doctors.

(7) The apparent greater effectiveness of contacts with colleagues during the early months was attributed to the greater uncertainty about the new drug that prevailed at that time. This interpretation is supported by comparisons of uncertain and clearcut situations of another sort; pairs of related doctors were found to be more alike in the drugs they use for essential hypertension than in the drugs they use for respiratory infections. . . .

CHAPTER 43

**GUNNAR MYRDAL, with the assistance of
RICHARD STERNER and ARNOLD ROSE**

The Principle of Cumulation

In social science we have been drawing heavily on the notions and theories of the much farther developed natural sciences, particularly physics. The notion of equilibrium, for instance, has been in all our reasoning for centuries. Actually it is present in most research of the present day, even when it is not formally introduced. In most social research, we have restricted our utilization of the equilibrium notion to that simple and static variant of it, the *stable equilibrium*. It is this equilibrium notion which is implicit in the sociological constructions of "maladjustment" and "adjustment" and all their several synonyms or near-synonyms, where equilibrium is thought of as having a virtual reality in determining the direction of change. We propose the utilization of *other equilibrium notions* besides this simplest one. For dynamic analysis of the process of change in social relations, it is highly desirable that we disengage our minds from the stable equilibrium scheme of thinking. The other types of equilibrium notions are often better descriptions of social reality than the stable one.

If we succeed in placing a pencil upright on its end, it is also in equilibrium, but an unstable one, a "labile status" of balancing forces, as we easily find if we touch it. No "adjustment," "adaptation," or "accommodation" toward the original position will follow the application of a push, but only an accelerated movement away from the original state of balance. A third type of equilibrium is present when a pencil is rolling on a plane surface—it may come to rest anywhere. A fourth type is what we might call "created equilibrium," that is, arranging a disordered pile of pencils into a box by intelligent social engineering.

The most important need is to give place in our hypothetical explanatory scheme to a rational recognition of the cumulation of forces. In one

From Gunnar Myrdal, *An American Dilemma* (New York: Harper & Brothers, 1944), pp. 1065-1067. Copyright © 1944 by Harper & Row, Inc., and reprinted by permission of the authors and publisher.

branch of social science, economics, these various types of equilibrium notions have lately been used with great advantage. The principle of cumulation has given us, for the first time, something which approaches a real theory of economic dynamics. We have referred to the theory of the "vicious circle" as a main explanatory scheme for the inquiry into the Negro problem. The following brief notes are intended to give an abstract clarification of the theory and a perspective on some of its future potentialities as a method of social research.

In considering the Negro problem in its most abstract aspect, let us construct a much simplified mental model of dynamic social causation. We assume in this model society of our imagination a white majority and a Negro minority. We assume, further, that the interrelation between the two groups is in part determined by a specific degree of "race prejudice" on the side of the whites, directed against the Negroes. We assume the "plane of living" of the Negroes to be considerably lower than that of the whites. We take, as given, a mutual relationship between our two variables, and we assume this relationship to be of such a type that, on the one hand, the Negroes' plane of living is kept down by discrimination from the side of the whites while, on the other hand, the whites' reason for discrimination is partly dependent upon the Negroes' plane of living. The Negroes' poverty, ignorance, superstition, slum dwellings, health deficiencies, dirty appearance, disorderly conduct, bad odor, and criminality stimulate and feed the antipathy of the whites for them. We assume, for the sake of simplicity, that society, in our abstract model, is in "balance" initially. By this we mean that conditions are static, that our two variables are exactly checking each other; there is—under these static conditions—just enough prejudice on the part of the whites to keep down the Negro plane of living to that level which maintains the specific degree of prejudice, or the other way around.

If now, in this hypothetically balanced state, for some reason or other, the Negro plane of living should be lowered, this will—other things being equal—in its turn increase white prejudice. Such an increase in white prejudice has the effect of pressing down still further the Negro plane of living, which again will increase prejudice, and so on, by way of mutual interaction between the two variables, *ad infinitum*. A cumulative process is thus set in motion which can have final effects quite out of proportion to the magnitude of the original push. The push might even be withdrawn after a time, and still a permanent change will remain or even the process of change will continue without a new balance in sight. If, instead, the initial change had been such a thing as a gift from a philanthropist to raise the Negro plane of living, a cumulative movement would have started in the other direction, having exactly the same causal mechanism. The vicious circle works both ways.

The Negroes' "plane of living" is, however, a composite entity. Let us, while retaining our major assumptions, approach a more realistic conception by splitting up this quantity into components, assuming that the cumulative principle works also in their causative interrelations. Besides "relative absence of race prejudice on the side of whites," we introduce a number of variables: levels of "Negro employment," "wages," "housing," "nutrition," "clothing," "health," "education," "stability in family relations," "manners," "cleanliness," "orderliness," "trustworthiness," "law observance," "loyalty to society at large," "absence of criminality," and so on. All these variables, according to our hypothesis, cumulate. In other words, we assume that a movement in any of the Negro variables in the direction toward the corresponding white levels will tend to decrease white prejudice. At the same time, white prejudice is assumed to be, directly or indirectly, one of the causative factors effective in keeping the levels low for the several Negro variables. It is also our hypothesis that, on the whole, a rise in any single one of the Negro variables will tend to raise all the other Negro variables and thus, indirectly as well as directly, result in a cumulatively enforced effect upon white prejudice. A rise in employment will tend to increase earnings, raise standards of living, and improve health, education, manners, and law observance, and *vice versa;* a better education is assumed to raise the chances of a higher salaried job, and *vice versa;* and so all the way through our whole system of variables. Each of the secondary changes has its effect on white prejudice.

If, in actual social life, the dynamics of the causal relations between the various factors in the Negro problem should correspond to our hypotheses, then—assuming again, for the sake of simplicity, an initially static state of balanced forces—*any change in any one of these factors, independent of the way in which it is brought about, will, by the aggregate weight of the cumulative effects running back and forth between them all, start the whole system moving* in one direction or the other as the case may be, with a speed depending upon the original push and the functions of causal interrelation within the system.

Our point is not simply that many forces are "working in the same direction." Originally we assumed that there was a balance between these forces and that the system was static, until we introduced one push coming in at one point or the other. When the system starts rolling, it is true that *the changes in the forces*—though not all the forces themselves—work in one direction; but this is because the variables are assumed to be interlocked in such a causal mechanism that a change of any one causes the others to change *in the same direction,* with a secondary effect upon the first variable, and so on.

We may further notice that the "balance" assumed as initial status was not a stable equilibrium at all—of the type which is tacitly assumed in the notions of "maladjustment," "adjustment," "accommodation," "social lag"—and, further, that in our scheme of hypotheses there is not necessarily assumed to exist any new "balance," or "equilibrium," or "harmony" toward which the factors of the system "adjust" or "accommodate." In the utilization of this theoretical model on problems of actual social reality, the initial state of labile balance, which we assumed for simplicity in our demonstration, will, of course, never be found. What we shall have to study are *processes of systems actually rolling* in the one direction or the other, systems which are constantly subjected to all sorts of pushes from outside through all the variables, and which are moving because of the cumulative effect of all these pushes and the interaction between the variables.

CHAPTER 44

WILLIAM F. OGBURN

The Hypothesis of
Cultural Lag

The thesis is that the various parts of modern culture are not changing at
the same rate, some parts are changing much more rapidly than others and
that since there is a correlation and interdependence of parts, a rapid
change in one part of our culture requires readjustments through other
changes in the various correlated parts of culture. For instance, industry
and education are correlated, hence a change in industry makes adjustments necessary through changes in the educational system. Industry and
education are two variables, and if the change in industry occurs first and
the adjustment through education follows, industry may be referred to as
the independent variable and education as the dependent variable. Where
one part of culture changes first, through some discovery or invention and
occasions changes in some part of culture dependent upon it, there frequently is a delay in the changes occasioned in the dependent part of culture. The extent of this lag will vary according to the nature of the cultural
material, but may exist for a considerable number of years, during which
time there may be said to be a maladjustment. It is desirable to reduce the
period of maladjustment, to make the cultural adjustments as quickly as
possible.

A first simple statement of the hypothesis we wish to investigate now
follows. A large part of our environment consists of the material conditions
of life, and a large part of our social heritage is our material culture. These
material things consist of houses, factories, machines, raw materials, manufactured products, foodstuffs, and other material objects. In using these
material things we employ certain methods. Some of these methods are as

From William Fielding Ogburn, *Social Change* (New York: Viking Press, 1922),
pp. 200-212. Copyright 1922 by B. W. Huebsch, Inc., 1950 by William Fielding Ogburn,
and reprinted by permission of the Viking Press, Inc.

simple as the technique of handling a tool. But a good many of the ways of using the material objects of culture involve rather larger usages and adjustments, such as customs, beliefs, philosophies, laws, governments. One important function of government, for instance, is the adjustment of the population to the material conditions of life, although there are other governmental functions. Sumner has called many of these processes of adjustments "mores." The cultural adjustments to material conditions, however, include a larger body of processes than the mores; certainly they include the folkways and social institutions. These ways of adjustment may be called, for purposes of this particular analysis, "the adaptive culture." The adaptive culture is therefore that portion of the nonmaterial culture which is adjusted or adapted to the material conditions. Some parts of the nonmaterial culture are thoroughly adaptive culture such as certain rules involved in handling technical appliances, and some parts are only indirectly or partially so, as for instance, religion. The family makes some adjustments to fit changed material conditions, while some of its functions remain constant. The family, therefore, under the terminology used here is a part of the nonmaterial culture that is only partly adaptive. When the material conditions change, changes are occasioned in the adaptive culture. But these changes in the adaptive culture do not synchronize exactly with the change in the material culture. There is a lag which may last for varying lengths of time, sometimes indeed, for many years.

An illustration will serve to make the hypothesis more clearly understood. One class of material objects to which we adjust ourselves is the forests. The material conditions of forestry have changed a good deal in the United States during the past century. At one time the forests were quite plentiful for the needs of the small population. There was plenty of wood easily accessible for fuel, building, and manufacture. The forests were sufficiently extensive to prevent in many large areas the washing of the soil, and the streams were clear. In fact, at one time the forests seemed to be too plentiful, from the point of view of the needs of the people. Food and agricultural products were at one time the first need of the people, and the clearing of land of trees and stumps was a common undertaking of the community in the days of the early settlers. In some places, the quickest procedure was to kill and burn the trees and plant between the stumps. When the material conditions were like these, the method of adjustment to the forests was characterized by a policy which has been called exploitation. Exploitation in regard to the forests was indeed a part of the mores of the time and describes a part of the adaptive culture in relation to forests.

As time went on, however, the population grew, manufacturing became highly developed, and the need for forests increased. But the forests were being destroyed. This was particularly true in the Appalachian, Great Lakes and Gulf regions. The policy of exploitation continued. Then, rather suddenly, it began to be realized in certain centers of thought that if the policy of cutting timber continued at the same rate and in the same manner, the forests would in a short time be gone and very soon indeed they would be inadequate to supply the needs of the population. It was realized that the custom in regard to using the forests must be changed and a policy of conservation was advocated. The new policy of conservation means not only a restriction in the amount of cutting down of trees, but it means a more scientific method of cutting and also reforestation. Forests may be cut in such a way, by selecting trees according to their size, age and location, as to yield a large quantity of timber and yet not diminish the forest area. Also by the proper distribution of cutting plots in a particular area, the cutting can be so timed that by the time the last plot is cut the young trees on the plot first cut will be grown. . . . There of course are many other methods of conservation of forests. The science of forestry is, indeed, fairly highly developed in principle, though not in practice in the United States. A new adaptive culture, one of conservation, is therefore suited to the changed material conditions.

That the conservation of forests in the United States should have been begun earlier is quite generally admitted. We may say, therefore, that the old policy of exploitation has hung over longer than it should before the institution of the new policy. In other words, the material conditions in regard to our forests have changed but the old customs of the use of forests which once fitted the material conditions very well have hung over into a period of changed conditions. These old customs are not only not satisfactorily adapted, but are really socially harmful. These customs of course have a utility, since they meet certain human needs; but methods of greater utility are needed. There seems to be a lag in the mores in regard to forestry after the material conditions have changed. Or translated into the general terms of the previous analysis, the material conditions have changed first; and there has been a lag in the adaptive culture, that is, that culture which is adapted to forests. The material conditions changed before the adaptive culture was changed to fit the new material conditions.

•

The foregoing discussion of forestry illustrates the hypothesis which it is proposed to discuss. It is desirable to state more clearly and fully the points involved in the analysis. The first point concerns the degree of adjustment or correlation between the material conditions and the adaptive nonmaterial culture. The degree of this adjustment may be only more-or-less perfect or satisfactory; but we do adjust ourselves to the material conditions through some form of culture; that is, we live, we get along, through this adjustment. . . .

Another point to observe is that the changes in the material culture precede changes in the adaptive culture. This statement is not in the form of a universal dictum. Conceivably, forms of adaptation might be worked out prior to a change in the material situation, and the adaptation might be applied practically at the same time as the change in the material conditions. But such a situation presumes a very high degree of planning, prediction and control. The collection of data, it is thought, will show that at the present time there are a very large number of cases where the material conditions change and the changes in the adaptive culture follow later. . . . It is not implied that changes may not occur in nonmaterial culture while the material culture remains the same. Art or education, for instance, may undergo many changes with a constant material culture.

Still another point in the analysis is that the old, unchanged, adaptive culture is not adjusted to the new, changed, material conditions. It may be true that the old adaptive culture is never wholly unadjusted to the new conditions. There may be some degree of adjustment. But the thesis is that the unchanged adaptive culture was more harmoniously related to the old than to the new material conditions and that a new adaptive culture will be better suited to the new material conditions than was the old adaptive culture. Adjustment is therefore a relative term, and perhaps only in a few cases would there be a situation which might be called perfect adjustment or perfect lack of adjustment. . . .

CHAPTER 45

MORTON A. KAPLAN

Essential Rules and Rules of Transformation

The equilibrium states of going systems, such as political systems, may be described in part in terms of what can be called their essential rules.[1] Essential rules describe the forms of behavior that maintain the equilibrium conditions of the system. In a "balance of power" international system, the essential rules specify that nations pursue additional capabilities: if necessary, fight wars for that purpose; limit the indemnities levied on defeated nations; treat all other nations as acceptable alliance partners; and oppose nations or alliances that seek predominance in the system. Alliances are transitory and limited to immediate objectives in this system. Of course, these rules do not need to be followed in every case for the equilibrium of the system to be maintained, but if they are not followed in general, the system can be expected to change. Thus the rules are regarded as essential.

Different international systems are characterized by different essential rules. Thus the loose bipolar system is not characterized by transitory alliances that are oriented toward immediate and shortterm objectives. Instead, blocs are formed within the system, and the nations that join these blocs subordinate immediate interests to bloc interests. Since members of the opposing bloc are not potential future alliance partners, certain limitations of objectives *vis-à-vis* those nations that would have characterized behavior in the "balance of power" system are not to be expected in the loose bipolar system.

If some dramatic change occurs in a system—*e.g.,* the rules are not followed, the number or types of actors change, relative or absolute capabilities change, etc.—the system undergoes transformation. That is, the old equilibrium becomes unstable and is replaced by a new equilibrium. One of the

---

[1] Morton A. Kaplan, *System and Process in International Politics* (New York: John Wiley & Sons, 1957), pp. 9-10.

objects of the discipline of international politics is to understand the linkage between the starting state of the system and the change it undergoes if it becomes unstable. Statements that link changes in the behavior of the system to other changes in the system are called the transformation rules of the system, for they specify—if only probabilistically—the changes that are to occur if a particular disturbance affects a particular state of the system.

The transformation rules may be related to the essential rules. The essential rules of a system constitute an equilibrium set. If it becomes impossible to follow one of the rules, at least one other of the rules will necessarily change also. If one relates these changes to the parameters of the system, the transformation rules can in some cases be derived as applications of the theory. For instance, although the evidence for the deduction is not complete, one would deduce from the theory of the "balance of power" system[2] that the changes in Europe after 1870 would incline the system toward rigid rather than flexible alliances and to unlimited rather than limited wars.

The seizure by Prussia of Alsace-Lorraine from France after the war of 1870 set in motion a transformation of the "balance of power" international system. The French public reacted in an outraged way that made it difficult or impossible for the government to reconcile itself to the loss. As a consequence, Germany could not, in the foreseeable future, expect to have France as an alliance partner. Since one of the reasons for limitations of objectives in the "balance of power" system is to optimize the number of potential coalition partners who are able to protect a nation against dismemberment, this constraint ceased to operate with respect to France and Germany. In addition, the potential number of coalitions or alliances was greatly reduced as a result of this and other occurrences. As a result, the system of alliances became rigid. This forced other changes in national objectives and alliance behavior that produced a transformation of the system and that helped produce— although the actual explanation is more complicated than this—the loose bipolar system.

Growing ideological issues and international political movements also made the normal functioning of a "balance of power" system difficult and perhaps impossible. As the national power of the Soviet Union grew after the Second World War, the organizational relationships of the Communist states and the operations of local Communist parties in non-Communist states made the normal alliance arrangements of a "balance of power" system inappropriate and helped to produce a transformation to a loose bipolar system.

The cohesion of the Communist bloc gives that bloc a distinct organizational advantage, if other major nations do not form an antagonistic bloc. This is reinforced by Communist organizations within the democratic nations,

---

[2] For a discussion of the theory of the "balance of power," see Morton A. Kaplan, Arthur Burns, and Richard Quandt, "Theoretical Analysis of the 'Balance of Power,'" *Behavioral Science*, V (1960), No. 3, pp. 240-252.

which may be able to prevent foreign policy measures that are "rational" from an external point of view. If a counterbloc were not formed, one would expect the Communist bloc to secure enormous international victories, which would transform the system in still a different way, that is, in the direction of hegemony.

The formation of the bloc system is not the end of the transformation process that produces bipolarism. The rules governing nonintervention that were followed in the "balance of power" period were also related to the problem of optimizing alliance potential. If alliances become rigid or blocs are formed, the constraints maintaining the rule of nonintervention must weaken. On the other hand, the introduction of nuclear weapons—because of their enormous destructive power—introduces a new factor making for limitation in war, which compensates to some extent for the elimination of the constraint that ceased to operate with the failure of the principle of flexibility of alignment.

If we examine the present loose bipolar system, it is possible to see a number of factors that may produce an eventual transformation of that system. The problems arising from the development and spread of nuclear weapons may necessitate forms of supranational organizational control that change the nature of the international system. If these weapons are not controlled successfully, there may be a nuclear war that produces other kinds of transformation. If the war is a minor one, it may merely serve to emphasize the dangers of the age and may induce the major nations to accept controls that increase the powers of international organizations. However, the war may end in the victory of one side which may then seek to exercise a form of international control that prevents future nuclear wars. Whether such an attempt at hegemony would succeed would depend upon the completeness of victory, the organizational means at the victor's disposal, and the nature of its policies.

The number of possible transformations would be quite large, and efforts at exact prediction would not be worthwhile here in the absence of specification of the relevant variables. The transformations, however, would be the product of efforts at regulation and control carried out by nations and other organized groupings in an effort to maintain certain desired values. The general process that occurs during such transformations could be viewed in terms of Ashby's concept of ultrastability.[3] Ultrastable systems may be said to "search" for stable patterns of behavior. They are capable of recognizing the failure of existing patterns of response and of making changes in themselves that permit them to respond differently. The old patterns are rejected because they fail, and new organizational means and behavioral patterns are adopted. A series of changes may be made until some equilibrial pattern is discovered which is relatively stable, that is, which can be maintained despite disturbances in the environment.

---

[3] W. Ross Ashby, *Design for a Brain* (New York: John Wiley & Sons, 1952), p. 98.

If one examines the present system of international politics, one can see that relations between the United States and the USSR are only partly competitive. Each may desire an eventual international system in which its values predominate. But each is forced to search for patterns of behavior with which the other can live. Indeed, the uncommitted nations participate in this colloquy also. The more radical uncommitted nations are attempting to support a pattern of behavior that permits force to be used only against "colonial" regimes. The US rejects this on the ground that the criterion is insufficiently compelling and that the exception threatens the general rule. The Soviet Union attempts to secure adoption for the rule that intervention is permissible only in behalf of "popular revolutions." The major nations will find it impossible to agree on some of these rules, and such disagreement will serve to focus conflict. Other rules may succeed in satisfying sufficient of the interests and values of most of the parties of the dispute and may come to characterize more-or-less stable aspects of the period. This does not imply that these rules are fair in some abstract or arbitral sense, but that agreement—whether explicit or implicit—is reached on them.

The process by means of which this occurs is an ultrastable process in which a vast and complex social system finds a level of behavior that can be maintained. Any effort to understand these complex systems requires consideration of the ultrastable aspects of the process. This does not imply, however, that ultrastability is an explanatory concept. Equilibrium may be used as an explanatory concept when dealing with mechanical systems because there are independent measures for forces, etc. When we deal with ultrastable systems, we cannot use the concept in an explanatory way, for we lack independent measures. The concept is instead a directive for research. That is, it directs our attention to system properties that are either self-maintaining or that are maintained for external reasons.

There is, of course, no necessary value in any particular equilibrium. And ultrastability focuses our attention on change and transformation. Neither equilibrium nor change possesses any metaphysical value in itself. Attention to equilibrial aspects of systems has some pragmatic value, however. Generally, the factors that maintain equilibrium are more restricted than those which break it down, that is, only a few variables need be included in the theory that explains equilibrium. Thus theoretical development is more likely when attention is turned to problems of equilibrium and less likely when turned to problems of disequilibrium. If one possesses a good equilibrium theory, moreover, he may be able to predict what happens when a factor in the environment upsets the equilibrium, that is, he may discover the transformation rules of the system, since a specific question is being asked, rather than a diffuse set of questions. Reverse inferences are much less likely. Thus, in general, the concept of equilibrium may have a productivity for theory and for research that concepts which focus on disequilibrium and change lack—at least, where the subject matter is exceptionally complex and cannot be subjected to even semicontrolled experiment or good comparative analysis. It is not necessary to state that if the concept is reified and if the possibility of disequilibrium is neglected, there may be exceedingly harmful results of both a theoretical and practical nature.

HUMAN INITATIVE IN
SOCIAL CHANGE

Change Guided from "Above" and Initiated from "Below"

Introduction

How is change guided, directed, formed? Can master minds and hard working planners guide societal processes? Can elites impose their direction? What role do "the people" play, and what role might they acquire, in controlling the forces which shape their lives?

Charles Lindblom represents the pessimistic conservative school of thought, which despairs of planning, and above all, central adjustment of persons not ordered by any rule, central management or dominant common purpose. The advantage of mutual partisan adjustment in the U.S. and the Western democracies (over central planning) is that any value that any, even relatively small, number of citizens moderately or strongly wishes to see weighted into the policy-making process will be weighted at some value significantly above zero, Lindblom holds. On some counts, partisan mutual adjustment, as compared to central coordination, reduces the possibility that a set of decisions are so arranged as to constitute a gain for no one and a loss for some. Central decisions are often incompetent, noncentral decisions, exploitative. In any system of partisan mutual adjustment the weights given various values vary from one decision-making situation to another, and the weights in one situation will often correct deficiencies in earlier weights. In policy choices, partisan mutual adjustment will often so weigh values as to achieve, after the decision, a wide endorsement of the value weights implicit in the decision, despite the absence of prior agreement on weights. Other things being equal, the more widely shared a value, interest or preference, the heavier its weight in partisan mutual adjustment. Similarly, the more intensely held a value, interest, etc., the heavier will be its weight. This is a view which has recently regained a following and, whether one agrees or not, one surely must be acquainted with it.

Ralf Dahrendorf contrasts Lindblom's "laissez-faire" world, with that of the planned one. According to Dahrendorf there are two very different patterns of social organization both of which are rational. The first is the liberal, in which rationality is a quasi-economic term, meaning maximum yield for minimum cost. This market model assumes that individuals are rational and will not act against their own interest. Every increase in the rationality of the political process will necessarily increase the utility of this process for the people involved. In theory, utopia comes about naturally and automatically, since, if social forces simply take their course they will produce the best possible political solutions at any given time.

Plan rationality addresses itself primarily to the solution of social problems, and, at its most ambitious, assuming benevolent intent, it strives for nothing less than the construction of the perfectly just society. Ideal plan rational orientation is complete predestination and leaves no room for individual decisions. In the actual world, however, no plan can overcome the difference of power and preference. Plan rationality makes no allowance for conflict, especially for the opposition of powerful interest groups. According to Dahrendorf, it is the flexibility of market rationality in dealing with social conflict which makes it the superior choice of open, democratic societies. Market rationality is concerned with the rules of the game. In contrast, the other pattern—that of central planning—sees rationality as the setting of substantive social norms.

James Coleman and his associates move the discussion, in their often cited report, to the question of maleability, how changeable persons and institutions are. The preceding generation put great faith in the perfectability of the human race and the role of education in achieving it; the findings of Coleman *et al.* have raised serious questions on both counts. Their data showed that family background is much more strongly related to pupil achievement than quality of school. Variations in school facilities, curriculum and teacher quality have only small effects on children's success in school. However, though gains and losses are not dramatic, the achievement of minority pupils depends more on the schools they attend and less on family background than does the achievement of majority pupils. While 20% of the achievement of Negroes in the South is associated with the particular schools they go to, only 10% of the achievement of Southern whites is so correlated. More important are certain characteristics of the peer group; in particular, the achievement motivation of one's fellow students.

Pupils from families with strong educational backgrounds are generally high in achievement motivation and such pupils tend to perform well no matter what the family backround of their fellow schoolmates. But if a minority pupil from a home lacking in educational strength is placed with schoolmates with strong educational backgrounds, his achievement is likely to be higher than it would have been had he been put with others like himself. This finding has clear implications for the policy of racial desegregation of schools. It indicates that aside from being democratic, hence, normatively correct, school desegregation can be expected over the long run to have important utilitarian payoffs as well, by stimulating the achievement motivation and school performance of minority pupils.

If education is often not effective, broad as well as fundamental changes may be required to advance many of the new societal goals. Revolution has often been advocated as one way to gain such changes. If the advocated changes are blocked rather than accepted by the regime, a revolutionary potential is created, and the social movements are likely to become revolutionary movements. Note, though, that Brinton, studying the uniformities of revolutions, sees revolutionary movements as originating not in the despair of totally crushed groups, but in the discontent of groups on their way up whose further ascent has been wholly or partially blocked. Usually, many intellectuals and some members of the upper classes desert the existing regime and join the revolutionary forces. When forces, so fortified, are confronted with a government that is inflexible and inefficient, a revolution is likely to occur.

According to James C. Davies revolutions are most likely to occur when a prolonged period of objective economic and social development is followed by a short period of sharp reversal. The all-important effect on the minds of people in a particular society is to produce, during the former period, an expectation of continued ability to satisfy needs—which continue to rise— and during the latter, a mental state of anxiety and frustration when manifest reality breaks from anticipated reality. The actual state of socio-economic development is less significant than the expectation that past progress, now blocked, can and must continue in the future. Dorr's Rebellion of 1842 and the 1917 Russian Revolution, as well as several other major civil distrubances and revolutions, are cited as fitting the J-curve pattern.

Ralph Turner ties guidance of social change to the values, symbols, images, and ideologies which take root in the minds of the people, their leaders, and the social movements which congeal around them. Any major social movement both depends upon and promotes some normative revision —the change comes in perceiving a problem no longer in terms of misfortune, but as an injustice. Major eras in history have differed in the dominant sense of injustice underlying major movements of the time and dictating the main direction of social change. The liberal humanitarian era was characterized by insistence on expanding opportunities for people to participate in ruling themselves. The socialist era concentrated on demanding that the essential material needs of life be satisfied. The liberal humanitarian ideology no longer has the capacity to rouse populations to revolution or reform. The socialist conception of injustice is likewise losing its vitality. The new source of indignation is that people lack a sense of individual worth—a peace of mind that comes from personal dignity and sense of identity. The new symbol is alienation as a deep psychological state. Historically, all such revisions of the nature of injustice have been connected with a rising class. In this era, however, constituency is no longer a socio-economic class but an age group. The new movements have not yet formulated solutions to the problem. Prior to development of such a formulation protest can only be aimless.

Will the core force of societal change in the foreseeable future now be age, not class? Will the educated form a new interest group? What *positive* direction will their change-orientation take? Many answers have been suggested to these and other questions raised here. The systematic student of social change will surely be in a better position to evaluate them than those unfamiliar with the works collected here.

CHAPTER 46

CHARLES E. LINDBLOM

Rational Policy Through Mutual Adjustment

Coordination through Mutual Adjustment

A simple idea is elaborated here: that people can coordinate with each other without anyone's coordinating them, without a dominant common purpose, and without rules that fully prescribe their relations to each other. For example, any small number of people can through a series of two-person communications arrange a meeting of them all; no central management is required, nor need they all have originally wanted to organize or attend the meeting. When two masses of pedestrians cross an intersection against each other they will slip through each other, each pedestrian making such threatening, adaptive, or deferential moves as will permit him to cross, despite the number of bodies apparently in his way. Similarly, the representatives of a dozen unions and the management of an enterprise can coordinate with each other on wages and working conditions through negotiation.

On an immensely larger scale coordination also is often achieved through mutual adjustment of persons not ordered by rule, central management, or dominant common purpose. An American consumer of coffee and a Brazilian supplier are so coordinated. The market mechanism is, both within many countries and among them, a large-scale, highly developed process for coordinating millions of economically interdependent persons without their being deliberately coordinated by a central coordinator, without rules that assign to each person his position relative to all others, and without a dominant common purpose. Market coordination is powered by diverse self-interests. Scholars can hardly fail to note the possibilities of coordination

Reprinted from Charles E. Lindblom; *The Intelligence of Democracy: Decision Making Through Mutual Adjustment*, The Free Press, N.Y., Collier-Macmillan, London 1965, pp. 3-4, 226-245.

through mutual adjustment of partisans in the market, for a long tradition of theory has produced an increasingly refined explanation of the process.

Similarly, to speak a language is to follow rules. But innovations in language—usages that depart from existing rules—are coordinated by mutual adjustment among persons who have no necessary common interest, not even in the improvement of the language. Each person on his own reacts in one way or another to an innovation; the result is that the innovation either fails or is given an agreed meaning or use. It has then been made a coordinate part of a complex system for communication. . . .

The Problem

There being no criteria wholly adequate to guide the coordination of decisions and, consequently, an unavoidable "arbitrary" element in complex decision making, one can nevertheless ask whether the arbitrary elements might in some way be more reasonably, judiciously, or "better" handled in central decision making rather than in partisan mutual adjustment. Such a question forces us to look into the way in which partisan mutual adjustment achieves a weighing of conflicting values. . . .

The Advantages of Mutual Adjustment as Against Central Planning

In partisan mutual adjustment in the United States and in the Western democracies almost any value that any even relatively small number of citizens moderately or strongly wishes to see weighed into the policy-making process will be weighed in at some value significantly above zero.

We do not mean by this proposition that every value of the kind referred to in the proposition achieves some minimum of effect on each decision taken, but only that it significantly affects some decisions. Typically, such a value is given a respectful hearing by important participants in policy making, including agencies, executives, and legislators, wherever its advocates wish. The number of interests to which every legislator and executive must give the most careful and respectful, even fearful, attention, is extremely large; it is all the larger when it is remembered that what he does not attend to in one decision situation he must typically attend to in some other. He may disregard the watchmakers in acting on tax reform, farm policy, reform of the judiciary, or military aid to Laos, but he must then attend to their requests for tariff protection. For many values an allocation of authority to an agency, sometimes the creation of a new agency, will assign specific responsibility for the protection or pursuit of that value, as, for example, when a concern for equality of job opportunity leads to the establishment of a Fair Employment Practices Commission. In all this we are briefly elaborating well-known characteristics of the American political system, which is conspicuously open to participation in decision making at an enormous number of points.

If one can imagine a highly centralized decision-making system, it would be easy to imagine important values consistently being neglected, as, for example, in Roosevelt's "centrally" prepared analysis of and decision on packing the Supreme Court. Central decision making harnesses no powerful motivations to insure that all important values are permitted to affect policy, just as, as we have seen, it is weak in motivation to collect and analyze information; indeed this is, in some opinions, one of the merits of centrality. By contrast, in partisan mutual adjustment every group, agency, party leader, executive, and legislator who finds a prized value neglected in decision making is motivated, because each is a participant in decision making, to see that it is weighted in. Moreover, while opponents of that value can resist its heavy influence on decisions, it is almost impossible to shut it out completely. To be sure, again, it can be shut out of any given decision among many; but it can always find its way into some other decision that is part of the pattern of decisions that constitutes policy.

If we imagine a central coordinator urging all interested parties to call their concerns to his attention prior to his authoritative and conclusive decision on their conflicts, he can still give zero weight to any given value even if it is deeply prized by an important segment of the society. He can do so through any one of a number of errors in his grasp of his complex problem; but he can also do so because, in his final and inevitably arbitrary resolution of the conflict in which he must inescapably suppress some values for the benefit of others, he may deliberately decide to give some value a zero weight. The veto may or may not appear in partisan mutual adjustment, but in centrality it is inescapably a potentially paralytic force.

Because, on any given issue, only a few citizens are ordinarily politically active, through interest groups or otherwise, it is easy to believe that only a few interests are represented in policy making. There exists, however, in such a democracy as the United States, a representative function performed by citizens for each other, quite aside from the formal representation of citizens through legislators. On most issues most citizens "let John do it"; they are not practitioners of do-it-yourself in politics. And John does it. And, although there are differences in the pattern of preference or values between the politically inactive, on the one hand, and the active, on the other, the active in all their variety represent in policy making much of the pattern of interest or value of the inactive. . . .

On some counts partisan mutual adjustment, compared to central coordination, reduces the possibility that a set of decisions are so arranged as to constitute a gain for no one and a loss for some.

Given the fallibility of central synopsis, it will often be the case that a complex enough central decision worsens, by its errors, the position of all concerned. There is in central decision making no highly motivated check to see that at least one interest is well served by a decision. A central coordinator may be a Jack of all values and master of none. He is not committed to any one of those values whose conflicts he is charged with resolving, but is committed to their compromise on some terms. If, in rearranging the relation among the values by a coordinating decision, it turns out that all interests lose, it is not necessarily apparent to him that this is the case.

In partisan mutual adjustment, on the contrary, no move is made unless it is believed to be advantageous to at least one decision maker who is highly motivated to understand and protect his own values. For in partisan mutual adjustment only partisans make moves; and partisans initiate moves only when they believe it to be to their advantage to do so.

The character of the criticism of central and noncentral decision systems indicates that, cautiously as this last proposition has to be put, it may indicate an extremely significant difference between the two. Central decisions are often criticized for errors that cannot be defended by reference to anyone's interests; noncentral decisions are criticized for sacrificing someone's interests to someone else's. Central decisions, in short, are declared, when criticized, to be incompetent; noncentral decisions are declared to be exploitative.

Military decision systems, being highly centralized, illustrate the possibility that central decisions will not simply err in that they achieve a poor weighing of values in conflict, but will commit errors that sacrifice all the conflicting values. The Maginot Line, Pearl Harbor defense, and the employment of the Russian Fleet in the Russo-Japanese War are not criticized because they sacrificed too much of some values in order to achieve others, but because they were disastrous for all the values with which the decision makers were concerned.[1] By contrast, complaints against non-central decision making—such as political bargaining over farm price supports—allege that values of the public at large are unnecessarily, unfairly, or unwisely sacrificed to those of a subgroup, such as farmers. . . .

In any system of partisan mutual adjustment the weights given various values vary from one decision-making situation to another, and the weights in one situation will often correct deficiencies in earlier weights.

It is a mistake to think that certain interests, preferences, or values are garrisoned in such a way that they fixedly enter into all policy determinations with invariable strength. Variations in influence, of course, are not simply at the option of the interested parties concerned, as that example might indicate. Against their will, trade unions, for example, probably affect monetary policy in the United States substantially less than they do wage and hour policies.

---

[1] This is not an argument that military decisions ought not to be highly centralized, but simply an observation about a characteristic of centralized decision making.

Variability is also achieved because any given participant adjusts the values he himself brings to bear on that adjustment in which he participates. The shift in dominating values from, say, full employment and price stability for considering policy on taxation, to, say, equity, in dealing with minimum wage legislation is accomplished not simply because the two policy areas call on different groups of participants in partisan mutual adjustment, but also because some of the participants common to the two situations shift their standards of relevance. No one achieves satisfactory skill in bringing all his value to bear in important ways on any one decision or area of decision making; hence an essential prerequisite for making evaluative tasks manageable is to be selective in values made pertinent to any one decision or group of decisions. In our political system we shift values both by shifting participants and by shifting the attention of given participants. Many legislators and executives have to shift their attention simply because they take part in extremely large numbers of widely different kinds of decisions. . . .

In policy choices partisan mutual adjustment will often so weigh values as to achieve, after the decision, a wide endorsement of the value weights implicit in the decision, despite the absence of prior agreement on weights.

Partisan mutual adjustment is adapted to a situation in which there is conflict of values. This calls to mind the difference between synoptic central coordination and partisan mutual adjustment. In the face of unresolved value conflict we cannot specify how central coordination is conceived as operating; but, since partisan mutual adjustment is an adjustment among partisans each of whom pursues his own values, coping with value conflicts is built into the very model of the process. In the face of conflicts over the proper weights to be given values the various devices of partisan mutual adjustment nevertheless bring participants to decisions or resultant policies. Negotiators, for example, find a way to agree on a decision, even if all negotiators hold to different value weights; or if X unilaterally manipulates Y, X and Y are coordinated to a degree despite their value conflicts; or if X defers to Y, they are coordinated without agreement on values.

Thus, as is not the case in central coordination, unresolved value conflict is no barrier to decision in partisan mutual adjustment. And once the decision is reached or a resultant state of affairs is reached as a result of various partisan moves, the weights on values implicit in that decision or state of affairs will then often and only then be very widely endorsed.

Why are the decisions widely endorsed *ex post* if not *ex ante*? One reason is that actually reaching the agreement or resultant state of affairs through partisan mutual adjustment will often legitimize what has been reached and the value implicit in it.

If partisan mutual adjustment took the form of a conflict of naked power, the participants thus attacking each other unrestrained by conventions, it would hardly be an accepted process. But the process is highly conventionalized, as is indicated not only by the heavy dependence of power on authority, but also by the participants' acceptance of various rules of the game that have the effect of civilizing the conflict. Hence there will be some decisions widely endorsed simply because they emerge from partisan mutual adjustment. Many of us will endorse both the decision and the values implicit in the decision—say, to increase the benefits of old age insurance, believing that the decision is an outcome of a process that we find accept-able. Some of us may be equalitarians, others inequalitarians, some advo-cates of the welfare state, others advocates of a tight rein on government expenditure; but on the specific problem of how to reconcile values in con-flict over a specific issue of how much and when old age benefits should be liberalized, we will endorse the value resolution implicit in the decision taken, lacking any ground for complaint in view of the process by which the decision was reached. . . .

Other things being equal, the more widely shared a value, interest, or preference, the heavier its weight in partisan mutual adjustment.

This proposition is intended to assert a significant dependence of the weight given a value on the number of people who share it. Because it does not deny other factors in weights, it is not a very controversial proposition and needs only brief discussion.

All participant decision makers in partisan mutual adjustment are greatly influenced by the numbers of people advocating any given value. For legislators and executives this follows from their selection through elections. For agencies it follows from the authorized responsibilities of the agencies laid upon them by legislators and executives. For party leaders it follows from their desire to win elections. For interest-group leaders it follows from their competition for followings.

If this is plain enough, it can be suggested as an hypothesis that all deci-sion makers in government accept a convention or rule of the game accord-ing to which the numbers of citizens supporting a value is accepted, other things being equal, as a valid consideration in weighting. To some degree it appears that any participant in the process will acknowledge through deference, calculated adjustment, negotiation—and generally through his response to manipulated adjustment—some right of any other decision maker to prevail to the extent that he is taken as "speaking for" large numbers of citizens. . . .

Again, we do not deny that other factors than the number who share a common value are powerful determinants of value weights; we want only to make a place for widespread sharing as one of these factors.

Other things being equal, the more intensely held a value, interest, or preference, the heavier its weight in partisan mutual adjustment.

Again, the proposition is hardly controversial. To bypass the argument that intensities cannot be interpersonally compared, the proposition can be read to mean that an individual's more intense preferences will count for more in influencing governmental decisions than will his less intense preferences, and that if two individuals, A and B, have preferences with respect to value x that weigh equally, then a changed and more intense preference of A with respect to x will count for more than B's preference with respect to x.

Intensity is an important determinant of weight because, other things being equal, decision makers will be activated on those questions on which citizens feel intensely. Their intensity of feeling will be represented in their voting behavior and in their commitment to interest-group leaders. A system of partisan mutual adjustment is, of course, one in which citizens and decision makers, responding to intensity of feeling on a value, can influence the decision making process at many points. And since indication of intensity is willingness to expend energy to realize the value in question (though other factors influence the expenditure of energy too), it is almost impossible to deny, in a system of partisan mutual adjustment, as it could be denied for a highly centralized system, that intensity does not necessarily, other things being equal, result in heavier weight to the intensely prized value. . . .

•

Nothing about these features of partisan mutual adjustment disqualifies the process as a possibly acceptable method of coordination, and for most people each will be taken as a merit.

CHAPTER 47

RALF DAHRENDORF

Market and Plan

There are two very different patterns of social organization, both of which might plausibly be described as rational. One is the liberal pattern. In liberal thinking, rationality is a quasi-economic term. It seeks a maximum yield at a minimum cost—for example, a maximum of individual happiness with a minimum of political decision. The social order rests on the assumption that this kind of rationality guides the individual as well, so that as a rule people will not systematically act against their own interest. It is further assumed that every increase in the rationality of the political process will necessarily increase the utility of this process for the people involved. According to this view, then, if social forces are simply allowed to take their course, they will produce the best possible political solutions at any given time.[1]

It is on this point that the critics of liberal rationality find it least persuasive. Indeed, for at least a century critics of various schools have assigned the quality of rationality to quite a different pattern of social organization. On the grounds that the liberal pattern leads to chaos, they urge that the powers of human reason be applied to the task of designing and building the just society, or, more modestly, to solving certain social problems. To these critics rationality consists in the consideration of every step along the way from a problem to its solution, and in the creation of suitable organizational conditions for keeping problems under control. Solutions do not come about by themselves, but only as a result of controlled and controlling action.[2] Whether we try to solve the problems of our world

---

From Ralf Dahrendorf "Market and Plan" *Essays in the Theory of Society*, Stanford University Press, Stanford, California. 1968, pp. 217-231.

[1] Among contemporary liberal political theorists, Milton Friedman (*Essays in Positive Economics, Capitalism and Freedom*) probably comes closest to this undiluted eighteenth-century liberalism.

[2] Communists apart, probably the most extreme representative of this view was Karl Mannheim. See "Planning for Freedom" in this Reader.—The Editors.

with market-rational or plan-rational methods is a serious question, with manifold implications and consequences.

Market-rational political theory concerns itself with the forms, procedures, and personalities of political competition, but leaves out of consideration the substance of this process, namely what the competing parties or candidates stand for. The holding of elections, their timing, the system by which votes are translated into seats, when and how parliament is constituted, how the president is selected—all these are rules of the game in the market sense, with their ultimate sanction, perhaps, in a constitutional court. What market-rational theory cannot as readily deal with are questions involving substantive norms: questions like whether workers must be represented to a certain extent in parliament, whether private property is permissible, and whether or not to allow private nursery schools.

The plan-rational orientation, by contrast, has as its dominant feature precisely the setting of substantive social norms. Planners determine in advance who does what and who gets what. The ideal plan-rational orientation leaves no room at all for individual decisions, or indeed for conflicting decisions. Instead, the plan—assuming it is benevolent—successfully anticipates all needs, prescribes the means of satisfying them, and relates ends and means unambiguously to each other. In such an orientation, rules of the game are in principle as superfluous as substantive norms are in a market-rational approach; there is no game, but merely the controlled working out of predetermined processes. . . .

But the time has come to end such contrasts, for the distinction on which they are based, at least as it has been presented so far, is much too simple for the political analysis of any given society, or indeed for even the beginnings of a modern political theory. It is not just that reality is more complex than such simple types, that obviously no pure market-rational or pure plan-rational society exists. Nor is it merely that certain combinations of the two principles are possible. I mean something different and more fundamental here: Plainly there is some force that persistently interferes with the pure realization of market-rational principles, something that makes it impossible to play the market rational game according to purely formal rules. This force can be identified: it is power, and the social consequences of power. Because there is power, i.e., because there are rulers and ruled, there are always inequalities of participation in the regulated game of the political process, and there are always people interested in translating the rules of the game into substantive norms that create or perpetuate privilege. Because there is power, the political process is not a game. Because there is power, this process is not a strictly market-like process; what it has of market rationality is restricted by plan-rational requirements and inevitabilities. . . .

It becomes apparent that in all decisive questions there can be no such thing as equal chances of participation in the political process. Under all conceivable social conditions, the market is a fiction; the game always takes place in front of city hall. Whoever finds these remarks regrettable or depressing should reflect that the market is but one of the many versions of the utopia of powerlessness, of which neither modern political theory nor modern political practice seems to tire. The notion of the market shares with other utopias the impossibility of accounting for the necessity, the direction, and indeed the origin of change. What happens in the market is a constantly repeated game that is sufficient unto itself. Only a *deus ex machina*, the entrepreneur or the political leader, can initiate change in the market, and even then one cannot predict what direction change will take. At this point, the pure market theory of state and society comes close to pure determinism.

The structures of power in which the political process takes place offer an explanation not only of how change originates and what direction it takes, but also of why it is necessary. Power always implies non-power and therefore resistance. The dialectic of power and resistance is the motive force of history. From the interests of those in power at a given time we can infer the interests of the powerless, and with them the direction of change. Here is the nexus where norms are laid down, called into question, modified, and called into question again. Here is the source of initiative, and thus of the historicity—and that means the vitality, the openness, the freedom—of human societies. Power produces conflict, and conflict between antagonistic interests gives lasting expression to the fundamental uncertainty of human existence, by ever giving rise to new solutions and ever casting doubt on them as soon as they take form.

Such considerations lead to what one might call a sociologically refined concept of market rationality, a concept that resembles pure market rationality in name only. The game whose rules we have so often referred to is never a game of equals. To be sure, the inequalities between players take various forms, and there are ways of reducing them to minimum (as market rationality demands), but even in the most favorable circumstances the game remains a conflict. To say this is by no means to disparage the principle of market rationality, which has now become a metaphor; on the contrary, this may well be its noblest application. But it does lead to a much more subtle and complicated notion of a rational social order than the one suggested by market rationality in its pure form.

Plan rationality clashes with social reality in a special way. As a claim to certainty, plan rationality always implies an absolute claim to power. But reality resists such claims. Resistance and opposition do not disappear just because the ruling groups want to see them disappear; the plan that does not tolerate contradiction does not for this reason remain uncontradicted. Thus, any real plan-rational behavior must conclude many a compromise with reality.

All such compromises, including arrangements for recruiting planners, for discussing matters of substance, and for generating criticism, are necessarily included in the plan itself, which thus takes on market-rational aspects. The generating of criticism—i.e., the planning of opposition to one's own power—is an especially absurd business that has provided pointless extra worries for such enlightened despots of the modern world as Atatürk and Nasser.[3] For plan rationality always creates a precarious state in which the planning of resistance is likely to accelerate rather than prevent revolutionary upheavals. Functioning plan rationality requires a dubious combination of terror and institutionalized market factors, a combination that can respond to unexpected changes while restricting the people concerned to the narrowest possible range of freedom. Whether such plan rationality in the social and political order can gradually give way to market-rational conditions is one of the great questions of our time, and one to which I see no clear answer.

Our sociologically refined market rationality seems clearly worth striving for. If it does not create absolute freedom—and the very idea implies the nonexistence of society—the metaphor of the market still guarantees more freedom than any other idea in the history of political theory. Its strength lies in its recognition of social conflicts, and thus of the fundamental changeability of any society. More than the most perfect plan, this approach makes social change controllable. To the market rationalists, change takes place all the time, but gradually; patterns and forms remain, and society is never overpowered or engulfed. To be sure, this kind of control is precarious: since the only chance of creating a perfect social order lies in a readiness to put down threats and bar innovations, a market-rational order is by no means substantively perfect. Nonetheless, the principle of market rationality, with its sense of the reality of social structures and the uncertainty of all human knowledge in matters of value as of fact, is more conducive than any other principle to an open society and a free people.

Since these remarks have been very abstract, it may be useful to conclude by briefly indicating how they may be applied beyond the confines of sociological para-theory, political analysis, and political theory. Let us take West German society as an example. Economically, at least, the Federal Republic was founded on market-rational principles; in a broader social sense, however, its leaders have had no theoretical principles at all. Over the years, and especially since 1963, economic market rationality has been increasingly restricted, while in the social field plan-rational approaches have increasingly come to the fore. For Socialism has no monopoly on plan rationality; fascism, too, was plan-rational in essential respects, and so is

---

[3] Both actually tried to organize opposition to their own policies—within limits, as one would expect.

the "formed society," based as it is on substantive norms.[4] Where we might
have expected a critical analysis of how the market-rational rules of the
game operate in German society, and an attempt to create the necessary
conditions for their operation (or to abolish these conditions where they are
superfluous), we find ideologies of stagnation, i.e., attempts to avoid confronting the uncomfortable multiplicity and changeability of things social.
The resulting authoritarianism is plainly dangerous, and to liberals intolerable. There will probably be no effective liberal opposition within the traditional parties. The question has accordingly been raised whether Germany
might not do well to emulate France in this respect, and encourage the
formation of small, exclusive political clubs that can formulate precise
proposals and bring pressure to bear for their adoption.

The application of our considerations of rationality to West Germany is
comparatively obvious; the social and political problems of the Federal
Republic are far from subtle. By contrast, the problems facing nations with
highly developed liberal traditions and institutions seem to me much more
significant. For everywhere today it is being asked whether the traditional
democratic institutions as such can still accomplish what they once accomplished. Parliamentary debate, opposition, the mechanisms for generating
political initiative, the principle of elections—all these are in crisis. What
lies ahead?

In a situation of this kind it is useful to remember that the future of
liberty is as little tied to the specific institutions of parliamentary democracy as its past has been. Parliamentary institutions are but one historical
manifestation of the market-rational principle; and it is perfectly conceivable that they should lose their meaning in time and give way to new institutions designed to accomplish the same ends. Only the barest glimmer of
such a radical change in political theory can as yet be detected, though the
need for such a change may well be more urgent than our tired political
leaders—and their often no less tired ideologists—would have it. When the
time comes, it will be necessary above all to remember that the principle of
freedom lies in what we have called the sociologically refined concept of
market rationality. With this concept it may become possible at last for
modern society to find rational ways of recruiting people for political leadership, of developing political initiative, of institutionalizing resistance.
Only one thing remains certain: that if the new rationality is to be compatible with human freedom, it must be market rationality.

---

[4] The "formed society," *formierte Gesellschaft,* was Chancellor Erhard's attempt to
emulate President Johnson's "Great Society." Although the term was never elaborated
beyond a few general statements, it clearly referred to an organization of divergent
interests and groups along the lines of a corporate state. Erhard's combination of
liberalism in economic matters and anti-modern romanticism in social matters echoed
such heroes of his as Wilhelm Vershofen and Wilhelm Röpke.

CHAPTER 48

JAMES S. COLEMAN, et al.

Enhancing Equality of Educational Opportunity

A. The Present Situation

In its desegregation decision of 1954, the Supreme Court held that separate schools for Negro and white children are inherently unequal. This survey finds that, when measured by that yardstick, American public education remains largely unequal in most regions of the country, including all those where Negroes form any significant proportion of the population. Obviously, however, that is not the only yardstick. The next section describes other characteristics by means of which equality of educational opportunity may be appraised. . . .

Segregation in the Public Schools

The great majority of American children attend schools that are largely segregated—that is, where almost all of their fellow students are of the same racial background as they are. Among minority groups, Negroes are by far the most segregated. Taking all groups, however, white children are most segregated. Almost 80 percent of all white pupils in 1st grade and 12th grade attend schools that are from 90 to 100 percent white. And 97 percent at grade 1, and 99 percent at grade 12, attend schools that are 50 percent or more white.

More than 65 percent of all Negro pupils in the first grade attend schools that are between 90 and 100 percent Negro. And 87 percent at grade 1, and 66 percent at grade 12, attend schools that are 50 percent or more Negro. In the South most students attend schools that are 100 percent white or Negro.

Reprinted from *Equality of Educational Opportunity* by James S. Coleman et al. A publication of the National Center for Educational Statistics, 1966. Excerpt taken from pages: 3, 8-12, 20-22, 28-32, 325.

School Characteristics[1]

Facilities

Careful study reveals that there is not a wholly consistent pattern—that is, minorities are not at a disadvantage in every item listed—but that there are nevertheless some definite and systematic directions of differences. Nationally, Negro pupils have fewer of some of the facilities that seem most related to academic achievement: They have less access to physics, chemistry, and language laboratories; there are fewer books per pupil in their libraries; their textbooks are less often in sufficient supply. To the extent that physical facilities are important to learning, such items appear to be more relevant than some others, such as cafeterias, in which minority groups are at an advantage.

Programs

Just as minority groups tend to have less access to physical facilities that seem to be related to academic achievement, so too they have less access to curricular and extracurricular programs that would seem to have such a relationship.

Secondary school Negro students are less likely to attend schools that are regionally accredited; this is particularly pronounced in the South. Negro and Puerto Rican pupils have less access to college preparatory curriculums and to accelerated curriculums; Puerto Ricans have less access to vocational curriculums as well. Less intelligence testing is done in the schools attended by Negroes and Puerto Ricans. Finally, white students in general have more access to a more fully developed program of extracurricular activities, in particular those which might be related to academic matters (debate teams, for example, and student newspapers).

Teachers

[As to] characteristics which offer rough indications of teacher quality,

---

[1] All of the findings reported in this and the following section are based on responses to questionnaires filled out by public school teachers, principals, district school superintendents, and pupils. The data were gathered in September and October of 1965 from 4,000 public schools. All teachers, principals, and district superintendents in these schools participated, as did all pupils in the 3d, 6th, 9th, and 12th grades. First-grade pupils in half the schools participated. More than 645,000 pupils in all were involved in the survey. About 30 percent of the schools selected for the survey did not participate; an analysis of the nonparticipating schools indicated that their inclusion would not have significantly altered the results of the survey. The participation rates were: in the metropolitan North and West, 72 percent; metropolitan South and Southwest, 65 percent; nonmetropolitan North and West, 82 percent; nonmetropolitan South and Southwest 61 percent.

including the types of colleges attended, years of teaching experience, salary, educational level of mother, and a score on a 30-word vocabulary test: The average Negro pupil attends a school where a greater percentage of the teachers appears to be somewhat less able, as measured by these indicators, than those in the schools attended by the average white student. . . .

Student Body Characteristics

Clear differences are found on these items. The average Negro has fewer classmates whose mothers graduated from high school; his classmates more frequently are members of large rather than small families; they are less often enrolled in a college preparatory curriculum; they have taken a smaller number of courses in English, mathematics, foreign language, and science.

On most items, the other minority groups fall between Negroes and whites, but closer to whites, in the extent to which each characteristic is typical of their classmates.

Achievement in the Public Schools

The schools bear many responsibilities. Among the most important is the teaching of certain intellectual skills such as reading, writing, calculating, and problem solving. One way of assessing the educational opportunity offered by the schools is to measure how well they perform this task. Standard achievement tests are available to measure these skills, and several such tests were administered in this survey to pupils at grades 1, 3, 6, 9, and 12.

These tests do not measure intelligence, nor attitudes, nor qualities of character. Furthermore, they are not, nor are they intended to be, "culture free." Quite the reverse: they are culture bound. What they measure are the skills which are among the most important in our society for getting a good job and moving up to a better one, and for full participation in an increasingly technical world. Consequently, a pupil's test results at the end of public school provide a good measure of the range of opportunities open to him as he finishes school—a wide range of choice of jobs or colleges if these skills are very high; a very narrow range that includes only the most menial jobs if these skills are very low.

Table 48-1 gives an overall illustration of the test results for the various groups by tabulating nationwide median scores (the score which divides the group in half) for 1st-grade and 12th-grade pupils on the tests used in those grades. For example, half of the white 12th-grade pupils had scores above 52 on the nonverbal test and half had scores below 52. (Scores on each test at each grade level were standardized so that the average over the national sample equaled 50 and the standard deviation equaled 10. This means that for all pupils in the Nation, about 16 percent would score below 40 and about 16 percent above 60).

Table **48–1**

Nationwide Median Test Scores for 1st- and 12th-Grade Pupils, Fall 1965

| | Racial or ethnic group | | | | | |
Test	Puerto Ricans	Indian Americans	Mexican- Americans	Oriental Americans	Negro	Majority
1st grade:						
Nonverbal	45.8	53.0	50.1	56.6	43.4	54.1
Verbal	44.9	47.8	46.5	51.6	45.4	53.2
12th grade:						
Nonverbal	43.3	47.1	45.0	51.6	40.9	52.0
Verbal	43.1	43.7	43.8	49.6	40.9	52.1
Reading	42.6	44.3	44.2	48.8	42.2	51.9
Mathematics	43.7	45.9	45.5	51.3	41.8	51.8
General information .	41.7	44.7	43.3	49.0	40.6	52.2
Average of the 5 tests	43.1	45.1	44.4	50.1	41.1	52.0

With some exceptions—notably Oriental Americans—the average minority pupil scores distinctly lower on these tests at every level than the average white pupil. The minority pupils' scores are as much as one standard deviation below the majority pupils' scores in the 1st grade. At the 12th grade, results of tests in the same verbal and nonverbal skills show that, in every case, the minority scores are farther below the majority than are the 1st-graders. For some groups, the relative decline is negligible; for others, it is large.

Furthermore, a constant difference in standard deviations over the various grades represents an increasing difference in grade level gap. For example, Negroes in the metropolitan Northeast are about 1.1 standard deviations below whites in the same region at grades 6, 9, and 12. But at grade 6 this represents 1.6 years behind; at grade 9, 2.4 years; and at grade 12, 3.3 years. Thus, by this measure, the deficiency in achievement is progressively greater for the minority pupils at progressively higher grade levels.

For most minority groups, then, and most particularly the Negro, schools provide little opportunity for them to overcome this initial deficiency; in fact they fall farther behind the white majority in the development of several skills which are critical to making a living and participating fully in modern society. Whatever may be the combination of nonschool factors— poverty, community attitudes, low educational level of parents—which put minority children at a disadvantage in verbal and nonverbal skills when they enter the first grade, the fact is the schools have not overcome it.

Relation of Achievement to School Characteristics

The first finding is that the schools are remarkably similar in the way they relate to the achievement of their pupils when the socioeconomic background of the students is taken into account. It is known that socioeconomic factors bear a strong relation to academic achievement. When these factors are statistically controlled, however, it appears that differences between schools account for only a small fraction of differences in pupil achievement.

The schools do differ, however, in their relation to the various racial and ethnic groups. The average white student's achievement seems to be less affected by the strength or weakness of his school's facilities, curriculums, and teachers than is the average minority pupil's. To put it another way, the achievement of minority pupils depends more on the schools they attend than does the achievement of majority pupils. Thus, 20 percent of the achievement of Negroes in the South is associated with the particular schools they go to, whereas only 10 percent of the achievement of whites in the South is. Except for Oriental Americans, this general result is found for all minorities.

The inference might then be made that improving the school of a minority pupil may increase his achievement more than would improving the school of a white child increase his. Similarly, the average minority pupil's achievement may suffer more in a school of low quality than might the average white pupil's. In short, whites, and to a lesser extent Oriental Americans, are less affected one way or the other by the quality of their schools than are minority pupils. This indicates that it is for the most disadvantaged children that improvements in school quality will make the most difference in achievement.

All of these results suggest the next question: What are the school characteristics that are most related to achievement? In other words, what factors in the school seem to be most important in affecting achievement?

It appears that variations in the facilities and curriculums of the schools account for relatively little variation in pupil achievement insofar as this is measured by standard tests. Again, it is for majority whites that the variations make the least difference; for minorities, they make somewhat more difference. Among the facilities that show some relationship to achievement are several for which minority pupils' schools are less well equipped relative to whites. For example, the existence of science laboratories showed a small but consistent relationship to achievement, and table 48–2 shows that minorities, especially Negroes, are in schools with fewer of these laboratories.

The quality of teachers shows a stronger relationship to pupil achievement. Furthermore, it is progressively greater at higher grades, indicating a cumulative impact of the qualities of teachers in a school on the pupil's achievements. Again, teacher quality seems more important to minority achievement than to that of the majority.

Finally, it appears that a pupil's achievement is strongly related to the educational backgrounds and aspirations of the other students in the school. Only crude measures of these variables were used (principally the proportion of pupils with encyclopedias in the home and the proportion planning to go to college). Analysis indicates, however, that children from a given family background, when put in schools of different social composition, will achieve at quite different levels. This effect is again less for white pupils than for any minority group other than Orientals. Thus, if a white pupil from a home that is strongly and effectively supportive of education is put in a school where most pupils do not come from such homes, his achievement will be little different than if he were in a school composed of others like himself. But if a minority pupil from a home without much educational strength is put with schoolmates with strong educational backgrounds, his achievement is likely to increase.

This general result has important implications for equality of educational opportunity. For the principal way in which the school environments of Negroes and whites differ is in the composition of their student bodies, and it turns out that the composition of the student bodies has a strong relationship to the achievement of Negro and other minority pupils. . . . Of the many implications of this study of school effects on achievement, one appears to be of overriding importance. This is the implication that stems from the following results taken together:

1. The great importance of family background for achievement;
2. The fact that the relation of family background to achievement does not diminish over the years of school;
3. The relatively small amount of school-to-school variation that is not accounted for by differences in family background, indicating the small independent effect of variations in school facilities, curriculum, and staff upon achievement;
4. The small amount of variance in achievement explicitly accounted for by variations in facilities and curriculum;
5. Given the fact that no school factors account for much variation in achievement, teachers' characteristics account for more than any other —taken together with the previously reported results, which show that teachers tend to be socially and racially similar to the students they teach;
6. The fact that the social composition of the student body is more highly related to achievement, independently of the student's own social background, than is any school factor;
7. The fact that attitudes such as a sense of control of the environment, or a belief in the responsiveness of the environment, are extremely highly related to achievement, but appear to be little influenced by variations in school characteristics.

Taking all these results together, one implication stands out above all: That schools bring little influence to bear on a child's achievement that is independent of his background and general social context; and that this very lack of an independent effect means that the inequalities imposed on children by their home, neighborhood, and peer environment are carried along to become the inequalities with which they confront adult life at the end of school. For equality of educational opportunity through the schools must imply a strong effect of schools that is independent of the child's immediate social environment, and that strong independent effect is not present in American schools. . . .

B. Enhancing Equality of Educational Opportunity by School Integration

An education in integrated schools can be expected to have major effects on attitudes toward members of other racial groups. At its best, it can develop attitudes appropriate to the integrated society these students will live in; at its worst, it can create hostile camps of Negroes and whites in the same school. Thus, there is more to "school integration" than merely putting Negroes and whites in the same building, and there may be more important consequences of integration than its effect on achievement.

Yet the analysis of school factors described earlier suggests that in the long run, integration should be expected to have a positive effect on Negro achievement as well. An analysis was carried out to seek such effects on achievement which might appear in the short run. This analysis of the test performance of Negro children in integrated schools indicates positive effects of integration, though rather small ones. Results for grades 6, 9, and 12 are given in Table 48-2 for Negro pupils classified by the proportion of their classmates the previous year who were white. Comparing the averages in each row, in every case but one the highest average score is recorded for the Negro pupils where more than half of their classmates were white. But in reading the rows from left to right, the increase is small and often those Negro pupils in classes with only a few white pupils score lower than those in totally segregated classes.

Table 48-3 was constructed to observe whether there is any tendency for Negro pupils who have spent more years in integrated schools to exhibit higher average achievement. Those pupils who first entered integrated schools in the early grades record consistently higher scores than the other groups, although the differences are again small.

No account is taken in these tabulations of the fact that the various groups of pupils may have come from different backgrounds. When such account is taken by simple cross-tabulations on indicators of socioeconomic status, the performance remains highest in those schools which have been integrated for

Table **48–2**

Average Test Scores of Negro Pupils, Fall 1965

		Reading comprehension—Proportion of white classmates last year			
Grade	Region	None	Less than half	Half	More than half
12	Metropolitan Northeast	46.0	43.7	44.5	47.5
12	Metropolitan Midwest	46.4	43.2	44.0	46.7
9	Metropolitan Northeast	44.2	44.8	44.8	47.1
9	Metropolitan Midwest	45.3	45.2	45.3	46.4
6	Metropolitan Northeast	46.0	45.4	45.8	46.6
6	Metropolitan Midwest	46.0	44.7	44.9	45.1

Table **48–3**

Average Test Scores of Negro Pupils, Fall 1965

Grade	Region	Grade of first time with majority pupils
9	Metropolitan Northeast	1, 2, or 3
		4, 5, or 6
		7, 8, or 9
		Never
9	Metropolitan Midwest	1, 2, or 3
		4, 5, or 6
		7, 8, or 9
		Never
12	Metropolitan Northeast	1, 2, or 3
		4, 5, or 6
		7, 8, or 9
		10, 11, or 12
		Never
12	Metropolitan Midwest	1, 2, or 3
		4, 5, or 6
		7, 8, or 9
		10, 11, or 12
		Never

the longest time. Thus, although the differences are small, and although the degree of integration within the school is not known, there is evident, even

Math achievement—Proportion of white classmates last year			
None	Less than half	Half	More than half
41.5	40.6	41.1	44.5
43.8	42.6	42.9	44.8
43.1	43.5	43.7	47.2
44.4	44.3	44.1	46.6
44.0	43.4	43.6	45.6
43.8	42.8	42.9	44.1

Proportion of majority classmates last year				
None	Less than half	Half	More than half	Total
45.9	46.7	46.9	48.1	46.8
45.2	43.3	44.4	44.4	44.8
43.5	42.9	44.6	45.0	44.0
43.2	. . .	. . .	. . .	43.2
45.4	46.6	46.4	48.6	46.7
44.4	44.1	45.3	46.7	44.5
44.4	43.4	43.3	45.2	43.7
46.5	. . .	. . .	. . .	46.5
40.8	43.6	45.2	48.6	46.2
46.7	45.1	44.9	46.7	45.6
42.2	43.5	43.8	49.7	48.2
42.2	41.1	43.2	46.6	44.1
40.9	. . .	. . .	. . .	40.9
47.4	44.3	45.6	48.3	46.7
46.1	43.0	43.5	46.4	45.4
46.6	40.8	42.3	45.6	45.3
44.8	39.5	43.5	44.9	44.3
47.2	. . .	. . .	. . .	47.2

in the short run, an effect of school integration on the reading and mathematics achievement of Negro pupils.

CHAPTER 49

CRANE BRINTON

The Anatomy of Revolution: Tentative Uniformities

We have studied four revolutions which on the surface seem to have certain resemblances, and deliberately avoided certain other types of revolution. Our four took place in the postmedieval Western world, were "popular" revolutions carried out in the name of "freedom" for a majority against a privileged minority, and were successful, that is, they resulted in the revolutionists becoming the legal government. Anything like a complete sociology of revolutions would have to take account of other kinds of revolution. . . .

When all necessary concessions are made to those who insist that events in history are unique, it remains true that the four revolutions we have studied do display some striking uniformities. Our conceptual scheme of the fever can be worked out so as to bring these uniformities clearly to mind. We shall find it worthwhile, in attempting to summarize the work of these revolutions, to recapitulate briefly the main points of comparison on which our uniformities are based.

We must be very tentative about the prodromal symptoms of revolution. Even retrospectively, diagnosis of the four societies we studied was very difficult, and there is little ground for belief that anyone today has enough knowledge and skill to apply formal methods of diagnosis to a contemporary society and say, in this case revolution will or will not occur shortly. But some uniformities do emerge from a study of the old regimes in England, America, France, and Russia.

First, these were all societies on the whole on the upgrade economically before the revolution came, and the revolutionary movements seem to originate in the discontents of not unprosperous people who feel restraint, cramp, annoyance, rather than downright crushing oppression. Certainly these revolutions are not started by down-and-outers, by starving, miserable people. These revolutionists are not worms turning, not children of despair. These revolutions are born of hope, and their philosophies are formally optimistic.

Second, we find in our prerevolutionary society definite and indeed very bitter class antagonisms, though these antagonisms seem rather more complicated than the cruder Marxists will allow. It is not a case of feudal nobility against bourgeoisie in 1640, 1776, and 1789 or of bourgeoisie against proletariat in 1917. The strongest feelings seem generated in the bosoms of men—and women—who have made money, or at least who have enough to live on, and who contemplate bitterly the imperfections of a socially privileged aristocracy. Revolutions seem more likely when social classes are fairly close together than when they are far apart. "Untouchables" very rarely revolt against a God-given aristocracy, and Haiti gives one of the few examples of successful slave revolutions. But rich merchants whose daughters can marry aristocrats are likely to feel that God is at least as interested in merchants as in aristocrats. It is difficult to say why the bitterness of feeling between classes *almost* equal socially seems so much stronger in some societies than others—why, for instance, a Marie Antoinette should be so much more hated in eighteenth-century France than a rich, idle, much publicized heiress in contemporary America; but at any rate the existence of such bitterness can be observed in our prerevolutionary societies, which is, clinically speaking, enough for the moment.

Third, there is the desertion of the intellectuals. This is in some respects the most reliable of the symptoms we are likely to meet. Here again we need not try to explain all the hows and whys, need not try to tie up the desertion of the intellectuals with a grand and complete sociology of revolutions. We need simply state that it can be observed in all four of our societies.

Fourth, the governmental machinery is clearly inefficient, partly through neglect—through a failure to make changes in old institutions; partly because new conditions—in the societies we have studied, conditions attendant on economic expansion and the growth of new monied classes, new ways of transportation, new business methods—these new conditions laid an intolerable strain on governmental machinery adapted to simpler, more primitive, conditions.

Fifth, the old ruling class—or rather, many individuals of the old ruling class—come to distrust themselves, or lose faith in the traditions and habits of their class, grow intellectual, humanitarian, or go over to the attacking groups. Perhaps a larger number of them than usual lead lives we shall have to call immoral, dissolute, though one cannot by any means be as sure about this as a symptom as about the loss of habits and traditions of command effective among a ruling class. At any rate, the ruling class becomes politically inept.

The dramatic events that start things moving, that bring on the fever of revolution, are in three of our four revolutions intimately connected with the financial administration of the state. In the fourth, Russia, the breakdown of administration under the burdens of an unsuccessful war is only in part financial. But in all our societies the inefficiency and inadequacy of the governmental structure of the society come out clearly in the very first stages of the revolution. There is a time—the first few weeks or months—when it looks as if a determined use of force on the part of the government might prevent the mounting excitement from culminating in an overthrow of the government. These governments attempted such a use of force in all four instances, and in all four their attempt was a failure. This failure indeed proved a turning point during the first stages and set up the revolutionists in power.

Yet one is impressed in all four instances more with the ineptitude of the governments' use of force than with the skill of their opponents' use of force. We are here speaking of the situation wholly from a military and police point of view. It may be that the majority of the people are discontented, loathe the existing government, wish it overthrown. Nobody knows. They don't take plebiscites *before* revolutions. In the actual clash—even Bastille Day, Concord, or the February Days in Petrograd—only a minority of the people is actively engaged. But the government hold over its own troops is poor, its troops fight half-heartedly or desert, its commanders are stupid, its enemies acquire a nucleus of the deserting troops or of a previous militia, and the old gives place to the new. Yet, such is the conservative and routine-loving nature of the bulk of human beings, so strong are habits of obedience in most of them, that it is almost safe to say that no government is likely to be overthrown until it loses the ability to make adequate use of its military and police powers. That loss of ability may show itself in the actual desertion of soldiers and police to the revolutionists, or in the stupidity with which the government manages its soldiers and police, or in both ways.

The events we have grouped under the name of first stages do not of course unroll themselves in exactly the same order in time, or with exactly the same content, in all four of our revolutions. But we have listed the major elements, and they fall into a pattern of uniformities: financial breakdown, organization of the discontented to remedy this breakdown (or threatened breakdown), revolutionary demands on the part of these organized discontented, demands which if granted would mean the virtual abdication of those governing, attempted use of force by the government, its failure, and the attainment of power by the revolutionists. These revolutionists have hitherto been acting as an organized and nearly unanimous group, but with the attainment of power it is clear that they are not united.

The group which dominates these first stages we call the moderates. They are not always in a numerical majority in this stage—indeed, it is pretty clear that if you limit the moderates to the Kadets, they were not in a majority in Russia in February, 1917. But they seem the natural heirs of the old government, and they have their chance. In three of our revolutions, they are sooner or later driven from office to death or exile. Certainly there is to be seen in England, France, and Russia a process in which a series of crises—some involving violence, street fighting, and the like—deposes one set of men and puts in power another and more radical set. In these revolutions power passes by violent or at least extralegal methods from Right to Left, until at the crisis period the extreme radicals, the complete revolutionists, are in power. There are, as a matter of fact, usually a few even wilder and more lunatic fringes of the triumphant extremists—but these are not numerous or strong and are usually suppressed or otherwise made harmless by the dominant radicals. It is therefore approximately true to say that power passes on from Right to Left until it reaches the extreme Left.

The rule of the extremists we have called the crisis period. This period was not reached in the American Revolution, though in the treatment of Loyalists, in the pressure to support the army, in some of the phases of social life, you can discern in America many of the phenomena of the Terror as it is seen in our three other societies. We cannot here attempt to go into the complicated question as to why the American Revolution stopped short of a true crisis period, why the moderates were never ousted in this country. We must repeat that we are simply trying to establish certain uniformities of description and are not attempting a complete sociology of revolutions.

The extremists are helped to power, no doubt, by the existence of a powerful pressure toward centralized strong government, something which in general the moderates are not capable of providing, while the extremists —with their discipline, their contempt for half measures, their willingness to make firm decisions, their freedom from libertarian qualms—are quite able and willing to centralize. Especially in France and Russia, where powerful foreign enemies threatened the very existence of the nation, the machinery of government during the crisis period was in part constructed to serve as a government of national defense. Yet though modern wars, as we know in this country, demand a centralization of authority, war alone does not seem to account for all that happened in the crisis period in those countries.

What does happen may be a bit oversimply summarized as follows: emergency centralization of power in an administration, usually a council or commission, and more-or-less dominated by a "strong man"—Cromwell, Robespierre, Lenin; government without any effective protection for the normal civil rights of the individual—or if this sounds unrealistic, especially for Russia, let us say the normal private life of the individual; setting up of extraordinary courts and a special revolutionary police to carry out the decrees of the government and to suppress all dissenting individuals or groups; all this machinery ultimately built up from a relatively small group—Independents, Jacobins, Bolsheviks—which has a monopoly on all governmental action. Finally, governmental action becomes a much greater part of all human action than in these societies in their normal condition; this apparatus of government is set to work indifferently on the mountains and molehills of human life—it is used to pry into and poke about corners normally reserved for priest or physician, or friend, and it is used to regulate, control, plan, the production and distribution of economic wealth on a national scale.

•

In all of our societies the crisis period was followed by a convalescence, by a return to most of the simpler and more fundamental courses taken by interactions in the old network. . . . The equilibrium has been restored and the revolution is over. But this does not mean that nothing has been changed. Some new and useful tracks or courses in the network of interactions that makes society have been established, some old and inconvenient ones—you may call them unjust if you like—have been eliminated. . . .

CHAPTER 50

JAMES C. DAVIES

Toward a Theory
of Revolution

In exhorting proletarians of all nations to unite in revolution, because they had nothing to lose but their chains, Marx and Engels most succinctly presented that theory of revolution which is recognized as their brain child. But this most famed thesis, that progressive degradation of the industrial working class would finally reach the point of despair and inevitable revolt, is not the only one that Marx fathered. In at least one essay he gave life to a quite antithetical idea. He described, as a precondition of widespread unrest, not progressive degradation of the proletariat but rather an improvement in workers' economic condition which did not keep pace with the growing welfare of capitalists and therefore produced social tension.

A noticeable increase in wages presupposes a rapid growth of productive capital. The rapid growth of productive capital brings about an equally rapid growth of wealth, luxury, social wants, social enjoyments. Thus, although the enjoyments of the workers have risen, the social satisfaction that they give has fallen in comparison with the increased enjoyments of the capitalist, which are inaccessible to the worker, in comparison with the state of development of society in general. Our desires and pleasures spring from society; we measure them, therefore, by society and not by the objects which serve for their satisfaction. Because they are of a social nature, they are of a relative nature.[1]

Marx's qualification here of his more frequent belief that degradation produces revolution is expressed as the main thesis by de Tocqueville in his study of the French Revolution. After a long review of economic and social

Reprinted from *American Sociological Review* 27 (February 1962) no. 1, pp. 5-15.
[1] The above quotation is from Karl Marx and Frederick Engels, "Wage Labour and Capital," *Selected Works in Two Volumes,* Moscow: Foreign Languages Publishing House, 1955, vol. 1, p. 94.

decline in the seventeenth century and dynamic growth in the eighteenth, de Tocqueville concludes:

> So it would appear that the French found their condition the more unsupportable in proportion to its improvement. . . . Revolutions are not always brought about by a gradual decline from bad to worse. Nations that have endured patiently and almost unconsciously the most overwhelming oppression often burst into rebellion against the yoke the moment it begins to grow lighter. The regime which is destroyed by a revolution is almost always an improvement on its immediate predecessor. . . . Evils which are patiently endured when they seem inevitable become intolerable when once the idea of escape from them is suggested.[2]

On the basis of de Tocqueville and Marx, we can choose one of these ideas or the other, which makes it hard to decide just when revolutions are more likely to occur—when there has been social and economic progress or when there has been regress. It appears that both ideas have explanatory and possibly predictive value, if they are juxtaposed and put in the proper time sequence.

Revolutions are most likely to occur when a prolonged period of objective economic and social development is followed by a short period of sharp reversal.[3] The all-important effect on the minds of people in a particular

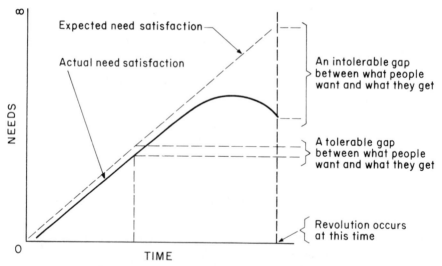

FIGURE 50-1. Need Satisfaction and Revolution

---

[2] A. de Tocqueville, *The Old Regime and the French Revolution* (trans. by John Bonner), N. Y.: Harper & Bros., 1856, p. 214.

[3] Revolutions are here defined as violent civil disturbances that cause the displacement of one ruling group by another that has a broader popular basis for support.

society is to produce, during the former period, an expectation of continued ability to satisfy needs—which continue to rise—and, during the latter, a mental state of anxiety and frustration when manifest reality breaks away from anticipated reality. The actual state of socio-economic development is less significant than the expectation that past progress, now blocked, can and must continue in the future.

Political stability and instability are ultimately dependent on a state of mind, a mood, in a society. Satisfied or apathetic people who are poor in goods, status, and power can remain politically quiet and their opposites can revolt, just as, correlatively and more probably, dissatisfied poor can revolt and satisfied rich oppose revolution. It is the dissatisfied state of mind rather than the tangible provision of "adequate" or "inadequate" supplies of food, equality, or liberty which produces the revolution. In actuality, there must be a joining of forces between dissatisfied, frustrated people who differ in their degree of objective, tangible welfare and status. Well-fed, well-educated, high-status individuals who rebel in the face of apathy among the objectively deprived can accomplish at most a coup d'état. The objectively deprived, when faced with solid opposition of people of wealth, status, and power, will be smashed in their rebellion as were peasants and Anabaptists by German noblemen in 1525 and East Germans by the Communist élite in 1953.

Before appraising this general notion in light of a series of revolutions, a word is in order as to why revolutions ordinarily do not occur when a society is generally impoverished—when, as de Tocqueville put it, evils that seem inevitable are patiently endured. They are endured in the extreme case because the physical and mental energies of people are totally employed in the process of merely staying alive. The Minnesota starvation studies conducted during World War II[4] indicate clearly the constant pre-occupation of very hungry individuals with fantasies and thoughts of food. In extremis, as the Minnesota research poignantly demonstrates, the individual withdraws into a life of his own, withdraws from society, withdraws from any significant kind of activity unrelated to staying alive. Reports of behavior in Nazi concentration camps indicate the same preoccupation.[5] In less extreme and barbarous circumstances, where minimal survival is possible but little more, the preoccupation of individuals with staying alive is only mitigated. Social action takes place for the most part on a local, face-to-face basis. In such

---

[4] The full report is Ancel Keys *et al., The Biology of Human Starvation,* Minneapolis: University of Minnesota Press, 1950. See J. Brozek, "Semi-starvation and Nutritional Rehabilitation," *Journal of Clinical Nutrition,* 1 (January, 1953), pp. 107-118 for a brief analysis.

[5] E. A. Cohen, *Human Behavior in the Concentration Camp,* New York: W. W. Norton & Co., 1953, pp. 123-125, 131-140.

circumstances the family is a—perhaps the major—solidary unit[6] and even the local community exists primarily to the extent families need to act together to secure their separate survival. Such was life on the American frontier in the sixteenth through nineteenth centuries. In very much attenuated form, but with a substantial degree of social isolation persisting, such evidently is rural life even today. This is clearly related to a relatively low level of political participation in elections.[7] As Zawadzki and Lazarsfeld have indicated,[8] preoccupation with physical survival, even in industrial areas, is a force strongly militating against the establishment of the community-sense and consensus on joint political action which are necessary to induce a revolutionary state of mind. Far from making people into revolutionaries, enduring poverty makes for concern with one's solitary self or solitary family at best and resignation or mute despair at worst. When it is a choice between losing their chains or their lives, people will mostly choose to keep their chains, a fact which Marx seems to have overlooked.[9]

It is when the chains have been loosened somewhat, so that they can be cast off without a high probability of losing life, that people are put in a condition of proto-rebelliousness. I use the term proto-rebelliousness because the mood of discontent may be dissipated before a violent outbreak occurs. The causes for such dissipation may be natural or social (including economic and political). A bad crop year that threatens a return to chronic hunger may be succeeded by a year of natural abundance. Recovery from sharp economic dislocation may take the steam from the boiler of rebellion. The slow, grudging grant of reforms, which has been the political history of England since at least the Industrial Revolution, may effectively and continuously prevent the degree of frustration that produces revolt.

A revolutionary state of mind requires the continued, even habitual but dynamic expectation of greater opportunity to satisfy basic needs, which may range from merely physical to social to the need for equal dignity and justice. But the necessary additional ingredient is a persistent, unrelenting threat to the satisfaction of these needs: not a threat which actually returns people to a state of sheer survival but which puts them in the mental state

---

[6] For community life in such poverty, in Mezzogiorno Italy, see E. C. Banfield, *The Moral Basis of a Backward Society*, Glencoe, Ill.: The Free Press, 1958. The author emphasizes that the nuclear family is a solidary, consensual, moral unit (see p. 85) but even within it, consensus appears to break down, in outbreaks of pure, individual amorality—notably between parents and children (see p. 117).

[7] See Angus Campbell *et al., The American Voter*, New York: John Wiley & Sons, 1960, Chap. 15, "Agrarian Political Behavior."

[8] B. Zawadzki and P. F. Lazarsfeld, "The Psychological Consequences of Unemployment," *Journal of Social Psychology*, 6 (May, 1935), pp. 224-251.

[9] A remarkable and awesome exception to this phenomenon occurred occasionally in some Nazi concentration camps, e.g., in a Buchenwald revolt against capricious rule by criminal prisoners. During this revolt, one hundred criminal prisoners were killed by political prisoners. See Cohen, *op. cit.*, p. 200.

where they believe they will not be able to satisfy one or more basic needs. Although physical deprivation in some degree may be threatened on the eve of all revolutions, it need not be the prime factor, as it surely was not in the American Revolution of 1775. The crucial factor is the vague or specific fear that ground gained over a long period of time will be quickly lost. This fear does not generate if there is continued opportunity to satisfy continually emerging needs; it generates when the existing government suppresses or is blamed for supressing such opportunity.

Two rebellions or revolutions are given considerable attention in the sections that follow: Dorr's Rebellion of 1842, and the Russian Revolution of 1917. Brief mention is then made of several other major civil disturbances, all of which appear to fit the J-curve pattern.[10] After considering these specific disturbances, some general theoretical and research problems are discussed.

No claim is made that all rebellions follow the pattern, but just that the ones here presented do. Both of these are "progressive" revolutions in behalf of greater equality and liberty. The question is open whether the pattern occurs in such markedly retrogressive revolutions as Nazism in Germany or the 1861 Southern rebellion in the United States. It will surely be necessary to examine other progressive revolutions before one can judge how universal the J-curve is. And it will be necessary, in the interests of scientific validation, to examine cases of serious civil disturbance that fell short of producing profound revolution—such as the Sepoy Rebellion of 1857 in India, the Pullman Strike of 1894 in America, the Boxer Rebellion of 1900 in China, and the Great Depression of the 1920s and 1930s as it was experienced in Austria, France, Great Britain, and the United States. The explanation for such still-born rebellions—for revolutions that might have occurred—is inevitably more complicated than for those that come to term in the "normal" course of political gestation.

Dorr's Rebellion of 1842

Dorr's Rebellion[11] in nineteenth-century America was perhaps the first of many civil disturbances to occur in America as a consequence, in part, of the Industrial Revolution. It followed by three years an outbreak in England that had similar roots and a similar program—the Chartist agitation. A

---

10 This curve is of course not to be confused with its prior and altogether different use by Floyd Allport in his study of social conformity. See F. H. Allport, "The J-Curve Hypothesis of Conforming Behavior," *Journal of Social Psychology,* 5 (May, 1934), pp. 141-183, reprinted in T. H. Newcomb & E. L. Hartley, *Readings in Social Psychology,* N. Y.: Henry Holt & Co., 1947, pp. 55-67.

11 I am indebted to Beryl L. Crowe for his extensive research on Dorr's Rebellion while he was a participant in my political behavior seminar at the University of California, Berkeley, Spring 1960.

machine-operated textile industry was first established in Rhode Island in 1790 and grew rapidly as a consequence of domestic and international demand, notably during the Napoleonic Wars. Jefferson's Embargo Act of 1807, the War of 1812, and a high tariff in 1816 further stimulated American industry.

Rapid industrial growth meant the movement of people from farms to cities. In Massachusetts the practice developed of hiring mainly the wives and daughters of farmers, whose income was thereby supplemented but not displaced by wages. In Rhode Island whole families moved to the cities and became committed to the factory system. When times were good, industrialized families earned two or three times what they got from the soil; when the mills were idle, there was not enough money for bread. From 1807 to 1815 textiles enjoyed great prosperity; from 1834 to 1842 they suffered depression, most severely from 1835 to 1840. Prosperity raised expectations and depression frustrated them, particularly when accompanied by stubborn resistance to suffrage demands that first stirred in 1790 and recurred in a wave-like pattern in 1811 and then in 1818 and 1820 following suffrage extension in Connecticut and Massachusetts. The final crest was reached in 1841, when suffrage associations met and called for a constitutional convention.

Against the will of the government, the suffragists held an election in which all adult males were eligible to vote, held a constitutional convention composed of delegates so elected and in December 1841 submitted the People's Constitution to the same electorate, which approved it and the call for an

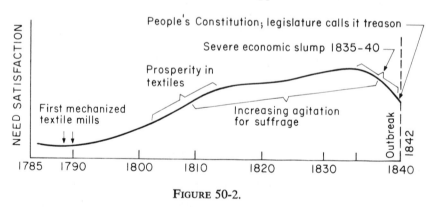

FIGURE 50-2.

election of state officers the following April, to form a new government under this unconstitutional constitution.[12]

These actions joined the conflict with the established government. When asked—by the dissidents—the state supreme court rendered its private judgment in March 1842 that the new constitution was "of no binding force

---

[12] A. M. Mowry, *The Dorr War*, Providence, R.I.: Preston & Rounds Co., 1901, p. 114.

whatever" and any act "to carry it into effect by force will be treason against the state." The legislature passed what became known as the Algerian law, making it an offense punishable by a year in jail to vote in the April election, and by life imprisonment to hold office under the People's Constitution.

The rebels went stoutly ahead with the election, and on May 3, 1842 inaugurated the new government. The next day the People's legislature met and respectfully requested the sheriff to take possession of state buildings, which he failed to do. Violence broke out on the 17th of May in an attempt to take over a state arsenal with two British cannon left over from the Revolutionary War. When the cannon misfired, the People's government resigned. Sporadic violence continued for another month, resulting in the arrest of over 500 men, mostly textile workers, mechanics, and laborers. The official legislature called for a new constitutional convention, chosen by universal manhood suffrage, and a new constitution went into effect in January, 1843. Altogether only one person was killed in this little revolution, which experienced violence, failure, and then success within the space of nine months.

It is impossible altogether to separate the experience of rising expectations among people in Rhode Island from that among Americans generally. They all shared historically the struggle against a stubborn but ultimately rewarding frontier where their self-confidence gained strength not only in the daily process of tilling the soil and harvesting the crops but also by improving their skill at self-government. Winning their war of independence, Americans continued to press for more goods and more democracy. The pursuit of economic expectations was greatly facilitated by the growth of domestic and foreign trade and the gradual establishment of industry. Equalitarian expectations in politics were satisfied and without severe struggle—in most Northern states—by suffrage reforms.

In Rhode Island, these rising expectations—more goods, more equality, more self-rule—were countered by a series of containing forces which built up such a head of steam that the boiler cracked a little in 1842. The textile depression hit hard in 1835 and its consequences were aggravated by the Panic of 1837. In addition to the frustration of seeing their peers get the right to vote in other states, poor people in Rhode Island were now beset by industrial dislocation in which the machines that brought them prosperity they had never before enjoyed now were bringing economic disaster. The machines could not be converted to produce food and in Rhode Island the machine tenders could not go back to the farm.

When they had recovered from the preoccupation with staying alive, they turned in earnest to their demands for constitutional reform. But these were met first with indifference and then by a growing intransigence on the part of the government representing the propertied class. Hostile action by the state supreme court and then the legislature with its Algerian law proved just enough to break briefly the constitutional structure which in stable societies has the measure of power and resilience necessary to absorb social tension.

The Russian Revolution of 1917

In Russia's tangled history it is hard to decide when began the final upsurge of expectations that, when frustrated, produced the cataclysmic events of 1917. One can truly say that the real beginning was the slow modernization process begun by Peter the Great over two hundred years before the revolution. And surely the rationalist currents from France that slowly penetrated Russian intellectual life during the reign of Catherine the Great a hundred years before the revolution were necessary, lineal antecedents of the 1917 revolution.

Without denying that there was an accumulation of forces over at least a 200-year period,[13] we may nonetheless date the final upsurge as beginning with the 1861 emancipation of serfs and reaching a crest in the 1905 revolution.

The chronic and growing unrest of serfs before their emancipation in 1861 is an ironic commentary on the Marxian notion that human beings are what social institutions make them. Although serfdom had been shaping their personality since 1647, peasants became increasingly restive in the second quarter of the nineteenth century.[14] The continued discontent of peasants after emancipation is an equally ironic commentary on the belief that relieving one profound frustration produces enduring contentment. Peasants rather quickly got over their joy at being untied from the soil after two hundred years. Instead of declining, rural violence increased.[15] Having gained freedom but not much free land, peasants now had to rent or buy land to survive: virtual personal slavery was exchanged for financial servitude. Land pressure grew, reflected in a doubling of land prices between 1868 and 1897.

It is hard thus to tell whether the economic plight of peasants was much lessened after emancipation. A 1903 government study indicated that even with a normal harvest, average food intake per peasant was 30 percent below the minimum for health. The only sure contrary item of evidence is that the peasant population grew, indicating at least increased ability of the land to support life, as the following table shows.

---

[13] There is an excellent summary in B. Brutzkus, "The Historical Peculiarities of the Social and Economic Development of Russia," in R. Bendix and S. M. Lipset, *Class, Status, and Power*, Glencoe, Ill.: The Free Press, 1953, pp. 517-540.

[14] Jacqueries rose from an average of 8 per year in 1826–30 to 34 per year in 1845–49. T. G. Masaryk, *The Spirit of Russia*, London: Allen and Unwin, Ltd., 1919, Vol. 1, p. 130. This long, careful, and rather neglected analysis was first published in German in 1913 under the title *Zur Russischen Geschichts– und Religionsphilosophie.*

[15] Jacqueries averaged 350 per year for the first three years after emancipation. *Ibid.*, pp. 140-141.

Table 50–1

Population of European Russia (1480–1895)

	Population in Millions	Increase in Millions	Average Annual Rate of Increase*
1480	2.1	—	—
1580	4.3	2.2	1.05%
1680	12.6	8.3	1.93%
1780	26.8	14.2	1.13%
1880	84.5	57.7	2.15%
1895	110.0	25.5	2.02%

* Computed as follows: dividing the increase by the number of years and then dividing this hypothetical annual increase by the population at the end of the preceding 100-year period.

Source for gross population data: *Entsiklopedicheskii Slovar,* St. Petersburg, 1897, vol. 40, p. 631. Russia's population was about 97% rural in 1784, 91% in 1878, and 87% in 1897. See Masaryk, *op. cit.,* p. 162n.

The land-population pressure pushed people into towns and cities, where the rapid growth of industry truly afforded the chance for economic betterment. One estimate of net annual income for a peasant family of five in the rich blackearth area in the late nineteenth century was 82 rubles. In contrast, a "good" wage for a male factory worker was about 168 rubles per year. It was this difference in the degree of poverty that produced almost a doubling of the urban population between 1878 and 1897. The number of industrial workers increased almost as rapidly. The city and the factory gave new hope. Strikes in the 1880s were met with brutal suppression but also with the beginning of factory legislation, including the requirement that wages be paid regularly and the abolition of child labor. The burgeoning proletariat remained comparatively contented until the eve of the 1905 revolution.

There is additional, non-economic evidence to support the view that 1861 to 1905 was the period of rising expectations that preceded the 1917 revolution. The administration of justice before the emancipation had largely been carried out by noblemen and landowners who embodied the law for their peasants. In 1864 justice was in principle no longer delegated to such private individuals. Trials became public, the jury system was introduced, and judges got tenure. Corporal punishment was alleviated by the elimination of running the gauntlet, lashing, and branding; caning persisted until 1904. Public joy at these reforms was widespread. For the intelligentsia, there was increased opportunity to think and write and to criticize established institutions, even sacrosanct absolutism itself.

But Tsarist autocracy had not quite abandoned the scene. Having inclined but not bowed, in granting the inevitable emancipation as an act not of justice but grace, it sought to maintain its absolutist principle by conceding reform without accepting anything like democratic authority. Radical political and economic criticism surged higher. Some strong efforts to raise the somewhat lowered floodgates began as early as 1866, after an unsuccessful attempt was made on the life of Alexander II, in whose name serfs had just gained emancipation. When the attempt succeeded fifteen years later, there was increasing state action under Alexander III to limit constantly rising expectations. By supression and concession, the last Alexander succeeded in dying naturally in 1894.

When it became apparent that Nicholas II shared his father's ideas but not his forcefulness, opposition of the intelligentsia to absolutism joined with the demands of peasants and workers, who remained loyal to the Tsar but demanded economic reforms. Starting in 1904, there developed a "League of Deliverance" that coordinated efforts of at least seventeen other revolutionary, proletarian, or nationalist groups within the empire. Consensus on the need for drastic reform, both political and economic, established a many-ringed circus of groups sharing the same tent. These groups were geographically distributed from Finland to Armenia and ideologically from liberal constitutionalists to revolutionaries made prudent by the contrast between their own small forces and the power of Tsardom.

Events of 1904–5 mark the general downward turning point of expectations, which people increasingly saw as frustrated by the continuation of Tsardom. Two major and related occurrences made 1905 the point of no return. The first took place on the Bloody Sunday of January 22, 1905, when peaceful proletarian petitioners marched on the St. Petersburg palace and were killed by the hundreds. The myth that the Tsar was the gracious protector of his subjects, however surrounded he might be by malicious advisers, was quite shattered. The reaction was immediate, bitter, and prolonged and was not at all confined to the working class. Employers, merchants, and white-collar officials joined in the burgeoning of strikes which brought the economy to a virtual standstill in October. Some employers even continued to pay wages to strikers. University students and faculties joined the revolution. After the great October strike, the peasants ominously sided with the workers and engaged in riots and assaults on landowners. Until peasants became involved, even some landowners had sided with the revolution.

The other major occurrence was the disastrous defeat of the Russian army and navy in the 1904–5 war with Japan. Fundamentally an imperialist venture aspiring to hegemony over the people of Asia, the war was not regarded as a people's but as a Tsar's war, to save and spread absolutism. The military defeat itself probably had less portent than the return of shattered soldiers from a fight that was not for them. Hundreds of thousands, wounded or not, returned from the war as a visible, vocal, and ugly reminder to the entire populace of the weakness and selfishness of Tsarist absolutism.

The years from 1905 to 1917 formed an almost relentless procession of increasing misery and despair. Promising at last a constitutional government, the Tsar, in October, 1905, issued from on high a proclamation renouncing absolutism, granting law-making power to a duma, and guaranteeing freedom of speech, assembly, and association. The first two dumas, of 1906 and 1907, were dissolved for recalcitrance. The third was made pliant by reduced representation of workers and peasants and by the prosecution and conviction of protestants in the first two. The brief period of a free press was succeeded in 1907 by a reinstatement of censorship and confiscation of prohibited publications. Trial of offenders against the Tsar was now conducted by courts martial. Whereas there had been only 26 executions of the death sentence, in the 13 years of Alexander II's firm rule (1881–94), there were 4,449 in the years 1905–10 in six years of Nicholas II's soft regimen.[16]

But this "white terror," which caused despair among the workers and intelligentsia in the cities, was not the only face of misery. For the peasants, there was a bad harvest in 1906 followed by continued crop failures in several areas in 1907. To forestall action by the dumas, Stolypin decreed a series of agrarian reforms designed to break up the power of the rural communes by individualizing land ownership. Between these acts of God and government, peasants were so preoccupied with hunger or self-aggrandizement as to be dulled in their sensitivity to the revolutionary appeals of radical organizers.

After more than five years of degrading terror and misery, in 1910 the country appeared to have reached a condition of exhaustion. Political strikes had fallen off to a new low. As the economy recovered, the insouciance of hopelessness set in. Amongst the intelligentsia the mood was hedonism, or despair that often ended in suicide. Industrialists aligned themselves with the government. Workers worked. But an upturn of expectations, inadequately quashed by the police, was evidenced by a recrudescence of political strikes which, in the first half of 1914—on the eve of war—approached the peak of 1905. They sharply diminished during 1915 but grew again in 1916 and became a general strike in February 1917.[17]

Figure 3 indicates the lesser waves in the tidal wave whose first trough is at the end of serfdom in 1861 and whose second is at the end of Tsardom in 1917. This fifty-six year period appears to constitute a single long phase in

---

[16] *Ibid.*, p. 189n.

[17] In his *History of the Russian Revolution*, Leon Trotsky presents data on political strikes from 1903 to 1917. In his *Spirit of Russia*, Masaryk presents comparable data from 1905 through 1912. The figures are not identical but the reported yearly trends are consistent. Masaryk's figures are somewhat lower, except for 1912. Cf. Trotsky, *op. cit.*, Doubleday Anchor Books ed., 1959, p. 32 and Masaryk, *op. cit. supra*, p. 197n.

which popular gratification at the termination of one institution (serfdom) rather quickly was replaced with rising expectations which resulted from intensified industrialization and which were incompatible with the continuation of the inequitable and capricious power structure of Tsarist society. The small trough of frustration during the repression that followed the assassination of Alexander II seems to have only briefly interrupted the rise in popular demand for more goods and more power. The trough in 1904 indicates the consequences of war with Japan. The 1905–6 trough reflects the repression of January 22, and after, and is followed by economic recovery. The

FIGURE 50-3.

final downturn, after the first year of war, was a consequence of the dislocations of the German attack on all kinds of concerted activities other than production for the prosecution of the war. Patriotism and governmental repression for a time smothered discontent. The inflation that developed in 1916 when goods, including food, became severely scarce began to make workers self-consciously discontented. The conduct of the war, including the growing brutality against reluctant, ill-provisioned troops, and the enormous loss of life, produced the same bitter frustration in the army.[18] When civilian discontent reached the breaking point in February, 1917, it did not take long for it to spread rapidly into the armed forces. Thus began the second phase of the revolution that really started in 1905 and ended in death to the Tsar and Tsardom—but not to absolutism—when the Bolsheviks gained ascendancy over the moderates in October. A centuries-long history of absolutism appears to have made this post-Tsarist phase of it tragically inevitable. . . .

Other Civil Disturbances

The J-curve of rising expectations followed by their effective frustration

---

[18] See Trotsky, *op. cit.*, pp. 18-21 for a vivid picture of rising discontent in the army.

is applicable to other revolutions and rebellions than just the ones already considered. The American Revolution itself fits the J-curve and deserves more than the brief mention here given. Again prolonged economic growth and political autonomy produced continually rising expectations. They became acutely frustrated when, following the French and Indian War (which had cost England so much and the colonies so little), England began a series of largely economic regulations having the same purpose as those directed against New York in the preceding century. From the 1763 Proclamation (closing to settlement land west of the Appalachians) to the Coercive Acts of April, 1774 (which among other things, in response to the December, 1773 Boston Tea Party, closed tight the port of Boston), Americans were beset with unaccustomed manifestations of British power and began to resist forcibly in 1775, on the Lexington-Concord road. A significant decline in trade with England in 1772[19] may have hastened the maturation of colonial rebelliousness.

The curve also fits the French Revolution, which again merits more mention than space here permits. Growing rural prosperity, marked by steadily rising land values in the eighteenth century, had progressed to the point where a third of French land was owned by peasant-proprietors. There were the beginnings of large-scale manufacture in the factory system. Constant pressure by the bourgeoisie against the state for reforms was met with considerable hospitality by a government already shifting from its old landed-aristocratic and clerical base to the growing middle class. Counter to these trends, which would *per se* avoid revolution, was the feudal reaction of the mid-eighteenth century, in which the dying nobility sought in numerous nagging ways to retain and reactivate its perquisites against a resentful peasantry and importunate bourgeoisie.

But expectations apparently continued rising until the growing opportunities and prosperity rather abruptly halted, about 1787. The fiscal crisis of the government is well known, much of it a consequence of a 1.5 billion livre deficit following intervention against Britain in the American war of independence. The threat to tax the nobility severely—after its virtual tax immunity—and the bourgeoisie more severely may indeed be said to have precipitated the revolution. But less well-known is the fact that 1787 was a bad harvest year and 1788 even worse; that by July, 1789 bread prices were higher than they had been in over 70 years; that an ill-timed trade treaty with England depressed the prices of French textiles; that a concurrent bumper grape crop depressed wine prices—all with the result of making desperate the plight of the large segment of the population now dependent on other producers for food. They had little money to buy even less bread. Nobles and bourgeoisie were alienated from the government by the threat of

---

[19] See U. S. Bureau of the Census, *Historical Statistics of the United States, Colonial Times to 1957,* Washington, D.C., 1960, p. 757.

taxation; workers and some peasants by the threat of starvation. A long period of halting but real progress for virtually all segments of the population was now abruptly ended in consequence of the government's efforts to meet its deficit and of economic crisis resulting from poor crops and poor tariff policy.[20] . . .

One negative case—of a revolution that did not occur—is the depression of the 1930s in the United States. It was severe enough, at least on economic grounds, to have produced a revolution. Total national private production income in 1932 reverted to what it had been in 1916. Farm income in the same year was as low as in 1900; manufacturing as low as in 1913. Construction had not been as low since 1908. Mining and quarrying was back at the 1909 level.[21] For much of the population, two decades of economic progress had been wiped out. There were more than sporadic demonstrations of unemployed, hunger marchers, and veterans. In New York City, at least 29 people died of starvation. Poor people could vividly contrast their own past condition with the present—and their own present condition with that of those who were not seriously suffering. There were clearly audible rumbles of revolt. Why, then, no revolution?

Several forces worked strongly against it. Among the most depressed, the mood was one of apathy and despair, like that observed in Austria by Zawadzki and Lazarsfeld. It was not until the 1936 election that there was an increased turnout in the national election. The great majority of the public shared a set of values which since 1776 had been official dogma— not the dissident program of an alienated intelligentsia. People by and large were in agreement, whether or not they had succeeded economically, in a belief in individual hard work, self-reliance, and the promise of success. (Among workers, this non-class orientation had greatly impeded the establishment of trade unions, for example.) Those least hit by the depression —the upper-middle class businessmen, clergymen, lawyers, and intellectuals—remained rather solidly committed not only to equalitarian values and to the established economic system but also to constitutional processes. There was no such widespread or profound alienation as that which had cracked the loyalty of the nobility, clergy, bourgeoisie, armed forces, and intelligentsia in Russia. And the national political leadership that emerged had constitutionalism almost bred in its bones. The major threat to constitutionalism came in Louisiana; this leadership was unable to capture a national party organization, in part because Huey Long's arbitrariness and demagogy were mistrusted.

---

[20] See G. Lefebvre, The Coming of the French Revolution, Princeton: Princeton University Press, 1947, pp. 101-109, 145-148, 196. G. Le Bon, The Psychology of Revolution, New York: G. Putnam's Sons, 1913, p. 143.

[21] See U. S. Bureau of the Census, Historical Statistics of the United States: 1789–1945, Washington, D.C.: 1949, p. 14.

The major reason that revolution did not nonetheless develop probably remains the vigor with which the national government attacked the depression in 1933, when it became no longer possible to blame the government. The ambivalent popular hostility to the business community was contained by both the action of government against the depression and the government's practice of publicly and successfully eliciting the cooperation of businessmen during the crucial months of 1933. A failure then of cooperation could have intensified rather than lessened popular hostility to business. There was no longer an economic or a political class that could be the object of widespread intense hatred because of its indifference or hostility to the downtrodden. Had Roosevelt adopted a demagogic stance in the 1932 campaign and gained the loyalty to himself personally of the Army and the F.B.I., there might have been a Nazi-type "revolution," with a pot-pourri of equalitarian reform, nationalism, imperialism, and domestic scapegoats. Because of a conservatism in America stemming from strong and long attachment to a value system shared by all classes, an anti-capitalist, leftist revolution in the 1930s is very difficult to imagine.

Some Conclusions

The notion that revolutions need both a period of rising expectations and a succeeding period in which they are frustrated qualifies substantially the main Marxian notion that revolutions occur after progressive degradation and the de Tocqueville notion that they occur when conditions are improving. By putting de Tocqueville before Marx but without abandoning either theory, we are better able to plot the antecedents of at least the disturbances here described.

Half of the general, if not common, sense of this revised notion lies in the utter improbability of a revolution occurring in a society where there is the continued, unimpeded opportunity to satisfy new needs, new hopes, new expectations. Would Dorr's rebellion have become such if the established electorate and government had readily acceded to the suffrage demands of the unpropertied? Would the Russian Revolution have taken place if the Tsarist autocracy had, quite out of character, truly granted the popular demands for constitutional democracy in 1905?

The other half of the sense of the notion has to do with the improbability of revolution taking place where there has been no hope, no period in which expectations have risen. Such a stability of expectations presupposes a static state of human aspirations that sometimes exists but is rare. Stability of expectations is not a stable social condition. Such was the case of American Indians (at least from our perspective) and perhaps Africans before white men with Bibles, guns, and other goods interrupted the stability of African society. Egypt was in such a condition, vis-à-vis modern aspirations, before Europe became interested in building a canal. The rise of expectations can be frustrated successfully, thereby defeating rebellion just as the satisfaction of expectations does. This, however, requires the uninhibited exercise of brute force as it was used in suppressing the Hungarian rebellion of 1956. Failing the continued ability and persistent will of a ruling power to use such force, there appears to be no sure way to avoid revolution short of an effective, affirmative, and continuous response on the part of established governments to the almost continuously emerging needs of the governed. . . .

CHAPTER 51

RALPH H. TURNER

The Theme of Contemporary
Social Movements

The main question is just what contemporary social movements are all about and what they signal with respect to major changes in our social system.

Movements and Injustice

Two main points are preliminary to the analysis that is to follow. First, any major social movement depends upon and promotes some normative revision. In case of movements having the greatest significance for social change this normative innovation takes the form of a new sense of what is *just* and what is *unjust* in society. This is quite different from merely saying that the leaders and followers of a movement discover a problem and seek to do something about it. The problem may have existed for a long time or it may be of relatively recent origin, and awareness of the problem may predate the movement by centuries. The change we are speaking of is represented in the difference between conceiving of a problem as a *misfortune* and conceiving of it as a state of *injustice*.

The sense of misfortune and the sense of injustice can be distinguished by the difference between *petition* and *demand*. The victims of misfortune petition whoever has the power to help them for some kind of aid. The victims of injustice demand that their petitions be granted. The poor man appealing for alms is displaying his misfortune. The Poor People's March on Washington to demand correction of their situation expressed a sense of injustice.

A significant social movement becomes possible when there is a revision in the manner in which a substantial group of people look at some misfortune, seeing it no longer as a misfortune warranting charitable considera-

Reprinted from *The British Journal of Sociology* Vol. XX, No. 4, Dec. 1969, pp. 390-405.

tion but as an injustice which is intolerable in society. A movement becomes possible when a group of people cease to petition the good will of others for relief of their misery and demand as their right that others ensure the correction of their condition.

Injustice and Historical Eras

The second preliminary point is that major eras in history have differed in the dominant sense of injustice which underlay the major movements of the time and dictated the main direction of social change. . . . We shall speak of the era dominated by the liberal humanitarian movements giving way to the more recent era shaped by the socialist movements. We suggest that the power of both the liberal humanitarian and the socialist conceptions of injustice has been largely exhausted. We shall seek to identify a 'utopia' or a new central theme which is capable of arousing the enthusiasm and focusing the energies of discontent in the era that is only now beginning to take shape.

If we look at the two eras specifically in terms of the major new conception of injustice which dominated the movements, we see first that in the American and French revolutions people asserted the right to be ensured the opportunity to participate in ruling themselves. Such specifics as freedom of speech, freedom of assembly, freedom of the press, were all incident to and justified by insistence that people should no longer merely petition to be heard, but that institutional arrangements should be so revised as to ensure that all people could be heard and participate in governing themselves in some tangible and dependable way. It is characteristic that the fundamental injustice of denying some people a full voice in determining their own destiny was the touchstone which would supply solutions to all the other important problems of the era. Give people the right to vote and the freedom to speak, to read and write and discuss their respective interests, and the problems of poverty and other avoidable misfortunes would be well on the way to correction.

The socialist movements retain the symbolism of freedom and participation but subordinate them to a new sense of injustice. For the first time the fundamental right of people to demand that the essential material needs of life be provided for them was recognized. To the liberal humanitarians of the late eighteenth and early nineteenth centuries poverty was a misfortune and gross inequalities in material wealth and comfort might be regarded as unfortunate. But they were certainly not to be treated as injustices. The arguments of the New Deal era in American history incorporate the difference between the older liberal humanitarian philosophy and the newer socialist conception of fundamental injustice. The New Deal was essentially a victory, albeit a limited victory, for the view that freedom of the liberal humanitarian sort without an underpinning of material security is meaningless. The New Deal incorporated reforms reflecting the assumption that a society is obligated to provide for the material wants of its people, and that its people have a right to demand that these wants be met. . . .

Injustice in the Contemporary Era

If we look at the contemporary era consisting of roughly the second half of the twentieth century, I think it has become quite clear that the liberal humanitarian ideology no longer has the vitality to rouse great populations to the active pursuit of reform or revolution. The contention that the socialist's conception of injustice, the demand for assurance of material wants or even for material equality is declining in its vitality, may be more difficult to substantiate. Nevertheless, a rather strong impression can be drawn from events in many spheres to suggest that as an accepted principle, the injustice of material want has become commonplace so that it draws ready assent without arousing excitement and enthusiasm for its implementation.

The New Conception of Injustice

It is the central thesis of this paper that a new revision is in the making and is increasingly giving direction to the disturbances of our era. This new conception is reflected in a new object for indignation. Today, for the first time in history, it is common to see violent indignation expressed over the fact that people lack a sense of personal worth—that they lack an inner peace of mind which comes from a sense of personal dignity or a clear sense of identity. It is not, of course, a new thing that people have wondered who they are, nor that people have wondered whether man and man's life are worthwhile. The Old Testament contains poetic complaints about the meaninglessness of life, and the insignificance of man. Although this concern has been before us for millenia, the phenomenon of a man crying out with indignation because his society has not supplied him with a sense of personal worth and identity is the distinctive new feature of our era. The idea that a man who does not feel worthy and who cannot find his proper place in life is to be pitied is an old one. The notion that he is indeed a victim of injustice is the new idea. The urgent demand that the institutions of our society be reformed, not primarily to grant man freedom of speech and thought, and not primarily to ensure him essential comforts, but to guarantee him a sense of personal worth is the new and recurrent theme in contemporary society.

These new views are perhaps most fully embodied in the doctrines of today's New Left. Well before the Vietnam war became the central preoccupation there were expressions of outrage against the depersonalizing and demoralizing effect of modern institutions, ranging from the family to the university and the state.

The main symbol of the new era is *alienation*. Here is a fine example of the way in which a term is borrowed from an earlier era but assigned new meaning. We know that the socialist movements borrowed the term democracy, but when we examine what they mean by a democratic government it is quite clear that it has little to do with the conception employed by the liberal humanitarians. Similarly, the concept of alienation is borrowed from Marx. It had original reference to the specific relationship of the labouring man to his work. In one way or another it meant simply that a man's work no longer mattered to him as it had in a handicraft era when he could take pride in his accomplishments, with various psychological overtones that made it more than simple job dissatisfaction. But the new meaning refers to a deeply psychological state. Man's alienation is now a divorcement of the individual from himself or the failure of the individual to find his real self, which he must employ as a base for organizing his life. Alienation has thus been transformed into the designation for a psychological or psychiatric condition which is quite different from the most important usage during the socialist era. . . .

The Nature of the Constituency

In each major era the fundamental circumstance that has made possible the development of a revised sense of justice has been the rise in power and general standing of some major class. None of the great movements has been the product of groups who were moving downward nor of groups in abject powerlessness, poverty, or despair. The liberal humanitarian movements were movements of the rising industrial and business classes. They had been growing in economic power and in wealth, but their resources could not be fully converted into commensurate power and social status because of the traditional power of landowning and aristocratic classes. The liberal humanitarian movements may be regarded, first and foremost, as the readjustment through which industrial and business classes were able to throw off the traditional power of the aristocracy and the landed gentry and to assume the station in society toward which natural developments had been moving them. The specific way in which injustice was defined reflected the nature of impediments to realization of their full status by these rising classes. They already had the economic resources: all they needed was the freedom to capitalize on them. Hence, they had no occasion to think of economic deficiencies as a matter of injustice. The solution to their problem lay in undermining the monopoly of political power in the hands of the aristocracy. Hence, it appeared from their own perspective that the fundamental injustice in society was the failure to grant full participation by all the people in self-government.

The socialist movements seem to have been associated with the rising status of working classes in the societies where they prevailed. The conditions of industrial life had in fact improved the position of the labouring man. But at the same time by making him an employee of large concerns that might lay him off whenever it suited their concerns, the system had created a fundamental insecurity about economic conditions which prohibited the worker from exploiting to the full the relative wealth which he was in fact experiencing. The fact that the idea once established was then extended to the impoverished does not change the observation with regard to the source of this kind of thinking.

If my interpretation of what is happening in contemporary society is correct, we are seeing a new type of entity in society as the constituency for the dominant movements of our era. In the two previous eras the constituencies have been largely socio-economic classes, though this has been by no means clear-cut and exclusive, especially in the case of socialist movements. In the contemporary era, however, the major readjustments which are being made in society no longer concern socio-economic classes but concern *age groups*. The most striking phenomenon of the last quarter-century has been the increasing authority and independence and recognition accorded the youthful generation. The rapid changes in society have meant that the technical expertise of the young is often superior to that of the more mature. Having gained considerable power and autonomy and comfort, young people now demand that the system be changed so as to remove the last restrictions to their assumption of an appropriate condition in society.

The problem of alienation and the sense of worth is most poignantly the problem of a youthful generation with unparalleled freedom and capability but without an institutional structure in which this capability can be appropriately realized. Adolescence is peculiarly a 'non-person' status in life. And yet this is just the period in which the technical skills and the new freedom are being markedly increased. The sense of alienation is distinctively the sense of a person who realizes great expectations for himself yet must live in a non-status.

For the movement to effect pervasive change in the institutions of society the new sense of justice must make substantial inroads outside of the movement's constituency. For this to happen, the problem at issue must not appertain exclusively to one class or age group. Political participation and economic justice had wide relevance in the eighteenth and nineteenth centuries. Today alienation is understandable to other groups than youth. The new dense of injustice can become the leaven for vast social changes because adults, the elderly, minority groups, and other organizable segments of society can see many of their own problems in the terms set forth by youthful activists.

From Chaos to Focused Movements

It is crucial to observe that the new movements have not yet discovered or formulated solutions to their problem. The liberal humanitarian movements formulated the solution to their problem as one of seeking political representation with related guarantees of freedom of speech, assembly, and press. The socialist movements defined their problem and identified the solution as either the dictatorship of the proletariat in the communist version or some form of welfare state in more moderate socialist versions. The contemporary movement is discovering the problem of alienation, is expressing indignation against society as the source of that alienation, but has not yet discovered or agreed upon a solution to the problem.

It is important to recognize that all conceptions of rights are myths in the sense that they are practically unattainable. The important circumstance permitting a movement to develop and to focus its activities effectively so as to bring about reform is that people essentially agree to believe in a falsehood. They agree not to notice that the programme they accept would not actually be more than a limited step in the direction of the ideal of justice that forms the background for their movement.

Prior to the establishment and acceptance of the movement's fiction there can be little more than aimless protest, and the general pattern is one of disruption. Within each era, anarchy comes to be one conception, though a passing one, of the solution to the problem. Anarchy would bring an end to the restraints on the business and industrial classes. Anarchy would destroy the rule of the capitalist over the worker. Today, anarchy looms large as a theme in the new movements, promising a way to free youth from the restraints imposed by their elders. Students of contemporary protest have often interpreted the activities of youthful protesters and black power advocates as anarchistic. But if our inference from previous developments is correct, anarchy looms large during that preliminary stage after a new conception of injustice has taken hold within a core group, but when there has been no agreed-upon programme as yet for the reform of the injustice in question.

Within the next decade or two we look for the emergence of some widely accepted schemes for the elimination of alienation in society. These schemes will surely involve a somewhat more satisfying status for the young. The penetrating social critic will, of course, see that the schemes can never guarantee freedom from difficulty in attaining a personal sense of worth. But the important thing will be that members of the movement's constituency come to agree upon the fiction that the schemes proposed will actually do away with alienation. However, until such time as a programme does achieve agreement, we must expect a continuation of anarchistic themes, of apparently random disruptive protest, of apparent blatant power plays and increasingly widespread attacks upon modern society in all of its aspects.

Associated Developments

It may seem strange to seize upon a problem that is expressed by only a rather small group of people and to place so much weight on the revolt of students in the face of all that is going on in modern society. However, I believe this step is justified and can be at least rendered plausible by calling attention to certain other developments. . . .

The civil rights movement, is partly a matter of winding up the unfinished business of the liberal humanitarian and the socialist movements. But there are at least two features which are striking about the contemporary civil rights movements that are not so apparent at an earlier period. First of all, the present activist movements among blacks are the movements of youth. They represent a rejection of the more mature leadership of a decade or two ago. The middle-aged Negroes are often caught in ambivalence, between hoping that some good may come from violent protest, yet fearing for their own total loss of control over Negro youth.

The second observation is that the theme of achieving human dignity and a sense of personal worth is beginning to play a larger and larger part in the ideology of Black protest. Carmichael and Hamilton's book on Black Power is predominantly the demand for an identity which can give the ordinary individual dignity and self-respect.[1] The repudiation of integration is an assertion of personal worth, renouncing the idea that a black would demean himself to the extent of wanting to be accepted among whites. The emphasis is upon the desire to make the identity 'Black' a matter of pride which can be the base for a sense of social worth.

Finally, there remains the question whether an age group can launch and carry a major movement for the reform of society in the way that an economic class can do so. Normally an economic class is one's life long membership group. The age group is intrinsically transitional, unless its span is artificially extended by the refusal to move on to a way of life appropriate to the next stage. It is very possible that youth movements are inherently abortive and can never be more than pawns in the service of other movements. Certainly most youth movements in history have been used by other groups rather than serving their own ends. However, a change can well be under way. In recent times the period of youth has been starting earlier in

---

[1] Stokely Carmichael and Charles V. Hamilton, *Black Power: The Politics of Liberation in America,* New York, Random House, 1967.

life. High schools are beginning to show the same activism as colleges. And even junior high schools are no longer immune to organized youthful protest. Similarly the upper limits of youthfulness have been extended. The longer and longer periods of college associated with graduate school have stretched the period of ambiguous status for many. If it is to be assumed that most movements cannot count on their activists remaining so for more than a decade, then there may well be an abundant supply of people who will spend from one to three years in high school and from six to ten years of college as minions of some youth movement. . . . Hence youth may be for the first time an adequate constituency to carry the major movements that shape the character of social change in our society during the second half of the twentieth century.

Index

Abortion, 185
Absolute monarchy, 222
Absolution, power of, 50
Absolutism, 529, 530
Acceptance of invention, 454–455
Achievement:
    goal, 162–164
    McClelland on, 161–174
    motivation, 71
    sources of, 172–173
    tests, 507, 508
Achieving Society, The, McClelland, 162
Activation level, 152
Active societal units, 145, 154–156
Active society, 154, 155–156
Active Society, The, Etzioni, 70
Activism and schools, 542
Adaptability, 196
Adaptive culture, 478–480
Adjustment, 480
    mutual, *see* Mutual adjustment
Administration, 41, 47–49
Adult education, 234
Africa, integration in, 11
African Nationalist Pioneer Movement, 400
African political systems, 278
Agriculture:
    cotton, and racism, 397
    and economic development, 269
    Rostow on takeoff and, 297*n*
    subsistence, 272
Alexander II, 528, 529, 530
Alexander III, 528
Algerian law, 525
Alienation, 5
    in the active society, 155
    and equality, 157
    as symbol of new era, 538–541
Allport, Floyd H., 523*n*
Allport, G. W., 378*n*
Almond, Gabriel A., 156*n*, 279*n*, 324*n*, 333*n*
America, *see* Canada, South America, United States
American Dilemma, An, 408
American Indians, 136, 533

American Medical Association, 461
American Revolution:
    anatomy of the, 514–518
    and injustice, 536
    and the J-curve, 531
    physical deprivation as a factor in the, 523
American unions, 115
Analysis, sociological, 66–67
Analysis of change, functional, 87–99
    criticisms and examples of, 95–99
    functional system, definition of a, 88–92
    methods of, 94–95
Anarchy, 540
Ancient Society, Morgan, 132
Angell, Robert C., 195*n*
Ankermann, 142
Anomie, 264, 280
Anthropology:
    and the evolutionary hypothesis, 133
    and personal disorganization, 358
    and selective culture change, 336
    and theories of change, 69
Antoinette, Marie, 515
Apaches, 136
Apter, D., 279*n*, 336*n*
Arabians and science, 14–15, 19
Argentina:
    economic development in, 150–151
    modernization of individuals in, 343–359
    takeoff for, 290, 291
Aristocracies, 28
Aristotle, 429
Aron, Raymond, 101*n*, 242
Ascent, linear, *see* Linear theory of history
Ascription, 79
Ashby, W. Ross, 483*n*
Ashramas, 334
Assembly line, 236
Assets, 151–153
Atatürk, Kemal, 503
Atomic Energy Commission (AEC), 146
Atomization, 5
Australia and achievement level, 171

Austria, Great Depression in, 523
Authority:
   and charisma, 44–45
   and power, 107–108
   succession to, 45–47, 51
Autocracy, Tsarist, 311–312
Automation, 236
Autonomy, 410, 419–420

Badgley, John H., 320*n*
Baker, A. W., 387*n*
Balance of power, 481–483
Bales, R. F., 277
Banfield, E. C., 522*n*
Baptists, 223
Barber, Bernard, 149*n*, 178–179, 199–209
Bascom, W., 337*n*
Bavelas, Alex, 371–374, 376
Beecham, 10
Beer, G. R. de, 381*n*
Behavior, modification of individual, 366
Belgium, 186–187
   takeoff date for, 290
Bell, Daniel, 69*n*, 115*n*, 241–250 *passim*
Beme, Kenneth D., 365*n*
Bendix, Reinhard, 265–266, 277*n*, 310–319, 336*n*, 526*n*
Benedict, Ruth, 133
Bennis, Warren B., 365*n*
Berdyaev, Nikolai, 226
Berelson, Bernard, 147*n*
Berlin, East, 103, 104, 112
Berna, James, 337–338
Bettelheim, Bruno, 242, 244, 248, 251
Bhave, Vinoba, 340–341
Binding, Karl, 443
Biological:
   model for social organizations, 379–382
   theory of history, 6
Bipolarism, 482–483
Birth control, 189
Black Death, 119
Black Muslim movement, 400
Black power, 540, 541
   See also Negroes
Bloch, Marc, 200*n*
Boeke, J. H., 272*n*
Bonaparte, *see* Napoleon
Bongiorno, A., 26*n*
Bonner, John, 520*n*
Boredom, 448
Bourgeoisie, 531–532
   and capitalism, 40
   Marx and Engels on, 32–39
   and revolution, 202–203
Boxer Rebellion, 523
Brauer, Jerald C., 225*n*
Breese, Gerald, 431*n*

Brinkmann, Carl, 101*n*
Brinton, Crane, 101*n*, 491, 514–518
Britain, *see* England
British General Strike of 1926, 103, 104
British unions, 115
Brozek, J., 521*n*
Brutzkus, B., 526*n*
Brzezinski, Zbigniew, 242–258 *passim*
Buber, Martin, 226
Buchanan, Norman, 286*n*
Buchenwald, 522*n*
Buddha, 45
Bull of Apis, 45
Bureaucratic state, 214, 217–218, 221–222
Bureaucratization, 316–319
Burgess, Ernest W., 178, 191–198, 429
Burhoe, Ralph W., 138
Burke, Kenneth, 117*n*
Burma, 320, 322, 327, 330, 331
Burns, Arthur, 482*n*
Business drive, 161–174
Buttrick, John A., 286*n*
Byron, George, 24

Caesar, Julius, 124, 125
Callard, K., 321*n*
Calvin, John, 5, 296
Calvinism, 411
Campbell, Angus, 522*n*
Canada:
   and achievement level, 171
   economic development in, 150–151
   takeoff for, 290–292
Cancian, Francesca, 67–68, 87–99
Cannibalism, 10
Capet, Hugh, 220
Capital:
   imports, 295
   knowledge as, 236
   wealth, 58
Capitalism, 275
   military, 128
   and technology, 40–41
Carmichael, L., 374*n*
Carmichael, Stokely, 541
Carnegie, Andrew, 412
Cartwright, Dorwin, 365*n*
Casimir the Great, King, 213
Caste system:
   Barber on the, 199–203
   Gusfield on the, 337–338
   Mosca on the, 216
   Park on the, 394
   Rose on the, 397
   Weber on the, 48–49, 51–52
   See also Stratfication systems
Catherine the Great, 526
Catholic immigrants, 224

Catholics, 223, 226–227
Central planning, 494–496
Centralization, 125
Change:
 beginning of social, 423
 Cancian on, 87, 91, 94–95
 functional analysis of, 87–99
 functional theory of, 72–86
 group dynamics and social, 371–378
 objective of, 375
 social, 65–66, 107, 114–122
 technological, 116
 theory of social, 65–66, 114–122
Changes of systems versus changes within
 systems, 118–119, 122
Charisma:
 hereditary, 46–47
 routinization of, 4, 43–53
Charlemagne, 219, 220
Chase, J. W., 410n
Chiang Kai-shek, 174
Chile, modernization of individuals in,
 343–359
Chin, Robert, 365n
China:
 and birth control, 189
 Boxer Rebellion in, 523
 and charisma, 46–48, 52
 Davis on, 189
 economic development in, 174
 as an irrigation state, 136
 and loanable funds, 293
 McClelland on, 174
 Rostow on, 293
 Steward on, 136
 takeoff date for, 290
 Weber on, 46–48, 52
Chinese population in the United States,
 394
Circulation of elites, 28–29
Cities:
 and Gesellschaft (society), 58–62
 proliferation of, 431
 Toennies on, 58–62
 See also Urbanization
Civil Rights Act of 1964, 404
Civil Rights Acts, 403
Civil rights movement:
 Bendix on, 315
 Etzioni on, 152
 Rose on, 396
 Turner on, 541
Civilization:
 Comte on, 14–19
 early, 135–136
 Spengler on, 3, 22–23
Clark, Colin, 286n
Class struggle:
 Marx and Engels on, 32–39
 Toennies on, 60

Class system, *see* Caste system
Classicism, 23
Clerical function in modern organization,
 391–392
Cochise, 136
Cohen, E. A., 521n
Coherence, 10–13
Coleman, J. S.:
 on developing nations, 279n, 282n,
 324n, 333n
 on diffusion of a new drug, 426, 457–
 472
 on educational opportunity, 490, 505–
 513
 on Nigeria, 276n
Coleman, McAlister, 115n
Collectivities, 158–159
College and university attendance, 234
Colonialism, 279, 280, 282
Colonization, 217
Comhaire, Jean, 337n
Commons, enfranchisement of the, 14, 19
Commune, medieval, 33, 220
Communism:
 and Christianity, 173
 McClelland on, 173
 world, 319
Communist Party:
 discipline of the, 312
 and the Russian Revolution, 205
Community:
 organization, 55
 Toennies on, 54–62
Competition, free, 34
Comte, Auguste, 3, 6–7, 14–19
Concentration of population, 431
Condorcet's theory of history, 4
Conflict, social:
 Coser on, 114–122
 Dahrendorf on, 100–103, 106–107,
 109–113
Conflict-theory model, 109–111
Congo, takeoff and the, 291
Congregationalists, 223
Congress of Racial Equality (CORE),
 399
Consciousness, 30–31
Consciousness II, 260
Consciousness III, 239, 248, 259, 260
Consensus, 154, 155–157
Consensus of functions, 13
Conservation of forests, 478–479
Construct, ideal-type, 268
Consumption:
 under differentiation conditions, 278
 by households, 86
 Riesman on, 413
Contemporary, as defined by Spengler, 25
Contemporary social movements, 535–
 542

Contraception, 185
Contract, norms of, 75
Control, 154
Control, span of, 388–391
Coordination, market, 493
Corporate:
    intervention, 126
    liberalism, 245, 246, 255
Coser, Lewis:
    on intellectuals, 149n
    on social conflict, 101n, 104n
    on social conflict and the theory of so-
        cial change, 68, 114–122
Costa Rica, 186–187
Coulborn, Rushton, 200n
Counterculture, 239, 247–252, 257–260
Counterrevolutionary theory of youth,
    242–245, 247–251
Creative disorder, 256
Crisis period in revolutions, 517
Cromwell, Oliver, 517
Crowe, Beryl L., 523
Cultural lag, 437–438, 440
    hypothesis of, 477–480
    in the United States, 437–440
Cultural setting for invention, 453–454
Culture:
    adaptive, 478–480
    folk, 56–57
    role of, 6
    Spengler on, 3
Cultures, life cycle of, 20–25
Curve of rising expectations, 530, 531
Cybernetic capacities, 146–149
Cyclic theory of history, 3–5

Dahrendorf, Ralf:
    and functional analysis, 87n, 98
    on market and plan, 500–504
    and social organization, 489–490
    and the structural-functional theory,
        67–68
    toward a theory of social conflict, 100–
        113
Dalai Lama, 45
Darrow, Clarence, 227
Darwin, 131, 137, 138
Darwinism:
    Social, 311
    Spengler on, 21
Das Kapital, Marx, 62
Davies, James C., 491, 519–534
Davis, Kingsley:
    on class mobility, 337n
    on demographic aspects of moderniza-
        tion, 177–178, 183–190
    on functional analysis, 92n
    on nationalism, 274n
    on urbanization, 431n

Davis, R. C., 387n
Dawson, 344
De *followed by* name, *see* name
"De facto" segregation, 407
"Death of Ivan Ilyitch, The," Tolstoy,
    419
Death rate, *see* Mortality
Decentralization:
    Etzioni on, 150
    Haire on, 389
Decision, 373
    group, 374, 376
Declaration of Independence, 233
Defense budget, 152
Definiteness, 13
Degeneration, 142
Dell, Floyd, 195n
Demand, limited, 308
Demobilization, 152
Demographic transition, the, 183–190
Demoralization, 538
Department of Defense, 146
Depersonalization, 537–538
Depression, 532
    See also Great Depression
Desegregation:
    school, 407
    See also Race relations
Determinism, economic, 129
Deterministic system, 88–89, 95
Deterministic theory of history, 7
Determinists, 5
Development, economic, 269
Development of society, 3
Dialectical conflicts, 4
Differentiation, 263–264, 265, 269
Differentiation, social, 10
Differentiation, structural:
    Parsons on, 72, 78–79, 83
    Smelser on, 269, 271–277
Differentiation model, 67
Diffusion:
    crosscultural, 140–144
    intracultural, 457–472
Diffusionism, 70, 140, 143
    British school of, 143
    German-Austrian school of, 142
Directed, inner- and other-, 410–420
Discovery, 451
Discrimination, *see* Race relations
Discussion network, 462
Disequilibrium, 484–485
    See also Equilibrium
Disorganization, personal, 358–360
Displacement, 141–142
Disraeli, Benjamin, 315
Diversification, population, *see* Popula-
    tion diversification
Divorce, 192
Doob, 344

Dorr's Rebellion, 523–525, 533
Dreeben, 348*n*
Drifting society, 154, 157
Drucker, Peter F., 180, 232–238
Drug, diffusion of a new, 457–472
  and characteristics of physicians, 460–461
  as an example of social process, 457–472
  and physicians' contacts with colleagues, 461–464, 470–472
  and processes of diffusion, 464–469
Durkheim, Emile, 75
  on contract, 75, 328
  on integrative mechanisms, 277
  and organic solidarity, 82
  and social morphology, 429
  sociological theories of, 100
  and welcoming disorder, 441
Dynamics, group, and social change, 371–378

East Berlin, *see* Berlin, East
East Pakistan, *see* Pakistan, East
Eckardt, Roy, 229
Economic:
  control, 56
  factors, role of, 6
  organization, modern, 307
Economist, 115
Education, 177
  adult, 234
  Barber on, 208
  in colonial areas, 309
  Drucker on, 232–238
  and the educational revolution, 232–238
  equal opportunities for, 208
  Keniston on, 241, 252
  and the knowledge sector, 257
  and modern men, 347–348, 349–350
  and modernization of individuals, 343
  in periods of development, 271
  and racial equality, 505
  Smelser on, 271
  and youth, 241, 252
  See also Schools
Educational opportunity, enhancing equality of, 208, 511–513
Egypt:
  castes in, 216
  cultural history of, 22, 143
  Davies on, 533
  as an irrigation state, 136
  Kroeber on, 143
  Mosca on, 216
  and revolution, 533
  Spengler on, 22
  Steward on, 136

Eisenhower, Dwight, 224
Eisenhower administration:
  and desegregation, 402
  power of the, 125
Eisenstadt, S. N.:
  on modernization, 266, 320–332
  on structural change, 280*n*
Eisner, Kurt, 44
Elite, power, 126–130
Elites:
  circulation of, 26–29
  decision-making, 149–150
  Eisenstadt on, 331–332
  Etzioni on, 149–150
  Gusfield on, 340–341
  in India, 340–341
  Mills on, 124, 126–130
  and modernization, 331–332
  Pareto on, 26–29
  See also Ruling class
Ellis, Howard, 286*n*
Emerson, Ralph Waldo, 233
Empires, 136
Empirical histories of firms, 382–392
Endogenous conflicts, 101–103
Engels, Friedrich, 32–39, 519*n*
Engels' theory of history, 4, 7
England:
  and achievement level, 171
  Barber on, 199–203, 206–207
  Bendix on, 310
  and business drive, 166–167, 169
  change without revolutionary upheaval in, 8
  Drucker on, 235
  and the educational revolution, 235
  Etzioni on, 147
  Great Depression in, 523
  ideologies in, 310
  and information collection, 147
  McClelland on, 166–167, 169
  Marx and Engels on, 37, 38
  Pareto on, 28, 29
  revolution in, 514–518
  Rostow on, 286
  Steward on, 131
  stratification systems in, 199–203, 206–207
  takeoff for, 290–292
  unions in, 115
English Revolution, 514–518
Entrepreneurs:
  Rostow on, 294–295
  sources of, 295–297
Environmental theory of history, 6
Epigenesis model, 67
Episcopal Church, 223
Equality, 157
Equilibrium:
  Cancian on, 93, 98

Coser on, 120, 122
Kaplan on, 481–485
Keniston on, 240, 253
MacIver on, 443–444
Mills on, 126
Myrdal on, 473–474
Parsons on, 73–74, 76–77
quasistationary, 375–376
set, 482
Smelser on, 66–67
stable, 473, 475
Erhard, Chancellor Ludwig, 504n
Essential rules, 481–482
Establishment, 245
Ethic of work performance, 316
Etzioni, Amitai:
on the active society, 370n
on group dynamics, 365n
and societal guidance, 70, 145–160
Euripides, 24
Evans-Pritchard, E. E., 155n, 278–279
Evolution:
cultural, 137–139
of functions, 12–13
human, 131–132, 137
multilinear, 69, 133–138
See also Neo-evolutionism
Evolution and Man's Progress, Shimkin, 138
Evolutionary hypothesis, 133
Evolutionists, 131–133
Exchange system, 272
Exogenous conflicts, 101–103
Expansion in an organization, horizontal and vertical, 385–387
Explosion, population, *see* Population explosion
Extremists in revolution, 517

Factories and modernization, 348–351
Fair Employment Practices Commission (FEPC), 402, 403, 494
Families, types of, 191
Family, 191–198
Family life, 58–59, 61, 62
Fascism, 503
Faunce, 344n
Federal Republic, *see* Germany, West
Feith, H., 320n
Feminine role, 82, 273
Feudal system of industry, 33
Feudalism, 16
Barber on, 199–203
Mosca on, 214, 217–221
Riesman on, 415
Feuer, Lewis:
and the counterrevolutionary theory of youth, 242
and historical inevitability, 251

on the psychopathology of youth, 248
on student rebellion, 244
Finance during the takeoff period, 295
Firth, Raymond, 92n, 96n
Flacks, Richard, 256n
Folk culture, 56–57
Foreign aid, 161
Forestry, 478–479
Formal schooling, *see* Education
Fortes, M., 155n, 278–279
Foy, 142
France:
balance of power and, 482
Barber on, 199–203
birth rate in, 178
and business drive, 169
Drucker on, 235, 237
education in, 235, 237
Etzioni on, 147
Great Depression in, 523
information processing in, 147
Kaplan on, 482
McClelland on, 169
Marx and Engels on, 38
Mills on, 124
Mosca on, 220
Pareto on, 28
revolution in, *see* French Revolution
stratification system in, 199–203
takeoff date for, 290
Frazer, James, 132
Frederick II of Hohenstaufen, 219
French Revolution, 241, 514–518
changes during the, 203
and injustice, 536
and the J-curve, 531
and social conflict, 103
Freud, Sigmund, 252–253, 412
Freudians, 366
Friedman, Milton, 500n
Friedmann, Georges, 116n
Friedrich, C. J., 314n
Fromm, Erich, 419
Functional:
analysis, 87, 90, 91–99
analysis of change, 87–99
system, definition of, 89–92
theory of change, 72–86
See also Structural-functional theory
Functionalism, 68
Cancian on, 92, 95, 98
Functions:
consensus of, 13
evolution of, 12–13

G (functional system property), 89–99
Gammanym, example using, 459–472
Gandhi, Mahatma:
and nationalism, 340

and nonviolent resistance, 399
and tradition, 266
Garden of Eden, 4
Garfinkel, 344*n*
Garrison, Winfred E., 224*n*
Garvey movement, 400
Gaulle, Charles de, 355
Geertz, Clifford, 87*n*
Geiger, Theodor, 101*n*
Gemeinschaft, 5, 8, 54–62
 See also Community
General Electric Company, 165
General Motors, 389
Generalization, basis of, 72
Genghis Khan, 137
Germany:
 balance of power and, 482
 and business drive, 169
 Drucker on, 237
 Kaplan on, 482
 Keniston on, 241
 McClelland on, 169
 Marx and Engels on, 38
 Mills on, 125
 Mosca on, 219, 221
 Nazism in, 241, 523
 Pareto on, 28
 the ruling class in, 28, 219, 221
 takeoff date for, 290
Germany, East, *see* Berlin, East
Germany, West, 503–504
Geronimo, 136
Gesellschaft, 5, 8, 54–62
 See also Society
Giant, possible size of the, 380
Gille, H., 190*n*
Gluckman, Max, 101*n*, 155*n*
God, 228–231
Goethe, Johann Wolfgang von, 20–24
 passim
Goode, William, 337*n*
Government, centralized, 283
Government intervention, 126
Grabbe, P., 374*n*
Graebner, 142
Graicunas, 389–390
Great Britain, *see* England
Great Depression, 523
 See also Depression
Great Society, 504*n*
Greece, 28
Greeley, Andrew, 251
Group:
 decision, 374, 376
 discussion, 374
 dynamics and social change, 371–378
Growth:
 of organizations, 379–392
 sectors, types of, 298
 self-sustained economic, 285–300

Gulick, L., 389*n*
Gumperz, John, 339*n*
Gusfield, Joseph R., 266, 333–341

Hagen, Everett E., 70–71, 336*n*
Hailsham, Viscount, 149*n*
Haire, Mason, 366–367, 379–392
Haiti, 515
Hamilton, Charles V., 541
Hampshire, Stuart, 246
Hannah, W. A., 320*n*
Hansen's Law, 226
Harrison, S. E., 279*n*
Hartley, Eugene L., 371*n*, 523*n*
Hauser, Philip M., 424, 428–442
Hawaiian Islands, 395
Hayden, Tom, 245
Health measures, public, 288
Hegel, Georg Friedrich Wilhelm, 124, 314–315
Henry III of Franconia, 219
Henry IV, 219
Heraclitus, 412
Herberg, Will:
 on labor unions, 115*n*
 on religious revival, 180, 223–231
Hereditary charisma, 46–47
Herskovits, M., 337*n*
Heterogeneity, 10–13
Hield, Wayne, 87*n*, 98
Higher education, 259
 See also Education
Hinduism, 335
Hippie, 257, 436
Histories of firms, empirical, 382–392
Hitler, Adolf, 125, 441
Hoagland, Hudson, 138
Hobbesian problem of order, 98
Hoffman, Abbie, 245
Holmes, Oliver Wendell, 441
Homer, 16, 233
Homogeneity, 10–13
Homology theory of history, 24–25
Horizontal expansion in an organization, 385–387
Hoselitz, Bert F., 268*n*, 274*n*, 335*n*
Human History, Smith, 143
Hungary:
 Dahrendorf on, 111, 112
 Davies on, 534
 social conflict in, 111, 112, 534
Hunters, 134–135
Huygens, Christian, 17

Ibo tribe, 336
Ideal-type construct, 268
Ideas, role of, 6
Illia, 151

Immigration and population diversification, 434
Imperialism, Marxist-Leninist theory of, 102, 205
See also Neo-imperialism
Imperialists, 233
Impersonality, 5
Implosion, population, see Population implosion
Imports, capital, 295
Index of simultaneity, 467–469
India:
  birth control in, 189
  caste system in, 48–49, 51, 216
  Davis on, 189
  Gusfield on, 266, 334–335, 337–341
  McClelland on, 174
  modernization of, 266, 334–335, 337–341
  modernization of individuals in, 343–359
  Mosca on, 213, 216
  Rostow on, 293
  Sepoy Revolution in, 339, 523
  Smelser on, 276, 279
  takeoff date for, 290
  Weber on, 40, 48–49, 51
Indians:
  American, 136, 533
  Pueblo, 411
  South American, 10
Individual:
  approach to propaganda, 374
  modification of behavior, 366
  rights of the, 3
Indonesia, 320, 322, 327, 330, 331
Industrial order, 3
Industrial organizations, 379
  empirical histories of, 382–392
Industrial Revolution, 166–167, 522
Industrialization, 265–266
  and economic development, 269
  and ideological change, 313–315
  and modernization, 177
  and race relations, 396–398
  and takeoff, 292
Industry:
  Comte on, 19
  Marx and Engels on, 35–36, 39
  Toennies on, 62
Inertia, 76n–77n
Infiltration:
  Kroeber on, 141
  Mosca on, 216
Inflation and takeoff, 293–294
Injustice, 536–539
Inkeles, Alex, 266–267, 342–361
Inner-directed, 410–420
  definition of, 411–412
Innovation, 447–450

conditions for, 448
  among physicians, 466
Input-output model, Leontief, 298, 299
Instability, 521
  See also Stability
Institute of Family Relations, 198
Institutionalization, 76
Integrated:
  housing, 406–407
  physicians, socially, 463–466
Integration:
  Smelser on, 269, 277–280
  Spencer on, 13
  See also Race relations
Intellectuals, 515
Intensity of feeling, 499
Interlocking directorates, 126
Interracial marriages, 407–408
Invention, 451–456
  acceptance of, 454–455
  classifications of, 452–453
  cultural setting for, 453–454
Involvement, degree of, 372
Irrigation state, 135–136, 138
Islamic nations, 170
Israel:
  Etzioni on, 155
  modernization of individuals in, 343–359
  Weber on, 46
Italy, 221

Jack the Giant Killer, 380
Jacoby, E. H., 281n
Jacqueries, 526n
James, William, 450
Japan:
  Davis on, 185, 189
  the demographic transition of, 185, 189
  Eisenstadt on, 331–332
  elites in, 331–332
  Gusfield on, 336
  Keniston on, 255
  Rostow on, 293
  takeoff for, 290–292
  Weber on, 47, 52
Japanese population, 394
J-curve of rising expectations, 530, 531
Jefferson, Thomas, 233
Jefferson's Embargo Act of 1807, 524
Jesuits, 15
Jewish Americans, 152
Jews, 223, 224, 226–227, 400
John, King, 220
Johnson, Alvin, 140n, 447n
Johnson, Lyndon, 404
  and the Great Society, 504n
Johnson administration, 403
Joint Chiefs of Staff, 126

Julian, Emperor, 15
Juridical epoch, 18

Kachin society, 97–98
Kahl, 344
Kahn, Herman, 242, 247, 248
Kaldor, N., 296n
Kallen, Horace M., 425, 447–450
Kaplan, Morton A., 427, 481–485
Kaplan, Norman, 149n
Katz, Elihu, 426, 457–472
Kautsky, John, 339n
Keniston, Kenneth, 181–182, 239–260
Kennedy, John F., 146
Kennedy administration, 402–403
Kepler, Johannes, 17
Kerr, Clark, 101n
Keynes, John M., 240, 296n
Keys, Ancel, 521n
Kierkegaard, Soren, 226
King, Reverend Martin Luther, 399
Kingdom of God, 4
Kinsey, A. C., 198
Kinship units, 81
Kitt, Alice S., 120n
K. K. K., *see* Ku Klux Klan
Knighthood, 200–201
Knowledge sector in modern society, 250–258
Koontz, H., 390n
Koppers, 142
Kornhauser, Arthur, 123n
Kroeber, A. L.:
    and the analysis of change, 70
    on diffusionism, 140–144, 425–426
Ku Klux Klan (K. K. K.), 368, 404–405
Kulturkreise, 142–143
Kulturkreislehre, 142–143
Kuznets, Simon, 271n, 286n

Labor:
    markets, 80
    migratory, 273
    unions, *see* Unions
Labour Government, 207
Lag, cultural, *see* Cultural lag
Laissez-faire, 310–311
Land:
    Mosca on, 213
    Riesman on, 416
    in Russia, 526–527
    See also Property, Rent
Landis, Benson Y., 224n
Law:
    Toennies on, 59
    Weber on, 41
Law and order, 394
Law of the three states, 18–19

Lawson, James, 400
Layoff, 388
Lazarsfeld, P. F., 522n, 532
Le Bon, B., 532n
Leach, E. R.:
    and functional analysis, 92n
    on the Kachin society, 96–99
    and modernization, 320n
Lefebvre, G., 532n
Legitimation, 79, 81–82
Leibniz, Gottfried von, 21
Leisure, 417–418
Lenin, Nikolai:
    and equality, 312
    and power, 124–125, 517
    and the rate of change, 205
Leo III, Pope, 219
Leonardo da Vinci, 455
Leontief input-output model, 298, 299
Lerner, Daniel, 333n
Levy, Marion J., Jr., 92n
Lewin, Kurt, 365–366, 371–378
Lewis, W. A., 269n
Liberal:
    humanitarianism, 536–541
    pattern of thinking, 500
    theories of man, 239–242
    See also Neo-liberals
Life cycle of cultures, 20–25
Lindblom, Charles E., 489, 493–499
Line personnel, 382–392
Linear theory of history, 3–5, 14–17
Linton, Ralph, 425, 451–456
Lipset, Seymour Martin, 241, 277n, 526n
Literacy, 341
Livingston, A., 26n
Loanable funds, supply of, 293–295
Locke, Harvey J., 197n
Lockwood, David, 87n, 104
Long, Huey, 532
Loomis, Charles P., 54n
Lorimer, Frank, 430n
Louis XIV, 221
Luddite movement, 243, 244, 245, 250
Lumpenproletariat, 38

McCarthy, Joseph, 369
McClelland, David C., 70–71, 161–174
Maccoby, Eleanor E., 371n
MacIver, R. M., 424, 443–446
McLennan, John Ferguson, 132
Macro-sociological analysis, 370
Macrosociology, 145, 159
Madagascar, integration in, 11
Magna Carta, 220
Malays, feudalism of the, 16
Man, modern, 344–353
Man for Himself, Fromm, 419
Mannheim, Karl, 436n, 500n

March on Washington, 399
Maritain, Jacques, 226
Market:
  coordination, 493
  economy, 177
  world, 33
Market-rational political theory, 502–504
Marriage-counseling centers, 198
Marriage Council of Philadelphia, 198
Marriages, interracial, 407–408
Marriott, McKim, 276, 279
Marshall, Alfred, 100
Martinet, André, 92n
Marx, Karl, 412, 533
  and alienation, 538
  on class struggle, 32–39
  and determinism, 360
  on feudalism, 117–118
  on materialism, 30–31
  on wages, 519n
Marxism, 69
  questioning of, 254
  and youth, 242
Marxist-Leninist theory of imperialism, 102, 205
Marxist theory of history, 4–8
Masai tribe, 336–337
Masaryk, 529n
Mass:
  approach to propaganda, 374
  culture, 177
Materialism, 30–31
Matossian, Mary, 281n, 339
Mayo, Elton, 115n, 365
Mead, George Herbert, 313–314
Medicine, practice of, 457
Melman, Seymour, 115n
Menzel, Herbert, 426, 457–472
Merton, Robert K.:
  and behavioral science, 147n
  and bureaucracy, 117n
  and functional systems, 87n
  and relative deprivation, 120n
  and sociology of knowledge, 149n
  and the structural-functional approach, 105n
  and technological change, 116n
Mesopotamia, 136
Metaphysical epoch, 18
Methodists, 173, 223
Metropolitanization and the population implosion, 430–431
Mexico:
  and achievement level, 171
  Drucker on, 235
  education in, 235
  Eisenstadt on, 331–332
  elites in, 331–332
  as an irrigation state, 136
  Steward on, 136

Middle Ages:
  Coser on the, 115
  Marx and Engels on the, 36–37
  Mosca on the, 218–219
Migration of Negroes, 397–398
Migratory labor, 273
Milbrath, Lester W., 159n
Milieu, personal, 123
Military:
  capitalism, 128
  clique, 129–130
  decision systems, 496
  epoch, 18
  establishment, 125–130
Mill, John Stuart, 310
Mills, C. Wright:
  evaluation of, 68
  and industry, 115n
  on the sources of societal power, 123–130
Minnesota starvation studies, 521
Mobility, individual, 276
Mobility in undeveloped areas, 307
Mobilization, 152–153
  social, 328–329
Model, definition of a, 88
Model for social organizations, biological, 379–382
Moderates in revolution, 517
Modern:
  man, 344–353
  personality, 267
Modernization, 177–182, 263–267
  Gusfield on, 333–341
  of individuals, 342–361
  political, 320–332
  theory of, 268–284
  variations in, 270–271
Modification of behavior, individual, 366
Monarchy, absolute, 222
Moore, W. E., 271n, 335n
  and industrialization, 265, 268n
  on motivational aspects of development, 301–309
  on the theory of social change, 65
Morality:
  Mosca on, 214
  Toennies on, 54, 59–60
Morgan, Lewis H., 4, 132
Mormonism, 43
Mortality, decline in, 183–190
  causes of, 184–185
  consequences of, 185–188
Mosca, Gaetano, 179, 210–222
Mosely, Philip E., 156n
Motivation:
  achievement, 71
  Lewin on, 372
  possible theories of, 301–309
Mowry, A. M., 524

Muhammed, Elijah, 400
Multifactor theory of history, 7
Muslim Brotherhood, 400
Mutual adjustment:
    advantages of, 494–499
    coordination through, 493–494
    partisan, 495–499
Myrdal, Gunnar, 426, 473–476

NAACP, *see* National Association for the Advancement of Colored People
Nagel, Ernest, 87, 88–89
Napoleon Bonaparte, 15, 25, 124, 524
Narayan, Jayaprakash, 340–341
Nash, Manning, 337n
Nash, N., 269n
Nasser, Gamal Abdel, 503
National Aeronautics and Space Administration (NASA), 146
National Association for the Advancement of Colored People (NAACP), 146, 399
Nationalism, 264
    roles of, 274–275
    in Southeast Asia, 281
    and tradition, 340
Nazism, 241, 523
Negative dominance roles, 109n
Negro Americans, 152
Negro Revolt and population diversification, 434–435, 439–440
Negroes:
    Barber on, 208
    and caste in the United States, 208
    migration of, 397–398
    occupational training for, 398
    Park on, 394
    plane of living of, 474–475
    problems of, 396–409, 474–475
    and slavery, 394
    as students, 506
    and technological change, 398
    and voting, 405–406
    See also Race relations
Nehru, Jawaharlal, 354
Neo-evolutionism, 134–138
    See also Evolution
Neo-imperialism, 246
    See also Imperialism
Neo-liberals, 251
    See also Liberal
New Deal, 127, 536–537
New Left, 537
Newcomb, T. H., 523n
Newcomb, Theodore M., 371n
Newman, K. J., 321n
Nicholas II, 528, 529
Niebuhr, Reinhold, 226, 228n
Nigeria:
    and British colonialism, 336
    and business drive, 170–171
    Gusfield on, 336
    McClelland on, 170–171
    modernization of individuals in, 343–359
Nixon, Richard, 146
Nobility:
    Barber on, 201–202
    Davies on, 531–532
Norm, 75
Northern Presbyterians, 223
Northern Student Movement (NSM), 399
Norton-Taylor, Duncan, 230

Objective consciousness, 256
Occupational training for Negroes, 398
O'Donnell, C., 390n
Ogburn, William Fielding:
    on change, 426–427, 432n
    and cultural lag, 437, 477–480
Old Testament, 251, 537
Open-class stratification system, 199, 203–209
Opportunity factor, 83
Optimism, 209
Organic solidarity, 82
Organization:
    clerical function in modern, 391–392
    expansion in an, 385–387
Organizations, growth of, 379–392
Organski, A. F. K., 333n
Oriental-American students, 508–509
Origin of the Species, Darwin, 138
Other-directed, 410–420
    definition of, 414
Ottenberg, Simon, 337n
Otto I of Saxony, 219
Overmanaged society, 154, 156–157
Owen, 24

Painter, Sidney, 200n
Pakistan, 320, 322, 327, 330, 331
Pakistan, East:
    modernization of individuals in, 343–359
Panchayati Raj, 341
Pareto, Vilfredo:
    on the circulation of elites, 26–29
    and political change, 3–4
    sociological theory of, 100
Park, Robert E.:
    and ethnic groups, 366–367
    influences Wirth, 429
    on the race-relations cycle, 393–395
Parkinson, 391
Parliament Bill, 29
Parsons, Talcott:
    on change, 65–67

on change of system versus change within system, 119
and a differentiation model, 263
and functional analysis, 92
on a functional theory of change, 72–86
and the Hobbesian problem of order, 98–99
and the integration of sociological theories, 100
and the structural-functional approach, 105n
as translator of Weber, 40n, 43n
Passive societal units, 145, 154–155
Passive society, 154–155
Patterned relation, 74–75
Patterns of Culture, Benedict, 133
Pauker, G. Y., 320n
"Peace of mind," 229–230
Pearsonian correlation, 347n
Pendulum theory of history, 4
People's Constitution, 524–525
Peron, Juan, 151
Perry, 143
Personal:
    disorganization, 358–360
    milieu, 123
    worth, 537
Personality:
    flexibility of, 196
    modern, 267
Personnel, line and staff, 382–392
Peru:
    and achievement level, 171
    as an irrigation state, 136
Peter the Great, 317, 526
Philip, André, 101n
Philip Augustus, 220
Philip II, 15
Physicians:
    characteristics of, 460–461
    and contacts with colleagues, 461–464, 470–472
    innovation among, 466
    socially integrated, 463–466
Piaget, Jean, 252–253
Pirenne, Henri, 116n
Pitts, J. R., 330n
Plan-rational political theory, 502–504
Planning, central, 494–496
Plasticity, 252
Plato, 24
Ploughback process, 294–295
Poland, 222
    business drive in, 165
    Dahrendorf on, 111
    McClelland on, 165
    Mosca on, 212–213, 222
    ruling class in, 212–213
    social conflict in, 111

Polarization in society, 420
Political Systems of Highland Burma, Leach, 96
Political theory, 502–504
Poll tax, 406
Population, 288
    concentration of, 431
    diversification, 432, 434–435
    explosion, 178, 430, 433
    implosion, 430–431, 433–434
Positive dominance roles, 109n
Postindustrial society, 245
Poverty of Philosophy, The, Marx, 121–122
Power, 501–502
    and authority, 107–108
    and business drive, 169
    Dahrendorf on, 107–108, 501–502
    development of the means of, 124–130
    Etzioni on, 151–153
    McClelland on, 169
    Mills on, 124–130
    Mosca on, 216
    and the ruling class, 216
    sources and mobilization of, 151–153
Power elite, 126–130
    in the United States, 126–128
Precipitant, 443–446
Prejudice, *see* Race relations
Presbyterians, 223
Primogeniture, 47
Production:
    under differentiation conditions, 278
    Marx on, 30–31
    Marx and Engels on, 34
Proletariat, 527
    Marx and Engels on, 32, 34–39
Propaganda, approaches to, 374
Property, 416
    See also Land, Rent
Protestant ethic, 5
    Calvin introduces the, 5
    influence of the, 296
    replaced, 368
Protestant Ethic and the Spirit of Capitalism, The, Weber, 7
Protestantism, 42, 274–275
Protestants, 223, 224, 226–227
Protospirituality, 21
Proudhon, polemic against, 117–118
Psychic strain, 358–360
Psychological theory of history, 70–71
Psychosomatic Symptoms Test, 358–359
Public:
    education, *see* Education
    health measures, 288
    opinion, 60, 61
    schools, *see* Schools
Pueblo Indians, 411
Puerto Rican students, 506

Puerto Rico, 189
Pullman Strike of 1894, 523
Purges, 111, 206
Pursuit of Loneliness, The, Slater, 248
Pye, L. W., 320*n*

Quandt, Richard, 482*n*
Quasigroups, 109

R&D, *see* Research and development
Race relations, 393–395
    and industrialization, 396–398
    and Negroes, 400
    and the social morphological revolution, 435
    violence in, 400
    and World War II, 400–401
    See also Negroes
Racism, 405, 439–440
    Keniston on, 255
    in the United States, 255
    white, 439–440
    See also Race relations
Radcliffe-Brown, A. R., 93*n*
Radical politics, 258
Radicalism, 244
Rapoport, Anatol, 100*n*
Rationalism, Occidental, 41–42
Rationality, 500
Reactionaries, 38
Rebellion, 120
Redfield, Robert:
    and the "little community," 436*n*
    and syncretism, 336*n*
    and transmission speed of a signal, 392
Reflections on Violence, Sorel, 114
Reforms, 522
    suffrage, 525
Reich, Charles, 245, 248, 250–251
Relation, patterned, 74–75
Religion, 177
    Herberg on, 223–231
    Toennies on, 54, 57
Religious values, secularization of, 275
Renaissance, 115
Rent, 213
    See also Land, Property
Research and development (R&D), 146, 148–149
Resistance, 141
Resources, external, 161
Revolution:
    American, *see* American Revolution
    anatomy of, 514–518
    crisis period in, 517
    Dahrendorf on, 100, 110
    and elites, 29
    English, 514–518

extremists in, 517
    French, *see* French Revolution
    Industrial, 166–167, 522
    Keniston on, 241
    Marx on, 30–31
    Marx and Engels on, 38
    moderates in, 517
    Pareto on, 29
    and the ruling class, 515–516
    Russian, *see* Russian Revolution
    social, 431
    as social conflict, 100, 110
    social morphological, 429–442
    theory of, 519–534
Revolutionary theory of youth, 245–252
Riesman, David, 368–369, 410–420
Rights of the individual, 3
Rivers, 143
Robertson, D. H., 300
Robespierre, Maximilien de, 517
Roman Catholics, *see* Catholics
Romanticism, 23
Rome, 23, 124
    Marx and Engels on, 32
    Mills on, 124
    Mosca on, 216
    Pareto on, 28, 29
    Spengler on, 23
    stratification systems in, 28, 32, 216
    Weber on, 46
Roosevelt, Franklin D.:
    and possible revolution, 533
    and the Supreme Court, 495
Roosevelt administration, 402
Röpke, Wilhelm, 504*n*
Rose, Arnold:
    on the Negro problem, 396–409
    and the principle of cumulation, 473–476
    and race relations, 367–368
Ross, Professor, 393
Rostow, W. W., 264–265, 285–300
Roszak, Theodore, 245, 246
Rousseau, Jean-Jacques, 313, 314
Routinization of charisma, 4, 43–53
Rule of genius, 44
Rule of St. Benedict, 233
Rules:
    essential, 481–482
    transformation, 482–485
Ruling class:
    Mills on, 129–130
    Mosca on, 210–222
    and revolutions, 515–516
    See also Elites
Russell, Jane, 229
Russia, 49, 125, 275
    and achievement level, 171
    and balance of power with United States, 484

Barber on, 204–206
Bendix on, 311–312
business drive in, 169–170, 173–174
direction of change in, 156–157
Drucker on, 234–235, 237
education in, 234–235, 237
Eisenstadt on, 331
elites in, 331
and the environmental theory, 6
Etzioni on, 156–157
growth process in, 286
ideologies in, 311–312
labor unions in, 312
land in, 526–527
McClelland on, 161, 169–170, 173–174
Mills on, 125
Mosca on, 213
revolution in, *see* Russian Revolution
Rostow on, 286, 293
slavery in, 526
Smelser on, 275
stratification systems in, 204–206
takeoff for, 290–292
Weber on, 49
Russian Revolution, 241
anatomy of the, 514–518
background of the, 526–530, 533
Ryan, Edward, 342n

Sanskritization, 338
Sartre, Jean-Paul, 420
Savings, 289
Sayeed, K. B., 321n
Scalapino, Robert, 336n
Schmidt, Father, 142
Schneider, Harold, 337n
Schneider, Herbert W., 223n
Schools:
    and activism, 542
    and desegregation, 407
    segregation in the, 505–508
    See also Education
Schuman, Howard, 342n
Science:
    Barber on, 208
    Comte on, 19
    Toennies on, 57, 62
Scientific knowledge, 40–41
Sears Roebuck, 389
Secularization of religious values, 275
Security, 50
Segregation:
    "de facto," 407
    in the public schools, 505–508
    racial, 394
    See also Race relations
Seligman, Edwin R. A., 140n, 447n
Sen, K. M., 334n

Sepoy rebellion, 339, 523
Sexual Behavior in the Human Male,
    Kinsey, 198
Shannon, L. W., 282n
Shils, Edward, 241
Shimkin, Demitri B., 138
Simmel, 104n
Simon, Herbert A., 148n, 317
Simpson, George Gaylord, 134
Simultaneity, index of, 467–469
Singer, Milton, 334n
Slater, Philip, 245, 247, 248
Slavery, 18
    Park on, 394
    in Russia, 526
Smelser, Neil J.:
    and differentiation, 263, 265
    and functional analysis, 92n
    and a theory of change, 66
    and a theory of modernization, 268–
        284
Smith, Adam, 431
Smith, David H., 342n–358n *passim*
Smith, G. Elliot, 143
Smith, Joseph, 43–44
Social change:
    beginning of, 423
    group dynamics and, 371–378
    theory of, 65–66, 114–122
Social conflict, 114–122
    Dahrendorf on, 100–103, 106–107,
        109–113
Social differentiation, 10
Social disturbances, 269, 280–283
Social morphological revolution, 429–442
    consequences of the, 435–440
Social-movement society, 155
Social movements, contemporary, 535–
    542
Social organizations, biological model for,
    379–382
Social structure, 123
Social System, The, Parsons, 65
Social systems, structure of, 74–76
Socialism, 503
Socialist movement, 536, 539–541
Socialization, 254
    Inkeles on, 351–352
Societal guidance, theory of, 145–160
Societal units, 145
Society:
    chaotic, 428–429
    from community to, 54–62
    contemporary, 428–429
    development of, 3
    evolution of, 9–13
    models of, 105
    polarization in, 420
    postindustrial, 245
    technetronic, 242–245, 250–251

Toennies on, 54–62
view of, 365
Sociogram, 463
Sociological analysis, 66–67
Solidarity makers, 326
Sorel, George, 114, 116
South America and achievement level, 171
South American Indians, 10
Southern Christian Leadership Conference (SCLC), 399
Soviet Union, *see* Russia
Span of control, 388–391
Spencer, Herbert:
on the evolution of societies, 9–13
on the levels of functioning in man, 133
and the linear theory of history, 3–5
Spengler, J. J., 271*n*
Spengler, Oswald:
and the cyclic theory of history, 3, 5
on the life cycle of cultures, 20–25
Sputnik, 237
Srinivas, M. N., 338
Stability:
Cancian on, 95
Keniston on, 240
Parsons on, 73, 76
political, 521
ultra-, 483–484
Staff personnel, 382–392
Stalin, Joseph, 441
Stalin Allee, *see* Berlin, East
Standard achievement tests, 507, 508
Standard Metropolitan Statistical Areas (SMSA'S), 434
Standard Oil Co., 450
Starvation studies, 521
State coordinates, 89–99
Status quo, 4, 444
Sterilization, 189
Sterner, Richard, 473–476
Steward, Julian H., 69–70, 131–139
Stolnitz, George J., 183*n*
Stolypin, Peter, 529
Storer, Norman W., 149*n*
Stouffer, 120*n*
Strain:
psychic, 358–360
in society, 306
Stratification systems, 199–209
See also Caste system
Structural changes, 124
Structural differentiation:
Parsons on, 72, 78–79, 83
Smelser on, 269, 271–277
Smelser's definition of, 271
Structural-functional analysis, 97–98
Structural-functional theory, 67–68
Cancian within the, 67
Dahrendorf on the, 103–106

Dahrendorf outside the, 67
See also Functional theory
Structural unemployment, 123
Structure, concept of, 72–73
Structure of social systems, 74–76
Struggle, class, 32–39
Stryker, Sheldon, 335*n*
Student Nonviolent Co-ordinating Committee (SNCC), 399
Students for Integration (SFI), 399
Stutz, U., 51
Subsistence agriculture, 272
Succession to authority, 45–47, 51
Sudan, 320, 322, 330
Suffrage reforms, 525
Sufrin, Sidney C., 115
Sukarno, 327
Sumner, 429, 478
Supernatural theory of history, 6
Comte on, 16
Supply, limited, 308
Supreme Court:
on civil rights, 396
and desegregation, 505
and housing segregation, 406
on integration, 76
packing the, 495
and race relations, 401–402
support for civil rights, 368
and trusts, 450
Sweden:
and achievement level, 169, 171
takeoff for, 290, 291*n*, 292
Switzerland, 235
Syncretism, 336

Tacitus, 52
Takeoff, 285–300
definition of, 291
Eisenstadt on, 320–321
inner structure of, 292–299
of national independence movements, 152
table of dates for, 290
Tariff, 425
Tariff protection, 494
Tax, poll, 406
Tax system, 208
Taxation, 218
Technetronic society, 242–245, 250–251
Technism, 256–257, 259
Technological change:
Coser on, 116
and Negroes, 398
and unions, 116
Technological unemployment, 398
Technology:
and economic development, 269
role of, 6

Tension in society, 306
Tenure, 388
Tests, standard achievement, 507, 508
Theological epoch, 18
Theory, convergence of sociological, 100
Theory, market-rational political, 501
Theory, plan-rational political, 501
Theory, structural-functional, 67–68, 103–106
Theory model, conflict-, 109–111
Theory of change, functional, 72–86
Theory of dependence, 310–311
Theory of history:
  biological, 6
  Condorcet's, 4
  cyclic, 3–5
  deterministic, 7
  Engels', 4, 7
  environmental, 6
  homology, 24–25
  linear, 3–5, 14–17
  Marxist, 4–8
  multifactor, 7
  pendulum, 4
  psychological, 70–71
  supernatural, 6, 16
  Weber's 4–8
Theory of imperialism, Marxist-Leninist, 102, 205
Theory of man, liberal, 239–242
Theory of modernization, 268–284
Theory of motivation, possible, 301–309
Theory of motives and consequences, 301–302
Theory of organized cooperation, 302–303
Theory of revolution, 519–534
Theory of social change, 65–66, 114–122
Theory of social conflict, 100–113
Theory of societal guidance, 145–160
Theory of youth:
  counterrevolutionary, 242–245, 247–251
  revolutionary, 245–252
Thomas, Norman, 230–231
Thompson, D'Arcy, 380
Thoreau, Henry David, 399
Three states, law of the, 18–19
Tillich, Paul, 226
Tinker, H., 321n
Tocqueville, Alexis de:
  and the French Revolution, 519–521
  on inequality, 314–315
  on revolutions, 533
Toennies, Ferdinand, 177, 429
  on community and society, 8, 54–62
  and the linear theory of history, 5
Toffler, Alvin, 242
Tolstoy, Leo, 419
Totalitarian:

  societies, 156
  states, 111–112
Totalitarianism, 317–318
Toynbee, Arnold, 117n
Trade unions, *see* Unions
Tradition, 140
Traditionalism:
  Bendix on, 310
  Gusfield on, 333–341
  Weber on, 53
Training for Negroes, occupational, 398
Transformation, structural, 159
Transformation rules, 482–485
Transmission speed of a signal, 392
Trotsky, Leon, 529n, 530n
Truman administration, 402
Trusts, 450
Tsarist autocracy, 311–312
Turkey:
  and elites, 331–332
  takeoff date for, 290
Turner, Ralph H., 491, 535–542
Tylor, Edward B., 132

U Nu, 327
Ultrastability, 483–484
Unemployment, 66
  structural, 123
  technological, 398
Unions, labor:
  American, 115
  British, 115
  in coalfields, 115
  and reduction of inequality, 208
  Russian, 312
  and security of workers, 116
  and wages, 37
United African Nationalist Movement, 400
United Nations, 76n
United States:
  and achievement level, 171
  and balance of power with Russia, 484
  change without revolutionary upheaval, 8
  cultural lag in the, 437–440
  education in the, 233–234
  family characteristics in the, 191–192
  governance of the, 437–439
  Great Depression in the, 523
  Indians in the, *see* American Indians
  industrialization of the, 286
  population characteristics of the, 188
  power elite in the, 126–128
  and the prolitarian, 38
  Pullman Strike of 1894, 523
  racism in the, 255
  religious identification in the, 227
  religious revival in the, 223–231

and research and development funds, 146
revolution in the, 514–518
stratification system in the, 208–209
takeoff for the, 290, 292
unions in the, 115
University of Virginia, 233
Urban League, 399
"Urbanism as a Way of Life," Wirth, 429
Urbanization:
    Burgess on, 193
    and economic development, 269
    and the population implosion, 430–431
    Rose on, 397
    Smelser on, 278
    See also Cities
Urwick, L. F., 389n
U.S.S.R., *see* Russia
Utopia:
    Dahrendorf on, 502
    Etzioni on, 155
    Turner on, 536

Values, conflict of, 497
Van der Kroef, J., 274n
Veblen, Thorstein, 120, 317
Venezuela, takeoff and, 291
Venice, 222
Vershofen, Wilhelm, 504n
Vertical expansion in an organization, 385–387
Vested interests, 120, 122
Vietnam war, 537
Violence:
    in race relations, 400
    Sorel on, 114
Von Stein, Lorenz, 315
Voting and Negroes, 405–406

Wage incentives, motivation of, 305, 307–308
Wagner, Richard, 24, 25
Walinsky, L., 320n
Wallin, Paul, 196n
War, 394
    See also Vietnam war, World War II
War economy, permanent, 128–130
Warrior class, 212–214
Washington, George, 412
Weber, Max, 100
    on authority, 108
    and bureaucracies, 317, 318
    and economic behavior, 334
    and ideal-type constructs, 268–269
    influence of, 69, 316n
    and the Protestant ethic, 335
    and Protestantism, 274–275
    on the role of ideas in history, 40–42
    on the routinization of charisma, 43–53
    and a theory of history, 4–8
    and a theory of societal guidance, 151
Weil, Simone, 226
Welfare-warfare state, 245
Wellemeyer, Fletcher, 430n
Wesley, John, 173
West Germany, *see* Germany, West
Westermarck, Edward, 132
Wheeler, R., 321n
White, Leslie A., 134
White Citizen's Councils, 368, 404
White racism, 439–440
Wiesner, Jerome A., 149n
Willcox, 429
Williams, L. F. R., 321n
Williams, Robin M., Jr., 225n
Williamson, H. F., 286
Wilson, James Q., 152n
Wirth, Louis, 429
Women, status of, 82, 273
Work, meaning of, 416–417
Work performance, ethic of, 316
World War II:
    and power structures, 127
    and race relations, 400–401
Worth, personal, 537

X, Malcolm, 400
Xenophobia, 275, 281

Yoruba, 170–171, 358n
Youth, 436
    counterrevolutionary theory of, 242–245, 247–251
    movement, 539–542
    revolutionary theory of, 245–252

Zander, Alvin, 365n
Zawadzki, B., 522n, 532
Zulu, 358n